FOR LU 1992.

The Alex Quartet

Alex
Alex in Winter
Alessandra: Alex in Rome
Songs for Alex

Tessa Duder

Auckland
OXFORD UNIVERSITY PRESS
Melbourne   Oxford

Oxford University Press, Walton Street, Oxford OX2 6DP
Oxford   New York   Toronto
Delhi   Bombay   Calcutta   Madras   Karachi
Kuala Lumpur   Singapore   Hong Kong   Tokyo
Nairobi   Dar es Salaam   Cape Town
Melbourne   Auckland   Madrid
and associated companies in Berlin   Ibadan

Oxford is a trade mark of Oxford University Press

Text © Tessa Duder 1987, 1989, 1991, 1992
Setting © Oxford University Press 1987, 1989, 1991, 1992
This edition first published 1992

All rights reserved. No part of this publication may be reproduced, stored in a retrieval system, or transmitted, in any form or by any means, without the prior permission in writing of Oxford University Press. Within New Zealand, exceptions are allowed in respect of any fair dealing for the purpose of research or private study, or criticism or review, as permitted under the Copyright Act 1962, or in the case of reprographic reproduction in accordance with the terms of the licences issued by Copyright Licensing Limited. Enquiries concerning reproduction outside these terms and in other countries should be sent to the Rights Department, Oxford University Press, at the address below.

ISBN 0 19 558263 2

Printed in New Zealand by GP Print
Published by Oxford University Press
1A Matai Road, Greenlane
PO Box 11-149, Auckland, New Zealand

ALEX

Author's Note

Anyone familiar with the fine sport of swimming in New Zealand during the period described will detect some historical liberties. For dramatic reasons, the locations of championship meetings during the period have been slightly changed, and for reasons of simplicity race distances have been given in imperial measurements.

New Zealand school students sat School Certificate around age fifteen, at the end of the Fifth Form, and the following year were either accredited or required to sit the Sixth Form examination of University Entrance.

Passing reference is made to some of the outstanding champions of the time – the Australian freestyle swimmers Dawn Fraser, Lorraine Crapp, Jon and Ilse Konrads, the English backstrokers Judy Grinham and Margaret Edwards. Apart from these, all characters are entirely fictitious.

Prologue

I have always known that in another life I was – or will be – a dolphin. I'm silver and grey, the sleekest thing on fins, with a permanent smile on my face. I leap over and through the waves. I choose a passing yacht to dive under and hear the shouts of the children as I emerge triumphant close to the boat.

Right at this moment, I'd give anything for that freedom. I am a pink human, caught in a net of ambition and years of hard work. In a few minutes I will dive into that artificially turquoise water waiting at my feet. A minute later I'll be either ecstatic or a failure.

I stare at my toes, which are white with fright. How will I ever get my legs going with feet of marble? I step from one foot to the other. My arms describe drunken windmills. I'll need all the oxygen I can get: I breathe in long slow lungfuls. My heart is already pumping away as if it has gone berserk.

I hear 'In Lane three, Alexandra Archer' and something else, which is lost in cheers. Automatically I step on to the starting-block. 'In Lane four, Maggie Benton,' in the lane I wanted to be in, should have been in. Cheers and shouts for her, too. More than for me, or less? I have never been able to tell. What does it matter, anyway? I stand head down. Nothing will make me look at her. Since we hugged goodbye this morning we have avoided each other, carefully not being in the dressing-room at the same time, not meeting in doorways, sitting well apart in the competitors' enclosure. I hope she is feeling as ghastly as me.

We all step down. I walk back to the chair where a woman in a blazer waits to take my track suit. My hands are shaking so much that I can't get my fingers latched on to the tab of the zip. She helps me. Yes, I did put my swimsuit on under all this, my most special pair. People haven't, in the past, from nerves.

Then comes the gold chain, bearing my most precious possession in all the world, Andy's pearl, his tear. It goes deep into my track suit pocket, along with his parents' telegram.

I'm cold, so cold . . . appalled at what I have to do. I stand tall, centre stage, on the first rung of the starting-block. Under the night sky, I feel almost naked. Just me, the body Alex, fit, ready, dangerous.

A whistle blows somewhere. I climb up to the block, as to a guillotine. Shouts and cheers echo around the packed stands. 'Maggie', 'Alex', 'Come on, Maggie', 'Go Alex'. Then, silence falls like a curtain.

I make a last adjustment to the cap clinging to my ears, a last swing of the arms, shake of the feet, shrug of the shoulders. I hear the breakers of my nightmares crash on the nearby beach. I need a pee.

'Take your marks.'

I curl my toes carefully around the edge of the block. It's a relief to bend my knees. I crouch down, hearing the wrench of cartilage in knee joints, and look along the fifty-five yards of smooth blue water in front of me. Up and back we'll go, flat out. I feel tired already.

Heads or tails? This throw is for you, Andy.

Beside me someone starts to move.

Bang!

Alex, you're dead.

Maggie's got a flyer on you. A glorious flyer.

You're beaten before you even start.

1

It all began years ago. I'm a veteran at fifteen years and two-and-a-half months, a seasoned campaigner with countless races under my belt, and the subject of much journalistic purple prose, which charts my ups and downs. This last year, it was mostly downs. Those reporters have had a field day with Maggie and me! And how I get it in the neck at school when they write something!

Monday last week was bad, the worst yet. Start of a new term, a new year, everyone at school, frisky with holiday gossip and sizing up the new teachers. A long piece on Maggie and me appeared in the morning paper. I'd biked along to the pool, done my usual training, and come home sodden with pool water, eyes a delicate shade of pink, to peaches and cereal, steaming bacon and eggs with fried potato, four slices of toast, and hot chocolate to drink. Try doing two and a half miles' hard swimming before breakfast and you'd need more than a cup of coffee, too.

Dad waited until I'd finished my last bit of toast, and the others had all been shooed off to get ready for school. 'You'd better have a look at this.'

'Look at what?'

'Remember that reporter from the women's page? Came to see you last week.'

'The orange sack dress, and very high stilettoes?'

'That's her. Here's the result.' He handed me the paper. I didn't like the expression in his eyes. 'Did she tell you she was going to see Maggie as well?'

'No, she did not.'

My eyes were still blurred with chlorine. Through the haze I recognized a ghastly photo of myself taken by the photographer who'd sat in the armchair picking his teeth and reading a book, while his wig-wearing mate had asked her silly questions. Then he asked me to sit on the verandah with the family dog in a stupid Hollywood starlet pose, and when I refused, he got all surly and grumpily fired a few flashbulbs. It wasn't a bad picture of the dog, or of the verandah.

Silly questions get silly answers. What had possessed me to answer them? Or had I, indeed? The reporter hadn't been taking shorthand, I'd noticed that much.

'SWIMMERS HAVE FEMININE INTERESTS TOO!' the headline proclaimed. I looked up at Dad. He was studiously marmalading his toast. Over at the bench, both Gran washing dishes and Mum cutting lunches had their backs turned, but I knew they were listening and waiting.

'Life is not all stop-watches for Auckland's two brilliant girl swimmers who meet at the national championships in Napier next week to settle which of them goes to the Rome Olympic Games in August.

'Despite their gruelling training programmes, which mean four hours a day in the pool, fifteen-year-old Maggie Benton and her great rival of many years, Alexandra Archer, retain their interest in more traditional feminine matters.'

(Maggie first, again. Well, that's fair enough. Maggie's the famous one, I'm more what you'd call notorious. Nevertheless . . .)

A spiel about the pretty, slim Maggie followed, about her dark gamin hairstyle, which suits a swimmer's life as well as being very stylish, her love of nice clothes, her devoted mother and immaculate house full of interesting Eastern curios, her cute younger sister and her father an importer. 'Maggie wishes she had more time for boyfriends and parties, but enjoys going to the movies, reading, sewing her own dresses, listening to Elvis and Pat Boone records, and reading *Seventeen* magazines.' Her photo showed her doing just that, with devoted mother (fresh from the hairdresser) peering proudly down from behind. 'Eventually she wants to do a secretarial course, maybe some modelling, and travel. Maybe she will do something connected with the tourist industry, since she was brought up in Singapore and has travelled with her parents around Asia and Australia.'

Of course, we all want to travel. Now Maggie may be the person I most want to beat in this entire world (perhaps for the equal pleasure of beating her mother), but I actually like her. She's shy rather than stand-offish, quite funny when she gets going, and certainly not the 'yes-Mother-no-Mother' little drip I once thought.

And she's always been generous on those occasions when I have beaten her, and she's not nearly *that* gormless.

'And what about her arch-rival, Alex Archer, who is also vying for the Olympic nomination? "Alex and I get on quite well out of the water," says Miss Benton. "But I suppose I must have a killer instinct that comes to the fore when we line up for an important race." (What a load of rubbish. Maggie just swims, she always has. She is more interested in times than beating people. And no one our age talks like that.) Mrs Harold Benton, her attractive youthful mother, listening proudly to her acclaimed daughter, adds, "Maggie has a wonderful race temperament. She is very calm and determined. We are feeling very confident about the championships next week and the Olympic nomination that will follow." '

The hell it will. With dread, I came to my part. According to the reporter, I live in a comfortable old house where I am the eldest of four children. My mother, Mrs James Archer, a devoted 'home-maker', works hard to provide the extra big meals that I need, lots of steak and vitamin C. (Translation: big girls need feeding up.) My grandmother, Mrs Albert Young, lives in a bed-sitting-room especially built on for her. She tends the large vegetable garden and chicken-run out the back, and sews our clothes. Father works in the Post Office. He was a fine swimmer and tennis player in his day, a backstroke champion. The younger children (James 12, Debbie 9 and Robert 4) are all proud of their famous big sister. My parents are pleased with my achievements, but try to encourage the other children as well, and my activities do not run the entire household. (I'll say!)

The next bit made me choke. 'Besides her swimming prowess, Alex is an outstanding senior student and a prefect at her school. This year she hopes to qualify for university entrance. She represents the school in hockey, and takes a leading role in school theatrical productions as a talented musician and dancer, having passed advanced examinations in piano and ballet. She has temporarily suspended most of her other activities outside school hours to concentrate on her bid for Olympic nomination. Her training regimen includes calisthenics and weights, which she greatly enjoys. She says she has not yet decided on her future, but one possibility is the study of law. Or perhaps she'll "just get married and have lots of children".'

I looked up into Dad's eyes. He'd been waiting for me to get to that bit.

'Just get married! Just get . . . what! I never said anything of the sort.'

'You didn't?'

'I most certainly did not.' I tried to remember what I had said. '*She* asked me if I might get married and have children and was I worried about having big shoulders and difficult childbirth after having done so much sport. I said of course not, I'm a fit healthy female, what more did doctors want? And one day I might get married and I might have kids *if* I felt like it. Then I said it was a myth that girl swimmers got big shoulders. They were swimmers because they had strong shoulders in the first place, although not all, you only have to look at Maggie. She's only five foot five, even if she has got hands like paddles and takes two sizes bigger than me in shoes. And both my parents were tall so it was hardly surprising that I was five foot ten and one-quarter and you're quite tall yourself and do people ask you about difficult childbirth all the time. She looked a bit po-faced at that.'

Over at the sink, Gran was chuckling away. 'No wonder she's giving you a hard time,' she said.

But Dad wasn't smiling. 'Alex, I thought you'd have learned by now. The less you say to reporters the better.'

This time I didn't merely choke. I stood up, knocking over the chair, waving the paper with rage. 'Listen to this. "Miss Archer, who is five foot ten and of Junoesque proportions, says she misses the parties and dances and movie-going that her school contemporaries enjoy. 'Most of the boys I meet,' she says, 'seem rather scared of me.' " '

'You said *that?*' asked Mum, wiping down the table.

'It wasn't. I didn't. Gran, stop laughing, please. She . . . she asked me all those stupid questions and I said yes and no and I suppose so and maybe sometimes. I did not *say* them. Well, I wasn't going to tell her about Andy, was I, or those other things? Once upon a time, there was a very tall princess who had a very tall boyfriend called Andy . . . Heck, Dad, she did all the talking, then she turned it all around. I don't even know what Junoesque means. I bet it's something rude.'

'Junoesque? Tall, stately. Juno was . . . who was Juno, Helena?'

'Roman goddess, consort of Jupiter, the Roman god of victory.'

My mother is a lady of few words, but she knows a lot. It's all that reading, two hours every night, through stacks of library books piled beside her special armchair. This time I was too angry to be impressed.

'I couldn't give a damn who she was.'

'Alex, I'm *sorry*,' said Dad. 'But from the women's page . . . Next time you'll have to be more careful.'

'She might have said Amazonian. They were female warriors,' said Mum. I glared at her.

'She makes me sound like some sort of freak.' I read on. It got worse and worse. ' "Usually talkative and forthright in her opinions, Miss Archer was uncharacteristically tight-lipped when asked about her rival Maggie Benton. 'I'd rather not say anything about Maggie. We can't both go to the Games, that's all.' " That makes me sound as though I don't like Maggie, like we have some sort of feud, but I do like her, even if I can't stand her bloody mother, and that's just not fair.' I looked down at the table so that Dad wouldn't see that my red-rimmed eyes were now brimming over with tears as well as pool water.

'Well. A subtle hatchet job,' said Dad. 'At least there's an implied compliment. All that space, more than Maggie if it comes to that. The lady might not approve of you, but at least she finds you and your family environment interesting. Laugh it off.'

'Laugh if off! I'll be the laughing stock of the school today. And there won't be a next time. Thanks, Mum,' I added, as she handed me a neatly-wrapped lunch.

'Your friends will know it for the artificial nonsense it is,' she said quietly. 'Most of them probably won't even have read it. Allow yourself to be amused, Alex. It's not important.'

'It's important to *me*. This . . . this *rubbish* . . . That's *me* she's talking about.' And I stomped out of the room and ended up seething on my bed. I thought I had become thick-skinned, but I did not relish the thought of walking into the cloakroom at school, and worse, into morning assembly. It's not that I'm completely green at seeing my name in print. I've had to get used to things being written about me, sometimes by male sports journalists who normally cover rugby or rowing and think swimming is a kid's sport. Even with the regular swimming reporters, it hasn't always been flattering, when I've had bad patches and Maggie's had the upper hand – 'MISS ARCHER BEATEN AGAIN', 'DISAPPOINTING SWIM', 'ALEX

ARCHER DISAPPOINTS'. There have been predictions that Maggie will win this or that race, loads of stuff about the golden girl Maggie and a steadily diminishing few paragraphs about disappointing old me.

Mum was, as usual, right. Most of my friends had not read the paper; those who had, thought it was a hoot. The few staff who mentioned it were scathing. 'That hypocritical nonsense in the paper this morning. Not one bit like you, Alex,' said the Head as we walked together along the corridor to History class. Coming from her, this was indeed a small victory from shame.

'It wasn't me, Miss Gillies,' I said. 'The interviewer did nearly all the talking.'

'And then put it all into your mouth?'

'Yes.'

'A common distortion. Journalists with preconceived ideas, hearing what they want to hear, and inventing the rest. It was a remarkably shallow piece of writing, wasn't it, especially given your considerable difficulties last year. But tell me, do your male friends quote "seem rather scared of you", unquote? Your friend Andy, did he, even a little?'

She had stopped in a patch of sun, just outside the classroom door. A long row of school photographs, teams of this and that, stared at me as I got my thoughts together.

'Andy . . . didn't, no, not at all. The others . . . well, I train mostly with boys, just boys in our squad. I've had lots of trips away with teams. Andy I'd known for about five years before we, before . . . If I wanted to talk to him, I rang him up. Why not? Life's too short to wait for the phone to ring or some boy to decide he wants to take you out.'

On the rare occasions when Miss Constantia Gillies smiled down from her full six feet two-and-a-half inches, it was as if a lighthouse beamed at you. I got the full treatment.

'Alex, you remind me of the wild gels of my university days in England, in the twenties. They waited for nobody, least of all men. Today, we seem to have gone backwards. There's far too much emphasis placed on the skills of self-adornment, and "home-making", whatever that means, and flirtation.'

'I'm no good at flirting.'

'I can imagine. Neither was I.' Her black gown, about twice as long as any other teacher's in the school, created quite a draught as she swept into the classroom. Before the chatter and scraping of chair legs died away as the class stood, she added cryptically, 'But I was *wonderfully* tall.'

Tallness. I suppose there's such a word. 'The tallness of her,' Gran used to say when I began to grow and kept on ever upwards. 'You poor child' was another sigh, until one day I couldn't stand it any longer and sat Gran in a chair and told her firmly that I liked being tall. She got the message.

Once, it was my shortness and fatness that worried Gran. When I went to my first swimming lesson, it was a round little nine-year-old body that lined up shivering with five others on the side of the pool, my black woollen swimsuit already hanging half-way down my thighs.

Dad had decided that I should be taught to swim. The logical place was the outdoor Olympic Pool, only a two-section tram ride distant from our house. My teacher, and later coach and friend, can remember that first time very well, as he once told a reporter. 'She floated high like a dead fish and within two lessons was going like a Bondi tram. She learnt the breathing technique in one lesson. Some kids take two seasons. She had long arms, even longer legs, a resting pulse around fifty and the urge to win: champion material if I ever saw it. She always had to be first and furtherest out from the side of the pool. She was a pain in the neck in that class, so I moved her in with a lot of twelve-year-olds.'

I spent most of those summer holidays at the pool, romping, diving, jumping, swimming for hours on end after my lesson. Mum would bring James and Debbie (Robert wasn't born then) and set herself up with book and picnic basket on the terraces above the pool. I saw older kids training, up and down, up and down. Soon I could do several lengths without stopping, hoping that Mr Jack, a portly and seemingly permanent fixture in baggy shorts, panama hat and grey plastic mac by the side of the pool, noticed me. If he did, nothing was said until the start of the following summer, when I had had my first two lessons in a class of twelve-year-olds. On the way home in the car, Dad asked me if I'd like to go in a race at an inter-club meeting at the indoor pool in town. Mr Jack thought I'd go like a bomb.

It was not a good start. Actually, it was a disaster. Dad virtually had to haul me bodily into the building, I was so nervous. They spelt my name wrongly in the programme. Surrounded by kids in track suits who all seemed to know each other, I nearly froze to death waiting for my race, wrapped only in a towel. I upset the starter by insisting on diving from the side of the pool rather than from the starting-block. The dive itself was a belly flop. When I finally got going, it was straight into the lane ropes. The water was a thick warm soup of salt and chlorine that stung my eyes. But I untangled myself, and set off again, eyes shut, cheeks aflame, and swam so fast through the wash that I overtook the other seven in the race three feet from the finish and forgot to stop.

They allowed me and Dad home from hospital sometime after midnight. The X-rays showed nothing broken. The hand which had hit the wall at ninety miles an hour was the worst bruised, but I had a good purple egg on my forehead, too. At impact, the pain had been so intense that I must have blacked out for a bit and sunk like a stone. My disappearance from view was long enough to cause two stout female officials to leap into the pool fully dressed, and apparently very nearly banging themselves together like a pair of cymbals as they jumped. By this time I was on my way back up towards air. The middle-aged mermaids landed on top of me, stockinged legs and white knife-pleated skirts thrashing around like demented jellyfish. I got hauled to the top. Or maybe we hauled each other.

Dad took charge then, and Mr Jack, and an ambulance person with a black peaked cap and a bag, who felt my pulse and put my arm in a sling in case it was broken. Towels, clothes, and our pale blue Morris Oxford car appeared from nowhere. I remember a nearby official's comment: 'Silly kid, but did you see her *go*! I've never seen such acceleration.' I remember, too, the baleful looks of my two rescuers, permed hair afrizz, peeling off their heavy wet blazers, and shaking the water from their stop-watches. Through the hum of excitement around the crowded pool came a snigger or two. Make the most of it, I flung silently at them as I was carried out, this is my first and last appearance here. Not until Mum pulled the sheet over my slinged-up arm and turned out the light did I allow myself a tear.

Embarrassment was not an unfamiliar sensation, even then. Something about me always seemed to invite attention: I found myself chosen to be leader of this or that, the class captain, giver of the morning talk, organizer of this team, thanker of that speaker, Alex'll do it, she won't mind. Did they think I had no nerves at all? I seem to be incapable of blending in with the landscape, even less with a crowd.

It's not just my tallness. I only have to look in a mirror to see that mine is not an especially pretty face, with my father's rather large nose, and a pointy chin. There is nothing special about my hair, which is short and wispy and what Gran's magazines call dark blonde (read: mouse). I am, however, regarded as photogenic. 'Big smile' call photographers, not easy when I've just lost another race to Maggie. Or there's this obsession with legs, pin-up stuff like World War Two calendars. As I've got older and my legs longer, I've refused to stand propped against pool ladders with one leg bent like Betty Grable.

I suppose I did – and do – talk more than most, and my voice, unhappily at times, seems to carry; but aged nine I was no taller than most of my class mates. The tallness came later. In my first few years in ballet class I was even considered a 'short leg'.

Not long before that fiasco at the pool, there had been another, my first appearance on stage; also my last, I swore at the time. I was supposed to lead a troupe of Daisies on stage for our dance in my ballet teacher's annual concert. It was very grand. A proper theatre was hired, with a great swishing curtain. Our mothers had to make costumes, and we had proper stage make-up. The seniors pranced around in tutus. Only the tinkling piano and scratchy record-player set up in the orchestra pit spoiled the illusion.

Things began badly, first when Mum made it clear the whole family was coming. Dad was going to run me to the theatre an hour earlier, but by the time he'd discovered a puncture and changed the wheel on the car, I got there with only ten minutes to spare to find Miss de Latour nearly beside herself, and punctures no excuse at all.

What happened was hardly my fault. It wasn't that the person working the record-player got the wrong record, only that he put the needle down about a quarter of the way through, and with unbelievable ill luck, right at the point where the first theme was repeated. Of course, I would never have started had I heard strange music from the pit. I skipped confidently out; after a few bars I realized that we were well out of phase with the music.

A real pro, as Miss de Latour told me later, would have gone on regardless. We would, she said, have finished the dance well after the music had finished. The father working the record-player might have been able to give us some more music. It would have been messy, but the audience, recognizing adult bungling, would have forgiven us. It was clearly going to take her a while to forgive me taking the law into my own hands. I had stopped in mid-*pas-de-chat*, put hands on hips, and not once, but twice said to the man below in the orchestra pit, 'You got the music all wrong. Can we start again?' I nearly brought the house down. At that point Miss de Latour high-heeled her way on to the stage, bundled all the bewildered Daisies off, and made some light-hearted comment to the amused audience. In the dress circle, most of my family were under the seats, except for my darling three-year-old sister, who yelled 'There's Alex, she looks funny,' as I shuffled off.

It was the last straw. Second time round, the dance went okay, but I was sick of the whole thing. Curtseying to the applause at the end, I caught a glance from the record-player man. If looks could kill, I'd have gone down like a Dead Swan. I fled from the stage the wrong way, pushed past a flutter of false eyelashes waiting to go on, and in the empty make-up room plastered my face with greasy cold cream and returned my face to normal. I changed into my clothes, crept out the stage door, and into the spare seats at the very back of the dress circle, where I glowered away alone while the senior students did their Little Swans and Bluebirds and the whole of *Peter and the Wolf*. I envied the girl dancing Peter in Russian peasant breeches and cropped hair, she was very nimble with her red boots. One day I'd be Peter: brave, adventurous and famous.

'I loved the Daisies, dear,' Gran said kindly from the front seat of the car. The rest of us, including Mum, were all squashed into the back in layers. 'You danced very nicely.'

I don't want to dance 'nicely', I fumed inwardly, ignoring the snorts from various quarters. I want to dance like a Bluebird, superbly.

'Mind you,' Gran was going on, 'with those legs, I don't think you'll ever . . .'

'What's wrong with my legs?'

'Too long! Not yet, but look at your parents!'

Sabotaged on all fronts, I can remember thinking, 'I don't want to be tall. I don't want to always have to lead the stupid Daisies or whatever. I want, I want . . . ' but I didn't really know what it was I wanted. Except not to have people laugh at me.

My fingertips slice open the water. Briefly I'm an arrow, piercing the blue with every muscle taut, making the most of the thrust from the block.

I dare not trust my mid-flight ears. I think I heard the whistle for a false start. From bitter experience I know I cannot assume anything.

Legs begin to kick. The first strokes, and then with both relief and disgust I'm pulled up short by the rope. It's like a physical blow, rasping roughly across my arms and sending shock waves juddering down to my feet.

Damn and blast! False starts break the spell, break confidence, break rhythm, everything! One often leads to two, and then we're all in dead trouble.

We swim slowly back, trying to get shattered nerves together. Blast and damn you, Maggie; but at least that's one race you're not going to win with a flyer. In the water, a fair fight.

'If there's a break, go with it. Don't waste energy on getting angry.' Mr Jack's last words, among others. 'Use the time in the water to relax. Get out last. Keep them waiting those few seconds. Maggie will be just as thrown off balance.' So she will; so she is. Maggie hasn't done a false start in years. She's rattled.

I look at no one as I haul myself out last, shaking the water off my arms. The starter, immaculate in white, is already waiting to give his pep talk. Already I can feel the coldness seeping through my feet. A sweet man, but get on with it. We line up the second time.

'Take your marks.' We bend down, and then someone does it again. Maggie stays poised on the brink, so do I. The rest have gone in. Tears of frustration blur my vision. And fear: break on the third time and you're out, Alex, finish, kaput. A humiliating way to let you down, Andy.

The crowd has nearly gone wild. Again the pep talk, though this time we are allowed to get towels and track suit tops for a laughable attempt at staying warm. 'Take it easy, girls. Next one who breaks is out. I'll hold you till every last one is rock steady. There'll be no flyers here.' I look over to where Mr Jack and Dad are sitting, but there is only a blur of faces, eyes, spotlights. This is the event of these nationals, my long-awaited clash with Maggie, the fight to the death. A capacity house, fanfares, overture and beginners please. Reporters' pens dipped in blood. I badly need a pee.

Toes around the block. A dreadful hush. I am cold through and through, literally trembling at the knees, devoid of any thought. I only know that I must not allow myself to break; neither must I be so cautious I get left behind at the starting post and throw that vital fraction of a second and the race away.

'Take your marks!'

An intolerable silence. There's not a movement. About five hours pass. My ears are out on stalks.

Bang.

We hit the water as one. This time I notice that the water feels warm, a sure sign of creeping coldness.

We're off to see the Wizard . . .

2

I suppose it was just as well that the first time I was beaten by Maggie I was already established as Auckland junior champ and record-holder, with brilliant prospects for the future, or so the papers kept saying. Otherwise, I might not have put up with playing second fiddle for so long.

Through three summers I had cut a swathe of firsts and set more than a few local and national records. I trained about two and a half miles a day (twice a day in the long holidays). I wore my first Auckland rep royal blue blazer and went off singing
   My eyes are dim
   I cannot see
(not, in our case, from old age, but from badly chlorinated salt water)
   I have not bought my specs . . . with . . . ME
in rattly chartered buses with jovial drivers and chaperones to other towns, there to be billeted with swimming families. I learnt to swim straight, even in old pools of black, insect-ridden water; wind-swept, ill-lit, unheated, unhygienic, with cracked concrete surrounds and slimy wooden changing sheds full of the bugs that gave you athlete's foot.

I learnt what it was to be cold most of the time, waiting in the rain until ten at night for my final race, sodden towel over sodden tracksuit over sodden swimsuit over goose-pimpled body. I certainly learnt to stop when I came to the end of the pool. In freestyle, no one could touch me. I even won the odd backstroke, butterfly or medley race, putting a few noses out of joint. I learnt how to cope with victory.

The joyride ended one day in August, 1956, in the front room, listening with Dad to some fantastic new world records being set over in Queensland, Australia, during the run-up to the Melbourne Olympics. Dawn Fraser was triumphant in the sprint, beating her great rival Lorraine Crapp. Mum, as usual, was in the kitchen,

Gran was with her, knitting a sweater for one of us while watching Robbie learning to walk, and the other two were climbing trees outside. Dad turning the knob on the radio was saying quite nonchalantly:

'Four years from now, Alex? Rome?'

I shrugged. I wasn't going to let on I'd just been making that promise to myself. I'd be nearly sixteen, just right if all those amazing Aussies were anything to go by.

Even more carelessly, he continued, 'A little competition wouldn't be a bad thing.'

'What competition?'

'You're hoping to get to the junior nationals this season?'

'Yep.'

'And win a place in the sprint titles?'

'Try,' I lied. I knew from people's times, I had every chance of at least a place. If my times kept improving as they had last summer, I could even beat the fifteen-year-olds. Or so, with all the arrogrance of a not-quite twelve-year-old, I thought.

'Mmm. I hear from Mr Jack of a girl who's just arrived from Singapore. New Zealand parents, but she was born there.'

I wasn't actually all that interested, and moved to the piano.

'Name of Maggie. Maggie Benton. She's been swimming in races since she was two.'

'Since *when?*'

'Two, so I'm told. They swim all year round up there, every day. Kids learn to swim before they can walk, literally.'

I slid fluently up and down a B flat major scale, pianissimo.

'I'm told she's very fast. Strong build, not as tall as you, but wiry. Big feet. A worker. Fast.'

Another scale, A major. 'How fast?'

'Times are up to yours.'

A very loud and fast scale this time, A minor. Dad evidently felt he had done his duty, or perhaps he knew when to leave me alone, for I heard the door open. 'You need some competition, Alex, if Rome really is your aim. I think she'll provide it.'

A nonchalant arpeggio or two. 'Good,' I said.

The Olympic Pool opened at the end of October in a northerly gale that went on for days. Several yachts were wrecked in the harbour, and a bitter wind blew me off my bike, but nothing could keep me out of the pool. Under a massive black umbrella and grey plastic mac, doling out the daily half-mile stints of this and quarter mile of that, Mr Jack asked me if I'd met the newcomer, Maggie Benton.

'Who's she?' I knew perfectly well. Dad's warning had been niggling.

'Girl from Singapore, might give you a run for your money this season. Didn't your father mention her?'

'Oh, yes, vaguely. Did you say half mile straight, quarter kick, quarter arms only, quarter length sprints, twenty width sprints?'

He nodded. I went. In that wind, it was too cold to stand around, even to glimpse this Maggie Benton. There were only five or six people in the pool battling against the wind and waves, heavy going for the first outdoor swim of the season.

Two or three lengths into the half mile straight, I became aware of a female form, in black racers like me, several lanes away. I was not shaking her off. It was not a feeling I was used to, or that I liked.

At the end of the half mile, I leaned against the wall. It was not easy to see through the driving rain, but I knew talent when I saw it, heading off down the pool again. Easy arms, good rhythm, power. Some people just look right in the water; I know I do, and so did this girl.

Maggie Benton, herself.

We got used to each other, training on opposite sides of the pool, with her coach and his squad over the other side. We said polite hellos and goodbyes, and when we met up in the changing-room talked a bit about school and life in Singapore and where she lived now, but not much more. While maintaining an outward nonchalance, I watched her closely. She was smaller than me, wiry, even stocky, neat in everything, pretty too, in a *Seventeen* model sort of way. She didn't seem to talk much to anyone. Those first few weeks, until we all got some tan, she was even whiter than the rest of us. 'Tropical pallor, but don't let it fool you,' said Mr Jack. Her stroke rate was faster than mine, and I could see she knew what hard work was.

I also noted a stop-watch being expertly wielded by a well-dressed lady, always clacking round the concrete in high heels, obviously her mother. Not discreetly enough, however; Mr Jack had already noticed that she was clocking my time trials. I knew by now that behind his Tweedledum appearance and jolly Aussie teddybear act lay the sharpest pair of eyes and ears around the pool. 'Some nerve!' he said. 'And some joy she'd be having, too. Her length sprints are about point five faster than yours.'

'How do you know?'

He looked around, innocent as Winnie-the-Pooh. 'Ssshh.'

'You've been timing her, too!'

'What me? A sneaky thing like that? Never!' But his eyes were looking past me and I noticed a slight jerk of the hand tucked inside his raincoat. Up the other end of the pool Maggie had just finished a length sprint. 'Never! Besides, the time to crack the whip'll be next week.' After a decent interval, he looked at his stop-watch. 'That, by the way, was thirty-two point one seconds. Not bad for the end of a session. She's consistent.'

I was both dreading and looking forward to our first race. At least, we would both know then where we stood. Maggie had already appeared at a couple of club meetings; Dad had insisted that I give them a miss because I had so much on at school, a Gilbert and Sullivan musical, and other end-of-year and end-of-intermediate-school functions. My absence from the first few meetings and her times had already been noted in the press reports. 'NEW JUNIOR STAR' stated one headline after Maggie's first swim, which to my considerable annoyance happened to be an unofficial Auckland record for the distance as well. I read that 'the first clash between Miss Benton and the current Auckland title and record holder Alex Archer is awaited with great interest', and was noticeably quiet at breakfast that morning.

Maggie won, of course, by point three of a second. Why do I say 'of course'? I had lined up for that first race full of confidence. We exchanged a few words, amiably enough, as we awaited our race, a hundred yards over three lengths. I took note of the greater volume of cheers for me, mostly from our squad mates, when our names were called out.

She won. I led to the first turn, led to the second, and she fought me like a tiger all the way up the last lap. By then I knew I'd gone too fast too soon; knew that my training so far that season wasn't enough to sustain the pace. I was still tired from being

Ruth in the three performances earlier that week of the *The Pirates of Penzance*, our end-of-year production.

This time on stage I'd been in my element, and thrilled to bits when various teachers asked if I'd considered a stage career later on. I had, actually, and rather liked the prospect (after the Rome Olympics). All that leaping around in pirate costume in the second act, brandishing a sword, and projecting the patter song which had taken myself and the two boys most of the year to learn . . .

This particularly rapid, unintelligible patter
Isn't generally heard, and if it is it doesn't matter
Matter matter matter matter matter . . .

It was a good end to my two years at intermediate school.

But stage performances and swimming races don't mix. In the final yards of the race against Maggie I died. The announcer confirmed my fears. True, we'd both broken the Auckland record in the process, but that was little comfort.

We went to our first national championships together in February of 1957. Auckland's brilliant juniors, they called us, future senior champs, future Olympic Games team members with prospects for Rome. Reporters relished this rivalry. We got used to them hanging around, wanting quotes from us or our coaches. We were used to our frequent races during the season, used to each other. Or rather I got used to being second most of the time and to Mrs Benton's sickly smiles sweeping round the pool when Maggie won.

At the championships Maggie made a clean sweep, but I made her work for it. Less than half a second in the quarter-mile, point three in the two hundred and twenty yards, point one in the sprint. The crowds were enthusiastic, the Press likewise. Our clashes became headline news. Returning to Auckland, I turned the tables with one glorious one hundred and ten yards win in March, and further redeemed myself by setting a new national junior record to boot. Mrs Harold Benton did not smile at all that night.

Strange things happened to my body that third form year. I was twelve, so I will not bore you with the usual things that happen to twelve-year-old girls. Unlike my schoolmates who talked behind the bike sheds, I'd always known about babies and periods and wet dreams and French letters and things, which proved Mum (who'd been a nurse and could talk about such things) had done a better job than most. Fortunately, my periods soon settled into a regular routine, hardly noted from month to month except that on those days I took care not to hang around in my swimming togs. Maggie was rather less fortunate – some months she got such bad cramps that she had to take a couple of days off training.

And we both got rosebuds. Again I was glad that my Mum, unlike most, did not immediately whisk me off to a shop for my first bra. Lots of mothers could hardly wait to get their daughters all harnessed up, my friend Julia's for one, and Mrs Benton. Mum waited until I asked, the last girl in the class. I hated the loss of freedom. I went braless around the house, and even my togs, those awful limp cotton things we wore then, became something I enjoyed wearing. At the pool, in the water, I could be free.

I grew in all directions that winter. Soon I was nearly as tall as Mum, which is saying something because she is five feet ten and a half inches. Part of me rather hoped that I might equal her, which I never quite did; a sad part of me knew that I had grown past the point of no return for ballet, or even the stage as a career.

By the start of the next season, I was a strapping five foot seven and still growing and I'd decided if I couldn't play the part of Portia I was going to be a lawyer.

We had another baby in the house. Debbie had just gone off to school and along came another boy, christened Robert Albert after my long-dead grandfather. Mum smiled serenely from the chair where she seemed to spend most of her time plugged in to the baby. Gran washed nappies and cooked and mended and ironed and gardened and fed her hens. Dad worked long hours to get extra overtime pay, and helped with the shopping. For the rest of us, life went on as usual. If it sounds a bit mean to say I wasn't much affected by a new baby brother, that's the way it was. Naturally I was pleased, but I'd been through the baby bit twice before, and there was never any suggestion that Robbie's arrival should have any effect on my routine. Life went on; there were always clean pressed clothes and big meat pies, roasts, lemon custard puddings, and muffins or cheese scones when we got home from school.

It was Gran I worried about, and Mum did too, but nothing anyone said made the slightest difference. When she wasn't working away at the sink or ironing board, or pegging out clothes, Gran was in her little bedroom, which had become a tiny factory, producing beautiful baby dresses, pink and white, occasionally pale lemon, with elaborate smocking, the sort Royal babies are photographed in. Not for Robbie, obviously, but to sell in a very exclusive baby shop in town.

Sometimes I helped her with the more boring jobs like turning the sashes right side out and sewing on the delicate mother-of-pearl buttons which went down the back. She made them in batches of about twenty at a time. I thought it was a pretty hard way to earn money, but she seemed happy enough. When I asked her once who got the money between what she got for each dress and what I knew they cost in the shop, she simply didn't hear the question. I also wanted to ask what she did with the money she did earn, because she certainly didn't spend it on herself, but the look in her eyes warned me off. A long time later, I found out. We were two of a kind, Gran and me.

Next summer, Christmas of '57, came and went, more of the same. Maggie won all the national junior titles going, set records in every event, and narrowly missed selection for the Empire Games in Cardiff. I was an honourable second. How I pushed her to all those records!

And again, at the very end of the summer, I got everything right just once. I needed that sprint record badly. I'd been seriously thinking of retiring gracefully, and telling Mr Jack I'd had enough. It wouldn't be easy, I was his star pupil, his first real champ. I'd be failing him, too. The papers were generous: 'After a season of pushing Maggie Benton to one title and one record after another, Alex Archer hit form with a brilliant sprint performance at the Olympic Pool last night. She trailed her great rival at the halfway mark, but fought back splendidly to win by a fraction in record-breaking time, confirming that her potential for Rome is virtually as good as that of Miss Benton.'

'Just shows what you can do after four months' solid training,' said Mr Jack. 'Give me a year of your life, and the sky's the limit.'

But how could I, even for Rome? I was too busy. That year, 1958, I got an Honours pass in my piano exam, and although I knew that I could never be a professional dancer, I still loved my lessons and flew through the exam. I got involved in the junior musical production, which was a very boring version of *The Emperor and the Nightingale* especially written for schools, with fake oriental music and slanty eyebrows. I shuffled around as a courtier, singing a solo and saying my few lines through a long drooping moustache that fell off on the first night in the middle of my song and temporarily put the chorus out of action with the giggles.

In the winter term I played hockey in the school Junior First Eleven team. School exams were a pain, but I got respectable marks with a minimum of work. The days were so packed, I hardly saw the family. Through the winter, Dad took me to training at five thirty am (my first winter training, with the eye problems that went with it). I ate breakfast after the rest of the family, got home from school/lesson/rehearsal just in time to have a meal, then disappeared for homework, or piano practice. Weekends were almost as bad, though I occasionally escaped from Jamie and Debbie squabbling and Robbie throwing three-year-old tantrums and went out to help Gran with her baby dresses. I was as happy as a sandboy, and riding for a fall.

There's my story up to the end of 1958. I'm fourteen years and one month old, five foot ten and one-quarter inches, about to go into the Fifth Form to sit School Certificate, which I don't expect to fail. I'm a 'brilliant prospect' for Rome, a talented stage performer and musician, and I've a reputation for saying what I think. I'm popular in the swimming crowd. I train with the boys because they make me go faster. I don't have time for 'normal feminine pursuits' like dating, or buying clothes or records. Besides, with all my lessons/petrol/pool entrance money/track suits/trips away, and three other children coming up behind, there's no money spare for Elvis the Pelvis. I've a working relationship with Maggie, but don't ask me what I think of her mother. I hate coming second, though I've had plenty of practice at it.

Can I have 1959 again?

Warm water, glaring underwater lights, and the black shark that is Maggie right alongside me. Surprisingly, my arms feel good, rhythm feels good, at one with the water. It's not always so, especially after false starts; five seconds into a race your chest can be tight, arms sluggish and legs like lead. Then it's hard going all the way, fighting the water, fighting pain and anger.

Anger. Now there's an interesting sort of fuel. After the events of today, I'm fairly loaded with it, and taking off like a rocket. Ten yards down and still I've not taken a breath.

We're spread out in a line across the pool. Soon, about a third of the way down, one head will be seen by the crowd to be marginally in front, the point of the arrow. It must be me. But beware, not only Maggie, but the complete outsider who could beat us both to the turn and then hang on like grim death. Unlikely, but not impossible. In sprints, settled in hundredths of a second, stranger things have happened.

People ask me what I think about when I'm swimming. Right now I hate everyone. I hate Maggie and what she might yet snatch from my grasp, and even more I hate adults who jump to conclusions and spread untrue gossip.

First round is to me. On this lap, where the water is smooth, I can see Maggie's white bathing cap cruising along when I take my first breaths. Hey, Andy . . . I'm about a hand's breadth in front.

There's a long way to go yet, Alex.

3

MEMO TO MYSELF. AIMS FOR 1959.
- *Become national sprint champion. You can. It just means beating Maggie.*
- *Pass my Grade seven piano, ballet exam, School Cert.*
- *Get in the First Eleven hockey team.*
- *Shut my big mouth. Be nicer to the brats.*
- *Look after Gran.*
- *Stop growing. I'm tall enough.*

Signed: Alexandra Beatrice Archer
1 January, 1959

Enough for one year. I folded the page carefully, buried it under my mattress, and mused. Even as I wrote that summer morning, with the sun streaming in the window on to my hair (only just dry from training, and acquiring a distinctly greenish tinge from chlorine), I felt weighted down, not with all my goals, but with something else, something new I couldn't define. It wasn't just the previous late night, a New Year's Eve barbecue at one of my swimming friends. I had the feeling that I wouldn't want to know what a crystal ball might tell me about the year ahead.

We'd had a pep-talk at the end of the year about choosing our exam subjects and 'setting yourself realistic goals'. Who'd said that? Not The Gillies, for sure. No, it was Nipples, Miss Hunt, who wore tweed suits with very skimpy sheer blouses, took English and was supposedly the 'Vocational Guidance Counsellor'. 'You must decide, girls. Do you want to strive towards degrees, diplomas, achievements, to be a *career girl*? Or the greater and more realistic satisfaction of motherhood and family?'

Realistic? To win a national title at fifteen? Plenty of Aussies had, Ilse Konrads for one. To be an Olympic rep? There was a team going, someone had to be lucky. To want to do law, to do something challenging? I knew two boys from the school where

Andy went who wanted to be lawyers. Why not me? To do something worthwhile with my life, earn more money and have less worries than Dad does? Why not? A husband, children, a nice house somewhere, maybe I could have those as well.

Why did our teachers tell us how marvellous it was being a good wife and mother, when they themselves were not? Did that mean they considered themselves failures? But some of them had pretty interesting lives: for their holidays they travelled overseas, went climbing, tramping, skiing, wrote books. It didn't make sense.

We'd all been asked what we wanted to do when we left school. Many of us would be fifteen soon, said Nipples, and would be assessing how many more years of schooling remained. It was to be hoped that we would all want to try at least for our School Certificate, an important qualification for the jobs open to girls. Some would go on to University Entrance, one or two might even want to try for a university scholarship in their Upper Sixth Form year. She made a scholarship sound both dull and unattainable.

We had all sorts in our class. Sober sorts like me; dizzy sorts who hung around milk bars after school, with or without bright red lipstick; tough types with stained tunics and pony-tails, serving time until their fifteenth birthday when we wouldn't see them for smoke; several who were in with the private school set and spent their entire August holidays skiing and their May ones going to private dances (the record was twenty-two invitations for two weeks of holidays, but then she was both stunning of face and reputedly 'fast').

In response to Nipples' bored voice reading out the class list, we all mumbled our ambitions, some truthfully, some not. A few said they might end up working in a shop, or a factory as a machinist or packer or something. The usual replies were training college, nursing, secretarial college, home science, and then travel. One said journalism, two or three arts degrees, one fine arts. I said law, but I was the only one who did.

Even my close friend Julia, who I'd known since we started primary school together and wanted to be a doctor more than anything in the world, said nursing. 'Why did you say that?' I demanded after class. 'You don't want to be just a *nurse*.'

'Nothing wrong with nursing.'

'No, but . . . you come top in maths, chemistry, biology, Latin, the lot. Anyone can be a nurse.'

'Maybe.' She refused all further discussion on the subject, until she came around a few days before Christmas to bring me a present. Her father, she told me wheezily, had insisted that he couldn't afford to put two sons through university *and* a daughter through medical school. Naturally it was more important that James and Charles, etcetera. Besides, she was his most precious only daughter and he didn't approve of women doctors. 'That's rot,' I said. Her brothers were both creeps, and were going to be creepy things like accountants and stockbrokers. 'And you just took that as gospel?' I asked.

'Mum agreed with him,' said Julia. 'She said she couldn't bear the idea of me going away to Dunedin for six years to cut up bodies. She just wants to keep me at home, or at least in Auckland. And then Dad trotted out my asthma. I'd not be strong enough for years of swot and stress, dissecting rooms and lab work and operating theatres, and wards full of cancer patients and loonies and neurotic women and dying children. That's what he said, his words.'

'But nursing's just as hard, harder in some ways. Mum has always said it's the nurses who take the real brunt. Front line troops and all that.'

'Try telling that to my parents. What I haven't told them or even you yet, is that I want to do obstetrics, deliver babies, do research into methods of childbirth. I know they would say, I'll never get a night's sleep.' She shrugged, bitterly, wheezily, looking lost, the shadows under her eyes darker than usual and her jawline puffy. The more I heard about other peoples' parents the more perplexing it all was. Julia might have been asthmatic, but it wasn't as bad now as when she was in primary school and there was no doubt about her brain, she'd won every science prize going as long as I could remember. I hugged her and wiped away her tears and rubbed the knobbles up and down her thin back until the wheezing noise had quietened down a bit. 'Julia, don't lower your sights.'

'There's been the most almighty row already. Dad shouting and telling me how cruel I am, upsetting Mum like that, can't I see all she wants is my happiness.'

'You've got two years yet. It won't make any difference to what subjects you do for School C, will it? I don't know why you told them so soon.'

'It just slipped out. We had a sort of uncle visiting from Australia, a second cousin of Mum's, something high up in insurance on transfer back here for a year. Somehow I told him, and it came out at the dinner table, you know . . . I suppose he thought they might be proud of me, or something . . . '

'Well, they might learn to be.'

'Not my father. He'll use my asthma . . . '

'Haven't the doctors always said you'll grow out of it? And aren't there all sorts of new drugs coming through? There'll be a way,' I said, but without total conviction. Her father was a factory manager, a tough nut to crack.

'I'm sorry, but it's nice of you to ask me.'

'Miss Archer, I don't think you understand,' said the man calling long-distance from somewhere near Wellington. 'Our new pool is the best in the North Island. This Gala Opening is the climax of three years' fund-raising. We've lined up water ballet, diving, gymnastics, bands, marching girls, a carnival queen contest, even a rock 'n' roll group. Our Member of Parliament will be there, and the Mayor and . . . '

'If you've got all that, you don't need me.'

'Oh yes . . . '

'It's only four days before the nationals. I'd have to taper off my training a week earlier, and I haven't got that sort of time.'

'We're relying on you and Miss Benton. A Grand Invitation one hundred and ten yards, climax of the evening, sneak preview to the championships. In country areas like this, our people seldom get the chance to see a duel between two such great rivals.'

'Is Maggie coming?'

'Yes, she accepted immediately. Actually, we were hoping that you might come down together.'

Not on your nellie. With her mother? 'I can't.' Disconcerted by his persistence, I added, unwisely, 'Put her against the boys.'

A horrified silence. 'Boys? Girls don't swim against boys.'

'I'm joking, Mr . . . Sorry I didn't hear what your name was. I'm known for my funny sense of humour.'

'My name is Cleverly. Well, naturally, we'd pay your airfare, and my wife and I would be delighted . . . '

'I can't race Maggie four days before the nationals. I'll just be getting over the Auckland champs, which everyone says she's going to win anyway. I'm sorry.'

He tried a last tack. 'We've already had the posters printed.'

Oh, help. I wavered. Perhaps I *could* go straight from there to the nationals in Wellington. Who with, and how, and where did I stay when I got there? It would only work if Dad was prepared to come with me, and he was in the middle of his two weeks' annual leave right now and he'd never before been able to get any extra time off, even when Mum had babies. But surely the poster was Mr Cleverly's problem, not mine. He should have asked sooner.

He sensed my hesitation. 'Couldn't you come down with Miss Benton and go straight on to your championships? Or fly down and we'll fly you home the next day? It's just one event, one exhibition race . . . ?'

With Maggie it was never just that, and especially now. 'I'm sorry. These nationals are too important to me . . . '

'To give something back to the sport that supports you?'

'That's not . . . ' very fair, I was saying, to myself.

'I'd like to speak to your coach, if you don't mind. Can I ring him at the pool?'

Did I have any choice? 'Yes, any time. He's the assistant manager there,' I said wearily. Three weeks to the nationals. Training was a twice daily ordeal and time trials a nightmare. I was having sunburn problems, and sinus problems, and rash problems with my swimming togs. Maggie's time trials were getting better and better. The Auckland champs next week were going to be a Maggie Benton benefit, I knew already. I didn't need some smooth-talking organizer on my back as well.

'I'll ring him right away,' he said, adding, 'perhaps I should have rung him first.' And the line went dead. I went to find Dad in the garden. 'Unfortunate timing,' he grunted, in between swipes at the hedge with a nasty-looking sickle. 'A hard decision for you, but I've no doubt the right one. These people . . . how do you get through to them?' He paused, maybe to emphasize his next words. 'Be prepared for some flak.'

'The right decision, Alex,' said Mr Jack when I saw him at the pool later in the day. 'I had to tell that persistent fellow to stop putting the acid on. You don't race to order, mine or anyone else's.

He should, of course, have gone through the proper channels first, rather than coming to you direct. But the result would've been the same. Be prepared for some flak.'

'That's what Dad said.'

'I mean real flak. Our friend's taking it higher. Centre officials and Press. Pressure will be exerted. You'll be accused of bad sportsmanship, among other things.'

Across the pool, Maggie was resting between time trials and getting an earful from her mother, who was using her stop-watch quite openly now and writing my times down in a little book.

'I *can't* go.'

'Agreed. I'll support you. I'll talk to any Press who come stirring. You, my girl,' he poked a stubby finger, 'would be advised to say nothing.' Behind the genial smile, the warning was clear. 'Now, half mile straight, two quarters time trial, four two hundred and twenties . . .'

And a thousand length sprints, I thought wearily, as I looked down the pool for a free lane and patted down the large piece of sticking plaster under my arm which covered a patch of raw skin, the chafing of tens of miles. Why do I do it?

That was a question I asked myself more than once in the next few weeks as I pushed Maggie to new junior records in all the Auckland champs, and we both put in some long hard grind in preparation for the nationals. The rest of the country was on holiday, sporting in the sun.

The flak from my refusal to race against Maggie in the Manawatu gala had been short, 'a storm in a teacup', as Mum said mildly, but some sharp things were said by various officials in the papers. Mr Jack did his bit to defend me but it all read as though I was a spoilt brat. A centre official, upright in navy blazer and indignation, arrived during training one night and kept Mr Jack in the office and us waiting for nearly half an hour. 'Sorry about that, team' was all he'd say when he returned to finish our time trials. 'Keep smiling, Alex,' he added when we'd mercifully finished, and Andy and I were sitting gasping on the side of the pool. 'Interesting, really. You need officials to run the races, just like they need swimmers to compete. But it's not the officials who get up at five in the morning, day in, day out, and they need to be reminded of that, occasionally. The problem comes when money starts talking. It seems those people have spent a fair whack on their pool opening. You were the only thing money couldn't buy. My God, Alex, that man Cleverly didn't offer you any, did he?'

'No, course not.'

He whistled, a long tired phew of relief. There was more to being a coach than just standing on the side of the pool dishing out schedules. Mr Jack absorbed all my worries like a big comfortable sponge.

'Do you think I should go?'

'No. But next time don't talk to these people, officials, organizers, what-not. Put them on to me, straight off. That's what I'm here for.'

One night I found myself in the changing-sheds with Maggie. It may have been deliberate; generally we preferred to change at different times. She had parked her English dress and the beautiful American petticoat which made the dress stick out like a lampshade unusually near my limper version and Gran-made sun-dress. As we dried and dressed, we exchanged pleasantries, but this day there was more. She was a neat girl, was Maggie, controlled in everything she did, but she seemed to be taking her time rolling up her towels. Finally, she said, 'I'm sorry you're not coming to that thing in Manawatu next week. You could've come in the car with us, and then on to Wellington.'

'Oh, well, you know why. It's been splashed about the papers enough,' I said ungraciously.

She dried her dark curls in front of the mirror, carefully arranging the fringe and side bits in kiss-curls like Audrey Hepburn. 'I hate long car trips. It would've . . . '

She dried up. I looked at her sharply from under my own spiky hair. Would've what? Been nice, been fun? Perhaps, with only a much younger sister, she would've actually enjoyed my company, any company, deflecting for a while the unrelenting beam of her mother's attention. 'It's even longer in the bus.'

'Yes, but there's lots of singing. And getting out to buy fish 'n' chips and fizzy drink, things I'm never allowed 'cause Mother thinks they're bad for me. And games and . . . '

I looked at her even more curiously. Come to think of it, Maggie only rarely went on the bus trips. Usually her mother took her in their great big Austin car. 'You sound like you don't much want to go yourself. They'll make a big fuss of you. Queens in white kid gloves and the Member of Parliament. Bands and marching girls. Lovely.'

She pulled a face at the mirror. 'A lot of pompous speeches, and strange people. And fuss. I hate fuss.'

She did? I had always thought she coped with fuss remarkably well, always pleasant to reporters, obliging to photographers, polite to officials; unlike me, who was known to have been terse with all three. 'Then why did you say you'd go, straight off, the man said.'

'It wasn't straight off. We talked about it first, then we rang Mr Upjohn and he accepted for us. Mum thought I should.'

'The lying hound! That man, I mean,' I added hastily. So she'd done everything right, been through all the proper channels. 'And I suppose she thought I should, too.'

'Yes, um, no, I mean . . .'

'She said as much in the paper.'

'That's only her. In your position I'd have done the same.'

In *my* position? But there was no irony in her voice, no sideways smile, nothing to suggest she was playing games with me. She meant just what she said. I relented a bit.

'You'll enjoy it when you get there. They're good kind people really, if you don't include that Mr Clever Dick. Three years raising money, it's a big thing for them.' It wasn't original: Mum's contribution, actually, to our family discussion on whether I should have gone. (Verdict: Not guilty.)

'I suppose so. Still, I wish you were . . . well, see you.' As she zipped up her bag and left abruptly it occurred to me for the first time that Miss Maggie Benton, Olympic prospect, soon to be *Weekly News* cover girl and darling of the Press, could actually be rather lonely.

Well, Maggie went off to be the star turn at the opening, while I trained like a mad thing during the final run-up to the nationals: thousands of sprints and starts and turns. Fat lot of good it did me. Maggie, rested, cheerful and confident, was already in Wellington when we arrived after a dreadful bus trip that took over twelve hours. Half the team sick, and the bus getting slower and slower, finally grinding to a halt. Electrical problems or something. By the time we arrived, we were all dying of hunger, or boredom; or frantically trying to sleep.

It was a rotten start to the week, too. The champs were at a new pool, but four events and two relays were more than enough, with heats and finals morning and evening. Sure, I had the minor satisfaction of edging out two former rivals in my best times ever, and Mr Jack was full of theories that this was exactly what he wanted in the two-year run-up to Rome. And, again, the wiser reporters said nice things about me as well, but it was Maggie who climbed to the top of the victory dais.

After the nationals it was straight back to school, where I was treated (just for a morning) as a returning hero rather than the 'also-ran' that I thought I was. Four silvers in national senior titles were enough to warrant special mention at assembly, with La Constantia in full flight, burbling on at great length about individual achievement and all-round ability and hauling me up on the stage to be gawked at by seven hundred pairs of eyes.

'A credit to the school, Alex. Well done and good luck,' she finished. Hearty round of applause from the serried ranks of black gym tunics while I shuffled about in front of the senior teachers lining the stage like a row of smiling black cats, all smug and comfortable.

Had I but known, it was not to be long before the claws came out, mine as much as anyone's. Soon America would shoot two monkeys into space, the Chinese would march into Tibet, and Aucklanders would queue to see Dame Margot Fonteyn dance *Giselle* with the Royal Ballet and/or hear Billy Graham. In the same month, the Auckland harbour bridge would open for business, I would go to my first dance and someone would whisper that Alex Archer was really rather a mannish sort of girl with her broad shoulders and flat chest and slim hips and long legs, always hugging other girls after her races – and nothing would ever be quite the same again.

Concentrate!

One hand has brushed the corks that make up the lane ropes. That might cost me a hundredth of a second, and the race. Can't you swim straight, even now, just once, Alex, your last chance?

Concentrate! The turn is coming up. It must be nothing less than perfect. Races and trips have been decided on a single turn.

Into deeper water, darker blue glass. On both sides, through the criss-cross patterns of underwater lights, are bodies hard at work. I'm leading.

And not only by a hand, more an arm's length. What has happened? 'Go out hard,' Mr Jack said. (I've done that.) 'Pile on the pressure.' (That too.) 'You'll need every bit you can get for the return journey, flying blind.'

The turn, idiot! Where are the red lane markers, the black lines on the bottom of the pool, to judge how far? I have a moment of sheer panic that I've missed them and am about to slam into the wall. I'm nine years old again.

I got all three turns right in the two hundred and twenty yards two days ago. It was one of those races where everything clicked. That, and pushing myself past the pain barrier into a silence where I swear I heard Andy call my name, was why, contrary to all expectations, I won it! The quarter-mile on Tuesday had been Maggie's. I had to win the two hundred and twenty to stay in the running. One each, then, and Mrs Benton up to all sorts of mischief. Why can't you just leave Maggie and me alone to slog it out?

This is the decider, here and now, for Rome. May the best woman win, and her mother go to hell.

Despite the false starts, I'm feeling good. I'm flying over the water with that delight in my own speed, my own power, which only comes when everything is right. Make the most of it. The pain, the real work is yet to come.

Five yards to the turn. Right or left arm will touch? Alarm bells ring. Prepare to dive!
Help me, Andy!

4

'Who will you ask?' said Mum, as I stared at the blue frilly-edged card that waited for me after school. Three girls – one of them Maggie Benton – were inviting Miss Alexandra Archer and Partner to a dance to be held at some cabaret I'd never heard of, 20 May, 1959. RSVP by 10 May.

'What did she ask me for?' I said. 'I'm not in her crowd. And she's still fourth form.' It was a small satisfaction to me that she was.

'Don't you want to go?'

'Suppose so.' Translation: No I don't, because I'm scared stiff. Who with, and what do I wear, and how do you foxtrot let alone quickstep! I half-hoped that Mum would tell me, as she always had before, that I was still too young for teenage dances; it was different for Julia or my classmates who were mostly a year older. Mum was, however, saying nothing of the kind. She was off on a tangent of her own.

'Makes me feel quite old.'

'What does?'

'Daughter going to her first dance. Mine was a country hop, I was fifteen and taller than you. All the girls huddling down one side of the hall and the boys down the other, glaring at each other. Kids screaming up and down on the white powder they put down to make the floor slippery. Dads out the back with the beer, Mums watching their daughters like hawks.'

'Sounds like nothing has changed,' I said, thinking of a certain mother I knew.

'Ancient band of piano, sax and drums. Awful. And if your partner was the boorish sort, and most were, or you were unusually tall or even if you weren't, he'd sneak out the back for a beer. You'd end up a wallflower. Fate worse than death.'

'Did anyone actually dance?'

'Oh yes, enough. Quite often women together, fed up with sitting around waiting.'

'Mum, I don't think I want to go to Maggie's dance. It sounds too . . . too grand for me.'

'Oh dear, Gran was so looking forward to making your first formal dress.'

'She can do that later. Fifth Form, Sixth Form dance or something. Anyway, who could I ask?'

'Andy, surely? Well, think about it, Alex. I mean that about a dress. And Dad'll teach you to do the foxtrot. With all your ballet, you'll pick it up in two minutes.'

Clever old Mum. And cunning. She'd answered all my worries. Of course I could ask Andy, my swimming and special friend since primary school days, three years older and just a bit taller than me. He was in his last year at school sitting scholarship exams. He'd done all sorts of sports: First Fifteen rugby in the winter, tennis, a bit of water polo, surfing, but mostly swimming and yacht racing. Since we were juniors, we'd trained together during the long summer holidays once exams were over. I chased him on time trials up and down the pool. He usually made the Auckland champs finals; he was my keenest supporter as I progressed towards national level. We'd shared lots of things: books like Homer's *Odyssey* and Kingsley Amis' *Lucky Jim*, radio Goon Show jokes, and music. While most people were falling over Elvis, Ray Charles, Bill Haley and the Comets, Dean Martin, Pat Boone, even Little Richard (serious question: why are all pop stars men?) he introduced me to Noel Coward, Gershwin and Errol Garner, and I introduced him to ballet and musicals. We shared great ambitions. I was the only person in the world who knew what he really wanted to do. His father thought it was medicine, but I knew differently.

I knew Andy could dance, because he'd complained bitterly two or three years before about his father making him learn ballroom dancing. Then he'd actually enjoyed it, and I felt . . . jealous? Still a child, which I suppose I was then.

I decided to go to Maggie's dance when I heard several others in the swimming crowd had also been invited. Andy was happy to oblige. I went shopping with Mum and Gran for material and a pattern. Dad marched me around the living-room and pronounced me a 'quick learner', (to my disgust) 'easy to lead', and I wrote a formal letter in my best handwriting on stiff paper. 'Miss Alexandra

Archer thanks Maggie Benton, Susan Clarkson and Tania James for their kind invitation . . .'

Maggie was simply holding out the hand of friendship, I reassured Julia, who seemed to think there was some ulterior motive behind the invitation. I couldn't for the life of me imagine one, and neither could she, when pressed. I hadn't seen Maggie in weeks. The season had fizzled out, and we were taking a break. Training, when it started again at the beginning of the May holidays, would be for real, with heavy distance work, calisthenics and weights.

Not that I was twiddling my thumbs. I had end-of-term tests at school, hard work at my new piano pieces, ballet twice-weekly and rehearsals for *The Wizard of Oz*, the current school show, which somehow I'd auditioned for and ended up in. We'd had the first trials for the hockey teams; I saw myself going straight from Junior to Senior First Eleven, right half.

Maggie's dance, middle weekend of the holidays, loomed. Gran and Mum talked on about their first dances, putting your hair up and stuff on your eyelashes and biting your lips to make them pink; country hops, rugby club socials, church dances and city balls; debutantes, hovering chaperones and men in white gloves and patent leather dancing pumps. It all sounded a long way from waltz and rock 'n' roll at a 1959 teenage dance. The kids, home and fighting fit, didn't let a day go past. Andy, my friend, had suddenly become 'the boyfriend'. Like dogs, they knew their victim.

'What's that for?' Andy, done up in suit, tie, pink carnation but no Brylcreem because he knew I hated the stuff, was holding out a small bunch of flowers.

'You, clot.'

'How did you know I was wearing pink?'

'I asked you last week.'

So he had, a special phone call, for this very reason. I'd been rather rude, demanding why he wanted to know.

'You put it on your left shoulder,' he said.

'I do?' The brats all danced around the hall, jeering, while Andy pinned the silver-wrapped stalk to my dress, and I prayed my breath smelt okay and the Tangee Natural lipstick was on straight and I hadn't overdone the mascara. 'Hey Mum, the boyfriend's brought flowers, oooh,' shouted Robbie, while Jamie did an Elvis: 'A *white* (wiggle of hips) 'sports coat' (another wiggle) 'and a pink car-

NATion', until Dad appeared to rescue me ('That's enough Jamie,' in the low voice he kept for last warnings) and shake Andy's hand. 'Nice to see a man is punctual.' Mum and Gran leaned against the archway at the other end of the hall, giving me a final once-over. It was a nice dress, coral pink satin cotton, with a boat neckline, wide belt, and full circle skirt. Even with the extra pounds I'd put on in the lay-off from training, it had crossed my mind I could almost pass for something out of *Seventeen*.

But I simply couldn't understand why I, used to standing up in front of crowds of people, was feeling such stage fright. And with Andy! It was ridiculous, although he did look mildly uncomfortable himself.

'Off you go then,' said Dad through the commotion. I sailed grandly through wall-to-wall family, clutching my white nylon stole as the brilliant May night hit my bare arms.

'Chilly,' I said, making for the car door. Andy was quicker and beat me to the handle. 'I can do that.'

'No, let me.'

He'd taken me home from training in his mother's Volkswagen many times. 'You've never opened doors for me before,' I said.

'I've never taken you to a d-d-dance before.' We fell into the car and an uneasy silence. The VW didn't run to a radio.

I've been cherishing – Through the perishing
Winter nights and days – A funny little phrase
That means – Such a lot to me
That you've got to be
With me heart and soul
For on you the whole – Thing leans.

It was easier singing Noel Coward than talking, so I took the cue,

Won't you kindly tell me what you're driving at
What conclusion you're arriving at?

I'd noticed before that, when singing, Andy didn't stutter, even the d words, which were sometimes d-d-a problem before he found another word to use. He sang the answer,

Please don't turn away – Or my dream will stay
Hidden out of sight
Among a lot of might-
Have-beens!

and together we sang the rest of 'A Room with a View' which got us safely to the driveway of the cabaret. Cheerful groups of four and six at a time were getting out of other cars. I'd turned down Andy's offer of going to someone's house 'for drinks' beforehand. I began to fuss with bag and stole and white nylon gloves and skirts.

'Now, Alex Archer. You sit right there.'

'Why? We're going inside, aren't we? Isn't this the place?'

'The rules say a girl waits for the car door to be opened by her escort. Here beginneth the gospel according to Mrs Richmond, chapter one, verses one to t-t-sixty, read to me at great and tedious length before I left. So wait, damn you.'

Andy got out, locked his door, and came round to open mine with an Elizabethan flourish. I stepped out, Marilyn Monroe from her limousine, Audrey Hepburn on a Roman holiday – no, Junoesque Jane Russell was nearer. Who you kidding, lady? Music was already coming from the hall, and figures could be seen moving around inside.

'Now you take my arm,' he said.

'So I don't trip on the stones in my high heels and fall over? Or get raped and pillaged on the way?'

'That's right.'

Our eyes met, and we both broke out laughing.

'This is ridiculous,' I snorted. 'Let's get on with it.'

'Lead on.'

Running the gamut of the reception committee in the foyer was another matter. There was Maggie, lady-like in pale blue taffeta and pearls, her escort a Brylcreem ad, the other hostesses also desperate to do the right thing in front of their parents. It was a film set: chandeliers, flowers, silk dresses, hairdos, dinner jackets, air thick with perfume, the band playing Glenn Miller. This was a teenage dance! Fourth and Fifth Formers! I caught some stage whispers. 'That's Alex Archer. The swimmer. Big girl, huge,' that sort of thing. Maggie seemed pleased to see us. Mrs Benton was overboard with joy. After a quick once-over lightly of me and partner, her smile was warmth itself, her outstretched hand regally limp. My hands were cold, but hers was colder, a little broomstick of bones.

'Alex dear. How *well* you're looking.' (Translation: You've put on weight.)

'You know Andy Richmond?'

'Yes, of course. I've seen you training with Alex many times, haven't I? You're the young man who's hoping to do medicine. How nice of you both to come.' (Translation: I do my homework. Your partner is approved.)

We were saved by a blast from the band. 'Do go through,' she piped. 'The ladies' cloakroom is over there.' Her eyes were already on the next guests to be given the royal welcome.

Andy, nodding thanks for favours bestowed, took a firm grip on my elbow and steered me down the foyer's green swirled carpet. 'Spare me! Where's her tiara? You go in there,' he muttered, nodding towards a closed door marked Powder Room. 'The holy of holies.'

'The what?'

'The cloakroom. You leave your things in there.'

He knew what I was going through. It wasn't his first dance; he knew it was mine.

Inside there was much swishing of taffeta and plumping up of well-padded bosoms and straightening of stocking seams and re-glossing of mouths. I knew not one carefully-prepared face. For the first time in my life I was feeling my tallness, aware of curious stares in the mirror. The family was playing Monopoly at home tonight. I wished I was there.

Andy proved as easy to dance with as Dad. It was odd, being so close to someone, whose body (in swimming togs) I knew so well. I was just beginning to relax when a short gent in tails rushed into the middle of the room, all bonhomie and bright ideas. The snowball and excuse-mes passed as bad dreams, but at least I wasn't left standing, rather the opposite. Grasped by a lanky, acne-ridden youth with a fake English plum accent for the dance where they spun a beer bottle and if it pointed to your corner you were out, I prayed for the bottle to point at me. As the numbers dropped, and the little gent got more and more red in the face, my jitters rose. The waltz rhythm was completely beyond my partner; not that he was aware of it, as he held me rigidly at arm's length and talked about the harbour bridge being opened next week.

'They're having this walk across the bridge. A once-only chance for the proles.'

'Oh really?'

'Are you going?' he asked.

'Ah guess ah might.'

'Are you American?'

'Oh yes, ah come from Milwaukee.' It was the first place that flashed into my mind.

My prayers were finally answered. The bottle pointed and we were out. We slunk to the edges. I couldn't regain control of my hand. Andy, bless him, steered his partner round towards me as the winners were declared.

'How'd ya be?' he muttered.

'Awful.' I didn't know Andy's partner, frolicsome in pale pink polka-dotted frills and remarkably high stilettoes. We all grinned bleakly at each other.

'Sorry,' I said to Plum, 'What d'ya call yourself?'

'Christopher. Christopher Allardyce.'

It would be. I'd had enough, and since Polka-dot's arm was twined up Andy's, I had to escape by myself. I needed some fresh air and a pee, and to extricate my hand from the damp grip of Mr Allardyce.

'Excuse me, I need to visit the bathroom,' I heard myself say. Andy's face was a picture.

'The supper waltz is soon,' said Andy as I disengaged. It was all I could do not to wipe my hand on my dress.

'And?'

'May I have the pleasure?'

'Oh. Yes. Thanks.' Remembering, 'Sure, baby.' I had to cross acres of slippery floor, through couples standing stiffly round waiting for the next dance to begin. One boy seemed to move deliberately into my path, and his hips brushed along mine. 'Not bad, honeybun,' he breathed beerily into my ear. A cheeky hand cupped itself under the curve of my buttock, or would have, given fewer layers of petticoat. Thrown off balance, I went over on the side of one flimsy white sandal. Something gave. It was a strap, broken. I bent down, picked up the shoe and walked with as much dignity as I could summon into the sanctuary of the Ladies, and on into an empty toilet. If the overheated fumes of hairspray, deodorant, perfume and BO didn't knock you out first, there, at least, was privacy.

One strap pulled away and a whole shoe useless! Who designed these things? And who bought them, more fool me. As I stared at the shoe angrily, I heard the outside door swing open.

'Look at my stockings. Ripped to shreds. What a *clod*hopper! I'm going to have blue toes for a week.'

More of the same, two or three of them lamenting certain partners with feet like pile-drivers and girls who waltzed past drawing blood with stiletto heels spiking into unsuspecting ankles. I was beginning to wonder if dances were all they were cracked up to be.

'And I've got a bone to pick with mine, slimy creature. That gorgeous tall girl, the swimmer, I saw him when she went past.'

Uhh?

'You mean Alex Archer? Maggie's swimming pal? What a figure!'

'If you want to be six feet tall and built like a tank.'

'But you watch the boys, the looks she's getting.'

'Little do they know.' Darkly.

'Know what?'

Voice lowered. 'Well, you know.'

'I don't know.'

'Well . . . those great shoulders and slim hips. More like a man if you ask me. I've heard it said . . .' the voice faltered, for maximum effect.

'What?'

'I've a friend at her school who says it's no accident she always winds up being a male in their school plays. Apparently, she's always hugging the girls after races. And she's got this very special friend Julia at school. Imagine Maggie and Alex Archer in the same race. Hardly fair, really. Maggie's half the size.'

I could either wait until they'd gone, or throw a spanner in the works. Ears on fire, I decided I'd heard enough. Taking off the other shoe, I flushed the toilet, rearranged my dress, and stepped grandly out. It was worth it if only to see their faces. Such a rush of blood upwards. One was a proper little dumpling in scarlet lace and black gloves to her armpits, the other all crimpy permed and hung about with diamante. Barefoot, I smiled sweetly at them both before padding over to wash my hands. Within five seconds they'd snapped their clutch bags shut and fled.

My own cheeks were none too pale, either, flushed to a deep mottled purple under the terrible neon lights. From the pile of bags and stoles, I found the little evening bag Mum had lent me, got out a comb and forced myself to look myself in the eye. My hands were shaking. Is *that* what people were saying? Did they say it of Julia too? Was it peculiar to hug when you wanted to congratulate someone; odd to rub Julia's back when she got wheezy?

The door swung open again to admit another girlish gaggle,

cackling away. Their shiny faces swum in the mirror, one vaguely familiar from Maggie's swimming squad.

'Hi, Alex. How's things?'

If I ever needed my acting talents, it was now. 'Fine, thanks', I said. In the mirror I saw my gay, brittle smile and glinting eyes, and below them the wide ('great') shoulders I had been rather proud of.

'You cold? You're shaking.'

'Am I?'

'It's the supper dance next. Where're your shoes?'

I pointed to the floor. 'Come apart.'

'You poor thing. What're you going to do? You can't go around in your stockinged feet.'

'Why not?' I snapped, surprised that even she seemed to think it so important. 'Do I have any choice?' I swept past her out into the foyer, where the first person I saw was the faithful Andy, waiting just along from the door. I almost ran at him.

'Where're your shoes?'

'Why are people so obsessed with my shoes? One broke.' He was looking at me closely. 'Well, I didn't do it on purpose, did I? Stupid things. Someone pushed me over.'

'You all right?'

'Of course I'm all right. I'll just have to go barefoot for the rest of the evening, that's all. Do you mind too much? If people want to think it's because I can't bear being tall . . .'

'What's . . .?'

'. . . and I feel an overwhelming desire to be a normal female size, that's their business.' My voice was shrill. I couldn't help it.

'OK, OK. Let's d-d-dance. It's the supper waltz.' I felt a strong arm around my waist; I was being propelled towards the dance floor. I'd been about to ask him to take me home.

'That pill,' he said into my ear, 'what's-his-name, with the English accent . . .'

'Christopher something. What about him?'

'Frightfully put out, when I asked you to supper. He had the same idea, I could see a mile off. Muttered something in his beard and walked off.'

'Tough.' At this range he could see the tears in my eyes. I kept my face well turned to the left.

'You dance well, Alex. Much better than most.'

'Thanks.'

'What's with the Yankee accent? He wanted to know, were you an American F-Field Service scholar.'

'Stow it, Andy.'

I knew I was still shaking, and that Andy was aware of something peculiar going on. Then I saw one of my accusers, she of the tomato-red lace and heavy eyebrows, dancing with the dark fellow who had pushed me over. I glared at them both. Her eyes dropped immediately, he winked and leered. I made sure I was still glaring when she looked over again, with such a smirk on her face that the thought occurred that I might have been meant to overhear what I did, revenge for her boyfriend's finding me baggage worth handling. Cheap. And cruel. And yet – how many other tongues wagged? Why, why?

I put on a good show, with my stockinged feet and breaking heart, receiving curious looks and laughing it gaily off; through asparagus rolls, cheerios on sticks, chocolate log and fruit salad at supper; meeting a lot of people that Andy seemed to know; through the statue dance (I accidentally-on-purpose over-balanced very early on); and the last half hour of rock 'n' roll where, with things loosened up a bit and me past caring, I learnt very quickly how to rock around the clock tonight. Fast footwork and pirouettes were called for, and ballet came in handy. Andy could be forgiven for thinking I was enjoying myself; it was a dance of defiance, with skirts swirling high around my hips, and my long legs bared to stocking-tops and even suspenders for any who cared to look. One who did was Plum, lurking in the entrance with a cigarette drooping from his lips, and a twist to his mouth that said that rock 'n' rolling was beneath him. 'You made a hit there,' murmured Andy. 'Get me away,' I said, and instantly found myself in the thick of the crowd, away from his hungry eyes.

'Straight home?' Andy said, as the balloons came down after 'Auld Lange Syne' and all the little boys chased around popping them in their partners' ears.

I nodded. I'd needed all my stamina to last this long. A last visit to the Ladies to get my things and it would all be over. That was achieved, mercifully, without seeing anyone I knew. Maggie was at the door, saying goodnight. So, unluckily, was her mother. She still looked fresh and grimly gracious, not a permed hair out of place.

'Alex dear, wonderful to watch you dancing barefeet. Quite the belle of the ball.' (Translation: You were conspicuous. It is not done.)

'My shoe broke, Mrs Benton.'

'You must take it back.' (Translation: And get better ones.)

Andy intervened then, with loud thanks to all and sundry for a wonderful dance. I said about two words of thanks and left him to it. Down the steps and (painfully) across the gravel in my stockinged feet, and shortly the crunch of shoes catching up with me.

'That woman is a pain.'

'She also hates my guts. But Maggie's OK.'

'Where was f-f-father amongst that lot?'

'Overseas, on business. He's not around much.'

'Maggie didn't look as though she enjoyed her own d-d-dance much either, poor kid.'

Kid? Did Andy see me as a child, too? I was, after all, only a few months older. Too much had happened too fast. I could think only of getting home, to my own bed. I couldn't open the car door because Andy had to unlock it, a tedious wait in the bitter moonlight, which set me shaking anew. Then there was all the chivalrous bit again, before Andy drove off and there was another uneasy silence.

Couldn't they see that the only reason why I took male roles in school shows was that being at a girls' school someone had to.

And what about our Third Form year and getting swept up in the fashion for declaring your undying love for a certain senior girl? Mine had been Leonie, dark and Spanish-looking, a prefect, promising singer, lead in school shows, captain of tennis, A-team netball, now studying at the School of Music. I would have done anything she asked me. From the great heights of the Fifth Form I now knew this was simply innocent heroine-worship. It was love, of a kind. Everyone knew hero-worship went on at boys' schools, why not at girls'?

I suspected that two of the little thirds currently felt that way about me, nudging each other in corridors and thinking themselves unnoticed when they followed me home from school. But had I smiled at them, would that have set tongues wagging? Had it already? And my own classmates, old friends since primary days – did they edge away from me when I had to be a man in plays, or avoid contact in sardine assemblies, or wonder about the hug when you won a hockey match or holding hands for games? I knew they didn't. It was crazy! I hugged people because I was pleased for them, winning things, or it seemed to help when someone was in tears about something. I rubbed Julia's back at school sometimes because it seemed to help her wheezes. So what?

As we turned into my street, I remembered I'd been dreading the last bit, the kiss in the car or at the front door that was much discussed at school. Maybe Andy didn't even want to. ('Little did they/he know!') But he just sang a sad little song, *The party's over, It's time to turn out the lights*, as he pulled up outside the house, did his final escort duties, and gave me a brotherly hug on the front doorstep. 'Thanks for asking me, Alex. See you Saturday night, around six?'

'Saturday?'

'The Sixth Form dance? We've been asked to Jeff's place beforehand.'

'Oh yes. Thanks.' The thought did not thrill me much.

Mum's reading light was still on. 'Enjoy yourself?' she whispered as I bent to kiss her goodnight and put her book on the cluttered table beside her bed. 'Beaut,' I lied.

Looking ahead through my bow wave, I see the glint of blue tile.

In the end it's instinct that determines which hand will touch, plus a few years' experience! Maggie's flip I know to be neater, with her shorter legs, and more reliable; mine is less dependable, but when it really works, fantastic.

It's that sort I need. Right now. The right hand touches, slides down the wall. Follow it down, legs shoot over. If it's a good one, feet will be close to the wall for a good strong push-off.

I'm over! I've seen a flash of black in the lane next door. My legs thrust backwards, hopefully sending me off towards the finish like a catapult. I'm Archer and Arrow again, taut from fingertip to toe-tip.

But you've slipped, Alex! Your toes have not gripped the wall. Your push-off makes the best of a bad job, but is feeble compared with what it could have been. An eighty per cent push. Your leg reminds you that a few months ago it had problems of its own. You know without looking that the black torpedo in the next lane has done one of its neat, reliable turns and thrust itself into the lead.

Damn you, Maggie. And damn you even more, Alex's feet, for costing you the trip to Rome. Six years' work, sliding sideways off a patch of tile.

All you watching and yelling people, cheer for me no longer.

Alex has blown it. I can just hear the radio announcer . . . 'They've turned, Miss Archer just slightly ahead, a magnificent first lap, under thirty seconds, there could be a record here, no it's Miss Benton who comes out in front, what a magnificent turn, half a yard ahead now as they begin to stroke . . .'

Alex has blown it. She is screaming and crying too, with anger and shame. You fool!

The first stroke, a breath because my lungs are bursting and there's worse to come, and even though Maggie is now on my blind side

I can see enough out of the corner of my right eye to know that she has a full yard on me.

I'm sorry, Andy. My gift – resolutions, intentions, determinations – was not enough.

5

It's not every day your city declares open the harbour bridge it has been dreaming about for a hundred years, planning for over ten and building over five. The week after Maggie's dance we talked, read, heard about nothing else in the newspapers, on radio: our new bridge that some thought was more elegant than Sydney's, and others thought looked like a coathanger, and with only four lanes was going to be too small even before it was opened, and shame that they'd had to do away with footpaths so people couldn't walk over and admire the view. Rows of smug old men – mayors and politicians, city council and harbour board members – stared daily out of the newspapers. I noted that one of them was called P. N. R. Allardyce and had exactly the same self-satisfied expression as his nephew.

Andy had been right about Maggie and her dance. She'd hated every minute of it, she told me at training two days later in an unusual burst of confidence.

'I'd have given anything to take my shoes off too, but you know what Mother's like. She made me get these English shoes. Looked nice, but hurt, even in the shop. Two other girls had broken heels . . .' (So I wasn't the only one) '. . . and one broke her bra strap and we couldn't find a safety pin. They were all so embarrassed they went home.' (What?) 'Then Briar, from my class, lost her petticoat completely. The elastic went. Christopher Allardyce, her partner' (oh yes?) 'was so embarrassed he left her in the middle of the floor and she had to step out of it and pick it up and screw it into a little bundle, which wasn't very little, all those gathers and frills and hoops and stiff net and stuff, and walk off all by herself. At least he could have danced her to the side, somewhere near the Ladies, the swine.'

'Poor her,' I said. 'I met Christopher, very proper he was. In fact, a proper drongo.' We were getting dressed, leisurely for once, because Maggie was clearly needing to get it all off her chest to someone.

'He wanted to know who the American girl was, the tall one, with the legs like a chorus girl. Danced like Cyd Charisse, he said. Beat's me – well, he'd had a few, whiskies and that, with the adults. He got very angry when he heard Briar had already gone home with some friends. Don't blame her, do you? Then some guy had an asthma attack and had to be taken home, and someone else's partner arrived drunk and started to abuse the waiters, and then we had to throw out two carloads of gatecrashers. Susan's Dad took charge, threatened to call the police. Trouble is, they were friends of Susan's, you know . . . And my silly mother is saying if that's supposed to be the best band in Auckland she'll eat her hat and she asked them not to play rock 'n' roll and they did, and she's threatening not to pay the caterers because there wasn't enough food.'

Her silly *what?* I looked at her in the mirror as we both slicked down our wet hair, astonished. 'There was plenty of food, Maggie. And I thought the band was great.'

'So did I. Trouble is, Mother thinks she's still in Singapore. She gave lots of parties there, cocktails at the club and that. Always sitting round drinking gin. I wasn't sorry to leave.'

Well! Behind the scenes of what I'd taken to be a typical dance, overdone with formality and starch, had been all sorts of dramas. Was life always in layers, like water, clear on the surface but more murky and dramatic and complicated the deeper you got? I still couldn't work out why they bothered, people like Maggie's Mum. Who were they trying to impress?

'Sorry, I didn't mean to . . .' said Maggie.

'Sorry for what?'

'All that about my awful dance. Boring really. But at school, that's all they talk about, dances, gossip . . . With you, here, it's a relief, I don't have to . . .'

'Try so hard?'

She nodded, embarrassed. 'Thanks,' I said. 'I'll take that as a compliment.' But I knew what she was trying to say. Here in the pool, in the water, among our swimming friends who were a pretty mixed bunch, she could be herself, judged on her own terms, not those set by her mother or the private school she went to. Minus all the trappings, we met as equals.

The boys' school Sixth Form dance was a much less stuffy affair, with no over-dressed parents hanging around and only a small disturbance by some gatecrashers, which the teachers on patrol dealt with swiftly. There was a great band, Bill Haley-style rock 'n' roll music, very loud, nearly all night. Andy and I danced ourselves into the ground. I knew lots of girls from my school. Dress went all the way from diamante, strapless and gloves, to circular skirts or even a few jeans, pony-tails, cardigans worn back to front and eyelids full of liner. Gran had made me an emerald green skirt to wear with a slinky black top, a four-inch wide black elastic belt, and I borrowed Mum's black low-heeled shoes, plain as ballet shoes, ideal for twirling.

I enjoyed this dance as much as I'd hated Maggie's. Three days after hearing all those awful things the hurt remained, but only as a dull ache somewhere deep inside. Let them think what they pleased. Dancing with Andy was all I needed, getting lost in the pulse of the music, looking only for his eyes and the strong hand which would propel me into yet another pirouette.

It all started, really, that night, not with anything soppy like whether or not he opened car doors for me (we'd agreed I was perfectly capable of opening my own) or the way he said goodbye at the front door (just another hug), but in the shared exhilaration of the dance. And going home he suggested we do the 'Great Once-Only Walk' across the new bridge the following day.

Half the city was expected, but it seemed as though the *whole* city had turned out, well wrapped up against the cold south-westerly wind. We kept bumping into people we knew, swimming and school friends; even Mr Jack and his equally buxom wife who ran the pool tuckshop and was known to us all as Mrs Jill, both puffing from the long walk up one side and down the other. Not Maggie. She'd hinted at training that morning that in her household 'The Walk' was being regarded as an exercise for hoi polloi; besides, her mother thought it was bad for her swimmer's legs to walk that far. 'Come with Andy and me,' I suggested, but a trip had been arranged to visit relatives on a farm near Hamilton.

We walked right over, about two miles, to the toll plaza and back up to the top, where we stopped to lean over the rail. The water shimmered a long way beneath. It would be so easy just to swing a leg over the rail and fly off, join the seagulls below.

'Would you live, do you think?' I said.

'Might. D-depend on the way you hit. As hard as concrete, they say, from this height. Imagine your thoughts, going down. I can think of pleasanter ways to d-d- snuff it.'

We looked across to the city's gentle green hills. 'Last, loneliest, loveliest, exquisite, apart . . .'

'Who said that?'

'Rudyard Kipling, about Auckland. A poem called "Song of the Cities". He did a grand t-tour of the Empire in 1891. My English teacher's mad on Kipling, trots it out in his best Gielgud. Rest of it's pretty dreary. There's better Kipling.

'If you can keep your head when all about you
Are losing theirs and blaming it on you . . .'

He went on, through the whole thing . . .

'If you can fill the unforgiving minute
With sixty seconds worth of distance run,
Yours is the Earth and everything that's in it,
And – which is more – you'll be a Man, my son!'

He laughed. 'Sorry about that, Alex. Girls didn't run, let alone swim, in Kipling's d-day. And no one needs to tell you how to fill your unforgiving minute.'

'Sixty seconds worth of distance swum would be more like it.' The amazing view of the harbour, this clever person beside me who could quote Kipling and win prizes for physics and play the trumpet and wanted to go to sea, despite what his father thought, it all went to my head. I felt reckless and exhilarated. I grabbed Andy's hand. 'Let's run down.' We went haring off down towards the city side, dodging among the crowd, which by now had thinned a bit, shouting greetings to friends we saw in the opposite two lanes. Grannies smiled at us, as they did to children. Our pace dropped to a brisk walk. I realized I was still holding his hand. And enjoying it.

The car was miles away. The road got steeper, and though we were both breathless, I was puffing less.

'You'd better come back to training,' I said.

'That's a sore point. No swimming, no skiing at August, no more trumpet. I'm allowed to play rugby this year, that's all.'

'That's crazy. You'd stay fitter if you kept on swimming. What about injuries? You go and dislocate your shoulder or something? Or get your head stamped on, at the bottom of a scrum.'

'You know the old man.'

Bad-tempered, bossy, not quite an All Black in his day, forever talking abour Springboks and Lions and the team he didn't quite make in 1928 or whenever, and his latest golf score. I knew him. Determined that Andy was going to scale the ultimate twin pinnacles of New Zealand manhood, as a doctor *and* an All Black, and all outside activities during this scholarship year forbidden to that end.

'I'm surprised he let you out twice this week to go to the dances,' I said.

'He d-didn't. He's away, on business, and Mum, well . . . she's all for a bit of social life. And someone's got to look after you.'

'I beg your pardon. I can look after myself very well.'

'So sure? You worry me.'

'Why?'

'Your swimming's one thing, what about all the rest. Maggie *only* swims. Hasn't anyone ever t-t-said you could beat her hands-down every time if you *only* swam?'

'Mr Jack has hinted as much. Dad . . .'

'Only hinted? He's supposed to be your coach, for heaven's sake.' His hand was gripping mine tightly.

'Mr Jack understands, that's why he's a good coach. He doesn't think the world starts and finishes with swimming . . . neither do I . . .'

'It does for Maggie. And her parents. That's why she keeps winning.'

'He knows me, that I have to . . .'

'Be all things to all people?'

I yanked my hand from his grip. 'It's not that. I just . . . like being *in* things. It's important.'

'Why?'

'Well, I might be asking some questions too, like why are you letting your old man run your life, putting his foot down about this and that . . . everything except rugby which is the most stupid dangerous game ever invented, guaranteed to land you up in hospital sooner or later . . .'

'OK, you tell me.'

'Because he's got great plans for you. "You'll be a Man, My Son!" Except that he doesn't know that you have no intention of trying for medical school and boy, are you in for . . .'

'Don't shift it all on to Dad, Alex. You don't do me justice when you say that. I've got my own plans. I've got to get accepted into the Navy first. I wasn't much of a trumpeter so that doesn't matter. Skiing will wait, so will swimming till next season. And rugby's not so horribly dangerous, senior club's a bit rough, perhaps, but not school . . .'

'I hate it.'

'You're just jealous.'

'I wouldn't waste my time.'

'Anyway, you're side-stepping.'

'I'm not.'

'Why hasn't your old man put his foot down with you, then, or your Mum, who can be as solid as a rock when she chooses?'

'Because, because . . .'

'Because they know you wouldn't listen. Or they don't take your ambitions very seriously? They know, *I* know you want to do law. And what about the Olympics next year?'

'They do take me seriously! No one else does much, but they do. Look I'm only Fifth Form. You're doing scholarship. Give me a chance!'

'Breeze through School Cert. Breeze through University Entrance, breeze through life. Yeah, you will, Alex, because you're you, for a while.'

In the silence he took my hand again. We'd reached the car.

'Whether you'll breeze your way into the Games team is another matter. Has it occurred to you that you might not?'

'Of course it has. Where do you think I've been all these years? Second, time and time again.' You're a liar, Alex Archer. You do expect to beat Maggie, when the chips are down next February. You keep telling yourself that when you *really* start trying . . .

'But up till now there has not been too much at stake, has there?' he persisted.

'Only a medal or a title or a record or two.'

'Not a black blazer, a trip to Rome. How badly do you want it? I sometimes wonder. You know, I do worry about you, Alex Archer,' he said gently. Leaning forward he pinned me up against the side of the car and kissed me. On the mouth.

Back to school for the winter term, traffic jamming up daily on the new bridge, six am training now part of my daily routine – and strife not two days into the first week.

On the Hockey notice-board was the list of people selected for the First Eleven. My name was not there.

Some mistake, surely? In the place I'd mentally reserved for myself, right half, was B. Selwyn: Sixth Former. Last year in the Second team, stolid enough but *no* dash, no inspiration, just a reliable stick that stopped balls, and fed them back to the forwards. I'd shot a few goals from right half last season, which I doubted she'd done.

Underneath I noticed the Second Eleven, with A. Archer as right half.

'Barbara Selwyn? Well, what d'ya know!' I heard Julia's voice saying, dimly.

'None other, ' I said.

'But you were a dead cert.'

'Apparently not.' I was now seeing through hot eyes that two or three from my last year's Junior team had made it straight into the First. I'd seen enough. 'I've got a rehearsal, see you.'

Julia came after me. 'Alex, that's not fair. Even I can see Barbara's not exactly nifty on her pins.'

'Apparently she's better,' I said walking fast through the lunch-time groups, and unintentionally straight past Miss Edwards who had done this to me. Julia, sensing that I wanted to be left alone, didn't try to keep up. I nearly turned on the spur of the moment to ask Miss Edwards why she'd chosen Barbara ahead of me, but pride said, don't ask for more hurt, Alex. I could give up hockey altogether, but it might look as though I'd given up in a huff, and I didn't want that to be said. And I enjoyed it too much to give up. It only meant two practices a week and a game on Saturday mornings.

At the first practice game before school the next day, I lined up with the Second team, chirpy as they come. Made nice noises to Barbara, who obviously could hardly believe her luck, and played like a demon. There was no chance of my team beating the First, but I put our only goal in the net. Put that in your pipe, Miss Edwards.

'Played well, Alex,' she said, as we stumbled muddily from the field, red-faced and panting, me less than most. 'Could you stay behind a moment?'

It turned into a monologue. 'You might be a little disappointed, Alex. I imagine you'd hoped to make the First team this winter. But you do have two more seasons at school, assuming you're staying into Upper Sixth, and Barbara is in her last year. Admittedly, she's not as fast or as fit as you, but she's very reliable and works hard and it means a lot to her. Also we felt that with all your activities both in and out of school, you have enough pressure as it is, and in the Second Eleven you can enjoy your hockey without the strain . . . '

I heard her out, mumbled a few understanding noises, which made her feel better, and probably kidded her that I was not hurting all the way down to the toes of my muddy boots. Yes, Miss Edwards, I'm very used to being second best, Miss Edwards, but in swimming I'm second best to a top-flight lady. I'm also regarded by some as a second best specimen of femininity around the place — except that Andy not only kissed me so many times I lost count on that day of the bridge walk, but also, later in the car, very gently traced the outline of my breast with his fingers, deliciously reassuring me of my femininity . . .

Actually, what I'm really getting tired of is people who think they know what is best for me. Andy's well-meaning, no doubt, but he's three years older. Does life have to get so serious in the Fifth Form? And there's Mr Jack, asking bluntly when I turned up to training one morning with a massive bruise on my shin, had I considered giving up hockey this winter, given the risk of injuries, and did I want to give myself a fair crack at Rome? A Greek chorus from Dad in the car on the way home. Even Mum, more subtle again, and Gran sighing into her cup of tea everytime I helped her with her sewing, which admittedly was not very often, 'You're so busy, Alex, so busy. I don't know how you keep going, I just don't.'

Yet they supported me, to the hilt, all of them, and Rome was miles away yet. Dad enjoyed coming to training with me before dawn; he swam too, while I trained, and said the exercise was good for him. We came home to cereal and Mum's steaming cooked breakfast, eggs, bacon, sausages, fried bread. Before school to hockey practices, lunch-times to rehearsals, after school to piano or ballet. Early meals so that I would have the evenings free for homework and piano practice. I was let off drying dishes, which I knew irked all the kids, especially Jamie, who's about as loud-mouthed a twelve-year-old-boy as you'll find anywhere, but they dried them just the same.

Then one Saturday morning early in June I collected a really vicious ball at close range from a stick wielded by a twelve-ton Tessie. The whole team from some country school up north was big, like me, but this girl playing left back outdid all of us, and when she took a swipe at the ball, watch out. It rose above the mud and landed just behind the pad on the side of my right leg, and when I came back to earth and tried to pick myself up and found I couldn't walk things really started to come unstuck.

The doctor at casualty didn't look much older than Andy, but he had black smudges under his eyes, and his hands, as he ran them over my leg, seemed to be shaking slightly, which Mum told me later came from working over ninety hours a week as a house surgeon and being on call practically all the time and paid an absolute pittance.

'Comminuted fracture of the fibula,' he intoned, peering up at the X-ray. The pompous manner and glasses didn't go with the haircut, which was almost a teddy boy's duck's tail. 'Fortunately the bone is in good alignment. Plaster for six to eight weeks will be necessary.' He might have been reading today's sharemarket prices.

'It can't be. What's comminuted?'

'It is. Comminuted means several cracks. See for yourself.' He pointed to the paler lines on the X-ray. I looked down at my swollen leg, plum-coloured, horribly aching and still muddy, then up at Dad.

'It *can't* be, please.' I felt Dad's hand on my shoulder.

'Young lady, when I tell you your fibula's sustained a comminuted fracture and that plaster from foot to above the knee is necessary, that's exactly what I mean.' He was now looking at me squarely for the first time. The panic in my eyes must have stirred up something from the depths of his weariness. 'I played hockey myself once, with similar results. I'm sorry.'

He started writing on his bits of paper, then looked up. 'Alexandra Archer? Are you the girl who swims?'

I nodded, head down so that he couldn't see my eyes, as the implications began to sink in. No hockey, no ballet, no training even. Maybe out of the production at the end of term. Staggering around on crutches. All for a lousy Second Eleven match against a brutal lot of overgrown country bumpkins. I felt sick.

'Swimming's the best thing to get your leg back into shape when all this is over,' he said more gently. 'Are you training at the moment?'

'I was until today.'

'Get yourself a good physiotherapist. Couple of months, you'll be back in the water. Now, the nurse will wheel you into plaster room.'

'Couple of months!' I cried to Dad later as he helped me, weighted down with a plaster from knee to toe, out to the car. 'Couple of *months*!'

Andy came round later in the afternoon. I was reclining in state on my bed, flowers arranged by Mum, Dad's transistor radio to hand, fresh grapefruit juice, a bell in case I needed anything, and kids and/or Gran coming when I rang. Very sorry for myself.

'Your Dad rang me. Bad luck,' he said. He was standing back from the bed because various brats were sniggering in the hall outside.

I shrugged, feeling somewhat foolish. Recently, it was me giving him advice about risks of injury. He would not have forgotten.

'Or a slight relief?'

'What's that supposed to mean?'

'Accidents can make d-d-decisions easier for you.'

'Shit, Andy, so you think I decided to have an accident? You think I *chose* to stand in the path of that over-sized bullet and bugger up my ballet, the school show, not to mention my training and the little matter of Rome next year?'

'Not exactly . . .'

'If that's all you can say I'd rather you didn't come.'

'Ok, I'm sorry, tactless, heartless, cruel, all that. I'm truly sorry, Alex. Is it sore?'

'Yeah. And *boring*.' I'd not cried, really cried, to anyone yet, to Dad or Mum or Gran fussing around, and certainly not in front of the kids, and I'd not meant to cry in front of Andy. But tears came from nowhere and I just couldn't help it.

He said nothing for about five minutes, but just held my hand at first. Then when the waterworks went on and on, he got up and shut the door so that no prying eyes would see him give me a long strong cuddle, smoothing back my hair, planting kiss after kiss on my wet brow.

He was right, of course: part of me was rejoicing. Two whole months' relief from climbing out of bed in total blackness at five thirty, from eyes being gouged by chlorine; permanent respite from the Second Eleven hockey team. The other part of me knew only too well that come the next nationals Maggie would have two months' more training on the clock, and no matter how hard I trained I might never catch up.

'If you're ahead after the turn, don't let up. If you're not, my only advice is put your head down and go furrit.'

I am now going furrit, Mr Jack, truly I am. Breathing every second stroke, because I've used up nearly all my puff on the first lap and the going's getting rough.

This part of the race I loathe. The tops of your arms are aching, and every breath is your last gasp and you've yet to go into the overdrive where you forget you're dying and the only thing that's left in the world is getting to that solid wall at the end.

There's always the stupid hope that Maggie will somehow slow down, take a mouthful, hit a lane-rope, get a stomach cramp – anything. But she never does. She swims like a true pro. As Andy says, 'That's why she keeps winning, because swimming is her life.'

Hasn't it been my life? So much so that I've been obsessed by it, even to the point of not noticing that Gran was fading away to a shadow, and Julia had just a wee problem with that Australian uncle of hers.

I'm not going to make it. It's all been too much, really. I'm retiring as of now. Good luck for Rome, Maggie. I'll find someone who's got a television and watch you on that.

Don't give in, Alex. Never give in. Forty yards to go yet.

Andy, have pity.

I can't keep this up.

6

I had long known that Dad and Mr Jack had little chats about me and my training on the phone or while I was ploughing up and down the pool, but the Monday after my plaster went on, Mr Jack came around in the evening and there was a big chat in the front room.

Eventually I was called in, by this time quite wound up. They both looked very solemn as I swung my crutches through the doorway and eased myself on to a chair. Mr Jack was shaking his head slightly as though he couldn't quite believe what he was seeing.

'Evening, Mr Jack.'

I got a rueful smile. 'Well, Alex, where do we go from here?'

'I'm not going anywhere, am I? Well, I went to school today and very boring it was too, answering the same question over and over again. I can't train for six weeks and my ballet teacher has had a go at Mum because I can't be in her recital in October, and Miss Edwards at school is feeling all guilty and . . . '

'Alex . . . '

' . . . and my piano teacher is angry because it was my right leg and not my left and if it had only been my left I could have worked the pedal and taken my exam and . . . '

'Alex!'

' . . . I can't do gym or calisthenics or go to any dances or places.' I could hear myself burbling on like the babbling brook. 'All I can do is boring homework and play the piano without the pedal and twiddle my toes. Oh no, that's not all, I can't be the Scarecrow in *The Wizard of Oz*, but I can be the Tinman because he's stiff-legged anyway and Miss Macrae, who's producing the show, said today that what you lose on the swings you gain on the roundabouts . . . '

I petered out. Smiles, the patronizing adult sort, were being exchanged.

'Alexandra Archer, would you do me a favour?' said Mr Jack quietly.

'Anytime.'

'Pull your head in. Stop talking and listen.'

'Sure.' I was on uncertain ground here.

'It's June, June the eighth to be precise, 1959. Right?'

I nodded, despite myself, I was interested in what was coming.

'The nationals are next February, right? The nominations for Rome will be sometime after that? Now, those dates aren't going to change. No one and nothing's going to wait for your leg to get better or you to . . . '

'I never thought they would.'

'No, but do you realize you've only seven months to prepare for those nationals. *Seven* months, from now.'

Put like that, I hadn't, but I also wasn't going to let on.

'In that time you've got to work your leg back into shape, put in some solid training and sit School Certificate. Your father has made it quite clear, between August and October, exams will come first. After that you've got about three and half months.'

'What we are saying, Alex,' said Dad, 'is this. If you want to get to Rome, you must plan now. Because of this little set-back, ballet and hockey are out. They should stay out, at least this year.'

I was silent. All this seriousness was getting to me. And give up ballet? Didn't they know how much I loved dancing?

Mr Jack said, 'Alex, do you want that trip to Rome?'

I nodded.

'How badly?' he persisted.

'Badly. But . . . '

'Before you go any further, I'd better say that all this was probably a blessing in disguise.'

'Hardly.'

'Your father has asked me for my considered opinion of your chances next February. Well, here it is, straight. Three silvers, but not close enough to Maggie to be considered for Rome.'

'You'd coach me, thinking that?'

'Sure. I'd do my professional best for you. But there's only so much I can do or say. It's basically up to you.'

The genial smile and twinkling eyes had gone. He was in dead earnest.

'So, I think it's time for you to tell me, no, both your father and me, just how much you are prepared to give up.'

After a pause I said, 'I don't actually have much choice, do I?' I sounded surly, but I was not enjoying being put on the spot.

'In the long term, you have plenty. In the short – yes, you still have some,' said Mr Jack. 'You can't train in the water, but you can train out of it. We can work on a programme of weights, use these weeks to strengthen arms and upper body. We'll need good physio advice when the plaster comes off. The hockey team will manage without you, your ballet teacher's recital likewise. And you can get more shuteye than usual.'

My eyes met Dad's briefly. Mr Jack clearly knew quite a bit about my home life, more than I imagined. My late nights, usually catching up on homework or music theory, were a source of some friction between me and Mum. She was a night owl herself, and she'd see the light on under my door and come prowling in asking how much more I had to do. I always halved the estimated time and hoped she wouldn't notice, but I suspect she did.

'You say . . . I wouldn't have beaten Maggie at the nationals . . . ?' I said.

'Not unless you cut down, no. You might have surprised me,' he added with a slight smile, 'as you've surprised me before.'

'*If* I do as you've planned it all out . . . with Dad . . . what are my chances?'

'Good.'

'Just . . . good? That's all?'

'What more can I say? I can't say yes, Alex, you'll beat her hands down, your chances are great, because you know as well as I do that Maggie's a tough little cookie and she's got the advantage of a mother who's prepared to work hard and fight hard and spend money to see her daughter on the victory dais. Maggie is single-minded and a worker, and she doesn't bend under pressure. Your advantage is your greater natural talent, your height, your long limbs and . . . I'm bound to say, your talents in directions other than swimming. A buoyant personality, which can count when the chips are down. Many outstanding athletes are just that, rather special people. They often go on to success in other fields. You will, in due course.'

Such eloquence rather bowled me over. I sat quietly, trying to take all this in.

'So it's not going to be easy, Alex. And I can't guarantee success. You might do all we ask of you, and still see Maggie as the only nomination for Rome.' .

'I'm going to be two months' training behind her, for a start . . .'

'Only in a sense. OK, this is a set-back, but all the years you've put in already, they're not wasted, Alex. Your hockey training, the suppleness and control from ballet, rhythm from your music, all helps . . .'

'Oh good,' I said somewhat bitterly; my leg was aching and it sounded like I had a pretty uphill battle ahead of me.

Mr Jack stood up. 'Think about it. You don't have to make any decisions right now, Alex, except one. Do you want to start on weights next week?'

'Yes.' I didn't hesitate. All this sitting around talking was driving me bananas.

'Good. I'll get some equipment, and a programme nutted out. Thanks Jim, see myself out. Don't get up, Alex. T.T.F.N.'

'Ta-ta for now,' I called. Dad saw him off, with more chat out at the car, while I sat on, thinking, my Tinman's leg stuck out to one side. I had much to think about.

I was not, according to Mum as nurse, a good patient. I bored the whole family rigid complaining about having to be helped into a bath and being driven to school and having to ask someone to carry my schoolbag. In winter, between classrooms, between home and school, there was the problem of keeping plaster dry and toes warm. People horsed around with my crutches, and drew silly pictures on my cast. I had to sleep with my leg on a pillow. Later I had to poke down inside the cast with a knitting needle to get at itches.

Sympathy became boring too. I hated being so conspicuous in assemblies and getting on buses, and I have to admit that more than a few people got a thick ear when they tried to help. Wobbly at first, I soon learnt to speed along the school corridors faster than people could walk.

I wasn't seeing much of Andy, who was head down into books and rugby scrums. At home I sat for long periods in my room, listening to the Goon Show and working away with the weights Mr Jack had brought around. I could do lots of floor exercises like bending from the waist, frontwards, sideways, back, or lifting my torso off the floor and holding; or even lifting my legs and holding – murder on stomach muscles with the extra weight of the cast.

Not rushing out to training at five thirty, I had time to listen to my radio when I woke. On the early news, it was rugby and the All Blacks all the time, a real blow-up because they'd announced that the team going to South Africa next year would be without any Maori players, to keep the South Africans happy. There'd been a petition and a march on Parliament by six hundred students in Wellington and it seemed there wasn't any middle ground. Either you thought the arrangement was OK, or you thought the team shouldn't be going at all under those terms.

Andy and I, to his father's disgust, shared the opinion that the team shouldn't be going.

'And protestors, students, dangerous riff-raff should all be locked up,' his father stated during a steamy discussion in the Richmond kitchen. The three of us were doing the dishes after a Sunday roast with all the trimmings. With Andy being an only child, meals at his place were quiet adult affairs, with English china and napkins in polished silver rings and butter knives, unlike the noisy battlefield that I was used to at home.

'Because they're standing up and being counted? Come on, Dad,' said Andy.

'Politics shouldn't be brought into sport,' droned Mr Richmond for about the eighth time, rubbing the Spode dinner plate ever more vigorously. 'If you haven't been to South Africa . . .'

'. . . you've no right to pass judgement,' joined in Andy.

'Just so.'

'Dad, why should we have to conform to their rules?'

'Because we are their visitors, their guests. Because it is the best arrangement for all concerned, including our Maoris themselves.'

'Imagine how you'd feel if you were one of the Maoris left out, after all that training,' I said.

'You'd be old enough to understand the complexity . . .'

'I don't think it's complex at all. I think it's very simple,' I said.

'Really.'

'It's a New Zealand team, isn't it? We send our best team, just like we do to the Olympics. If the South Africans don't like who we select, that's their . . .'

'A simplistic line of reasoning. Fallacious. Quite unrealistic.' He was going to blind me with words.

'If I thought my hard training all went for nothing because a lot of politicians . . .'

He laughed. 'Oh, I know you're a good swimmer, sweetie, but what would you know of training?'

'Pardon?'

'You young things, kids, slips of girls, you don't know what training is. A few lengths of a pool, I daresay. A spot of sunbathing in your bikinis.'

'Dad . . .'

I waved him down. There was a dangerous silence. 'Tell me about training, Mr Richmond.'

'We'd come in, every muscle aching, covered with mud, exhausted . . .'

' . . . but happy,' I put in politely.

'Exactly. Seven o'clock in the morning and the frost not even off the grounds. Passing practice, line-outs, until you're bent double. Practice after dark, mud and rain. A sense of trust in your team-mates . . .'

'Real man's work,' I said.

He looked at me suspiciously. My face was as blank as I could make it. Inside I was shouting '*balls!*'

'Well, time I went, Andy,' I said, hanging up my damp tea-towel and slotting crutches under armpits. I hoped I could contain my anger until I got outside, before I said something really rude, or threw a plate at him. 'Goodbye, Mr Richmond. Excuse me, but I must go and', I couldn't resist, 'do some real girl's work.'

He looked round from re-lighting his pipe.

'Lifting weights, about two hundred pounds each. Didn't you know they're introducing women's weightlifting at the Olympics next year?'

I had the satisfaction of seeing the lighted match pause and his mouth drop, just a little. For a moment I think he might have believed me.

'Alex, wait,' said Andy as I swung off down the path on my crutches, somewhat in danger of over-reaching myself and ending in a heap on the road. He was still wiping his hands on the frilly yellow apron. 'Pay no attention . . .'

'I don't.'

'He doesn't know what he's talking about.'

'I'll say. That rot about *real* training . . .'

'Look, you know he knows nothing about it. He took no interest in my swimming, never came to the pool once, not one carnival. He's never seen a training session in his life.'

'I bet he comes to *all* your rugby games.'

'Yes, and after years of shouting at me from the sideline even he's beginning to realize I'm not going to be another d-d-Don Clarke.'

Interesting. A male version of Mrs Benton.

'I can open my own car door, thank you.'

Somehow I managed door, crutches, getting inside, hauling crutches in after me. Andy watched initially, then shrugged and went around to get in the driver's seat. By the time he had started up the car I was laughing.

'Did you *see* the expression on his face as we left. I shouldn't tease him, but . . . Oh hell, I forgot to thank your mother for lunch.'

'She won't mind. I'll tell her. I think she's quite glad that somebody argues with the old man other than me. She gave up years ago.'

We laughed all the way home. No, that's not strictly true, we took a slight detour and parked behind a tree in the park. Thirty minutes of kissing and petting (not heavy, the lighter version), and I went home in the best humour I'd been in for days.

Although we talked about the All Black row in the cloakrooms at school, with most of us thinking along much the same lines, in class it hardly rated a mention. An All Black team was going to South Africa minus a few Maoris, so what? Girls' schools hardly need concern themselves with male sports, even the one that everyone agreed was the country's national religion, and Maori culture was an annual trip to see the canoe in the museum. Miss Gillies was more concerned with getting through the exam syllabus. In English, where current events were sometimes discussed, Miss Hunt was currently putting us all to sleep with her very correct readings of *The Mill on the Floss* and Gray's 'Elegy in a Country Churchyard'.

Most of us were connected in some way with *The Wizard of Oz,* since the school prided itself on its productions. Through July we rehearsed three lunch-times a week and one afternoon after school. My mishap had thrown Miss Macrae only temporarily off balance. 'My dear Alex, my Scarecrow,' she had boomed when I hobbled into rehearsal the week after the break. 'You auditioned so brilliantly. Where will I find another Scarecrow?'

Miss Macrae was in her Laurence Olivier as Hamlet pose, hand to brow, musing. She wore plain suits, a Joan of Arc hairstyle, and her voice (in the best British tradition, trained at the Royal Academy of Dramatic Art) could be heard all over the school.

'Tinman, that's it,' she declaimed. 'You can be the Tinman. We can paint your plaster cast silver.'

'I'll be out of it long before that.'

'How long?' Not only did she look like Joan of Arc might have done if she'd reached fifty, she had once played Joan on the London stage. That was about all we knew. How she'd ended up teaching Dramatic Art at a girls' school in Auckland, New Zealand, none of us ever found out. 'But you'll not be dancing, I fear. Not Scarecrow dancing.'

'Doubt it.'

'Janice can be Scarecrow. She'll make quite a good fist of it, I daresay. If your leg's up to it, we'll put in an extra dance for you.'

I was not thrilled. I thought the Tinman a creep, unlike the Scarecrow, who was a character of some spunk. And every time I'd seen the film, which was now four, it had disturbed me that the Tinman actor had nearly died because of all the toxic silver stuff they had used on his skin. But as with the Second Eleven hockey I felt certain obligations, stupidly, and I was enjoying the whole production far too much to pull out now.

So Tinman I was. I somehow failed to tell them at home until we were into the round of full run-throughs coming up to dress rehearsals in August. Eyebrows went up into heads when I started mentioning weekend rehearsals, and Jamie made rude comments about me supposedly cutting down on my activities, including pulling out of the school show. I would have been wiser not to take on Tinman. But I was in too deep.

The grand ceremony of taking off the plaster, scheduled for the second week of July, was an anti-climax. At the hospital there was much fuss with X-rays and cautionary pep-talks from yet another young doctor suffering from exhaustion. In the plaster room an orderly with arms like a truck driver and Elvis kiss curls expertly wielded a gigantic pair of hedge clippers. On the slab all lay revealed. A pathetic shrivelled leg, hairy, pale, scaly and noticeably smaller than the other. Also two knitting needles I'd lost in my frantic poking for an itch. 'Ugh' I thought, then 'Aaaaaah' as I had a good scratch. If I thought I could put on a shoe and walk out, I had a shock coming. A nurse rolled bandage around my leg from knee down. Then it was crutches again, peg-legging it down the hospital steps.

I was so impatient to get training again, that if I'd known then that it would be another three weeks of bandage, crutches, and sessions with the physio, I'd probably have stepped under a bus there and then.

I knew now it was the water I had missed more than anything. I needed that swirl of water around my body, the actual touch of cool water on skin, the feeling of flying, of lightness, and of power. Even on my least inspired days of training, I always had a little frolic, dolphin-diving in the shallow end, or a long moment of lying on my back, weightless. They say our bodies are two-thirds water, but water seemed to have got into my soul, too. When I couldn't swim, I felt starved.

At the end of the second week, I became so desperate I made Andy put down his books for an hour and drive me to the pool for a swim. On a quiet Sunday aftrnoon I hoped no one else we knew would be there. We unwound the bandage in the car and I tried to walk into the pool as normally as possible.

Cleopatra in her asses' milk had nothing on me. With Andy hovering around to make sure I didn't slip on the wet concrete, I got to the side of the pool and dangled my legs into the water. Beside me Andy sat, too. If he'd known what I was thinking he would have run a mile, but this was the first swim we'd had together since . . . since we'd moved on to the kissing plane. All that distance, those years we'd trained together, but today I was bowled over by his beauty when he stood on the block, dived cleanly in, did a lap and came back to slither the last few yards under water and emerge like a water-god at my feet. This beautiful boy, not quite a man, wants to kiss me, share himself with me, loves me? I could hardly believe my luck. 'Come on,' he said, smiling. That was a swim I shall always remember. Slipping into the shallow end, feeling the cool water slither up my back, over my shoulders, through my hair, I wondered how I could have gone for so long.

It felt like a million years. I did a few laps without kicking, taking care to push off with one leg only. Andy swam alongside me. There was only an occasional twinge and we made a reasonable job of putting the bandage back on. I made sure my hair was very dry before I got home.

When Andy suggested a trip to Helensville for a hot swim the following weekend, I got grudging permission from Mum to go, and all sorts of conditions. The chance of another fun swim with Andy was too good to miss. It was to prove another bad decision.

If you really mean business, you have to keep it up, Alex, and more.

Am I gaining on her, Andy? Pinned her back a hand's breadth, a finger, a fingernail even?

This is for real, maybe the first race in my life at total one hundred per cent effort, where desperation and rage have added their fuel to ambition, and afterwards I will be able to look Mr Jack and Dad and Mum and Gran and the kids and Miss Gillies and Maggie and even Mrs Benton in the face and say I could not have tried harder.

Breathing is uphill and every arm stroke a circle of pain. My legs, shaved so carefully in the shower tonight, are tingling, almost as though being massaged by the water. It's a feeling I've not had often; a signal that my body is about to go into another gear.

I think I'm gaining. I can no longer see much. I dare not upset my rhythm and take a breath to the right. I never learnt to breathe right-handed. It always felt as awkward as breathing to the left was natural. The water is choppy and I can't tell whether the arms and legs flailing away next door are ahead or even with me. But I think I'm gaining.

Andy, tell me, I need to know. Am I? Am I?

7

It wasn't the first time I'd been to the hot springs at Helensville. Every winter, once or twice, we went as a family for a Sunday treat, leaving Gran behind for what she called a nice day's peace and quiet to herself. We'd come home water-logged, cooked like lobsters, the car windows steaming up and Deb and Robbie asleep on the slow journey home in the dark. But this was the first time I'd been allowed to go with friends.

They turned up early Saturday afternoon at the front door – Andy, his friend called Keith Jameson and a tiny smart miss called Vicki, who smoked a cigarette while the rest of us went through the hellos and goodbyes with Dad. Andy had warned me Keith was a gruff, prickly sort of guy, but good value, really, the best maths scholar the school had seen for years, set to be top of the class, and then do engineering next year. He was also rather strange-looking, short with heavy gnomish eyebrows that almost met in the middle.

Andy and I slotted ourselves into the back seat of the pale blue Morris Minor car. Our long thighs lay the only way they could, crossways and close. We hadn't even got to the end of the road before his arm was around me.

We left pleasure behind at the gate though, as Keith was not the relaxed driver that Andy was. Through several orange lights, one which was undoubtedly red, around corners on squealing wheels, nipping out to overtake and back as oncoming cars sped towards us, we were soon hurtling along the country highways. Keith drove that Morris like the Triumph TR3 he said he was saving for.

'You OK? You're very quiet,' murmured Andy. If he was puzzled, so was I. Was this sort of driving normal?

About forty minutes later, although it semed like forty hours, we pulled up with a scrunch outside the pool complex. As we got out, dust was still rising from where the brakes had grabbed the gravelly road. I felt more than slightly ill. Vicki's cigarettes, and those she had lit for Keith and passed to him without a word, hadn't helped.

For once, the swim failed to work its soothing magic. The thought of the drive home terrified me, even as I felt the relaxing effect of the hot water on my wasted leg, even as Andy pulled me down into the blue for a lengthy underwater kiss until we both had to surface for some fresh air.

In the dressing-room Vicki and I small-talked about her boarding school. She spent quite a bit of time on her face and hair, which she'd not allowed to get wet. When we finally came out, Andy and Keith were sitting at a table with a pile of hamburgers and chips already going cold. 'Women!' sighed Keith. 'Take all day.' Vicki ignored him, and lit another cigarette. I decided to ignore him, too; swimmers, male or female, can change their clothes faster than anyone in this world. They get a lot of practice at it. I ate, listening to talk of their school, the All Black thing, cars, more All Black thing (Keith thought the team should go), more cars, more rugby. It seemed all Keith and Andy had in common was playing in the school First Fifteen.

'I'm not too struck on his driving,' I muttered to Andy as we walked in pairs to the car park. 'Couldn't you drive home?'

After a pause, Andy said, 'He's all right.' Afterwards I learnt that to have made such a suggestion, man to man, would have been a deadly insult.

The sky had clouded over since we were in the pool, and it was trying to rain. We sped past the town's small cluster of houses, shops, garage, dairies, a church; little sign of life except for the pub where, with only fifteen minutes to go before closing time, the six o'clock swill was in full swing. The car park was full and the place inside clearly jammed to the doors with men, getting down as much beer as possbile.

'Man, great idea,' said Keith, throwing the wheels into yet another small skid. The car had barely stopped before he was out and gone. 'Come on, Andy, one for the road.'

'Where does that leave us mere females?' I said

'Sitting waiting for half an hour,' muttered Vicki.

'Won't be long, just get a couple of bottles,' said Andy, hesitating before he walked off towards the sounds of male laughter.

It was a good ten minutes before Andy emerged, followed a minute or so later by Keith, laughing, swinging a brown paper bag which contained two more bottles. Keith expertly prised off the tops, and handed a bottle over to Andy. Vicki and I were expected to be happy with occasional swigs.

'No thanks,' I said to Andy's offer. He looked a bit sheepish, as well he might. The time had come. 'Keith, could you drive a bit slower, please. I felt sick before.'

He was about to turn the ignition key. 'What?'

Once had taken enough girding of loins, to repeat it took more. 'Could you slow down a bit?'

'Did I hear right?'

'Alex gets carsick,' said Andy hastily.

'Sorry to hear that.' We left the pub behind. 'Just make sure you do it out the window. Mum's car.' Although I was right behind him, I could see his elbow raised for another swig at the bottle. I wished he'd put both hands on the wheel.

I was trying to think what to do or say next when we came around a corner. A farmer and his dog were moving a few cows before nightfall. Vicki saw them momentarily before Keith did, her yell coming just before the howl of the brakes, the skid narrowly missing the dog, and the fearful stop about six inches from a cow's nose. I don't remember the words, only the flow of abuse between the farmer and Keith, who seemed to think that roads were built solely for cars and not cows. Vicki added some surprisingly ripe expressions of her own, about Keith. It would have been funny if I hadn't been so frightened.

'Get your bloody cows off the road,' shouted Keith. The cows had withdrawn to one side and the car was already accelerating. 'Stupid bastard.'

'Take it easy, Keith,' said Andy

'Bloody farmers. Think they own the place.'

Over eighty-five miles per hour and I'd reached the end. If I don't get out now, I thought, I'm not going to get home at all.

'Keith, please stop.'

'Why, baby?'

'I'm not your baby and will you please stop.'

'Be sick out the window.'

'No. If you don't stop, I'm going to be sick right over the top of you.'

There was a silence, but no reduction in speed, if anything his foot went down a touch. He flicked the car lights on. Andy's arm was tight around my shoulders.

'Keith . . .'

'Shut up, Vicki.'

'I mean it,' I said. 'Your car will stink for a week. Not to mention you.'

I could almost hear him thinking. He was caught now, between me and Vicki and his mother. His mother's anger won, with her added potential for doing inconvenient things like banning the car. If she knew how he drove, she wouldn't be letting him have the car at all.

'Keith, you'd better stop,' said Vicki. I could feel Andy's tension, and embarrassment too. I was probably breaking all sorts of unwritten male rules.

Of course Keith couldn't just stop like normal people. He threw both his feet at the floor. It wasn't quite a skid, but uncomfortable enough to make his point, with Vicki thrown against the dashboard and Andy and I against the front seats.

Silence, except for a distant dog barking and the car idling. Vicki looked around at me, pulling at her cigarette, scared stiff. Keith was taking another swig of beer. In the rear vision mirror, our eyes met.

'I'm getting out.'

'Suit yourself.'

'I will. I can think of better ways . . .'

He laughed. 'Aren't you going to be sick first?'

'I might, I might not. When I've got my bag out of the back, you can go.'

I looked back inside at Andy. I could hear his mind ticking over, too. Go with her, bad leg and all? or lose face with his mates? No doubt Keith would tell all of them over a beer how Andy had gone after some feeble jittery *girl*. You've got about three seconds, Andy old chum – but I was also pleading for support. After two and a half seconds, I got it.

'Hang on,' he said levering himself with some difficulty towards the open door.

'You're not going too?' incredulously, from Keith.

'Yeah.'

'Don't be such a prick. Let her walk.' I wasn't meant to hear the next bit, but I've got these great ears. 'Silly cow.'

'I can't.'

'Why not?'

'For Pete's sake, Keith, she's only just out of plaster. God knows how we're going to get home.'

Keith shrugged and took another swig. 'Your problem.'

'I don't know what's got in to you.'

From the look I saw Vicki give him, I guessed there was some sort of long-running row going on, which would explain much. Their problem. I was past caring, shaking all over and already wet from the light drizzle. I put my parka on, slung the two bags over my shoulder, turned my back on the car and started walking.

'See you Vicki,' I said. 'Hope you get home all right. I hae me doots.' She peered through the windscreen: two huge eyes giving her the look of a startled doll. The car revved off into the dusk; within seconds the red tail lights had disappeared around the next corner.

The noise seemed to take a long time to fade, leaving a damp stillness that suddenly made me feel very lonely, miles from anywhere. I still didn't know how angry Andy was with me, nor did I particularly care. He'd gone with Keith into the pub, hadn't he?

The dog had stopped barking. I continued walking, but slowed as rage and tension seeped out of me. Andy caught me up, firmly relieving me of both the bags and taking my hand. My leg, only two days out of the last bandage, tired quickly. Even walking on the grassy verge I couldn't disguise the sound of a slight limp.

His voice was more resigned than angry. 'Alex, you do make things . . .'

'Difficult?' My voice went up and up. 'Embarrassing? Tiresome? Silly cow? Is that what you think, too? Did you really want to stay in that car and get killed?' I yelled.

'It wasn't as bad as that . . .'

'Oh yes it was. He's an absolute maniac. He'll kill himself one day, you see. And probably a few others as well.'

We walked along in silence. It was already too dark to see anything more than shapes. A warm tide of relief and gratitude went through me when Andy put his arm around my waist and tried to take some of the weight off my leg.

'Thanks, mate.' My face was wet with both rain and tears. A few more steps and I stopped, because I needed the comfort of his strong arms, to reassure myself with a very hard kiss that I was still alive. 'Thanks. For . . .'

'Alexandra.' Like something out of an old silent movie, he put his finger across my lips. 'My Alex.' He started to laugh. 'Alexandra the Great.'

'That was Alexander.'

'Some talk of Alexandra, and some of Hercules,
Of Hector and Lysander and such great names as these.'

'Idiot.' Another (wonderful/amazing/unbelievable/incredible) kiss, our bodies pressed hard together all the way down. 'I didn't want to die. Not like that. Nor you.' So why was I still feeling so fearful, for me, for him?

'No.'

'Hold me, Andy. Make me stop shaking.'

It doesn't seem very sensible, remembering in the cold light of day, but we lay down in the wet grass on the side of the road and had a good long and very damp kiss, the drizzle falling on our parkas, our faces, my bare outstretched legs, until the stillness was broken by a car in the distance. We let the first one go. And the second.

When I got out of Keith's car, I knew there were two choices: either walk to a farmhouse or hitch a ride from a passing car into somewhere where we could ring Dad. Weighing up concern for my silly leg against the feeling I never wanted to get in a stranger's car again, the leg won. Andy declined the first three offers of help, men driving home from the pub. The fourth was a woman with a boy about Jamie's age. All we needed was to be dropped off at the next phone box, said Andy, and my father would come and pick us up.

The phone box was near a fish and chip shop in the next small block of shops. Unfortunately we didn't know that there was another fish and chip shop with a very similar name in the next suburb and mistakenly we told Dad only that Keith's car had broken down.

All my memories of that night are now a jumble. Andy and I sat in the warmth of the shop, playing the odd record on the juke box as we got more and more worried about Dad. When he finally turned up we knew at once that there'd been trouble: an accident about four miles back towards the city. The ambulance had already gone when he came across tow trucks, traffic officers, red lights flashing, the wreck of a pale blue Morris Minor, and some sort of farmer's jeep it had collided with. It had taken him a while to find out they'd taken only three off to hospital, two teenagers thrown from the Morris, beer bottles inside, asking for trouble, and the driver of the jeep. The traffic officer couldn't or wouldn't say how badly hurt or what their names were. He'd got confused, poor Dad, in his panic, and gone to the wrong fish and chip shop at first, and worried when he couldn't find us . . .

We stopped near the Morris Minor and the jeep, those dreadful flashing red lights that hurt your eyes, and a traffic officer squatting outside our car and wanting all sorts of details from Andy – names, addresses, age. Just why we'd been left behind was thankfully not asked. Andy could tell them about Keith, but we knew nothing about Vicki when it came to the point, other than her first name. I sat zonked in the front of Dad's car, staring fascinated at the two mangled cars, imagination running riot with mangled bodies, pity for Vicki. How badly hurt were they?

And yes, there was more than a touch of self-righteousness. If I hadn't . . . if Andy hadn't . . . When the questions had finished and Dad started us on the homeward journey, Andy's hand sought mine from the back seat and held it very tightly all the way back to his place.

Apart from weeping on Mum's shoulder when we got home, I never told anyone. Neither did Andy, in fact I don't think he told his parents at all. Dad somehow found out the next day which hospital they were in. Andy went to see Keith's mother, but she was at the hospital and when he finally got her on the phone she could hardly put two words together. The report in the paper on Monday morning confirmed that two teenagers thrown from a car on the Helensville highway after a two-car collision early Saturday night were in a stable condition in hospital. The seventeen-year-old boy had sustained two broken legs and multiple cuts, the sixteen-year-old girl thrown through the windscreen had facial injuries and a broken arm. The driver of the other car, a local farmer, was in a comfortable condition with cuts and abrasions.

In my family, only Jamie saw the picture of the two cars and put two and two together. After his first few awkward questions, he was told as little as possible and sworn to secrecy. Gran fussed over me even more than usual, although it should have been the other way round because we all knew she wasn't particularly well.

Mum commented that it would have made a nice little story for the papers, my escape. I fear I was very rude, both about her even thinking such a thought, and about reporters who would probably have agreed.

I'd decided, even before Andy hinted when he rang the day after, not to go anywhere near Keith in hospital. The time would come, he said. Right now Keith was a pretty mixed-up lad, with his legs in traction and inclined to blame the farmer in his jeep and, slightly, me and Vicki, for what had happened. Me? Well, you'd upset him, hadn't you, being rude about his driving, and the row with Vicki had been going on for days. Maybe one day he'd appreciate a visit. Well, I said, I'll send a note, just saying I'm sorry he was hurt and get better soon. If he thinks I'm trying to score a point he's stupider than I thought.

I cycled over to the hospital to see Vicki after school, or rather what I could see of her face. Those huge eyes peered at me with a strange expression, not hostile, rather, dare I say, the same look as in the eyes of the little third formers who follow me round. Neither of us could say much – she because of the bandages, and me because I hate hospitals. I just didn't know *what* to say, and I couldn't stop wondering what she looked like behind the bandages. Everything I tried sounded wrong. After a few false starts, I took her hand, and then a nurse stopped at the end of the bed. My face must have been all doom and gloom for she said, 'Not as bad as it looks, fortunately. One of the luckier ones. She'll be OK, there'll be a scar or two across her forehead, which her hair will hide.'

Vicki was still holding my hand. 'I wish,' she said. 'What?' I said leaning over to hear. '. . . I had your . . .', 'Shush,' I said. I had a nasty feeling she was going to say something like courage or confidence or stuff like that. 'I'm just pig-headed. Look after Number One, I do.' After a pause she said, 'Keith had some flowers sent.' I followed her eyes to a magnificent heap of roses, carnations, the works. It was a nice way to say sorry, despite that nonsense he'd told Andy, which I certainly wasn't going to pass on. Spoil someone's face for life, even just a scar hidden by hair; save your own face with your mates. If she still liked him, after this, good luck to her. One of these days he might grow up. Driving-wise, he might not.

There are strange things going on around me. I am aware of some late-night talks between Mum and Dad, and I overheard enough one night to guess they were arguing about Gran, and, although I couldn't see the connection, an overdraft out of control. But Mum has these great ears too, and when she heard the wooden floor creak as I went past on my way to the bathroom the voices stopped.

Gran herself never stops – working or telling everyone how well she is. Then why do I notice one day how thin her arms are sticking out from the cardigan?

Back at school I am sufficiently subdued after the Helensville trip for Julia to ask if I'm OK, I seem pretty quiet these days, and how's my leg. 'Good, good,' I say, referring only to the leg that was almost back to normal size with careful nursing by Mr Jack and his physio friend. But I feel Julia is hiding something, just like I am hiding Helensville. All these secrets are getting on my nerves.

I didn't even hear from Andy for a couple of weeks. I knew he was working hard for end-of-term exams, but it was more than that. He'd withdrawn, as I knew I had. Then there was a phone call one night and an invitation to meet at the American milk bar after school.

'Very daring of you. My parents aren't all that keen . . .'

'I need a break. I need to see you, without family, kids. Please.'

'Five o'clock. I've got rehearsal till then.'

When I hitched my bike to the lamp-post outside, he was already waiting at one of the tables. We ordered Rangitoto Special sundaes and as he brought them over to the table I noticed he was limping himself.

'What's up with the leg?'

'Hamstring. At the weekend.'

'Rugby game?'

'Yes.'

'I'm sorry. Not a good year for legs.'

He had the grace to smile as he said, 'Bit of a relief really. I wasn't going to make the rep trials anyway, but D-D- the old man wouldn't believe that. And he's on my back about swot, exam marks . . .'

I nodded. There was an awkward silence as we both dug through the scarlet sauce into the ice-cream below. 'Could've been worse,' I said pointedly.

'I very nearly didn't get out of the car that night . . .' he said.

'I know.'

'It was only your leg that . . .'

'Was it?'

'You were being so damn righteous. You know, if nothing had happened, Keith would never have let me forget it.'

'If you say so. I wouldn't know. I don't know what goes on between males, except that it seems pretty weird sometimes. All than boloney about it being everyone else's fault but his . . .'

'What I'm trying to say, if you'll only let me get a word in edgeways, is . . . I owe you some thanks.'

After a bit, I said, 'Would you really have left me there, if I hadn't had a bum leg, on the side of the road, miles from anywhere?'

'I was pretty angry with you. You put me in an impossible situation.'

'I was angry too, mate. Encouraging him into the pub . . .'

'Not true.'

'You didn't stop him. You didn't say a damn thing.'

'What did you expect me to do. T-take his car keys away?'

'Why not?'

'He drives no worse . . .'

'That *can't* be true. Two broken legs, one girlfriend scarred for life and I don't know about the farmer, how he's getting on. Two wrecked cars.'

Andy was silent.

'He doesn't seem like your type at all.'

'Meaning?'

'Girls at school say he's wild, moody. And randy. Doesn't like it when anyone objects.'

'That figures, up to a point. Do they also say that his father walked out two years ago with a secretary seventeen years younger. That his Mum has to work full-time, that his younger sister is a mongol, expensively looked after in some home, and the middle one a real handful, climbing out of windows at night to go to dances?'

I took refuge in my sundae. 'No.'

'He's going to design the most graceful, slender bridges ever built, his words, true. He's got a scrapbook of every stage of the harbour bridge being built. Every weekend, five, six, years, taking pictures. Plays the guitar, belongs to the CND, worries his head silly about bombs . . .'

An interesting guy, under the tough Marlon Brando exterior.

'He was showing off that night. He'd had a row with Vicki.'

'I guessed.'

'You were famous. And taller than him.'

'So somehow I'm . . .'

'No, of course not. I didn't mean that, Alex.'

He looked so wretched that I took pity. 'No. Well, how's he getting on?'

'Comes out of hospital next week. Pity about the rep team. He'll still beat us all in the scholarship exam, though, with no work,' he said ruefully.

Catch a falling star, put it in your pocket,
Keep it for a rainy day . . .

Some noisy chewing-gum types in jeans and leather jackets had come in and started up the juke box.

'Aren't people . . . amazing . . . what they do, what they've done. You never know, do you, what goes on.' I licked the last of the sauce off the spoon. 'I'm full!'

'Disgusting. You've got a bit of weight aboard, Alex.'

'Come on – I've only been back training a couple of weeks. And pretty gentle at that.'

'You mean two miles instead of four.'

'Not even that. And no ballet or hockey.' Alex, you're at it again. Playing it all down when you know you're up to your eyebrows.

'So what else have you got on?'

'School C. Piano exam in November. Oh, and *Wizard*.'

'What wizard?'

'Didn't I tell you. I'm the stupid Tinman, with my face all silver. Our annual production. The usual shambles.'

'And A. A. in full cry, yet again. I don't know how you find the time.'

'You sound like my grandmother.'

'Strange choice of show for a girls' school, isn't it?'

'You haven't heard Miss Macrae who's producing it. She has a real thing about musicals, which she says are the most exciting development in popular theatre since Shakespeare. Shows that run for years and then films, she says, that give pleasure to millions. She's played us lots of recordings – *West Side Story*, *My Fair Lady*, *Salad Days*, *Gigi*, *Guys 'n' Dolls*, even *The Wizard of Oz* . . . What we're doing is a watered down version of the film. "If I only had a heart". . . my song.'

'Sure I'll come, silver girl. It'll suit you.'

He meant all my silver medals. 'Beast.'

I am! I can, Andy! I'm closing the gap.
Breathing each stroke now, because I've no breath left for anything else.
Too late? Thrown away at the turn, with that feeble push-off?
But I'm feeling good, strong. I'm riding up over my bow wave. One race in five, perhaps, comes this surge, this incredible sensation that I'm being pulled, propelled through the water by some invisible force, not just my own muscles.
I'm in overdrive, relentless. Pain has gone. I know I can do it now. I'm almost flying.
Coming to get you, Maggie Benton. This'll teach you, Maggie Benton, bringing coaches in from Australia for special coaching all to yourself and not telling anyone. Only that you'd gone out of town to train for the week before the nationals. It took a few days for the grapevine to shake out the news that the coach you'd had in Queensland last August holidays just happened to be in the same place the same week. Funny that.
I hate to spoil your little plans, Mrs Benton, but Aussie coaches or not, Maggie's not going to win this race. You can spend all the money you like, but when we get in the pool we're all equal.
You can't blame your equipment like most other sports, or the weather, or being put off by someone screaming instructions from the sideline. There's just your body and a whole lot of water to get through faster than any other body. Your body, and your will, against hers.
You're not level yet, Alex. She's holding you off. She's not beaten yet. Oh, what's twenty seconds of agony after what you've been through in the last eight months? Don't chuck it away . . .
Andy, I hear you. But I'm hurting like hell . . .

8

If Andy, or my family, or Mr Jack, or the teachers at school all thought that, at last, Alex had settled into some sort of reasonable routine, they were being successfully fooled, as intended. End-of-term meant exams, the *Wizard* in the last week. My early morning three miles, twice-weekly calisthenics, daily weights and minimal piano practice were going on as well. I was beginning to wonder myself how I had ever fitted in hockey and ballet.

Winter storms raged as I cycled hither and yon. After the initial pleasure of being back in the water, training had quickly become a grind, especially with a lot of arms-only stuff while the leg got stronger. Maggie and I ploughed up and down on opposite sides of the indoor pool over in town, where there'd been that first race all those years ago. The warm salt water, heavily chlorinated, was still a problem there. Goggles always filled up with water and were not an answer. We tried castor oil, all sorts of chemists' potions, but how could anything work when it just got washed out? It took all my courage to dive into the water each morning, knowing that after a length my eyes would be stinging like after some nasty medieval torture. We had over two months of this, until the freshwater Olympic Pool opened in October.

I knew I was slipping behind in class. I could hardly see my books, let alone a blackboard, for the first part of each morning. All lunch hours and even study periods were *Wizard* rehearsals. Exams loomed, and the only time I had for extra work was during rehearsals when I wasn't needed (which wasn't often: Tinman didn't say all that much, but was on stage a lot) or late at night. A towel along the bottom of my door hid the strip of light sometimes until one or two in the morning.

Only the daily escape into the merry old land of Oz kept me sane. On stage I could forget everything: the very word Helensville, the exams, training, red-hot eyes, the silly leg, which still ached occasionally. But not Andy, even though I hadn't seen him for weeks because he was in the middle of exams; I thought about him *all* the time between phone calls with a sort of exquisite ache. If that's what falling in love feels like, then I'd fallen.

Even with the *Wizard* I knew I was skating on thin ice. I'd learnt my lines in a hurry and at dress rehearsal still needed three prompts, less than some, but in my book inexcusable. And that morning I'd woken from a nightmare where, fully-dressed as Tinman I'd spent the half hour before curtain-up frantically trying to cram the lines into my head, knowing that I'd never do it and would be left standing speechless and humiliated.

Backstage before the first night was the usual shambles. Fathers still hammering scenery, third-former Munchkins everywhere, violinists tuning up, flutes piping, Miss Macrae's voice echoing around the classrooms, which had been turned into dressing-rooms, squads of mothers and teachers helping with make-up. I was a nervous gibbering wreck, again unusual for me.

Inside the costume (silver lamé breeches and shirt, silver socks, sandshoes and gloves, breastplate of cardboard painted silver) and watching my face disappear, I wondered, and not for the first time, what the hell I was doing here.

'Alex, you look superb,' Miss Macrae was booming at me, with various Munchkins staring awestruck at her handiwork. I had just put the helmet, shaped like a funnel, on top of it all. My face was silver with eyes heavily rimmed in black, Charlie Chaplin style, two dinky black eyebrows like little boomerangs, and a red rosebud mouth. My nose was tipped in black and I had some rivets along my jaw line. Almost a clown face. I had vanished, without trace. Towering above the Dorothy, who was a third former, and the pint-sized Lion, and Janice equally unrecognizable as the Scarecrow, I felt like some bizarre statue, a metallic lighthouse with legs. What *am* I doing here?

I don't remember much of the first night. The land of Oz must have worked its magic. The ability I knew I had (and indeed counted on) to rise to the occasion, along with native cunning – and a little bit of luck – got me through. Young Dorothy sang like an angel, almost as beautifully as Judy Garland. My songs passed in a daze, the audience loved the tiny Lion with her deep voice, and the witches, green-faced and grotesque, brought the house down. Through the curtain calls and cries of great, marvellous after the final curtain, stumbling through to the classroom and wiping my face clean, it still felt dream-like. Andy was out there somewhere; but it didn't seem to matter one way or the other.

I dressed slowly, apart from the others, saying little, knowing I looked pale with heavy rings under my eyes, which no amount of cold cream could remove. Was it vanity or self-protection that an echo from another dressing-room had made me choose a very frilly, feminine blouse?

In the corridor outside, I found Andy, smart in tweed sports coat and polo neck. The object too of much giggling and heavy breathing from passing third formers, as well they might.

'Alex, was that really you? Splendid stuff.'

'I don't remember much.' I might have looked wan, but inside, seeing him, I was tingling all over.

'I didn't know you could sing, too.'

'Neither did I. Take me home, please.'

'Aren't your family here?'

'I wouldn't let them come tonight. Tomorrow.' Around us swarmed Munchkins, in street clothes but flaunting their make-up proudly. 'Get me out of here.'

Going home, I could barely speak. Andy chattered on about the show, full of enthusiasm. Outside the house, I could only sit limply when he leaned across and with cool fingers traced the outlines of my face, my pointy chin, hairline greasy with cold cream; hardly romantic.

'A very special girl.'

'No.'

'Yes. Fragile, for all her apparent strength. Needs tender loving care.' He leaned across and kissed me gently. 'Go get some sleep, sweet maid.'

Weak at the knees, I got slowly out of the car. 'You're not going training in the morning,' he stated.

'Yes, I am.'

'My God, Alex, give yourself . . . '

I was half-way up the drive. 'I have to.'

'According to who . . . '

'Me. Don't spoil it Andy. Goodnight, thanks for coming.'

Dad had other thoughts. I slept through the alarm and he didn't stir me. I woke, with a dreadful taste in my mouth, at eight thirty.

Dad and the others had already gone, and Mum and Gran were standing either side of the washing machine feeding clothes through the wringer, up to their elbows in suds.

'Why didn't you wake me? I'll be late for school.'

'I think not,' said Mum quietly. 'Porridge in pot, lunch on bench, clean shirt in your room, twenty minutes in hand.' As I stared at her, stupid with sleep, she added. 'Mr Jack agreed. You need sleep more than training this week.'

It was a Jack-up. Ha! I was furious. How dare they decide for me. I stomped off to my room to get dressed. In the mirror I saw two bags under a pair of eyes, closely followed by A. Archer, Tinman Extra-ordinaire. The very thought of tonight, and tomorrow night, and the last night, made my blood run cold.

At school, those who'd seen the show were complimentary. Still in my dream-like state, I survived the next two nights. I even survived with my family there, but knowing that I sang and spoke my lines without much conviction, not up to Miss Macrae's expectations. Before bed the night they came, I had a heavy argument with Dad about training, him trying to be logical, understanding and so on, but ending with him flatly refusing to wake me or take me, actually forbidding me to go training until the show was over. I knew in my bones he was right. I was pretty near some sort of flash-point.

Andy rang before breakfast on Friday to see how the show was going. He'd finished his exams and, with holidays about to start, was feeling like celebrating.

'I'm coming tonight,' he said.

'You can't. You haven't got a ticket.' Why was I so reluctant for him to be there?

'I'll get one at the door.'

'It's the last night, sold out.'

'Then I'll hang around outside. There's sure to be a single seat or standing room somewhere. Afterwards we'll do something special, how's that?'

Over-ruled, I was silent. I'd got through three nights, but I was full of foreboding about the fourth.

'Alex, you still there?'

'Sort of. See you.' I put the phone down, and went along to breakfast. There was a funny sort of atmosphere in there too.

'Where's Gran?'

'Not feeling too good. She's staying in bed today,' said Mum. 'Jamie, take this tray in to her, will you?'

'I'll go,' I said, earning a most weird look from Jamie. Gran was propped up in bed drinking tea, surrounded by piles of unfinished baby dresses. She looked about seven hundred years old.

'You shouldn't be running round after me. You look so tired, Alex.'

'Don't talk rot, Gran. Here's some breakfast. Mum says you've got to stay in bed.'

Surprisingly, she didn't protest.

'What's wrong with Gran?' I said to Mum.

'She needs a rest.'

'You should ask,' said Jamie.

'Meaning?'

'Nothing.' Breakfast passed, the usual grizzlings about who was drying the dishes. Mum seemed preoccupied, I gave her a hand with the lunches. Dad left earlier than usual.

'Try to get a sleep after school,' Mum said.

'I can't sleep in the day.'

Mum slammed down the bread knife. 'God help me, I'm surrounded by obstinate women. I've practically had to chain Gran into her bed. And you walk around looking like a zombie, but you're above sleeping.'

Such explosions were rare. 'OK, OK. I'll have a rest.'

'Poor little Alex,' said Jamie nastily from the sink. 'Never lifts a finger. So who's in bed with overwork, trying to earn money to pay for all her lessons and being in sport and shows and trips and things . . .'

'Jamie,' shouted Mum, an even rarer event. 'You will stop immediately.' Usually it would have been me first in the debate, but this time I was too weary and too thunderstruck to do anything other than gape at Jamie. I was to blame for Gran in bed, getting so thin? Is that where all the money she earned went? Rows between Mum and Dad? An overdraft out of control?

I took a silent ten seconds or so to gather up my sandwiches, then I walked out of the kitchen, aware that Mum was trying to regain control of herself, and Jamie was probably both scared and pleased at what he'd said. I sank on my bed, and saw Mum's figure in the doorway through tears.

'Why did he say that? How would he know anything about it?'

Mum sighed. 'Dad and I had a row last night while you were at school, about money as usual. I can only assume he heard a bit, behind the door. We should have driven off somewhere in the car and had it out . . . '

'So it's true?'

'Only partly. The money Gran earns from her dresses helps pay for your lessons, coaching fees. Jamie's too, and there'll be extra things for the others as they get older. We've always wanted you to have every oppor . . . '

'Why didn't you tell me? She slaves away out there . . . '

'Gran's a very proud little lady, Alex. Her whole life has been family, since Dad died, helping me, helping us. She's made of stern stuff. Napier in the 1920s, raising children through the Depression, the earthquake, it was a pretty hard road if your husband's shop fell down, *and* he took to drink.'

Dad? My grandfather? You never knew, did you?

'I'm going out to see her.'

'Alex, if you really want to help her, you'll say nothing about money, or her working herself to a standstill, so you can swim . . . '

'It all seems so . . . so, pointless, now.'

'What does?'

'Just trying to swim faster than Maggie, when Gran looks like she does out there. If that's . . . '

'I told you. She's as tough as old boots. Two days in bed, she'll be back at her sewing machine and nothing I, you or anyone can do will change that. So, we've got to use very subtle methods to lighten her load.'

'Like me giving up swimming.'

'That would be the worst thing. Her reward is your success, your achievements. She just loved the show last night. When you win the nationals, she'll be in seventh heaven knowing that in her own way she's helped you get to Rome.'

When, she said, not if. 'Thanks, Mum,' I said, giving her a big hug. 'Can I go and see her now?'

'Just . . . belonging, is all she needs. I couldn't manage without her – well, I could, lots do. But she knows what it means to me, her help . . . And please don't say anything to Jamie.'

Gran had not touched her breakfast. Sleeping, she looked only about two hundred years old. I bent down and kissed her cheekbone, which was the least lined part of her face. 'Sleep well.' She grunted, her eyelids moved. 'See you after school, Gran.'

Despite my own extra hours' sleep each morning, by mid-morning I was feeling so tired, and still upset by what I'd heard, I was almost light-headed. I saw Miss Macrae looking at me in assembly; later she bailed me up in the corridor. Was I all right, and then some nice stuff about my stage presence, comic timing and generosity to my fellow performers. I hardly knew what she was talking about. Was it obvious I was on a tightrope?

There was no understudy, therefore no escape from tonight. The Lion, Daphne, and Scarecrow, Janice, were both sixth formers, gaily riding the wave of success and (unknown to me) anticipating some high-jinks traditional on the last night. Yet even they, when I walked into our dressing-room that evening, took one look at me and burst forth.

'You OK?'

'You sick or something? You look awful!'

'Thanks, pals, for those heart-warming words of encouragement. Guaranteed to make a girl feel just fine.'

Julia was in our room too, in her green Emerald City garb, looking at me critically as I started to undress. Not the frilly blouse tonight; I had more important things to worry about.

'Stop gawking at me, Julia. I'm fine.'

She made a doubtful face, but didn't say anything. As I put on the silver socks, breeches, shirt, there was a lot of chat. Clearly the others were out to enjoy this last performance. I'd just be glad to get it over.

'My God, look at you.' One of the witches came through the door. If her green make-up had been bizarre on previous nights, now she looked positively macabre. The atmosphere of last night recklessness made me even more determined to get through the show unscathed. I was enough of an idiot in my silver clown face, without making it worse. Mercifully, I did not have to insist that only Miss Macrae do my make-up. Skilfully, professionally, even soothingly, her fingers smoothed on the silver goo (imported especially, guaranteed non-toxic), obliterating the dark shadows. I was almost beginning to like hiding inside this Tinman.

The Kansas farm, Munchkinland and Scarecrow's song came and went. Janice was in top form. Watching in the wings as my scene drew closer, I put the two halves of the breastplate on and got one of the chorus to tie the bows holding it together. I heard a snort and snigger behind me, and titters, which must have been audible to the audience. I turned around.

'What is it?' I mouthed.

Eyes are all I remember, glinting with malice.

The curtain had closed on the witches. I had about ten seconds of music to get into position. I stormed on to the stage, where Dorothy and Scarecrow were standing ready.

'What is wrong with me?' I demanded.

They looked at me blankly.

'Tell me, otherwise I'll walk right off this stage, now, and not come back.'

In the pit outside, the orchestra faded out. The stage manager was frantically signalling to the curtain operator not to pull the curtains. The audience shuffled in the silence.

'Tell me, or I leave.'

But I was too late. The curtain had begun to open. I had two seconds to decide: leave or continue and take the consequences. Four lines into the scene, they were supposed to discover me behind a bush. I just couldn't leave them there on the stage, looking silly. I leapt into my rigid, rusted-up Tinman position on the side of the stage.

Janice began the scene, outwardly fine but eyes wary. By now my adrenalin was flowing nicely. I decided, whatever was on my back, I'd act them all off the stage. I heard my voice calling for oil in a heavy Texas accent. I deliberately manoeuvered Janice upstage so that she could see my back. When I turned to look at her, I had the satisfaction of seeing that behind her Scarecrow make-up she was nearly beside herself. Serve you right, I thought, unfairly no doubt. Little Dorothy was wide-eyed, more terrified than amused, clearly wondering what was going to happen next.

I turned my song into a soft shoe number, putting in all sorts of nimble steps, totally out of character, and belted out the final phrases in a voice to rival Ethel Merman, 'If I on-lee-had-a-HEART.' Then with my arms outstretched for the final note, a long high E, I swung around and presented the audience with my back.

The laughter and clapping went on for so long that I was obliged to turn around and follow Miss Codlin's lead to sing the song again. Even the orchestra, who'd sat through umpteen boring rehearsals, was nearly falling off its collective seats. Before that, however, I muttered to Janice under the applause what the hell they were laughing at.

'You'd rather not . . .'

'Tell me,' I hissed.

'Campbell's Soup,' she muttered. 'Made in Hong Kong. In red paint.' In the wings delighted faces watched in tiers.

Not so funny, I thought sourly. Have you ever tried to keep a straight face when all about you have completely lost their cool? I suppose professional actors have to be able to do it. I now decided to see if I could, too. As I heard the orchestra begin the four-bar intro, I thought, I'll show you. So I belted out the song again, giving the Codlin Moth a hard time, and made up a quite bizarre little dance, with comic *pas de chat* and silly arabesques. As the *coup de grâce* I did an almighty jump and finished with the splits. Ever seen a Tinman do the splits? No? This one shouldn't have either because getting to my feet again I felt a distinct pull in my leg.

It was unforgivable, really. Dorothy and Janice stood there bent double, the audience by this time laughing with them, as one does when actors have got the giggles. I stood snapped rigid into my Tinman pose, while all hell broke loose. The longer I stood, the more they laughed. It became a test, to see if they could break me. But swimmers spend hours every day staring at the bottom of a pool, switched off, thinking of nothing in particular. After a while, I was actually enjoying the control I found I had.

Thank God my family aren't here. Andy – oh shit!

From the wings, I heard a stage whisper, Miss Macrae, 'Get on with the scene, Dorothy.' Eventually she did, with me still the po-faced injured party. The audience seemed to find everything I said hilarious. I tried out an English accent, then broad Aussie and broader Scots. When the Munchkins came on they were supposed to be all nervous about the hazards of the journey to the Land of Oz but the scene was ruined. When we finally got on to the Yellow Brick Road, my nerve was beginning to go, but I was up to my silver neck in it now. We swung through that number like we never swung before. It was written as a trio with chorus, but it became my dance. This time I was a tipsy marching girl. The Munchkins didn't have a show.

I have to hand it to Miss Macrae. She'd already decided there'd be an interval and sent a message to the Codlin Moth. As I stood gasping behind the closed curtain, hearing the torrent of applause, I knew Miss Macrae, who'd played Joan of Arc on the London stage, could have destroyed me for ever. But she merely held back the surge of excitement with a raised hand and said quietly, 'Ten minutes' interval, girls, to calm down a little.'

I felt a hand take mine. Although Miss Macrae had not finished talking, Julia led me offstage through rows of grinning teeth and into the classroom. She sat me on a chair, knelt and undid the fastenings of the breastplate.

It was worse even than Campbell's Soup and Made in Hong Kong. Painted in large black letters, a heart with an arrow stuck through it said A LOVES A. Where my bottom would have been was a card, stuck on crudely with chewing gum. I remember someone pressing up against me in the wings. This one read HANDLE WITH CARE.

I swear the flush was visible through the silver. With just a little fight left in me before I crawled into my hole, I snatched the breastplate from Julia and bent it across my knee. Then I hurled it into a corner.

'Take that bloody thing away, burn it or do any damn thing you like with it, but piss off, all of you . . . ' – this for the benefit of a few faces that had appeared at the door. 'Leave me alone. I'm going home.'

'Alex.'

The steely voice boomed through my rage.

'And you can stick your wizard . . . '

'Alex, sit down, please.'

Deflated and shaking, I sat. I had the wrong costume on, I was the Scarecrow minus all his stuffing. There was an ominous pause while Miss Macrae walked into the room. People have been expelled for swearing at teachers.

'Before a race, I'm sure you do this, Alex. Singers also, musicians. Hands on diaphragm, deep breaths, feel that rib cage expand, shoulders steady.'

The Tinman had rusted up for ever.

'Alex, ten deep breaths, with me. One, two, three . . . ' I matched her rhythm. 'Good, now ten more.'

She stood behind me and expertly massaged my shoulders. And I, traitor that I was, thought she's enjoying this, a chance at last to touch me. But her strong fingers were easing away the tension.

'So tight! Now listen to me, Alex, you've got a performance to finish . . . '

I jumped like a cat. 'No.'

'Relax, let yourself go.' Her fingers both hurt and eased me. 'You have an obligation, mainly to yourself but also to the rest of us . . . '

'I can't.'

'I believe you can.'

I looked up. In the mirror was this unlikely pair, the silver clown with staring glazed black eyes, the middle-aged woman with short grey hair above. It wasn't me in there, it was someone else. I was at home, in bed.

'How could they?'

'It wasn't only you.'

'Why me?'

'You were just the first, believe me. Lion had a pair of wings sewn into her costume, and for Scarecrow, well, I shudder to think what they were going to do with a string of sausages. Intestines, possibly. Our Wizard had secreted about her person, under her cape, a dead fish, a golf umbrella and a tiny third former dressed as a chicken. Highly unprofessional and irresponsible. I shall find out who was involved.'

'Too late now. I've ruined everything . . . '

'No, you haven't.' She stopped massaging and pulled up a chair to sit very close to me. 'Alex, you're very talented . . . '

'No,' I cried. 'It's all a lie, I fail, every time.'

'Nine out of ten professional actors could not have survived on that stage tonight. Your control was quite breath-taking. And that was a very funny dance. Will you believe me when I say it was brilliant, I haven't laughed so much for a long time. If I didn't personally think that law, court work, or maybe politics, was the most suitable career for your undoubted gifts once you've got all that sport out of your system, I should recommend that you trained for the stage. Despite your height, or even carrying your height to your advantage.'

'That wasn't me,' I muttered.

'Oh yes it was,' she smiled, 'You, with your inhibitions loosened by anger and defiance and embarrassment. Most people need booze to enjoy themselves quite as much as that in public. Actors need years of experience. Women find it particularly hard. There's a reluctance to take the risk of making a fool of yourself.'

I was silent. Enjoy myself? Had I? Oh, yes, I'd ridden that wave of audience approval with guns blazing.

'I did make a fool of myself, didn't I?'

'Look at me, Alex. The answer is no. You played to the gallery, you carried it off superbly. Now, I'm asking you to use that discipline, that control I've just seen, to finish the show. There'll be no more pranks.'

Something in my eyes must have signalled, I'll try.

'Good girl.' She stood up, hands on my shoulders, almost as though trying to knead her will, her strength and her experience into me. 'The audience will expect more of the same. Don't get rattled. Just play it as we rehearsed. They'll soon settle down.'

Brisk, booming voice again. 'Janice, get the cast on stage for me. Alex, you sit quietly for a few minutes.'

'No, I'm coming.' I saw a smile before she left. Julia had moved across to pick up my battered armour. 'Not much we can do about this, Alex,' she said, trying to flatten out the cracks. 'You'll just have to keep your front to the audience.'

That won't be difficult, I thought, standing wearily, while Julia tied on the breastplate.

'You'll be fine,' she said. I checked myself in the mirror. I still had the oddest feeling that it was someone else inside that costume, behind the silver mask. 'Come on.'

Keeping to the back, I caught a few curious looks, nudges, and giggles as we assembled behind the curtain. The second act, Miss Macrae announced briskly, was to proceed as rehearsed. Anyone rash enough to try any more pranks on stage would be severely dealt with.

Then it was house lights again, orchestra and back on to the Yellow Brick Road. I was back into my dream-like trance of the previous nights, just going through the motions. After my initial few lines, the audience seemed to sense I'd done my dash and shifted their enjoyment to Daphne's wonderful husky, petrified Lion and later the witches.

Final curtain, speeches, thanks, bouquets, I stood as inconspicuously as my height and a silver face allowed. As soon as it was all over, Julia had my hand again. 'Let's go.' In the dressing-room she started to undress me.

'You'll make a wonderful nurse,' I mumbled. 'But an even better doctor.'

'Hush.' Then harshly to a swarm of excitable people trying to get in through the door, 'Get out all of you. No one's allowed in here for ten minutes except those needing to change.'

'Who said?'

'I said. Alex is not well. Now scram.' I heard the door bang. 'Rabble we can do without.'

I seemed powerless to help myself. I obeyed her orders like a dummy. Stripped to bra and silver breeches, my hair scraped back from the silver mask which looked like one of those Greek tragedy masks on our school Shakespeare books, I surveyed myself in the mirror and began to laugh. It was not a good moment for the swell in the noises from the corridor outside as the door opened and shut, a male voice saying firmly, 'I'm her brother.'

There stood Andy.

Some brother. By now I was laughing fit to bust.

Julia moved first, with a dressing-gown which she slipped around my shoulders.

'She's cold and exhausted,' I heard her say. 'And she's about to have hysterics.'

I roared at my reflection. Ha ha *ha*, ho ho *ho*, the Merry Old Land of Oz, get lost. Hysterics, what's that. The Tinman is cracking up. I scooped up a great dollop of cold cream from a pot and threw it at my face. I rubbed at the silver mask. The stuff went in my eyes, ears, hair, very quickly becoming a nasty molten mess.

'When a man's an empty kettle, he's always on his mettle,' I sang. Another scoop of cold cream. 'And yet I'm torn apart.' I threw the dressing-gown off. ' . . . I could be kinda human, If I Only Had a *Heart*.' Ethel Merman again. There was a sinister silence in the corridor now. Were they all listening? Julia and Andy were moving towards me, coming to get me. If I noticed anything at all, it was the expression on Andy's face, aghast, as I spat out what I had to say.

'I'd be tender, I'd be gentle, I'd be awful sentimental – you know what they say, Andy . . . ? Because I always . . . have to be, wind up a male in these charades, they think . . . do you know what they think, they *think* I'm a bit odd, I'm nearly six foot tall and built like a tank, and I've got this funny tenor voice . . . What do you think, Andy? I shouldn't be swimming against proper girls like Maggie, that's what they say. Perhaps I'm a neuter. Isn't there a word, hermaph . . . hermaph . . . Oh, I could be kinda human if I only had a . . . '

Andy had grabbed one sticky hand, Julia the other. My knees buckled as they forced me back on to a chair.

Now I knew they were coming, the tears I'd held back for days and weeks, even months since Maggie's dance. I heard Andy's voice. There was a towel in his hand. 'Alex, sweet maid. Hold her hands, Julia. Alex, please, Alex, let me . . . '

I was draped across the chair, my head thrown back. I felt the tension literally dripping out of me. Fingers were gently wiping my face clean, as soothingly as Miss Macrae had put the stuff on.

'Nearly gone now, Tinman, for ever,' Andy said. Mothers talked like that to their children, soothing away a nightmare, a hurt. I'd done it myself, to various brothers and sisters. 'Nearly gone, rest now.'

If only I could. 'I'm going training in the morning.' If I kept this up, I could train in my own tears.

'We'll see.' Mothers said that too, fobbing off. 'There now. Sit up, Alex . . . '

I looked at myself again. There were still black smudges where my eyes should have been, globs of cold cream in my hair, but mostly I was me again. I wept afresh, on to the shoulder of Andy's nice sports coat.

'We've got to get some clothes on her,' said Julia. 'She's shaking, but whether from cold or . . . '

'He's seen me in bikinis before,' I sniffed. 'Don't be prudish, Julia. And don't talk about me as though I'm not here.'

'I'm not,' Julia began indignantly.

'If you're going to be a doctor, you can't be prudish. Andy here, now he's not going to be a doctor, he's going to sea, aren't you Andy? Funny that, both your parents . . . Julia thinks she's going to have to be a nurse, but that's only her silly father. I think you're very brave, Julia. I can't *stand* the sight of blood.'

'She's away with the fairies,' I heard Julia mutter. 'Do you think we should call a doctor?' How sharp were all my senses, especially my great ears which heard far too much. I heard the door open and shut again.

'Get some clothes on, Alex,' said Miss Macrae brutally. 'Time to go home and sleep. Holidays as of now, three whole weeks, thank God.'

Julia was on hand with shirt, jumper, skirt, shoes.

'I'm very proud of you, Alex,' said Miss Macrae. 'That took courage.'

I could only wail, but I was running out of tears.

Julia said, 'This is her boyfriend, Andy Richmond.'

'Good, you take her home as soon as we can get some clothes on her. Come on, Alex, help yourself. Make a fuss of your girl, Andy. She needs it. We all need reassurance from time to time when we think we've gone off the rails . . . '

I was down to sniffing and snuffling now. I had never felt more totally drained in my life.

'One day when you win a few gold medals, or you're making a name for yourself in court, or whatever you choose to do, I'll think back to tonight. Raw talent, off the leash. You'll remember it too, Alex, and chuckle.'

I wasn't smiling yet. But Andy was.

'Don't laugh at me,' I whispered, pathetically. 'Please, Andy, don't laugh.'

He was staring at me, remembering. 'I wouldn't have believed it possible. If a Hollywood talent scout had been here . . . '

'Don't.'

'Will you listen just for once? Can't you believe I'm so proud of you I could burst? That I stood there at the side and just marvelled? What are you afraid of?'

'It's a female problem,' said Miss Macrae. 'Reluctance to make a fool of herself. I did it, often enough. I know what it takes.'

I looked at her, with her severe grey fringe and tailored suit. She looked more like an off-duty hospital matron.

'I always got the character parts, blacked up for minstrel shows, pantomime horses, Cinderella's ugly sister, Noel Coward revues, lots of ghosts, witches – *Macbeth*, the opera of *Hansel and Gretel*. A riotous version of *The Taming of the Shrew*, in a red wig.'

Katherine the Shrew, Miss Macrae?

'Now, Andy Richmond, take your girl home. Leave all your stuff, Alex. Julia will look after it.'

We went out a side door, to avoid Munchkins and others. Andy treated me like a sick patient coming home from hospital and I wasn't going to protest. Truth to tell, I felt as though I'd been through some kind of storm at sea, washed up, some ordeal by fire, melted down. I also knew I wouldn't be training tomorrow, because I didn't think I'd wake for about three days.

Some things I do know, Andy. Round about here, races are won or lost. Maggie, for the first time in her life, too, is swimming this race to win. Never mind what the stop-watch says. And she's increased her stroking rate.

I've gained, yet still she holds me off. Half a yard, a hand? Are my arms that much longer when it comes to the final lunge for the wall?

No, they're not. I've mighty long arms, like an albatross, a wing span of over two yards, but that's not long enough.

Round about here races are lost, Alex. Oh think ahead, sweet maid, to the wall, to Rome.

That Aussie coach sitting out there with Lady Benton. He might ask me to join his squad in Queensland . . . what about a scholarship to an American university . . .

Put that in your pipe, Mrs Benton. Oh I'm slipping, I'm slipping, I'm going backwards for Christmas . . .

Alex, you're not concentrating. Your stroke rate – can you move it up a notch?

9

When Mum puts her foot down, which is not often, it goes down hard. I woke up after two solid days' sleep, getting out of bed only to pee and sit silently at the family table to eat some food. Mum, with Gran back on her feet ('I am *not* staying in there another day, Helena,' I heard her indignant voice) was in no mood for discussion. Messages had been taken, from Julia and Miss Macrae and also Miss Gillies, to see how I was; Alex is fine, thanks, I heard Mum say on the phone, catching up on sleep and going away for a few days. I was? I was about to do what I was told.

'Your father has taken three days off work,' she said quietly after tea on Sunday night, cheese on toast around the fire. We were in for two weeks of school holidays for the brats, three for me. I'd planned on catching up with training, weights, some extra piano practice, and swot, with School Cert only two months away, and miles of notes to revise.

'Why?' Dad never took time off work, even to come to champs and things. He just couldn't. He had two weeks' holiday a year and that was that.

'I've rung up your Auntie Pat. You can use their beach house.'

'Mum, I've got to start *training.*'

'I've already spoken to Mr Jack,' said Dad. 'He agrees that what you need right now is a complete break. We'll be back Wednesday night. You can start Thursday.'

I thought, I can't stand people organizing my life for me, but I knew a brick wall when I saw one.

'Andy is coming, too,' said Dad.

'*What?*'

'Don't say what, please Alex. I spoke to him yesterday. He's got permission from his parents, provided he brings his books and does four hours' a day.'

'Dad!'

'What's the matter? I thought you two got on well.'

'You seem to have me all sorted out.'

'That's right,' said Mum. 'This time we have, and about time. Three days of sea air will do you a power of good.'

'I breathe sea air all the time. Auckland's surrounded by sea . . .'

'You know what I mean, Miss Smarty Alec. Blow away the cobwebs. Go for long walks along the beach, read, sleep. I know your leg's not entirely right yet but . . .'

I had my marching orders.

How can you have two totally opposite feelings about the same thing? I was thrilled down to my boots that Andy was coming – and horrified as well. After last Friday night, I thought I'd never be able to look him in the face again. In the car going home, I'd been like a zombie. I knew it, but just couldn't help myself. I'd muttered to myself, and my head kept falling off my neck.

There'd even been a reception committee waiting: Mum and Dad, apparently alerted by a phone call from school. I was helped out of the car like a cripple. Dad would have carried me inside, but he wasn't a giant and there was, frankly, too much of me.

Everyone was deliberately cheerful, speaking too clearly and a touch too loud. What had happened wasn't directly mentioned.

'Bed for you, Alex,' said Mum. 'Cup of tea, Andy?'

So, after I'd had a shower and washed the remaining smudges off my face, they'd all sat around in my bedroom drinking cups of tea and eating digestive biscuits and talking about the Queen having another baby and Krushchev visiting America and the second rugby test against the British Lions in Wellington. Unreal.

Then I fell asleep, just like that. As I went, I heard Mum saying, 'My poor Alex. I'm afraid some people have to learn the hard way.'

Andy: 'She was very *very* funny . . .'

Mum: 'What happened?'

Andy: 'Well, . . .'

I gave a tiny scream, 'Shut up Andy,' but I was out for the count.

We picked Andy up at half past eight on Monday morning, fortunately without getting involved with his parents. I'd climbed out of bed still feeling zonked, and apprehensive about Andy coming.

When I saw him, I felt much better; what a fine-looking young man, Gran muttered as she came out with me to the car to say goodbye, and he was too. Three days of him, all to myself!

Dad was like a kid wagging school. I suppose when you have two weeks' leave a year, anything else is a bonus.

'Good weather predicted,' he said. 'South-westerlies, occasional showers, mainly fine. Brought your togs, Andy?'

'I never thought to.'

'Pity. Bracing stuff, August swimming. I grew up only a stone's throw from the beach. We had a thriving life-saving club, swam the year round. Well, a few of us did. I've often wondered if that helped when it came to swimming around in the Atlantic when my ship . . . '

'D-did you serve in the navy, sir?'

Then they were away, all the way out to the coast, or rather Dad was, pleased to find someone interested in his war-time exploits, being torpedoed in the Atlantic and later missing his ship in Crete or somewhere, and the ship going down with all hands two days later. Of course, Dad didn't know that going to sea was all Andy had ever wanted to do, and Andy didn't know that Dad hardly ever talked about the war, and that he should count himself lucky.

I watched the bungalows slip by, content to sit in the front and let Dad's quiet voice put me to sleep. Andy lent over the back of the seat and gently rubbed the back of my neck. I liked hearing them talk, my two favourite men (not forgetting Mr Jack, of course): men's talk. Andy talked about the Sea Cadets he'd been in at school. He was rather sorry that compulsory military training had been stopped last year and he didn't have to go off and do his three months as a naval trainee.

'Sorry?' said Dad. 'Most young blokes I know . . . '

'It's because I want to go to sea,' said Andy in a rush. 'It's all I've ever wanted.' (So now two people know.) 'But my parents want me to do medicine. I've got to t-tell them soon that I'm not going to.'

After a silence, Dad said, 'Will that be difficult?'

'Very.' I felt the finger rubbing my neck stop, as though it was thinking about the problem. 'That's why I want to get good scholarship marks, then I'm in a strong position to convince them I'll get accepted for officer training. Midshipman cadets go to D-D-England, to Dartmouth Naval College, first.'

You'll be going away, Andy? I couldn't bear it. I will wait for ever. My eyelids and my brain closed down as we started the climb up the hills to the beach and the beach house beyond. I'd not been out to the west coast in years. Perhaps this whole junket wasn't such a bad idea after all.

Three days suspended in time. The house was a very small wooden box snuggling up against the hillside, about two hundred yards back from the beach. There were two rooms. One had four bunks, four lumpy pillows, a wooden chest of drawers, that's all. We hung our coats on hooks behind the door. The other room had a wood-burning stove, an enamel sink, some very plain cupboards, a worn table and rickety chairs. Battered tin billies, a frypan that had seen better days, crockery and eating utensils that might have belonged to some old great-aunt, circa 1890. Two 'Beautiful New Zealand' calendars (1953, 1956), two armchairs, fishing gear stacked in a corner and some horrible curtains completed the decor. There was no telephone and no electricity. Water came from a large tin tank beside the house, and the toilet was a long drop in a tiny outhouse twenty yards away.

Dad was rather rude about his sister, Pat, my aunt. 'Married into all that money. Obvious they haven't spent much of it here.'

'I like it as it is,' I said. It was true. I really liked the plain wooden walls and the kerosene lamps flickering away at night. We lit the wood stove late each afternoon and by tea-time it was as warm as toast. Dad did all the cooking: sausages and fried eggs on Monday night, shepherd's pie on Tuesday.

Andy tried, mainly in the early mornings while I was still asleep, but he didn't get much work done. Dad said he, for one, was happy pottering, and might do a spot of fishing later, so Andy and I went for long meandering walks along the beach. There was hardly anyone around, fishermen casting with long lines from the rocks near the car-park, a few like us, just walking, kids scrambling up and jumping down the high dunes of black sand.

On our last day, we soon left them all behind, walking slowly, barefoot through the shallows, kicking at the froth and feeling the suction around our ankles as the waves were pulled back into the ocean. My leg gave me no trouble. Ahead of us the mighty beach swept in a clear curve until it disappeared into the mist. And offshore the surf rolled and broke against a hard blue sky. Hundreds of miles to Australia, thousands to anywhere else.

If Andy was thinking how small my worries were against that seascape, he was right. I could feel myself unwinding.

We found a sheltered crater in amongst the black dunes and sat down for the lunch we'd put together, Marmite sandwiches, cheese, a carrot each, some biscuits Mum had sent with us, a thermos of tea.

As he munched, Andy smiled.

'What's the joke?'

'I was just thinking . . . you won't like this . . . of you on that stage.'

I was already on my feet, brushing the crumbs off my jeans and packing up the thermos.

'You'd better get this straight, Andy Richmond. You mention *The Wizard of Oz* ever again and I'll . . . '

'What? Refuse to see me?'

'Yep.'

'You wouldn't do that. I'm the best friend you've got.'

'That doesn't mean you can keep on teasing and hurting me any old time you want.'

'It means', he said, grabbing my wrist and pulling me towards him, 'I'm going to kiss you like this and not even the famous Alexandra is going to protest.'

How could I, anyway. My legs had given way beneath me and we'd fallen into the sand. I was underneath, helpless, loving it.

When we'd both run out of breath, he said, 'There, Alexandra, now kiss me back.'

One thing led to another and with anyone less strong, I might well have gone, as my older classmates at school so delicately put it, the whole hog. But Andy had firm views about some things and this was one of them. I suppose I did, too, when it came to the point. So we went only half-way.

Pity really, because the sensation of wind against my bare breast and Andy kissing it softly was almost too much for me.

'I want to ask you something,' he said.

'Fire away.'

'If you'd rather not . . . '

'Try me.' He hadn't shaved this morning, and his chin was rough, like sandpaper, a cat's tongue.

'Do you remember saying, after the show, that last night when you were . . . upset . . . you said, people are saying you're odd. Being tall, and good at sport, and you, quote, "always have male roles in these charades" . . . '

After a long while, I said, 'Did I say that?'

'Something like.'

'Hmmm. Do you remember Maggie's dance? That's what I overheard in the Ladies'. Some little cat and her friend. A friend at her school, quote, "says it's no coincidence she always winds up a male in school shows," unquote. And "she's always hugging girls, and giving her very good friend Julia back rubs" . . . '

'No wonder you came out pink.'

'Do you blame me? Julia's asthmatic, you know that. What am I supposed to do, never touch her when a massage seems to ease it?'

He had pulled back my bush shirt further and was stroking the other breast as well.

'Boys get it, too,' he said. 'Anyone who's not your average guy. Show an interest in music, theatre, smart clothes, poetry, art – you're suspect. Even hockey or soccer is unmanly. If you wanted to be an interior designer, or a ballet d-dancer or a hairdresser – you'd be called a *girl*, absolutely beyond the pale. Real men play footie, or watch it, and prop up the bar until six. Then they go home and listen to the radio to find out how much they've lost on the horses, swear at their kids and beat up their wives.'

'You like jazz and Gershwin and Noel Coward . . . '

'I keep that very quiet. And I play in the First Fifteen, which puts me beyond suspicion. Anyway, I thought it might help, well, to know you're not alone in this. Others get knocked too, people who are different and successful. You gotta get cut down to size. I've a teacher at school, a real larger-than-life Englishman, who says it's a New Zealand national pastime.'

'It's worse still for girls. No one's really expected to have great ambitions. Nearly all my class are going to do nursing or teaching or secretarial work, travel a bit, catch a husband and disappear for ever into the suburbs.'

'What about Julia? She's going to do medicine, you said.'

'Her father says he can't afford to put her through university, as well as two brothers. She'll end up nursing, you'll see. Girls are expendable in the end. The Head at school says it wasn't always like this, girls being talked out of careers, out of higher education. At least *you* are encouraged, great things are expected, great scholarship marks. At our school they won't even let the Upper Sixth girls *sit*. Only a few people are encouraging me: Mum and Dad, some of the teachers at school.'

'I am.'

'OK, you. The rest think I'm crazy to want to do law. And then people say, because you want a proper career so that you're independent and you happen to be tall and have broad shoulders and can swim a bit, that you're not feminine. Career girls are hard, selfish and not true women.'

'I wish you'd told me at the time why . . .'

'Not likely! I wouldn't have told anyone, ever, except for . . .'

He propped himself up on his elbows and smiled down. 'It doesn't matter a d- tinker's cuss, does it, what people say. You know what you are. *I* know. Lordy, how I know! Oh, Alex, I could . . .'

He had never kissed me with such force, nor, it must be said, I him. I had a sudden vision of Deborah Kerr in her famous beach scene, rolling round in the surf. There must be something about beaches.

'Wow,' I said when I could get a breath. 'What are you grinning at?'

'How could anyone even think it? When you can kiss like that? Oh Alex, sweet maid, will you wait for me while I sit these lousy exams?'

'Will you wait for me while I sit mine? And plough up and down a swimming pool?'

'And while I go to Dartmouth?'

'And while I go to Rome? And get my degree?' It sounds for ever, an awful long time, is it fair to ask anyone to wait that long?

No answers were needed. Some time later we shook the black sand out of our hair, packed up the lunch things, I did up my shirt and we walked back along the beach. Dad wasn't ready to head for town yet, he said, grimly casting his line into the water swirling below the rocks, because he'd promised Gran he wouldn't return without a fish. So we walked slowly on up the headland.

We lay silently for a very long time, just lying in a patch of long grass and looking out to sea, picking out the king waves rolling towards their final magnificent ending against the rocks. Andy's

Alex

arm was around my shoulders, and we drew warmth from each other as the sun slid towards the horizon, a chill in the air reminding us it was still only August.

What lay ahead for us? I felt like I was leaving something behind on that beach, saying goodbye to something. I don't know, my childhood perhaps, the carefree life? Tomorrow, tonight, we'd be back to the reality of routine, work, swot, train, towards the hardest goals we'd ever set ourselves. Here, on this craggy headland, watching the sun slide towards the sea and the sky change colour, only the sad, magic *now* mattered. We must have slept . . .

'He's caught something.'

Blinked awake, I could see the figure far below us on the slab of rock, the rod bending. 'Dad'll be pleased.'

'Look!' said Andy as the figure staggered backward and the rod nearly bent in half. 'He might need help.'

'You go on, Andy. My leg, I don't want to . . . hurrying . . .' And by the time I got down the steep path, the fish had been landed: a handsome enormous snapper. It was thrashing around so much that Dad was having difficulty holding it down for the *coup de grâce*. I couldn't watch. Rock against skull, thud, thud, thud.

'A beaut, Mr Archer,' said Andy. They both looked like grinning kids.

'Ten pounds at least. Baked snapper tomorrow night, squeeze of lemon, enough for everyone. You'll have to come and share it with us, Andy.'

I was more sorry for the fish. Did there always have to be winners and losers? I turned my back on the rocks and the surf and the pale green sky, even on Andy to whom I'd said a sort of temporary goodbye up there on the headland, and began to walk up the road to the beach house. It was time to go home and get on with it.

Did you say stroke faster, Andy? I'll try, oh I'll try, though my lungs are bursting.

Through the splash, through bathing cap tight against ears, I can hear the roar of the crowd. It must be loud.

They don't care who wins, not really. It's just a good race to them, another good battle, like gladiators in the Roman arena slogging it out. One dies, one will live, they don't care which.

But Mr Jack cares, and my family cares like hell, even Jamie in his own funny way, and Andy does, would have, does.

You care, Alex . . . more than anyone, you care, says Andy. So get cracking.

How much does she still have, Andy? Between me and Rome, me and oblivion – between Maggie the winner and me the loser . . .

10

I thought the schedule Mr Jack doled out at five thirty the next morning was a bit rough for the first morning back, convalescent leg and (shush) sort of nervous breakdown (just a little one, nothing too serious) and all. 'One mile straight, half arms only, we'll keep off the kicking . . .' so it went on, up to three miles. He didn't bat an eyelid. Neither did I. Two can play that game. I got in and did it.

The water felt and tasted like salt soup and after about three lengths I knew I was back to the medieval eye torture again. My arms ached, and worse, I seemed to have caught a cold, maybe from the one swim we'd had with Dad out at the beach, which was freezing cold and the surf looked from water level absolutely monstrous. When I finally climbed out of the pool I thought my head was on fire.

Among the few other serious swimmers ploughing up and down I noticed no sign of Maggie, and said so to Mr Jack.

'You've got to know sometime. She's in Aussie for three weeks.'

'Doing what?'

'Training up in Queensland, with some of the Aussie squad.'

'She can't do that.'

'Why not? It's a free world.'

'Because . . . they don't coach Kiwis over there.' What I meant was, it isn't fair. Maggie hadn't told me she was going; I could hardly blame her.

'Perhaps no one ever asked before. Maggie's Mum did, apparently. So there she is.'

Being sharpened up by one of the best coaches in the world, no doubt at some considerable cost. How badly Mrs Benton wanted that Olympic blazer for Maggie; time and money were no object. If it wasn't for me, she'd waltz in. No wonder Mrs Benton hated me so.

That explained the morning's heavy schedule. I knew I was being watched, to see how I could take it.

I could take it – the programme of sprints and time trials (arms only, because my leg was aching a bit) that followed at four thirty, and again twice the next day, and into next week. The eyes and the sinus problem didn't get any better, but I'd become used to that pain.

Two or three hours' swot when the blur cleared and I could actually see the print in my books, and an hour's piano practice daily, bed at the same time as the youngest kids, the holidays ground on.

Andy was incommunicado, head down into his books, although we caught up by phone every two or three days. I began to wish someone had told me I had to give up training for exams. Every time the sting in my eyes got so bad I thought I really couldn't bear it, I pictured Mrs Benton sunning herself by the side of a pool in Queensland, sipping a gin and tonic, talking earnestly to the Aussie coach, and Maggie keeping up with those Aussie whizz kids in that nice clean pale blue sunny sparkling *cold* water that didn't leave your eyes burning like coals.

Far from the picture of Queensland health, Maggie looked grim when she walked into the pool the first morning back after the holidays. Resting at the end of my first half-mile, I saw her come in alone, say a few words to her coach, but none to anyone else and get straight down to business.

I hoped, being naturally curious, we'd end up in the dressing-room together. I'd just finished my hot shower when she came in.

'Hi Maggie. How was Queensland?'

I thought she might be bashful, or embarrassed, but I was wrong. She looked at me briefly and then started peeling her togs off. Her hip bones were sticking out, and her arms thinner.

'OK.'

'I heard you'd gone. What a tan, lucky you!'

'It won't last long.'

'Hard work? Harder than here?'

'Not really. Just more people, crowded lanes. Each coach had his own special time.'

'Nice clear water, I bet. Your eyes'll have to get used to this soup all over again.'

She didn't reply. I decided I'd tried hard enough to be pleasant. We finished changing in silence. 'See you,' I said casually as I left. Be like that.

If I thought I was the only one with problems, I was wrong again. Gradually, word got about – as it always does – that Maggie had a few, too.

Like having a monumental row with her mother in Australia because she wanted, among other things, to go to a drive-in movie with an Aussie swimmer she'd met, and wasn't allowed. Like her coach here being upset that he wasn't consulted about the Aussie junket. And Mrs Benton coming back loaded with schedules that didn't quite fit in with his ideas, and how he and Mrs Benton had had a row (on the phone the night before Maggie had reappeared at the pool), and she'd threatened to send Maggie to Mr Jack for coaching. And the only reason Maggie was not continuing training in Australia was because she had to live a certain time in New Zealand to qualify for Olympic nomination, and so on. All good clean fun.

Knowing all this, a small bit in the paper during the week was interesting for what it didn't say. 'AUSTRALIAN EXPERIENCE FOR MAGGIE BENTON' was the headline. 'Olympic swim hopeful Maggie Benton returned this week after three weeks' intense coaching with the famed Australian squad in Queensland.

'Her mother, Mrs Harold Benton, said that Miss Benton had gained invaluable training and time-trial experience alongside swimmers who were expected to make strong bids for the Australian Olympic team next year.

' "They were very impressed with her improvement and her potential. She was offered a place in the squad, which is of course a great honour, but she has her own coach here and her schooling has to be considered."

'Miss Benton has resumed normal twice-daily training. Arch-rival Alex Archer has also started training after suffering a hockey injury to her leg in June, which kept her out of the water for six weeks. They are expected to have their first clash at an invitation meeting on 24 November.'

'Would've been interesting', Mr Jack said the morning this

appeared and he told me about Mrs Benton threatening to send Maggie to him for coaching. 'Both of you together.'

By what divine right did Mrs Benton assume that he'd automatically take her darling Maggie for coaching?

'No thanks,' I said. 'If that happens, I'm retiring. It's me or her.'

I was not joking. The winter seemed never-ending. Swot was never-ending. Early training, the same three miles day after day, seemed pointless. My leg still ached. Eyes were permanently red-rimmed and sinuses permanently stuffy. Calisthenics, without Andy to do exercises with, was a bore. Weights got heavier. Piano lessons, with little practice to speak of, were a sham. School was dreary, my family too noisy, Gran too busy with her baby dresses and Andy so deep into his books he'd disappeared from sight.

I really had begun to wonder if it was worth it, when Maggie plainly had it sewn up. Why didn't I just gently fade out, not enter for meetings, forget about Rome. Or 'announce my retirement' – one story, one photo, promptly forgotten. Alex, the might-have-been if only she'd stuck at it.

At least Maggie and I were talking again. It turned out that she'd hated Aussie. The coach had talked down his nose about our little Kiwi cousin and got rather upset when she'd beaten one of his bright hopes in a time trial. Whereupon her mother had got in on the act and talked about paying him good money ('Alex, I could have died, right on the side of the pool they were') and she was known thereafter as the Kiwi-dragon lady. The swimmers themselves were OK, but the only one who really understood was the boy she'd not been allowed to go out with. She was still writing to him and if all went well they'd both be in their Olympic teams next year – 'Ooops,' said Maggie. 'That wasn't very tactful, was it?' 'That's OK,' I said.

Maggie told me all this, because we understand each other, even though her mother and reporters and everyone else seem to think that because we both want the same thing and only one of us can have it, we can't be civilized to each other. Let's face it, when you train in the same pool, use the same dressing-room, line up for the same races together as long as we have, you'd have to have a lot of stamina to be anything but civilized.

She still has something, Alex. You'll have to try harder.
  I can't.
  I think you can.
  It's not fair, for a trip to hang on the result of one race!
  Consider yourself luckier than the Americans. They have trials for their Olympic teams. It doesn't matter if you hold a world record, if you get beaten in the trials, that's it. One trial, one race, one chance.
  Perhaps they might send both of us?
  It's possible. Your times are good enough.
  Even if she wins this, I hold the national record.
  You're on your way to another.
  You're kidding.
  Honest. First lap was under thirty seconds. Turn wasn't too hot, you lost about point four there . . .
  And lost the race.
  Oh no. She's only got about six inches on you now.
  That's all? No kidding?
  That's all. Dig in, girl . . .

11

At school, as the third term swung into action, I kept a low profile. There were a few remarks in the first assembly about the great success of the production, with some outstanding work by soloists, etcetera. People round me looked sideways, sniggered, nudged each other; I looked blankly at my shoes and ignored them.

Auditions were being held for a revue to be put on during the last week of term after exams. To my own surprise I was tempted. It was to be extracts from musicals: *South Pacific, Oklahoma, My Fair Lady, West Side Story,* even something called *The Sound of Music* which had lots of kids in it and was in rehearsal and due to open on Broadway in November. A friend who had something to do with stage management had written to tell Miss Macrae the music was superb, he was sending some of the songs, including a delightful number called 'Doh-Ray-Mi'.

I thought of Andy and how I'd love to sing a Coward song, as a sort of gift. Miss Macrae bailed me up; how would I like to do just one solo, and perhaps a trio? There'd only be a few rehearsals in the last two weeks when exams were over and everyone was just having fun and packing up for the holidays. I agreed.

Our end-of-second-term exam marks came back. Moderate in most, brilliant in none, and History, where I'd usually been one of the top two, a disaster. Not even a pass, forty-one in fact, about thirteenth out of twenty. When the mark was read out, with rather undue emphasis, if felt like an actual blow. I put my head down on the desk, and looked at no one. When it was time for break I walked outside to the fartherest corner of the playing-fields.

Julia caught me up, put her hand on my shoulder.

'Don't.'

'Alex, it's only a silly test, a practice run.'

I strode on, towards blurred trees. 'Go away, Julia.'

'Wasn't that the exam you fell asleep in? No wonder. You probably did half of it quite well. Forget it, Alex.'

How could I? The shame! I'd lost the security of knowing that even without much effort I could end up somewhere near the top. Worse, perhaps even really trying, I might not get the School Certificate marks I wanted . . . That would be a bitter pill. I'd *always* been in the first three.

We'd reached the boundary trees. I slumped down on to one of the surface roots. 'Leave me alone.'

'Your other marks weren't so bad . . . '

'Five weeks to School C . . . '

'For heaven's sake,' said Julia. 'What does getting School C mean to you? Nothing.'

'Of course it means . . . '

'Just one easy tiny step up the ladder towards fame and fortune. You don't expect to fail, now, do you?' Her voice was rich with scorn. 'I'm sick of you, Alex Archer, moping round the place, grizzling about training and swot and all the other things you choose to do. Some people actually have to *work* just to pass. Some people work and still don't pass.'

'I am not some people.'

'Oh no, we're special we are. Look, Alex, you've got everything going for you. You can do anything you want, you're good at every single thing you try, your parents worship the ground you tread on . . . '

'They don't.'

'Oh yes, they do. If you decided you were going to be the first woman Prime Minister or fly to the moon they'd say fine, Alex, how can we help.'

'All right, I'm lucky . . . '

'Don't you notice anything? I rang you last night, with some great news, but you came rushing into class late, forgetting me completely . . .'

She had rung too, sounding most peculiar, promising to tell all before school.

' . . . expecting everyone to excuse you because *you've* been *training*, and forty-one for History is of course far more important. Oh, the shame, not to be in the top few . . . '

She'd put her finger right on it, perceptive Julia.

'What the hell does it matter?' she went on. 'How would you like to be sitting School Certificate knowing that your whole future depended on it? My whole future, being a doctor – three hundred marks, and a scholarship, that's the deal with Dad . . . '

'What are you talking about? What deal?'

She was flushed, breathing noisily, trying to get the air in and out of her lungs, and I knew an attack was coming. It all came out then, about this second cousin from Australia, who'd seemed so nice, so interested in her career. About him coming to the house one Saturday when she was alone, and her feeling very uncomfortable. Nothing specific, just . . . Anyway, there'd been several occasions and then he went skiing too, with the family, and he kept getting on the tow bars with her and putting a protective arm around her, and then yesterday, he'd been there again, after school. Mum was out shopping in the car, and he tried to kiss her and had actually started undoing his fly, but he didn't choose his moment very well . . . 'Dad came out of his study, we didn't know he'd come home early from work. I rushed off to my room, and I heard a bit of a row between them, but then they both came in, Cousin Mario full of apologies, didn't know what came over him, would never happen again, and my dear father playing it down. Mario was just feeling affectionate, and he *was* half-Italian as if somehow that excused him, and I mustn't tell Mum because it would upset her, she was very fond of Mario. Well, after I stopped crying I'd had a bit of time to think, and I thought what would you have done, all I could think of was you might have given him the old knees up or socked him in the jaw because you're a whole lot bigger and stronger than me . . . Anyway, Dad seemed so concerned not to upset Mario or Mum, never mind about me, that I suddenly thought, I'll keep quiet in return for being allowed to apply for medical school.'

'You didn't!'

'I did. Dad was furious but Mario, all smarm and cringe, persuaded him that I should be allowed to try. To save a bit of face he had to say three hundred for School C, *and* a scholarship . . . '

'That's steep.'

'But it gives me something to aim at. I don't think either of them believe I'll make it. But I will.'

My quiet friend Julia, who would have believed it? She looked so pleased with herself I had to give her a hug.

'So that's all. Dad would kill me if he knew I'd told you. He was still pretty angry at breakfast this morning. He was even angrier when I produced a piece of paper with all this written down and asked him to sign it, in front of Mum so that he couldn't protest.'

'You did? Oh boy.'

She shrugged as I chortled. 'Mario's going back to Australia. The funny thing is, I felt dirty, ashamed, as if it was somehow my fault. How was I so brave, Alex?'

She shook one of her little yellow pills into her hand, and popped it under her tongue. I gave her a back rub until they took effect, and until her heart had stopped racing.

'How? Does it matter? You did it. I'm so proud of you – and sorry for being such a pain.' If people saw us together under the trees and wanted to think strange and weird thoughts, well, it's all in the mind, as the Goons keep telling us.

I remember reading some actress saying that a woman's greatest pleasure is taking her corsets off at night. I wouldn't know because I've never worn corsets, but it's fairly obvious she hasn't sat exams, because there's nothing like the feeling of joy and relief you get as you hand in your last exam paper.

My last one was Music, with six others. Even as we agreed it was the last exam we'd ever sit – there was only University Entrance next year and all of us expected to be accredited – I knew I personally was talking nonsense. If I was going to do law there'd be four or five years of exams, tests, essays.

Today, however, I am free, free, *free*. Julia still has two to go, and she's so grimly determined to get her three hundred marks she's working like it's going out of fashion. I've arranged to meet Andy at the Olympic Pool because he had his last scholarship exam today and we are going to celebrate in the sparkling clean blue champagne water. I am floating with freedom – no hockey, no swot until one in the morning, no ballet, no piano (I did that exam two weeks ago and strangely was quite pleased with a modest Pass Plus), no teachers reading out forty-one for History, no school shows except for the little revue, not even any school because we have two weeks off as a reward before the last two weeks which are a fun time anyway. Then it's the long holidays and Christmas and the run-up to the nationals where I am going to do brilliantly and beat Maggie and get nominated for Rome.

That's what I thought. I'd sorted myself out, stopped trying to do so much, staggered through what Dad has called 'a difficult year'. Now I had only to train, with the gorgeous Andy alongside, up and down the lengths that make up my daily three miles. And when training is finished we can lie in the sun and talk to our hearts' content, and if there is no one too near we might kiss and he'll serenade me with Noel Coward.

Or so I thought.

Mr Jack and Dad had planned my programme and my races carefully between now and the nationals. An invitation club meeting in three weeks, on 24 November. Another, three weeks later. Then a long gap over Christmas/New Year when I'd put in some really hard slog. Taper off a little for the Auckland champs which start on 15 January. Four events in that. Then the final run-up to the nationals in Napier starting 10 February. As usual, I'd be missing the second week of school.

Normally, Mr Jack would have wanted more races than this to sharpen me up, but he'd decided that I'd only meet Maggie at the big events, which would no doubt be of some interest to the papers. Therefore I'd be sharpening up with lots of time trials against Andy and the boys of the squad; no inter-club meetings or long bus trips out of town.

My first appearance/performance was not a success. Nothing actually went wrong. I didn't fall off the starting-block, or jump the gun, or muff my turn. I didn't foul the rope or hit my head on the end of the pool, or swallow a mouthful or get cramp. I didn't get the evil eye from Mrs Benton. It wasn't pouring with rain, or freezing cold or blowing a gale up the pool. I didn't have to wait until ten thirty at night. I did have my favourite togs on.

Maggie just started off better than last season, that's all, while I started off worse. I did sixty-eight point one seconds, two seconds down on my best one hundred and ten yards, that's a lot. While she, sharpened up by her Aussie experience, did a sixty-six seconds, point two faster than her best last season, a record.

I felt like I was swimming through glue. Towards the end I felt the first stabs of cramp in my left calf. I was still carrying a few pounds of extra weight. I was only half-way fit . . . I felt stale. Already.

'For a first outing . . .' said Mr Jack, staring at his stop-watch.

'Not good. Lousy in fact. Alex could do better. In ten weeks' time, will she pull through? Will she make it? Will she achieve her heart's desire? Listen to the next thrilling episode . . . '

'Pipe down, Alex,' said Andy, sitting next to Mr Jack, looking equally grim. Dad on the other side completed a dismal trio, the Marx brothers at a funeral. 'You talk too much at times.'

Of course I do, because I can't bear the sound of my own silence. It howls failure at me, and asks me why I bother, when Maggie will be a perfectly splendid rep for her country, very trim in her black blazer. It reminds me of everything my family has done to get me this far, not forgetting Gran who works her fingers to the bone and helps Mum the way I should help her if I were ever at home, nor the brats whom I hardly see and who don't see as much of Dad as they might because he's always driving me to training or someplace else . . .

Not even Andy gripping my hand tightly helped to soothe my awful premonition that things were not going to improve.

Nothing is simple, everything gets complicated, and even the following day got out of control. 'Come sailing,' Andy said, as we were leaving the pool after the race. 'You need a blow-out. You're getting too earnest. Again.'

'Don't you start.'

It wasn't a day I would have chosen for my introduction to small boats, to find out what made Andy, the future sailor, tick. I held things while Andy rigged the yacht, with what he described as a twenty-knot westerly rattling the sail in anticipation. Only the male of the species, and mad ones at that, seemed to be out on the harbour today.

'Get in,' he yelled. 'Port side, hang on to the jibsheet.'

'What side? The what?'

'That rope there.'

It was all go: movement, wind, waves, spray, rocking, noise, tangles, shouts, total confusion. Andy was pushing, leaping, climbing in, leaning over the stern, pulling ropes, the boat already taking off. I was, as they say, totally at sea.

'Stack out,' he yelled, and when I looked blank, 'Lean out, balance. That's better. Yippeeeeee.'

I could even laugh with exhilaration, and not a little fright. We were screaming away from the beach, leaning over, plunging into the waves so that within seconds my shorts were soaked. Of Andy the sailor, grinning, balancing tiller, ropes, stacking out so that he seemed to be attached to the boat only by his toenails, seemingly in superb control, I was in complete awe.

I thought, even as yet another wave came up to drench my backside, I could get quite keen on this.

'Where're we going?' I yelled.

'You choose.'

'I don't mind. How do you change direction?'

If we'd stuck to the sailing lesson, it would have been a wonderful day. We tried tacking, reaching, running, even my first hair-raising gybe, and then set sail for North Head and around the corner, Cheltenham Beach for lunch. We lay in the sun to dry out a bit, and then walked up North Head. The seascape glittered, silver and turquoise, at our feet. Dozens of the big keelers were heading for the city, returning from the islands of the gulf. The city volcanoes lay round and green in the haze. 'Kipling said it all, didn't he, in five words,' said Andy. 'There's not a harbour like it.'

Being so busy sailing, I'd been able to forget last night's terrible race, until, for reasons best known to himself, Andy chose to remind me on the return journey, when we were reaching comfortably back towards Orakei.

'I felt for you, last night. You looked so sluggish, not like you at all.'

'Not now, Andy.'

'I hate to see you . . . '

'Lose? I've done that plenty of times, even if only to Maggie.'

'No, I mean, working so hard, flogging yourself, for what? You're investing an awful lot of time . . . '

'Wouldn't you, if you had the chance of a trip to Rome? What are you trying to say? Are you ever so gently advising me to get out, now? Don't you think I'm going to make it?'

'It's not that.'

'Then what is it?' Oh, he'd touched a nerve. 'Did you bring me sailing just to show me what I'm missing, and hint that I'm wasting my time doing four miles a day because it's as clear as the nose on your face . . . '

'Alex, calm down.'

I didn't even stop to see how far we were from a beach.

'I will not be told to calm down. And if that's the way you feel . . . I can do a bit more training, right here and now.'

Somehow I got out of the boat, fell, dived, I don't know. Andy's horrified face flashed by. The water felt warm. I came up spluttering, saw the beach, trees, houses that looked as near as any others, and began swimming. In shorts and sweater, with the chop of the waves, it wasn't easy. I knew even I would begin to tire pretty quickly.

'Alex!' I heard shouts, the rattle of the boat nearby. Andy must have turned quickly. *'Alex.'*

I stopped swimming and began to tread water. Some people did harbour races for fun. Was it the season for sharks?

'Alex, get in.'

'No.'

'Get *in*.'

'I'm training.'

'You're just being bloody-minded, pulling a stunt. Now get in. You can't swim that far . . . It's over a mile . . . '

'Rubbish,' I spluttered, though I suspected he was right. I was tiring just with the effort of keeping my head and clothed body above the chop. I started to take my sweater off, but even that meant treading water very fast. 'I swim . . . twice as far . . . every morning.'

'Not out here, you don't.'

Being bloody-minded, and angry, I swam over to the boat, threw in my sweater and set off again, now in shirt and shorts. The water didn't look that bad.

'Alex.' There was real anger in his voice. I must have swum for fifty yards, no more, when I heard his voice again, closer. I stopped and looked up.

He was furious, afraid, all at once. 'You can't run away for ever. *Get in.*'

'I'm not . . . ' but I'd caught a mouthful, and when he held out the paddle, I hung on to it with some relief.

'You can't run away, you can't always be in control, and you can't always get what you want . . . OK, be pig-headed, get swimming, if you don't make it, for the rest of my life I'll be the guy who took his girlfriend sailing and d-drowned her.'

I coughed and spluttered.

He yelled. 'Just because I said something you didn't want to hear. Can you do *that*, Alex?'

I knew I couldn't. And the tide was carrying us out, away from the waterfront. Against chop, wind and tide I had no show. I let go the paddle and swam to the boat.

'Get in over the stern.' Somehow, pulling, kicking, hauling, dragging myself and being dragged, I got back on board. In the wind I was instantly cold, and there was a long red gouge down my thigh where I'd dragged over a screw or something sharp.

'There's a parka up front. Wet, but it'll keep the wind off. Put it on.'

But I could only sit, shaking, rocking, as the boom flogged to and fro. We looked at each other, and had the same thought, for in the bottom of that madly rocking boat, two very wet and tired people had a long and grateful cuddle.

'We do choose some funny places,' I said. 'You *know* why I'm trying for Rome. Why do you have to cross-examine me, as if I'm in court? Why does anyone do anything?'

'They climb Everest because it's there. What did Ed Hillary say, "We knocked the bastard off." '

'Rome's my Everest then. I can't give up now. After six seasons . . .'

'I know, but it's hard for the people around you . . . '

'That's no reason . . .'

'Allow me some concern, Alex. You're so damn stubborn, sometimes you're right, but not always. You were right about Helensville. You were wrong just now. The sea doesn't respect anger or any sort of arrogance. The sea will always win.'

I could see how far the tide had taken us. I wouldn't have got home against that. 'OLYMPIC SWIM PROSPECT DROWNS IN HARBOUR' . . .

He gave me the bailing tin, and began pulling in ropes to get the boat sailing before we both froze to death. The brilliant sunshine was no match for the wind across my goose pimples. We gybed back on course and sat close together on the long beat home, thigh to thigh. I decided I liked Andy the Masterful, taking charge.

I've been thinking what you said about both of us going to Rome, Andy. I read something this week, that swimming commentator in the 'Weekly News', some old boy who's been doing it for years. Anyway, predictions:

'Whatever the outcome of the national titles, serious consideration should be given to sending both these talented girls to Rome. Their intense rivalry over five seasons has already inspired a new generation of juniors and can only go on benefitting the sport.

'Miss Benton has the more impressive score of titles and records over the seasons, and has proved herself a consistent and graceful champion. But time and time again she has been pushed to these achievements by the brave and determined Miss Archer, whose potential is, if anything, the greater. One must win the lion's share in Napier, but both should be considered worthy for Rome . . . ' Isn't that great?

Alex, you're d-dodging the issue, already looking for boltholes . . .

I am not . . .

Yes you are. Don't you realize you're absolutely neck-and-neck. Twenty yards to go and you're already justifying second place . . . hoping it will be good enough for Rome.

All right then, I am. I simply cannot go any faster. And I've got my period, a week early. My body is telling me something.

So? It has never worried you in the past. You've won races with your period before.

You know me too well.

Wasn't this win for me?

Perhaps I just haven't got what it takes, not really. I should've listened to you that day when I jumped off your boat, saved myself a whole lot of work. You were right.

I was wrong. But you've got to do it. No one can win for you. Oh, keep trying, sweet maid . . . Hold on . . .

12

The last two weeks of school were always fun, and did I need it, some light relief to counteract training morning and night, as heavy as it had ever been, weights and calisthenics daily. Over the other side of the pool, Maggie ploughed up and down solo, did her time trials against the stop-watch and her mother's constant presence.

Only knowing that Andy would be there, diving in with me, alongside in the water for length after length, made it bearable. I had to work hard to keep up with him. Looking back, those few weeks in November, despite that awful first race, I was never happier, freer. I had a birthday, with Andy included in a family party. His present was a single pearl on a gold chain.

At school we had no lessons to speak of, instead, class discussion, films, trips to the art gallery, packing up books, extra swimming and tennis time, rehearsals for the revue, almost holidays already.

On the last day of term, at prize-giving, we'd find out the prefects for next year. Drawing up our own lists, it seemed everyone thought I was a dead cert. A wee voice inside said perhaps they'd do the dirty on this dead cert like they did with the hockey team; my turn in 1961, in the Upper Sixth, when I'd been, or not been, to Rome.

First rehearsal for the revue was posted for lunch-time the first day back. One perfomance only, an hour long, Miss Macrae told her singers in the Music Room. The sixth formers who'd been accredited had been working on some skits and funny songs. 'Alex, Janice,' she called, 'What about a couple of numbers from *Oklahoma*, "Oh What a Beautiful Morning", "Surrey with the Fringe on Top" or "I'm Just a Girl Who can't Say No". Who'd like to have a go at that? Alex?'

Beside me, Julia snorted. I did not appreciate the unsubtle dig. That Alex was light years ago. (If she is, said my wee voice, what are you doing here? Shut up, I can have a bit of fun, I told the voice firmly. It's all in school time, Mum and Dad need never know.)

'You talked about a Noel Coward song. I'd rather do one of those,' I said.

'Very well. Janice, you can do *Oklahoma*, have a look through the score here. You saw the film, didn't you? Alex, what about "Mad Dogs and Englishmen"? Or "Don't Put Your Daughter on the Stage, Mrs Worthington"?' She flipped through the book of Coward songs.

One thing, as it always does, led to another. Before I knew where I was, it had been decided thus: an upper sixth former, with a Clara Butt foghorn, would do 'Mad Dogs and Englishmen' dressed in a solar topee and plus fours. Another who was learning to sing properly with beautiful vowels like Julie Andrews would sing 'I'll See You Again' in a long slinky dress. Then I'd come on for the Worthington song dressed à la 1930s, in a check suit and bow tie, with my hair Brylcreemed back. 'You'll make a handsome young man, more so now you're taller,' said Miss Macrae, who'd known me since Third Form. Alarm bells went off. They continued jangling while the group threw round some more ideas.

'Can't I do one of those Gertrude Lawrence numbers, romantic, in a dress?' I asked plaintively. Miss Macrae didn't even hear me. Then some sixth former I wish I'd killed on the spot said 'Why doesn't Alex do her song dressed as you, Miss Macrae, she'd bring the house down, you're always saying the stage is no career for anyone with any sense. In one of your suits and her hair grey and a cushion down her front . . .' She stopped, face scarlet, hand to mouth and we were all relieved when Fish-face threw back her head and roared with laughter. It was decided.

And why, you are asking, did I put my head in the noose once again. Various reasons. One, my time trials were so dreadful I really did need something to make me laugh. Two, I wanted to make an audience laugh again. Three, I dreaded even trying, but surely this was foolproof, taking off a teacher most people thought was a bit of a joke. Four, I can't resist a challenge. I'm a show-off, all right then, a great show-off, but aren't all performers, and showing off is also an urge to share, and what is so wrong with that? I intended to do the song well, even dressed as Miss Macrae with a cushion down my front and feeling a great ninny.

The song was a long one and took me a couple of nights to

learn, *sotto voce* so that no one could hear noises coming from my bedroom. I had two practices with Miss Codlin in the music room. The words were fun to sing. No wonder Andy was a fan of Coward.

> *She's a bit of an ugly duckling*
> *You must honestly confess,*
> *And the width of her seat*
> *Would surely defeat*
> *Her chances of success . . .*
> *On my knees Mrs Worthington,*
> *Please, Mrs Worthington,*
> *Don't put your daughter on the stage.*

How I put it across would be left to me, said Miss Macrae. I could work it out with some of the others. 'Watch the way I walk. How do I sit in a chair, legs crossed, apart? I use my hands a lot, gestures? My large voice, how will you get the impression of that across in a song? We'll have to let down the hem of one of my more repellent suits. Make-up won't be hard, a few lines here and there. Hair greyed, would you mind cutting the fringe a little shorter? A cushion, as Jane so rightly said, down your front. Well, this will be a new experience for me, too.'

Which brings me, reluctantly, dreadfully, to the morning of 2 December, a date which is for ever carved into my heart. Sunday morning, early training as usual. I cycled out of the house, sun already up, a bonus after all those gloomy pre-dawn sessions through the winter and spring. Andy was not at the pool, but then he didn't come to every single session, and he had some sort of school function last night to which, as a prefect, he was obliged to go. Three miles, time trials marginally better, although I could tell Maggie's over the other side of the pool were better again.

No plans for the rest of the day, apart from training again at four and a loose arrangement with Andy to take a picnic lunch somewhere. We might drive over the bridge and have lunch on North Head again, watching the yachts, and then go for a swim.

I knew from the minute I walked in the back door something was odd. No kid's breakfast session blaring *The Story of the Little Red Engine* or Danny Kaye singing 'Tubby the Tuba' through the house. No kids, not even out playing in the garden on this lovely summer morning.

Gran in the kitchen, clearing up breakfast, but no welcome to speak of. Just a little bent back at the sink washing dishes, saying: 'Your Mum wants to see you in your bedroom, Alex,' in response to my 'Where's everyone?' She sounded a bit sniffly. I hoped she wasn't getting a cold, because sometimes they went to her chest.

What had I done? Had Mum found out about the Macrae thing at school? Surely it wasn't that serious, just a bit of fun . . .

Mum was sitting on my unmade bed. Something was up, I could see that. 'Sit down, Alex. Shut the door.'

'OK,' I said lightly. 'What's up doc?'

One thing about Mum, she comes straight to the point.

'I had a ring from Mr Richmond this morning. Andy was knocked off his bike around eleven o'clock last night, riding home from a school function. A drunken driver in an E-type Jag, leaving a party, no lights on, came tearing out of a driveway at fifty miles an hour. He didn't have a chance. He died on the way to hospital.'

'No.'

'I'm sorry, Alex . . .'

'No. Not Andy, never. He heard the car coming and stopped just in time . . . He's in hospital, broken legs, the car only ran over his legs. Soon fixed . . .'

Mum had moved over and was kneeling at my feet, looking up at me. 'Alex, he died on the way to hospital. There was nothing that could be done. The driver of the Jag didn't even stop . . .'

I stared down at her. All I could see was her brown wet wise eyes, waiting for me to crack. The rest was darkness, ringing noises in my ears, the crash of chrome on metal, crunch of tyres running over bones, blood, blood and more blood . . .

'No!'

'Alex, my baby . . . Come here . . .'

I slid down off the chair into her arms. Gran told me later I screamed. Well, so what. I can remember folding myself into the smallest ball possible and burying myself in Mum's enclosing arms. We sat there, on the floor, for hours, rocking, drowning in my tears.

You can only cry for so long. When every tear had been rung, I'd filled several of Dad's large hankies that she thoughtfully produced. Wise Mum. And when you can't bear the grief, you make arrangements.

'Can you run me over to see his parents?'

'Now?'

'Yes.'

I don't remember much of that visit, except certain very vivid details. His mother was in a state of shock, just sitting in a chair. Mr Richmond shook me silently by the hand. I was about to embrace him, but the phone rang. Three calls later, with me sitting beside Mrs Richmond and getting absolutely no response from whatever I said, not even from taking her limp hand and holding it tightly, it was clear the best thing I could do was go home. I didn't wait for him to come off the phone. Some impulse took me along the corridor and along to the bedroom, Andy's Room with a View. I opened the door and stood for a while waiting for my eyes to get accustomed to the shadows. It was like I was taking a photograph, capturing every detail. This was one room I'd not been in. Going along with his father's idea of what was proper, we'd always gone to the study when we wanted to talk.

The bed had not been slept in. Stuff lay everywhere as in my room. A large transistor radio, yesterday's towel on the floor. Balsa wood aeroplanes, made when he was a child, hanging from the ceiling; even more models of ships and pictures of ships, warships and sailing ships. Hadn't his parents realized? Text books on physics, marine engineering, maths, war stories, sea books and ship books, Lawrence Durrell, Kingsley Amis, Robert Graves' *Greek Myths*, books everywhere. Behind the closed curtains lay the famous View across the harbour. 'Last, loneliest . . .' How terribly true.

I looked again at the bed, made but crumpled with the imprint of someone who'd put his feet up for a while. Right next to the alarm clock, in a modest frame, was a photo of me. I put it in my shirt pocket.

Mr Richmond was still on the phone, so I walked quietly past, gesturing goodbye. He put his hand over the receiver, 'Just a moment, sorry, Alex . . . toll calls. Do you have to go? Thank you . . .' and had to blow his nose before he could continue. I kissed him on the cheek and felt the tremor under his skin.

Returning home to a subdued Sunday lunch, with the family being abnormally polite to each other, training again that afternoon – I'd turned to ice. The strange thing was that people didn't say *anything*, most people anyway. Everyone knew we'd been going steady for the best part of six months. Apart from Mr Jack, who looked almost as dreadful as I felt, and Julia, and a few others, most people avoided me, their eyes looked away. It was almost

Alex 131

as though it had never happened, Andy had never existed. Even Maggie was speechless. She mumbled a few words at the end of training. She was, I realized, embarrassed.

It was the same at school. Groups of two or three talking, suddenly silent. Andy had been well known, like you'd expect when he was six foot two and played in the First Fifteen. Julia shielded me with the knack of knowing when a touch of her arm would help.

I suppose it got around the staff room. We suspected the staff knew a good deal about our out-of-school doings, especially different pupils like me. Miss Gillies called me into her study and talked directly about the tragedy of young death. 'People will tell you you'll forget. They're wrong. Even if this young man had not turned out to be your future partner, you won't forget.' She said it with such conviction I believed she had been through it herself. There'd been two wars, so it was pretty likely. Who would ever know?

Miss Macrae didn't mince words, either. She made me talk about him, about the dreadful unfairness of being in the wrong place at the wrong split second of time, why him, why, *why*? 'Life is not fair, Alex. You are just learning a little earlier than most, and harder.' But I felt better after the tears. 'You won't, of course, be doing Mrs Worthington. It was a good idea. Maybe next year. I'll still be around.'

But I won't, I thought. I'm going to Rome. For him. I'm going to Rome.

I sat with Mum and Dad at the back of the church for the funeral, staring at the dark wooden walls and the rows of relatives and business friends in black suits, a large contingent from his school in their navy school shorts, lots of men who were obviously teachers. Some uncle also with a stutter (a family thing?) gave a dreary speech, gloomily recounting Andy's achievements in 'his tragically short life'. I just wept, I couldn't stop and I couldn't care who saw me. When the very long coffin went by at the end, carried by Mr Richmond and a lot of elderly men, I thought I was going to explode with anguish.

'Rest in Peace,' the man said. How could he, when he hadn't said goodbye and every cell in his body must have been screaming *'This is it'* the split second before the Jaguar hit him and turned him in another split second from a beautiful young man with the body of a Greek god into a bloody corpse.

He would have known, in that last point five of a second. I know how long point five of a second is, the difference between winning and losing, living and dying. If only . . . It makes no sense. Did I save you, Andy, from certain accident at Helensville, only for this? Good choices, bad choices, dark fate, confusion, muddle, all a jumble. And now they carry you past me . . .

Somehow I made it to the car, running from the church via a side door before the hoards of dark suits came down the aisle. I sure wasn't going to go to the crematorium, nor stand around talking and laughing outside the porch, as I'd seen people do at funerals, and even less go to the house to watch his mother, and drink tea and eat cream cakes and make polite conversation. Mum and Dad followed. Mum said I blacked out in the car. I don't remember. I didn't go back to school that day. I went to the pool and swam and swam and swam, maybe something over seven miles, until I was exhausted.

In the sleepless nights that followed I turned from being a sweet maid into an ice maiden, not a very nice person at all. I hung for endless hours in that state half-way between sleep and wakefulness, with a blue Morris Minor and an E-type Jaguar coming straight at me, missing me but leaving me standing on a stage strewn with corpses, like the last act of *Hamlet*. Reading didn't help because the same image kept getting between me and the page. The radio finished at midnight. I took to making myself cups of hot chocolate at three and walking round the garden. I did calisthenics for half an hour, working up such a sweat that I needed to take a shower before getting back into bed. One night I even ended up in Mum's bed, terrified out of my skin, appalled at the thought of another two hours' nightmares before dawn broke and I could reasonably go training.

There were, I decided, two things I could do for Andy. The first was rather weird. I had no idea where it came from or if I had the courage to see it through.

The second was more straightforward. For Andy I'd train harder than I ever trained in my life. Every time trial would be an ordeal, maximum effort, every length a test. For Andy I would beat Maggie at the nationals. Being realistic, it would be part of the plan that she'd probably win the Auckland titles first, though I'd give her a run for her money. But the nationals would be all or nothing.

Alex   133

And when I heard my name among the Olympic nominations later in February, it would be my silent private memorial, my gift.

The other thing I was going to do for Andy would be short and sharp, all over and done with next week, three days before the end of school. I found Miss Macrae and asked if it was too late for me to do a song in the Coward bracket for the revue.

'Changed your mind, Alex?' she said, looking at me curiously.

'Not the Worthington thing. Could I do perhaps one of the quieter songs, a duet, like "Room with a View".'

My voice was as nonchalant as I could make it, but my heart was pounding.

'I don't see why not. Let's see, Lorna is doing "I'll see you again". That would fit in well, you as the young man as we suggested earlier.'

'OK,' I said. She looked puzzled, but said nothing more.

Only Julia knew why. I had to tell her, tell someone, to keep myself sane.

'Alex, you're mad,' she said. 'What if you break down? You look so awful, all that training and no sleep. You've lost weight. Look at the bags under your eyes. I tell you, you'll never get through it.'

'Yes, I will. They didn't make me laugh before, remember . . .'

Julia shook her head, wearily. Looking after me was tiring. She'd lost weight herself after working herself into the ground for her exams. What Julia didn't know was that I was in a strange way looking forward to seeing myself as a young man, if only for an hour. Some sort of tribute? Defiance in the face of those rumours? But as Mum had said, among much else these past few days, we all have our own ways of dealing with grief. Many people get to forty, even older and never have it touch them closely, never see a body or weep until they can weep no more. Some go to church, others escape to their office to work, or rush round doing housework, smiling merrily, fooling everybody except the voice inside that talks to them at night. If mine was to get up and sing his favourite song, so be it.

And the fact that this time I'd *chosen* to wind up playing a male, so that catty little girls and their mothers might again whisper Alex Archer has too many male hormones – that no longer mattered. Andy's gift to me was his breath on my lips, his rough chin on my breasts, telling me (as if I ever really doubted it) that I was everything female. I mightn't be very feminine, but boy, was I female.

People could think what they pleased. If that was something else you had to learn, growing up, again so be it.

I learnt the song in a night, remembering snatches of it from earlier days.

A room with a view – and you,
With no one to worry us,
No one to hurry us – through
This dream we've found,
We'll gaze at the sky – and try
To guess what it's all about
Then we will figure out – why
The world is round.

Simple enough, but also deep enough for me at this time.

. . . and sorrow will never come,
Oh, will it ever come – true,
Our room with a view.

Rehearsals were fitted in among all the other things going on in the last week of school. Miss Macrae seemed quite happy with my small contribution. Dress rehearsal was pretty patchy. We all hoped the skits would go better on the day. Janice, in red gingham with a very low bodice, made a good job of Ado Annie's song, 'I'm just a girl', and Clara Butt's 'Mad Dogs' wasn't too bad, either, though I think I'd have done it better. I didn't have a costume yet – a double-breasted suit was being provided by someone's elder brother, about the same height as me.

I was to sing the song downstage right, with Julie Andrews in a soft twilight lighting effect. I wanted something romantic. The school would think it wet, corny even.

Performance was timed for one forty-five. We had a final rehearsal that morning. I could feel the atmosphere getting super-charged, as it did that final *Wizard* night. Me, I was cold as stone.

I put on the shirt and the tie and the suit, which fitted remarkably well. Anyway, I didn't have to move much, just lean against the window frame, and sing. It would all be over in two minutes.

Miss Macrae was directing make-up again, though being only fifth formers upwards most of the girls were doing their own, heavy-handed because when else do they get the chance to plaster it on and mothers not complain? I'd already slicked my hair right back with Brylcreem when I presented my face to her. 'Foundation as usual, then come back.' I did that. My face was set hard as a statue. Julia appeared in the mirror, checking me. I gave her a cold male smile, if there is such a thing, and ignored her. Miss Macrae sat me down in the chair. 'Let's see, won't need much, not with your bone structure, those cheekbones, like Katherine Hepburn. Slightly heavier eyebrows, no lips. Little shading here, and here. Sideburns, no, not in 1930, but just a suggestion of male hair here. Moustache?

'No.'

'I told you you'd make a handsome young man,' she said, as I stood up. 'Alex, are you all right? You're very quiet.'

'I'm fine.'

A tall young man stared back at me from the full-length mirror. Pale, interesting, quite elegant actually, like something from an old movie. What had she said about cheek-bones? I'd never really noticed.

And the suit did fit well. I'd always felt comfortable, even felt a sense of freedom, in the male gear I'd worn for shows over the years. Well, I thought, I don't see why men should have the monopoly on freedom, why girls should have to totter round in tight skirts and stilettos, from now on I'm wearing slacks, jeans, shoes I can run in if I want or need to.

'Not bad,' said Julia's voice. 'I could fall for you. You've got a nerve, Alex. I just hope . . .'

'Sssh,' I said. To everyone else in the room I was just Alex doing a song, one of many. Nothing special. It would be counted as rather a boring number.

'Break a leg,' she said. Not a particularly apt remark, all things considered, I thought, as I trooped along the corridor to the school hall with the others.

By the time my turn came I was sweating through the grease-paint. I debated with myself whether I should throw a faint. The school would never miss my number in a thousand years. There was no programme. They'd never know.

Your choice, Alex. Live with it. Which is more choice than Andy had, in that point five of a second. No choice at all. The choice was made by that drunken slob. Andy, innocently riding past on his bike, lost on the first and the last throw of the dice.

Oh Andy, it would have been better if you had fallen off the bridge that day when I first began to love you. What did you say? 'Pleasanter ways to d–d–snuff it.'

It was a good audience, already in holiday mood, ready to laugh at anything. Julie Andrews finished with a top A, everyone clapped loudly because she was the only girl in the school learning singing properly, and she was going to be an opera singer. I was already leaning against the French windows in the shadows. The song, thank goodness, was in a low key, so that I'd sound like a very light tenor.

Four bars introduction. At two and a half bars, a split second before the light came up on me, I have to admit I very nearly threw in the towel and fled. Instead I swallowed hard, and began to sing.

I've been cherishing
Through the perishing
Winter nights and days . . .

I heard a rustle go round the hall. Julia told me afterwards that the first impression was that they'd got one of the boys from the school along the road, some new hunk on the scene, until someone whispered, 'It's Alex!' Me, after that first rustle, I heard nothing, not even Lorna singing her part. I was in Andy's bedroom, looking out over the harbour.

We'll watch the whole world pass before us
While we are sitting still
Leaning on our own window sill . . .

There was no question of breaking down or tears or making a fool of myself not finishing the song. I sang it like I never sang before, just for Andy, wherever he was now, and for whatever we might have shared. And I knew the audience, even a lot of adolescent schoolgirls, were with me, because when we finished, there was a little hush before they began clapping. It wasn't much, it was even a little puzzled, but I was satisfied.

I went straight back to the classrooms, not waiting to see the rest of the revue from the wings as all the rest were. Julia, faithfully, was there waiting.

In silence I handed her the suit, which she hung up for me. I took off the shirt and tie, the shoes. Methodically, slowly, with complete control, I removed the make-up, and put my school uniform back on. I think she was quite scared of me at that point. To tell the truth, I was quite scared of me, too.

I went into the cloakroom and got out the bottle of shampoo I'd brought with me. We weren't supposed to use the hot water, but I washed my greasy face and then my greasy hair in the basin. I towelled my hair dry and combed it. 'There,' I said.

'I cried,' said Julia, finally. 'Do you know that, you terrible girl, tears and tears. I stood at the back of the wings because I couldn't bear to look at you. Just your voice . . .'

I didn't want to know. Julia had had a soft spot for Andy, she'd even been out with him once, last year, but this was between Andy and me.

Right now I was going home, I was not waiting for the final curtain call with streamers and three cheers for whoever and could Julia please tell Fish-face that I wasn't feeling well and had gone home.

My first gift to Andy had been delivered. Now I intended to put my heart and soul into the second. As they say, we can do the impossible while you wait. Miracles take a little longer.

What a fool! I've just remembered, Andy. The race nearly gone and I've only just flicked up, she can't see me either. We're both flying blind!

That's right, you chump. Don't think you're the only one with the handicaps. Maggie's frightened out of her tiny mind.

She's never.

This time she is. She knows you've got longer arms than her. You can lunge for the wall.

I should take up fencing.

You could try winning this race first. Ten yards. The crowd is going wild.

I can see them when I turn my head, people on the side of the pool, arms waving . . .

Don't worry about them. Say after me . . . First, Alexandra Archer . . .

First, Alexandra Archer . . . I'm dying, Andy. My arms are falling off . . . I stopped breathing about a minute ago.

13

From the day school finished, three days after the concert, my times started to improve.

We closed the year with the flourish of prize-giving, where Julia and I trooped up far too often: she won all the Fifth Form science prizes, me prizes for English, drama, Latin, music, senior swimming champ, the Fifth Form Belinda Parr Memorial Shield (who was she?) for all-round ability and leadership. I was also mentioned in dispatches by Miss Gillies, best wishes of the school in my quest for Olympic nomination, think of her training while the rest of us are sunbathing . . . Laying it on a bit thick.

Training was still a grind, but it had become a grind with purpose and some of my old pleasure in the feel of the water had come back. I looked forward to training sessions, rather than dreading them, especially the early morning ones with the pool clean and smooth and blue, and only a few people there. Now I trained alone.

Perhaps I'd become some sort of a masochist, or perhaps I'd just been lazy before, but I almost welcomed the pain, the gasping for breath towards the end of a time trial. Mr Jack tried hard to look unimpressed as he checked his stop-watch each time, but the little nod of his head told me he was pleased as he wrote times and heart-rates down in his book and drew curves on various graphs.

I was on an upward curve again. It had been a long time coming.

My second clash with Maggie, the weekend after school finished, was encouraging, too. It was a fine summer night for once. We had two events, two hundred and twenty yards first, then a hundred and ten yard invitation, with the best seniors still around and a couple of promising juniors (I'd been one once), which had been put on late in the programme as the 'highlight' so that people would stay and see us. There'd also been talk that Maggie might be near to a national record, as she'd been edging close to it in training.

Mr Jack had firmly told me just to cruise through the two hundred and twenty yards treating it as a warm-up. Maggie never cruised through anything; she always swam against the clock. So when we turned for the last lap of what I thought had been an easy race, I was astonished to find myself right up with her. Twenty yards from home and we were still together. Ten yards and she had the edge. Five yards and I was not so sure. We touched together, but when the timekeepers and judges had come out of their huddle it was Maggie by point two.

'Nice swim,' said Mr Jack when I'd changed into dry togs and joined him to get instructions for the sprint. Dad, alongside, looked pleased too. 'Looked good, easy. Better than I've seen you for some while.'

'Felt good.' Further down in the enclosure I could see Maggie with her coach and her mother, heads together. Mr Jack followed my gaze, but did not say anything.

'You can wind it up for the sprint. Go out fast, settle down, throttle back just a bit after the turn, dig in the last half length. Don't expect a miracle. Maggie's exceptionally fit and sharp for so early in the season. *But* . . . I am greatly encouraged, Alex.'

The last time we sat in this same place, less than a month ago, there'd been another person here. I'd been another person then, too: a child who talked too much. Now I knew too much.

By the time the sprint event was due, some forty minutes later, I had run the whole gamut of depression and elation: hope that I just might be able to turn the tables on Maggie and despair that her Aussie training would count in the end. Yet I had her rattled. She kept clear of me as we assembled for the event. She tried the old trick of keeping us all waiting just a little longer than polite, slowly peeling her track suit off, while the rest of us stood by our blocks and shivered. I stood windmilling my arms and smiling. According to the papers, it was she who was supposed to be breaking the record, not me. Her burden. I had enough of my own.

A perfect start, and again I felt good. She was on my left, so I knew that I had edged ahead as we neared the turn, maybe half a yard. A perfect turn; this was all too good to be true. I felt so good I forgot to throttle back. Pain set in, but I felt I was using it to ride the wave, not fight it. I dared not take a right-handed breath to see if I still led, but there was a black shape right up with me. To win this race would put me right back in the picture.

I touched. Maggie touched too, but as I lay back on the ropes I saw my timekeepers straighten up smiling. One old friend gave me the thumbs up. There was a certain amount of commotion around the pool.

'Good swim, Alex,' said Maggie.

'Thanks.' She looked cheerful enough, but I wondered how she felt, really. If anything, she had more at stake and more to lose, publicly anyway.

The announcer's voice came over loud and clear. 'First, Miss A. Archer, swimming for . . .' The rest was lost in cheers. As I climbed out of the pool, an old friend, who'd been standing on the side of the pool as a timekeeper for as long as I could remember, showed me the stop-watch. 'It was sixty-six point three,' she said. 'Only point three off Maggie's record. A grand swim. You deserved that.'

I glowed, I danced back into the changing-room and out to see Dad and Mr Jack. Point three! In all fairness Maggie still had a slightly faster unofficial time and tonight she'd been off form. But I'd proved I could!

I was back in the picture, literally, with both papers splashing headlines and a head-and-shoulders of me. 'MAGGIE BENTON DEFEATED', said one. 'MISS ARCHER WINS', said the other. 'Surprise win to Miss Archer at last night's invitation meeting', 'brilliantly judged race', 'hitting form after a disappointing season', 'fulfilling earlier promise', and 'fine clashes expected at the Auckland and national championships later in the season'. 'Their rivalry is as intense as that between the great English backstroke swimmers Judy Grinham and Margaret Edwards in recent years,' said one commentator. 'Which of them wins the national titles in February and subsequently the Olympic nomination will be a seasoned and worthy competitor.'

Mr Jack, true to form, didn't go overboard, but I knew he was delighted, behind his warnings that this race was a mere stepping stone, it was the nationals now, less than two months away. A lot of distance had to be clocked up between now and then.

For the first time in my life, I had nothing to do but swim.

That's not strictly true, either. There was Christmas, only a few days away, and New Year. I was spending much more time with my family. Julia was away with her family. When I wasn't at the pool I was at home, helping with Christmas things like making hundreds of mince pies and writing cards, and doing the annual visit to some of Gran's cronies around the place. ('My, what a big girl you've grown,' like Red Riding Hood's wolf.) I looked after the kids while Mum and Gran went shopping. Then Gran looked after them while Mum and I went shopping, or I looked after Gran while Mum took the kids shopping.

Gran had a Christmas rush on with her baby dresses, and helping her in the afternoons between lunch and training gave me the solitude, the time that I needed. We would work in silence, just the sounds of her Singer sewing machine whirring away, the kids playing outside in the tree-hut, flies buzzing in the windows. If Gran noticed that sometimes my hands were still and my eyes wet, she didn't say anything.

I think I began to get a reputation among the swimming crowd for being remote, a bit weird even. It wasn't intentional. I just didn't have much to say to Maggie or anyone these days. The pressure was on her too, with her mother's stop-watch clicking off her time trials and mine too, and engaging her coach in long conversations, while the rest of his squad hung about. I listened to Mr Jack, did my usual, sometimes with the boys in the squad, but usually alone, and went home.

Sometimes I took a book and lay in the sun for half an hour or so after training. But I had to be careful of sunburn, of peeling and blisters, which chafing togs could turn to sores. And the image of Andy was still too vivid; every time I walked through the ticket office I thought of him, saw his long frame leaning against the rail around the pool, waiting for me. Every time I stood on the block, psyching myself up for yet another three miles, his long shape was there in the water. When I lay on the terrace I heard his voice, remembered our rare kisses when no one was around, still so recent. Tears came then, too. For the first time in my life, despite all my family and easy friendships among the swimming crowd, I felt like someone separate. Last. Loneliest.

Christmas Day dawned brilliantly. Although the pool didn't open until mid-morning, I woke early anyway and joined the kids tearing their Christmas stockings to pieces. We found all sorts of tiny goodies, sweeties, cherries, grapes, and an orange in the toe, which Gran told us, every Christmas, was an English custom going back to the time when an orange was an incredible treat, imported at great expense from Spain or Italy. 'You kids in this land of fruit, you don't know what it's like to taste one orange, the only fresh fruit through an entire English winter. My mother knew, before she emigrated out here.'

Mid-morning it was church. As a family we went only at Christmas and Easter, and for what Mum called 'Hatches, Matches and Dispatches', which I suppose is better than not at all. Gold, yellow and white flowers were everywhere, and ladies in hats, and the long service was made longer by much hearty singing of carols. Twenty days since I last sat in a church; and there were still tears left inside me.

Home to help Mum and Gran prepare the turkey; the table set with holly and pohutukawa flowers picked from the old tree in the garden, colour scheme of green and crimson and white. Lunch went on for ages, with far too much to eat and toasts to all, and Gran raising her glass to 'absent loved ones and friends'. She meant mostly grandfather Albert, who'd gone under to drink and the Depression, and Mum's parents who lived down south, but I saw Mum look at me and raise her glass.

After all the presents were opened, and tables cleared and dishes washed and kids shooed out to the garden, Dad and I got in the car. Dad hesitated before he turned the starter.

'You're sure . . .?'

'They're expecting me. I rang a few days ago and asked when they'd like me to visit, if at all. Mrs Richmond said come Christmas Day, for afternoon tea.'

'That was thoughtful of you, Alex.'

It had cost me something, to ring up Andy's mother and find out that no, they were not going away, and yes, they'd like me to call around four on Christmas Day.

'How long do you want?' said Dad as he pulled up outside the house.

'Maybe half an hour. I'll walk down to the beach.'

'Outside the dairy then, half past? I'll wait.'

'Thanks, Dad.' I pushed the car door shut. I'd eaten too much but that was probably not the only reason I was feeling slightly ill.

The house had a closed-up look. Venetian blinds down, garage door shut. Even the door chime sounded muffled.

Mrs Richmond opened the door so smartly that I knew she'd been watching out for me. 'Come in, dear.'

How can you say happy Christmas? I said nothing but hello. Besides she looked awful, I was shocked. She'd become a little old lady, still upright, carefully dressed in powder blue twinsets, but haggard. Less prim people might have wanted a comforting hug, but I was wary and she held out a formal hand to shake. 'Come in, come in.'

I followed her into the darkened living-room. The View from this Room was shut out by blinds. Mr Richmond rose from a leather chair and greeted me equally formally. I handed over the small present of chocolates I'd brought with me.

'Alex, good to see you. Sit down, please.'

There was a slight awkward silence. Then I thought this is not on, I'm doing to them what other people have done to me, hiding their embarrassment behind silence, dodging the issue. I took a deep breath.

'I wanted to tell you . . . that I've been thinking of Andy, and of you, since . . . You probably know I'm not a very religious person, but in church this morning I said some prayers. Some of them were for you, because I just can't imagine what it would be like . . . And worse at Christmas, with everyone's little kids pulling crackers and opening presents, all the talk of babies being born and goodwill and stuff . . . Anyway, I prayed.'

Mrs Richmond was sitting primly as usual, looking at her feet. The trolley beside her chair was beautifully set for tea and covered with a flimsy embroidered throw-over thing.

Mr Richmond spoke first, with just the hint of a smile on his face. 'Thank you, dear, for your prayers. We need all the help we can get. It has not been easy.'

'Christmas is a sham,' said Mrs Richmond suddenly. 'We've just had Christmas dinner with my sister and her husband, their children of course are grown and overseas. Kind of them, I know, to make the effort, but . . .'

She stood up abruptly. 'Would you like tea, Alex?'

'Yes. Yes, please.'

Mr Richmond watched her leave, and took refuge in stoking

his pipe up. 'Very hard for her, all this. Andrew was her whole life.'

I heard myself say, 'Funny how people don't say anything. Your boyfriend gets killed and they talk about the weather.'

'Embarrassment. Fear of saying the wrong thing, making it worse.' He took a deep puff of his pipe and looked hard at me. 'You had more than a soft spot for our Andrew, didn't you?'

'I suppose . . . more than.' Some loyalty to Andy prevented me from saying we had an agreement to wait for each other, a sort of engagement.

He nodded, almost as though he'd read my mind. 'You'd have been good for him, too. You've a streak of ambition, a toughness that he lacked.'

Ambition for his goals, or his father's? What do I say? Rightly or wrongly, I decided what was the point, a sad father should keep his dream, so I said only, 'He knew what he wanted. And we were good for each other.'

Mrs Richmond returned with a magnificent silver teapot. I was getting the favoured nation treatment. The conversation turned to my swimming, my win against Maggie, my hopes for Rome. I was offered asparagus sandwiches and home-baked afghans. After I turned down a third cup of tea, Mrs Richmond said, 'Please could you come, Alex. I have something . . .'

I followed her, along the corridor to the closed door of Andy's bedroom. She stood for a moment, then slowly opened the door. 'Please . . .' Her gesture indicated that I was to go in first.

I was none too keen, but I had no choice. The curtains were still drawn and there was an unlived-in smell, musty, slightly old socks. When my eyes got used to the gloom I saw that nothing had been touched since my first visit, right down to the wet towel on the floor.

'I haven't been in here since the night he died,' she said softly behind me. I said nothing, what on earth could I say. I thought of taking her hand, but when I turned to look at her, I saw only the impassive face of a woman who'd hidden her feelings all her life. So now she stood with blank face, while God knows what went on in her mind. I might have been the only person whose shoulder she could cry on, but for her it was too late.

We stood there for maybe a minute, although it seemed like an hour. 'Thank you, dear,' she said, moving to close the door.

'Clearing out the room is something I was dreading. Coming with you has helped.' She might have been talking about having to do a spot of spring-cleaning.

'Could I help?' I longed to fling wide the curtains, take my last look at Our View.

'No, thank you, dear. It's my job and I'll do it in a day or so.'

She will too, with her back upright and her heart broken into tiny pieces; tidily and methodically, till not a trace remains of the person that Andy had been. All his dreams, in cardboard boxes. I needed fresh air.

Mr Richmond met us in the hallway. I thought it was a good moment to leave, but as I started to speak Mrs Richmond interrupted me.

'Just a moment, Alex. I'd like you to have . . .' I didn't hear the rest, because she was walking back down to Andy's room. She went in without hesitation this time, and a few seconds later came out carrying the large transistor radio, which she held out to me without a word. I wasn't sure what she meant.

'Andrew would have liked you to have this.'

'Oh no, I couldn't . . .'

'Please, he would . . .'

'It's very kind, but . . .'

'He treasured it.'

Mr Richmond said, 'Alex, please. He worked hard for that, driving a van for the local grocer after school.'

Something I hadn't known. And you say he lacked ambition, drive, I thought. Not him.

'Well, I . . . shall treasure it too,' I said. I had to get out, and quickly. 'Please, I must go . . . Dad's waiting . . . Um, goodbye . . . Thank you . . .'

To my departing back, Mrs Richmond called, 'Come and see us again, Alex. When you're passing . . .?'

It wasn't a very gracious exit. I turned at the bottom of the steps and waved. They were standing in the porch, each in a separate space. I almost ran down to the beach, although the transistor was quite heavy and I didn't want to bang it on anything. It was inside the half hour, but Dad was waiting. I put the radio on the back seat, and climbed in the car.

'What's that?'

'His mother gave it to me.'

Dad just nodded wisely. I didn't feel very wise about anything. We drove to the pool in silence, for which I was grateful. 'I'll put it in your room. Do you want picking up later?'

'I'll walk.' It was a fair distance home, but I needed time to myself. I was beginning to need the isolation of training, just me and the water and the black lines on the bottom of the pool, back and forth. That Christmas afternoon I discovered you could cry and swim at the same time, and no one would know. A pale face and blood-shot eyes they'd put down to swimming pools and hard work.

From Boxing Day the days started to wash into each other. I hardly knew what day of the week it was. New Year's Eve came and went. I turned down a party with some of Mr Jack's squad, and Mum let me off the family affair after the barbecue in the garden when all the kids played spotlight with torches and insisted on staying up until midnight.

I went to bed early and heard nothing. Sleep was coming easier these nights as the nightmares were less frequent and I was physically so tired, clocking up between four and five miles a day if you added my two sessions together, plus weights and forty minutes' calisthenics.

The Auckland champs in the second week of January attracted a lot of interest because apart from Maggie and me there were others, especially a couple of boys, with hopes for the Games team. But the weather was pretty terrible for mid-January, with a nasty wind turning all the swimmers blue and blowing up the skirts and raincoats of the women officials stoically doing their jobs night after night at the end of the pool.

Times were slow. The press tried to turn my races with Maggie into great clashes. I tried hard, and there was less than point seven in all the events, but there were too many events, what with heats and finals, and club relays, and I didn't try my hardest, not really. Mr Jack didn't *quite* tell me to be happy for once with silvers, but that was what he wanted, too: to lull Maggie into a false sense of security. So I read the headlines in her favour with hardly a twinge. And there were some promising juniors, particularly a young man brilliant at the new dolphin butterfly, who threatened to steal the limelight as we had once done. Good for them!

24 January, and the dreaded letter was sitting on my bed when I got home from training. Julia had already rung to say she was coming round at eleven, but she wouldn't tell Mum what she'd got. I shut the door and slowly opened the envelope.

English 88. History, well well, 74. Latin 68 (not bad for a terrible paper). Maths 79 (surprise, surprise). And Music 91 (and so I should, after all that piano theory).

Not bad, all things considered. Yes, I'm pleased, I decided. Family were very pleased. Mr Jack when I saw him later at the pool was pleased. I sent a little message to Andy. He was pleased, too. But Julia bounced in the door ecstatic.

'Tell me.' She'd done it, it was only a question of by how much.

'My top four – three hundred and seventy-two.'

I realized I'd forgotten how to laugh, to cry for pleasure, to shout for joy.

'Three hundred and seventy-two – for *four* subjects?'

'Yes.'

We danced, yelled, shrieked around the kitchen. Mum and Dad, who knew nothing of Julia's situation, thought we'd gone mad and all the kids came rushing in to see what the commotion was.

Later, in my bedroom, I said, 'What did your father say? That's better than either of your brothers.'

'Funny, you know, he was actually quite pleased, although *they* weren't. He's started telling all and sundry, "My clever daughter, brilliant at science you know, is going to do medicine." Em-*barra*-ssing!'

'The old rogue. Well, he just had to get used to the idea, didn't he?' I hadn't felt so warm inside for months. Julia was walking on air, brown as a berry after her holiday, the dark shadows under her eyes as faint as I'd seen them in years. 'Oh, I'm happy for you,' I said, giving her a bear hug.

'How are *you*, Alex? You've got an awfully lean and hungry look about you. And dangerous. Maggie, watch out. How's . . . the other thing?'

'All right. No, it's not all right. I think too much. But I don't feel so angry now, just . . . sort of grim. Dangerous, if you like.' I also said it lightly, but it wasn't a bad word to describe how I felt these days.

A couple of days later I got a strange phone call from Mrs

Richmond, which had me right back to anger and anguish, weeping on my bed for a long while, banging my fists against the pillow at the cruelty, the unfairness, the waste, and my loneliness. She thought I'd like to know that Andy's scholarship results had just arrived in the mail. Somehow, someone had boobed; it had not got through to Wellington, what had happened. He'd gained excellent marks in maths, biology, geography, physics and chemistry and won a National Junior Scholarship.

First, Alexandra Archer. Second, Alexandra Archer. Ninety-fifth, Alexandra Archer . . . Also ran, Alexandra Archer . . . Go, Alex, Alex, go . . .

You can hear the crowd, Alex? It's pandemonium down there, Alex. Your father's on his feet, Gran's actually standing on the bench, jumping up and down, Mr Jack is still sitting on his butt biting the quicks of his nails. He can't bear to look.

I bet Mrs Benton can't either.

She's gone very pale. The Aussie coach beside her has just said something about that Archer girl's got courage, great fighter, and she's just bit his head off. He's come right back at her and says he knows real talent and spirit when he sees it, and Mrs Benton thinks he's getting at Maggie, putting her down, and no one's ever done that, ever, and for once in her life she's speechless.

Serve the woman right. Though not fair to Maggie.

Maggie's scared out of her brain. Not really of losing to you. She's got a lot of time for you . . .

It's mutual.

Her mother's face. Disapproval, disappointment, written all over. That's what Maggie's afraid of, guilt, letting her mother down. It's going to take her another whole year to come to terms with it, not until . . . No, I mustn't say that, not yet.

I've beaten her before . . .

This time is special. It has become more than just a swimming race to you. Why else are you pushing yourself past your limit . . .

True. Oh Andy, when will it end . . .

You're doing well. Courage . . .

Alex   151

14

'You'll do it,' said Mum as we hugged out by the car. 'It's written in your stars, in your eyes.' She had tears in hers, Mum the serene, the unflappable, the big strong nurse whose shoulder everyone else cried on. 'I'll be listening to the radio, but ring me anyway, each night.'

Gran did the kissing rounds too, just as wound up as I was, in her way. First time back to Napier in fifteen years, so naturally she was excited. She'd come up to help Mum when I was born (Dad had gone back to his ship and the war), and somehow, apart from going back for a few weeks to sell her tiny flat, had just stayed.

During family talk at tea about Napier one night, I'd suddenly thought, why isn't she coming with us? Because she couldn't, she said when I asked her later; couldn't leave Mum, leave the kids, she had too many baby dress orders to meet, and anywhere where would she stay. Haven't you friends? 'They're all dead or moved away,' she said, adding, 'I suppose there might be old Lillian,' and I caught a whiff of longing before she closed the conversation.

The real reason, of course, was money. She hated getting presents, new clothes, anything spent on her. She'd no more listen to Mum and Dad than she would to me, except perhaps . . . So I drew some money out of my savings account and bailed her up in her room. 'For you, for Napier,' I said firmly, closing her hand around the notes.

'You can't do that.'

'I can and I have. I don't care whether you use it to stay in a hotel, or with old Lillian or whatever. It's yours.'

'I can't possibly. . . .'

'Oh yes you can. Look at me.' The tough old warrior's eyes were glinting, with hope as well as tears. 'You can, Gran. You've been helping me, all of us, for years and it's about time you had a holiday.'

'I don't need holi . . .'

'We all need holidays. Gran, if you don't come, I shall be personally hurt, offended, rejected . . .' She looked up to see whether I was serious or joking. I was both. It was a mean trick, but it worked. We spoke the same language, Gran and I. 'Do you want me just to mention it to Dad, casual-like? You'd rather like to go back to your old haunts?'

It took a lot to silence Gran. She nodded, and busied herself at her sewing machine because she thought that way I'd not see how moved she was.

I lost the battle over the front seat of the car, though. When I opened the door for her, she simply climbed in the back, and smiled triumphantly. 'Drive carefully, Jim,' called Mum through the open window.

We waved to the farewell committee as Dad backed down the drive. The brats, still with breakfast Marmite on their faces, were all yelling 'Good luck, Alex,' as they followed the car and chased us along the street. It was Saturday morning, and I'd already done my two miles. Dad had taken a whole week's leave. I had special permission to travel down with him, rather than in the team bus, which was also leaving this morning but would take much longer.

I hadn't ever swum in Napier. Down the Great South Road Gran talked darkly of the road between Taupo and Napier. 'Fit only for mules. Our radiators used to boil, so we'd have to stop half-way up and wait for an hour.' 'But that was the 1920s, Gran,' I said. 'You were driving an old jalopy. A 1956 Morris Oxford, surely . . .' 'You wait.'

By the time we got to Taupo five hours later, I was almost past caring. Dad drove slowly and the unsealed bits of road through the forests slowed us down, too. We had Mum's bacon and egg pie and thermos tea in Taupo, on the edge of the lake, after a gorgeous swim in the cleanest, purest water I have ever seen, I didn't swim any distance, maybe quarter of a mile out into the lake over neat rippling ridges of white sand.

Although the schools had been back a week, there was a holiday atmosphere here, with lots of children in the shallows, and people my age fooling around and diving off a raft moored about a pool's length offshore. We sat in silence watching them.

Dad said, 'You've forgotten what it's like, haven't you?'
'What?'

'To frolic like that. Carefree, no stop-watch. You go for a swim and it's a training session, half-way out into the lake.'

'A measly quarter mile?' I lay back on the hot sand.

'All this striving, driving, I sometimes wonder where my little daughter has gone.'

There was a long silence. 'And what about the wolf whistles?' he said, teasing.

'Dad!' As if it mattered, now. The sleek fit, the vivid emerald colour of my one decent pair of togs made a change from boring black racers. If grinning lads can think of nothing better to do than lie around and gawk . . .

Below us on the water's edge a tall guy was rigging his yacht. Both boat and figure not unlike, if I half shut my eyes . . . If, if! I knew that poem of Kipling's. Apart from the 'You'll be a Man, my son!' bit, it was something to hold on to.

If you can make one heap of all your winnings
  And risk it on one turn of pitch-and-toss,
And lose, and start again . . .

Dad was talking. 'Alex, I want you to know . . . Whatever happens, I'll be proud of you.'

Not knowing what to say, I nodded.

'You've come through these past months . . . I haven't said much (he never does, Dad), but I've watched. I'm proud of you already.'

Gran's hand, on my other side, took mine and squeezed hard.

'She'll do it, our Alex,' she said. 'I know she will.'

'Time to go,' said Dad. I never did see the full extent of Gran's dark hills on the Taupo-Napier road. Warmed by the sun, and lulled by the slow rhythm of the car around bend after bend, twisting and turning at ten miles per hour, I slept all the way to Napier.

We arrived at dusk, just as they turned the lights of the Marine Parade on, and drove slowly past a skating rink, sound shell, gardens, statues, aquarium, lamps reflected in small pools, and that mighty row of Norfolk pines you see in every picture of Napier. Behind was the beach, strictly scenic, with dangerous Pacific dumpers crashing noisily down on to stones.

On a warm Saturday night, people were out and about; crowds of teenagers, some fairly ordinary, others in big American cars, were heading to Saturday night flicks. Right up one end of the beach, near the port, almost under the headland, Gran pointed out the pool. It was closed. Posters, here and elsewhere in the city, proclaimed the New Zealand Swimming Championships. 'See our Olympic prospects compete for nomination: Maggie Benton, Alexandra Archer . . .'

Dad saw me into my room at the team hotel, only a street away from the pool. 'You're room seven, with a Miss Davidson,' said the woman at the desk downstairs. 'Originally it was a Miss Benton, but her mother insisted she go in the suite with her. They arrived two days ago, such a nice girl. I keep reading about her in the papers. I imagine you know her quite well.'

'Quite well.' From her slight sniff I could imagine what had happened. Dad was smiling, too.

'And just as well,' Dad said as we humped my bags up the stairs. 'For once I agree. The officials who did the allocations must be out of their minds. Hopeless!'

'Oh, I don't know.' But Carol Davidson was OK. She was a breaststroker, a race apart.

It was another room with a view – across roof-tops to the Norfolk pines and the ocean beyond. I hardly heard Dad as I stood at the window, remembering another room.

'You'll be all right then?'

'What? Oh, yes, 'course. Thanks, Dad,' as he kissed me goodnight. 'Hope your place is okay. Look after Gran.'

Dad, after that long drive, looked tired, too. 'See you at nine, at the pool.'

I fell into bed and surprisingly, despite sitting in a car all day, slid straight into sleep. Around eleven the team bus arrived and I heard people finding rooms. As she threw herself into bed, Carol muttered something about a puncture and never wanting to see another hill in her life. After that I kept waking, tossing on the bed, which was too narrow and too soft, dreaming of waves falling, trees falling, a yacht, a bike, a boy falling, myself falling, swimming through air, falling, in lazy floating slow-motion, always downwards like the regular thud of the breakers along the nearby beach.

Sunday, Monday, only light training now, a mile or so, tapering off, with lots of sprints, starting practice, turns until my head was full of water. Hundreds of competitors jostling for pool space, stop-watches, coaches, reporters, parents' gossip and predictions. Dad and Mr Jack watched my training from the back of the stands, quietly avoiding the general team activity. Mrs Benton sat by herself on the other side.

I knew my new reputation: iceberg, unforthcoming, unfriendly, crazy, gone a bit odd. Juniors kept clear. So did Maggie. Officials didn't stop me for chats as they'd once done and reporters got the cold shoulder. I was having only three or four hours' sleep a night, yet I felt as fit as I'd ever done, hungry, lean and, yes, dangerous.

Tuesday, opening night, and Maggie won the four hundred and forty yards, by point seven. It was my worst event, and the one I least expected to win, but Thursday I knew I *had* to win the two hundred and twenty yards to remain in the hunt for Rome. For the freestyle crown it was best of three.

I swam the race according to Mr Jack's instructions; feeling good, I knew from the start I could do it. The last lap was the hardest I'd ever swum. Maggie was on my breathing side. She didn't yield an inch, and at the end there was only point four in it. But I knew I had won. It was a national record, two minutes twenty-three point one seconds. One each. As we heard the result in the pool, Maggie gave me a hug and we both grinned for the photographers. The smiles on Mr Jack's moonface and Dad's cragface were worth every last gasp. As for Gran, her little back was ramrod straight.

But there was the first hint of the price I had to pay, the forthcoming game. Leaving the pool at the end of the night, Mrs Benton (never mind, 'Congratulations, Alex') walked straight past me in the foyer, and again in the hotel dining-room. OK, I thought, I'm invisible. Watch me win an invisible gold. Play rough.

I put a call through to Mum and heard general family jubilation, whoops and cries, at the other end. They'd all been listening to the radio. It was a good feeling, and so was reading the paper the next morning, until I got to the bit about predictions for the sprint title. 'Miss Benton, because of her greater consistency over the past four seasons, must start as the favourite.'

The very thought of Saturday sent shivers up and down my spine. I would have only one chance, like a singer having to hit a stupendous top note without cracking or the ballerina doing the Rose Adagio in *Sleeping Beauty* and holding her *attitude* on one pointe for many breath-taking seconds. She couldn't wobble over and then say to the audience, 'I'm sorry I'll do that again.'

The performer has one chance. One heap of all her winnings . . . Friday, for me a rest day. Dad, Gran and I went to visit some relatives in Hastings for lunch. Dad thought, Mr Jack thought, and I agreed that I needed to get away for a few hours after training in the morning. I got special permission from our team manager Mr Upjohn, and the chaperone Mrs Hooper, who seemed to be having a few problems keeping track of one particular sixteen-year-old with a mind of her own. I hardly remember a thing about the visit: the family, the house, the lunch, the countryside, anything. Does that sound crazy? But I *was* crazy by now, obsessed with that unforgiving minute that lay ahead.

Five yards Alex. Maggie's as desperate as you are. Her stroke has disintegrated a bit. Her mother is frozen, still as a stone, white-faced. She thinks it's all over.

My stroke went out the window ages ago. I feel like some sort of crazy windmill.

Looks good to me. I've always loved watching you swim, Alex, the sheer power of you. I get the same feeling watching dolphins in the sea out from the beach.

I was thinking of dolphins earlier.

Wait till afterwards, concentrate on what you're doing. Three yards, Alex, she thinks she's got you . . .

Andy, help me, please . . . I want, so badly . . . to win.

15

I didn't go to the Friday evening session to cheer Carol and the other Aucklanders on. Neither did Maggie, and I think most of the other people in the team understood why, although one or two eyebrows were raised, notably Mr Upjohn when I told him I wanted to get an early night. He said of course Alex, but his eyes gave me another message. You could always tell those officials who'd been competitors themselves, or who had children of their own competing. He had neither. I'd heard Dad say he'd come in the side door, to improve administration.

After tea, in that same cool hour before dusk as the night we'd arrived, Dad, Gran and I went for a walk along the Marine Parade. We wandered through the gardens without talking much, and read the legend of Pania under the bronze statue. Sitting, smiling Pania of the Reef, sea-woman, part-taniwha, married to human Karetaki but drawn back to the sea to live with her family. Many people had been drawn, as I was now, to stroke the smooth polished bronze. Her limbs were full and strong. Give me some of your strength, Pania. Already I had the sinking feeling in my stomach and still there was a whole night and day to survive.

Carol had promised not to wake me when she came in, but she needn't have worried. I'd gone to bed at nine thirty, and ninety minutes and almost a whole book later I was still wide awake.

'Silver! Look.' She held up the medal, delighted with herself. She had hardly dared hope for the bronze, and had swum two seconds faster than her own personal best. I sat up, shared her joy, and heard other fates and fortunes. Then I must have yawned. 'Hell, I'm sorry, Alex, you're all wide awake now.'

'I was wide awake before,' I said. I was beginning to have a very unwelcome suspicion. It was another ten minutes before I could bring myself to get out of bed and investigate.

'Oh no, no! Damn, damn, damn.'

'What's the matter?' When I didn't reply, she said sharply. 'Alex?'
I came out of the bathroom. 'My period, a whole week early. I haven't even brought any . . .'

'Here.' She rummaged round in her suitcase. 'Stress, I suppose. Don't you take those pills? In our squad, we all do.'

'My coach reckons there's no proof that you go slower with a period. I've swum good times with and without it. So why upset all your hormones? He doesn't go for pills.'

'Not even vitamins? Everyone does that. The Aussies eat them like sweeties, by the ton so they say.'

'Sure, that's different.'

'There's a rumour going round, pep pills, some of the guys from . . .'

'Carol, please can I go to sleep? Thanks for the doings.' I turned my back on her. I didn't want to hear about whoever might be taking pep pills because that was just plain stupid, as well as illegal. We'd heard enough from overseas to know that pep pills sent you all the way up and then crashing all the way down, and in the long run did a lot of harm.

But I was not nearly as sure about periods affecting your times as I'd sounded. Damn, damn! It was a complication I didn't need. But not an excuse either. I decided not to tell anyone, not Dad or Mr Jack, who always knew my monthly cycle exactly. There'd be no excuses, no justifications, no complications, if I could help it.

Fate had other things in store. Carol finally got to bed, turned her light out, I suppose about eleven thirty. I willed my eyes to close, willed myself to sleep. It was a warm night, and I seemed to be either too hot under one blanket or not quite warm enough with just a sheet. I heard the breakers' regular drumbeat, a distant clock strike midnight, and some more people (adults) walk along the corridor outside and say noisy goodnights and bang their doors shut.

Then I must have slipped into a sort of sleep for a few minutes before I was standing on a starting-block, then swimming round in the sea and between me and the shore was this gigantic surf, not the rolling kind which you could, with luck, ride to safety, but the evil dumping kind, which makes a point of hurling its victims head-first into the sand, breaking every bone before washing your body ashore, and now I have to choose between the surf and a school of sharks, I am Tinman again, crumpled silver tossed ashore, but look what else the surf throws up on to the moonlit sand, Miss Macrae in full costume as a witch from *Macbeth*, with blacked-out teeth, more skull than face, Andy in school uniform, but covered with blood and his handsome face set in a smiling death mask, terrifying in its smoothness and perfection, and a female body, broken and twisted by the force of the sea, which I recognize as myself . . .

I sat up in bed, rigid. Carol told me in the morning she'd heard me cry out in my sleep, a loud wail that had penetrated down to her marrow. Slowly the images, so dreadfully clear, faded. I got out of bed and stood, shivering, sweating, at the open window. The street below was deserted and most of the lights along Marine Parade out. I could hear the crash of those breakers on the beach, and a persistent song in my head.

A room with a view – and you,
With no one to worry us,
No one to hurry us – through
This dream we've found . . .

Some dream! I had a snowflake's chance of sleeping. If I thought backwards, the dream, its waves, its vision of death, would overwhelm me again, and next time it would be worse. If I thought forwards, it was to tomorrow's task, just a swimming race, for heaven's sake, and yet so much more than that. I had to concentrate on the present to stay sane. Carol, although she'd been stirring when I woke, was back out for the count, silver-satisfied, snoring lightly. I knew I either had to go for a swim or go mad. I needed water to clean my mind, and stretch my aching body.

I put my track suit on over my pyjamas, and unhooked a pair of old racers and a towel from the clothes-line we'd rigged up by the window. My sandals made a flip-flop noise, so I carried them. In my very peculiar state, I had no idea where I could swim, but I just had to get my body into water somehow and feel the rhythm of the stroke that had carried me over so many thousands of miles over the years. It might have to be, it could surely not be, the sea . . .

I was cunning enough to remember to snib the door so that it wouldn't lock behind me, and to take some considerable time to creep down the wooden stairs and open the main door. The night wasn't cold, but how I shivered. I walked straight down to the beach. There wasn't a soul around. I sang silently, for some comfort . . .

> . . . *high above the mountains and sea.*
> *We'll bill and we'll coo – ooo-oo,*
> *And sorrow will never come,*
> *Oh, will it ever come* . . .

No use going to the pool, Alex. That will be shut. It took all my resolve to walk through the gardens and on to the shingle, to confront the merciful emptiness of those breakers. I knew as I sat there that I had too much sense to swim alone, now or at any time. My nightmare had been true in one respect: those waves were short, nasty killers. That was why there was a pool right by the beach. 'SWIMMER DROWNS ON EVE OF BIG RACE – The body of Miss Alexandra Archer, strong contender for Olympic swimming nomination, was found on the Napier foreshore this morning. Police say there are no suspicious circumstances . . .' It would look like I'd cracked up under the strain. I couldn't do that to my family. To Mr Jack, whose tubby chubby face when I won the two hundred and twenty yards had been wonderful to behold. Nor to Maggie either. And not to Andy, up? out? there beyond the horizon.

Perhaps there was a way. I sat, trying to blot out the vision of waves and death with the more obvious and very beautiful image before me of a full moon reflected on the water. Nothing but ocean between me and South America. Perhaps . . . I was unhinged enough to consider climbing over something to get into the pool. I began to walk along the beach.

Then a car drove along the road. I stopped and hid in a shadow, needlessly, I suppose since my track suit was dark blue. The car stopped, too, outside the pool. I crept on to the grass skirting along the walls of the pool building, furtive as a cop peering melodramatically around corners in a gangster film.

Whoever had got out of the car had gone inside the pool's main office, and turned a light on. That meant someone with a key, some person who might let me have a dip.

I walked quickly towards the main door, and peered inside. A man in a blazer was standing behind the counter, busy with something.

'Um . . . Excuse me.'

He jumped a mile. 'Who's that?' He thought I was a burglar or something.

'Um . . . Excuse me. Could you – would it be possible . . .?' You idiot, Alex, of course he'll say no. And then where will you be? Some further native cunning made me stop talking and walk quite boldly into the foyer.

With the light behind him, I could only see that he was about Dad's age, neatly dressed in blazer and tie. I recognized him as the pool manager, usually behind the counter when we arrived at the pool each morning. I'd heard he'd been a good swimmer in his time. He was still fit looking, good-looking, not one of those who'd gone to seed. Surely he'd recognize a damsel in distress. He certainly identified me smartly enough.

'Alex Archer, isn't it?'

'Yes, um . . .'

'What are you wandering around for, this time of night? Don't you see enough of pools? You should be in bed asleep.'

'I should. But I can't.' I must have sounded pretty desperate.

'Nerves? Your big race is tomorrow night. Well, tonight, actually. Stage fright, can't sleep?' He looked hard at me. 'You're not sick, are you? Fever? Do you want me to call a doctor?'

'No, it's just . . . nerves. Bad dreams. Please, I've got my togs. Can you let me have a swim? Just a short one, five minutes?'

He finished whatever he was doing in the drawer. 'I'm not usually here this time of night, you know. I was on my way home from the officials' do at the hotel in town.'

We'd heard, over the years, about the officials' get-togethers. That explained the banging doors after midnight at the hotel.

'Please.'

'I'd a funny feeling I'd not locked up the till properly.'

'Please. Two minutes.'

'Go on then,' he said gruffly. 'But it'll have to be in the dark. I don't want the police over here.'

'I don't mind,' I said, already half-way through the pool entrance. I changed in the shadows in about ten seconds, ran along to the starting end and dived into the blackness.

I've never swum in the dark before or since. But I knew as soon as I hit the water it was the right thing for me, that night. After two laps I felt cleaned out; the pounding of my heart and dreaded pictures in my head had gone. I thought only of my body and its power through the water, the rhythm of my stroke, which was so ingrained into every cell of me. Half of the pool was in shadow, the other in moonlight; I swam in and out of moonbeams.

I knew he was watching me. After six lengths it occurred to me that he'd be wanting some sleep too, with the pool open for training at six and heats at nine-thirty. I could have gone on for miles. I saw Andy clearly now, his face relaxed and brown, smiling down at me as he had that day on the headland.

Behind a stairway, I put my pyjamas back on, and track suit, and wrapped the towel around my head like a turban.

'Thanks.'

'Thanks for the demo. Before, you looked like being at the end of your tether. In there, you swim like a mermaid. Feel better now?'

'Much.'

'What would you have done if I hadn't happened to be here?'

'I don't know. Climbed over the wall, probably. No one would ever have known.'

'Risky.'

'Yes.'

'Your big race, I've got my money on you after that two hundred and twenty yesterday.'

'Thanks.'

'Sometimes I'm glad my own kids don't want to get into this game. One's seven, full of beans, hasn't learnt to breathe yet, but she can go. You'd be surprised what I see here from my office.'

I thought of Maggie, and others. 'No, I wouldn't.'

'Yourself? Who pushes you – parents, coach, club, press, peer group?'

'Not my parents. They've never pushed me. Or Mr Jack.'

'OK, OK. Bill Jack's a nice bloke.'

'I push myself.'

'I believe you. Well, it's getting late. I'll run you back to your motel.'

'It's only one street away.'

'Can't have girls wandering around . . .'

'I'd rather walk.'

'I insist. What if you got set upon between here and the motel? Good-looking wench like you. I'd be for the high jump. Your Mr Upjohn'd have my guts for garters.'

He didn't mean it, but I was now starting to imagine things, quite unfairly, and those things included not getting in his car. So I took off, running in my bare feet.

I was back at the motel driveway before I heard the car engine. From the safety of the gate I saw him cruise past, no doubt checking that I was safely home. He waved and decided to give a little toot.

Two yards, Alex. There's nothing in it, nothing. You just need a fingernail that's all. Oh, Alex, stretch, reach . . .

God's teeth, Andy . . .

For me . . .

I'm dead, Andy. I have nothing left.

You have, a fingernail, that's all you need . . .

I haven't even got that. I bit them all off years ago. You know how awful my nails are . . .

For God's sake, shut up. You are so near a record, over a second off.

You're kidding me again.

Listen, woman, would I lie?

I've shot my bolt . . .

Don't be crude. Just throw yourself at the wall . . .

What do you think I'm doing?

Reach for a star, Alex. The one I'm holding out . . . The gold one with a record and Rome written on it . . .

16

One thing I learned during the events of that day: apparently sensible people will believe anything they're told. They won't or don't want to stop and say 'Hey, wait a minute, is this what it seems?' They jump right in the cactus to conclusions.

In my innocence, feeling relaxed after my moonlit swim, I had crept in the hotel front door, shut it with great care and silence, tiptoed up the stairs and into room seven. What I didn't know, until later when I sorted it all out with Maggie, was that her mother couldn't sleep either. She'd got up and was walking round the room having a cigarette when she heard the car toot. So she looked out the window and under the street light saw me running in the driveway with my hair all bedraggled, saw the car and a person wave in a friendly fashion and drive off. What's more, the toot had woken Maggie, also sleeping only lightly.

At breakfast, over the far side of the dining-room, I saw Mr Upjohn and Mrs Hooper in deep discussion. I was feeling terrible, because with wet hair it had still taken me ages to get to sleep and then I'd woken at the crack of dawn with my heart pounding. But at least I hadn't been carted away screaming, which is what might have happened.

I'd tried to read, got up, went for a walk down to the beach to watch the sun rise out of the sea, and came back to breakfast as soon as the dining-room was open. My heat was early in the programme, so I wanted to get my food down, my body in good working order.

Dad and Gran came in shortly after breakfast. 'You look pale, Alex. How did you sleep?' 'Not so bad.' I wasn't going to tell them, was I, or about the ache in my tum, which could have been nerves or an unusual period pain. We walked over to the pool.

'Good morning, Miss Archer,' said the man behind the counter, with a tactless wink. 'How are we today?' he said, staring hard, so that I frowned, and mumbled 'Fine, thanks.' He didn't look too good on four hours' sleep either. Dad, thankfully, was preoccupied with getting money out of his wallet. But Mrs Benton standing there in the foyer, she noticed the wink, and the long steady gaze, as I later discovered. The smile on her face should have been a warning to me.

In broad daylight, the pool looked quite inviting. Only a few early-birds were already in. I wanted plenty of time to warm up, time for a few slow lengths to settle my stomach and some sharp sprints to get my arms going. Mr Jack was there. If he looked concerned at my pale face, or the fact that out of the blue he'd been summoned to an urgent meeting with Mr Upjohn up in the committee room, he didn't show it. Today he was all optimism and Aussie good humour.

I did my warm-up, changed into second best togs as if in a dream. I sat with Dad and Gran for a while, and then went and found a distant spot in the competitors' enclosure. I was avoiding Maggie, and she me.

Ten minutes before the session was due to begin, I saw Mr Jack come back and join Dad. Then a reporter, a young guy from one of the bigger papers, came over. He was new to the game this season, but had seemed friendly.

'Any comment, Alex?'

'On what?'

'The meeting that's just been held.'

'I don't know anything about a meeting.'

'On your midnight escapade?'

'My *what*?'

'Gallivanting, so they say. There's talk of disciplinary action.'

I was speechless. Utterly. Then I heard myself say, cold and supercilious as a fish, 'I have no comment. I have a race in ten minutes and I'd be obliged if you'd leave me alone.'

'You mean to say you didn't know about the meeting?' I knew that look, amused, wicked, so full of malice. He knew I didn't. Coming from an evening paper, he wanted a quick quote, a good strong reaction from me to whip up a story before his mid-day deadline. I'd learnt a few things at last. As I turned away, staring at the race that was in progress, he went on, 'I gather there was some doubt as to whether you'd be allowed to swim this morning.'

'Go away.' I could have been a lot ruder. When he didn't, I got up and moved, catching Maggie's eye – such a strange expression, half pleading, half pity, trying to tell me something but this was neither the time nor the place.

Maggie's heat was called. She did a great sixty-five point six seconds, a national record. In the sunshine, surging through the still water, it looked so easy, effortless, beautiful. She was roundly applauded. By this time I was as angry as I'd ever been in my life. Allowed or not, I'm here, I'm swimming and nothing and nobody will stop me! I stood on the block with my head lowered, feeling like a clap of thunder. I swam the race in a fury, oblivious of the other girls, finishing about three seconds clear. When I looked up my timekeepers were grinning and nodding at me like a pack of demented monkeys – sixty-five point two. I'd gone one better, and broken her record.

No, please, no. I don't want it, not now. It will hang around me like a dead weight in the final tonight. I'd never yet done a good final after a fast heat. Heats didn't matter a damn, it was only the final that counted, in the end. And now I'll be in the wrong lane, the blind lane.

I climbed from the pool, feeling sick. People said great swim, and clapped me on the back, but I could only think of getting to the sheds. I gathered up my towel and track suit and ran. A photographer tried to take a picture, but I ignored him.

In the toilet, I was violently ill. I stayed there, until the shaking had at last started to subside. Outside, I heard the usual chatter of competitors coming and going. Mrs Hooper's voice called 'Alex? Alex, are you all right?' 'Yes,' was enough to send her away. I was so cold.

'Alex?' I recognized Carol's voice. 'Alex, you in there?'

'Yes.'

'Message from your Dad. Great swim. Please join him as soon as possible.'

Too right I'll join him, and Mr Jack, and find out what's going on. I caught a glimpse of myself in the mirror as I came out, and wished I hadn't. Then I saw Maggie, clearly waiting for me. She beckoned me into a narrow passageway between two sets of lockers.

'Alex, that was a great time.'

'Thanks.' What was all the secrecy?

'I won't get another chance.'

'To do what?'

She looked very uncomfortable. 'Well, before tonight . . . if I'd known what it'd lead to, I'd have stopped her, somehow.'

'I don't understand.'

'Reporting you to the manager for being out with Mr Phillips.'

'Mr who?'

'Mr Phillips, the pool manager.'

'Is that his name?'

'You don't know his name?'

'Of course I don't. I never even spoke to him until last night. Well, hardly. Just hello, goodbye, that sort of thing.'

'Then what . . .? Mother was awake standing at the window having a cigarette. She gets nervous for me, you know. (Really?) She saw the car, you waved goodbye, he drove off tooting. That's what she felt she had to tell Mr Upjohn. Upholding team reputation, all that stuff. I did try to tell her it was none of our business. After all, if you wanted to spoil your chances by . . .'

'Listen, Maggie. I was having nightmares, real shockers, you know? Perhaps you don't. I was desperate enough to go for a walk, desperate for a swim to try to calm down before someone took me away in a straitjacket. You know that feeling, you need water, it's like you're addicted to it?'

She nodded.

'I saw a light on in the pool. Mr Phillips was there, checking something in the office, the till or something. He takes his job seriously, you've seen that. He'd just come from the officials' party and didn't need much persuading. It's his pool, he's the manager. I had a short swim, in the moonlight. It was great. I had togs on, it was all very proper. He offered to run me back to the motel, but I walked. He was just checking that I got home safely. I did, and I got about two hours' sleep last night. That's all.'

She didn't say anything. Then Maggie did something that gave me hope, whatever happened in the final, even if her mother succeeded in having me 'disciplined' and my name smeared, and my hopes for Rome dashed. She stepped forward and we embraced for a long understanding moment. A couple of juniors happened to pass the end of the passageway and stood there with their mouths open at what must have been the touching sight of two great rivals hugging like sisters. I couldn't give a damn who saw us, or what they thought of the fact that both of us were crying.

'Good luck, Alex,' she whispered. I knew she didn't mean for the race itself, but for that other battle, against people, hypocrisy, jealousy, pomposity and gossip. She wanted a fair fight tonight, and so did I. I heard Mrs Hooper's voice again, calling me, and the moment was over.

It was no doubt already all over the pool, this lie about my gallivanting. Feeling like death, I walked boldly out along the concourse, to where Dad, Gran and Mr Jack were sitting. 'Congratulations,' followed me all the way, and a few whispers too.

They looked very serious.

'Great swim, Alex,' Mr Jack said finally. 'Just great.'

'Then why aren't you celebrating,' I said bitterly. 'Do you believe what they've told you?'

'No.'

'Good. Because if they've told you I was out having some sort of date with Mr Phillips they've got it all wrong.'

'Keep your voice down, Alex,' said Dad.

'I'll tell you what happened.' I did, just as I had told Maggie. They looked relieved, amused, despairing all at once. I think Mrs Benton had overplayed her hand, because it seemed I'd actually been seen getting out of the car, and the toots (plural) had been loud enough to wake Maggie, which was, according to Mrs Benton, an unacceptable form of gamesmanship. From her, that was rich!

But I had to eat some humble pie. Even if I wasn't actually out painting the town red, I'd still been out doing something I ought not to. Little girl swimmers of fifteen shouldn't be out of their safe little beds at midnight.

'Well, where do we go from here?' said Mr Jack, sounding rather weary. 'I had hell's own job persuading them that you had to be allowed to swim in the heats. There would have been a full-blown scandal otherwise, which would obviously have rebounded on them when they heard the true facts. One or two were all for suspending you then and there.'

'Without hearing my side of the story?'

'Yes.'

'But that's a kangaroo court.'

'Alex, sit down,' said Dad.

Mr Jack actually laughed. 'True, Alex, Cecil Upjohn as judge, jury and executioner. But don't underestimate his power. I've got a lot of talking to do. I've got to get alongside Ron Phillips quick. I want you to get out of the way, and say nothing to nobody.'

'But . . .'

'Better still, Jim, Mrs Young. Take her away in the car. Out to Cape Kidnappers, anywhere. No, that's too far, but you know what I mean. Go to the Saturday afternoon flicks if it's the only way you can relax, take your mind off things. Anything!'

I sat silently. I wasn't to be allowed to speak for myself.

'Don't you trust me, Alex?'

'It's not that.'

'What is it then?'

'Just, well, I got myself into this mess . . . Surely all I have to do is explain . . .'

'And this time you've got to trust me to get you out of it. Explaining is not enough. You need Ron Phillips to back up your story. You'll need to eat a bit of humble pie about going for walks in the middle of the night. You're not the first young swimmer to fall foul of officials, you know. They know all about it in Aussie, and I wasn't born yesterday. I know what drove you to the pool last night. I wish to God you hadn't. But you did, and now I'm going to find Ron, so get lost, both of you, pronto. Excuse me, Mrs Young,' he said, with a momentary twinkle at Gran.

'T.T.F.N.,' I said, rather naughtily under the circumstances.

'Get out of here. By the way, I reckon you'll both break the record again tonight. But you'll crack it the most. Now get.'

I love you, Mr Jack. Gold in record time. You still have faith I can do it, despite everything.

It was a long long day. We went back to the motel. I changed from track suit into the jeans I wore most of the time now. We went for a little walk into town because I had to find a dairy that sold what I needed for a period coming a week earlier than expected.

The ache in my tum had gone, but it had been nothing compared to the sick feeling I now had to live with. I had two battles on my hands: one only I could win, one I must trust someone else to win for me.

Lunch in a hotel was subdued and I had to force myself to eat the steak and mashed potato I knew I had to eat. Tonight I'd be down to glucose tablets. Gran and Dad talked about the old days, the people she'd been visiting during the week; it was like a conversation overheard in a bus, not quite understood.

We bought some orchard fruit, peaches and watermelon, and ate them on the return journey, finishing up on Bluff Hill, the headland overlooking the port and beach front. Dad got Gran talking, this time about the great earthquake of 1931 when large bits of land rose from the sea and others fell into it, and the whole central city area was wrecked. Gran's story was gloomy, because Albert's shop had been completely destroyed and their house damaged. Lots of people, about two hundred and fifty, had died the day it happened, buried, burned, trapped, many known to Gran, or children or parents of her friends. Today, in the sunshine, it looked like a sleepy seaside town with a small port and a nice waterfront.

Time dragged. I rejected the idea of a Saturday matinee, the aquarium, going back to the hotel for a rest. I wanted a quiet beach, shaded, cool, away from people, which we found to the north of Bluff Hill. Dad miraculously produced a lilo out of the car and blew it up, and Gran threatened me with a smacked bottom if I did not rest on it. Sounds of seagulls, children and the sea lulled me into a deep dreamless sleep for nearly two hours. I woke feeling woozy, but I was over the worst of the waiting period, and after that things began to improve.

Around five thirty we went back to the hotel, to find a note left at the desk by Mr Jack.

'All's well. Complaint dropped. For Pete's sake Alex, *don't* talk to any reporters. See you for tea, 6 pm.'

I looked at Dad. If I looked half as relieved as he did . . . I could only grin feebly. He just shook his head, despairingly. 'I don't know, Alex. Always skating on thin ice.'

I would meet Maggie tonight, in a fair fight. A reporter, my malicious friend from the morning session, turned up and was firmly told by Dad I had nothing to say.

When Mr Jack joined us in the dining-room he was grinning from ear to ear. Over a large mixed grill, while I toyed with an omelette, he explained that my friend Mr Phillips had been as outraged as me, when he heard what was being hinted at behind the closed doors of the committee room. He had his own reputation as pool manager at stake. It was his first such job and he didn't intend to let some gossiping woman and a self-righteous official ruin him. So, of course, his story tallied exactly with mine, and

I knew I had been wrong to suspect his motives for offering me a lift home.

'They accepted his explanation. I think they even learnt something about the pressures swimmers can get under. He told them, when you appeared in the office, you looked like a ghost. He seriously thought you were on the verge of a breakdown. A quick dip, if that was all you wanted, seemed a simple enough way of getting you back on the rails. He'd intended to have a word with me in the morning. When you powered off to a new national record there didn't seem to be much point.'

Curtain down on another saga. I seem to attract attention, trouble, gossip, talk. Was it always going to be like this?

'The dreams. Were they that bad, Alex?' Dad said gently.

'Yeah.'

'Do you want to tell us?'

'No.' The images had already faded, and I had no intention of trying to pull them back into focus. What I needed now was some time to myself. 'Excuse me, I'll be back, half an hour.'

They did not follow me. Our room was empty. Carol had finished her events and was away having fun. On the dressing-table was a huge pile of telegrams: from Mum and the kids, from Miss Gillies, staff and pupils; from Miss Macrae (Go, and catch a falling star [John Donne] Marcia Macrae); from Julia, and other classmates; from Auntie Pat and Uncle Ernie; from Miss de Latour who had never forgiven me for growing so tall; from my piano teacher; and incredibly even one from Keith! There were telegrams from relatives I barely knew and the neighbours on both sides and several up and down the street as well, and some of Gran's friends who we visit each Christmas. So many people taking the trouble!

One of the last I opened read, 'To a true champion, our thoughts and love, from Tom and Elizabeth Richmond.' I lay on the bed, looking at it with wet eyes, for quite a time.

It is time to go. I get up, and under the shower wash my hair. It will be wet again soon, but I must be shining clean for the moment when I strip my track suit off, stand on the block, face my audience and my opponent and my task.

This is opening night, this my dressing-room. Instead of the costume of another identity, the make-up that hides, and changes, I am paring myself down to essentials. Slowly, with care, I shave armpits and legs, even thighs and arms below my elbows, which is something I've not done before. I must be sleek as a dolphin.

Before the mirror I stand for just a moment: I see a lean female body, with small firm breasts, a flat stomach, wide shoulders, eyes a bit wild, cheeks a bit gaunt. I look fit, battle-scarred, prepared.

Around my neck is Andy's single pearl, a tear-drop.

My costume is a pair of practice togs for warm-up, track suit, although the night is warm. Carefully packed along with towels, caps, glucose and tampons are my precious togs saved for tonight, for luck. I also pack a dress, petticoat and shoes, because there is usually a party on the last night.

I wonder how Maggie is feeling. Then I think of her mother and one or two others who've directly tried to cut me down to size, to be the also-ran, the normal teenage feminine girl, and a few more who've tried indirectly, and I allow myself a big broad smile.

My stomach is churning, my hands are even trembling a little as I comb my hair, but above all that, I feel tall, strong, invincible. I stand for a last moment, savouring the peace of being with myself. Once I close the door of Room Seven behind me, I become public property. There will be the quiet anxious faces of Dad and Gran and Mr Jack, reporters, photographers, all those people, a glimpse of Mrs Benton, the awareness of Maggie. I fold up the Richmond telegram and put it in my track suit pocket, next to my heart.

Lead on, Andy. I'm ready.

Epilogue

I'm nine years old and it's my first race again and I'm swimming so fast that I try to swim right through the end of the pool.

Two strokes, one. I'm swimming up a waterfall. I'm at the bottom of the sea. I've drowned.

I've touched, with an arm I swear grew five inches. Later I'll find all my fingers are bruised.

All movement stops. It has stopped in the next lane too, where Maggie lies on her back gasping like a fish in extremis. I can hear nothing, see nothing. I hang over the lane ropes. I will never swim another race as long as I live. I don't think I'll survive to tell the tale.

Gradually, I'm aware of a crowd on its feet, applause, cheering; thankfully, because my body is making most peculiar noises as I draw in great lungfuls of air. I am strangely uninterested in the result.

Liar, he says. Anyway, you know, don't you?

Do I? Dare I?

Yes, you'll dare anything now.

It was supposed to be my gift to you.

It was. You gave me yourself, the greatest gift of all. Now stand up. You're the champ. Enjoy the rituals. Maggie wants to congratulate you. You can enjoy being friends now. You're both going to Rome, you know, but don't tell her just yet.

You knew? All the time?

Of course.

Through all that? Killing myself . . . You knew?

My gift was hope. Arrivederci. I loved you, sweet maid . . .

Andy?

Arrivederci . . .

Before you leave me, I love you too . . .

Alex in Winter

Part One

TO get from the floodlit water up on to the victory dais was not really a very great distance. It involved only the swimmer climbing from the shallow end of the pool, drying off, regaining some sort of normal breathing, blinking eyes into focus; waiting while the judges and timekeepers went into their huddles. A minute perhaps, or in this case nearly three, longer than the race itself. And then, as the announcer called the placings, two steps up on to the top level of the dais.

The new champion was seen to falter.

Hard-bitten journalists watching through binoculars from the Press box above the starting end thought they had an even better story about to break.

'What's wrong with the kid?'

'I've seen some burned out young in this game,' said a bald veteran of forty years' experience covering every sport known to his paper's readers, 'but . . . it was only a sprint, for Chrissake. Two laps!'

'She can't even get out of the pool.'

A silence fell in the Press box while the unplaced girls climbed out, leaving only Maggie and Alex, longer than was usual, while the crowd's clapping merged into an excited buzz. Alex groped for the side of the pool; lay across it like a stranded fish; tried once, fell back and tried again, taking her weight on her rigid arms, hanging suspended with her head down on her chest, until she'd gathered the strength to heave a knee up and crawl on to the side of the pool. She sat slumped on the edge with her eyes closed while an official in whites and blazer, concern in every curve of her motherly figure, squatted down beside her and slung a large towel and track suit top around her shoulders.

At her feet, Maggie eased her own quite different pain by swimming away, a few strokes of backstroke, filling her ears with water, shutting out the sight and sound of a standing ovation which she knew was not for her.

'Do they have a doctor at these shows?' said one of the reporters.

'Bound to be, somewhere in this crowd. Or the St John's

ambulance people. But she's standing, at least!'

'Women's 100 metres freestyle.' The announcer's voice abruptly silenced the three thousand people who had come to see this race and who — since they could not separate the two swimmers at the finish — had not been disappointed. He paused dramatically, spinning out the moment. On the Napier beach, a hundred yards away, Pacific waves crashed noisily on to the black and grey stones.

'First — the new New Zealand champion — from Auckland, Miss Alex Archer ...'

The crowded stands and terraces exploded with cheers, applause, whistles and banners.

'She's not going to make it.'

'She's a zombie. Look at her face.'

'Oh, God,' said the veteran. 'I've had enough of watching kids kill themselves in the name of sport.' He put down his binoculars, took a long pull on the scraggy remains of a roll-your-own cigarette, and looked around the huge crowd now on its feet, still cheering and clapping. 'Blood sports, in effect. The Romans have a lot to answer for.'

The only woman reporter, herself once a sprint champion, as tall as Alex and ten years older, said, 'You're being melodramatic. She's all right.'

The veteran, thinking of his nine-year-old granddaughter who had just started training and who worshipped the ground Alex walked on, stubbed out his fag and reluctantly took up his binoculars. Alex had put on the bright blue track suit top, smoothed back her hair with the comb the official gave her, and slowly made it to the top step of the dais. She was standing erect, staring ahead. The image was close and clear enough to expose tears, a gaunt face drained of colour, eyesockets deep in shadow, the pulse beating fast in the side of her neck, and chest still heaving. Photographers' flash bulbs went off below, but she gave no sign of having noticed, even less of smiling for the camera.

'Bill Jack's not very happy,' said the veteran swinging his glasses on to the trio of Alex's coach, father and grandmother, whose anxious expressions contrasted sharply with the smiling faces and clapping hands on all sides. 'There's something funny going on with that kid. If I were her parents I'd be worried.'

'Time, a new national record, sixty-four point nine,' boomed the announcer, unable to keep the delight out of his voice. As the cheers and applause again rose into the soft February night air, the face in the circular image of the glasses was seen to smile slightly.

'She earned that,' said the woman reporter.

'What's that she's fastening round her neck?' said another.

'Some sort of gold chain, a pearl, I think.' Probably very special in some way, but she wasn't going to tell her cynical male colleagues that.

'A bauble.' This younger reporter put down his binoculars, disappointed that Alex was controlling whatever turmoil was going on inside. It looked like the hoped for front page human-interest story (a faint, breakdown, stretcher case perhaps) wasn't going to eventuate. He leaned forward, smirking slightly as he peered through the glasses. 'Fine pair o' legs! If I was in the business of advertising stockings, I'd grab those legs. Figuratively speaking, of course.'

'Would you now.' The woman reporter looked sideways, not relishing the thought of future evenings spent sitting in Press boxes with this slimy newcomer, with his loud tie and over-oiled hair. 'Exploitation, the old story.'

'Rubbish. Women love it, the implied promise, if you wear our nylons you too can have legs like that. That girl could get a job as a swim-suit model tomorrow.'

'For your information, Ross, Alex is a schoolgirl and an amateur and bound to the amateur code. And she's got better things to do with her life than advertise nylons or swim-suits.'

'But you have to admit it's a spectacular body. Now Maggie there, neat enough little figure, bit muscular in the calves perhaps, too flat in the chest. Doesn't hold a candle.'

'She. A young woman, not a body.'

'Oh, come on . . .'

'Second,' interrupted the announcer, 'the previous title-holder, Miss Maggie Benton, in a time of sixty-five seconds.'

'A tenth of a second! Well, I certainly couldn't separate them,' said the veteran, his fingers carefully rolling another cigarette from shreds of tobacco and a leaf of thin paper. 'We might see a protest from the mother. She's not looking too pleased over there.'

'Naa, it was clear enough.' The implication of better eyesight did not escape the veteran, catching the woman reporter's amused glance. Ross went on, unperturbed, 'Now isn't *that* a touching sight.'

To those still watching closely, Alex's eyes were seen to have flown open at the mention of Maggie's name. She was looking down, extending a hand and stepping down to the lower level as the two came together and hugged closely. It was clearly spontaneous, not set up for the photographers whose flash bulbs caught the moment. The woman reporter said sharply, 'You're new to this game, Ross. You don't know what those two have been through, for years. They're actually good friends.'

'I don't believe it.'

'It's a fact. And if you think Alex looks a bit overwrought, she's had a rough spin these last few months, apart from what happened last night. I didn't rate her chances of winning very highly. Perhaps you should also know that she had something going for a lad who was killed in a hit-and-run road accident, about nine weeks ago. Bowled off his bike by a drunkard. She used to train with him.'

'Really?' said Ross. The woman caught the interest in his voice.

'Off limits, Ross. Alex won't tell you anything on that score. You'll leave it strictly alone if you know what's good for you.'

Ross did know, from deliberately upsetting Alex just before the heats that morning, telling her in the calculated hope of an angry quote to catch his midday deadline, that she was under threat of being suspended and disqualified from competing. She had told him to go away, two polite words of profound contempt. He had admired her control, for a kid.

The third placegetter had climbed on to the dais. The crowd, knowing the ritual, was silent for the fanfare being played by two young trumpeters from the town band, but burst forth again in prolonged clapping while the three girls were handed their medals by the local mayor.

'I'd pick both of them for Rome,' said the veteran. 'Maggie is sane enough, nice uncomplicated sort of kid, as long as her mother stays out of the picture. But our Alex there . . .' He thought he'd seen it all: bright kids in high-pressure sports, swimming, athletics, gymnastics, tennis, in football and rowing teams; kids shoved forward by pushy parents, fired up by ambitious coaches, manipulated by empire-building, mealy-minded officials; twelve-year-old puppets, specializing too soon, pushed too hard, bored and burned out before they even left school.

Hadn't he seen it all time and time again, and growing worse in recent years? Shaking his head now, watching closely as the three girls came off the dais, Alex last, still moving slowly, too slowly — he wasn't so sure. Bill Jack, he noted, had taken the unusual step of forcing his way on to the crowded concourse to lead her away from the engulfing press of photographers, officials, young swimmers, and applause which had broken out yet again, louder and longer than he had heard around a swimming pool in years.

I just won the race of my life.

Overcoming a battle to the death with officials and a certain mother, no sleep, my period a week early, two false starts, hitting the lane ropes and a disastrous turn, I still did it!

At the finish the world went into weird slow motion. (Strange, did nobody else notice?) I suppose I stood on the victory dais with the gold medal in my hands while the trumpets played. I think I was crying, I can't really remember getting up or getting down. Mr Jack was somewhere around. Then I vaguely remember being congratulated and hugged by the most unlikely people and interviewed for the papers and the radio. God only knows what I said, 'cause I don't. I was photographed, but I remember now, I insisted only with Maggie because the result could have gone either way and she was still smiling, admittedly a bit wan, but that's more than I could say for her mother. I rang home and heard my Mum actually weeping and the brats cheering at the other end of the phone. Dad and Gran were over the moon, crying too.

I am more than likely to be nominated for the Olympics in Rome, six months away.

So why can't I sleep? Why, hearing a town clock strike one, am I once again lying on this lumpy motel bed listening to my room-mate snore? And why am I sweating from a nightmare, just as bad as last night's which drove me to a midnight swim and nearly got me disqualified from the sprint and any chance of Rome altogether. Isn't it all over, this crazy yearning?

And the dreams! There are two versions, but always the same components: Andy, me, his yacht and more wind than we can handle. In one version we are sailing perilously along, but laughing and singing, thrilling to the speed. There's a gust which lays us on our ear. Andy is caught off balance, falls overboard, The boat recovers, I sail on. He doesn't come up. The water turns a sinister streaky dusky brown.

If that isn't bad enough, the second is worse: this time the boat does capsize, in slow motion. This time it's me that goes, deep deeply under, tangled with ropes and sails and wires that grow tighter around my neck my arms my chest and that's when I wake up sweating, gasping, telling my room-mate that it's nothing, sorry I yelled, woke you up, go back to sleep. I don't want to remember any more, please God, no. Andy was run down by a car, two months ago. I went to his funeral, and saw that awful long box being carried past me. I saw the dent on his bed where he'd had a nap a few hours before he got mashed up. I spent part of Christmas day with his parents. I have trained myself into the ground for him. I won tonight's race for him. It's over.

There's something else bugging me.

After all the final relays and victory ceremonies and speeches were done, I'd stood holding court at the cup-of-tea-and-sausage-roll party for officials and senior swimmers held in the clubrooms above the pool. It wasn't intentional; I was literally pinned into a corner by officials who were old friends, several reporters, other swimmers, all wanting to talk or get me to sign programmes or autograph books. Over their head I could see Mr Jack with a group of coaches, Dad and Gran talking to Maggie with a few officials. I was glad they were talking to her; they knew as well as anyone how she was feeling, being pipped at the post. They'd had a lot of practice with me, over the years.

I was relieved when Dad suggested that Gran was a bit tired and was I ready to leave? I knew there was a group of swimmers planning to go to a milk bar, maybe walk along the beach and stay up until dawn, to unwind after our months of hard training, but that wasn't for me, tonight. My victory smile was already wearing thin.

'Yes, I'm ready,' I said, but beside my elbow a very patient young male reporter from the local paper wanted a few minutes, Miss Archer? Somewhere quiet, he said, politer and more earnest than any reporter I'd ever met. Tomorrow morning, I suggested, but he was sorry he had another assignment tomorrow morning and afternoon was no good as I'd be on my way back to Auckland. Would I mind, only a few minutes? So we went along the passage, to a sort of alcove. All the lights were still on. It was after about ten minutes, during a long silence while he was busy trying to remember his shorthand and I was busy trying to stay awake, that I heard the voices coming along the corridor.

'Here's the committee room. Pity about the sprint title.'

'Indeed, Albie, a great pity. Ten yards out, even five, I thought young Maggie had the race sewn up. Great shame for the kid. It's made the nominations difficult.'

With the huge crowd gone from the spectator stands, the officials and swimmers' party thinning out, and the reporters off to drink at a hotel with a friendly and not particularly law-abiding publican, the selectors could be forgiven for thinking they had the place to themselves.

Not that stocky Albie Jones would have noticed a stray competitor anyway. Half a lifetime as a primary school headmaster and swimming official had made him impervious to children, except inside schoolgrounds in controllable lines. Swimmers he saw only as meticulous entries in his personal register of local and international times.

'As title-holder Alex must now have the prior claim,' said Cyril Upjohn, his official's blazer straining across a pigeon chest and a well-padded backside. He paused outside the door that was being held open for him, and poked a match down into the bowl of his pipe, before continuing.

'I can't say I like the girl, really. Too much to say for herself, too inclined to argue, a bad influence on juniors. I dislike tall women, even young ones. I don't want her in Rome.'

'Well, as the likely manager, Cyril,' said the miniature headmaster, also immaculate in whites and a blazer, 'you'll have to cope with her. Maggie, not Alex, and young Brett David was how I'd seen it.'

'Could be.'

'Not,' said Albie Jones, flipping open his precious file, 'not that either of them would make an Olympic final, on current times. We'll be lucky to see a swimmer in the team.'

'I think, Albie, we'll have to announce a delay. If Maggie can get that record down, substantially down, she'd be back as first choice. Ah, here's Brian, come in, come in. We were just discussing, postponement, do you think?'

A third elderly man in blazer and white trousers had been guided to the committee room by the resonant voices of men who were well used to making themselves heard. The door was closed. Half an hour, two pipes, an ashtray of cigarettes and six double whiskies later, they had formally confirmed the postponement that Cyril Upjohn had proposed in the first place. They drafted a brief Press statement, carefully, because this wasn't the end of their responsibilities, for release in Monday's papers, and returned to their hotel rather tired. If only that wretched girl hadn't pulled off a major surprise, (or, thought Cyril Upjohn, she'd managed to get herself properly disqualified last night), things would have been so much simpler and tidier.

The wrong place, the wrong time. And the wrong script, the wrong words.

Even when the door closed, I could still hear the ringing tones of my least favourite official and that small headmaster called Albie Jones, who minced around holding forth to anyone who would listen about times which had been done at the last European championships by obscure Hungarians.

'I've heard enough,' I whispered to the fascinated boy beside me. I took my sandals off and tiptoed as silently as I knew how down the echoing corridor and three flights of stairs. They might hear us, but once they'd climbed to their geriatric feet and opened the door, they'd never see or catch us or prove anything.

'You'd be wise to keep that to yourself,' I said, outside the pool's main entrance. My sixteen-year-old friend (who I noted had also taken his black shoes off) was panting and flushed, wondering how he could use this juicy bit of information. A scoop?! And also embarrassed for me, I think. It's not every day you get to hear home truths about what top officials think of their swimmers, and one in particular.

'Sounds as though you don't have many friends in high places, Miss Archer.'

'I don't. No that's not true. It's only Mr Upjohn who's got it in for me. But don't try anything clever. They'll get you, write to your editor, withdraw your Press pass, silence you somehow. Like they nearly got me.'

He probably knew; it had got around, rumours about Alex running round the town with a married man the night before the final. As if I'd be so *stupid!* I'd nearly not been allowed to swim in the final; I had been officially reprimanded for taking a midnight swim, which I needed to stop me going off my rocker on the night in question. They would like to have believed Mrs Benton's tittle-tattle version, pure invention. Then I could have been suspended and Maggie could have won easily and been nominated for Rome, and everyone would have been happy.

'I could write the story, informed sources say . . .'

'Please, forget it,' I said from the superior wisdom of my six seasons in swimming. 'They'll deny everything. You'll achieve nothing, except more trouble for me.'

'But you'd think they didn't *want* any swimmers . . .'

'Funny, I had that impression too.' He was flipping back through the pages of his shorthand. 'Can you read that stuff?' I asked.

'Sort of,' he said, blushing. 'I've only been learning for a month. Is that true, you wouldn't get into the Olympic final?'

'Who knows? Dawn Fraser's world record is sixty point something, there are lots around the sixty-three mark. Who can say what we might do, Maggie or me, or anyone, with the sort of competition people in Aussie, or England, or America, or Europe get all the time.' As usual, I was talking myself into a state. 'I'd better be going.'

'Can I use that as a quote?'

'Yes, you can say that it's amazing that New Zealand swimmers do as well as they do, *all* things considered.'

'Lack of competition ...'

'Lack of competition, official encouragement, training facilities, anything you like, make it up, that's what most reporters do. No, except what we just heard up there, that's for real, that's ... oh hell.' I was losing control. Even under the street lights I could see he was hurt. I had to trust this boy.

'Sorry, I didn't mean — what's your name?'

'Grant Davies.'

'Grant, look, I have to go. Please, don't drop me in it.'

'Thanks for your time, Miss Archer. And good luck ... with the nominations.'

'Thanks. Hope you've got enough.' He didn't deserve my scorn. He'd asked some quite intelligent questions, for a reporter, like what did I, a true amateur, think of the Australian and Communist countries' training camps which many people thought were a violation of the amateur code (envious, I said), and how much did my parents contribute to my success? Everything, I said; my parents, my little old grandmother who was born right here in Napier you know, even my brothers and little sister, they all did.

I went over to meet up with Mr Jack, Dad and the said little old Gran sitting on the edge of a raised flower bed, waiting for me. Outwardly the champ, a woman of the world. Inside I am seething, confused, sick at heart as we walk silently along the Marine Parade back to the hotel. The breakers crash on the nearby beach. It seems like twenty-four days, not twenty-four hours, since I sat on the beach last night and contemplated finishing it all. I have dreamed of this victory for months, longed for the security of the nomination in my pocket, my rightful due, the satisfaction of lining up for the next hurdle.

I've done it — and — nothing. Nothing.

Why is it always *me* — taking pity on a polite but insistent cub reporter in a tie and walk-shorts, giving him time and co-operation. If I'd been Maggie, say, my Dad would have said enough, no more, and taken me home to bed. And then I'd never have been sitting in that alcove behind a potted plant with my ears burning, when I should have been drinking tea quietly back at the hotel, enjoying my win, thinking of the amazing trip to Rome I'd just earned.

'I don't want her in Rome,' he said.

Andy, you have betrayed me.

On the long drive back to Auckland the next day they put my unusual quietness down to nervous exhaustion, the understandable anticlimax. Sunday night Mum had planned a celebration dinner, with Mr Jack and his wife as honoured guests. Sweet local bubbly, roast pork with crispy golden crackling and apple sauce, Mum's most magnificent pavlova, as big as a road sign. Excitable kids, Mr Jack at his jovial best, his wife plump and happy, Gran all fired up after her trip down memory lane to the town where she'd spent most of her life, and frequent phone calls of congratulations all meant I did not have to contribute much to the party. I smiled weakly at the toasts, and said thank you to the telephone callers and tried not to weep and to forget all the rest.

Dad woke me next morning from a groggy sleep with a cup of tea and the newspaper. 'School today.'

Through gummed-up eyes I saw the sports page, with a large picture of me and Maggie on the victory dais, taken from below to distort the length of our legs. A chorus girl, the sort of photo I'd got very cunning at avoiding, but not this time. Maggie, a head shorter, smiling manfully.

'Nice picture.'

'*Dad!* It's awful. Glamour puss stuff.'

'Sleep well?'

'Not particularly.' I scanned the report, which said some nice things about the superb duel we had fought, my fighting spirit in victory and Maggie's sporting spirit in defeat and how both of us should be nominated for Rome.

'Look below,' Dad said quietly. 'I'm sorry, you won't be pleased.'

And there, sure enough, was a small story that the National Selectors, Messrs C. D. S. Upjohn, A. R. V. Jones, and B. J. Webster, had announced that the Olympic nominations would be held open for six weeks until the middle of March, to give 'the small vein of candidates' a chance to improve their times. The general impression was that not one of us was good enough.

I heard Mum's voice from the doorway, unusually holding forth. 'No encouragement, no indication of possible candidates, no times to aim at, nothing. It's a disgrace. I sometimes wonder if these men ever stop to think what it means to youngsters who train five miles a day, who give their waking hours to their sport. And their families and coaches. They don't do it for a slap in the face.'

When I said nothing, but just went on staring at the paper, Dad said, 'Alex?'

'What?'

'Did you know about this? Did Mr Jack hear something?'

Was I that transparent? Gran had now arrived in her dressing gown; a third tired unsmiling face. 'Why do you say that?'

'You just don't seem surprised.'

'I'm not, are you? We've never actually been told, except for some vague notion about times good enough to get into an Olympic final. How can they know that, from four years ago, records falling all the time? It's guesswork. Sixty-four point nine, never mind a record, still three seconds behind Dawn Fraser. And two nominations for one stroke? Of course I knew.'

'Unconvincing,' said Mum, who'd given me a close once-over as she came to collect my dirty clothes for washing and had no doubt seen the pain in my eyes. 'Don't tell me . . .'

'Mum, leave it out.'

Gran, now sitting on my bed and rubbing my arm sympathetically, interrupted. 'Don't upset her, Helena. Naturally she's disappointed, aren't we all? Of course she'll get nominated. How could she not? She's the champion. It's only the others they're not sure about.'

Dear Gran, so sure and optimistic, and Mum so upset on my behalf, and Dad too, and now James and Debbie going on about it not being fair, and my cheesecakey picture grinning at me out of the morning paper, applauded and rejected on the same page. I can't tell you why I am screaming inside. It's worse than you will ever know.

'Alex, would you come forward please?'

Miss Constantia Gillies looked over the lectern, over the heads of seven hundred girls, towards the back of the crowded school hall. Morning assemblies compelled her, as principal, to face this spectacle daily. The uniform was dreary enough: white blouse and short socks, above-knee gym tunic belted around the middle (in summer, a dull blue, in winter, black; unflattering and demeaning, and the all-male Board of Governors resistant to any suggestion of change), black regulation shoes. Worse was the regulation short hairstyle, not touching the collar; most disturbing was the regulation expression, incurious and slightly hostile. Every morning she wondered about the effect of such clothes on young minds and spirits.

'Alex?' called Miss Gillies, putting her spectacles back on. Pupils thought this taking on and off was a spinsterish habit; a few staff knew it was her defence when the sight of massed girls became unbearably depressing.

She believed Alex had arrived at school today, a week late from the long summer holidays because of her triumphs at the national swimming championships. The school, already restless in the heat and sensing an interesting hitch, was shuffling. Eventually, a head with fairish hair cut unusually short could be seen above the others, moving slowly from the back. As Alex neared the steps leading up on to the stage, Miss Gillies began to regret her decision to call the child forward. A mention would have been enough.

'I agree, it was a mistake,' she said afterwards in the staff room to an angry drama teacher. 'But we hadn't seen her for over two months. How could we have known?'

'What she needs is less adulation, not more,' said Marcia Macrae, who had also watched Alex's progress towards the stage with mounting alarm. The sluggish walk, the sullen eyes, the atypical ungraciousness — all indicated anger and depression, either unresolved or caused by some new problem. She was not even bothering to hide her pain; this girl who had as much talent as any Marcia Macrae had ever taught. She was verging on thin rather than slender. She looked nearer twenty-five than fifteen.

'One must expect,' said Miss Gillies, 'some sort of reaction.'

'Naturally,' said Marcia Macrae with scorn. 'Reaction to success, sleepless nights, to pressure from all sides. To a grief as profound as any I've seen and only two months along its course. She needs very careful handling. Reinforcement of her social role, understanding of her anger and loneliness. Recognition that a girlfriend ostensibly outside the family can grieve as deeply as someone inside it. Encouragement to think about something else other than swimming.'

Miss Gillies sighed. 'What are her after-school activities this year?'

'Swimming, swimming and swimming. Oh yes, calisthenics, weights. From what I gather, reading this morning's paper, a probable trip to Rome in August, more pressure.'

'What about her ballet, piano?'

'Quit, as far as I know, more's the pity.'

'Well, there's no doubt about her accrediting prospects, provided she keeps up with the homework. Even allowing for two months away in August and September. Her School Certificate results were quite remarkable, all things considered. We can keep her on the fringes of choir, the musical production, any plays you might be planning, Marcia?'

Miss Macrae busied herself collecting up books for the next class, avoiding a direct answer. She had every intention of involving Alex in *something* during the second term, and on her return from Rome, if only as an antidote to all that training. Alex's gifts were too unusual to be watered down by her current mania for punishing herself in a pool.

'I'll talk to the parents,' said Miss Gillies, unfolding her long bird-like limbs to their full six foot two inches. She was always glad when the first two weeks of the school year were over, and staff and school had settled down to regular work. Depressed pupils were more commonly a problem in the winter term, or as exams approached. Around the large staff room, women in black gowns drained their coffee cups and responded to a loud bell signalling the end of break.

'Anything to keep that girl on an even keel,' said Miss Macrae bluntly. 'Frankly, she disturbs me.'

I had two days off training to settle down at school, 'before we have a final crack at that record, Alex?' Perhaps Mr Jack anticipated how awful school was going to be: torture, with gushing teachers and moony juniors hanging round the cloakrooms asking for autographs, wanting to carry my bags.

Then there was Miss Gillies hauling me up on the stage at

Monday assembly. I very nearly refused to go up; in the end, prodded on all sides by the people around me, I couldn't care if I went or not. I had to stand there, while La Constantia went on about courage and stuff and then presented me with two books, 'By Katherine Mansfield and Vera Brittain, strong, interesting women, both.' Dutiful applause. Yawn.

Julia, my wheezy and scientific friend, was harder to fool. She'd been away that morning at the dentist, but at lunchtime, when I thought I'd have some time to myself under the far trees of the playing field, she found me, and didn't waste any time considering we hadn't seen each other since Christmas.

'What's happened to your nomination? What was all that stuff in the paper about delaying the nominations until next month.'

'I don't know. I'll just have to do better, won't I.'

'Don't they tell you *anything*?'

'We read about it in the papers like anyone else.'

She waited but I know the interviewer's trick of silence, waiting for you to break and say what you meant not to say.

'That's rough,' she said, eventually.

I shrugged. So she went off on a tangent, talking about the special nursing home for unmarried mothers she'd visited during the holidays. Not the most cheering topic of conversation.

'Remember Jackie?'

I did — Jackie in our class who in the middle of last year had put on rather a lot of weight and vanished. Dark rumours told of a baby boy, adopted out, and her now working in a bank in town and, according to those who'd seen her, looking defeated and sad and ten years older than sixteen.

'I read about this place in a magazine, with discreet photos so you couldn't see the faces. Jackie had her baby there. One of mum's friends, her husband is a visiting doctor. So I got in touch and asked him to show me around. I told him not to tell Mum, of course.'

'Of course.'

'He was quite encouraging about me wanting to be an obstetrician, in a patronizing sort of way. When I asked if I could watch a birth, that was another matter. "Plenty of time for that, young lady, during your training ..." — went all stuffy and pompous, you know.'

'Yeah.'

She struggled on, her voice showing all the familiar signs of an imminent asthma attack. 'There was something creepy — all those huge dumpy girls. Twenty or thirty of them sitting around knitting bootees and matinee jackets. Pink for a girl, blue for a boy. Waiting for babies they're not allowed to keep.'

'Who says?'

'The doc' says. All the babies get adopted. There are plenty of people waiting, he said, specially for cute little baby girls.'

'Where're the fathers in all this?'

'Not even mentioned. They escaped, didn't they. Well, I suppose if you're lucky, you have parents who insist on a shotgun wedding, get you married off good and quick.'

'That's not luck, that's press-gang. No one's going to marry me off,' I said fiercely. 'I'm never going to get married, ever. As for babies . . .'

'You'll meet someone . . .'

'*Else*? You sound like my mother. No I won't.'

'What's the matter, Alex? You look awful. It's not just Andy. It can't be just the delay in the nominations.'

'*Just* Andy, isn't that enough?'

'I didn't mean it like that,' she said wearily, yet determined to prod me further. 'But you beat Maggie and you're going to Rome, what more do you want for heaven's sake, and you can't stay angry for ever.'

'Don't bet on it, and I won't be going to Rome, not if . . .' She had nearly succeeded! 'I'm just tired, all right? Dad's going on about feeling a bit flat after reaching the heights, etcetera, etcetera. Beware of the day you get your heart's desire.'

'If it's the trip to Rome, you haven't actually got it yet,' she said pointedly. 'When does the final Games team get picked?'

'May.'

'So, it doesn't apply. But there's something . . .'

'There's nothing.' I stood up, screwing the remains of my uneaten lunch into a tight ball and throwing it under the hedge. I saw surprise in Julia's eyes. 'I've got some stationery to get from the office.'

And there was the pill bottle, being unscrewed for the potent yellow tablets she took for an asthma attack. I knew what I was doing was inexcusable. I couldn't help myself.

'I haven't finished with you yet, Alex,' she called.

'Don't count on it,' I said, walking away fast. All this ambition to be an obstetrician was making her uppity. I could tell no one, *no one* about my eavesdropping. I wasn't about to tell Julia, friend that she may be, once have been. She could go and have her asthma attacks and do her good works somewhere else.

After school, I got on my bike and rode off smartly, to avoid Julia. I needed to swim, to wrap myself round with water, to loosen the tightness in my stomach. I'd been told to stay away from the pool, normally my bolt hole. I could go to the beach, any beach on the waterfront would do.

It took about twenty minutes of riding; or would have had I not gone straight through a red light and straight into the path of a car starting off with the green light. I heard his horn and his brakes scream in protest, heard the rattles as his car bounced back on to its springs. Another foot and I'd have gone underneath. As it was, I swerved myself, fell sideways, bike jangling, leg, elbow, forearm, hands grazing, scraping, sliding to a halt across stones, gravel, asphalt. What little it takes to cause such damage to human skin. I scrambled to my feet as cars piled up behind.

'Beating the gun?' I yelled at the driver, by now out of his car. He was an oldish man, someone's grandad, wearing a brown old man's hat, and I could see he was as shaken as I was. 'Trying to beat the lights? You nearly killed me.'

Pinpricks of blood were appearing in the large areas of raw flesh up my leg. I was so angry I was literally jumping up and down.

He said, 'You went through a red light, girlie.'

'Girlie? What sort of a word is that?'

'Are you all right?'

'No I'm not all right. I've got third-degree grazes and my bike is probably ruined. I suppose I should say thank you for not killing me. Drivers like you get away with murder.'

'You went through a red light,' he repeated, dumbstruck, as I swiped my hands along my tunic, ostentatiously flicked the blood from my legs and elbows (God, it hurt), picked up my bike, and inspected it for damage. All around the intersection faces were watching, people waiting at the lights or behind windscreens. I felt a total fool.

'Girlie, I'm sorry,' he said, grabbing my arm, knowing full well he was in the right. 'But it wasn't my fault ... I've seen you before?'

Yes, in a newspaper or two. This morning's for a start.

'I'm the Tinman from the Wizard of Oz. Knock me down, rub me down with sandpaper, beat me back into shape with a hammer, who cares?' I caught a final glimpse before I rode away. You read about people standing open-mouthed, well he was. I heard him shout something about taking me to a hospital.

I rode about a block before I began to shake so much I had to stop for quite some minutes before I could go on. Besides, I couldn't see the road for tears. Mum's kitchen grater couldn't have done a better job on my legs or elbows, scraped raw like a carrot. How they stung! That little episode was one hundred per cent my fault. Day-dreaming (and going at some speed) through a red light — and nearly another statistic, like ... How much pain had Andrew Trevor Richmond, aged 17, of Kohimarama, killed last night by a hit-and-run driver, how much had he felt? I concentrated on the pain. I was stinging all over; but at least there was nothing broken. I was alive, more's the pity.

There seemed to be no damage to my trusty bike, as we gradually picked up speed. The beach opened up in front of me. I propped my bike against a tree, and flopped on to the grass above the sand. The tide was nearly high, good for swimming, the sea calm, just a summer breeze. On the waterfront road behind, traffic sped past; before me were moored boats, a few people swimming, mothers with picnic baskets and naked babies. Girls sunbathing, dipping in prissy toes. Boys rigging dinghies, boys sailing dinghies.

Why had I come here, this beach? The last time it was blowing a twenty-knot westerly. The Cherub had taken off like a rocket, exhilarating beyond belief. Then for some reason I can't remember I'd got angry with Andy and leapt overboard, intending to swim home, but a mile in a choppy sea, against the wind and an outgoing tide, is not the same as a mile in a pool.

I remember, now. I'd got angry at his message, the real possibility of failure. 'For the rest of my life I'll be the guy who took his girlfriend sailing and d-d-d-drowned her. Can you do that, Alex?' he had yelled, the first time I'd heard him shout in anger. So I'd climbed in, and the sails flogged about while Andy climbed on top of me and we kissed so hard with relief and passion that later I found all sorts of bruises that come from trying to be passionate in a twelve-foot dinghy, and which caused some very ribald comments about love bites at school and at the pool.

The rest of his life. All two weeks of it.

I pulled my togs out of the bag, and looked for a changing-shed. It was down the other end of the beach, so I threw caution and school rules to the winds and changed right there, little caring about modesty, or the areas of bloody raw skin. The water would wash them clean.

Yes, but how they stung as I dived in! Salt water on grated flesh — it may be the best thing for healing, as Mr Jack said afterwards, but you pay a price. My whole body tingled, jangled, resonated like an out-of-tune violin on a very high note.

I'd swum a long way out, fast, furious, long past the nearest moored yachts, and the violin had dropped to a low throbbing beat, when I heard the voice.

'Alex!'

Even here, no peace? A yacht about to run me down as well? Above me a dinghy loomed, its white sail flapping, a gnomish face grinning at me over the side.

Keith Jameson.

'Thought I recognized you. There's only one girl who swims like that.'

How would he know, he's never seen me swim, except maybe that terrible night at Helensville last year; the night four of us went out for a hot swim and he smashed himself and his girlfriend up.

'Great swim in Napier. I read about it in the paper this morning. Did you get my telegram?'

'Yes. Thanks,' I said, treading water. I couldn't imagine why he'd bothered. I hadn't seen him since I climbed out of his car in high dudgeon before the Helensville smash-up, not even at Andy's funeral — had I been in a fit state to recognize anyone?

'Training for Rome, now, are we?'

'No.' I kicked myself into action and began to swim back to the shore. On my breathing strokes, I could see he'd got the yacht sailing and was following me in.

I waded ashore, panting, ignoring him, picked up my towel and patted carefully at my grazes, while he pulled the dinghy up.

'Like to come for a sail?'

'No thanks.'

'Another time? I don't start varsity lectures for another couple of weeks.'

'No.'

'How's your leg?'

'How's yours?'

Both of us had broken legs last year, me one from hockey and him two from his car crash. We eyed each other's legs. His were on the skinny side, and hairy, with prominent knobbly knees, but then he was a wiry type anyway. His eyes travelled up my legs, too slowly for comfort. I now noted the scar down the side of his face (multiple cuts, the paper had said) and more on his neck and shoulders. He hadn't been much of an oil painting to start with.

'You fall off your bike or something?'

'Yes.'

'Looks sore.'

'No.' At least he didn't fuss.

He was fiddling with something on the front wires holding the mast up, not looking at me. 'I crewed for him, sometimes.'

'Who?'

He glanced up, just briefly.

'Oh. I didn't even know you sailed.' I couldn't help asking, 'Is that his boat?'

'No, it's mine. His boat's still sitting outside the house, his parents don't know what to do with it but won't sell it. Too soon, I suppose.'

For all of us. I turned away, picked up my uniform and walked up towards my bike. I didn't feel like dressing on the beach with him staring at me. In his eyes had been the most curious expression, a mirror of my own mixed-up feelings.

He didn't follow. When I came out of the changing-shed the boat was gone. It might have been any one of the five or six dinghies with white sails out there. I envied them their smooth grace through the water, unlike swimming which is basically a lot of splash and hard work. I could be tempted into sailing, given different times and places and people and memories. Home, meanwhile, was a long tiring uphill ride away, and my grazes were wet and seeping blood and hurting like hell.

'Where have you been?' said Mum, preparing dinner as I clomped, very hot and very tired, through the kitchen towards the shower. Unfortunately there was no other way to get there.

'Out.'

'How's school?'

'Horrible. I want to have driving lessons.'

'When the pressure's off.' Peeling spuds, she paused and looked at me. 'Alex, what *have* you been doing? Look at your leg. And elbow!' I'd tried to keep my grated side out of sight, but you can't keep much from Mum.

'Nothing.'

'Nothing, and you've got grazes like that?'

'Like what?' Her jaw went stubborn. 'Riding round on my bike, if you must know. I fell off, that's all.'

Being a nurse she couldn't help it. She dropped her peeler and gave me the once-over. 'Must have been some fall. At least there's not much grit or stones.'

They've all been washed out by the sea, I thought, but I wasn't going to tell her that. My hair had dried to its normal wisps on the way home.

'After you've showered, I'll put some dressings on.'

'I'll be all right.'

'At least the elbow. It's still bleeding.'

'It'll stop. Don't fuss.'

She went back to peeling spuds, grimly. 'Maggie rang. Wants you to call back.'

I have nothing to say to Maggie, I thought as I retreated to the shower. We both know there is a rotten six weeks ahead. We'll have several more well-publicized races, seen by everyone as grudge matches, and we'll both be making extra record attempts as the only way left to convince Messrs Upjohn, Jones and Webster of our worthiness. Tenth of a second by miserable tenth of a second down towards Rome. Or sticking in a rut, growing desperate with failure. And being no saint, I'm certainly not going to tell her what I overheard, that if she managed to break my time 'substantially' she'd be back level pegging with me.

When I finally and reluctantly rang later, Maggie shamed me into an admission of shared disappointment. The selectors, she said, hadn't been much help, had they? From her weaker position, she could still say *I* deserved a nomination. 'We both do,' I said, admiring her generosity. Her mother, apparently, was furious, though I'd have thought she might also be relieved that the door was still open. I wondered if she'd started to pull strings, complain, and carry on. 'How's school?' I said. 'I didn't go today.' Interesting, couldn't she face it, the embarrassment of people saying, great race, Maggie, sorry you lost? She didn't elaborate; I wondered just what was going on in the Benton household.

Sorry, Maggie. You really are a much nicer person than me, and it will be great if we both go to Rome together. But this, meanwhile, is a parting of the ways.

In one of the city's older suburbs, on the lower slopes of a green terraced volcano rising up from the harbour, a vigil had been kept.

The house was typical of the area: two storeyed, with gleaming white weatherboards, set back from the street in a spacious garden of lawn, rose-beds, and old Empire trees planted a hundred years earlier by the gardener wives of settlers. Australian eucalypts, Indian deodars and English oaks stood alongside native tree-fern, cabbage-tree, puriri, kowhai, rimu, and pohutukawa.

It was perhaps also typical that the owner, the provider for this family, should be away overseas, in Singapore or maybe London, on one of his frequent business trips. Maggie was used to her father's absences, to his rarely being around to share her triumphs or her disappointments, and she would not have turned to him for comfort this night, either. At midnight, with a nagging headache from the long silent drive back from Napier, and unable to sleep, she had swallowed the two pills her mother gave her — aspirin, she was told — and been grateful to drift off at last into a restless sleep.

Joyce Benton spent the rest of the night among the carved rosewood furniture and fine Oriental vases of her living room, in preference to the large and lonely bed upstairs. She read, knitted, put on a long-playing record of Mantovani and sipped several gins. She dozed a little, confident that two of her own regular sleeping pills would keep Maggie's head on the pillow until mid-morning.

Mostly she just sat and thought, filling up the ashtray on the coffee table. She went endlessly over the selectors' options. Send just Alex, or send both, or send neither. She no longer had any illusions that Maggie could be the sole nominee. Training in Australia, expensive coaching; Maggie's talent, body and temperament nurtured as carefully as any thoroughbred — and still that uncouth, wretched girl had come out on top, sabotaging her Olympic plans. She had already booked her own air ticket and confidently written to Italian friends from Singapore days: 'You will of course remember our Margaret, once champion at the club. To our great joy and delight, after many years of hard work, we fully expect her to be selected to swim for New Zealand in the two freestyle events at Rome in August.' With any luck, an offer of accommodation would come by return.

If both girls are both nominated, she reasoned, both must be selected finally, or neither. The selectors would be unlikely to name one female swimmer, requiring two officials, both manager and chaperon, unless the case for sending that swimmer were irrefutable. Until Saturday night Maggie had enough edge over Alex to have been that one. Growing chill in her housecoat of ming embroidered silk, she got up to make a cup of tea. The first light of dawn meant the paper must be here soon.

When she finally heard the squeak of the boy's bicycle, she delayed walking down the drive to the gate, and delayed opening the paper she pulled from the letter-box. She stopped to smell some roses, and bent to pull out a few tiny weeds in the brick driveway. Inside the house, she put the paper on the sofa, poured another cup of tea, lit another cigarette and ran her eye over the front page. Yet more church leaders complaining about the exclusion of Maoris in the All Black tour to South Africa; yet more about Harold Macmillan and his 'winds of change' speech to the South African Parliament. Then she turned abruptly to the sports pages and quickly found what she wanted.

Cowards, she thought angrily, cowards hiding behind a smoke-screen of pompous generalities, prolonging the agony. It was also humiliating; these girls are not yet quite good enough, it told the world. But between the lines there was hope, a message that Alex's win on Saturday had not clinched the matter, and that Maggie was still in with a chance.

Joyce Benton sat on for another half an hour, chain-smoking, thinking, until Maggie's ten-year-old sister Isabel come wandering down the stairs wanting breakfast.

'Don't wake your sister,' she said. Why were you crying last night, said the child; I went to the toilet and you were down here crying. You were dreaming, said her mother sharply. Did Maggie, asked Isabel, get nominated? No one did, and won't be for another six weeks, said her mother. That's not fair, said Isabel. Six weeks *more*, creeping around, don't upset your sister, thought Isabel.

'Don't wake your sister,' said her mother. 'Your uniform is in the laundry.' Maggie could sleep herself out this morning. She would ring the school to explain.

Meanwhile, the delay could be useful, thought Joyce Benton as she carefully poached eggs and cut toast into even slender fingers. She would never get used to having to prepare her own breakfast, rather than having it brought to her on a tray with fine Chinese linen by the amah. The phone went several times, quite possibly Alex, she thought sourly, lifting and replacing the receiver. There were several carnivals planned, there must be time trials, record attempts, school pressures on Maggie made minimal; she must speak to the headmistress. As for Alex, there were a number of interesting avenues to be explored.

So, again the treadmill. School, training at five in the morning and again after school, sleeping badly, losing yet more weight; training and more training and my grazes, immersed twice a day in water, growing infected, scabby, itchy, slowly eventually healing; dreading upcoming races and record attempts in the full glare of publicity.

I am living two lives, two lies: the routine daily world of pain, dragging myself from pool to school to home, avoiding contact, snapping at almost everybody. Except Mr Jack. He doesn't say much either, but he's *there*, my anchor on the side of the pool, nodding quietly when I do a good time trial and ignoring the bad ones. I cry for no apparent reason. It's high summer, day after day of beautiful weather, but I'm either inside a classroom or ploughing through water. I get no joy from the sun.

Then there's the other, public life, the fantasy world of being 'a celebrity'. I refuse most of the requests I get, and know that most of the people think me ungrateful and arrogant for doing so. For example, please help our fund-raising campaign for a new swimming pool or school hall. Ten invitations to speak to women's groups and school assemblies, seven to give out the silver cups and certificates at swimming clubs' end-of-season prize-givings.

I write a lot of polite refusal notes.

Mr Jack will not allow me to avoid the Press entirely. I am, he says, a public figure: my fare to Rome will be paid by public money and for that I have certain obligations. I have two radio interviews and a colour picture taken for the *Women's Weekly*, to go with a long article about all the female Olympic hopefuls, athletes (who have already been nominated) and swimmers (who have not). 'Please,' the editor writes, 'could you also write something for our Teenage Pages — how you manage to be a champion sportswoman and still keep your femininity?' Sorry, no I couldn't, because I'm not an expert on femininity, and do not want to be reminded about my alleged lack of same.

There were nuttier ones, to open a garden fête and judge a baby competition, a teenage beauty queen competition, and a talent quest for the best Shirley Temple or Elvis Presley imitations — all of which filled me with horror. 'On the Good Ship Lollipop' would be *the* most nauseating song ever written, without a doubt; and I can't *bear* Elvis.

'Here's one I think you should accept,' said Mum, as I came in from training. 'A Mr Brookefield from Rotary rang, wants both you and Maggie to speak at a special luncheon next month.'

'Because her father is a member, I suppose.'

'That's not the point.'

'Tell them no.'

'I think you should.'

'Why?'

'Rotary is . . . influential. Very choosy about its members and its speakers.'

'We should feel flattered, you mean.'

'No I don't mean. For the sake of your sport, you should go. It's to honour the achievement of youth, he said.'

'And I suppose Mrs Benton will be there.'

'Very likely. We've been invited too.'

Could I stand it, after seeing her face the night I beat Maggie? I'd heard on the grapevine that there'd been some hard words hissed at Maggie's coach as my name came over as winner, and more as the crowd left the stands. The Aussie coach brought over at great expense had made the mistake of admiring my fighting spirit, and been virtually told to go back to where he came from.

Later that night she had walked past me twice, nose in the air, before dragging Maggie away from the party very early. At training since then I'd seen her only, by mutual agreement, across the other side of the pool.

'When is it, this Rotary thing?'

'March 27, in town. Lunch, then a panel discussion.'

By then the die would probably be cast. 'All right,' I said ungraciously. Had I known that Mr Upjohn would be there too, I would not have allowed myself to be persuaded quite so easily. Or at all. He had just been announced as the Manager for the swimming team to Rome, along with a Mrs Churchill from Christchurch, who I knew slightly, as chaperon. It struck me as very odd (and Mr Jack smiled when I said so) that they chose the officials before the competitors. I thought we were the ones who actually did the competing, that the Games were held for us. Did that mean they really did intend to send *someone*?

'Your hair needs a cut,' said Mum. 'If you're going to wear it that short . . .'

'Costs too much,' I said, flouncing out. 'You're always going on about money.' I looked at myself in my dressing-table mirror. She was right, it was all ends. I dropped on to my bed. Under the pillow was a small silver frame, courtesy of Gran, with the picture of me and Andy taken by Dad at Muriwai last year, just as we came back from a passionate lunch in the black sand dunes.

'Will you wait for me . . .?' I looked at it for a while, with a great empty hole where my heart should be.

So my hair needed a cut. Why spend good money when all they did was snip off bits around the ends. I could do that. So I sneaked a pair of Gran's dressmaking scissors from her room while she was helping chase Debbie into bed, and did the deed myself. I tried to even out the sides, and get the fringe straight; it turned out shorter and scraggier than I intended, sort of Roman. It'll grow, who cared.

Despite all those people out there who want me to judge this, open that or present the other, reassuring me that of course I'm going (with Mr Upjohn and Mrs Churchill) to Rome to swim against Dawn Fraser and see the Colosseum, I feel, I *know* that I am the most gigantic empty sham.

It was pouring summer rain on the asphalt of the netball courts outside, and the worms were out. Around me the Sixth Form English class groaned. Desk lids flew open noisily, with mutterings of 'Bor-ring . . . that old creep . . . George Bernard who? . . . here we go again, the Mackerel on her drama kick . . . wake me when the bell goes.'

'One of the greatest plays of the twentieth century,' Miss Macrae announced briskly. 'Settle down, girls. Alex, where's your book?'

I'd been gazing at her while all the scuffling was going on. Saint Joan — hadn't she once been Joan in London? And for some reason after that she'd stopped acting and become a teacher in the colonies? Today she was not in any mood for messing around. My fearsome haircut had occasioned only a long cool appraisal. 'Alex, are you with us? We haven't got all day. Have you looked at this yet?'

Shaking my head, I got out my Penguin *Saint Joan*. I had read it, the whole thing, including sixty-nine pages of Preface. It was funny and tragic and the bits in the Preface about women through history who wanted to wear men's clothes simply because they wanted to lead a man's life, either in disguise or by defying public opinion, was the first bit of good sense on the subject I'd ever read. And written in 1924!

'We'll go straight to the script, and come back to the Preface later,' Miss Macrae announced. 'Now come on girls, backs straight, you are about to meet one of the most fascinating minds in English literature.'

'Weren't you Joan once?' said a voice.

'Yes, I played Joan.'

'How did they burn you up on the stage, like when they burned Ingrid Bergman?'

'They didn't. Shaw's fire is more effectively described through the eyes of a young French monk and the English chaplain, her most implacable enemy. Put that letter away please Monica — or would you like to share it with the class?' The class grinned hopefully.

'In the film it was horrible. You could see . . .'

'We are studying Shaw, not Hollywood. Now who's going to read what?'

I knew what I wanted. But the parts came and went and I ended up Dunois. 'He's twenty-six,' said Miss Macrae, 'the French commander. Capable, good-natured, a staunch supporter of Joan. Alex, you can read that.'

And Joan went to Kathie who certainly had Shaw's 'uncommon face' but not much else. I loathed these class readings. Most people hadn't got a clue and it was wooden and tediously slow and no wonder people got put off Shakespeare and Shaw and Wilde and the other people we had to study. It struck me that Miss Macrae must have similar urges to stop people and say for heaven's sake put some life into it, read it as though you mean it. These are human beings talking. Kathie was pathetic, milk and water.

I sat back and listened with scorn, until at one particularly feeble bit which wouldn't have inspired an army of mice let alone French soldiers, I caught a very strange look from the teacher's desk, a flicker of a knowing smile that said, 'I agree. Painful. You'd do it better.' Yes, I thought angrily, and you couldn't even give me the pleasure of just reading the part, just once. Dunois didn't even appear until the third scene, which would not be in today's English period. Maybe in about three weeks at this rate. I put my chin on my cupped hands and ostentatiously dozed off, and had to be woken when the bell went. Miss Macrae equally ostentatiously turned a blind eye. I had another race with Maggie that night and needed the sleep.

When Maggie Benton beat Alex Archer for the third time in special invitation races up in Auckland, lowering the women's sprint record by three-tenths of a second and making sports headlines even in his local Napier paper, Grant Davies knew he could remain silent no longer.

'Maggie comes back fighting,' said the caption to a large picture in the Auckland paper which showed Alex congratulating an elated Maggie. Was he imagining despair in those wondrous grey eyes, Grant mused, sitting at the long reporters' desk in the newsroom, ploughing through the morning papers from all round the country. During that remarkable interview after her win at the nationals, he'd seen her dutiful, a little bored, and then, as they listened to the voices, seen her grow wide-eyed and flushed with determination to control her shame and anger. There was something distant and formidable about her, a larger-than-life quality which put out of reach any expectations a cub reporter like himself might have about getting to know her better, even had they lived in the same town. The accompanying report speculated yet again about the equal Olympic chances of each. Since the writer was no ordinary journo, but Norman Thompson, the country's best-known and most influential sports reporter, Grant took some comfort. Yet it was not enough to counter his growing sense of guilt and conviction that he had to tell someone what was going on.

Cub reporters don't normally get sent on assignments to Auckland, thought Grant, and so it turned out. The chief reporter was not impressed with a proposal that his admittedly brightest but also youngest and newest sports reporter should be sent to Auckland to cover an international tennis tournament. So it happened that Grant Davies, who'd never been outside Napier or slept in any bed other than his own, left the next morning ostensibly to go to work and from a telephone booth at the deserted Napier bus terminal rang in sick to the early duty newsroom copy typist. 'A bad dose of 'flu,' he said, surprised by his convincing croak, 'high fever, don't expect I'll be in for two or three days. Tell the Chief someone'll have to do my council meeting tomorrow night.' He knew, with his reputation for punctuality and completing assignments on time and staying away from the pub, a bit of a mummy's boy, he'd be believed without question. To his mother, he made a call saying he was going away unexpectedly to Auckland for a few days, his first big assignment, something to do with the All Black tour to South Africa. She was naturally very proud.

'I must be crazy,' he thought as the near-empty bus climbed over the unsealed, rutted and tortuous road to Taupo. What the hell am I going to tell Norm Thompson, who probably won't even remember that I sat behind him in the Press box at the national championships? That Alex Archer's chances of getting to Rome are nil, the chief selector hates her guts. She knows it, and I've heard it with my own ears. What can he, we, do about it anyway?

By Taupo, Grant had convinced himself that nothing much could be done and that he was on a wild goose chase. It would take all day to get to Auckland, and another whole day to get back. Napier was such a small damn place, his boss was bound to find out, or his mother. Yet he knew why he hadn't done the more sensible thing and used the telephone. He wanted to see what a city newsroom looked like, he wanted to see where the legendary Norm Thompson worked, and he knew from Norm's piece in the *Herald* that Alex and Maggie were both having their final record attempts during the coming week. And he couldn't live with himself if Alex with the steely grey wounded eyes missed out on the Olympic team and he'd not told someone what he knew.

Time is running out. At dawn training, and again as we finish at dusk, there is a feeling of autumn in the air. Between Maggie and me, training where possible at different times, it's frosty; between Mrs Benton (hanging round the pool like a bad smell) and me, it's positively polar.

We race together five times. Apart from old Norm Thompson in the *Herald* who keeps harping on that the selectors must send us both, the press writes a lot of nonsense about revenge, and organizers advertise the meetings as Olympics hopefuls fighting it out to the death. We win two each. Somehow I've stopped caring, until the last race which Maggie wins, taking a whole *substantial* point four off my record.

'I think we'd better have an official record attempt, Alex,' says Mr Jack, after the race. 'The pool's closing on Sunday. I'll ask for Thursday.'

On Thursday there's a small crowd of officials and swimmers gathered to watch. Not Maggie, though I see her mother sitting on the stands by herself. Come to gloat, stick pins in my wax effigy, I dare say. The water looks unfriendly too, and there's a chill wind blowing the length of the pool. I have a sore throat, I'm half a stone lighter, it doesn't feel right at all, and I miss her record by point one.

'So you missed. It's still a personal best, faster than Napier. And this is a slower pool than Napier, don't forget,' says Mr Jack as I climb hurting from the pool. 'It was a great swim Alex, and I know you can do a sixty-three. We'll ask for another crack at the weekend.'

He doesn't tell me that Messrs Upjohn, Jones and Webster would be there, along with a much bigger crowd (because word has got about) come to see both me *and* Maggie have our final desperate fling in the long-course pool.

We warm up on opposite sides of the pool, and join our coaches on opposite sides. Neither of us suggests we make a race of it. My whole family sits in a gloomy row, probably sick to death of me and who could blame them. I walk about, numb with nerves. I see Norm Thompson with a photographer and some young guy who looks vaguely familiar. Despite his neat clothes, there is something about him that says Press, and something about the way he stares that makes me uneasy. Where have I met him before?

'Who's going first?' asks the chief timekeeper. Neither of us can look up. I'm about to say, I'd rather go second when he says, 'Toss for it, then?' Too late. The seconds tick by while he finds a coin, flicks it, drops it, flicks again. Couldn't he have thought of something more appropriate, less flippant? Despite my dry togs and a jumper under my track suit, and socks, I'm shivering with cold. The sun has gone behind the stands; the water is a hostile flat icy blue.

'Maggie, call?'

'Tails,' she says.

He lifts his palm and we all peer at the Maori warrior squatting on a silver shilling, spear at the ready. 'Tails it is. Your choice, Maggie.'

'I'll swim second,' she says, and they all turn to look at me. Damn your eyes, Maggie. You would. I would have too, given the choice. I'm not quite ready to throw my last card. I'm feeling sick and my shoulders are tight, and annoyed that I cannot remember where I've met that face before. I go into the dressing room for a pee, and find myself retching over the toilet bowl.

When I come out, trembling, there stands Mrs Benton, combing her already immaculate perm. She looks at me in the mirror. I had not heard her high heels on the tiled floor. She is not there by accident.

'Are you all right, Alex?' she says, with more curiosity than concern. She almost certainly heard the unpleasant noises coming from the toilet.

I turn my back to wash my hands and sluice my sweating brow with water. Even if I was dying, you are the last person . . . I am not, not, *not* going to talk to you.

Napier! I remember now. The earnest lad with his carefully prepared questions, writing hesitant shorthand, his Adam's apple moving up and down behind a staid tie, the long silent corridor echoing with selectors' voices. Why am I bothering? As I lean over the basin, I am shaking uncontrollably all over.

'Are you well enough to swim, Alex? You look quite overwrought. If you were my daughter, I'd be putting my foot down.'

Since she has invaded my privacy, I'll make it worthwhile, give her something to remember. I retch disgustingly into the basin and spit out a mouthful of yellowish saliva as noisily and revoltingly as I know how. Not a pretty sight, I'm sure.

She waits. Then she says, quite blandly, matter-of-fact and all the more menacing for it, 'Maggie will swim well under sixty-four today, I believe. She did a sixty-three point nine at training last night. You may not have heard.'

Oh, I heard all right. You don't keep times like that secret. But I will *not* give her the satisfaction of a response. I straighten up, give her a brief, dismissive glance, wipe my wet face with my towel, have a final hoick and spit in the basin and walk out. Her face was as blank as her voice. Don't you know *yet,* Mrs Benton, I am a dangerous animal when aroused.

'Take your time, Alex,' murmurs Mr Jack as I stride over to the starting blocks and throw off my track suit. I watch myself from a great height checking my cap, swinging arms, shaking legs, filling my lungs with air as I walk around behind the block, back and forth, like a big caged cat.

The face beside Norm Thompson clicks into focus; he gives a sober sort of half grin and a small thumbs up gesture. Afterwards, I have to admit it was a good reminder of what's at stake and what I have to overcome. I storm up to the block and glare at the starter. I can't wait to get in the water. I have become a shark.

I know from the shouts and the timekeepers' faces that it's good. As they compare stop-watches, Mr Jack comes hurtling over and as he kneels down to show me his watch, his face is a joy.

'I make it sixty-three point eight,' says Mr Jack, hoarsely. When the official time is announced, he's spot on. I can't help looking over at Mr Upjohn, who is sitting in the front row of the stand with his chin in his hands, nodding thoughtfully as Albie Jones talks and searches through his files to make a point. He sees my look: Put that in your pipe. My complete family, all six of them, leave their seats and surround me.

Though it was her choice to go second, it's awful for Maggie, the cheers and general jubilation. Now the pressure is all hers. Her mother and coach are giving her final instructions, stupidly. She'd have been better walking about quietly, psyching herself up, concentrating on the two laps to come. I watch her curiously as she prepares, gives her mother her jumper, track suit bottoms, track suit top, socks. As she comes over to the block I think she's holding back tears. She looks very small in her black racers, and very lonely. She's slow off the blocks; but through the smooth water looks so fast and graceful that I'm struck with a sense of wonder that I must look every bit as powerful. I watch Mrs Benton at the turn — the lap time is clearly too slow. She goes stone-faced as people around us start shouting encouragement. Over the last ten yards I see the stop-watch held high, counting off the seconds — sixty-one, sixty-two, sixty-three . . . sixty-four? Sixty-three point . . . what? I can't watch. That a trip to the other side of the world should hang on a tenth of a second.

'Sixty-four point one,' says Mr Jack, unable to keep the glee out of his voice. Equalling her official personal best, but not mine.

'Of course I am relieved, and pleased. But I'm not so mean that I don't feel sorry for Maggie, who comes over to give me a hug with a grim rueful smile, mercifully unaware of her own mother's part in all this. Her mother, I note, (to whom I suppose I should be grateful) is ear-bashing the coach again. I see Norm Thompson talking to Mr Jack. The lad from Napier comes over, and shakes my hand.

'Grant Davies, from Napier,' he says, looking me dead straight in the eye. 'A great swim, better even than Napier.'

'What are you doing up in Auckland?'

'Interviews,' he says. 'Meeting people.'

'Interviewed Maggie?' I say. 'Or Mrs Benton? She's always got a lot to say.'

'I'm here for the tennis. But it's good to see you book your place for Rome.'

'Oh, yes? We'll see.' He'd kept his promise of silence, as far as I knew. I suddenly feel very tired of all these games and battles, and have to sit down. I've played my last card, Maggie. If I were you I'd have one further throw. She does try again, the next day, on the eve of pool closing. And equals my time. Mr Jack, who rings to tell me this, says that my advantage has narrowed down to the sprint title I won in Napier, against Maggie's greater reliability. You're a tough nut, Maggie old girl, a real battler.

Is this an official time, I ask, with proper timekeepers and all? Or just her mother and her drippy coach.

Official, he says. Cyril Upjohn was there. No doubt, I say, cheering her on. Are you suggesting out and out favouritism, Alex? I'm tempted to say yes, let me tell you about Napier, but what's the bloody point? I laugh into the phone before I hang up and start howling.

Bill Jack put the telephone down slowly in his small, sparsely furnished office at the pool, which featured only a large framed aerial photograph, rather garishly hand-coloured, taken during events at the 1950 Empire Games ten years earlier.

Today he was closing down the pool for the winter; it was an unsatisfactory and depressing note to end a season on. Swimming was supposed to be a fun thing, a useful and health-giving skill for children, but for his star pupil, and to only a slightly lesser degree, for Maggie, it had developed into an ongoing struggle that would have finished many an older competitor.

He was deeply disturbed by the bitterness in Alex's voice. 'So that's it,' she said. 'Perhaps the selectors will toss for it. Heads Maggie goes, tails I stay behind. Perhaps they just don't want me in Rome.'

He had at that point wavered, torn by respect for her secret, and anger at what he had two days earlier heard off the record from Norm Thompson turning up late in the afternoon, supposedly to watch training. A young reporter, Grant someone from the paper in Hawkes Bay, had turned up at the sports desk out of the blue, said Norm. Straight off the bus from Napier. He was a serious, unlikely young man, not your normal sports journo. He said he'd been with Alex the night of the nationals, an hour after her victory, and had listened to some dark and uncomplimentary statements on the part of the selectors. This would explain the delay in nominations and could be interpreted as a devious manoeuvre to favour Maggie, and put Alex out of the running. This lad, said Norm, had been sitting on this quite unusable story for several weeks, while Maggie closed the gap on her no doubt demoralized rival. Even now, I'm damned if I know what can be done, Norm had said, other than to pass it on as useful background to you, to use as you see fit.

She's not breathed a word of this to me, said Bill Jack hopelessly, watching Alex and Maggie and the few swimmers still left in the pool so late in the day, but it explained a lot. To aspiring swimmers, the selectors were the next thing to God almighty, their deliberations secret, and their decisions final.

Norm, snorting cynically, said well, I could tackle Cyril Upjohn but he's a slippery customer, would simply deny the lot, say it was the overheated imagination of a foolish young girl or an unprincipled reporter fabricating a good story. Young Grant said that Alex begged him not to tell anyone. Even if he'd tackled Cyril, and blown the story himself, it would only have backfired on Alex. She was quite right, a clever girl. Sorry, Bill old man, I hope your knowing helps get the kid to Rome. God knows she deserves it. My granddaughter goes ga-ga at even the mention of her name. I'm a bit of a fan myself.

In the end, after much thought, Bill Jack had decided not to tell Alex that word of her secret had got back, even though it had been passed on by people who believed in fair play and wanted to see her win her place for Rome. For whatever reason, she decided not to share her dark burden; not with him, nor apparently, with her parents. As if she didn't have enough on her young shoulders already. After Norm Thompson had left the pool, Bill Jack went out on to the concourse and felt a chill wind and tears prick his eyes as he watched over two lonely and troubled girls still ploughing up and down in the gathering autumn dusk.

―――――

'I'm bloody sick of this.'

'Jamie, mind your language.'

'Why's it not in the paper this morning?'

'Don't point your knife at me, little boy.'

'Why's it not?'

He's a persistent little creep.

'Because the selectors haven't decided, that's why.'

'Why not? They said six weeks, it's six weeks today and I'm sick of it.'

'*You're* sick of it!'

'Finished breakfast, Jamie?' calls Gran from the sink. 'I'd like some help with the chooks.'

Jamie makes another accusing stab with his breadknife at me.

'She was up at five, out at the gate, waiting for the paper.'

'I'm always up at five.'

'I saw you.'

'So?'

'Jamie, for heaven's sake, leave her alone,' says Dad from behind his newspaper. 'Go and help Gran.'

'You just want to get rid of me.'

'Too bloody right,' I shout. 'Piss off.'

Silence. Gran takes Jamie by the hand and leads him out. Mum and Dad are gritting their teeth. Debbie and Robbie are head down into their cornflakes. Since I can't eat a thing, I see no point in prolonging this.

'Alex...' Mum begins, overture to a familiar dirge. I could write the script: we know it's hard, it's hard on us too, please eat some breakfast, please stop cutting your hair in that awful way, please tidy up your room, please stop picking at the quicks of your nails, please stop swearing at your brother, please put your jeans out for a wash, please wear something normal for a change, like a dress, please try to meet your teachers half-way, please try to forget Andy, please...

'Forget it.'

The nominations were not in this morning's paper. They are not in tonight's *Star*. Oh, they know how to twist the knife, these people. They are not in Tuesday's papers, nor Wednesday's. I am not training, what's the point now, until I know one way or t'other. I can't sleep, can't eat. I sit in class in a daze, and after school dawdle home and lock myself in my bedroom. Sometimes I play the piano, every piece I've ever learnt and some of the songs from the shows I've been in. I'm missing my music, I realize. Once or twice I nearly ring Julia, but she's been pretty stand-offish. Maggie? What could we say to each other? More platitudes. Or to her bloody mother if she answered the phone? I sometimes get a clear picture of three men sitting round smoking pipes, Mr Upjohn using all his greasy charm to convince the others I should not be nominated. I don't want her in Rome. But I hold the title and share the record, how much is enough?

Mr Jack rings once or twice, he means well, but what can he say? Keith rings, because he actually noticed that Norm Thompson's last bit in Monday's *Herald* said that the nominations were expected this week, and noticed that it was dragging on. Strange.

Even stranger, a toll call from Napier along much the same lines, from baby-faced Grant Davies. 'Norm Thompson has promised me he'll ring you when anything comes through from the Press Association, so you'll get it early.' Why, I wonder, is old Norm promising favours to a cub reporter from Napier, young enough to be his grandson? I nearly ask him if he blabbed, but again, now, what is the point? 'You'll make it,' says Grant. 'Good luck.'

Thursday afternoon and I am nearly climbing the wall. After school the thought of my own company behind a locked bedroom door is too much, and I need a long sweat-making burn out. My bike finds its own way towards a certain house, a quiet side street. The garage is open. His parents must be out, in the Volkswagen where we once ... Through the open door at the back of the garage I can see into the garden, and his yacht, forlorn on a trailer. I don't know how long I sit there, until I hear a car coming up the hill: the throaty sound of the Volkswagen home for tea. I swing my bike around and grunt on up the hill, hoping they had not recognized me. If I ever needed you it was now, Andy Richmond. Why, why ... damn you, and Maggie and her sixty-three point eight and her miserable conniving mother and those pompous old selectors and the stupid Olympic Games, damn, damn, damn everything ...

That night the phone goes. Late. The house is asleep and I'm reading Tolstoy, *Anna Karenina*, and crying into the pages, because I know how it ends.

I know immediately who it is. I can't get out of bed.

Mum answers promptly, years (she says) of responding to cries of children, and patients when she was a nurse. She knocks on my door. 'Alex? For you.'

I can't move. 'Alex!'

'Coming.' It's all slow motion again.

'Do you want me to leave you alone?'

'Yes.' Please. I don't want anyone listening, watching. 'I'm coming.' She goes back to the phone and tells Norm Thompson she's coming, please hang on.

So I walk along down the dark hallway, only the dim night-light on above me. Mum has closed the door, but a strip of light tells me she's waiting. Pictures I haven't noticed in years appear sharp and important; the runner carpet is worn. Ahead lies the waiting phone on a small table. It takes me about a year to pick it up.

'Alex? Norm Thompson from the *Herald*.'
'Oh, hi.'
'It's just come through on the wire. You're in. Maggie too.'
Oh. I'm nailed to the floor.
'Congratulations. Well deserved. Are you there, Alex?'
'Oh, yes. Thanks.' I can barely get the words out. 'Ah, listen, would you ring Maggie for me? Please.'
'If you want. Got a number?'
'Ah, I can't remember. It's, um, Benton, Seascape Road, Remuera.'
'You wouldn't rather . . .'
'No. Just . . . thanks for ringing,' and I put the phone down very quickly before he can start to ask me for quotes and how I feel because I'm about to weep buckets, and it's Mum's bed that I weep them over, a ten stone, five foot ten and a quarter inch baby that creeps into her bed and cries herself to sleep.

The phone starts ringing before breakfast. Mr Jack is first, even before the paper arrives which means Norm rang him too; obviously so relieved and pleased his smile almost bends the telephone wires. He even hints that he might be able to save enough money to come to Rome. After that, the phone goes non-stop: women officials I've known for years, swimmers, neighbours, relations out of the woodwork on toll calls from Christchurch and Timaru and Napier and Nelson.

I can't get through to Maggie. She's engaged, or it rings once and then clicks off, a fault somewhere, infuriating. I'd always known, way deep down, I was going to Rome, and Maggie too. I want to share it with her.

It's in the paper, in black and white (I feared it might all have been a bad dream) along with some nice comment from Norm Thompson: the selectors are to be commended for doing the decent thing, etcetera. And yet — not much improved from days gone past. While I smile sweetly down the telephone, I hear the kids bitching at each other, and Mum short-tempered. The newspaper is full of 67 DEAD IN SHARPEVILLE after South African police fired on a whole lot of Africans, and MORE CALLS for our All Blacks not to go and play rugby in such a place.

I want to wag school, to escape Miss Gillies' gushing at assembly and the pack of Third Formers that follows me everywhere. I'm feeling guilty about Julia, and bad about being rude to Miss Macrae several times this week. Mr Richmond rings up to offer his congratulations and I find I don't have much to say to him either. 'Andy always knew you'd swim in Rome,' he says, reducing me to a speechless jelly. I seem to have run out of the right responses, the right words to say. Only Gran seems to have any idea of how confused I'm feeling, as I kiss goodbye and tears spring to my eyes. 'To thine own self be true,' she murmurs in my ear.

The weather has turned nasty — a howling nor'easter which is ripping all the leaves off the oaks and cherry trees unseasonably early, while Gran bemoans the state of the garden and Dad can't mow the lawn because it's too wet for our ancient motor mower. We have lit our first fire of the year. It's winter, but I didn't have a summer. Tomorrow morning there'll be the usual picture in the paper of a yacht torn from its harbour moorings and battered to pieces on the waterfront rocks.

I'm feeling a touch battered, a touch adrift myself.

Tomorrow morning I have to start training again.

Part Two

'TELL me,' said Joyce Benton lightly, 'about Alex.'

The question was primarily aimed at one of her guests, but there was a general reaction of surprise from the five women gathered for morning coffee in the spacious drawing room. Late summer roses, picked that morning during a short break in the rain, stood a little limply in silver bowls; the pale blue carpet and drapes perfectly set off the heavy black Oriental furniture.

'Surely,' said one, 'you know her well enough already, after all these years? This is a beautiful piece, Joyce,' she added, running her fingers over the ornate carvings of the huge coffee table. 'Singapore?'

'From Shanghai, antique,' said Joyce Benton. 'Only in the context of swimming, and now it's likely they'll be travelling together . . .'

'You must be so proud of Maggie,' cried another.

'Naturally, but she's worked for it, sacrificed a great deal. So has Alex, such a talented girl, I gather.'

She let the statement linger, not looking directly at her principal target. As she hoped, another took the cue.

'Isn't she a good friend of your daughter, Pauline?'

Julia's mother, leaning forward to pick up the Wedgwood cup, played for time. 'Well, she has been. They seem to have drifted apart of late. Alex has become so obsessed — no, perhaps that's not fair — single-*minded* about her swimming, she doesn't seem to have much time for her old friends.'

Mrs Benton nodded understandingly, and let the conversation flow on.

'What a wonderful experience for them both. Rome in high summer! My husband was there in '44 with the Allies, one of the first to enter the city. He's always wanted to go back, such a historical place, full of arches and tombs and churches, said he'd take me when . . .'

'I suppose there's a chaperon,' said another, tackling a hefty slice of chocolate log with her cake fork. 'I shouldn't be eating this, Joyce.'

'Certainly there is. A Mrs Churchill, from Christchurch. I haven't met her, but I'm told she's a very nice woman. Harold and I intend to be there too.'

'I know a Churchill, a lawyer in Christchurch.' Jane Sutherland dug deep into the moist confection on her plate. She was, if not the slimmest, certainly the smartest woman in the room, with aspirations as an organizer of fashion parades and some small successes with charity parades behind her. 'Perhaps his wife?'

'Quite possibly,' said Joyce Benton, knowing full well that the Churchill woman in question was a widow with two teenage sons, and earned her own living as a primary school teacher.

'It's a big responsibility, taking two very attractive girls to Rome. Christopher met Alex at a dance, oh, last May holidays. He was very taken with her. I gather she's very striking?'

Joyce Benton smiled warmly at Mrs Allardyce, whose husband was a member of the City Council and thus worth knowing. 'Very. Rather broad-shouldered, but so was Esther Williams, wasn't she? How does she manage at school, Pauline?'

'She did very well in School Certificate, Julia said, with practically no work. Over-committed, into everything. And last year she was learning ballet, until she broke her leg. Piano too, and getting involved in school shows . . .'

'Really, I didn't know that,' said Joyce Benton. 'In the chorus?'

'Alex in the chorus?' Pauline laughed. 'My dear, she's larger-than-life. We were there the final night of *The Wizard of Oz*. She nearly brought the house down.' On the whole, Pauline McGregor was not sorry Alex had stopped coming to their house; she found the child disconcertingly direct, even aggressive, a questionable influence on Julia, especially on Julia's unfortunate ambition to do medicine, which for some unfathomable reason her father was encouraging; but there was nevertheless something about the girl, something you warmed to.

'Really. So versatile, I hadn't realized. And what does she want to do with all this talent?'

'Law, I believe.'

'Law? That's most unusual. Few women do law.'

'That's probably why,' said Pauline rather pointedly. 'Though there's no doubt she's got the brain for it. She's a prefect too, a popular one. Almost certainly head girl if she stays for the Upper Sixth.'

'Well,' murmured Joyce Benton. 'I look forward to getting to know her better, now. She'll be a stimulating companion for Maggie in Rome.'

Mrs Allardyce said, 'I suppose they're both training very hard again?'

'They started yesterday, in that dreadful indoor pool in town. Twice a day.'

Murmurs of sympathy went around the room. Imagine. Such dedication, you too Joyce, up at five every morning.

'It's very tough. The final selection is about seven weeks away. I have no doubt both will get in the team.'

'How wonderful.'

'How will Maggie cope with School Certificate this year, if she goes to Rome?'

'We're not quite sure she'll even sit at this stage.' She took the chocolate log and orange sponge around a second time, noting how easy it was to persuade her plumper guests into a second — and third — piece, despite their protests and well-informed but ultimately ludicrous talk of diets. The conversation drifted off to other teenage sons and daughters, the dances that were being held in the May holidays, by whom and with whom and where. Television transmission was starting in June, and opinion was divided as to whether to acquire a set sooner, or later; expensive, of course, but having seen it overseas, wonderful for news items, and documentaries too. Of course, the Olympics would be televised. Joyce Benton hadn't given it much thought, since she and Harold were going to be there anyway.

And although it pained her to be reminded of that dreadful night of defeat in Napier, Joyce Benton had left lying casually on the coffee table a large print of the newspaper picture of Maggie and Alex with their medals. Jane Sutherland carefully squashed the last cream-moistened crumbs of chocolate log between the prongs of her fork, wiped her soft hands carefully on the linen napkin, and picked up the print. 'May I?' She scrutinized it closely. 'Good legs.'

'You should get the girls to model swim-suits in that fashion parade you're organizing for the school,' said Mrs Allardyce.

Joyce Benton, making a final round with the coffee percolator, smiled.

I am Alexandra, on her best behaviour.

'And on my left,' said the chairman, who was seventy if he was a day, 'two charming young ladies who I'm sure you'll agree will wear the New Zealand silver fern in Rome most graciously — Miss Alex Archer and Miss Maggie Benton.'

Heavy words, heavy atmosphere, all these men in identical grey suits below us, such a dismal room — high, dingy-cream ceiling, embossed with all sorts of ribbons and bows and flowers, and long tired curtains in a depressing pattern of browns and greens. How could anyone *choose* such designs, such colours? After the lunch — minuscule portions of stew and two veg, custard and tinned fruit salad, served by prim girls in aprons — cigarettes and pipes were being brought out, chairs pushed back and grey legs crossed for the floor show.

Maggie and I were both wearing specially pressed school uniforms. Mum even had my blazer dry-cleaned. There wasn't much I could do about my Roman haircut, or my bloodshot eyes. At a front table below the stage sat my parents, who looked shy and out of place, and Mrs Benton, who was being most uncommonly pleasant, dressed to kill in a silk dress, pearls, crocodile handbag and a hat with a little veil.

On the other side of the chairman at the top table sat — guess who — Mr Upjohn, introduced as 'a valued Rotarian, successful manufacturer, and leading sports administrator'. I must confess to being taken aback when he strutted in the door. You didn't win your little battle, I thought, nastily, as he went through the motions of warmly congratulating Maggie and me, hoping that we would all be enjoying a trip to Rome in August, with much bonhomie and chuckles. Anyone watching would have taken him for a jovial well-loved uncle.

We heard about forthcoming meetings and played some jolly after-lunch games, which involved members being fined for assorted 'sins'. Someone walked round and rattled a wooden box, and various members tried to cap each other's jokes and everyone chuckled heartily as the sinner paid up. I had to keep reminding myself that these were the city's captains of industry, our country's leaders.

After fifteen minutes of Cyril Upjohn on the glories of sporting endeavour, the Olympic movement, the amateur ideal, and our country's youth as the hope for the future, I was beginning to think Maggie and I were there for decorative purposes only. We had, I thought, been asked to take part in a panel discussion. He spoke glowingly of our careers, our rivalry, our achievements which put us into world class, our shining examples to juniors (oh yes?!), our worthiness to go to Rome representing our country, wearing the coveted black blazer. Well, he'd been nominated as manager, if we didn't go, neither did he. Then he got on to the need for money for training camps like those being run so successfully in Australia, for trips to Australian meetings, visits by top coaches, all to raise standards. I have to admit, he was very convincing.

Almost as an afterthought, he invited questions from the floor. A thin grey figure rose from near the back.

'Could I ask our young visitors — how do they feel about facing swimmers who have the advantage of these American sports scholarships or Australian training camps you've talked about?'

Mr Upjohn turned to Maggie, who looked pointedly at me.

'Scared,' I said, raising a few chuckles. Then because no one else said anything, I said, 'Well, they're sort of professional really. I don't see much difference between being paid an actual salary to train and big prizes if you win, or having all your expenses paid for you to train and travel and everything. It's the way it's going. Unless we go the same way we'll always be at a disadvantage.'

They seemed a bit nonplussed at that. In fact, I think they were generally nonplussed by these females at the top table, instead of the usual experts giving lengthy speeches on the state of the economy. I looked down at the sea of elderly male faces (several had their eyes closed, as in sleeping — the lunch had been too much for them) and said rather lamely, 'We'll do our best.' Then another figure rose.

'Mr Upjohn, can you tell us what the selection criteria were for these charming young ladies to be nominated?'

This should be interesting.

'We look at comparative times, assessing the potential for a swimmer to make it into the Olympic final of his or her event. It was very clear that only Miss Benton and Miss Archer had that potential.'

There was a silence.

'Can I say — that wasn't an awful lot of help,' I said. 'How can you assess finalists' times with world records falling like ninepins every year? It would have been easier, not just for me and Maggie but some of the others too, if we'd been given some actual times to aim at, no matter how tough they were.'

I looked over at Maggie, whose eyes had gone all huge. There was a rustle of interest among the suits, and Mum's head was shaking to and fro slightly. But Mr Upjohn was smiling genially at the audience, making it clear he had no intention of taking me seriously. 'We are well informed on current overseas times.'

'But how can you possibly guess . . .?'

'We are not dealing in guesswork, Alex.' It was a crocodile smiling at me. 'We simply prefer not to set times,' he said, end of discussion.

Another figure rose unsteadily to his feet. 'Miss Benton, you are remarkably slight for a world-class swimmer. Why do you think you have this talent?'

Maggie blushed, not so used to performing in public as me, Sixth Form prefect, survivor of school productions and general show-off. 'I don't know really,' she said. 'I just love the water, swimming . . . I don't mind the training . . .'

'She could swim before she was two, in Singapore,' I helped her. 'She trains very hard. She's got big hands and feet like flippers. She's a great fighter, the hardest person I know to beat,' I said, warming to her praises. 'More often than not, she's won.'

'Isn't it unfeminine for young girls to partake in such strenuous and competitive sports?' said another, younger man. Well, fortyish as opposed to eightyish. Mum's eyes were glinting with warning signals, and there was an encouraging smile on the face of the Mrs Benton tiger.

'Maggie, do you think we're unfeminine?' I turned and looked at her, staring into her hands, very embarrassed. He'd got me on the raw; besides it was a rude and tasteless question in the circumstances. 'I don't feel unfeminine, unless of course you're talking about these school uniforms which aren't exactly flattering, are they? Or is it for protection?'

I looked straight at him.

'Do you think we *should* be protected from training five miles a day and going to the Olympics, for our own sakes? Like the Maoris not going to South Africa with the All Blacks next month?'

'I take it then, Miss Archer, you have strong views on the South African question . . .?'

'Yes I do, especially after Sharpeville.'

I felt another rustle, this time of disapproval. But the chairman was on his feet. 'Gentlemen, honoured guests . . . Cyril Upjohn, Miss Benton and Miss Archer, such charming and spirited young ambassadors for our country . . . our time is up.' Asked to show their appreciation of a most interesting half hour, the audience applauded politely. Then it was more bowing and scraping at the top table before Maggie and I could join our parents. If Mr Upjohn was angry he didn't show it; he was charm itself.

'Strong stuff, Alex,' said Dad. He sounded more resigned than displeased. 'Most interesting,' said a Rotary man sitting with them. 'You would seem to have considerable experience in public speaking, Alex?'

'Only in plays and stuff at school,' I said. Mrs Benton was still sitting down, looking at herself in a powder compact. Then a reporter, young, female, and eager, appeared at my elbow. 'Please, Alex, just a few more quotes, what you'd have said if the chairman hadn't closed the discussion.'

'What about?'

'The All Black team.'

'Oh, well, I only think like lots of other people. Maoris are New Zealanders, aren't they? It's supposed to be a New Zealand team. Just like we send the best possible team to the Olympics.'

She was scribbling furiously. You are getting out of your depth, Alex.

'Sorry, I have to go.' I muttered something about five a.m. training, but it was really to avoid Mr Upjohn who was heading our way. I didn't think he'd stop at ticking me off in public if he felt like it. I gathered Mum and Dad around me to make our final thanks to the chairman for lunch etcetera, and left Maggie and her mother to chat on.

Out of those few scraps, the reporter managed to cook up a small story for the next day's paper. Olympic nominee supports Maori All Blacks. 'Swimmer Alex Archer, guest at a Rotary lunch in Auckland yesterday, spoke out strongly in support of Maori players being included on the forthcoming South African tour...' and a few direct quotes, reasonably correct. But the last paragraph read, 'National swimming selector Mr Cyril Upjohn said that while Miss Archer's views were her own and undoubtedly sincere, he believed that competitors from one sporting code should refrain from commenting on the internal affairs of another.'

'This is Keith.'

Just home from training, my eyes are so sore that just to close them while I talk is a relief. 'Hi.'

'I saw that bit in the paper about you.'

'Which bit?'

'Yesterday. About the All Black thing. Want to come on the march?'

'What march?'

'Up Queen Street. The Rugby Union's dug its toes in, the Government's a pack of lily-livered cowards. Not one of them will come out and say it, *do* anything. We need people, lots of people, to march, show them.'

'Who's we?'

'Citizens All Black Tour Association — I'm a member, lots from varsity are. From what you said in the paper...'

'I still don't know what you're talking about.'

'Didn't you tell those Rotary creeps that you supported no Maoris, no tour?'

'Yes, but...'

'So you'll march? If you believed what you said, you'll march. The date isn't fixed yet. I'll let you know.'

'Now wait a minute...'

'It'll be a weekend, a morning. I'll come and pick you up, eight o'clock.'

'I'll still be at training.' And I'm not ever driving with you again, mate.

'Where do you train, the Tepid Pool in town?'

'Yes, but ...'

'The march starts in Quay Street, just along from there.'

'I thought you approved of the All Blacks' going. That night at Helensville ...'

'I did then. I don't now. What time do you finish?'

My soggy brain is beginning to wake up. I am being bullied. Into the silence he says, 'Well, if you finish by nine that'll be fine. I'll wait for you outside. Be in touch. By the way, want to come sailing?'

That wakes me up properly. He'd caught me off balance about the march and all that political stuff, but sailing with him is another matter. 'No thanks.'

'Please yourself.'

'I will.'

'That day out with Andy, he said you were great. Good feel for the boat, nice touch on the jibsheets, 'til you jumped over.'

And that silences me properly. He is grinning, I can tell.

'Are you there? Alex?'

I put the phone down slowly. How much else does he know? The reason for our fight, and me jumping over? I was a stubborn little girl, who couldn't take advice — is that what Andy told him? I was hot stuff, not bad at kissing for a beginner, responsible for one or two bruises on that manly neck — did he tell him that too? I had thought, Andy Richmond, that what went on between thee and me was private. I was wrong, it seems.

'Who was that?' asks Mum passing the phone with a pile of clothes in her arms. 'Anything wrong?'

'No. Someone from school.'

I don't like the once-over I am getting, so I stand up and try to look businesslike. 'Where's Dad? When can I have a driving lesson?'

'I thought we'd been over all that.'

'I'm fifteen and a third, and all my friends ...'

'*All* of them?'

'Nearly all. Ninety-five per cent, with their licences *and* borrowing the car.'

'Your father and I don't approve of 15-year-old drivers. Most of your classmates are older than you. That's all there is to it.'

'But can't I *start*? I've got to learn some time.'

'When you've got fewer pressures on you.'

'That's rubbish. I'm not doing piano any more, or hockey, or ballet . . .'

'There are other pressures. And Olympics or not, you've got exams at the end of the year . . .'

I snort. 'Accrediting. No one misses accrediting except the real dummies.'

Her gaze is level and disconcerting. 'Alex, just occasionally your arrogance worries me.'

'Oh Mum . . .'

'I'm getting rather tired of you slopping round in jeans. And the state of your bedroom. It's my considered opinion that driving lessons . . .'

'Oh forget it.' I flounce up the hallway towards said bedroom, which I must admit is a bit of a mess. I intended shutting the door, but I am followed.

'I forgot — something rather more to the point. Mrs Benton rang this morning.'

'Her.'

'She was very pleasant. Said that she really didn't have a chance to congratulate you properly at the Rotary lunch.'

'What's she after?'

'You don't like her?'

'Not much.' Where would I start, mother dearest, if I was to tell you all the slights and indignities over the years? Have you forgotten what happened in Napier, only a few weeks ago? You couldn't have!

'She struck me as very sincere, said she was very pleased at the prospect of you and Maggie travelling together to Rome. Apparently she and her husband are planning to go too. They have friends there.'

'They would.'

'She's planning a surprise barbecue for Maggie's birthday, and to celebrate your nominations. Next Saturday I think, but an invitation will come in the mail. I told her I thought you'd be delighted to go.'

'Charmed.' For Maggie, yes I'll go. Because I've never actually been to Maggie's house, and I'm curious. And because no one asks me to anything much these days, except strangers with all their ghastly prize-givings and talent quests. And because I don't trust Mrs Benton one inch.

Maggie's house was grander than I'd ever dreamed, set amongst huge trees with large beds of spiky bare rose bushes. Mrs Benton grew roses, one good thing about her. I walked up the drive, with my inevitable damp hair because I'd come more or less straight from training, feeling like Cinderella without the ball gown. There was an impressive porch and inside the open door I could see lots of Chinese-looking vases and statues, blue and gold rugs and chunky black carved furniture which I supposed was also Chinese. It made my house look very homely and untidy, and Andy's house seem very proper and boring. Before I could pull the bell, Mrs Benton came trit-trotting down the staircase.

'Alex, so pleased you could come. Welcome, my dear. Maggie doesn't know a thing about it.'

'Isn't she here?'

'Her father's whisked her away to see some relatives. By the time she gets back, everyone should have arrived.'

Her eyes had quickly run down my clothes, and registered disapproval of my jeans, check shirt, floppy pullover tied around my waist, and flat shoes.

'I'm so glad you've come casually dressed, Alex,' she said, most graciously. 'For a barbecue after all.'

'That's what I thought too.' I smiled grimly, and thought if only you knew, there'd been an almighty row in the car when Dad had picked me up from the pool. He insisted on taking me home to change; I'd changed my shirt but stood my ground over jeans. Everyone will be in dresses and skirts, and the boys in ties, Mum had protested. Not me, I'm going *like this*, I hate skirts and why should I dress up for Mrs Benton — because she is your host — well I don't care, it's a barbecue and . . . go away, leave me *alone*, and Gran had put her skinny arm around my shoulder and pleaded with Mum and Dad to let me make my own decisions.

So there I was, in my jeans, shown through the house and out through French doors to a sort of courtyard with crimson bougainvilleas and pot plants all around; an uncle type decked out in a chef's hat and a rude apron standing over a sizzling barbecue, and about twenty others my age standing round with glasses of punch in their hands. The girls were dressed up to the nines, best satin cotton frocks and matching sandals, white cardigans because the air was nippy, hair set, some with pancake and eyeliner, and not one of them was more than five foot three.

Mrs Benton introduced me as if I was Maggie's best and most dearest friend, 'nominated for the Olympics too, with Maggie, you will all have heard about Alex'. I thought I was going to be sick.

'Well, well, the American, from Milwaukee,' said a plummy voice.

'American? What are you talking about, Christopher? This is Alex, Christopher Allardyce.'

'Of course. The tall and beautiful Alex, all the way from Epsom. We met at Maggie's dance, last year, didn't we?'

Oh gawd. Christopher, with a face like a turnip, with whom I'd done a travesty of a waltz at my first ever dance. Last year, last May to be precise, my childhood ago.

'Who were you with that night?' he said. 'I can't remember.'

Mrs Benton hesitated only slightly before stepping in and asking me what I would like to drink. Mercifully, someone heard a car at that point, and we all hushed, and in came Maggie and her father to much acclaim. There were more drinks and then the barbecue, which I have to admit was beautifully done, chicken and spuds done in silver foil. I managed to avoid being alone with Christopher until shortly before Dad was due to come and pick me up at nine-thirty.

He must have seen me looking at my watch, because he came sidling over at the first moment I was not quite part of a group, with what looked like a whisky in one hand and a cigarette in the other. 'The night is but young.'

'Not for me. I have to go.'

'Of course, you train at ungodly hours. How many miles a day?'

'About five.'

'Amazing.' He shook his head in mock wonder. Then he said

slyly, 'You didn't fool me, you know, Miss Milwaukee, 1959, with the yankee accent. Not for a minute.'

I looked at him straight, until his eyes dropped. 'Ah guess ah did. Otherwise you wouldn't have remembered it so-o clearly.' He drained the whisky glass, and I felt his free hand grope for mine. I remembered that hand, damp and knobbly. I drew mine away, and said, 'Tell me, what part of England did you grow up in? Somewhere in the Cotswolds? Oxfordshire? Kent?' Where else was there, where they spoke posh?

'Cambridge? Knightsbridge? Or Hertford, Hereford and Hampshire, hurricanes hardly happen,' I said, emphasizing the Eliza haitches in 'Rain in Spain' song from *My Fair Lady*.

'I was born here, actually.'

'Oh, so you're not English, ack-chew-ally,' I said sweetly. 'Just a Kiwi like the rest of us. I could have sworn, with that B.B.C. voice . . .' Too late, he got the point, and even blushed. But I'll say this for him, he was a stayer. Or just thick. He lit another cigarette from the one already in his mouth, and said, 'Can I take you home? I should be honoured.'

'My father's coming.'

'You could ring him . . .'

'No I couldn't. He's coming at nine-fifteen. Now.'

'Another time? May I ring? Could you stretch a point and come to the pictures some time?'

Oh gawd. 'I'm not . . .'

'Someone else? Are you going steady?'

Was it any of his business? 'I don't go out at the moment. At all.'

'Such dedication. You danced so beautifully that night, in your bare feet, as I recall. Who were you with again?'

There was only one way out of this.

'Andrew Richmond. Went to Auckland Grammar, prefect, First Fifteen, rep. swimmer, stuttered, only child, a gentleman, would now be aged eighteen. He died.' I didn't stop to see how he took it. If he was embarrassed, that was his problem. Besides the whole evening had been a disaster, despite, or because of, all the toasts that Maggie's mother, warmed up with gin, had proposed to our two wonderful Olympic girls, and the birthday cake-cutting, and the presents which Maggie had been made to open there and then, with my offering looking very insignificant. A celebration? Maggie didn't look all that thrilled, Mrs Benton had been so charming and generous and nice to me it made me want to puke, and I couldn't get out quick enough. With superb timing the front door bell went just as I turned away from Christopher Allardyce so that he should not see the tears running down my face; it was Dad, firmly declining offers from Mr Benton to come in and have a drink, to the rescue.

The letter was written on his business paper, Cyril D. S. Upjohn and Associates, Manufacturers and Importers of Quality Men's Clothing. An Auckland address, thick quality paper, almost like parchment, a fancy italic typewriter, dated April 4, 1960.

> *Dear Alexandra,*
>
> *May I first offer my sincerest congratulations to you on your nomination for selection as a member of the New Zealand Olympic team to Rome.*
>
> *As chairman of the selection committee, I have watched your development, and that of Maggie Benton, with great interest and admiration. I'm sure you are aware that your particular achievement, against considerable odds, in winning two national titles and the recent improvement in your times contributed greatly towards our final decision to nominate you both.*
>
> *I am sure that you also recognize the responsibility that the nomination places upon you, to uphold the fine reputation of the National Swimming Association, its officials and its membership. We expect the highest standards of conduct from our leading competitors at all times, both in and out of the water.*
>
> *May I wish you continued progress with your training in these six weeks leading up to the final selection by the Olympic selectors. As the nominated manager, I look forward with confidence to our joint selection and the resulting pleasure of accompanying you and Maggie to the Rome Olympiad in August.*
>
> *Sincerely yours,*

And signed in an unintelligible scrawl, Cyril Upjohn.
I'm glad that some instinct (survival?) that Saturday had led

me to check the mailbox as soon as I heard the postie's whistle. No one knows of the official-looking envelope addressed to me which now lies on my bed, while I stare at the letter and see it for what it is: a warning.

Keep your head down, Miss Alex.

Nothing political. No asking the selectors awkward questions in public. No rudeness to reporters or ill-informed comments about the All Black team or rumours about bad behaviour at school. Thou shalt be grateful and graceful in all thy public and private doings, otherwise thou shalt not be going to Rome.

It is not inconceivable that a nomination be withdrawn, or even a selection.

Between the lines, that's the message to little girls. The man can't stand tall women. He doesn't want me in Rome. He had to select me because I made it impossible for him not to, but he's going to make me pay the price of coming into line.

I tear the letter into little shreds. Then I take them out to the incinerator and burn them. Then I surprise Gran by offering to clean out the chooks' cage because hens are creatures of peace, and soothing to stroke, and because there no one can see my fury.

I stand stunned in the hallway from another late-night phone call, looking stupidly at the telephone in my hand.

My last anchor has gone. Now I'm completely adrift, without direction, in a sea of people who all want something from me I can't give. I don't know anything anymore, how to behave, what to say, how to react; even, or especially, the common courtesies at home, at school; all seem hollow and meaningless or sinister and threatening; everywhere in my life but with you, my anchor at the pool because you ask nothing of me except that I immerse myself in water and blank out my mind . . . become an automaton . . . and swim.

'I'll write, Alex,' Mr Jack said, 'or cable, soon as I can, and let you know when I'm coming back.'

And now he's gone, too, like all the rest in one way or another. Gone hurriedly to Australia because his old mother in Sydney who's had emphysema for some years has suddenly got worse, and he's flying out tomorrow morning on the first Electra flight from Whenuapai.

'I couldn't get much sense out of my sister when she rang,' he said, 'except that it's bad. I might be only a week, or several.'

Please don't go, I am yelling silently, I need you. I have five weeks' training before the final Olympic selections, and two sets of time trials and short-course record attempts scheduled to convince the overall selectors, if they still need convincing, that I'm not resting on my laurels — I need you.

The reality of my nomination — because, whatever else, I have the cutting from the newspaper pinned up beside my bed to reassure myself at five o'clock every morning that it's true — and you standing on the side of the pool as I plough up and down — those are the only things I know are real any more.

He would write out my schedules on the plane, and put them in the post. I'd like to have come over and seen you before I go, he said, but I've run out of time. He'd talk to my Dad, give him the low-down; since Dad still came with me in the mornings, he could take my times, and I had my log book right up to date, didn't I?

The afternoons — he'd thought of asking Maggie's coach to take me on — no thanks, I said — but decided to ask Steve, one of the younger coaches from another pool who didn't have any people still training. Was I happy with all that?

Happy? About to be cast adrift? Sure, I whimpered. You know Steve, don't you, Alex? He's good with his kids. And he lives pretty near you. Finishes work at four, so he's happy to give you a lift there and back.

He's not you, I thought.

'You've got about five weeks before the final selection. I'm sure I'll be back long before that. And we should have some official time trials in about three weeks.'

'Suppose.'

'Alex, I know this isn't easy for you. But you don't need anyone to crack a whip over you. I know that.'

'Please . . . don't be too long. I hope your mother's OK.'

'Thanks champ. T.T.F.N.'

'Ta ta, just for now,' I said sadly. It's the next morning, on the way to the pool that I begin to cry. In the dark, the rain beating on the windscreen, the car sluicing its way through great puddles caused by drains blocked with dead leaves, I turn my head away, pretending to doze off, and Dad doesn't notice. The pool, without the squat body planted on the bench with stop-watch, thermos of tea and morning *Herald*, seems an echoing treacherous space of nothing.

April passes in a haze of sore eyes, twice daily at those terrible baths, school in between. I'm a robot. Dad times my morning stuff, and Steve the after school session. We get word from Mr Jack that his mother is still hanging on — it turns out to be not quite as bad as they thought, not bad enough to carry her off, but she's on oxygen and can't last much longer. His voice on the long-distance call, at least what we can hear of it through the crackles, is flat and tired. The days, the weeks, drag by. Maggie does her stints on the other side of the pool, her mother continues to be pleasant. I am still wary.

Steve's OK, at first. He used to be a swimmer too, now has a young squad, not actually training at the moment because it's the winter lay-off period, two kids of his own, and a beer belly. He works peculiar shifts as a printer somewhere, so he picks me up from school and we go straight to the pool. We have Mr Jack's handwritten notes for each week's schedule.

About the third week of April I come in for some tongue-lashing.

'Next time, get your skates on, Alex. That wasn't good enough,' he says looking at the stop-watch as though it was going to bite him. I sit on the side of the pool with my chest heaving and my eyes out on red-hot stalks, knowing I have still another four 100 metre sprints at two minute intervals not to mention the ten one-lap sprints at thirty second intervals, and I hate his very guts. The next time it happens, though I know he is right, I shout back, with tears of rage in my eyes.

'Come on, Alex, put some ginger into it,' he says in tones of deep disgust. 'That's a pathetic effort. You're not trying.'

'I am bloody trying, leave me alone,' I shout, and storm into the dressing room, and refuse to get back in the pool or say one single word to him on the way home.

For a few days we get by. Then I notice the distances have gone up. I ask to see the schedules, he tries to distract me, I insist, and see that what he is telling me to do and what is written there by Mr Jack are two quite different things.

'You need more mileage, the Aussie girls are doing twice as much,' he says.

'They're not doing ten miles a day.'

'They're up to forty miles a week.'

'I'm doing five a day, seven times a week, thirty-five miles, exactly as I was told.'

'You're slacking, Alex. Afraid to push yourself just that bit extra?'

'I'm doing Mr Jack's schedule. Not yours. He's still my coach, whatever you might think.' I walk off, swearing softly, which I think he hears, dive in and complete the session. When I get out he has gone, telling the receptionist in the office that he never wants to set eyes on that bumptious kid Alex Archer again, and because I haven't any money on me to get a bus home I have to ring Dad at work, which is something only done in emergencies, and ask him to come and get me.

Even before we get home, Steve's been on the phone to Mum, saying he's had enough of my lip and can't cope with me any more, Olympic prospect or not, and good luck to her because I'm a sullen young lady with a few problems, and he's not surprised she's got a reputation for insolence and general bad behaviour, he only took her on because Bill Jack's a good friend, but he doesn't know how he's kept her in his squad all these years, and if she was my daughter she'd be in for a good hiding if she spoke to adults like that.

I know all this because Mum is so upset when we arrive home that she's not in the kitchen cooking tea but in her bedroom, and they forget to close the door before she pours it all out on Dad's shoulder. It's not that I am eavesdropping, I can just hear her voice and her crying all over the house. Gran gives the subdued kids their tea, I lock myself in my bedroom, and refuse to even answer Dad when he knocks. I have never, ever, seen Mum cry before, except pleased tears when I won something, and I don't ever want to again. I cry myself to sleep; I've given up everything, lost everything, lost everyone. For what?

When my alarm goes off at five a.m. the next morning, I can still hear Mum's crying in my head. Almost immediately, someone knocks on the door. 'Alex? We going?' 'Yes.' Somehow I manage to get vertical; I have to keep going, whatever happens, if I stop now I might never start again, Dad knows that, which is why he's up and ready to go, as per normal. I didn't clean my teeth last night. Ten minutes later we're driving through the dark. Dad doesn't say a single word about Mum or Steve. He doesn't need to.

So much for Steve. Dad now takes me twice daily, but we can't go until he finishes work at five, and we don't get home until nearly eight, by which time my eyes feel like they've been boiled in oil and I can do nothing more, after dinner, than crawl into bed and dread the ring of the alarm the next morning.

Two days after Steve threw in the sponge, Mr Jack rings and says his mother is on her last legs, they don't expect her to last the week, and how am I getting on? I suppress a strong desire to let fly, but what's the use? He can't come home anyway. I don't tell him about Steve. Everything's fine, I say, looking good for the time trials soon, I'm beginning to taper off, feeling good, feeling great. I'm a good liar.

There was one tiny pleasure that awful April, one only. A few days after we started reading *Saint Joan*, Miss Macrae called me to stay behind after class. I stayed in my seat, because I was barely awake after another dreary lesson spent bashing all the life out of George Bernard Shaw; the scene with Joan and the Dauphin at court. She planted her bulky backside on a nearby desk, and straightened the pleats in her grey skirt. She was not usually so ponderous, intimidating. Her voice, when she began, was curiously non-committal.

'I'm planning the production at the end of the year. For a change, I thought a Shaw evening — a scene from *Pygmalion*, some songs from *My Fair Lady*, an extract perhaps from *Caesar and Cleopatra*. There are too many male parts, and not enough talent for the whole of *Saint Joan*, but we can do excerpts, possibly three scenes.'

I shrugged. So? I may or may not be away in Rome for five weeks, and anyway she hadn't given me the chance to read Joan. It hardly concerned me.

'When do you know about Rome?' she said.

'Middle of May.'

'If you go to Rome, when is it?'

'About August 10, the games start August 25, the team comes home about September 20.' I realized, by rattling off the dates, I was betraying how much it meant to me.

'School holidays would account for three weeks of that. Well, it's just possible.'

'What is?'

'I'll put my cards on the table, Alex. Even if you go to Rome, with all the attendant disruption and excitement — could you manage between now and November to learn and rehearse three scenes?'

'What as?'

She looked at me in surprise. 'Joan.'

'Kathie's been reading it.'

'And badly. Painful for you, who could do it so much better. Excruciating for me, who has performed the role. Behind the don't-care leave-me-alone mask you are wearing these days, you were angry. Yes? I was relieved you still have some ambitions besides cutting minuscule slices off your swimming times.'

I shrugged again, hardly wanting her to know that she was right. Joan! Who said what she thought and obeyed her voices, lived briefly and gloriously and in the end got dragged off to die the way I sometimes wished someone would do to me.

'Think about it, Alex. Let me know next week. You might want to talk it over with your parents.'

I've stopped talking to them too, I thought, and they've stopped listening and anyway who in her right mind would refuse Joan.

'I know you're being particularly single-minded at present, for the first time in your life. I also believe that despite what you and most other people might think, you're still deeply grieving for your soulmate Andrew, at odds with yourself and everyone.'

I could only look out of the window. My soulmate. Grieving

— is this what grieving feels like? I'm not wearing black and weeping and wailing all over the place as they do in films, but my eyes were suddenly full of tears. A fake cough to stop them dripping down my cheeks didn't fool Miss Macrae for one minute.

'I think you're punishing yourself. Physically, mentally. Drowning yourself in water and pain. And another thing — why so long until the final selection of the Olympic team? This has been going on for months.'

'I don't know. It might have something to do with being in the wrong hemisphere, out of season.'

'I simply don't understand. To keep people in hard training, for so long — there's a lack of compassion somewhere. It'd be like having to learn the whole of Hamlet just for an audition, and seeing someone else chosen.'

She realized her lack of tact.

'You know what I mean. The papers keep saying you should be selected for Rome. Will be. Well, for the sake of your health, you've got to start thinking positively, *now*, about something other than a stop-watch.'

She stood up. 'Joan is a real challenge, believe you me. Think about it.'

I read the play again in class, while we were supposed to be doing a Latin prose. Even if it was only three scenes, it was a gift, a treasure, a plum of a part! I would probably never get the chance again. Joan had no time for pompous officials, she said what she thought and she wore what she pleased, and she did what her conscience and her passion and her ambition told her. And I realized, as I read on through break, and into History, that there had been something missing besides a social life, or a home life or anything other than a swimming life. I must have got very boring.

Unexpected visitors always annoyed Joyce Benton. She was used to the politer ways of the English country life of her childhood, where one normally first called by telephone to arrange a visit; or Singapore where the amah was trained to provide minimal hospitality to unannounced or unwelcome visitors until she was ready to appear. Here, women frequently popped in and out of each other's houses. Joyce Benton had made her dislike of the practice clear when she first came to live in Auckland. Now she was rarely disturbed during the hours when Maggie and Isobel were away at school, the quiet hours she filled with running her large house, supervising the housekeeper and gardener who came twice a week, and organizing the dinner parties demanded of her by her husband's business interests.

She had been hoping for this visit, however, and though given no warning, welcomed it. She put Jane Sutherland into a deep chair with a copy of Vogue and went out to the kitchen to make some coffee. Her tins were full of yesterday's baking; she deliberately selected chocolate iced afghans, cheese fingers; the most fattening.

'I hope you don't mind me popping in,' said Jane Sutherland, still perched on the edge of the armchair.

'Not at all.'

'I wanted to check with you first, before I ask Maggie.'

'Oh? Ask her what?'

'Well, some mothers might . . . your cheese fingers are superb, Joyce.'

'Thank you.' Joyce Benton waited patiently. Her guest had a laddered stocking, and no self-discipline when it came to food; if she wanted to get into the fashion game, thought Joyce Benton, Jane would have to make sure her city smart appearance went deeper than the expensive suit. It was the details she needed to attend to. And lose about a stone and a half.

'I had this phone call the other day. You know the girls who do dressmaking at school, making outfits for the parade in July? My daughter's doing so well. Well. Right out of the blue, I've been offered some of the new season's swim-suits. The 1961 California season, imagine that! They'd heard that our school's show was a little bit special. And I thought . . .'

Joyce Benton sipped her coffee. She was not going to be seen to enthuse.

'I thought, two wonderful young swimmers, wouldn't it be tremendous? Two Olympic models. We can make it a charity event, raise money for the Crippled Children or something.'

'You mean, you see Maggie as a model?'

'And Alex Archer. That photo I saw when I came for coffee — such fine girls, both of them, wonderful figures. I know Alex goes to that other school, but I'm sure, if it's for charity . . .'

Joyce Benton offered her animated guest more coffee, presenting a reaction of coolness, even reluctance.

'I don't know, Jane. Maggie's very young. Won't these all be very sophisticated garments?'

'Oh, but beautiful. I've seen them, Grecian styles, very classical, with little skirts, and South Sea Isle prints, the South Pacific look, big flowers, you know, gorgeous colours, even some with matching beach coats.'

'They sound lovely.'

'Oh, they are. And I'd just love to have Maggie and Alex . . .' Jane Sutherland was disconcerted by the lack of response. 'It's only a school thing, just the girls and a few parents. Perhaps you're worried about the time involved?'

'Not so much that.'

'Only one or two rehearsals, just to make sure the swim-suits fit and the girls know what to do?'

After a brief pause, Joyce Benton said, 'Let me discuss it with Maggie. After all, she is the one who's got to do it. More coffee?'

'Of course, naturally. Oh, yes please.' She held out her cup. 'I did enjoy your coffee morning the other week. How long before the final selection? How are the girls coping?'

'About three weeks. Maggie is coping very well, I feel. Alex, I'm not sure; she's looking very strained these days, losing weight. She was here for a barbecue recently, and didn't seem to fit in terribly well, though of course we did all we could . . . I do worry about the child.'

She got up to close a window. 'It's getting chilly, these days. I rather dread the winter, the incessant rain, the damp of this climate. Perhaps . . . leave it a while, your suggestion. After the selections are announced, maybe?'

'I'll have to let the man from the department store know.'

Oh, he'll wait, thought Joyce Benton. I only know George Sadler through Harold's business contacts, but it had been relatively simple to include him and his dreary wife in a recent cocktail party. He'll wait, because even 'a school thing' is good promotion for him; and it had been difficult to restrain him from the idea of mounting a whole fashion parade in his genteel but slightly shabby department store around the idea of Olympic models; quite against the amateur code, I had to explain, but maybe a school parade, no one could object to that. Incidentally, George, depite her rather flamboyant appearance, Jane Sutherland is still a rather . . . insecure little person, not very experienced. This is her first parade for the school. Her husband is rather a difficult man. Say that you'd heard the emphasis the school put on good grooming and dressmaking, and about their excellent annual parade. Let her think it was her idea.

'Delighted to see you. Thank you so much for calling,' she said coolly as she saw her guest to her car in the brick driveway. 'I'll be in touch.'

We swam into winter, into May, two weeks to go. Mr Jack was still away in Sydney, Dad faithfully clocking my time trials, the household ticking away as usual, though I saw precious little of anyone.

Maggie and I survived two official time trials, 100 metres and 400 metres; unofficial sprint records for us both but not allowable because they were done in a short-course salt water pool. The first time, I had the faster time by point one; the second time, Maggie did, by the same margin, but not enough to tip the balance in her favour. So I still had the edge; and Mrs Benton was still going out of her way to be charming when I let her get anywhere near me. We got small bits in the paper, about our heavy training schedules and these unofficial records 'reinforcing our claims for two places in the Games team', and 'keeping the pressure on the Olympic selectors'.

I'd lost another five pounds and my hip bones were sticking out.

The papers were full of the all-white All Blacks soon to leave for South Africa despite the petitions and general public outcry. I hadn't forgotten Keith's suggestion about the protest march, but I was simply too tired, and my eyes too sore to do anything except wait for him to ring back. Training, sitting in class, and using lunch-times and what free periods I had to read *Saint Joan* over and over — my life had come down to this.

Keith rang the night before the march, with only a week to go before the Olympic team was due to be announced. He was abrupt to the point of rudeness.

'Alex? You a starter? Nine o'clock tomorrow, outside the pool, OK, gotta go, seeya,' again leaving me holding the phone in amazement.

Sure enough, outside the pool there he was. For some reason of native cunning I hadn't told my parents what I was doing after training, other than 'meeting some friends, going to an eleven o'clock film in town'. Life had got so dull, they seemed to think *South Pacific* and the new wonders of the big screen were a good idea for a Saturday morning.

'What's wrong with your eyes?' I was beginning to find out Keith didn't waste time on the usual courtesies, like hullo, how are you, and goodbye. I hadn't been quite quick enough with my sunglasses.

'It's the water. Salt and chlorine mixed, then heated.'

'What about goggles?'

'I can't keep them on. The suction, it's like pulling out your eyeballs.'

'Christ.'

I looked a bit funny in sunglasses, 'cause it was overcast and wintry. Coming with wet hair from the fug of a heated pool, I was envious of the marchers who'd dressed warmly in hats, warm coats, gloves and handknitted scarves about nine feet long. Keith seemed to know lots of the students in duffle coats. We milled around a bit with families, vicars in dog collars, students; and Maoris, as you might expect, 'cause it was them, who were being left out of the team 'in their best interests,' who'd been insulted. The team was due to leave the next day.

Next to me as we assembled were two men wearing New Zealand blazers — Athletics, Olympic Games, Melbourne 1956. Keith, darting round, stopped briefly to shake their hands. 'Good-ta-seeya, mate,' almost as though he had some sort of status as an organizer. Then he grabbed my hand and led me almost to the head of the parade. I ungrabbed it, and without speaking slunk back a few rows. I was here, wasn't I? That was enough. There were times when I was conscious of my tallness, and this was one of them. I didn't want to be conspicuously here. We moved off slowly.

It's the first time I've been in a large moving crowd of people since last May, the day we walked over the harbour bridge and talked of Kipling and dying. As we approach the Ferry Buildings I see a blue Morris Minor parked on the far side of the road, and leaning against it, his arms folded, watching the parade, is Andy.

I'm swept on. It's the clothes that tell me I must be wrong — he would never have worn that scruffy jacket. But the height is the same, and the hair, and the relaxed folded arms, and the smile, and so is the voice that calls my name. I'm swept past, and in my hand my sunglasses are shaking and it's not because I'm cold.

The march went past the Central Post Office, up Queen Street lined with spectators who'd come to watch. The papers said later there were 2000 marchers and 3000 spectators. Ahead of us I could hear an African drum, and people were holding banners saying 'No Maoris, No Tour' and 'Sharpeville 128-0,' 'I'm All White, Jack' and 'We want no part of Apartheid.'

We'd just turned into Queen Street, when Keith remembered he had his own banner in his duffle bag. It was a long piece of cloth, with '1960 All Blacks the Shame of New Zealand' written in crude black paint. 'Here, hold one end of this,' he said.

'No.'

'Why not?'

'I don't want to. I'm here, I'm marching, and that's all I'm doing.'

'Women,' he said. 'Here, mate, take this,' he shouted across to an older man abreast of us. I may as well have carried the damn thing, because now I was walking directly behind it.

'You're a weirdo, Alex. You'll get up at a Rotary do in public and say your piece . . . even argue with Andy's cantankerous old man.'

'How did you know about that?'

'Well, it's obvious isn't it? We were . . . mates.'

'I can't imagine why.' That hurt; he drew breath to say something, then seemed to change his mind. 'Anyway, I don't want to talk about it.'

'You're still . . .?'

'Bitter and twisted? Of course I am. Maniacs behind wheels of cars — good people die and others get away with murder. What sort of logic is that? They didn't even find the guy who did it.'

'Yes they . . .' He looked at me over his end of the banner. 'Oh Christ, Alex, didn't you know?'

'Know what? I didn't make a point of finding out, no.'

It was more than that. I'd told my family, Julia, Mr Jack that I didn't want to know, anything more about who, or why, or what happened. There'd been a brief bit about a 'hit-and-run accident in Epsom last night, 17-year-old boy killed', and I'd not looked at the newspapers for weeks after that.

'They know who did it all right, except they think he's in Australia.'

Coming on top of what I'd just seen, or not seen, I was feeling sick to the very depths. And from those depths a mighty fury was beginning to stir.

'Oh, *great*. Scot-free.'

'Him, yes. After a fashion. His wife, no.'

'How?'

'It was her that rushed out, found him . . . dying. Neighbours too, 'cause of the noise, her screaming, and before that the row in the house, him drunk as a skunk, yelling and throwing things.'

'Keep politics out of sport!' yelled a voice, penetrating. I was under a street light, a dying boy in my arms.

'The guy worked in cars. So he knocked up a friendly panel-beater in the middle of the night, and had the car locked away in a garage half way down Great South Road. Paint job, number plates, the lot. The police found it eventually. They found paint chips, on his . . .'

'Don't!!'

'They think our friend crept back to the house that night, whipped up his passport and a few clothes and shot through to Aussie. His wife couldn't, or wouldn't, tell them anything.'

'She's protecting him? Knowing he's killed someone?'

'She's not obliged to tell the police anything. Or testify if they ever did get him to court, which they won't. There were no witnesses.'

'If they did? How do you know all this?'

'My mum works for a lawyer. The secretaries, well you know what this place is like, one of them knows the wife through kindergarten. Apparently she's gone to pieces a bit.'

'*If they did?*'

'Oh, manslaughter, drunken driving, failing to stop at an accident — be put away for a few years. Could you blame the wife, she's lost a husband, big house. Three young kids to support. And he's stuck in Aussie, can't come back, lost his job, his family ... one drink too many ...'

'One little mistake? Is that what you were going to say. Did he lose his life? You feel sorry for *him?*'

'Go back to school, little girl,' came a voice. 'The rest of you, go back to your pulpits.'

Poofters!

Traitors!

Cranks!

'Shame,' came a few softer voices of reason from the crowd, women's voices. 'Shame.'

'Keep politics out of sport!'

'You're a pack of girls!'

'Girls don't start wars,' I yelled. 'Or kill people with cars. And they've got too much sense to play rugby, with the Springboks or anybody else.'

There was some laughter, ironic cheers. A few people clapped. I saw Keith's expression change from worry to slight amusement.

'Go back to your kitchen, girlie,' came the same voice, but fainter, now behind us. Keith was looking at me. 'Alex, I ...'

'Drop dead,' I said. We marched on through friendlier territory. Most of the crowd seemed quite amused by the whole thing, as though they were watching the Santa Parade. We had marched on up the gradual incline of Queen Street before I could bring myself to speak again.

'You're all the same. In the end. You drive like a maniac, you've had accidents, plural, and damn near killed someone, but you close ranks, you're all the same. I suppose you're going to tell me poor bastard, wife playing around and mother-in-law and three snotty kids driving him mad, so somehow you can understand a guy blowing a fuse and firing up his Jaguar ...'

Now I know why I want to do law.'
'Alex, I'm sorry. I shouldn't have told you.'
'Well you did.'
'I thought . . .'
'Forget it.' I don't know why I went on marching, why I didn't just duck off out the side and catch a bus home. Perhaps I was just shell-shocked, all the old wounds opening up. Andy would have marched, we would have marched together, I know we would have. I had to go on. So we marched in silence to the bang of the African drum up the long straight road, ending up in a kid's playground, standing around among the swings and slides listening to lengthy speeches by church leaders, Maori leaders, union leaders, men in hats. After a while they began to get rather repetitive and boring. Keith had wandered off to talk to other people; I had sunk into a sort of apathetic daze, chilled to the marrow, sitting on a roundabout. I didn't see the press photographer until his flash had gone off and it was too late.

You *fixed* that, didn't you!'
'Christ, Alex, how . . .'
'You hauled me along for a bit of cheesecake, female support, Alex Archer on behalf of New Zealand's young sportswomen standing up and being counted. You tried to get me up in front of the parade, and to carry that bloody banner, and when you couldn't you fixed the photographer.'
'I swear to God I had nothing to . . .'
'You expect me to believe that, Keith Jameson?' I yelled down the phone. 'The Olympic team gets announced in a week. Because of you . . .' I choked.
The front page of the evening paper was shaking in my hand. What was making me especially angry was the posed sort of way I was sitting, without knowing it. With damp hair, sunglasses, I looked like some sort of outsize, sulky, brooding Grace Kelly. 'Olympic nominee, swimmer Alex Archer was among the marchers'.
'Someone must have told them. How did they know it was me?'
'Come on, a face as famous as yours? Cover girl of the *Women's Weekly*?'
'I was wearing sunglasses. I was just one of thousands.'

'And you thought you were incognito? Grow up, Alex. Press photographers have memories. And they know a pretty face when they see one. All those dour Presbyterians, scruffy varsity students — can you blame them picking you out?'

'That's exactly what . . . you didn't ask me to march because I believed in it. You asked me just to get extra publicity for the cause. Cheesecake, using models to sell, draped all over cars . . . you used me, Keith Jameson and I'll never forgive you.'

'Keep your hair on, woman.'

I saw Jamie's shadow against his bedroom door. Indeed the whole house had gone remarkably quiet as they all listened from behind doorways.

'Don't you woman me.' I have yet to run the gamut of my family, or Mr Jack when he comes back and finds out I've blown it, or Mr Upjohn who may now have found the weapon he needs to inform the main selectors that I am politically unreliable and a bad influence on juniors.'

'What's the matter with you anyway?' said Keith. 'Aren't you proud to be a leader? In twenty years' time no one will be going to South Africa to play *anything*, unless they change their appalling race laws. Ten years even, Olympics, rugby, trade, nothing, because of us, because of what we did yesterday. Talking and petitions aren't enough any more, we have to get out there. Protest, march, obstruct, get in the papers, make a nuisance of ourselves so that the politicians have to listen.'

'In twenty years' time I'll be looking back and thinking about the Olympic trip I missed out on.'

'Calm down, Alex. Are you seriously trying to tell me that one picture in the paper will ruin your chances? I don't believe it. This is 1960, not Orwell's 1984. You're entitled to your views . . .'

'Not if you're fifteen and female and you know damn well one selector has already got it in for you.'

'He's only one of how many, three?'

'If you *knew*, if you had any idea at all, what it's cost me to get this far . . .'

'I know one thing, Miss Alexandra Archer, and that is you've got a very high opinion of yourself. So what if your picture's in the paper doing something worthwhile, standing up against tyranny. Better than winning a swimming race, better than any medal. Andy knew that. Wouldn't he have been proud of you?'

'Don't you ever EVER say that name to me again.' I slammed down the phone, so hard that I probably cracked the casing. Gran was the first person to appear from the kitchen, wiping her hands on a tea-towel.

'I'll say it, Alex,' she said quietly, 'because you'll take it from me. Andy is proud of you, so are we all.'

'I won't get in the team, Gran,' I wept, sinking to a heap against the hallway skirtings. 'I won't, I won't, I won't.'

Everyone's abandoned me — Mr Jack's gone, Mum and Dad are pussyfooting and not talking to me, Julia's gone off with someone else, Keith is a bastard, and Andy who told me I'd be going to Rome — the unkindest cut of all.

Gran stroked my hair for a long time, wet as always because I'd only just come in from evening training when I saw the paper. The kids crept about as though someone was sick, the peas burned, and Mum stayed safely in the laundry doing the ironing.

'You'll be there.'

The next day Keith, along with about twenty-five others, rushes out on the tarmac at Whenuapai and flings himself down on the runway in front of the plane carrying the all white All Blacks. Earlier there was a bomb scare and the luggage was examined, and the captain led his team out after all the ordinary passengers singing 'Now is the Hour' which shows what total hypocrites they all are because they can sing a Maori song when they've left the Maoris behind. Because the Electra turns around and takes off extra quick, almost as though the crew knew what was planned, the protesters are too late to actually stop it, although the nearest gets within twenty yards, and they are left standing shaking their fists at the sky. I know about this because it's in the paper, and there he is, duffle coat awry, scarf trailing, legs planted wide in the grass, caught shouting and gesticulating, gnomish face scowling in frustration; and by then I've calmed down enough to see the funny side. See how you like *your* picture in the paper, Keith Jameson.

Mum and Dad must have decided I'd punished myself enough, because nothing is said about the cheesecake photo or even about me going protesting instead of to see *South Pacific*. An uneasy truce reigns in the house.

Maggie and I plough silently up and down the pool and exchange small talk when we meet in the dressing room, groping around for our clothes, blinded by chlorine, pink as lobsters. The days tick by, five to go, four. The team is being announced on May 25, the papers are full of the earthquakes and tidal waves in Chile, 1500 dead and 30,000 homeless, and the tsunami which is rushing across the Pacific towards our small defenceless country. People actually go down to the water's edge of the waterfront to watch it coming in, never mind getting on to higher ground. What they see is the lowest tide ever, a sea of mud stretching half-way to Rangitoto, before a fizzer of a high tide. Tsunami are too close to my nightmares in the few minutes of sleep I manage each night. The dreaded dream is back: going sailing with Andy, at first laughing and happy, but he is still jumping over the side never to surface and I'm still left to sail on alone.

It's school holidays, not that it makes much difference except that I can go training at six in the morning instead of five. Maggie, by some unspoken agreement, goes later in the day to both sessions, so that we avoid each other entirely. At home you could cut the atmosphere with a knife.

On the twenty-fifth of May I sleep in, a long, unusually dreamless sleep until after eight, which is late for me. Last night's paper has told us that the team is expected to be announced midday today: I have four hours to fill in. I can't hang around the house listening to the kids fight. A bike ride seems to be in order, and I have a score to settle.

It's only when I'm riding towards Andy's school that I realize I don't know exactly which house and which driveway it was that the Jaguar screamed out of that December night.

I haven't got any money on me for a phone box, so I go into a dairy which I know to be one of those friendly places where Mum cashes cheques every now and then. I persuade the man behind the counter to let me use his phone; I ring Keith's number.

He's not at home, of course, he's working down on the wharves during his holidays, earning vast sums of money, and his mother works too.

I know the general area, where it happened. One driveway has a large For Sale notice beside it. This would be a logical conclusion to the story I heard from Keith: the man fled to Aussie, the woman and her children gone to ground. Some ghoulish instinct has me searching for bloodstains on the road outside, but there's been a lot of sun and a lot of rain since that December night. Another instinct has me looking around to see that I am not watched, and pedalling myself slowly up the driveway, which is strewn with leaves driven into decaying piles and fallen branches. The trees and bushes are out of control, the flower beds gone to seed. It's an expensive house, the sort usually described as gracious, but empty. Broken toys in a scruffy sandpit, cardboard boxes lying round, a broken chair by the front door, evidence of the house being left in a hurry and with no thought for the next people. I walk along the porch. Except for a few boxes of rubbish, the rooms inside are empty. The garage door is shut, but being so tall I can see in through a small high window. Inside is a dark green car. Even though I can't see all of it, I know it's a Jaguar.

Perhaps it's just as well I can't see its bonnet, the sleek and dangerous sharp end that had killed him, because I think I might have lost all control of my temper, my senses, my self. I lose enough control of my temper to try to pull off the padlock that opens the side door of the garage. It's too strong; what I thought I might have done to the Jaguar had I been able to get my hands on it, I don't know. As it is, I have to let go a cry of despair that echoes round the courtyard. I have just enough control to know that neighbours might come to investigate; but not enough to stop myself picking up a large rock from the ornamental rockery in front of the house and hurling it at the side of the garage, too badly aimed to break the window; not enough to stop myself repeating the performance, twice more; enough awareness to be relieved that I am too angry to aim properly to alert neighbours to a sound of breaking glass; enough momentum to leap on my bike and free-wheel down the drive; enough sense to slow up at the bottom because the irony of me being knocked off my bike in the very spot would be too much; not enough control to go pedalling off down the road far too fast, considering I cannot see a thing for tears.

The score is not settled. What had I wanted, anyway? — to talk to the wife, feel sorry for the kids, recognize a blood stain on the road. I don't know, don't know. You told me, Andy, I was going to Rome. Was it just a weak man talking, telling me what I wanted to hear. Is Keith right when he says you wouldn't have made it to command a ship because you lacked drive, aggression, grit, you were too soft; things had come too easy for you? Have all these months been wasted? I'm up against forces I don't understand. Have you betrayed me? Did you know all the time I wouldn't get in?

Where have you gone?

While I am eating bacon and eggs for brunch, waiting for the midday news that will probably include the team, something happens in my head and I find myself telling Mum and Gran about Mr Upjohn and what I had overheard in Napier. 'I don't want her in Rome.' They look at each other, sort of helplessly.

'Why didn't you tell us earlier?'

'I don't know, Mum. I just couldn't.'

'Why?' persists Mum. 'Three months you've been soldiering on, and God knows that's not been the only problem. Why didn't you tell us at the time? Couldn't we have helped?'

'I don't know. I don't know. I don't know anything any more.'

I am crying, again, even before I hear I haven't made it into the team.

'Alex,' says Mum sternly. 'If you get in the team, no one will be prouder than your family, and no one knows better than us how hard you've worked for it. If you don't . . .'

'That'll be it,' I say. 'I'll stop as of today, training, swimming, for good.'

'I was going to say, whatever, we'll be just as proud for what you've achieved already. The greater achievement is sometimes to reassess goals.'

'She will make it, Helena,' said Gran testily, looking at the kitchen clock. It's five minutes before high noon. 'Shall I get the kids in from the garden?'

'No.' They both know I'd rather hear the worst without an

audience. Mum turns on the radio and we sit, Mum on one side, Gran on the other. Is this how a prisoner in the dock feels when the foreman reads out the verdict?

The fruity male voice drones on, events in Chile, South Africa, the Summit conference breaks down in Paris.

And then. 'Thirty-nine athletes and twelve officials have today been named for the Olympic Games to be held in Rome in August. They are ...' The announcer reads the list slowly, deliberately: the athletes, the cyclists, the equestrians, the fencers, the hockey players, is there no end to it?

The rowers, then 'Swimming. Manager, Mr Cyril Upjohn, of Auckland. Chaperon, Mrs Enid Churchill, of Christchurch.'

Someone is going. A female is going.

'Miss Alexandra Beatrice Archer, of Auckland. 100 metres and 400 metres freestyle. Miss Margaret Louise Benton, 100 metres and 400 metres freestyle. Weightlifting ...'

Like an old-fashioned heroine, I swoon.

Part Three

IT was a busy day for the Sports Desk, and Norm Thompson, clocking in only ten minutes late. As the Olympic team came clattering off the teleprinter machine at noon, the Sports Editor ticked off a list of interviews and pictures he wanted done that afternoon for tomorrow morning's paper. The announcement had happily come over too late for the evening paper, except for a tiny stop press in the final edition, so he expected plenty of space, on both the front page and an inside sports page.

'Murray Halberg and coach, and Peter Snell who's crept in the back door. The lady shot-putter, we've got her on file already. We need a bit of glamour . . . get the two girl swimmers together, Norm. Not a bad list, I suppose, no real surprises.'

Norm Thompson grunted, unimpressed with this off-the-cuff analysis. He was greatly relieved that justice and common sense had prevailed in the case of the two girls. It was not impossible that Alex could have missed out. The promising young butterfly swimmer hadn't made it; neither had the female runner whose half-mile times placed her among the world's top ten. Hardly a Games team had gone by without controversy, inexplicable omissions; the workings of selectors' minds remained a total mystery. He had some experience of the sort of despair and disillusionment the female half-miler would be feeling, years of work for nothing. Fortunately another reporter was being assigned to that interview, to probe and document her anguish for the nation's breakfast reading.

'You could get the cadet to go out to see young Archer and Benton. Attractive kids, he'd like that.' The Sports Editor looked at Norm across his ash-scattered paper-strewn shambles of a desk.

The cadet, thought Norm, was a lecherous little creep, if his behaviour with the copy typists around the news-room was anything to go by. He wouldn't wish that on young Archer and Benton. Besides, since her triumph at the nationals in Napier and her political notoriety of the past three months, he was curious about young Archer. In the light of what he'd heard from that boy from Napier, she'd taken a big risk in tackling Cyril Upjohn head-on at a recent Rotary lunch. It indicated either a high measure of self-confidence or a total and refreshing lack of political nous.

'No, I'll go myself.'

'I want a human interest slant, Norm. Two pretty faces for the front page. Bitter rivals turned team-mates, that sort of thing. Whistle up a photographer. You can do a think-piece on the overall team when you get back. They may want a sub-leader too.'

Do it yourself, you're the Sports Editor, thought Norm, although pleased to have the honour of pronouncing the paper's official line on the Olympic team, as he'd done regularly for the last twenty years. You're a lazy sod, he thought, looking down at this man in braces, with the gift of the gab and sharp line in suits, brought in seven years ago from a provincial paper to sit in the chair that he, Norm Thompson, might reasonably have expected.

Still, Sports Editors get chained to desks in noisy, neon-lit and badly-ventilated news-rooms, while he at least would spend this afternoon in the far more wholesome company of two young women with the world at their feet.

He rang to make a time to see Maggie Benton — 'No, she's not going training today,' said her so-couth mother. 'She's having a day off to celebrate with her father and I.' Me, thought Norm, a stickler for grammar despite his sloppy appearance. 'I'd like to get a picture of both the girls together, in togs, at the pool,' he said, and there was a long silence while a conference took place behind the muffled phone. Her voice, when it informed him that Maggie would be available at two-thirty at the pool, was polite but remote, as to a tradesman. 'She couldn't speak for Alex,' she said; 'Maggie had tried to ring, but her phone was permanently engaged.' No love lost there, he thought, a bundle of jealousy, a 'swimming mum' of the first water. He'd met plenty, in all sports. The male versions who hung around rugby fields were — if it was possible — the worst. He'd have to take a chance on driving out to Epsom and finding Alex at home and prepared to go to the pool for a picture.

He prised a photographer out of his dark room, and a battered staff Morris Minor, smelling of cigarettes and grubby raincoats, out of the carpark underneath the newspaper's central city office. The weather was unusually miserable for the end of May, raining and so dark he had to put on side lights to negotiate the traffic. Along the Archers' street, lined with plane trees, stood rows of fifty-year-old kauri villas and thirty-year-old California bungalows; comfortably bourgeois. Outside one of the shabbier villas, he drew up and left the photographer loading up his Rolleiflex while he went into the house.

The rain beat on the windscreen and time passed, longer than the photographer thought necessary to jack up the girl for a quick pic'. She was talking to her coach in Aussie, said Norm when he finally came back to the car. Good story — some drama, it seemed. Bill Jack's old mother finally did the decent thing and died yesterday, so he'd be back home after the funeral. Alex had been without her coach for the past six weeks, poor kid.

What about the picture, said the sleepy photographer, interested only in what he saw in his viewfinder. Took some persuading, said Norm, taking his time rolling a cigarette between brown fingers. Why, for God's sake? Just a kid, going to the Olympics, a mugshot's all we want, said the photographer.

Norm grunted. Highly strung, intense sort of kid. Been crying. Strange; the mother was a very pleasant sort of woman, large-boned, soft-voiced, no pretensions, three other kids eating lunch, school holidays; a tiny old crone hovering round, chooks out the back, gumboots in the hall, smell of baking, your average Kiwi family. Father does something in the Post Office, served in the Navy.

Rivetting, said the photographer sardonically. Norm started up the car. The mother will drive her to the pool at two-thirty, he said. The real story on Alex Archer he kept to himself. After the phone call from her coach, she'd pulled herself together with the poise of an old trooper. Yes, of course she was delighted to have made the team, along with Maggie.

He'd asked her feelings about the selections, those who'd missed out, the butterfly junior for instance. Yes, he deserved to go, she thought. How did she feel about other methods of selection, such as official target times or the one-off sudden death trials they held in America? Well, by being deliberately vague, that's how the selectors kept their power, she said quite blithely; they made up the rules as they went along and told the actual swimmers as little as possible. It was cuttingly, ironically true; also unprintable. Norm was not about to jeopardize any young athlete's career for the sake of a good quote. Across the Tasman, Dawn Fraser had been waging a very public running battle with officials for years, but she was a grown woman of twenty-two.

'I'm sure,' she went on, 'Mr Upjohn will be delighted Maggie and I have earned him a free trip to Rome.'

'That's off the record, of course, Alex,' he said gently, and he had been surprised by the challenging glint in her eyes. Fifteen or not, she knew exactly what she was saying.

What about their chances in Rome, she and Maggie? Dawn Fraser will win again, with Americans breathing down her neck. I'd like to make the final, she said. I think I can, on times, if I'm left alone to get on with the job. I can't speak for Maggie, though she's had a few chances I haven't, swimming in Australia. Not for the first time, Norm Thompson found himself intrigued by the cynical smile, remembering heaven knows what scandals as she gazed unflinchingly at him. Apart from what he'd heard from Grant Davies, there'd been other rumours over the past year or so; that boy who'd died as well as that storm in a teacup at the nationals, the stand-in coach who'd thrown in the sponge because she was 'impossible' to work with, and her public pronouncements about the All Black team to South Africa. Unwise, but no doubt shrewdly calculated. In ten, even five years' time, she'll be a hell of a woman, he thought.

After the announcement I was out cold for less than a minute. When I came to, it was to find Gran waving eau-de-cologne under my nose and the telephone receiver by my ear. Dad, who'd listened on his transistor at work, was on the other end. It seemed Mum had already filled him in about my eavesdropping problems with Mr Upjohn. Being Dad, he didn't waste time with a whole lot of 'if onlys'. 'You've done it, Alex.'

'We've done it.' I just felt exhausted.

My first phone call was to Sydney, but even while finding the number I had to take five long calls one after another and allow myself to be hugged by the kids who came rushing in from the garden, and neighbours who knocked on the front door. After the Sydney call, which gave me the equally good news that Mr Jack would be home in a few days, there was that reporter Norm Thompson at the door, jacking up a picture at the pool, and then the phone again, endlessly.

What demon made me keep Mum waiting out in the car for three or four minutes? Was it just vanity, carefully rubbing in some Max Factor erase stuff to get rid of the shadows under my eyes? I'd been using it quite often these days, even at school where make-up is *verboten*, because I couldn't bear the sight of myself in the mirror, all hollows and bloodshot eyeballs, like a European refugee.

Or was it some devil which made me engineer a grand entrance, keep all of them waiting? Anyway, it was two-twenty-five by the time I escaped from the telephone by leaving it off the hook, and two-forty by the time we arrived at the pool. Mum, who hates being late, was annoyed.

'You'll have to apologize to Mr Thompson and the photographer,' she said stiffly. 'I'll go and park the car.' Frankly, I was more interested in finding Maggie, since we had a lot to celebrate. I ran through the rain into the pool, and straight past the waiting group. Maggie was in her track suit. It was, surely the most natural thing in the world to want to hug and share our achievement. We'd both done it, together, and in our separate ways. So we hugged. The photographer took a picture. 'You won't use that,' I said, laughing.

'I hope not,' said Mrs Benton. 'You're late, Alex.'

'Sorry,' I said. 'The phone kept ringing, honestly.'

'Alex, this is our photographer, Graham Wills,' said Norm Thompson, who had come to the house earlier and quizzed me about a few things like selection processes. I don't think I was all that tactful.

'Hi,' I said, holding out my hand. Today I was giving a good imitation of a 15-year-old girl bubbling with excitement, partly because that's what they all expected and partly because I didn't like Mrs Benton's opening shots, and I needed time to find out why. 'Maggie, wasn't it awful, waiting while they read out all those other people, the fencers and rowers and everybody. I thought I would die.'

'I can't believe it. I didn't expect to get in.'

'Of course you did,' said Mrs Benton quickly.

'I'm glad . . . Rome, here we come,' I said. 'Rome! The other side of the world!'

'Can you get changed quickly, Alex?' said Mrs Benton. 'Our friend doesn't have much time, and neither do we.'

'Why, where are we going?' asked Maggie. Clearly it was news to her.

'We're meeting your father in town, and some business associates.'

'Sure,' I said, and left to get changed, puzzled at the change in her tone. She'd been rather friendlier of late. What she hadn't said today was anything like well done, Alex, congratulations, after all these years it's great you've both made it. Strange.

Even stranger, when I rejoined the group, was Maggie having some solo shots taken in her togs only, being asked to bend her knee a little more, tilt her chin up, weight on the right hip, no the right, smile now. Pretty, and posed, like a *Seventeen* model, and Maggie really embarrassed, I could tell. I couldn't understand why her mother allowed it, but the look on her face said she approved.

'OK, now together,' said the photographer. 'Alex, you're the taller, what about sitting on the railing, Maggie can stand in front.' He took a few steps back, remembered just in time he was on the brink of the pool, and positioned himself squatting on his haunches, peering down into his viewfinder. 'Great, good, what about an arm around your girlfriend, Alex?'

'No,' I said. He looked up. I shook my head. He didn't need to know that exactly a year ago the rumours had started: that being tall and broad shouldered and always hugging my girlfriends and playing male parts in school plays — I was a bit short on feminine hormones.

After a slight pause, he thought better of pushing me any further.

'Well, let's see. Just incline your heads a little towards each other. That's it, more. More. More. Two brilliant smiles, you're off to Rome.' I must still have been looking steely.

'Alex? Big smile. Bend that knee a little more.'

'No,' I said again. 'I'm a swimmer, not a beauty queen, which is patently obvious in these togs.'

He looked up at Mr Thompson. 'What's the matter with this girl?'

'You can take me as I am,' I said. 'I'm not Marilyn Monroe, and I don't intend to look silly trying.'

'You're being very childish,' said Mrs Benton.

To my relief, Norm Thompson took over.

'Looks fine to me, Graham. We'll probably only use head and shoulders anyway.'

'Good,' I said. Graham took a few more, without saying anything except 'Ready, here we go'. His bald head was shining with anger.

'Look,' I said, 'If we were 15-year-old male swimmers, you wouldn't be asking us to flex our biceps and look manly like Mr Atlas. You'd just take us as we are. That's all I'm asking, the same treatment.'

'Neurotic,' I heard him mumble under his breath as he began to put his equipment away in his bag.

'That's great, that'll be fine,' said Norm Thompson. 'Quite right, Alex, we don't want our Olympic athletes reduced to cheesecake, do we?'

'He gave it a good try,' I said, earning a look of darkest fury from the photographer. I don't suppose he was used to young females refusing to be pushed around into the approved moulds.

'I think we should go, Maggie,' said Mrs Benton. She'd had enough of me too. 'Oh, Mrs Archer, I didn't see you there.'

'Well, hullo, this is a big event, a big day. Maggie, well done, dear,' said Mum, hugging her. 'I'm very pleased you've both made it. Mrs Benton, congratulations to you too.'

'Excuse me, ladies. We're off,' said Mr Thompson. The photographer had already gone, without a backward glance. 'We've got others to see, some of the athletes. Thanks for your time. I'm sure the picture will be quite OK.' We all said polite goodbyes.

'Yes, we're very happy,' said Mrs Benton, turning to Mum, lying through her teeth. 'Now Harold and I can make our own travel plans. We were intending to go to Europe anyway, but of course, this is the best possible reason.'

'How wonderful,' said Mum. 'Someone to cheer for you, girls.'

'Maggie will be staying with us in Rome. We have some old

Singapore friends there, diplomats.'

'But . . . I'll be with the team in the Olympic village, with Alex.'

'I don't think so. You're too young.'

'Oh Mum! I want to be with the team.'

'Of course she does,' I said, lightly. 'There're five athletes going too, but they're all much older than us. I don't want . . .'

'What you want, Alex, and what Maggie's father and I think is best for her, might be two different things.'

'Mum, you can't . . . '

'We're not discussing this now. Go and get changed, please Maggie.' She'd certainly put a dampener on things. With a despairing glance at me, Maggie went slowly.

'She's just a child, not like this sophisticated young lady here,' said Mrs Benton.

'I'm only four months older than Maggie.'

Her brief silence spoke volumes. Then, 'I always enjoy your daughter, Mrs Archer.'

'I'm delighted to hear it,' said Mum, hoodwinked. 'So do we, despite her whirlwind life.'

I couldn't stand it. 'I'm going to have a swim, not training, just fun. Twenty minutes, OK Mum?'

'Can't keep her out,' said Mum, with mock resignation. I dived in and left them to it.

The photographer got his own back, in the end. The next morning I went training with Dad, and came back to the breakfast table to find Maggie and me on the front page. It was the one taken when I'd first rushed into the pool. I looked like a gorilla, enclosing Maggie in my great shoulders, teeth bared in a hideous grin. WATER BABIES CELEBRATE, said the heading. Some baby!

Dad and Mum tried to make light of it, as they'd done in the past when less then flattering things about me had appeared in the papers. 'They say there's no such thing as bad publicity.'

'What do I want publicity for?' I said.

'Didn't you realize the photographer was there?' said Mum pointedly.

'What am I supposed to do, creep around the place because some photographer might be lurking! Take it away!'

'Water baby,' sang my darling little brother over his porridge.

'I love you too,' I snarled and took my porridge into my bedroom.

Luckily I didn't have to face the masses at school for another week and by then it would be old news. But the phone calls, telegrams, interviews and visits continued for several days. I didn't want to see Keith at all, but he came anyway. He reminded me of all the things about last December, especially what he'd told me recently about the driver of the Jaguar, that I was trying to forget. We sat awkwardly around the kitchen table for ten minutes or so, then he got the message that I wasn't going to suggest we went somewhere where there weren't children, Mum and Gran coming and going, the radio going, a meal being prepared. He gave me up as a bad job and left.

Julia, however, could be useful, and I rather hoped she might bury the hatchet and turn up. We'd hardly spoken for months and I knew that she had sentenced herself to heavy swotting during the holidays, towards those brilliant science marks she had to achieve in November. I heard Mum say, 'Go on through, Julia,' and she appeared, uncertain, in the doorway.

'Great stuff, Alex. I'm really, really pleased.'

'Thanks.'

'That was a lousy picture in the paper yesterday.'

'I thought so too. It was revenge.'

She laughed. 'Who have you been upsetting this time?'

'Everybody. I'm past caring.' Help, I felt tears coming. 'Oh, hell, Julia, why can't people leave me alone?'

'It's obvious why.'

'Oh, I wish ... tell me. Why haven't I had a period for three months? All that Human Biology you do — can you tell me?'

She looked totally shocked. 'What!! You're not ...'

'Don't be stupid. I haven't been anywhere near a boy since ...' Still I can't say it, still I can't control the tears.

She put her arm around my shoulders as I wept. 'I don't know. Haven't you asked your Mum?'

'I can't talk to her any more.'

'Your Gran? No? What about your coach?'

'He's been away. His mother died.'
'When's he coming back?'
'This week some time.'
'Well, ask him. You might need a check-up. You *do* need a check-up, you're so skinny and scrawny I'm surprised your mother hasn't hauled you off already.'
'That drunken bastard, Julia, do you know he's shot through to Aussie? Killing, mudering someone, and he's going to get away with it? And his wife can't or won't say anything and doesn't have to.'
'Who are you talking about?'
'The driver of the car that . . .'
'Who told you?'
'Keith.'
'He would. The creep. The tactless, thoughtless, stupid little creep.'
'Did you know too?'
'Oh yes, I've known for months.' She waited for my tears to abate, which of course they did. 'I'm sorry, Alex, it's rotten. Oh, yes.' Changing the subject. 'My mum was at Mrs Benton's for coffee recently. She said the house is amazing.'
'Yeah, it is,' I said gloomily.
'She said Mrs Benton's a bit odd. She kept talking about you all the time.'
'All lies, I bet.'
'No, all compliments. Couldn't say a thing against you. Wanted to know more, since you and Maggie are going to Rome together.'
Mrs Benton knew all about me already. I didn't like the sound of this.

The house is full of things Italian. Mum has organized the kids into getting huge posters which line the hall, my bedroom, the kitchen — crude wobbly images of the dome of St Peters, the Colosseum, famous Roman arches, the leaning tower of Pisa, the canals of Venice and the great bronze Bapistery gates of Florence. She gets books from the library in heaps — every travel book that's ever been written — and brochures from travel agents, and reads them over meals. Dad has hauled out his diaries from his time in the Mediterranean during the war — his ship was based in Malta, he says, but he did visit Naples and some of the southern ports and went to an opera house, though he can't remember what he saw.

The music! The music teacher at school and Mum both get records of Callas and Tebaldi and Giuseppe di Stefano and the house rings with arias from *Butterfly, Tosca, Aida, Rigoletto, Traviata* until the neighbours complain and the kids go and play with their friends. Mum finds out that during the Games they are doing a massive production of *Aida*, outdoors, and so she gets a complete recording and for several nights we all sit down — not the kids — and listen to the whole thing, following the story and the words on a booklet that comes in the box. By the end I'm a jelly.

And the artworks! Mum gets books on Michelangelo and Leonardo and Giotto and we pore over them together. She gets a phrase book and starts practising Italian, jollying me along with her, which dissolves the kids into helpless laughter. 'Parlo Italiano.' 'Buon giorno, signora.' 'Scusi, signore, mi può dire che ora è, per piacere.' 'Certo, signore, sono le due e venti.' Etcetera.

And the clothes! The day I was selected Gran hauled out every pattern she has for me, discards most of them, and takes me into the material shop in town to work down her list of clothes I'll need. 'It's going to be hot, so mostly drip-dry cottons, none of those jeans, my girl' she says firmly. 'Girls look like girls in Italy. We want you to look nice too, don't we.' We come home armed with about ten patterns — dresses, skirts, shorts, tops — and as many lengths of material. Where she gets the money from in one fell swoop, I don't know. How she fits in all this extra sewing for me along with her programme of baby dresses and all the other things she does, is no mystery. I often hear the sewing machine whirring away when I'm up prowling the house at midnight, unable to sleep.

I wonder at all this love and preparation and sharing in my trip — but how can I ever shout at them all, it's no use, no use, turn off the record-player, take all the books away, rip down the posters; stop it, Gran, hunched over your Singer in the middle of the night, stop it, all of you, in my bones I know I'm not going. I've been betrayed once; don't lead me on, down a road that doesn't lead to Rome.

Dad and I took Mrs Jack out to the airport to meet Mr Jack, because she's one of those wives who doesn't drive. She was looking plumper than ever, hair specially done, but anxious. She was, she said, 'one of those people who eats'. The past weeks had seemed an eternity.

'Me too,' I said.

'I don't like the nights much. It's the first time I've been alone at nights.'

'Pity you couldn't have gone over too,' said Dad.

'Well, the fares aren't cheap, and someone had to look after the cats. Besides, I don't really . . . his family . . .' I thought, it's what people *don't* say that's interesting.

'The aircraft landed half an hour ago,' said the clerk at the TEAL desk. 'It was early, strong tail winds.' I looked around the airport lounge, a pretty bleak and cheerless place despite the people waiting for passengers. Three months and I'll be out here, going! I can say it now, going to Rome! Are you excited, Alex? If not, why not?

Mr Jack was one of the last out of Customs. He looked tired and thinner. We hung back, but over Mrs Jack's shoulder I saw him looking at me. He was never much good at hiding his thoughts, and what I saw was a frown of concern and disbelief, before a weary smile.

'Alex, champ, you made it,' he said, tears in his eyes, and mine too, as we had a good cuddle. 'Jim, good to see you,' he said shaking Dad's hand. He looked back at me, up and down, like a trainer might look at a racehorse.

'You've lost weight,' he said.

'So've you,' I said lightly. 'I'm sorry about your Mum.'

'It's been pretty rugged. Even if she'd had a good innings. Well, Alex, tomorrow morning? Down to work?'

'I haven't exactly been sitting around . . .'

'I can see that,' he said quickly. 'But it's different now. And better, we know where we're going. You've done a great job, Jim, and no doubt Steve too.'

'Ahhhh — well . . .' I said.
He looked up from checking his bags. 'Didn't work out?' I shook my head. 'Interesting,' he said, glancing sideways at Dad. 'We've some fences to mend, eh?'

It was more than that. Mr Jack was there on the side of the pool the next morning, at six, sure enough, and no one was gladder than me to see him there. But he told Dad he was shocked to the core by my gaunt appearance and hollow bloodshot eyes. And my surly manner hadn't improved, if anything, it was worse. He should have known that I'd rub Steve up the wrong way, and vice versa.

Worse, my stroke had gone to the dogs and he was amazed how I'd managed to produce the times I did in those final time trials, if *that* was how I was getting through the water. Finally, when did I have my last period; *four* months ago? Hardly surprising given stress and me being a stone less than my normal racing weight, and I still seemed, no don't say anything Alex, I just want you to listen; I think, Jim, the child is still pining, still grieving, and might need some professional help if she can't begin to cope with it soon. Anyway, I'm to have a complete medical check-up. This week.

All this was the night after he got home, another of those 'putting cards on the table' sessions. 'I'm not pulling any punches, Alex,' he said. 'You can hear everything I have to say to your father. It's too late for pussyfooting around.'

He looks about as tired and grey and old as I feel.

'I gather the team leaves for Rome on the tenth of August, which gives us just under three months. We'll cut back to once a day training, and make the other session weights and calisthenics. Just for two or three weeks, give her eyes a rest too. I don't suppose she's doing any stupid things we don't know about, like playing hockey?'

'Not that I'm aware.'

'Well, check up. Alex, please sit down.'

'Have I disappeared? Can't you see me sitting in this chair?'

'Oh, yes I can, and I remember about ten months ago sitting in the same chair looking at you with a broken leg, up to your thigh in plaster. Remember? And how did it get broken?'

Hockey, because I wasn't prepared to give it up.'

'And did any of us know what was going on?' He turned back to Dad. 'Talk to her school if necessary. She needs no extra pressures there. She needs to eat more, and sleep more. I'll increase her vitamins.'

'I'm not playing hockey, or any other damn thing besides swimming,' I mumbled.

'You're going to Rome, Alex,' he said, unperturbed. 'Worth it? Is life worth living?'

I couldn't reply, because I didn't really know the answer.

'You've got to decide. And soon.'

I make one decision the next day.

'I'm not going.'

'Alex, please.'

'If that silly cousin of mine goes and gets herself pregnant, why should we have to drive all the way to Hamilton for her wedding?'

'You don't know she's pregnant.'

'Oh, Mum. An invitation arrives dripping with gold for a wedding in two weeks' time. I saw the look you gave Gran. And Auntie Pat rang the other night, late, to break the glad tidings.'

'How did...'

'I heard Dad talking to her.' Does she assume that I *sleep* at nights? I'm sorry Pat, he said, very sorry, of course we'll come, you're having *how* many people? In the *cathedral*?

Mum's lips are twitching, despite herself.

'You're coming,' she says, pleasantly.

'I'm not. Wild horses...'

'Alex, on this occasion you're not being given the choice. The family is going, you're family, and that's that.'

I go into my bedroom, slam the door and literally pound the walls. I'm not ready for any wedding, shotgun or not, Hamilton or wherever, in a cathedral or a tent, in false white or brazen scarlet, with a baby or without a baby, with two guests or two hundred. Then I march out to see Gran in her little baby dress factory.

'Why is it so important, Gran? *Why?*'

Her tiny feet are pumping the sewing machine treadle, flat out. Against the windows on three sides of her bedroom, added on specially when she came to live with us, the rain beats, the bare peach tree branches clack.

'God, it's cold in here,' I say. No wonder she is wearing two jumpers and a great thick long cardigan over her skinny frame, tweed skirt, thick stockings and fluffy slippers.

'You can put the heater on.' A pitiful one-bar heater stands unused.

'Tell me *why*. No one would ever miss me.'

'Well. Your cousin's having a baby. Her parents are making the best of it, as yours would for you. No listen, Alex. Families close ranks at times like these. They honour the customs, they put on a brave face.'

'But we're not her family. Mum doesn't even like Auntie Pat.'

'Your father is her brother. That's family.'

'And we tag along.'

Gran nods, roaring up another yellow organza seam, down a pink one, up a blue one, pumping at the treadle like an ancient harmonium, expertly clipping the seams and threads away, while I sit on.

'It's ... I don't want ...'

The rhythm of the needle never falters. 'You fear the young couple might clearly be in love. You fear something worse, they might not be, it's an empty ritual. And you are dreading all those fawning, well-dressed strangers, "Virginia's clever cousin, I've read about you in the papers".'

She often surprises me, Gran.

'Yes?' She looks at me sideways over the top of her sewing glasses.

'They'll never miss me.'

'Your Mum 'n' Dad will.'

'I didn't think they cared, that much.'

She lets that one lie in the air between us. Nothing is said, but I feel deeply reproached, not harshly but sadly. Even you, Gran, I've finally got offside even with you.

I'm still not going.

I make another decision, first day back at school, when the combined smiles and whispers and pointed fingers and congratulations of too many staff and too many Third Formers become altogether too much.

'I'd like to try,' I tell Miss Macrae after assembly and all that *that* entailed.

'Good, splendid. I presume your parents are happy? You've discussed it with them?'

It's easier to nod. I'm sure they would be if I explained it to them; that it was only three scenes from a very worthwhile play and all I have to do before I go away is learn a few lines and go to a rehearsal once a week; and although you can see my permanent pink eyeballs, what you can't see is my brain getting pickled in salt water; of course they're happy.

It's only the first scene, where Joan first appears as a simple country girl and talks her way into an audience with the Dauphin; the short scene by the river, Joan as the soldier, waiting impatiently for the wind to change to begin the battle; and the Trial Scene, Joan as prisoner, defeated in battle and on trial for her life. Not the whole play, three shortish scenes.

There's another reason, too, why it's become important to me. After the May holidays, all that most people can talk about is the dances they went to, how many and where, who with, who other people went with and how often, and what they wore. People don't expect me to join in; they know I'm right out of the social whirl, that I wasn't invited to one single dance; they know I had a boyfriend, once; now they seem to know something else about me.

It's lunch break, inside because the rain is belting down, the macrocarpa trees around the playing fields are bending to the gale, the netball courts are under water and the hockey field is awash. Though it's against the rules, I've gone back into the classroom to read, to get away from the hen talk in the hall.

Julia sits herself down beside me. I know it's Julia because no one else bellows and wheezes like that.

'What you reading? Oh, *Saint Joan.*'

'Mmm.'

'I hear Miss Macrae wants to do some of it in her Shaw thing.' I grunt. 'Has she chosen people?'

'Mmmm.'
'Are you doing Joan?'
'Maybe.'
She's not impressed, I can tell by the silence.
'So why shouldn't I do Joan?' I say suddenly looking at her straight.
'Oh, no reason, if...'
'If what?'
She's horribly, embarrassingly embarrassed. What is she trying to tell me as she struggles for air?
'There's rumours.'
'There's always rumours.'
'Joan will make it ... worse.'
I understand. Type-casting, if you're ignorant enough to think there was something queer about Joan. So, rumours about my lack of femininity have surfaced again. Last year only Andy and Julia knew that I knew what was being said; only Andy ever dared raise the subject. Please, *not* again.

'Joan is not ... for heaven's sake, the first paragraph of the Preface, look here.' I wave a shaking book at her, oh, how the leaves of the little book are shaking. 'See, "the pioneer of rational dressing for women ... she refused to accept the specific ..."' I stumble twice over specific. Julia waits.

'And who from, this time?'
She is wheezing, pumping, fumbling with her pill bottle.
'My mother ...'
'Your *mother*? Oh, I see, she's upset and worried that one of her daughter's friends might be ... and warning you to stay away, that it?'

Don't make it any easier for her, will you?
'No, no. It's just, she heard ...'
'At another of those precious coffee mornings? Or little groups tittley-tattling over bridge?'

The bell starts ringing and some people open the door into the classroom. 'You're interrupting! Get out!' They have as much right to be in the classroom as I have, but they flee at least temporarily. I'm leaning over Julia's shoulder like a baddie threatening a goodie in a cheap Hollywood movie. 'Was it at Mrs Benton's?'

'No, I told you, she's all sweetness and light.'
That's what worries me. Don't relax yet. With head tipped back, Julia is trying to gather enough saliva in her mouth to swallow down the pill. If I had an ounce of human kindness in me I'd offer to get her a drink of water from the cloakroom.

She swallows, coughs and says hoarsely, 'Someone whose daughter goes to Maggie's school, Mum wouldn't say.'

'Naturally. Of course she wouldn't.'

I go back to *Joan*. My rigid fingers are still holding open the first page of the Preface ... *and innumerable obscure heroines who have disguised themselves as soldiers and sailors, she refused to accept the specific woman's lot, and dressed and fought and lived as men did.*

'Why did you tell me, Julia? What am I expected to do about it? Grow my hair. Get a boyfriend. Start wearing lipstick all the time. Throw a brick at all the Third Formers who follow me around. Prove something.'

'I thought you should ...'

'No.' Know, no, NO.'

'No one else'll tell you,' she bursts out, defending herself.

'So you've told me. You've *told* me. Now what?' I toss *Joan* inside my desk, slam down the lid, fling wide the door, push through the people waiting outside the door, ignore the booming voice of Miss Macrae following me down the corridor and take myself for another very long bike ride in the rain, skip calisthenics, fool Mum that I'm getting 'flu and end up cold, shivering, sleepless, tearless, sexless, friendless, hopeless, helpless, curled up rocking like a baby on the floor behind the locked door of my bedroom.

A skeleton called Alex gets up in the morning, goes to training, goes to school, hears nothing, says nothing, learns nothing, does nothing. Another cardboard person called Alex goes through the motions of appearing normal-if-a-bit-withdrawn; something tells her that she must.

The night before the wedding she tries to throw a sickie. Her sinus has been playing up genuinely, her eyes look as though she has some terrible medieval disease, and the idea of her poor pregnant cousin being hauled to the altar in white satin and lace sickens her. It'll be one of those weddings that ends up in Gran's *Weekly News*, BELLS RING FOR JUNE BRIDES.

'We'll leave after your training, about nine thirty,' says Mum. 'Pat's putting on a light lunch at the house beforehand.'

She's picking at her dinner, not hungry anyway.

'Eat up, Alex,' pleads Gran. 'Spinach makes your hair curl.' The idea of her with curls is so ludicrous she doesn't even bother to snort. 'Please, dearest.'

'There's 'flu around at school.'

Mum says nothing, but after dinner she arrives in her bedroom shaking down a thermometer. She had intended to cook the thermometer under the hot tap to read a hundred and two; Mum beats her to it. Her temperature is normal. Mum assesses her professionally. She knows that look.

'What are you going to wear tomorrow?'

'I'm not feeling well.'

'You're not looking well, but that's a separate issue. I'm asking you to come tomorrow, for your father's sake.'

'I've got nothing to wear to a wedding.'

'This do?' Mum goes out into the hallway and brings back a dress on a hanger, a simple pinafore in a soft plaid of blues and greens. Her fingers tell her it's fine wool, probably expensive. 'Should be warm enough, with a plain blouse underneath, your black court shoes.'

'Gran-made?'

Mum nods, her trump card. Cardboard Alex sighs, vanquished. It's a Simplicity pattern Gran has used for her before; she chose the material well, and probably spent her last pound on it. That's what she's been doing this past week, sewing a wedding pinafore on top of all those baby dresses and clothes for Rome. She had thought Gran was upset with her.

'I'm not wearing a hat.'

'I'm not asking you to.'

The voice on the telephone, thought Joyce Benton, belonged to someone who was flustered, who didn't understand the subtleties of negotiation, keeping doors open, gentle persuasion.

'She was very off-hand,' said Jane Sutherland.

'Yes, she can be, but what was the outcome?'

'Not exactly 'no', but well, indifferent. Rather rude, really. Unwilling to commit herself to a function so far ahead.'

'Six weeks?' Joyce Benton stared at the Chinese painting which hung above the telephone table in her hallway, her mind working hard on the implications of this setback. 'Well, it was a grand idea of yours, Jane.'

'Of course, we can still get the swim-suits and just Maggie will be fine, with one or two of the other girls. I'm sure we can find a suitable girl.' They may be prettier, she thought, but none of them have Alex's figure, her height and slenderness, her background of ballet; not to mention the coup of two Olympic girls. She'd been taken back by the girl's sullen voice, no life in it at all.

'You don't want me,' she had said flatly. 'I'm not the model type. You want ... you know, girls with waists and pretty smiles and curls.'

'Perhaps,' Joyce Benton was saying in her clipped remote way, '... what date have you set, Jane?'

'Last week in July. The 29th. A Friday afternoon.'

Cutting it fine, thought Joyce Benton. 'Maggie and I will be back from Queensland on the 24th.'

'You're going to Australia?'

'Tomorrow, you're lucky to have caught me. Maggie can't train another day in that pool. The specialist says she runs the risk of permanent damage.'

'Dear me, what to?'

'Her eyes. Every session is sheer torture. It's salt water, badly chlorinated and then heated. And they don't get any special privileges, the public jump in, get in the way.'

'It sounds appalling.'

'After two laps, Maggie can't even see. By the time she's done two and half miles, her eyes look quite dreadful. So we're going back to Queensland, the same pool and a rather special coach, where I took her last year.'

'Lucky girl,' said Jane Sutherland. 'I suppose Alex just has to ...'

Joyce Benton cut in sharply. It had crossed her mind that she could have offered to take Alex to Australia with Maggie; her family couldn't afford it; her conscience was clear. 'Jane, ring me when we get back. I really don't want to commit Maggie either. The team leaves for Rome on August the tenth, not a great deal of time, obviously.'

'Just one rehearsal, Joyce, and it's all in school time. Did I tell you the Head is delighted? We're sending out printed invitations and the money is going to the Crippled Children Society.'

'I'm so glad,' murmured Joyce Benton, weary. There was some way round this problem, she knew, but her immediate concern was tomorrow's departure for Brisbane. 'I think you're doing a wonderful job, Jane. Please excuse me, I have to go and pick up Maggie.'

Home after training, I find the house unnaturally quiet, with the three others farmed out for the day, and both Gran and Mum looking unnaturally smart. Gran has hauled out her 19-year-old brown tweed best suit, and a strange little hat, and Mum has an eight-year-old navy suit and (as they say in the *Weekly News*) 'white accessories'. There'd been some discussion as to whether Dad should hire 'morning dress', whatever that meant, but in the end he climbs into his one grey suit. I envy him his lack of fuss; the only frivolous decision he has to make is his tie.

Dressed up, we pass with a push. My pinafore hangs in interesting folds over hips that have never been slimmer. Mum produces some nice stockings and lends me black gloves and handbag to go with my black court shoes; I cut off a few spiky bits of hair and it looks worse than ever. Mum has also got Gran a spray of pink carnations to pin on her lapel, and a single white carnation for Dad as the bride's uncle. I sleep all the way to Hamilton, my head on Gran's bony, tweedy shoulder, smelling of Yardley's lavender water.

I haven't seen Auntie Pat's house in years. Not much of it is visible today, because a huge tent-like thing, decorated with golden ribbons and hanging baskets of yellow and white flowers, has been put up in the garden. 'They took a risk, in June. Lucky with the weather,' says Dad, as we walk up the driveway carefully lined with neat plants. The sunshine here is crisper, colder than home. Inside the house, which is boring brick and tile, the first thing I notice is a busy, bilious green, floral carpet arguing with all the wallpapers. The 'light lunch' for relatives from out of town consists of four tables groaning with sausage rolls, club sandwiches, sponge cakes, butterfly cakes, the *Edmonds Cook Book* come to life. She must have been cooking for weeks.

Cousin Virginia, plain to start with, looks as brittle as a celluloid bride doll. In guipure lace, satin, net and seed pearls, diamante tiara, the works; she's agreed to be a triumph. The dress has a twenty inch waistline and a Merry Widow girdle underneath, no concessions to a baby there. Her beehive hair-do, even from across the room, is stiff with beads of hairspray; make-up is a demure pink mask. I find myself staring at this Christmas tree fairy, wondering how she'd arrived at this point: the groping in a car, two weeks overdue, three, four; the telling scenes, him, both sets of parents; the tears over the alternatives of having the baby in disgrace and adoption, or a fast wedding before it shows; who had won, in the end? So there she stands. The Bride, on the happiest day of her life, pinned against the venetian blinds while the photographer sets up his gear. She sees me staring. I deserve a poked-out tongue, what I get is a terrible blank gaze in return. She makes my blood run cold.

Auntie Pat, in cream silk, is beside herself. The bouquets haven't arrived.

'Oh, here's Alex, *dear*, Helena, Jim, lovely to see you, thank you, all that way. We're all a bit, oh dear. One of the bridesmaids keeps feeling faint, one of *those* days. Oh, darling, you got in the team, well done, lovely to see you, Ginnie's *so* glad ..'

Ginnie's not with us at all, I think. Her bridesmaids, three of them, crowd the lounge, bulging in golden satin like ripe apricots, amid the stench of hairspray. Like Ginnie, they are not all that much older than me, and too carried away to take much notice of me in my plaid pinafore. I'd once thought that when I married it would have been in Grecian style like one of those old statues in the Museum. Plain white silk, straight and simple, not a flounce nor a shred of lace anywhere, flowers in my long hair, no jewellery, no veil; a man in white, with brass buttons, a naval sword. A garden wedding, under the pohutukawa and magnolia trees ...

A wicked echo of Julia's last words makes me pluck a white flower from the garden on the way to the church and poke it behind my ear. 'That's nice, dear,' says Gran, not understanding. 'Pretty.'

Somehow we all get to the cathedral, which is the biggest church

I've ever been in, full of flowers and people in silk suits and swathed turbans and furs and what I now know is called morning dress or penguin suit. Grey top hats, like the Ascot scene in *My Fair Lady*, and everywhere the smell of perfume and face powder and mothballs. There is a huge choir in red gowns, and a small thin person who turns out to be the groom, Ginnie's ballroom dancing partner, naughty man, who looks equally terrified.

We have to sit up the front, among 'family' on 'the bride's side'. The first thing that happens is that Virginia is forty-five minutes late. *Forty-five*. The organ plays, the choir sings, and sings again, a vicar makes two reassuring announcements and the guests, relishing the prospect of a complication, start to talk softly and turn around to see if anything's happening. Finally, Auntie Pat scuttles alone up the side aisle and collapses on the pew in front of us; hat feathers, fur stole, silk sleeves all a-quiver; what *has* been going on?

The organ pounds out the wedding march and we all leap to our feet and sing madly — Praise my Soul, the King of Heaven — before the bridge changes her mind completely or the groom gets fed up. I turn and look: behind several robed vicars walks a puce-faced Uncle Arnold with a veiled livin' doll leaning slightly on his arm, followed by the apricots, looking less than ecstatic. The service proceeds, formal and hushed and relentless, up and down for hymns, prayers, readings. Auntie Pat's glistening fur stole betrays her. 'With this ring, I thee wed . . .' Although we are only a few feet from Ginnie and her husband of a few seconds, we can barely hear her responses, while her mother weeps.

When the bridal couple walk down the aisle at the end, Ginnie is leaning slightly inwards in much the same way as she leaned on her father, smiling brilliantly as though her face had cracked. His face, little fox-trotting Mervyn, is darkly flushed. I feel very sorry for him, until I discover that 'family' are expected to follow the bridal party, solemnly in pairs. I cannot escape having to file out after Mum and Dad, arm in arm with tiny Gran, which must look hilarious. I snap my sunglasses on my head to cover eyes which are both sore and wet with tears of anger, and somehow we make it down the nineteen miles of rich ruby carpet, through a forest of curious eyes. Flowers in the hair are not a usual substitute for a hat, except on a young girl; I'm too tall for a girl but not a woman either.

Outside the cathedral and again back at the marquee begins the waiting: for family portraits; for the bridal party to go for formal studio pictures and come back an hour later; for the receiving lines. Meanwhile there are the waiters bearing silver trays of shallow glasses of French champagne, greetings, introductions, gushings, eyeings up and down. I don't fit in here, we don't, we four Archers from ordinary old Epsom, Auckland; among these rich silk suits that are quickly getting spotted with food, osprey hats snagged on tent poles, English stiletto shoes pegging their wearers into the damp grass, penguin suits smeared with spilt drink, squashed top hats and little fox faces hanging down the furred backs of well-fed and dotty old women. The coat off an animal's back is bad enough, but keeping its dried-up head, whiskers, eyeballs and all, is *disgusting*.

I stick close to Gran, but she is waltzed away to meet some old cronies, so there's only Mum 'n' Dad 'n' me crushed along with three hundred others into the marquee because that's where the food is, and outside a cold niggling wind is blowing away any warmth in the late afternoon sun. I overhear comments about 'bad form', which turn out to be not about racehorses, nor the haste of the wedding, but about Ginnie's lateness at the church. The reason why has not yet got about. People jostle past and say 'Oh, you must be Alex-who-swims, Virginia's cousin, going to the Olympics, how nice, dear. In August? Are you going Mrs Archer, no, well I hope the chaperon's on her toes, those naughty Italians; pinch your beautiful bottom they will, m' dear'.

I discover that a hard level stare registering no reaction works quite well; I am as tall as most men; they turn away puzzled, to more interesting topics like old Stanley's recent operation, or the price of lambs in the UK, or their wonderful flight up from Christchurch on the Viscount, the central North Island mountains sporting early snow and clear as a bell. The All Blacks have won their first few provincial matches in South Africa; whether or not the team should have gone without the Maoris is a dead duck, and Sharpeville never rates a mention. One or two men who read the sports pages say, oh yes, you and that Benton girl, good stuff, dear.

In the crush I get swept away from Mum 'n' Dad, towards the

billowing sides of the marquee. There is no one else my age and no other female hatless. Most of the three hundred range from middle-aged to ancient, except for a small group of Virginia's smart friends. When I can go no further, I'm up against a row of small chairs provided for the old ladies; like one myself, I sink gratefully down on the last vacant seat. The old dears next door go on nattering loudly; Ginnie always has been a bit of a problem; she was late, disgraceful really, because she decided two minutes before the bridal cars arrived that she'd rather have the baby adopted and not marry Mervyn, and poor old Arnold had to say it was a bit late for that, Virginia, with the Bishop and three hundred guests waiting at the church. Only threatening to disown her made her see sense, poor child. Dis-own? Throw out of house, write out of will? Always money, somewhere. I hate bullies. I know further why I want to do law. I find my eyes full of tears for her, and all those dumpy girls knitting bootees Julia once talked of, and myself who people consider too manly to want to have a baby, one day; Andy's baby, a boy, never to be. Fat, full tears brim over, drip down my cheeks. A youngish waitress comes over with a tray of glasses shaped like saucers. Up till now I've only had orange juice, and refused all food.

'You look as though you need one of these,' she says. 'It's not the end of the world.' She leans down and whispers in my ear. 'You'd be surprised how many weddings we do like this, two weeks' notice, bun in the oven already.' I knock back one glass and take another. 'Atta girl. Cheer up.' It's the French champagne that's been flowing like water for an hour. It's clean-tasting and fizzy; a third goes down like lemonade. It's a mistake.

'Charge your glasses, ladies and gentlemen!' So I do, because another waitress is pushing her way through the crowd, working her way along the row of flushed old ducks with a huge green bottle wrapped in a cloth. Even sitting down, I can't seem to hold my glass awfully steady. Some spills on to the grass. Perhaps someone pushed her elbow. Far away, past the solid wall of eye-level bottoms, I hear an ancient, quavery, male voice droning on. I catch about every tenth word — Virginia — our radiant bride — since a little girl. Words to that effect.

I can stand for the toast. 'The happy couple.' I have an extra one for the baby; a few people look round as though someone has said a terrible swear word, and mutter to each other. The bridegroom's speech I can't hear at all. I can still stand for the next toast, although as I do a hiccup escapes and I have a slight bout of coughing while people turn and stare. 'The bridesmaids, bless them,' and I add an extra sip for the bridegroom — poor little fox-trotting Mervyn because, with a mother-in-law like Auntie Pat, boy, is he going to need it.

I can hear the best man only too well, because he's fearsomely handsome like Gregory Peck and has an actor's voice to match. He flatters the bridesmaids to the skies and reads out some crude, tasteless telegrams, which *I* can tell don't go down too well under the circumstances, and so can the old ducks next door, who are by this time muttering and nudging each other and staring at me. The baskets of flowers and strings of coloured lights above me are now out of focus and rather small; I'm looking down the wrong end of a smudgy telescope. I am feeling both terribly ill and an urgent need to find a loo. I think I am going to be sick.

'The bride and groom will now cut the cake.'

I believe I am whirling into space; falling off my chair.

I believe I am making an effort to stay upright. Or maybe I'm trying to crawl underneath the tent flap out into the cool air. Or maybe, hearing the crack of wood beneath me, I am breaking my chair. Of course, built like a tank; she would! Or maybe I am actually vomiting French champagne on to the damp grass. I really can't remember.

I remember waking up. I'm juddering, convulsing, coming back from the dead. Someone is pushing my head down on to my knees. Voices boom in my ears.

'Stand back. Give her some air.' Male, in charge.

'What's wrong with the child?' Female, curious.

'Fainted, that's all.' Male, matter-of-fact.

'Just keeled over.' Female, startled.

'Or rather too much . . .' Female, whispering.

'Alex?' Mum, at last. 'Where have you been?'

'Ask a silly question . . .' Me, grinning.

I know it's her arm around me, her fingers taking my pulse, her voice requesting air and some help to get me outside. My head is spinning and I'm weeping quietly, as a woman's voice with a pommie accent, high-pitched like the Queen, penetrates all too clearly through the crowd noises.

'Isn't that Virginia's cousin, the Olympic girl from Auckland? Something of a madam, Joyce says. I do believe the child has been drinking.'

'Not at all,' says Mum loudly. 'This child has already swum six miles this morning.' You exaggerate, Mum! And she's not finished yet. 'She's a finely-tuned athlete, in extremely heavy training, not used to standing round for such long periods.' It's quite convincing, since I've actually been sitting for the past half hour.

'I'm training for Rome, ma'am,' I hear myself saying with great dignity, 'Maggie and I are both going to Rome. Together. Although, Maggie's in Australia and that silly prick of a selector, Mr ...'

'That's enough, Alex!' Mum's voice, her best nurse's voice, loud and cold. Her strong arms are pulling me to my feet. She's dealt with nutcases before.

'I want to lie down,' I say, as the marquee goes round and round above my head.

'Into the house,' says Dad. They walk one on each side of me while I sing *Three Coins in the Fountain* and the guests part like the Red Sea. Behind me, I hear, 'Ladies and gentlemen, your attention please. The bride and groom will now cut the cake.' I've almost certainly spoiled Virginia's big moment and Auntie Pat's grand wedding, the youngest guest blotto on French champers.

My feet won't work properly, but we're out of the marquee, and away from those voices. The cold dusk air makes me gasp. To give her her due, Auntie Pat comes rushing out behind us.

'Helena, I'm so sorry. This is most unfortunate, shall I call an ambulance?'

'Of course not,' says Mum. 'She's just a little faint. Her period on top of seven miles of training this morning and all this standing around.' *Seven* miles now and my first period in five months! Perhaps the back of my dress is stained and I don't know it. I didn't know Mum could lie like a flatfish.

After vomiting into a flower bed on the way into the house, I slept in a spare bedroom for maybe an hour and woke around eight with a throbbing head.

'Water,' I croaked to the upright little figure of Gran keeping watch on the end of the bed. I lay there for a bit. At least the room wasn't whirling round. Mum came in, and, rather unnecessarily I thought, took my pulse again.

'How are you feeling?'

'Fantastic.'

'Virginia and Mervyn are just leaving. After that, we'll be going too.'

'I'll get up.'

'You don't have to.'

'I want to.' And I meant it, to hold my head high and have the pleasure of looking right through those smugly disapproving people. I got vertical and nearly changed my mind.

'Good girl,' said Gran. We went quietly out to the front porch where Virginia was saying tearful goodbyes under the coloured lights, and Mervyn looked as though he'd danced his last waltz. Their car, decked out with ribbons, buckets, tins, and rude signs, waited below in the driveway. Virginia was dressed in a quite revolting going-away suit of orange, with nipped-in waist, matching hat, black gloves and the highest stiletto heels I have ever seen. Female squeals went up when she threw her bouquet towards the twittering bunch of apricot bridesmaids, ripe for the picking. One had already homed in on Gregory Peck, clutching at his arm. In the shadows no one took any notice of me when tears fell; I have seen Andy again, a face among the crowds down there around the departing car. Please, leave me alone.

And that might have been the end of an awful day, except that Auntie Pat, now that she had done her duty and gone through this charade, got stuck into the gin bottle. If we'd had any sense we'd have left half an hour earlier than we did.

'Just come and sit down for ten minutes,' she pleaded to Dad. 'I've hardly seen you, Jim.' Dad hesitated. 'And Alex, are you feeling better now?'

'Yes thank you, Auntie Pat.'

'Just go into the living-room, I'll be with you in a minute. There are a lot of people leaving.' So we small talked with other relatives until she came back with a large gin in her hand and collapsed on to the sofa next to Mum.

'Thank God that's over.' We all knew what she meant. She took a large swig, lit up another cigarette, and started to talk to Mum. From my chair alongside Gran, on the other side of the floral carpet, I saw Mum's smile getting more and more inscrutable, like a camel. Then quite suddenly, unusual for someone who is big and moves rather slowly, she heaved herself out of the sofa and made a beeline for me and Gran. Auntie Pat's voice beat her to it.

'Alex,' she cried. 'Come and talk to your Auntie Pat.'

I could hardly refuse. 'We're going,' Mum muttered as we passed. 'Say your goodbyes.'

But Auntie Pat was patting the empty seat beside her, and I had to sit down. She had never taken much notice of me in the past, and I saw no reason to get all palsy-walsy now.

'So tall and handsome, our Olympic girl. I don't see enough of you, do I? I was just telling your dear mother, it was such a shame you couldn't be a bridesmaid today.'

'Why not?'

'Virginia felt, it wouldn't have looked quite right, now would it?'

What was she talking about?

'Pity you got it from both sides. Your father was a beanpole at fourteen, like our father, and then he went and married your mother, who's no thistle-down is she.'

I'm not usually thick, but I still didn't know what that had to do with me not being a bridesmaid.

'Ginnie knew you'd understand. Not being a bridesmaid.'

As if it mattered, if it meant apricot satin. 'I don't mind.'

'Such a short man she's married. He says he's five foot eight, but you'd hardly know it. Anyway, it would have been, you know, rather like David and Goliath.'

'You mean, I'm Goliath?'

'Oh, dear, no,' she giggled, meaning yes. 'But you understand. I didn't think your dear mother did, quite . . .' She took another swig of gin. 'But then I didn't expect that she would.'

One thing I've learned this past year is that sometimes saying nothing is the best way of finding out what's going on. People can't bear the sound of their own silence.

'All that swimming, made you so bulky, those shoulders ...'
I think she actually shuddered.

'I like my shoulders.'

'And I hear you want to be a lawyer?'

'Yes.'

'Whatever for?'

'Use my brain. Help people in trouble. Know how to stand up to bullies. Bring murderers to justice.'

'My dear!'

'I might stand for Parliament. Earn enough money to buy a car, buy a house ...'

'A house? My dear, get a good husband, he buys the house. Like Ginnie, not so clever as you, I always knew that, but only eighteen and married already.' She didn't quite look at me as she said this. 'He mightn't look much, but his father's in furniture, the best business in town, antiques, real English quality — he's the "And Son", you know.'

Who cared? Perhaps Virginia was the smart one after all.

'Alex?' Mum's voice from across the room, sharply. 'We have to go now. Gran's rather tired.'

Auntie Pat's hand was on my knee. 'Take it from your Auntie Pat. Forget all that lawyer nonsense, dear. Men don't like girls with brains. Helena, you and Jim shouldn't encourage her ...'

'We don't, overly. Neither do we discourage her. Alex will decide for herself.'

'But how dangerous! All this sport, and then she wants to be a career girl as well, and you and Jim say nothing?'

'Pat, it's been a good day, a good wedding. You've done a magnificent job and thank you.'

'You'll regret it, when she's thirty and still on your hands.'

I said, 'When I'm thirty I'll be a lawyer and not on anyone's hands.'

'Don't let your mother down, Alexandra.'

'Let her down?'

'Mother of the bride ...'

'And you've done it superbly, Pat. Now ...'

'... that's all any mother wants, don't you, Helena?'

'What I want for Alex is something quite different and doesn't include a hasty marriage, however grand, at eighteen. Alex, go and find your father, please. Gran, we're going.'

'I do believe you're jealous of Virginia, not quite ideal circumstances, I know, but still only a year after being a deb ...'

I was rude enough to laugh.

'You can think that if you wish,' said Mum.

'I do. You were always ...'

'Pat, don't go on. You don't want to spoil your day, neither do I, any further.'

'Well, yes, Alex did steal a wee bit of the show, didn't she? One or two people have told me ...'

'One or two people have got it wrong, Pat, as they always do. Although in Virginia's case ... you are hardly in a position to start pointing a finger at my daughter. Now, where's Dad?' I'd been standing with my mouth open at this unleashing of claws, but one look at Mum's face told me to get moving. She went to get Gran, who was having her own animated last-minute goodbyes with some other old ducks.

I found Dad in the kitchen with Uncle Arnold and a group of penguins, into the whisky and beer and cigars.

'Mum wants you quick quick. We're going.'

'Now?'

'Right this minute, before she and Auntie ...' There were some curious males eyes resting on me in a way I didn't like, eager, gleeful.

'Gran's tired.'

'I'm coming.' But now Mum had followed me, and we were out of there in two minutes flat, goodbyes, thanks. As we drove off to waves and cries, I caught a last glimpse of Auntie Pat. Her hostess mask had gone, she looked exhausted, close to tears, her cream silk dress all crumpled.

Mum broke the silence. 'I went with the best of intentions, Jim. I'm sorry ... her prattle irritates me so, as it always did, and she was being inexcusably rude to Alex.'

'What about?'

'She called me Goliath. Virginia couldn't have me for a bridesmaid because I'm too tall. Men don't like girls with brains, and wanting to be a lawyer is positively weird.' But Dad found it rather funny; so, chuckling alongside, did Gran.

'She's jealous, always was, my poor sister. You're going to the

Olympics and Virginia's put them through the humiliation of a shotgun wedding. Well, it's not the end of the earth. Pat had all sorts of dreams. Ginnie was going to be another Rowena Jackson, but then she went into ballroom. She's a nice kid, but not all that bright.'

Mum said, her voice calmer. 'Give Pat her due, organizing all that in three weeks. Well, at least they didn't throw her out of the house. Some do.'

'He threatened to,' I said.

'Who did?'

'Uncle Arnold, that's why she was late, because she got cold feet and he threatened to disown her. Didn't you hear all the prattle?'

That silenced them. Then Mum sighed.

'I didn't like to ask. Poor Pat, Ginnie wed and gone, what's left?'

'A baby,' I said.

'She'll need something more than a grandchild to babysit,' said Dad, testily. 'She's only forty-six, for God's sake.'

Mum snorted. 'Well, let's see. Good works, meals on wheels. The house is immaculate and no weed dares poke up its head. She doesn't sew, doesn't knit, she's got everything money can buy, Arnold's away on business a lot and he's hardly a ball of fire. And he makes her account for every last penny of the housekeeping money.'

'Did you see all the presents?' said Gran. 'I have never *seen* such a display.'

'On the vulgar side, I thought,' said Dad, mildly. 'A bit overdone.'

We all fell silent. The oncoming lights were hurting my eyes so I snuggled up against Gran.

'You've never told us you wanted to do law, Alex,' said Mum suddenly. 'Why law?'

'Just do.'

'The power to change things, eh?' said Dad.

'Something like that,' I said sleepily.

I was drifting into sleep, feeling carsick. Tomorrow I might have a hangover.

'A finely-tuned athlete.' Mum, you did well. But something I heard in that tent is lying at the back of my memory, niggling me.

I recognized the paper immediately. The thick feel of it, the italic type, the pompous ornate letterhead, the smell of trouble.

'You'd better read it,' said Dad, as Mum shut the bedroom door behind me.

> Dear Mr and Mrs Archer,
> I am writing to you in strictist confidence, with the deepest regret that such a letter is necessary. I have thought hard as to the best course of action to take about this matter. With the best interests of all our young swimmers at heart, it seemed desirable that I should write to you informally and privately to express my concern.
>
> We have all watched Alexandra's career develop with great interest and admiration.

I've read that phrase before.

> Since her nomination in March, Alexandra has displayed commendable tenacity in her quest for Olympic selection. Sadly, this has not always been matched by behaviour which is commensurate with her abilities and performance.

'What does commensurate mean?' I asked.
'In line with, equal to,' said Mum.
'Why doesn't he say so?'
'Businessmen, academics and politicians like long words, Latin words, five words where two would have done,' said Mum.

> I refer to her public criticism of the selectors, her outbursts on the current South African All Black Rugby tour, and her participation in the protest march last month, resulting in some unfortunate publicity. Any one of these one could possibly overlook as evidence of the high-spirited personality we know her to be. However it has come to my attention . . .

'How?' I said.

> ... that at a recent social occasion in Hamilton she was seen to have consumed an amount of hard liquor hardly befitting a New Zealand sporting representative, particularly female, and in this state to have made further ill-considered remarks about officialdom, remarks which could be seen to be singularly lacking in gratitude to the administrators who give freely of their time and expertise to run her chosen sport.

'I only know of one remark,' said Mum. 'Were there others?'
'No,' I said, with more confidence than I felt.

> I am aware that her coach's absence, and the long waiting period between nomination and selection may have contributed. But now that she has, by her own admirable efforts in the pool, won her place in the team, I personally would be saddened to see her jeopardize her place by incidents out of the pool. I have to reluctantly say that should any further incidents like this occur, I shall be compelled to raise with the Olympic selectors and my fellow swimming selectors the question of her suitability to compete in Rome.
> Please understand that I write to you not in my capacity as a National Selector, but as a friend, and a parent myself, in Alexandra's best interests. Her talent is great and I know that, provided she exercises the self-control and behaviour expected of a young girl, she will be a worthy competitor in Rome. I look forward greatly to accompanying her, and Maggie, to Rome and carrying out my duties there as their manager. I hope you will accept this letter in the spirit in which it is written. I believe it would be preferable not to discuss the matter with Bill Jack; I have every confidence in your discretion and judgement as her parents to take whatever steps you feel appropriate. Neither is a reply necessary. The best reply would be that the period between now and our departure in August is free of controversy and further incident involving Alexandra.
>
> Yours most sincerely,
> Cyril Upjohn, Esq.

Ordinary family noises went on, Robert and Jamie scrapping in their bedroom next door, the radio in the kitchen while Gran finished the dinner dishes. Mum and Dad were both looking at their feet. Eventually I broke the

silence.
'Five hundred words to say, "Last warning, sweetie pie".'
'Correct,' said Mum, wearily. 'Has there been a first, Alex?'
'Who told him about the wedding?'
'Does it matter?' said Mum.
'Oh, it matters,' I said. I read the letter again. Then because Mum was smoking, I leaned over, picked up her silver lighter, and deliberately set one corner of the letter alight. We all silently watched it burn down towards my fingers. The flakey ashes fell on to my desk; I held the paper until it was burning my fingertips and I could blow the last flame away. I brushed the blackened tips of my fingers and licked them, feeling the heat on my lips. 'There,' I said. 'Mr Upjohn up in smoke.'
There was another long silence. Then Dad said,
'You shouldn't have done that, Alex.'
'He'll have a copy. He's bound to have a copy.' Then, because my normally sensible, all-knowing parents seemed to be at a loss for words, I said, 'Well, if there's nothing else, I've got homework to do.' I began to scrummage in the mess on my desk.
'Please. Alex. This can't go on.' Dad's voice, low, intense, with a catch in it.
'What can't?'
'For four months nearly, since the nationals — don't you realize you've hardly said a civil word to your family. We've had complaints from school, Miss Gillies and two of the staff, Julia has been around here expressing her concern, and that boy Keith, Mr Jack is worried sick. That letter — if the press got wind of it.'
'Why should they? It's private.'
'They will, if you continue to make scenes and ...'
'Alex Archer dropped from Olympic team, Mr Upjohn reluctantly announced today. I warned her, I sent her a letter. Young swimmer can't behave herself. Disgrace to the family name, letting the school down. Tart, show-off, loudmouth.'
'Alex!'
'Well if it's so bad, if I've been so dreadful to live with, why haven't you said something before? Do you know *why* I had two too many at that ghastly wedding ...'
'Alex, please ...'
'Because you shouldn't have made me go in the first place,

because you shouldn't have let me out of your sight, I hate crowds ... it was all a great lie, a great sham, a great act, like I am. It takes one to know one. So I had a drink or two. So I got a bit squiffy and passed out. So you had to remove me ...'

I stopped, because a cultured and penetrating English voice is ringing in my head.

'*Something of a madam*, Joyce says.'

Mrs Benton's name is Joyce.

'What's the matter, Alex? Please, please tell us.'

While I stare at her, Mum has knelt at my feet and taken my hands in hers and is desperately trying to reach me. I see her lips moving, and catch about every twentieth word: we've been trying so hard, all of us, to understand; Andy was a fine boy; but; my whole life ahead of me; asking so little; coming to terms; we've hoped, we've prayed, as every day has passed ... please, Alex, *try*.

I am trying, I scream silently. But how can you fight something so ... vicious. I can hear her now. 'Oh, Mr Upjohn, I thought you should know ...'

I haven't kept her precious daughter out of the team. So why is she still trying to destroy me?

I can't bear the sight of Mum's wet brown eyes any longer. I leave my desk, the room and the house. Mum doesn't like me walking round the streets after dark, but that night, I finally have to escape, from the suffocation of their worry, from the posters of Rome the kids have pinned up in the hallway and Gran listening to the Quiz Kids in the kitchen; from their common sense, their logic, their expectations, their impatience, coming to terms, pulling myself together, counting my blessings, and fleeing from their love; most of all, love.

So I run. Away, I suppose you could say. Through the rain, puddles, traffic lights, late Friday night shopping, cars, lights, people, reflections, water, rain, no idea where I'm going. Not the well-worn path to Julia's house, nor the forbidden, abandoned path to the Richmonds, nor the pool closed for the winter, nor the house For Sale, nor school. Nowhere.

Somewhere, because I'm wearing only a shirt and jumper and jeans now soaked through and getting heavier by the minute. I can think of only one person I think who might be glad to see me. I can't remember his number from that time I tried to ring him; his address will be in the phone book. Jogging now, I see a phone box in the distance. It's hard to focus on the tiny type. Jameson. Not all that far from Andy's place. A fair bike ride, a long walk.

A car pulls up alongside, a window is wound down. A wolf whistle.

'Like a lift, girlie.' I ignore him. He tries again, fifty yards on.

'Get lost.' And again, a hundred yards on, when the man in the front seat gets out and confronts me. He is shorter than me, twenty-ish, a bodgie, stovepipes, leather jacket, Elvis hair.

'I said like a lift.'

'And I said Get Lost. Go pick up a chick some place else.' He stands in my way, stretches out a hand. Even as I take a swipe at his face I'm thinking, oh, God, what now. A house to run in to? My hand is stinging, heart gi-donk gi-donk, as I run off.

'Bitch,' he yells. But I'm lucky; they don't follow — there are easier pickings in the American milk bar.

The cars thin out. House lights are still on. In a couple I see the black and white flicker of a television set against venetian blinds. I suppose it's television, I've never seen one except in a shop window; it started last month. House lights begin to go off, as sensible people go to bed, and still I walk.

Number 42 is down a right of way, small, weatherboard, no lights on. There's no car outside. I'm not so sure Keith will be that pleased to see me, but I ring the bell because I don't know what else to do. A light goes on, a shadow appears behind the glass front door. The door opens a fraction, because it's chained; suspicious eyes. I remember, his mother's separated, his father went off with a secretary.

'Yes?'

'Is Keith in?'

'No, he's — are ye not Alex, Alex Archer?'

'Yes. Can I ...'

The door has closed in my face. That's it. He's out and I'm not welcome, even here. Then I realize she's fiddling with the chain, cursing it for jamming; the door opens wide. Against the light, she's only a silhouette.

'Come in.'

'I'm soaked.'

'Nae matter. Take your sandshoes off.' It's a Scottish lilt; Keith has no Scottish accent. Have I got the right house?

'Mrs Jameson? I'm looking for ...'

'Aye. I know. Keith's out at choir practice. He's a game tomorrow, so he'll not be late.'

'*Choir* practice?'

'Aye. Well, that's what they call it, him and his engineering mates, Friday night at the pub. Hard cases.'

It's the right house. But she's pulling me in, organizing me out of my wet clothes, into the shower to warm up, into an old dressing gown — and not asking any questions. She's wearing a candlewick dressing gown herself, a couple of curlers in her hair, smells of Pond's vanishing cream, and I like her. She puts me in a frayed chair in the living-room and makes some tea; insists that I take an aspirin against a chill, and still doesn't ask me what I was doing frozen and wet and peculiar on her doorstep at ten-thirty at night. Then she says she must go to bed because she has to get up early for her Saturday job — do I want to stay the night, yes? Well I can have a blanket on the sofa, her daughter Jill is already asleep and Keith will be home soon, God and Dominion Breweries willing. She gives me a *Weekly News* to read and tucks me up with a blanket, turns out the top light and leaves. By this time I'm rather sleepy; maybe I hear the sound of a telephone clicking, a low voice, maybe I don't and care less. Maybe I hear the sound of the Morris Minor come down the drive, Keith letting himself in the back door, his mother calling him, voices. Maybe I'm aware of him standing over me for a few minutes. Maybe not. I wake with a great shudder before dawn, with no idea where I am. A small room, a different smell, frozen feet, breathing in cold damp air. Gradually it comes back: a letter, a long walk in the rain, hitting someone across the face, Keith's house, his Scottish Mum. I try to sleep again, but I have a tremble in me which won't go away. I get up, and wander through the dark house. I recognize

Mrs Jameson's room, the other bedroom must be Jill's or Keith's. The door is half open; there's enough light to see a shape in the bed. It smells like a male room; male clothes litter the floor. I sit on the end of the bed for ... ages, I don't know; strangely comforting, just waiting. Oh, this is the time I'm normally training. I chase away a little thought in my head that Mr Jack will be at the pool, waiting. And Maggie too, oh no, Maggie has gone to Australia again, hasn't she? I don't feel like training today.

Keith turns over, kicks me; prods again with his feet at this hard lump which won't go away; grunts and sits up; turns on his bedside light. We look at each other. He looks more like a half-baked gnome than ever. He's growing a beard and it's at the scraggy stage. I look around the room which is full of photographs and posters of bridges. Slender bridges, chunky bridges, the Auckland harbour bridge, Sydney, the Golden Gate. The man is obsessed with bridges. There's a guitar hanging on the wall, C.N.D. posters, books, varsity notes everywhere. Then he lies down again.

'I didn't know your mother was Scottish,' I say.
'Why should you?'
'You haven't got an accent.'
'Why should I?' Then, 'Go back to bed, Alex.'
'I don't feel like training today.'
'Don't then.' He turns over and looks at me.
'Do you want to come with me, to my footie match?'
'It's still raining.'
'So? A little bit of rain!'
'I've never been to a footie match.'
'Good. Always a first time. Part of your education. God, why did you have to wake me so early. My mouth's like an Ay-rab's armpit.'
'Too much singing.'
'What?'
'Choir practice.'
'Oh.' He grins. 'Choir practice.'
'I don't like that beard.'
'Neither do I much. Wait till it grows in red streaks.'
'Why red?'
'I'm a Scots bastard, aren't I? Mum was sort of red once.'

'What was your Dad?'

'Another bloody Scot. Go back to sleep.'

But I'm staring at a team photo on his wall. First Fifteeen 1959, fifteen fine young men, in rugby gear, boots, striped jerseys, hair cut for the occasion, combed slickly, arms folded, a rugby ball and some cups in front. In the front row is a face I knew.

Keith sees me looking at it. He sees the tears start to flood down my cheeks.

'Oh Christ,' he mumbles. He climbs out of bed, turns out the light and sits down beside me, puts his arm around me in the strong and wiry grip I might have expected. His half-pie beard is surprisingly soft against my forehead. For some long time we just sit, side by side against the bedroom wall, under the First Fifteen.

Through a sort of sleep, propped against the wall, I hear his mother get up, make breakfast, and leave on foot for whatever her Saturday job is. She doesn't fuss or pry into the bedroom to see what's going on. Eventually Keith disengages, goes to shower, comes back dressed in white football gear, and asks about breakfast. I've no clothes to wear. His sister, the boy-mad handful who climbs through windows, is much smaller, he says. Eventually, I settle on a pair of his jeans, a thick woollen Swandri shirt, gloomy khaki; he produces socks and sandshoes which also fit my big feet. In the mirror I look sort of neuter.

'It's going to be wet. You'll need a mac,' he says over a huge plate of weetbix and tinned peaches. 'My game's not till two, but I'm reffing a kids' game before, standing-in for a mate. Kids' games are fun.'

'Reffing?'

'Referee, hence the whites. Toast?'

'No.' The front of the *Herald* is telling me about rioting in the Congo and today the All Blacks play a game against Rhodesia which they are expected to win; the kitchen is freezing and needs a paint, even more than ours. 'Aren't you wondering . . . what I'm doing here?'

He gets up to wash his weetbix plate. 'Nope. You'll tell me in your own good time.'

I climb into the blue Morris Minor feeling oddly detached from the memories it holds.

'You driving yet?' he says.

'Parents won't let me.'

'Quite right too.'

'You're one ...' He's teasing. 'I thought you wrote this car off.'

'Mum and me bought another one.' You can't buy another face, you and that poor Vicki, I think, but I'm not in the mood to get into that. We're silent till we reach the car park outside the grounds. There's no chivalry here, no opening of car doors or umbrellas against the steady drizzle. He pulls his large bag of gear from the boot and throws me a thick brown oilskin.

'Keep dry. Here's a pound, to get in. I go thataway, you over there, that turnstile. See ya later, after my game, back here.' He's gone, long socks still white and snug around muscular calves.

'Thataway' means the players' entrance at the back of the tall and forbidding stands. He's right about one thing, today I want to be left alone, but I'm not quite sure how I ended up here of all places.

It's only when I join the men in the queue that I realize I'm wearing a sort of male uniform, and that no one is looking at me even once, let alone twice. I pay to go through the turnstile. On the field a boys' game is in progress, kids younger than Jamie, about ten. They look a bit like tiny Keystone cops, little feet twinkling often in the wrong direction, nowhere near the ball, until I realize there's nothing funny about the things that are being yelled at them from the sidelines.

'KICK the BALL, for God's sake. What's wrong with ya?' 'A bunch of pussy-cats.' 'A bunch of girls.' 'Put the boot in.' 'Pass, *pass*, PASS.' 'Jeez, the ref needs his head read.' 'Ya beaudy,' as one little boy shakes himself free from twenty-nine other little boys and pounds off down the field. But mostly, it's instructions and abuse, while the drizzle pours steadily down, and the kids' hair and clothes get plastered to their little bodies.

It finishes, and Keith runs on to the field, sparkling white, brandishing his whistle, with thirty more boys, a bit older. The barrage of insults from the onlookers around the field — I suppose fathers, teachers, uncles, the odd hearty-voiced mum — begins again. The ground is now beginning to break up; Keith's whites are splattered with mud, and the kids are beginning to slip and slide about. It's so funny that I start to laugh for the first time in weeks.

Two men beside me under a huge black umbrella turn and stare. 'What's so funny?' one asks eventually, when the sight of a lone female laughing to herself becomes too much for him. There's just the slightest suggestion that if I don't stop I might get asked to move on, so I decide to go up into the stands.

If it's funny to see kids slithering around in the mud after a ball, it's anything but when Keith finally, after another schoolboys' game, runs on with his varsity team in blue and white and a team of very large men, mostly Maori, in maroon stripes. After half an hour, they are all varying degrees of mud-coloured, slipping and sliding round. Keith could be any one of the thirty. Every scrum that goes down I think of the sprigged boots on the kitchen table this morning, and dread the man at the bottom who won't, can't get up. A few punches are thrown; scrums threaten, but don't quite turn into brawls. This is the game the All Blacks think more important than the Maoris and those 150,000 people who signed the petition. I suppose the first Test they just lost over in Jo'berg last week in front of 75,000 spectators looked as ugly as this, without the mud. No one can run more than five yards without being mauled or slipping over, the forwards barge at each other like enraged bulls, the backs like fighting dogs. The whistle goes interminably. The ambulance men are called out at least ten times, three or four players get escorted or carried off, the crowd around me yells, hiccups, boos, groans, bellows, chants, cheers, hisses, complains, roars. I suppose the Colosseum in Rome sounded like this.

At half-time I can stand the noise and the blood and the violence no longer. I get up to leave. 'Make a good front-row forward,' I hear behind me, and a few male sniggers. I'm stupid enough to look: a row of louts clutching made-up dolls and beer bottles are there and it's me they're all grinning at.

'Great game,' says Keith when he joins me in the car a good hour later. His face is ruddy and shiny from the shower, and the scars have been joined by a big, swollen, purple bruise.

'Was it? Who won?'

'Weren't you there? It was on the scoreboard.'

'Nope. I decided I didn't like watching people stamp each other on the head.'

'Come on, this is Eden Park. The very ground where the All Blacks beat the Springboks four years ago. The game of the century. "Listen, Listen, It's a Goal".'

'So what.' He is looking round for the car keys. 'I've got them.' He puts out his hand, then cocks his head when nothing happens.

'Don't play silly games, Alex.'

'Who's been doing just that! How can you go on playing if you're protesting against the tour?'

'Quite easily. I love the game, I hate apartheid. It's two *separare* issues. Now hand them over.'

In the enclosed space of the car I have smelt beer on his breath.

'No.' He puts his hands on the steering wheel and stares straight ahead.

'I've had one glass, that's all. The others are still in there at it.'

'So that makes you a hero?'

'I'm sober. Do I have to prove it by walking down that line on the road?'

'I'll drive.' Alex, you're a total fool. You don't have a licence and only five lessons from Dad under your belt.

'The keys.' He gets out of the car, and disdaining the rain wetting his dry clothes and dripping down his face, walks deliberately down a white parking line, one foot carefully after another; gives a sardonic old-fashioned bow. 'The keys.'

I'm too cold, I've no idea where to catch a bus and not enough money for a taxi, so I hand them over.

'Thank you,' he says, with heavy sarcasm. He drives sarcastically too, with elaborate stop signals, giving way where he doesn't have to, not more than 25 miles an hour.

'Where are we going?'

'Town. Want a milk shake? Or do you want to go home?'

'No.' We're outside a milk bar with the usual neon signs, juke box, next door to a pub. I might have known.

'I won't be long.'

'I've heard that before.'

'The team always meets here. I won't be longer than you getting a milk shake.'

'Prove it.'

'Pub closes at six anyway. Wait in the car.'

The creaming soda milk shake is the first substantial thing I'd had to eat all day. By the time it's finished I'm so angry I could throw the chairs around. How dare he, leave me here, while he gets boozed with his precious mates. I think of walking down to the pool, a bus home; letting his tyres down. Finally at ten to six I know there is a better solution.

The Public Bar is so crowded I have to push against the door. No one looks around as I elbow my way forward. They are all too damn busy getting as much beer down their ugly gullets before six. Despite the fuggy warmth of the place, there is nothing cosy about it; my wet sandshoes are on hard tiles, the walls are bare and painted a horrible pale green. Empty, it would be no more appealing than a public lavatory. The smell of beer, cigarettes and male sweat is overpowering, the noise presses on my head like a clamp. One man looks me straight in the eyes, registers surprise, shock, runs his eyes down what little he can see of my body, the boy's clothes don't go with the female face. Was I one of those skinny pansy boys with floppy wrists? I see him nudge his mate. It happens again, and again. I plough on regardless towards what must be the bar along the far side of the room. Keith, being on the short side, will be difficult to pick in this crush. By the time I see him, the place has gone quiet.

It is almost — almost — worth it for the look on his face as I push the last couple of yards. He is propping up the bar, a huge mug of beer in his hand, nearly full. I see shock and shame, and a flicker of regret as he puts his mug down on the bar.

'Hi,' I say finally.

'You're not allowed in here,' says a voice.

'Says who.'

'I say,' says the barkeeper, a squat tough character with a pock-marked face and piggy eyes. He has a sort of hose-pipe in his hand, filling up an unbelievable number of glasses in rows in front of him on the bar top. I'm surprised I remember all these details, but I do.

'Is there an actual law against women in bars?'
'Alex, we're going,' says Keith.
'Good. You said ten minutes.'
'On your way, girlie,' says the barkeeper.
'The missus wants you home, Keith old son,' mocks a voice. Keith is now pushing me, not with his hands because there's simply no room to put up a hand, but with his whole body. Body against body against body. I feel several wriggle and thrust against me as I am pushed towards the door. One deliberately blows a mouthful of smoke into my face, smiling as he does. Another rubs one of my short whisps of hair between his fat fingers. Another allows himself a long fruity belch, not quite in my face, but near enough.

But it is the smell I remember most, and the eyes which are mocking and merciless. Is this how Joan of Arc felt, surrounded by hostile angry men? And still the terrible silence until we are almost near the door and then the barkeeper delivers his punch line.

'Young tart. She should be ashamed of herself.'
The cold air hits me in the face. I am panting as though I'd just swum a hundred metre sprint, and my eyes are smarting from the smoke. So, I note, is Keith and his face behind the beard is a dark dusky red.

'God almighty, what ever possessed you, woman?'
'I don't like being kept waiting. You could have bought me a drink.'

He grips me by the shoulders. I think he is going to hit me, he is so angry. I notice I am, if anything, taller by two or three inches. Hit me Keith Jameson and you'll get it back with interest.
'Get this straight, you're under age as well as female, and you had no right ...'
'Under age, that's a laugh. So are you.' It's a stab in the dark, but I'm right.
'That's different.'
'Why? Because you play for Uni-varsity and engineering students think they're the bees knees.'
'I'm taking you home.'
'No you're not. Once was enough. How many jugs of that disgusting stuff have you had?'

He has me by the hand and is now pulling me along the street, around the corner. I am surprised at his strength. Several taxis are waiting at a rank and he propels me towards the first one, a big American tank.

'I'm taking you home.'

'No, please, I don't want to go home.'

'Why not?'

'None of your business.'

'It is my business when you choose my place to hide in.'

'I'm not hiding. Please, Keith,' I gasp, as he opens the taxi door with one hand, holding me firmly with the other. 'Please, please, don't, you're hurting, I can't ... go home, can't you see ...'

'Frankly no. Now get in.'

'No.' But he's too strong for me, when it comes to the point, and I'm pushed into the car. The seats are shiny and vast. I slither across, half on and half off the seat.

'Got a handful there mate,' says the taxi-driver sympathetically. I realize he is talking to Keith. 'Not nice to see a girl that age ...' He thinks I've been drinking.

'Half-wit!' I shout, 'It's him that's been ...'

'Shut up, Alex,' says Keith. 'I think it's time you told me what's going on.'

'Why bother, when you leave me to get pissed ...'

'Now look here ...' says the taxi-driver. 'I'm not obliged ...'

Keith interrupts, sharply. 'Please, that fish 'n' chip place half way up Queen Street.'

'A short fare,' grumbles the taxi-driver, but he pulls away from the rank, and negotiates the traffic coming in to the Saturday night pictures. Saved temporarily from the terrors of home, I run out of steam.

'You and I,' says Keith in a voice that brooks no nonsense, he'd make a good sergeant major, those officious eyebrows, 'are going to eat some fish 'n' chips, then we're going to the pictures. And hell, Alex, you're sexy when you're angry.'

The Saturday night pictures is one way to fill in the time with someone who may go off her rocker at any moment, but how could Keith have known what further torture he was putting me through. There am I, in my Swandri and borrowed men's jeans and muddy sandshoes, and there're all the couples, dressed up to the nines, the girls in their best coats and high heels, hair rollerset. The fish 'n' chips place isn't so bad, but at the cinema I skulk in the shadows, getting curious looks even there. Ironically it's *South Pacific*. By half-time I have stopped trembling and allowed him to hold my hand and agreed to go back to his place; his family will keep out of the way. We walk back up to the pub where he left the car. I'm grateful that he doesn't try to start a deep and meaningful conversation, and he drives normally. The house is quiet. He insists that I have his bed; he will sleep on the sofa; strangely, I trust him. Tomorrow, I think, as I drift into sleep surrounded by bridges, something significant might happen tomorrow. Today — if that's the way most men spend their Saturdays, at the footie and in the pub, they can have it.

I know the instant I wake, again at my normal time of five again wondering where the hell I am, what I have to do today; and it's not training because I seem to have lost my urge to swim every again, and it's not going home. It's the dream that tells me, the dream that has been haunting my nights; I have to find out what to do. Or can't do; the idea of peace, of shutting my tired eyes for ever ... why fight, for ever ...

Keith wanders in with the dawn.

'Mum and Jill won't wake for ages. Mum's only day off, she likes to sleep herself out. So,' he says, plonking himself on the end of the bed.

'Will you take me sailing this morning?'

'*Sailing?*'

'You offered, once.'

'That was summer. It's July. It'll be cold, looks like rain.'

'So. A little bit of rain.'

He grins, recognizing the echo, gets up and pulls back the curtains, revealing a grey sky, bare fruit trees bending to a good breeze. 'Marginal. And my boat needs a bit of work.'

'But nothing vital?'

'Suppose not. The gudgeon's a bit dicey,' he says, doubtfully.

'Scared? Too much wind?'

'Don't be daft.' But his eyes glint and I know he's taken the bait. 'Two up, we'll be fine.'

Dreamlike, I dress in my own clothes which I find washed and ironed on a chair, eat a piece of toast, help gather up oilskins, jumpers, sandwiches, the sail bags, the gear, and the boat itself on a trailer in the garden. The little Morris Minor makes heavy going of getting up the driveway.

It's the same beach and much the same wind as that other time, that other person.

'Twelve knots, at least,' says Keith, still dubious. The harbour looks grey and bleak; there's no one else out sailing, and only a couple of elderly women, well wrapped up, taking a Sunday morning walk along the beach. The tide is dead low, so we have to haul the trailer a long way down to the shallows. Keith takes an age to rig the boat; all the shackles are a bit stiff, he says. I'm cold already. My jeans are wet to the knees.

'Right. Where are we going?' says Keith, looking out at the choppy, murky green sea. In shorts and bare legs sticking out from bulky oilskins he looks top heavy. 'You'd have been better with shorts. Hop in. Or do you want to sail her?'

'Later.'

We get sorted out remarkably quickly and head up harbour towards the naval base. Even that has its memories, every place I turn.

'It's going to be a short sail.'

'Why?'

'Look at the sky.' It's overcast, but over the distant western hills is an ominous cloud, deep grey and menacing. Already the waves are breaking against the side of the hull and against our protruding backsides.

'Can I steer?'

He hesitates. 'First time?'

'No,' I lie. Andy had not suggested that I steer.

'I've steered before,' I say impatiently.

'OK. Slide behind me, take the tiller, give me the jibsheet, I'll keep the mainsheet.'

'What do I aim for?'

'Sail her full and bye.'

'What?' I have the tiller, we are sitting very close on the left rail and the sails are flapping wildly.

'See the sail lifting by the mast? Bear away to starboard a bit.

You're too close to the wind, sail on the main.'

I haven't the slightest idea what he is talking about, but I do something with the tiller and magically the sails stretch and curve and we take off like the clappers.

'That's it!'

I find I can hold her steady.

'We're really on a tight reach. Point her up a bit, towards the bridge,' says Keith. 'No, the other way.'

Damn and damn, speak English man! But the speed is fantastic; this is living dangerously; this is what I wanted; this is my dream. I see Keith looking over his shoulder at the approaching wall of grey.

'We should go back,' he shouts.

'Why? I like it. I want to sail under the bridge. You can tell me all about it.'

'It's too far. That squall . . .'

'A little squall.'

'There's twenty knots of wind in that squall,' he shouts. 'At least. Put her about.'

'I want to sail under the bridge.'

'Christ, Alex, do as you're bloody told.' He grabs the tiller and pushes it away. There's a large amount of noise and scrambling, ropes everywhere; he flings himself across the other side, but somehow we make it on to the other tack, pointing towards the cargo ships and tall cranes of the city wharves. I'm still in control of the tiller.

'We're going back.'

'Let's put the spinnaker up.'

'Don't be bloody silly.'

'Too much wind for Keithy-baby?'

He doesn't bother to respond. 'You'd better let me take her.'

'Why? I'm doing OK.'

'We've got to run off back to the beach.'

'Running away from a bit of wind.' But even as I shout, a gust catches the sails and lays us on our ear. Keith flings himself almost off the boat; the mainsail flaps; we straighten up a bit. There was rain in that gust as well as power and beyond the cranes the city has disappeared. I'm soaked, teeth literally chattering, every part of me vibrating.

'I want to take her.' There's panic in his voice, and I feel him start to push behind me.

'*Move!*'

'I'm OK.'

'You are not OK — and here's another one. Watch it. *Bring her up.*'

'What the hell does that mean?' But this time the gust is stronger again and though he moves fast, he's too late. The boom is already in the water, and I hear something crack sharply like a gun going off. 'Oh Christ.'

I'm caught off balance. I fall forward, downwards into the sea, tangled with the mainsheet. The water down here is sort of khaki green, I think. It's quite warm. I have a rope around my neck.

I am going to die.

Isn't that what I want?

The rope gets tighter. Now I've managed to get my fingers around wire, rope, something, trying to pull them away from my clothes, my body, my neck, but although I'm kicking my legs like fury to get to the surface, nothing is happening. This is how a fish feels in a net, a person grappling with a giant octopus. This is where I always wake up. This is why I bullied Keith to bring me sailing and why I probably hoped that the boat would somehow capsize, who will ever know, although something broke, I heard it . . .

I'm weightless and calm. Oh well, I think, a certain irony, on a number of counts. Serve you right, Keith old son, drowning me successfully where you failed to mangle me in your car last year; and Andy old son, making me get back in your boat because I felt sorry for you and in those days life was worth living. But that day I was never in danger, I have never been in danger, not real mortal *danger*, and now I am; and one third of me is saying that life has not proved worth living without you, and another third is saying that you weren't the strong person I believed you to be, and I'm tired of fighting you and everyone else who wants to tame me and I want some peace; and the last third is saying that I'd be a bloody fool and coward to sink to the bottom of the Waitemata Harbour here and now and let my enemies gloat — and I'm still struggling against the wire, the ropes, the heavy clothes holding me down, and my lungs are beginning to demand that they get some air from somewhere, otherwise it will be water that floods in, and curtains for Alex Archer.

In my dream this is where I wake up.

In my dream I'm in a frenzy. But now I'm resigned, *che sera sera*. Was this what I had always known? That teacher in intermediate school, remember? She said one in four of us sitting in the classroom that day would not reach the age of twenty, and we had all looked furtively around and firmly told Destiny to lay his sticky paws on cross-eyed Jocelyn over here, or that nasty lad Kevin at the back, or that tell-tale Sally with the nits in her hair ... but it was me all along.

I am not ready!

Dammit, despite everything, I have unfinished business and scores to settle and I'm bloody well *not ready*.

My hands are grabbing wood, rope, something smooth, the sail, desperately now. Oh God, help me. Why should he? He didn't help Andy. My head is pounding, oh I don't want that khaki water in my lungs ...

When I have to breathe in something, it's air I breathe, a great, gasping, spluttering, salty, beautiful lungful.

There are hills over there, and there, and waves and spray, and it's pouring black driving rain. The hull of the boat is high above me, and I'm trying to hold on to a tangle of ropes, finding out that being an Olympic swimmer is no guarantee that three wet woollen jumpers won't drag you down into the green murk, and there's no sign of Keith. I cough some more, and kick my feet like fury to stay afloat, and then a head surfaces near me and we look at each other.

'Jesus, Alex,' says a spluttering voice. 'Oh, Jesus, I thought you were a goner.'

He swims around to the stern, holds out a hand and pulls me over towards the hull. I hang on and splutter up water.

'Hang on tight. I couldn't find you, I thought ...' What about the three people you put in hospital after Helensville; or me popping up as a bloated corpse in two days' time, think about those. His free hand is pushing the hair off my forehead in a most strange manner. Then he heaves himself over and kisses me hard on the mouth. I taste salt, I feel his beard, the pressure of his teeth hard against mine.

'Get off,' I gasp, with only one hand available to do any pushing off, especially if he thinks I'm going to open my mouth. 'They say you're randy but this is ridic ...'

'Who does?'

'Girls at school.'

He smiles, and his gnomish face with its scraggy eyebrows and mangy beard, scars and footie bruise looks strangely gentle.

'That, my friend, was a kiss of thanks be to God.' He finds a better handgrip on the smooth wood of the hull. It's crunch time. 'Now tell me, what's wrong at home?'

'Nothing's wrong at home.'

'Then why ...?'

'I had to get ... my trip to Rome's under a wee cloud.'

'But you're going next month.'

'Possibly.' I have a coughing fit, tasting salt.

He gives a disbelieving laugh. The rain beats down harder still. It's a funny place for a tête-à-tête.

'That's not it.'

'Meaning?'

'It's time you got Andy out of your system.'

'I have.'

'So a picture of the First Fifteen sets you off? Look, he was my mate, I miss him like hell, the bloody waste ...'

'You could do the same, knock someone down any time, the way you drive ...'

'You don't give an inch, do you?'

'Yeah, well, isn't it about time we got this boat up and sailed home?'

'We can't. The gudgeon went. And I forgot the oars.'

'So what happens now?'

'We wait. A ferry just left from Devonport. We'll signal. And you're going to listen. Why do you think Andy wanted to go to Dartmouth?'

I thought that was my special secret? He coughs and spits up water and gets a firmer handhold to deliver his broadside.

'Sure, he liked the idea of the navy. Secure job, travel, glamour, smart uniform.'

'Not fair. It was the sea ...'

'It was also to get as far away as possible from his old man. Nothing was ever good enough. His marks. Girlfriends. They thought he should have been Head Boy, not just a prefect.'

I'm silent; he grabs at the hull again.

'You thought, just a pompous but basically kind old gent. I tell you, he had those two underfoot.'

'His mother, yes.'

'And Andy. The night he died ...'

'It was something on at school.'

'Not the whole story. We had our last exam that day, remember? We should have been celebrating, but he turned up at school looking like death warmed up. He told me his old man had started on at tea about him going to med' school. Wouldn't listen to any overtures about the navy. Pompous old sod. "We'll discuss it later, Andrew." So basically he was terrified to go home, hung about being a good boy helping the caretaker, *that's* why he was pedalling home at midnight and copped it.'

'Mr Richmond said it was eleven.'

'It was midnight,' Keith yells, spluttering. 'And if that old bastard doesn't know why ...'

The ferry motors past towards town, hard going against the driving wind and waves. Keith and driver exchange signals and we are close enough to see him talk into a microphone. Calling Coastguard.

I have never been colder in my life. I've even stopped shivering. I can't quite shape the words I'm looking for.

'Look,' says Keith. 'You and Andy might have made a go of it. I doubt it. He wasn't strong enough for you.'

I hear an echo of Mr Richmond when I visited them on Christmas Day. *You'd have been good for him.* How bloody ironic.

'Anything else ... tell me, that I should know?' I say.

'I'll talk about Andy any time you want. How the Third Formers worshipped him at school, six-foot, good-looking, in all the right teams. How he knew it, played on it. How he was hopeless with money. How he let people ride over him, too damn polite, you too. How he tried everything to get rid of that stutter, hypnosis even, because in the end you can't have naval officers who stutter.'

Alex in Winter

'No more,' I say, weeping freely at last for the person I only half knew. 'Stop it.'

He gets a fresh grip on the boat, but this time one of his deathly white hands is covering mine and I'm grateful.

'He was my mate too,' he says and there's a catch in his voice which I know is not from the salty grey waves surrounding us.

I suppose it was about ten minutes before a small white launch slowly motored alongside, and by then both of us were paralysed purple and even yellow with cold. Keith, with little help from me, had managed to get the boat upright, and the sails down, and we were both concentrating on simply hanging on to the side. The worst of the squall had passed. Two men peered down.

'Who's in the best shape?' one shouted.

'Me,' said Keith and he was right.

'We'll take the other chap aboard. You got a painter there?'

A rope came over, with a loop which went underneath my armpits. That was difficult enough, with oilskins and all, and it took both of them to haul me aboard because I had no strength to help myself and the waves made things difficult. 'Crazy kids, this weather, not a lifejacket in sight,' one grumbled. He had an English accent and looked like the bearded sailor on the de Reske cigarette packet. It appeared that we had interrupted them doing a spot of fishing.

I stood dripping on to his carpet and just looked at him.

'Get your clothes off, lad,' he said impatiently. 'Dennis, this kid's in a pretty bad way. How's the other one?' His mate was leaning over the side talking to Keith.

'Managing, just.'

'Young idiots. Come on, get them off.' All was slow motion, he helped me with oilskin and jumpers, while my personal devil, amused that for the second time in two days I'd been mistaken for a boy, waited for the moment when I got down to my bra. I wrapped the towel around myself before taking my bra off, and gave him a weak smile.

'Humblest apologies, miss. Just goes to show — I thought only some damn fool boys would be stupid enough to be out in the harbour today.'

'All in a good cause,' I said, feeling rather sleepy as he wrapped the blankets around me.

'I can't imagine what. Now curl up on that bunk and conserve what little body heat you've got. We'll have you ashore soon. Eat this.' He handed me some sort of chocolate bar, which I attacked greedily, because it was well past lunch-time and I'd had no proper food for two days.

'Your face is familiar.'

'No.'

'Funny. What's your name?'

'Alice. Alice Archibald.'

'Tom?' called the other one from outside. 'You free?'

'Coming.' So we rocked around on the harbour, and I'm ashamed to say I drifted off to sleep while poor Keith also got hauled aboard and they stripped him down too, and put him on the other bunk — and thus we made our ignominious way home.

Worse was in store. Through a state of half sleep, I heard a lot of business with bringing the launch into the jetty, and doing whatever had to be done to Keith's sad-looking Cherub. An ambulance was waiting, with a burly uniformed driver who came aboard and told us we were going to hospital to be kept under observation for hypothermia, whatever that was, whereupon I raised a great stink and told him we were perfectly all right and I wanted to go home where my mother was a nurse and could handle anything; so he checked us over and said we seemed to be a couple of fit young people and all right, he'd take us home.

Of the two evils, Mum's wrath, or the hospital where I'd almost certainly be recognized and have to give my name (thus the Press might get wind of Olympic swimmer admitted for observation after near drowning in sailing accident) — Mum was just slightly preferable.

Only just. Keith was provided with some of Dad's spare clothes and put in the car and driven home by Dad. Later I heard he'd got the rough end of Dad's tongue about taking me sailing, with the risk of injury and so forth.

As for me, I was put to bed, given scrambled eggs to eat.

Everyone talked softly as though I was sick, just recovering from an operation or something. No questions or explanations were demanded, which was bizarre.

Mr Jack was summoned.

After the pleasantries, we all sat and looked at each other in the firelight. The kids had been shooed off to bed, Gran was doing some hand sewing on some fine lemon-yellow cotton and Mum was smoking and knitting furiously. The battle lines were drawn, but no one wanted to fire the first arrow.

'Well, Miss Alice Archibald,' said Mum finally. 'We know this much. You've been with Keith. You stayed at his house. You went to watch a football match yesterday, and to the pictures last night. This morning you went sailing and nearly drowned yourselves.'

'That's about right,' I said, sure as hell not about to fill in the gaps. 'How do you know?'

'His mother rang us Friday night.'

'Oh, did she.'

'There are *some* responsible people around, Alex.'

'Helena,' said Dad sharply.

'Put it this way,' said Mum. 'We haven't been worrying unduly about you.'

Mr Jack saw my disbelieving smirk.

'It's true, Alex,' he said. 'I've had two whole mornings in bed, snoozing till seven.'

He shifted forward in his armchair. Here it comes, I thought.

'Something had to give. Are we back in business, Alex? Or are we going to put an end to it? Withdraw you from the team. I'll ring Cyril Upjohn tonight. Now. One phone call. That's all it will take.'

If it was shock tactics, it worked.

'What!'

'Don't say ...' began Mum automatically.

'You couldn't.'

'I could,' he said and it was my eyes which dropped first. There was a long, long silence.

'I wasn't born yesterday, Alex,' he said gently. 'I know about the letter, and what happened at the wedding. I know you went into a public bar last night ...'

'For God's sake,' said Mum, using her strongest oath. 'This is going from bad to worse.'

'How?' I said, conscious of a dark flush seeping upwards.

'A mate of mine — not your Keith — happened to be in there and rang me. He said you looked — fairly desperate. And you got a rough ride. True?'

I had closed my eyes against the memory. You could do nothing private in this bloody country.

'This Keith,' said Mr Jack gently. 'I don't know him.'

'He's all right,' I mumbled.

Mum interrupted sharply. 'I don't agree. That potentially disastrous trip to Helensville. Car crashes. Protest marches. As for going sailing midwinter, an act of irresponsible lunacy. He's not all right.'

'I got out of his car, didn't I?'

'What are you talking about, Alex?' Oh hell, Mr Jack never knew about that little incident, how close I'd come to disaster.

'I went marching because I believed in it.' They looked unimpressed. I took a deep breath. 'All right then, the sailing was my idea. I bullied him into it.'

'Why?' said Mr Jack, fixing me with a gentle smile. 'Hoping for an injury, an excuse not to train? Going with a friend of Andy's as a means of getting closer to him? Putting yourself at extreme risk ...'

'Dinghy sailing is not extreme risk,' I said loftily. 'Thousands of people do it.'

'Given certain conditions, it could turn out that way. It nearly did.' He didn't need to say the obvious next line: is that what you wanted? Nor the answer: yes. I mean no. Well perhaps I ... *No!* He sat back in his chair.

Tears were spilling down my cheeks, splashing on to my hands. I had just enough stuffing left in me to leave; not angrily; but slowly, sadly, suddenly very tired, empty.

There's a knock on the door.

'Go away.'

'Alex? I'd like to come in.'

The door opens slowly and Mr Jack walks in. He sits down heavily on top of the assorted bras, jumpers, old jeans, damp towels on the one chair. He makes no sign that the mess and the smell are rather bad. He sits there, on the edge of the chair, his two squat legs firmly planted in front of him, his pudgy fingers interlaced, thumbs going round and round. And then he tells me about the long drawn-out business of watching his mother die.

I notice how much weight he's lost, the deeper lines on his face. I've forgotten that he is grieving too. Those weeks without him — how petty my fights with Steve seem now.

'My sister didn't miss a chance to point out she'd been looking after mother for years. Then there've been arguments over the sort of funeral, the family furniture. I'm betting on problems with the will. I'm wishing now I'd taken Lorna over with me, at least try to mend a few fences.'

I remember what Mrs Jack had hinted at the airport.

'People say, sorry about your mother, Bill, know how you feel, and it makes me hopping mad, because how can they ever *know*. How can *I* know what you've been going through? I can't.'

There's a hush in the room.

'But then I get back and see you choosing to destroy yourself, it's more than I can cope with. My old Mum had had a good innings, but she had no control over her situation, none whatsoever. From the day they put her on oxygen, pain and hallucinations till the day she finally went. But you have.'

I am crying again.

'I think — something happened this weekend. Some sort of decision? Perhaps you don't quite recognize it as such, yet. I'm not asking you to tell me, except ... Am I right?'

I nod.

Then I say, 'When we capsized today, I thought I wasn't going to come up. I didn't want to ...'

He picks his way through the shambles on the floor, leans down and very delicately kisses my forehead.

'It won't all happen at once. We'll still have our bad days, you and me. But it's going to be all right, champ.'

Part Four

I HAVE decided to keep a diary, from now on; only five weeks before we go, Rome and all that. Mum says when I'm fifty I'll be jolly glad I did, to have something to show my grandchildren! So Gran rushed out and bought me a special sort of notebook, with a hard green cover. My Trip Book.

July 4 1960. Hullo Diary, good to know you. Actually enjoyed training today for the first time in ages. Only two days off — but it seemed like two weeks, two months, as though I'd been on holiday. Mr Jack has drawn up a new schedule — more medleys, to stop boredom setting in. He wants me to go for runs as well, and do more calisthenics and weights if I can stand it. Now, I can. Had postcard from Maggie in Queensland — she's due back in three weeks, lucky bitch, all that sparkling blue water. Mr Jack's heard rumours about the coaches there, that they don't get on, they train separately, spy on each other's squads, rows even, pathetic. Funny, I'm not worried about Maggie now — we're both going, we'll both do our best. Liar, I want to do better than her. Have enjoyed the break from Mrs B. Something on the postcard about a fashion parade at her school on the 28th. I remember some woman ringing weeks ago, something about some special bathing-suits from somewhere, me and Maggie, anyway, saying no. Perhaps it might be quite fun. And poops to all those rumours.

Keith rang tonight, to see how I was! He's got a derrible cold in the dose. I felt rather bad about that, for a while. But under that gruff exterior ... hope he doesn't get all randy and boring. Not that I need worry, really, he hasn't asked me out and I haven't got time or energy even if he did. Maybe just once? Perhaps later, after Rome?!

Riding to school this morning, I saw the first blossom out — pink blossom in the rain. I stopped just to look up close. I feel — is this corny, diary? — I'm seeing everything fresh, sharp, clean, as though a big weight has been lifted off my chest. Mr Jack is going to have a chat to Mr Upjohn, tell him about The New Look Alex. Toeing the party line and all that. Well, not so long to go now.

July 6. Bad news. Mr Jack once said he might have enough money saved to go to Rome. If I'd stopped to think about it, I should have guessed he'd used it all up going to Sydney. And he got a letter from the solicitor today to say that his sister's family are contesting the will and it's all held up, at least a year, so there's no hope of money there. His winter job doesn't bring in all that much, not enough to persuade the bank manager for a loan. When he told me, I made all sorts of silly suggestions about Mrs J. getting a job, and persuading the swimming association that we should have an official coach and he said fat chance of that, Alex; there are already two swimming officials for two swimmers. Funny really, I don't know why Mrs Churchill couldn't have been both manager and chaperon, (leave Mr Upjohn behind!) but Mr Jack says managers are always men and I don't see why a woman couldn't be a manager just as well.

July 8. Mr Upjohn came down to early morning training today the first time ever. Said he'd had a very useful chat with Mr Jack, and how was I feeling Alex? — fine, fine — and he was very much looking forward to setting off on our great adventure together. I guess it's a case, if you can't beat her, join her. He was so nice I began to wonder if what I overheard in Napier and the two letters had all been a bad dream, figment of my imagination.

July 9. We marked the Trial Scene for *Joan* at school today. We've done readings in class and I knew most of the lines, but it was really creepy; even surrounded by a lot of fat schoolgirls trying to be the Bishop and the Inquisitor and things, the words are so wonderful, so musical, so powerful it doesn't really matter who says them, and I felt just like I did in that pub, totally alone, daring to be yourself, different, surrounded by hostility. And then a very strange thing happened. When we got to the speech where Joan tells them to go take a running jump, the words are so beautiful and strong and defiant, something sort of took over. *Light your fire: do you think I dread it as much as the life of a rat in a hole? My voices were right.* I know Joan was talking about something much more important, like what she believes and how terrible it would be to be shut away in a prison breathing foul damp darkness for ever, but, well, it's an amazing cry for freedom and life and it just came out and when I finished the girls who were supposed to shout 'Blasphemy, She is possessed, Monstrous' and so on, just stood there looking stupid. There was a bit of an awkward pause and I felt a bit stupid myself because it was only a rehearsal and there's nothing worse than people overacting. But Miss Macrae stopped the lesson, and told the others it was time for a break which it wasn't, and told me to stay behind, and came slowly over to me and I believe her eyes were a bit moist. *Tears*, her of the plain suits and voice like a foghorn.

'I once swore, many moons ago, I'd never hear those words spoken on a stage again.' Something held me back from asking why. She'd tell me if she wanted to. But she only said 'Thank you Alex', wiping her eyes. I didn't know where to look.

'I suppose you have to do law?' and I said I did, with more conviction than I ever felt before.

Then quite on impulse, out of nowhere, I said, 'Julia says, it won't do my reputation any good, playing Joan,' and she gave me a long penetrating stare and then she started to smile.

'Julia really should know better, such nonsense,' she said, but kindly and then the bell rang. 'You will be a magnificent Joan.'

Maggie rang the day she got back from Queensland. She was fed up with Aussies lording it over her and scrapping among themselves, though Dawn Fraser was just amazing and actually talked to her several times like a real person, not a kid from New Zealand, and asked about her times and everything, and she'd even heard about you, Alex, really, and said she looked forward to meeting you in Rome.

I asked about the boyfriend she met last year. He hadn't made the Aussie team, she said sadly; it had all fizzled out, and he'd gone back to Perth which was over the other side of the entire continent. She was really, really glad to be home, even though it meant another two weeks' training with eyes out on stalks, and she had some fabulous Aussie clothes to show me. Her Mum had really gone to town in Sydney on the way home. You've picked up an Aussie accent, Maggie, I said — Seedney, listen to you; yes, Mum's working on it, she laughed.

It was a long phone call, because she seemed really keen to tell me everything and to hear what I'd been up to — nothing much, I said, just training, and more training, and my eyes were pretty bad but otherwise the last few weeks had been OK 'cause now it was close enough to believe we were actually going, and Mr Jack was beginning to cut back my miles slightly which was a relief. Letters had started appearing in the mail about travel plans and inoculations and being measured for uniforms and assembling in Auckland on August 9 — two weeks, fantastic wasn't it, incredible, can't believe it? Not forgetting boring old school, I said, getting so behind with my homework it wasn't funny, but the teachers were being pretty soft. I could do without all the sniggering about Italian boys and bottom pinching, and endlessly telling people of our stopovers — Sydney, Darwin, Singapore, Calcutta, Karachi, Beirut, Cairo, Rome, gosh, lucky you, they all gasp; tedi-ous, I said. She said she wasn't going back to school before we go — there was no point really — but, she said, there's this woman called Mrs Sutherland who rang two minutes after they got back, wanting to know if she and I could *possibly*; she knew it was asking a great deal of us, only two weeks before we go away; but *could* we possibly come over to Maggie's school on Friday afternoon and wear these fabulous American bathing-suits for her fashion parade. It was in such a good cause, the Crippled Children's Society, and she would just *love* to be able to send around a notice from school tomorrow saying that our two very own Olympic girl swimmers would model these beautiful garments. Honestly, Alex, she did go on and on, said Maggie. 'In the end I said I had to ask you.'

'What does your mother say?' I said.

'She ... strange really, she vaguely thought no harm in it, but I'd feel such an idiot, prancing round in those things. I don't want to. You'd be all right.'

'I've never modelled anything in my life.'

'Mum wasn't all that interested, she's rushing round, packing, getting tickets and everything. You know her and Dad are coming too.'

'I heard,' I said sourly. I had no proof that it was Mrs B who tattled on me about the wedding, but it figured and I intended to be as cold as a cucumber to her from now on. 'Oh, what the hell Maggie, a bit of fun. Ring the woman.'

Oh, Alex, you fool!

I didn't actually see Maggie until the Friday morning, because not being at school, she was able to train at civilized hours during the day, almost as though she was doing it for a job. Well, the Aussies are at training camps, and Maggie doesn't have to work 'cause she's got rich parents, I suppose one day there will be swimmers and athletes doing it as a job, being paid by the Government, perhaps, or getting prizes for winning, enough to live on. It's a strange thought.

Mrs Sutherland kept ringing me up, and I suppose Maggie too. I was a size 14, wasn't I? but the company supplying the garments were sending both 12s and 14s, so there'd be one that should fit. Could I bring a pair of white shoes with highish heels, 'cause bathing-suits always look so much better with shoes on, don't they. No, I couldn't and wouldn't, I said. But in beauty contests they always ... that's beauty contests, I said, I'm sorry Mrs Sutherland but if you want me you'll have me in bare feet or not at all. There was a stunned silence. Game, set and match to me, I thought, easy really. I'm getting wise to bullies in my old age.

I didn't actually tell my family what I was up to, except that I was going to Maggie's school to talk to juniors about going to the Games. Perhaps I was a bit bashful, unwilling to have the kids jumping round teasing me about being a model and walking like Marilyn Monroe, and would they have to pad my bosoms 'cause I wouldn't be able to fill them up by myself. I don't know, anyway, it was a mistake. Maggie and I were due at her school for a trial run about ten, so we both went training an hour later than my usual, and for the first time we actually trained together. Her coach had got the huff about her going to Australia, and so she's working to her Australian coach's schedules again. Mrs B didn't come into the pool. We compared our schedules and found they were quite similar, so we swam together and did some time trials together.

It was so wonderful having someone alongside to pace me, I wished we'd trained together a long time ago.

In the changing-room afterwards I heard a sharp intake of breath. I turned from doing my jeans up to find Maggie sitting on the bench, bent over, looking rather odd.

'What's the matter?'

'Nothing. Just the gripes.'

'Period?'

'Last week.'

'Nerves about this afternoon, I bet.'

'Oh, sure. I wish I'd said no.'

'Maggie, are you all right?'

She slowly resumed getting dressed. 'I had it once or twice in Aussie. It'll go. Mum says it'll go and it always does, with an aspirin or two.'

'My Mum says any pain in the gut should be investigated.'

'No, it's all right, truly.'

If I were her, I'd be dead scared about appendicitis too, right now. But she said it had gone, and I believed her.

I had never actually been in Maggie's school, which was grand and brick, with wonderful trees all round. I had managed to say hullo and goodbye to Mrs B, driving us there in her Super Snipe, without actually looking her in the eye. Mrs Sutherland was all over us like a rash. The togs were hanging on a rack in a classroom backstage, and we both gaped at creations of lycra and net and Grecian drapes and South Sea Island prints, ruches and tucks and insets and skirts. One or two were okay, I suppose, but I thought most of them horrendous and wished with all my heart that we had not got ourselves into this.

There was a large amount of talk and carry-on, clipboards at the ready, and girls parading round in their suits and dresses made in dressmaking class. It appeared Maggie and I were to wear ten garments each; some mothers would be on hand to help us change quickly. We tried each of the ten on, resulting in a lot more discussion about the absolute necessity of padding the cups with cotton wool (I reluctantly had to agree), accessories, bags and straw hats and beachcoats and jewellery until I could have screamed. Walking down the catwalk was rather strange. I'm used to standing on starting-blocks in front of three thousand people; walking down a school hall in the bikini which was the climax of the swim-suit bit left me feeling very exposed.

Lunch-time came, and I wanted to go home, but Mrs Sutherland had thoughtfully organized lunch. The parade started at one thirty, so we could rest in the senior common room until we were called. The senior common room was like a railway station, because half the senior school wanted to come and see their mate Maggie back for the day and wish her luck for Rome and also cast an eye over her notorious friend from that other school. After about twenty minutes of that, I knew I had to go for a walk or blow up. Maggie was looking decidedly pale and said she'd stay, you go Alex, don't forget to come back, she called.

Well, I walked around the grounds for a bit and went back inside at one o'clock as I was asked.

'Where's Maggie?' I asked Mrs Sutherland.

'I'm sorry, Alex, she's gone home.'

'Gone *home*?'

'Her mother insisted that she wasn't well. I tried Alex, oh dear, we'll just have to make the best of it, won't we. I've got a Sixth Former to wear Maggie's costumes, but it won't be the same, will it?'

'Thanks a bundle,' I said. But because I knew about her stomach-ache this morning, I believed it to be true, and I feared it might be appendicitis. I knew that I had to go through this terrible farce alone. Had to? I could have walked away, but I'm not a quitter. It was for a good cause.

Images and memories now go hazy around the edges.

I do remember another argument with Mrs Sutherland over make-up. The Sixth Former was so thrilled with being Maggie's stand-in and actually modelling a bikini, showing off her body beautiful to the assembled hall of parents and teachers and pupils gathered to raise money for the Crippled Children, that she allowed Mrs Sutherland's sidekick to go overboard. I took one look at the pancake, precise eyebrows, and heavy black lines drawn around her eyes for the latest Vogue doe-eyed look and flipped.

'You can forget that stuff,' I said.

'The lights . . .' began the woman, damp sponge and paintbrush at the ready.

'Not on your nellie.' So Mrs Sutherland was called over and we had another row and she danced up and down, a little plump pudding on her high heels, and told me I was being quite neurotic, and I said I'm here, Mrs Sutherland, I'll wear your bathing-costumes for the Crippled Children but I'll not look like a tart of twenty-five for anyone; whereupon, the Sixth Former danced around a bit too, in her first costume of gold lamé in Grecian mode, and called me a few names. Mrs Sutherland burst into copious tears and made me feel a total heel, because it's a terrible thing to see an adult who hasn't got a clue how to handle people, totally out of her depth. So we reached a compromise — I put on a bit of make-up and combed my hair into a sort of Audrey Hepburn pixie look, while the sidekick stood and sneered, and the parade began only fifteen minutes late.

The bathing-suit bit came at the end, after wall-to-wall teenage fashion, introduced by the honeyed tones of Mrs Sutherland in her best black compere's dress, while the dressmaking teacher fussed over each petrified girl as she waited behind the curtains for her name. Then it was our turn, the Sixth Former in stilettos you could kill someone with at twenty paces, and me in my bare feet sporting bosoms I never knew I had. Please welcome our Olympic girl, Alex Archer, who has kindly consented to join us today, and so forth. We got lots of claps and gasps when the bikinis appeared; you had to be *very* daring to wear a bikini as brief as these, showing your navel.

I was vaguely aware of hearing the brand name mentioned in the commentary; a tiny alarm bell started ringing. I was not aware (because of the coloured spotlights that some father was training right into our eyes, and the general confusion of music and applause) of a photographer taking pictures without flash, with an extra fast film. I should have been.

I rang Maggie that night after training to see how she was. It was a rather confused conversation. She was fine, the pain had gone; so why had she run away and left me, at *her* school too. She hedged a bit, and then told me her mother had changed her mind about allowing her to model swim-suits, but she thought it was more tactful to tell Mrs Sutherland she wasn't well. I suppose she said it was cheap, or something like that, I said, and Maggie laughed with surprise; how did you know? I know your mother, I said. Anyway, it was over, and they'd raised a hundred and fifty pounds for the Crippled Children, and Mrs Sutherland was over the moon.

The weekend passed uneventfully — just Gran ironing, yet again, all the cotton clothes she had made, and Mum getting the best family suitcase out of the hall cupboard, and more letters arriving to tell us about team meetings and photos to be taken in the domain, and booklets about Rome. The All Blacks had won another game in South Africa.

Monday morning, the first day of August, our Olympic world begins to fall apart.

I come home from school to find Gran has taken a message from Mr Jack. Would I be prepared to stay on after training tonight, please, for an appointment with Mr Upjohn?

'What does he want,' I ask before I start training. Mr Jack doesn't know either, but he didn't like the tone of Mr Upjohn's voice when he rang. I assume, he says, there's nothing you're hiding from me? Only Maggie's stomach-ache, I think naïvely, and that's not really my problem and it's probably not a problem at all, just nerves, tension.

Mr Upjohn arrives wearing his new black New Zealand Olympic blazer, with Rome 1960 on the pocket, and there's trouble writ large all over him. I'm still in my old track suit, and feeling rather cold. He marches down the concourse and over to where we are standing, and launches his rocket.

'Can you explain this?' he says, fumbling with the flaps of a large brown envelope. He holds up a photograph. Mr Jack and I stare at it.

'Well?'

Mr Jack sits down heavily on the form where he has sat for two winters watching me train. I know what he is thinking: six years, blown. Vanity, ah vanity, all is vanity.

'Well?' Mr Upjohn says impatiently. 'I'm waiting.'

The look I get from Mr Jack wounds me more than any words could. Reproach, incredulilty, resignation — he raises his hands and drops them as if to say, 'I give up'.

'Do you realize what you've done, Alex?' Mr Upjohn demands. 'Do you realize the implications of this? Wasn't the last warning enough? Don't you realize, child?'

I'm beginning to. But I cannot speak, because I'm burning fire all over as I look at what seems to be a press photograph, eight by six. Two girls simper out of it. One is rather glamorous, posing as in cheesecake, high heels, a brief bikini; under the bright lights, the doe-eyed look didn't look too bad. The other is, though barefoot, taller, slimmer, less posed, amateurish, rather bored. Me.

I take it, stupidly. The name and address of a photographer is stamped on the back, and a slip of paper has been pasted. 'Alex Archer (left) teenage swimming champion and Olympic hopeful, appeared at a charity fashion parade in Auckland last week. The glamorous swim-suits are by Rose Marie of California.'

'How in the name of heaven has this arrived in my office, Alex?' My silence is getting to him. 'Well? Have you nothing to say for yourself?'

'Not much, 'cause you won't believe me, anyway.'

'We'll ignore that.'

'I didn't see a photographer. I wasn't asked about photographers, no one warned me, no one told me, no one said anything about the Press.'

'Haven't you learned by now, Alex, that *everything* you do is potential news?' says Mr Upjohn.

'It was only a school thing. Last Friday, at Maggie's school. Some stupid parade, their dressmaking teacher and some jumped-up parent who saw herself as a fashion co-ordinator. Maggie and I...'

'Maggie too?' He gulps. 'You can't be serious.'

'I am, though her silly bitch of a mother changed her mind and took her away at the last minute and left me in the lurch.'

'Alex, you will show some respect...'

'Why? She hates me, it's mutual.'

'At least she had some sense about this — this *charade*.'

That's strange, I'm thinking. Why did she? Had she worked out that any picture of me or Maggie in someone's bathing-suits could be seen as advertising? Could get us wiped out of the Games team, no longer true amateurs. Maggie was putting all that on, about a pain in her guts? I don't believe it. I know you too well, Maggie Benton. Do I? The devilishness of the idea is too much. I subside on to the form next to Mr Jack.

Mr Upjohn is relentless. 'Look at you, baring your midriff to the world.'

'You mean my belly button? And a bunch of schoolgirls and their snotty parents isn't the world.'

Mr Jack stirs. 'That's beside the point. How did you get this picture, Cyril?'

'I got a phone call this morning from Norm Thompson at the *Herald*. It turned up on the desk of some Fashion Editor. She thought he'd like to see it, thank God he was bright enough to see the implications and ring me.'

'Who else, do you suppose?'

'Probably every newspaper in the country.'

'You can stop it.'

'I've tried that, already. I've spent the entire day on the telephone, toll calls all over the country, the Press Association, every magazine, every advertising agency I can think of. I've pleaded with editors, bullied them that the picture is under embargo, threatened them with legal action if they use it.'

'So what's the problem?' I say, cheekily.

'The problem is, Alex, that this picture has brought the swimming association into disrepute and you may no longer be an amateur.'

'Even if it never gets used anywhere?'

'I believe that may be so. I shall have to consult my fellow members of the executive committee. It will mean an expensive special meeting.'

'Even if,' asks Mr Jack suddenly, 'it could be shown there was malicious intent, that Alex has been the victim of some scheme to discredit her.'

'I can't believe that. And the fact remains, she was there, in those ... immodest and revealing scraps, parading round in front of a large sign, blatant advertising. See for yourself.'

Out of focus it may be, but the name is legible. It is filtering through that Mr Jack is treading the same path of suspicion as me. So I've nothing to lose, now.

'I've been set up,' I shout. 'I know who it was and I know why. You never wanted me in the team, and she's been trying for years ...'

'I will not stand for such ...'

'Perhaps the two of you, in cahoots ...'

'Alex!' It is Mr Jack, a squat figure of fear and fury standing before me. 'I see your father waiting out in the office. You'll go home and you'll watch your step.'

'I always knew ...' I say, defeated.

'If you persist, Alex,' says Mr Jack, implacably, 'it will be your loss.'

'What have I left?'

'You've got a lot of friends, Norm Thompson for one. If it wasn't for him, that picture would be all over this morning's *Herald*. You've got to trust them to get you out of this, again.'

He means my 'friend' Mr Upjohn, standing there with a face set in concrete, holding that photograph. It's bitter medicine.

I can't look Maggie in the face next morning at training, let alone her mother, although she makes an effort to be friendly. Naturally, if she thinks her plan has worked. I tell Maggie I'd rather train separately. The water feels like glue; Mr Jack looks as though he's been there all night.

Mercifully, the picture is not in the *Herald* when we get home. I go to school, I go training again in the evening. I go for a fitting for my uniform. Various documents from the Olympic association arrive in the mail. I fend off questions from Keith and Julia, both well-meaning, trying to share how I must be feeling about this fantastic trip coming up, only a week now, golly.

This goes on for five days. Mr Jack keeps telling me to *hold on*. 'It's going to be all right.'

'What are they *doing*?' I keep asking.

'Taking legal advice, I don't know. Going through the proper channels. It's out of my control now, Alex. Sorry, but it is. I've got you out of scrapes before, but this one's gone beyond me.'

'It's inhuman. Why doesn't Mr Upjohn ring, tell me what's going on? I always knew he'd get me in the end,' I say with every bitter bone in my body. One night I line up for my fifth hundred metre time trial and something breaks inside me. I just stand on the side of the pool and weep for my foolishness and vanity, the stupid desire to prove that I was as feminine as the next female through something as basically meaningless and trivial as a school fashion show.

Two days before the team is due to assemble in Auckland, Maggie has a bad cold and another stomach-ache. This time it's bad enough to be checked out with blood tests, but they can't find anything, and after a good sleep it goes. Though I still can't look her in the eye, I hear the edge of panic in her voice. They think it's just tension, nerves.

I get a ring from Mr Upjohn.

It's not bad news, but not good news either. It appears that efforts have been made. The photographer has been tracked down; he was engaged by someone ringing on behalf of the school, no one quite knows who, and he was asked not to use a flash because there'd be plenty of light and teenage girls were a little sensitive about having their pictures taken! He was asked to forward the picture to selected papers; no paper, as far as he knows, has used it. All paths lead back to that foolish woman who was simply carried away with trying to raise money for the Crippled Children, but she's so upset and confused they can get little sense out of her. The shop which supplied the bathing-suits said it was her idea. The committee have accepted Mr Jack's assurance that I received no money, and that I was there for simple and worthy motives like wanting to help a charity.

If it was Mrs Benton, I think she must be sweating blood, waiting to see if her little plan is going to work. I'm surprised by the reasonable tone of Mr Upjohn's voice as he goes on to tell me that he believes there may have been some unfortunate dealings behind all this; nevertheless, they are having to take legal advice through the Olympic association in Europe. It may not be through until after we go.

'I'm sorry, Alex,' he says, amazingly. 'It's the best I can do. Obviously, you still have to travel, at this stage. I've been holding the Press at arm's length by threat of legal action, and saying absolutely nothing. I strongly advise you to do the same.'

Oh, don't worry, I assure him, I've been doing that all week. Except, I don't say, for Norm Thompson who comes down to training and has a long chat with Mr Jack, and I'm able to thank him for his help.

I honestly think that Mrs Benton is poised for the kill. If she can get one single newspaper to publish that picture and say underneath that I am wearing a bathing-suit by Rose Marie, I'm out. With her contacts, her money, her slimy husband, it shouldn't be too hard. I don't doubt she's trying, even as the days tick by. But the next day, she's got more important things to worry about than her obsession with Alex Archer, or even going to Rome for the Olympic Games.

I didn't find out until late next morning when Mr Upjohn appears at our front door, looking as though someone has pricked his chest with a pin. He's wearing a thick polo-neck jumper round his bullish neck. I believe he has come to tell me that I'm out of the team.

'Mrs Archer, can I come in?' he says with overbearing politeness. This is not the voice of my executioner, I think. It's the voice of someone who is seeing his little Olympic team falling apart at the seams. He waits until we're all sitting.

'Alex, I'm sorry to have to tell you, Maggie's ...'

Maggie? I grip my knees hard and challenge him with my eyes to get it over with. I've had one of these messages before.

'She's what?'

'In hospital. Early this morning, emergency surgery for acute peritonitis. I'm afraid she's on the critical list.'

'Oh, dear God,' says Mum beside me. 'Oh, no.'

'Her father rang me this morning. It appears she's had these pains ...'

'I know.'

They both look at me. 'You knew? Why didn't you say anything?' he says.

The unfairness of this makes me angry. 'How could I? I'm not Maggie's mother or sister or anything. She kept telling me it was OK, just a little pain, gripes, constipation, tension, nerves, nothing an aspirin or a laxative wouldn't fix.'

'Oh, God,' says Mum the nurse. 'The worst thing.'

'What's peritonitis?' I say.

'Inflamation throughout the peritoneal cavity sometimes due to a burst appendix, very dangerous,' says Mum. 'How long, the pain?'

'When she came back from Aussie. Said it'd started over there, came and went.' Looking back, I realize she was terrified to admit it was anything brewing. So, I dare say, was her mother.

What am I feeling? Relief that I'm still going, agony for her that she's not, guilt that I didn't bully her into going to a doctor; but then she did, and they didn't find anything; anger with her mother for not taking her seriously.

'Her father rang me this morning. Of course Rome is out. They've been with her all night.'

'Can I go and see her? Where is she?'

'A private hospital in Epsom. I doubt you'll be allowed. And the team assembles tomorrow.'

'Perhaps you'll have another bit of bad news before then, Mr Upjohn.' He actually looks hangdog. Mum stiffens, and looks puzzled.

'It's nothing Mum.'

I don't even want to go to Rome now. You can't have a team of one. Maggie, you can't die on me. You can't.

The hospital, a two-storey building among some lovely trees, is not all that far away from our house, so after he's gone, I announce I'm riding over to see Maggie, whatever he might say. There's only one way to find out if I can see her, and that's to go there. Mum offers a lift, because there's a freezing cold wind blowing, but I'd rather go alone. I pick the occasional pink blossom from trees along the way. In the car-park outside is the black Super Snipe I know so well.

The nurse at the reception desk does not look up when I approach the desk. The message is clear, children wait till I've finished. So I wait. I'll wait, madam, all day and all night if necessary.

'Can I see Maggie Benton, please?'

She looks up and her eyes narrow. 'I'm sorry. She's not allowed visitors except family.'

'I'm family. A close cousin. I've just arrived from Whangarei.' She looks me up and down suspiciously and I pray that she has not seen me on my bicycle through the glass doors. 'If you wait, I'll check with the sister.'

'I'll wait.' She dials a number and mutters into the phone. 'I'm sorry, Miss . . . ?' I murmur Benton. 'Maggie is not allowed visitors, and won't be allowed any for several days.'

'Her parents are here?'

'I believe so.'

'Good. Then I'll find them.' I head off down the nearest corridor, blindly, dropping petals off my little bunch of blossoms.

'Miss Benton! You can't see her. You're not allowed . . .' Try to stop me, you old crow, I think grimly.

I've walked down several corridors between buildings, trying to look as though I'm on some sort of official message, before I know I'm hopelessly lost. Most of the doors are forbiddingly closed; there's that hospital smell, musk and disinfectant in the central heating. There's no sign of a door marked Miss M. Benton, or her parents keeping their vigil in a corridor. Then I see a youngish nurse with a friendly face, and several red stripes on her white uniform.

'Please. Can you help me?'

'Maybe.' Scottish too, I note.

'I'm . . . I just need to see Maggie Benton, please.'

She looks at me hard, and I see a flicker of recognition, which is not all that surprising for people with good memories. 'I know you. You're off to Rome tomorrow, aren't you?'

'Day after. Oh please, tell me . . .'

'I'm sorry . . . you obviously know she was admitted last night and why. She's in some danger.'

'You mean she could die?'

She doesn't answer directly, which in some ways is worse than an empty reassurance. I suppose I hadn't really believed Mr Upjohn.

'It could be several days before we know. I'm sorry, Alex. I've read about you two in the papers.'

'How's she feeling, does she know, that her trip ...?'

'I think so, poor lass. She's pretty groggy, sleeping mostly, will be for days. There's a nurse with her all the time.'

'If she's sleeping, can I see her, just see her, stand in the doorway?'

She hesitates. 'I suppose so.'

'Is her mother in there?'

'She's not left since she came down from theatre. I imagine Mrs Benton would be glad to see you. People need support, at times like this.'

You imagine wrong, I think, following the white uniform, white shoes squeaking on the polished floor.

She gently pushes on a door which says 'No Visitors' and I see a hospital bed, a shape, tubes, drips, bottles of blood hanging upside down. A sleeping face which I can barely recognize, as white as the pillow case it is lying on. Two arms outside the covers tethered by tubes with blood and some colourless liquid running in, or out. A nurse standing at the washbasin behind the door, doing something that nurses do. A nice room, not awful, hospital green but shades of yellow, with carpets, pictures, flowers, bedside cupboard. And Mrs Benton sitting, notably upright.

'Mrs Benton?' says the nurse in a low voice. 'Alex just wanted to see her.'

She turns. I'm glad the Scottish nurse has shut the door and moved on. After a long blank stare, Mrs Benton turns her back on me. I've seen mothers like this before, too: pale and staring with big grey circles of fatigue under their unseeing eyes; hair flat and uncombed; determined not to crack. Beyond sleep.

'I just wanted to give her these,' I whisper, waving my tatty little bunch of blossoms in the air. 'What can I say, the trip won't be the same. Get better quickly. I'm sorry.'

She gets up deliberately and comes over. I'm being shown the door, shown out.

'Didn't you read the sign, No Visitors.'

'The nurse said ...'

'No Visitors. Maggie is desperately ill and you come crashing in, even here, Maggie at death's door, will I never get any peace from you?'

'She's not going to die.'

'It's fifty-fifty.'

'She's not going to die,' I whisper fiercely. 'She's not going to Rome, but she's not going to die.'

'That's what you wanted all along, isn't it. All the kudos, the glory. You didn't want to share it with Maggie.'

I am speechless. I can only look at the ceiling as two nurses squeak along the corridor outside.

'I think I'd better go,' I say.

'Please do.'

I'm looking at my big feet, feeling very large and far too healthy in my jeans and face flushed from riding while Maggie lies over there. There is just one thing I have to say.

'That day, the fashion parade. I didn't believe her when she told me she had a bad pain, why she went home. I thought it was some other reason.'

There is a long silence. 'Why are you telling me this? Alex?'

'I feel bad about it. I'd hate it if she thought I hadn't believed her. Maggie's one of the straightest people I know. I just want to put the record straight.'

Her face doesn't flicker. I open the door.

'I'll come again tomorrow, before the team meeting. I want to say goodbye.' I realize you could take that statement two ways. Her silence as she sits slowly down beside the bed confirms all my suspicions. She won't object to me calling again. She owes me that much.

I have dreamed for years of this day. Training for the last time in that repulsive water, going to school just to say goodbye to my class and the teachers, enduring Three Cheers for Alex at assembly. Finishing my packing, telling Gran yet again that of course all the things she's made for me are just wonderful. Collecting my schedules from Mr Jack, ringing Keith and Julia and a few others to say goodbye. Tonight is the first full team meeting, seeing all the others who have trained at their sports

for five or ten or fifteen years.
All I want to do is weep. It's all such a mess. It wasn't supposed to be like this. I feel stale and exhausted and anything but fit at training. School is a nightmare. I should be gloriously fit and on top of the world. I keep seeing Maggie lying there gaunt and white as a corpse, and hearing the humiliating judgement of some lawyer in Rome or Switzerland or somewhere deciding I'm for the chop.

Mum rings the hospital, because one of her old nursing mates works there, and finds out that Maggie is holding on, but only just. She's not making the improvement expected for someone who's an athlete, super fit; the heavy cold when she had the operation isn't helping. And when I go to see her, Mum comes with me, and stands quietly in the doorway while I go over to the bed and gently kiss Maggie's damp white forehead. Mrs Benton has sunk into the chair. She doesn't even look up.

The team meeting passes in a dream. There are all these men and only six women, and I'm the youngest by about ten years. Oh, Maggie. The manager talks of tickets, passports, vaccination certificates, and the thirty-seven pounds of personal baggage we are allowed, and seven pounds of sports equipment — what does a pair of racing togs weigh, three ounces? Tomorrow's plans. I can't take anything more in.

Monday, August 8.
Totally exhausted. No training. Mr Jack says I'll need all my strength for the trip tomorrow. Today was frantic. Medical examination. Collect uniforms, put them on for 'Meet the Press'. Norm Thompson has a big story about Maggie in this morning's paper. Maggie Benton ill, 15-year-old Swimmer Misses Out On Rome Trip. He tells me he's just rung the hospital again, no change. So also does Mr Upjohn, quite subdued. I like my chaperon, Mrs Churchill, she's cuddly. *My* chaperon. I get weepy again over my cup of tea. I'm the Water Baby of the team, some baby! When the team photo is taken in the Domain wintergardens, all the women have to stand together behind the managers. I'm the tallest, so I go in the middle. We have these *terrible* red hats and plastic granny handbags.

After lunch, the Civic Farewell at the Town Hall with Mr Robinson swallowed up by his mayoral furs, and some old men droning on for ages. We are the biggest team ever sent north of the Equator, costing £34,000. Wow. Mum and Dad take me to the team hotel. Tomorrow morning we'll be up at six, because the plane goes at nine-thirty from Whenuapai. They are coming out to see me off. I don't think I'll sleep tonight. Maggie is the same.

Saturday, August 13.
Somewhere, an hour out of Singapore.
Sorry diary, it's all been a bit much. These are just notes until I can concentrate a bit better. Let's see — late leaving Auckland, mechanical fault to plane, grey and raining as per usual, couple of hundred people to see us off. Entire family, Keith *and* his Mum, Mr Jack and Mrs Jack, Julia, all weeping and waving. Oddly, the Richmonds, who I feel guilty about not visiting. She's older. I remember Keith
telling me about the fights, Andy and his old man. Today, he's smoking a pipe and genial. Most odd, *Mr* Harold Benton, smooth as silk in a suit, kissing me goodbye. Maggie is holding on Oh, and that young reporter, Grant Davies, ticked pink because he's going to start work at the *Herald* next week. He was offered a job, quite a step up from a small-town paper. Says he's now a shorthand speed fiend!

Seedney — saw the bridge and city centre and Botany Bay from plane, not much else. After that, red sand and desert for *hours* to Darwin (hot), sea and islands to Singapore. They let me go up in the cockpit as we approached Singapore. The ships! Being the baby has some advantages.

Singapore was full of surprises. Started badly, after a fifteen hour flight, twenty hours without sleep: a mix-up, no bus to take us to hotel, long hot wait. You can't imagine what tropical heat is like until you're in it.
Raffles Hotel, fantastic. Green, shady, cane chairs to sit in. But a visitor there for me! I hoped it might be someone from the High Commission, with news of Maggie but it turned out to be some friend of the Bentons, yes, Joyce Benton who used to live in Singapore, their daughter Maggie. Mrs Benton had rung her last night! No change to Maggie. The woman was slim and smart, just what you might expect of a Benton buddy. I thanked her, said I was sorry, thinking

that was all, *but* she floored me completely by saying that
Mrs Benton had asked if she would take me away, let me
sleep in a decent bed, show me the sights, take me training at
Singapore Swimming Club, Maggie's old haunt. I just stood
and gaped. Mrs Churchill was happy to let me go; gave her
two days off looking after me. It was a wonderful two days.
Swam a bit at the club, which is vast, but too hot and too
full of people for anything serious. Visited Tiger Balm
Gardens, saw amazing street scenes, beggars, rickshaws,
laundry on poles out of windows, went to a fantastical
Chinese restaurant and had to learn to use chopsticks in a
great hurry at a restaurant so swanky that I wondered what I
was doing there. This lady, whose name was Josephine, had a
lovely house in green jungly gardens, amahs and gardeners, a
husband who worked in a shipping company. *And*, imagine
this, she'd known Mrs Benton at school in England. Seems
Mrs Benton was *very* bright, but her father was a mean old
Sir somebody, huge great house, servants, antiques, and no
money; didn't believe in educating women. Wouldn't let her
finish university, had to come home and look after her
cranky old Dad. Then she drove ambulances in the war and
got married and moved to Singapore. Classic case of wasted
talent, which turned out to be the Classics, Latin and Greek!
Great shame, she's a marvellous organizer, said Josephine, but
Harold's, well, you know, very demanding, and treats her
like a child. No wonder she wanted so badly to go to Rome.
I'm glad I know this. Anyway, the rest of the team went
berserk buying cameras and watches and radios in Change
Alley. Josephine took me shopping for a camera too — a
Zeiss, with money from Mr Jack. She bargained beautifully.
We put a call through to the Bentons just before going to the
airport — got Mr Benton. Maggie's not yet out of danger
because that cold she had last week has brought on chest
complications, which are causing concern, a sort of
pneumonia, he said. I sent all my love, thinking of you,
Maggie. Boy, is it hot here! We had to get out of the plane in
our uniforms, stockings, blazers and all, which stuck to us
with sweat. The child beggars upset me terribly, dirty, some
mutilated, amputated. And the dirt.

Sunday, August 14.
Darkness. Somewhere over India. Can't sleep. My watch says

two a.m. but that's nonsense, 'cause we took off from Calcutta at three a.m. after sitting in the plane for two hours while they refuelled. Temperature was 110 Fahrenheit inside the plane. If this is what it's like at night, daytime must be hell on earth. Got a cup of water and a towel and kept my forehead and arms wet, what else could you do? We are all looking very hangdog. Mrs Churchill's feet have swollen something terrible, some of the athletes' too, can't get their shoes on. The men are unshaven and smelly. There's a red streak outside, dawn somewhere. Karachi soon. Another sweltering place. We can get out of the plane here, they say. I can't wait ... Oh yes, one of the crew came back earlier and told us the All Blacks had drawn the Third Test in South Africa, so they lost the first and won the second and I'm glad they are not having it all their own way ...

I stopped writing. Something was bothering me. It crossed my mind that people sometimes say they have known when someone's died, from thousands of miles away. I think myself back to Maggie's little yellow room, the Scottish nurse, and poor sad Mrs Benton sitting there for the past five days with those terrible plastic tubes of blood. Please Maggie, if it's you, hold on, hold *on*. I closed my eyes, and said the nearest thing to a prayer I knew, and drifted off to sleep. The hostess, God bless her, didn't try too hard to wake me for breakfast, because she knew a sleep of exhaustion when she saw it, and it was only three hours since we had dinner in the middle of the night!

I woke to a change of engine noise, and my ears popping, and needed a pee. Both toilets were full, so I looked idly out the window on to a seaside city below, as brown and dry and dusty looking as Singapore was green. The hostess was busy tidying things up in the galley nearby. I grinned at her. What I got in reply was not the cheerful grin she's had since Singapore. Despite the chic uniform and smart make-up, she was not that much older than me, and she spoke with a broad Aussie accent.

'Do you get off here?' I said.

'I hope so,' she snapped, dropping something, slamming shut a cupboard.

I peered out the window again. 'I've seen that bit of the city before, a few minutes ago,' I said.

'I doubt it. The whole place looks the same. Dry as dust.'

'I suppose, sometimes you have to wait, go around again to wait your turn, or if you have a problem.'

'How ...?' The quick glance out the window gave her away. We both looked. Though we were fairly low, there was no sign of the landing-gear.

'Don't worry. Go back to your seat. Quickly.'

'But I need ...'

'You'll have to wait.' She rapped on the toilet doors. 'Please return to your seats.' And to me, *sotto voce*. 'Don't say anything, please.'

I could try my prayers, I thought, as I swung myself upwards towards my seat and climbed over Mrs Churchill. The plane was climbing again. Out the window I could see a green patch of sports field, a mosque, flat tops of buildings, streets, dry exhausted trees; then the airport and trucks driving round which we later found out were crash wagons with firemen and extinguishers.

Then the crew began to tear up the carpet in the aisle just ahead of us and fiddle round with bits of machinery thus revealed. Mrs Churchill turned to look at me.

'What's going on?'

'I think the landing-gear has stuck,' I said, and though it was stuffy, she deliberately got out her blanket and hid herself right under it.

Well, I thought, if it's curtains, they may find my last will and testament amidst the rubble and bits of flesh, so I got out Gran's My Trip Book and found a fresh page.

It wasn't Maggie about to die, it was me.

Years and years of expensively trained athletes, and the kindly granny from Christchurch hiding her head beside me, about to evaporate in a puff of smoke on a Karachi desert. I began to write, fast.

> There's a problem with the undercarriage, and it looks as though we might have to land on our belly, or go circling round the earth for ever. The crew hasn't actually told us yet, but they are scrabbling around on all fours in the aisle, doing something fairly vital from the looks on their faces. I know because I'm too jolly smart for my own good, and the

air hostess isn't smart enough yet to lie convincingly. So this is the last Will and Testament of the would-be lawyer, the one in four in the classroom who didn't quite make it to adulthood, Alexandra Beatrice Archer, aged 15 and nine months, being of sound mind and very sound body, but right at this moment very unsound indeed, wobbly in the pit of my stomach, and my bladder. I haven't got much to leave except the stuff in my bedroom and the kids are welcome to that *if* they can share it out without fighting. I'd like Julia to have my bike 'cause hers isn't all that marvellous, and Andy's transistor radio to go to Keith. If you find the drop pearl necklace I'm wearing now, can you bury it with whatever you find of me, please. At sea, I think, yes, sprinkle me somewhere near Rangitoto because of Andy and what he may or may not have done in the navy and because he was happiest sailing his boat.

And Maggie, old friend? I wonder where we'll meet again. Somewhere un-earthly very shortly or somewhere earthly in September, if you've won your battle and I've won mine. It's been fun, hasn't it, mostly. Thanks for a good fight. If you make it and I don't, keep at it — there's the Commonwealth Games in '62 and they think it might be Tokyo in '64. Good luck, my friend. The plane has gone very quiet, because it's fairly obvious there's a spot of bother. Mum and Dad, thank you for everything, doing everything you did to get me here, all the love and support that went with it. Perhaps once you've got over it, life without me will be easier, three normal children without that large girl rampaging around causing so much *trouble*. Gran, too, I know you worked yourself to the bone, burning the midnight oil, all those lovely clothes in my suitcase, such a damn shame. Wherever I'm going, I know that Andy will be there. He didn't tell me anything about an air crash, perhaps he thought it better not to, but nothing's as simple as that, is it? He said I was going to Rome, not that I'd get there. Who'd have thought that Maggie and I would come to this — her missing the trip and quite possibly dead, even as I write this if my intuitions were correct, or me maybe about to be snuffed out. I'm feeling surprisingly calm. I'd like to have played Joan. I'd like to have had a child. I'd like to have stood in a courtroom and fought for someone.

Mrs Churchill is a hump of quivering blanket beside me,

poor thing ... the crew are still active ... I've just looked out the window, and Glory Be to God, the wheels are sl-ow-ly appearing. There's a lot of activity on the tarmac as I see it for the last time, and we straighten up for the approach. The crew are running back to strap themselves into their seats ...

My heart was going gi-donk gi-donk again, 200 per minute as we came in to land, over yellow water, rivers, scrubby grass, mud-coloured villages, skinny tropical trees. We straightened up, came ever lower, touched, bounced, touched again, screeched, roared, bounced ... but it was all right, the plane was level and slowing and the crash wagons were converging on us, and a few people began to clap somewhere at the back. We have landed, gloriously, normally. Did I imagine the whole thing? Mrs Churchill has poked her head up. I should have gone to the toilet because the relief was so enormous that I knew I now must, or wet my pants. I undid my seat belt and climbed over Mrs Churchill and dashed, against all the rules, while the plane was still moving fast, past the hostess strapped to her seat, and into the toilet. I didn't know which to do first, sit on it, spew into it, but it was so small I could actually do both at once, into the basin.

By the time I had calmed down and splashed water all over my face and arms, the plane was moving quite slowly. The hostess was busy again, preparing to open the door, let the heat in. She managed a wan smile.

'The hydraulics went,' she murmured. 'They wound the jolly thing down by hand. You wouldn't read about it, would you?'

'You would in the newspapers. I've just written my will.'

'You can tear it up.'

We were ten hours on the ground in Karachi, while they fixed the plane. I couldn't bring myself to write my diary; I remember very little of being taken to a hotel to have a sleep in cool bedrooms, on white sheets, or of taking off again. Landing in Cairo and long waits in the airport lounge there; taking off again and flying at last over the Mediterranean which was every bit as blue as I'd been told.

The last leg, over rocky Sicily and the toe of Italy. Getting ready to step out at Rome airport; uniforms and trying to push swollen feet into stiff shoes. Out the window I can see villages, churches and cyprus trees: Praise Be, the Seven Hills of the city, the Colosseum, the Tiber itself. Someone thinks they are seeing the Olympic stadium, by the river. I look back down the plane. Everyone is craning against their seatbelts to see something out the windows. We've worked for this.

The landing, taxiing, breathing for the first time — pure Roman sunshine, clear and hot. There is a band to meet us, dark Roman men, playing something I recognize, the trumpet tune, the triumphal march from *Aida*! Everyone looks so tanned here — we are winter white, pallid. We don't look like a bunch of athletes and my knees for one are trembling as I walk down the steps to touch Roman ground.

A strange flat bus takes us to the terminal. All the signs are in Italian! There are banners and posters everywhere with the five circles of the Olympic emblem. Customs, passports, tickets, painfully sore feet in our too-tight shoes, swelteringly hot in our black woollen blazers.

But proud, oh yes, *proud*: I come from New Zealand, that's way over the other side of the globe. We have taken six exhausting days to get here, travelled longer and further than any other team. It has cost our country £34,000 to send us. We have earned our right to be here, each one of us. You can see New Zealand on our pockets, and the silver fern which is our national emblem, because ours is a very green country with bush and mountains and rivers, about the same size as Italy, but more spectacular, wilder, newer.

And these tears I'm crying are because I am here, I'm at the end of my tether and I still have a heavy weight at the bottom of my stomach. Maggie may be dead for all I know. I may never swim here, for all I know.

We are standing round as we've done in all the airports, waiting like sheep to be herded, but here, it is different. There are Press photographers and reporters because we are rather special guests, and I seem to get more than my fair share of attention, though

I'm past caring what I look like.

'Bella!' one of the photographers whispers as he looks down into his Rollei. 'Benvenuto!' 'Grazie,' I say.

There's a reception committee too, well-dressed men in lightweight suits, who turn out to be from our embassy here. I wouldn't have taken much notice of them, as they seem to be talking about serious matters to the managers, Mr Upjohn and people — except that I see him pointing me out and one heads my way.

'Alex Archer?'

'Yes.'

'I'm Colin Browning, attaché at the embassy here.' He is fair and almost too smooth, but wearing a little New Zealand silver kiwi pin on his lapel, one of us.

'Welcome to Rome. I hope you are not too exhausted.'

'Fairly,' I say.

'I've two messages for you, which I was told to make sure you got the minute you landed.'

Maggie has died. But he's smiling, he doesn't look like the bearer of bad tidings. Maggie is OK, but I'm out.

'A Mr Harold Benton was in touch with our office yesterday. The message is that your friend Maggie is fine, she's over the worst and doing well, going home from hospital in two or three days.'

Oh, Maggie. I just stand there. A week's real tears well up and overflow. He takes me gently by the elbow towards a seat by the window. Outside all sorts of big jets are parked — B.O.A.C., Qantas, Alitalia, Pan American, Lufthansa, Air France. Funny how you notice these things when you're steamed up.

Mr Upjohn comes over and sits down beside me, which I don't find especially comforting.

'That's good news to hear, Alex, isn't it?' he says. ''The other is equally good. Mr Browning tells me that the games association has cabled. You've been cleared. The circumstances were sufficiently cloudy. It will go no further.'

'I can swim?'

'You can swim.'

I fumble for a hanky, but Mr Upjohn anticipates me and hands me one. I see something in his eyes, respect maybe, which makes me feel that I don't need to keep avoiding him as I've done since we left; that I'm not alone with poor flustered Mrs Churchill in this strange place. I have in fact two people, stand-in parents, to look after me. His smile is not the smile of a crocodile any more.

'Well, team of one,' he says. 'I think we should get you some sleep.'

'It's the middle of the day,' I say. 'I'd rather go for a swim. Can I go to the Olympic pool?'

'Why not?' he says, and stands. 'We appreciate your help, Colin. It looks like they're moving out to the bus now.'

Lead on, I say. *Arrivederci Roma* is being played on the sound system. Arrivederci Andy, and Maggie-getting-better, and all my family still having winter over the other side of the globe. Until we meet again, I'll be giving it my best shot.

Through the swing doors, out of the terminal into the Roman sunshine, full of flowers and trees and young people wearing the clothes of summer and freedom and song.

To the Olympic village and the pool and whatever times I can pull out of my hat against girls who have had a summer's training, a summer's racing. The opening ceremony and meeting Dawn Fraser and seeing the Sistine Chapel and *Aida*.

Andiamo. Let's go!

Alessandra
ALEX IN ROME

Alessandra: Alex in Rome, the third book of the Alex quartet, could not have been written without the help of a number of people, especially:

The Literature Programme of the Queen Elizabeth II Arts Council, whose travel grant allowed me to undertake research in Rome; and Denise Almao, First Secretary of the New Zealand Embassy, for invaluable help while I was in Rome.

CONI, the Italian Olympic Games organization in Rome, where helpful library staff, especially Maurizio Bruni, allowed me access to printed material and to bear triumphantly away a video copy of the four-hour official film of *La Grande Olimpiade, Roma, 1960*.

D. Jack Lyons, life-long friend, for thirty years manager of the Olympic Pool, Newmarket, in Auckland, and a successful and influential swimming coach throughout; Piera Zigliani-Sexton; and Janice Webb, an Auckland singer and teacher much loved by her pupils and friends.

Staff members of the English Department of the University of Waikato, Hamilton, where I completed the quartet during 1991 as Writer in Residence.

Though set in Rome 1960, *Alessandra* remains a work of fiction. No New Zealand swimmer competed at the Rome Olympics.

Sports historians will know that the medallists in the women's 100 metre freestyle event were Dawn Fraser of Australia, Chris Von Saltza, U.S.A., and Natalie Steward of Great Britain. These, and other outstanding swimmers of the Games — Murray Rose, Jon and Ilsa Konrads, John Devitt, and Lance Larson — are mentioned, as well as the previous New Zealand Olympians Jean Stewart and Marrion Roe, and some of the outstanding athletes of the Rome Games, including the New Zealand gold medallists Murray Halberg and Peter Snell.

Otherwise, all characters are fictitious.

The most beautiful pool in the world

Where . . . how to begin, eh Alex, when in Rome?

I turned over the last entry in my diary very firmly, a whole lot of gloomy stuff about crashing at Karachi airport, the Last Will and Testament of Alexandra Beatrice Archer aged 15 years 10 months, but we didn't crash, obviously, and we made it triumphal to Rome, she lives to swim another day . . . so, on a clean white slate . . .

Sat . . . my damn ballpoint wouldn't write properly . . . **urday, August . . . 13, 1960.** I couldn't write properly, either. Teachers always complain about my handwriting but they'd have a fit at this. **2.30 p.m. Olympic Village, Rome, Ita** . . . Why has a large drop of water just trickled down the side of my long nose and plonked onto the empty page? Why is my hand shaking and even the date looks wrong?

Here's why, diary. Because I'm lying in bra and pants in stifling heat on a new bed in a new twin-bed room in the new Olympic village in Rome and somehow we've lost twelve hours and the dates *are* wrong. (My writing is really appalling, like a spider on the booze.) I thought we'd had Sunday in Karachi or Cairo or somewhere up at twenty thousand feet, but when we arrived it was still Saturday August 13th here and I am totally confused.

And now, more or less left to myself, stranded with a stranger in this hot, pink, and airless room, I'm about to let go another whole Niagara.

Copious tears for Maggie who is lying in a hospital bed hooked up to tubes of blood ten thousand miles away instead of being here sharing this room with me. And Andy whose gravestone I haven't yet faced up to visiting. For my fragile wee

Gran whose last bright smiling wave to me at the airport sent a shiver down my spine, and Mr Jack left behind because the officials back home think that coaches aren't all that important, though swimmers know better. For Mum and Dad because I know I've been hurting them for a long, long time and couldn't stop myself.

And yes, I'm crying for me too because after the long dismal winter, it's suddenly glorious hot summer and I'm here, after all, and I can compete in the Olympic Games, after all, and Maggie hasn't died and is going to live to swim another day too. Because I'm not used to feelings of such happiness.

Thankfully, my room-mate Zoe, a skinny high jumper from Wellington, has stripped naked, pulled her sheet up to her chin and gone straight to sleep, flat on her back, hands clasped across her chest like those medieval tombstones. Unlike a tombstone, she is snoring lightly. I hope it isn't a habit. The wooden shutters are making stripes of dusty heavy sunlight across the room. We've been told about these Italian afternoons, when the shops shut and the traffic crawls almost to a standstill and all sensible Romans retire inside to sleep or sit under a pine tree and drink wine.

Well, I'm not Roman and I've never been all that sensible at the best of times (you can ask my best friend Julia) and though I don't know whether I'm Arthur or Martha, laughing or crying, there's no way I can rest and only one thing I want to do now. One place I *must* go to remind myself who I am and why I'm here.

We had driven past the new Olympic pool in the cool, springy bus, on our way in from the airport. I think I was still in a state of shock, having just heard from some man from the New Zealand Embassy meeting us in the arrival lounge that Maggie was at long last getting better from her emergency peritonitis operation. *Also* that my name had been cleared of allegations that I'd unwittingly become a professional (modelling and therefore advertising swimsuits, would you believe?!) which I'm fairly sure was due to a nasty little scheme cooked up by Maggie's nasty mother to get me disqualified from the Games. My long winter and the journey to Rome have not been in vain.

Anyway, we thirty-nine supposedly fit but actually half-dead, very smelly athletes and twelve old officials were all put in this bouncy bus for the final leg to the Olympic Village. We drove too fast on the wrong side of a flag-lined motorway in a tide of tourist buses and peculiar cars and huge trucks with Italian names on the sides; along noisy tree-lined streets with trams and orange buses and motorbikes and scooters. The road signs, except for a few names like Roma, Napoli, Città del Vaticano, meant nothing. We jolted stop-start past terracotta buildings with brown shutters and wrought-iron lamps, over cobblestones and flagstones, through piazzas and around fountains with water streaming over streaky white marble horses, male bodies, animals, shells, all curving and wet and cool. We swung around the archways of the *actual* Colosseum, and then looked down onto jagged pillars and ruins which I guessed to be the Forum, the real Forum where Julius Caesar got stabbed in the back, and above, the brick ruins on the Palatine Hill where the Emperors lived. I wanted to get out there and then, and walk among them, touch, smell, feel, listen to them. When those stones fell over, New Zealand had no people in it, only birds. Then this amazing white, well hardly just a building, more a monstrous wedding cake, and streets hung with Olympic flags and banners and the pavements packed solid with tourists, here for the Games. To see us. We looked down on cheerful umbrellas, outside the Caffè di this and the Ristorante di that, where relaxed-looking people sat at tables, drinking and eating and watching the world go by. (Why can't we sit outside like that at home, in summer? Tables and umbrellas in Customs Street, why not?). This terrible sight broke the silence in the bus. 'I could use a beer,' one guy behind me said mournfully, followed by 'I'll say!' and a few longing grunts. I could use one myself.

Stopped at traffic lights, I felt even more like someone dropped in from outer space; closer, these people were so brown, so fit-looking, so brightly, elegantly dressed, so exactly Roman. They belonged. We flew alongside dusty green parks and across a white bridge decorated with statues, tall ornate lamp-posts, more flags, the greenish river below; alongside the river, till someone cried out loudly, 'There's the pool, Alex,' but

I was on the wrong side of the bus and caught only a glimpse of the scaffolding of some huge stands amongst the pines. 'There's the stadium, folks!' several cried, louder still, because whatever our sport, every single one of us would march there in the opening ceremony. So we all stood up to see a big white piazza bounded by hedges, flagpoles, trees, flat brick buildings, a blinding white obelisk. The bus screeched right to cross the river again, but through the back window we could see at the far end of that white piazza the curving flanks of a gigantic stadium sitting under a tree-covered hill. I was near the back of the bus. When I turned around to sit down again I could see pairs of male faces still peering over the green seatbacks, their eyes bulging. Apart from a few people, like the long-distance runner Murray Halberg, most of us were first-timers to any sort of Games, and all of those faces looked utterly dead scared to me. Then I thought of that immense stand of seats above the pool, and a familiar feeling of dread mixed with pleasure stirred in the pit of my stomach. Another five hundred yards under more flagpoles and between pale brown buildings and we were there, outside the main entrance to the village.

We were all too totally exhausted to speak. We hauled ourselves out of the bus, claimed our travel bags and suitcases weighing no more than 35lbs; stood around, dimly aware of our black blazers being eyed by very healthy-looking athletes sauntering past. We tried to listen to yet more instructions, were given identity cards, handbooks, maps of the village, maps of Rome, sightseeing brochures, timetables, programmes, more instructions as if we weren't saturated already. We bumped our bags off to the allocated apartment block, up the stairs, found our room and bliss! a bed of my own for the next three weeks. Fling open the orangey shutters, discover a view of parched brown grass between us and the next identical apartment block, unlock my bag, fling off clothes, collapse on bed. Truly horizontal. Aaaaaaah.

But I lay there, twitching, tingling all over, tight as a drum, trying not to listen to Zoe's complaints about the unbearable heat and shampoo leaking all through her suitcase and sore calves and swollen ankles and no team physio to massage them back into jumping shape. I tried to write my diary but that was no use, it just ended up making me want to cry.

While Zoe snored, I tried doing some silent sit-ups on the wooden floor, press-ups, some old ballet pliés and développés. Nothing worked. My body said I needed water, that stretching, soothing, powerful rhythm that is so ingrained in me.

My whirling mind was saying: something is going to happen to me here, in Rome, and not just the Games. Isn't that *enough*, Alex? No, something else, something *else*, much more mysterious, delicious, unpredictable, scary too . . . there's such music here, and singing and ruins and paintings and churches . . . something, waiting . . .

The pool hadn't been so far away, when we drove past. Walking distance, surely. Mrs Churchill had pleaded for an hour's rest, *please* Alex, before we go over to the pool. Even behind the closed door, next room to mine, I could hear her snoring tunefully, out for the count. I had no idea where to find Mr Upjohn, somewhere in the men's quarters. It crossed my mind that my two guardian angels might not approve, but it was broad daylight and only just down the road and I just couldn't wait.

It felt just like being a new chum, the first day at school, only more so. Being siesta time there were only a few athletes out and about, in twos and threes, in very brief shorts or wondrous strange track suits of every possible colour. I felt very alone, but I'd got used to that, this past year. I tried to look as though I knew exactly where the gate was, much too nonchalant and/or busy to say hullo, even to a tall girl in a green and yellow track suit with AUSTRALIA written all over it and therefore someone who spoke English, even possibly a swimmer, even possibly friendly.

At the gates set into a high wire fence, like a prison, a couple of guards looked me sleepily up and down, and lengthily examined my identity card. 'New Zealand . . . ah, la Nuova Zelanda.' They both had droopy eyes and moustaches, evil grins and guns hanging from their belts. *Guns* . . . to keep the women in or the men out? I'd never seen a gun up close in my life, let alone on a policeman. 'Si,' I said somewhat haughtily because I didn't feel like trying out my fifty words of Italian yet. 'Excuse me.' Smirking at me, he held onto my card a fraction longer than was necessary. 'Permesso,' I said firmly. I saw a grinning laconic gesture which said *be my guest*, and felt their eyes following. We'd heard about bottom-pinching Italian men too. I began to wish fervently that I'd put a skirt on, however crumpled, not this sleeveless top and pale blue shorts — and brought a hat.

The roads were wide, with few trees for shelter from the baking sun, and not much traffic, just a few orange buses and motor scooters. By the time I reached the bridge I was wet all over and longing for shade, but this was the Tiber I was crossing, on the Ponte Duca d'Aosta, whatever that meant. Beneath me was the Tiber of my Latin books, Romulus and Remus, Rome beginning as a collection of mud huts by the river, Tarquin the Proud, the Punic Wars, Hannibal and his elephants, and Augustus and Nero and Rome burning and all that.

Ye gods! Miss Binning, I remember! You would be a happy woman if you knew how much I remember. Two thousand-year-old water swirled below me, cloudy green round the piles, curving off downstream between low concrete pathways which looked scruffy and not much used, between trees and pale gold buildings that also looked as though they had been there since Rome began.

Crossing carefully at the lights, I was walking slowly now, partly because of the heat, partly because I wanted to prolong and relish this moment of discovery.

There, in that huge stadium ahead, in ten days, in my black and white New Zealand uniform, I'll march with four thousand other athletes.

And there, to the left, in the pool down there between two vast stands just coming into view, I'll swim in my black togs with the embroidered silver fern sewn on by Gran with her tiny even stitches. Twice, even if I don't get any further than the heats of my two events. I could see the trees around the pool now, as from the bus; the high diving platforms at the far end, the stands gradually opening up. Can you believe it, I was trembling. And then, shutting my eyes, with two last decisive steps to the railings . . .

. . . looking down onto the familiar shape of an Olympic-sized pool, people splashing in a clear blue, so dense it reminded me of Gran's blue-bag that she uses in the washing to make the whites whiter. Around it was a concourse of that dusky terracotta pink which even after only half a day in Rome I knew to be its special colour. Above both long sides towered these gigantic stands — ten times bigger than any pool at home. I saw them full of people and shivered. At the left-hand end was the separate diving pool, with the 10-metre tower that people braver than me throw themselves off. At the other end was a grassy slope with a huge blackboard where the results would be posted, (1st, A.B. Archer, New Zealand, dream on, Alex); underneath it a tunnel and behind it a red brick building with tall windows.

Behind the far stand rose the peak of a tree-covered hill which my map told me was the Monte Mario. I've seen lots of pools in my time: square, long, short, kidney-shaped, clean, scruffy, brand-new and very old; blue water, green, black, and all the shades in between; clear water, cloudy, murky, plain dirty, salt or fresh. This was as clear and sparkly as the world's bluest blue diamond, ringed by terracotta and dark green and without a doubt the most beautiful pool in the world.

It may sound strange, but I didn't go down immediately for that longed-for swim. I walked up and down the footpath enjoying the shade of the pines, the pleasure of the swimmers in the pool, lots of them children (not Swimmers, who only ever go up and down). According to my map, this was the Stadio del Nuoto, and the brick building next door was the Piscine Coni, with modern white pillars above an imposing set of steps. I followed a couple of brown-legged girls up, and found myself in a sort of lobby with bronze statues of naked men and glass walls looking down onto another pool: a smaller indoor one, the warm-up pool perhaps, with a spectacular mural of yet more naked men and horses up the far end and the left-hand wall of glass looking out over the Olympic pool.

No one really gave me more than a second glance as I sauntered back outside, but if I wanted a swim I had to find the entrance to the main pool, show my card, and find the changing-rooms. I realized I had no money.

ENTRATA was clear enough. I flashed my Games card

confidently, but the man inside the ticket office didn't seem inclined to let me in. 'Scusi, non capisco' I said when he finished talking. We looked at each other. Then, bolder, 'Desidero . . . ah . . .' and not knowing how to say 'a swim' I mimed the rest with my arms, breaststroke then freestyle. 'Per favore.'

'You are from New Zealand?' The man behind me wore the white shirt and look of an official. A short, square, sweaty Italian one who spoke English, but who wasn't all that friendly either.

'Yes. We've just arrived and I just want to have a swim.'

'There is special time for competitors. This is hour for the public.'

'I don't want to train. Just to have a swim please.'

'Competitors have special time.'

'I don't want special time, I just want to have a swim.'

'You are swimming competitor?'

'I'm an athlete.' It was true enough, as far as it went. Swimmers are athletes. I mightn't look much like a runner, but I could pass for a slimmer kind of shot-putter, or javelin thrower. He asked to see my identity card. I couldn't remember if it said what sport I was competing in. Apparently it didn't. 'Look, it's a hot day, I just want a swim.'

'New Zealand?'

'Si.'

'Beautiful country,' he said, examining my card minutely, as though he'd never seen one before or it might be forged.

'Si.' This was getting tedious, and making me cheeky. 'Molto bello.'

'Ah, parla italiano?'

'Non, I mean no and please can I go in for a swim? I'll pay, if that's the problem,' I said rashly. 'Per favore?' I said, holding out my hand for the card.

But somehow the little game had been played far enough. He looked at the man behind the counter and nodded. 'Thank you, grazie, molte grazie' I said, pulling my card from his pudgy fingers and scuttling through the turnstile before they changed their minds. These poolside buildings were concrete and tiles, and smelled of chlorine, just like all the others. I followed a girl through an archway marked DONNE and found myself in a large changing-room full of very brown people speaking Italian, loudly and very fast. For the first time in my life I felt bashful undressing, being a pale slug by comparison; however, I changed, put my top back on to cover what were obviously racing togs, and followed the same girl out to the pool.

The whole place was even more spectacular from the pool level. The stands looked vast, the surrounding pines and cypress trees black against the sky. I walked up onto the grass slope under the results board and spread myself in the sun, but my winter-white skin, already pink from the walk over, soon began to sizzle, and I had to move into the shade. I found myself dozing, half-dreaming of Andy, of lying with him in the sun at another Olympic pool over the other side of the world, lazily singing 'Summertime — and the livin' is easy', but without pain, just a gentle thankful sort of remembering.

Then I heard a loud announcement, not a word of which I understood, and the pool slowly began to clear. Public hour was over. The clock said 4.30. I couldn't dive in hurriedly; yet how long would it be before the competitors started to arrive and I could legitimately be here? Ah, Alex, how do you get yourself in these embarrassing situations?

I waited as long as I could. To my great relief, when there were only a few people left, a group of what were clearly Swimmers came out of the female changing-rooms, carrying the usual paraphernalia of towels and bags. It was obviously now Competitors' Time, so I slunk back into the empty changing-room, changed into another set of togs in the toilet, put on a bathing cap and strode out with a towel hiding my black bag, looking as though I owned the place.

Stupid, maybe, as if anyone would care really, but the last thing I wanted on my first day in Rome was long explanations involving Mr Upjohn and interpreters and an irate Italian official. Now, I had every right to be there.

At last, I had my swim. There were only four girls in the pool so far, churning away. The starting blocks looked higher above the water than at home, something I'd have to get used to. Anyone watching me probably thought I was just having a big languorous stretch or windmilling my arms the way swimmers do before they dive in, but it was actually a primitive and irresistible urge to lift up my arms to the trees and the sun and say thank you, God and everyone else, for getting me here safely.

The water was bitingly cold on my overheated skin. I felt weightless, and, though I knew it wouldn't last long, utterly wonderful. The water felt every bit as good as it looked, like swimming in champagne.

Until I felt someone jab rudely at my shoulder as I turned. I looked up to see Mrs Churchill's round red and angry face leaning over me. I was not in her good books.

'Alex, I could put you over my knee, I could,' she panted. 'Have you no idea of the trouble you've caused? I searched the village, I woke up Zoe, I couldn't find Mr Upjohn . . .'

Thank goodness for that.

'I've run all the way over here, I couldn't get past the man at the ticket-office . . .' She sat down on the starting block, sweating heavily, fanning herself with her handbag. 'I know you were dying for a swim, but I have to say, I'm disappointed in you, going off by yourself without permission, without even telling me.'

'You were dead to the world,' I said.

'You should have woken me up if it was that urgent. I thought we agreed we'd all have a little rest first. Alex, you are NOT to go roaming round Rome by yourself ever again, is that clear? And no, I didn't tell Mr Upjohn.'

I hauled myself out of the pool, smiling at the pun, and gave her a sloppy fishy wet hug which I knew she didn't mind because she was so hot and because she was just as much relieved as angry.

'Thanks Mrs C for not telling. Clever Mrs C. Sorry Mrs C,' and she too couldn't help a twitch of a smile. It would certainly have been easier to have come here together, but a hundred times slower by the time she'd huffed and puffed her way from the village to the pool. And she'd have spoiled it, that first sight of the pool I'd worked so long and hard to compete in.

'You should come in, Mrs Churchill,' I said. 'It's *beautiful.*' I dived back in, did a dolphin dive or two, a pirouette, just for the sheer joy of it. Mrs Churchill was not pleased with me but she couldn't help herself smiling. 'It's *gorgeous.*' When I thought of that grubby dark pool I'd trained in twice a day for the past six months, the salt and badly treated water that left me nearly blind after each session . . . I did another set of twirls and swirls and dives. I was the dolphin I'd always known I once was or would be.

The changing-room was another whole new experience. When finally my five days in an aeroplane caught up with me and suddenly I couldn't swim another length, I found the changing-room now full of people arriving for their second training session of the day. I pretended to be preoccupied with dressing, but I was a new chum to this scene. There was lots of chat in several languages (two, Italian and French, I recognized — heaven knows what the others were). They wore smart track suits and skin-tight nylon togs in every colour under the sun, even white. Only black, dark green, and dull maroon had made it to the colonies so far, and my black togs looked pretty baggy and wrinkly and boring by comparison with these.

Along the benches were bags proclaiming U.S.A. Swim Team, South Africa, Italia, Canada, Sweden, something that looked like Hungary, Romania. No Brits or Aussies, thank heavens, the people most likely to say hello to a Kiwi. The Americans, whose striped togs were much the nicest, obviously all knew each other very well, and talked loudly among themselves about the price of hair sets in the village, going to see the Pope at St Peter's next Sunday, and having their bottoms pinched by randy Italians, taking absolutely no notice of anyone else.

Overall, though, behind the chat there was a brittle sort of tension. In ten days time we'd all be lining up against each other, the Americans against each other, too. In here, just as at home only more so, people would be watching what they said about their schedules, how they felt, which muscles were strained, which were hurting, when their periods were due, whether their time trials had been brilliant or lousy.

As I caught sight of myself in a mirror, I realized I was the only person in the entire dressing-area who was horribly, winterishly pale. Alongside the olive Italians and the golden California girls, my skin had an unhealthy bluish tinge, except on my shoulders where I'd caught some sun already. Compared with these healthy brown specimens, I didn't feel much of an international athlete at all. I had an overwhelming urge to lie down on a soft bed and pass out.

But suddenly it hit me that there was something we did share — our size. Here, for the first time in my little life, despite my peculiar colour, I was normal. I was not the largest, tallest female in the room, the butch freak with the huge shoulders. This idea was so powerful that I sat down on the bench. I looked up at all these fantastic bodies in various stages of undress. We were birds of a feather. In countries where there were big swimming communities and lots of competition, these tall girls would train and race together and it probably didn't cross their minds; but there'd only ever been one of me, the 'big girl' — 'Juno-esque', a stupid reporter once called me — who'd always been so much taller than Maggie and the rest. Here five foot ten and a quarter was normal, just your common or garden female body. Normal, at last!

'You from Noo Zealand?'

I was caught off guard. The dark-haired girl next along the bench was pulling on a pair of red togs, and her bag said Canada. She sounded utterly amazed that anyone should come from Noo Zealand. 'Yes,' I said, bracing myself for another query about my bea-uuuu-tiful country or just how long was the bridge between Sydney and Auckland, which according to those who've travelled a lot is a standard question of friendly but very ignorant North Americans.

'Excuse me, but are you okay? You're so pale I thought . . .'

'I'm like this all the time. It's winter at home now.'

'That a fact? Do you get snow there?'

I had a great urge to say yes, Auckland was this very moment under ten feet of snow; but she was trying to be kind. She looked the sort of earnest type who might belong to a church choir. 'No, just rain, cold, gales, more rain.'

Was it obvious that I was suddenly feeling homesick, stomach-sick, tired-sick and on the verge of a second explosion of tears? As I stood up, the room started to swim. I sat down again, pretending to get something out of my bag, willing myself to stand and walk out of the dressing shed without the total embarrassment of falling over in a roomful of foreign-speaking strangers.

'When did you arrive? How many in your team?' she said as I fumbled with my things.

'Today and just me.'

'Just one? *One* swimmer!' Having just taken her glasses off, she peered down and examined me closely. 'Glory be! Poor you. By the way, I'm Barbara, I do backstroke.'

'I'm Alex, freestyle . . . um, excuse me . . . see you later . . .' Sorry, Barbara backstroker, if you thought I was unfriendly but . . . I made it to the door, steadied myself along the tiled corridor, launched out across the concourse to where Mrs Churchill was waiting to take me home, feeling very weak at the knees. I dared not even look at the pool which was now full of no doubt very famous people churning up and down breaking world records. The first day of school was over. Tomorrow I wouldn't be a new chum. The New Zealand swimming team asked her chaperone, very humbly, if they could possibly get a taxi back to the village.

Born on a thirteenth

'Go to Rome, young man,' said my teacher as we sat, an uneasy thirteen, at dinner three nights ago in Milan. Our number had been noted early in the evening; I alone welcomed it, for I was born on a thirteenth, and too many good and/or interesting things have happened to me on thirteenths to discount as coincidence.

Though I hadn't then been to Rome, I demurred. The city, I said, would be packed full of tourists and beautiful but brainless Olympic athletes. Ah, they all agreed, but consider, La Grande Olimpiade! Aspiring singers should know something about crowds and large audiences; particularly those who come from a country which has virtually no people in it at all! You'll understand something of Rome when you hear the crowds roar in the Stadio Olimpico, they said. Go to see *Aida* at the Terme di Caracalla, outdoors, in the moonlight, they said. *Aida!* I needed little more persuading.

Even better, it transpired that Enrico, one of the older students also at dinner, was driving down to Rome, taking two days, returning a car to an aunt, and then going with her on holiday to Scotland, of all places, somewhere cool, quiet, and raw. The upshot was a seat in a splendid 1947 Alfa Romeo to Rome, and an empty apartment to stay in when I got there.

My only duties would be twofold; to help get the pair of them out to the airport on Saturday morning, she being an elderly and nervous traveller who liked courtiers about her to carry bags; and to feed an equally ancient Pekingese dog called Turandot who has apparently never left the apartment, which is near the Terme di Caracalla, for fifteen years.

I write this, in that apartment, on a thirteenth (August 13), beginning a new journal. My English, I suspect, skipping through eighteen months and nearly five hundred pages of my last journal, the chronicle of a Kiwi innocent abroad, has acquired a formality of tone which would raise eyebrows in the Land of the Long White Shroud; unless there has been a miraculous change since I left which actually encourages schoolboys and grown men to speak in sentences. To voice an opinion on something, anything, other than rugby and race horses.

This apartment is the epitome of cool Roman elegance, huge and sparsely furnished (cf a New Zealand house of wood with its china cabinets and colonial clutter), yet I don't feel lonely, just very privileged, surrounded by paintings, furnishings and porcelain of restrained beauty. Enrico's ancient aunt turned out to be less ancient than he pictured, but tall and patrician, not unlike a Roman version of Virginia Woolf, and not long retired as principal flautist with one of the Rome orchestras.

I received my standing orders for the dog Turandot, which resembles a bedraggled sheepskin slipper, and was given a brass key large enough to lock up the Victor Emmanuel II memorial. We left the apartment in a cloud of deep gloom — the fates had decreed that she would not, of course, return from this holiday. She hoped that the plane would at least honour her immortal soul and crash on Italian heads, not the chilly Swiss, the unmusical English, or worse still, the French. Her other nephew Ruggiero knew the bank where her will was kept. He would settle her affairs, as she was laid to rest in a common foreign grave. Enrico, a tenor, was becoming more than slightly hysterical.

As chauffeur for the day, I stylishly drove the Alfa Romeo to the airport and back, to stable it permanently in the garage below. Mercifully, from what I experienced of Roman traffic today, the car does not go with the apartment. By the time I put both my passengers on the plane, I was wondering if all our stars were foretelling disaster.

Except — this is a thirteenth. Reluctant to tackle the traffic until I'd had a beer and studied a street map, I wandered over to the arrivals lounge, reminded, by all the flags and music, that this is Rome in festive mood, that the Olympics start in about ten days. Perhaps I might see some of the teams arrive, a film star, a head of state. I can spend hours people-watching, and I am on holiday.

Curiously, or perhaps not for a thirteenth, it was during that hour that I saw the New Zealand team emerge from Customs — the largest, indeed the only group of Kiwis I have seen since my departure. If they'd come direct, it wasn't surprising they looked so travel-worn, trailing shoulder bags and black blazers, with the dazed eyes of a bunch of idiotic herded sheep. There were about forty men, at a guess; mostly smaller physically than I would have imagined, probably athletes and hockey players, about my height; older men who were obviously officials; short but brawny types who must have been weightlifters and boxers, with pugnacious noses and tight shirts; a couple of giants.

The six or seven women were in better shape. One was much younger than the others, and stood apart. Very tall, very slim but broad in the shoulder, long arms, maybe seventeen or eighteen. Very short hair, but she wore the drab uniform with a certain grace, more than the rest of them put together; also utterly and defiantly miserable. A distance runner, javelin thrower maybe? A swimmer?

As I watched, a well-dressed man, one of the welcoming party, went across and spoke to her. He was solicitous, but whatever was said looked like bad news; he led her crying to a seat. Unlike most girls, she wept openly, not trying to conceal her need. Something from home, a death, an accident, a reason to turn around and fly straight back? But after one of the officials joined them, I wasn't so sure. As she recovered from the tears, her face cleared like a flower opening after rain. Everything about her sang, vibrated with life. She looked as though a great weight had been lifted off those superb shoulders.

I went out of the swing doors. I could pass for an Italian bystander, of which there are always plenty. Behind my dark glasses, I saw the team straggle out to the bus, heard snatches of English: Cripes it's hot, complaints about swollen legs and entreaties to the manager to stop for a beer. I had forgotten how strong the Kiwi accent is, how raw the vernacular. I had no desire to speak to them, to identify myself as a countryman, even to wish them luck.

The girl came among the last. Closer she was, as were they all coming from a New Zealand winter, extremely pale, with dark rings under her eyes, but somehow triumphant too. She looked straight through me, clearly not a girl who smiles at strange men, but her eyes were warm, a curious grey-blue; indeed her whole face was curious, strong, not pretty, with wide-set eyes under a pair of straight eyebrows that owed nothing to the current fashion for plucking, and splendid bone structure. Not a typical New Zealand face, if there is such a thing; for a girl, too direct, too calculating. The rest of the team looked only barely alive, but she actually bounced up the steps. I watched her move down the bus, find an inside seat. Even from there, I could feel the force of her personality as she talked with the older woman next to the window. A chaperone, probably.

I had not intended to make contact with the team. Two or three Italian contacts, maybe, none very compelling; I may follow up the offer of a Vespa motor scooter. I have a week to see Rome, and then a few extra days to see some of the Games events if I can get tickets. Perhaps the opening ceremony, some of the athletics, the fencing, gymnastics, the swimming. Maybe she is a swimmer. I don't intend to make contact.

Staking out the territory

That first night I went to bed while it was still daylight and Zoe and all the others were having dinner. I slept for thirteen hours. No 5.30 alarm, no nightmares of Andy drowning, car accidents, swimming in glue or making a fool of myself on a stage; my first total zonked-out sleep for two years. Mrs Churchill got all peculiar about the idea of me missing dinner, but the very thought of food and another roomful of strangers made me feel ill.

Besides, I had this new and heady sensation of lightness. No one here knew anything about me or my times or the fact that I'd never swum in an international race in my life. No one expected me to win a medal or even get into the final. Back home, they knew I was up against Dawn Fraser and the American wonderkids and they just wanted me to do my best. I went off to sleep naked under a sheet, light-headed and smiling.

I'll never know if the bells were real. Did I dream them, the bells ringing at dawn, the magical beginning of the third act of *Tosca* when the shepherd boy sings to his sheep? I listened to the record at home often enough. Or did I really hear the distant bells of the city, St Peter's and the rest, all on different notes, calling? Real or dreamed, no matter, I slid blissfully back to sleep, hearing bells.

'Alex? Are you alive? Wake up.'

Behind my eyelids I registered light, warmth, sweet female smells, my own hot smell. Voices outside, not English, traffic, car horns. Where on earth was I?

'Alex!' An older voice, worried. A weight sat on my bed. Someone had hold of my toe. *'Alex?'*

I'd become paralysed in the night, I'd picked up polio in Calcutta, I was about to be carted off to an iron lung.

I prised a sticky eyelid half open, and saw a prim lady with fuzzy grey hair and glasses, wearing a white embroidered blouse of the sort bought in Singapore. Mrs . . . Churchill, ah, *right*, my chaperone and I'm in Rome for the Olympics.

'How do you feel?'

I'm in Rome to swim in the Olympics!

'How do you feel, Alex?'

'She's okay, Mrs Churchill. Look at her grinning.' That must be Zoe, my high-jumping room-mate, sounding quite chirpy.

'It's breakfast time, Alex. You must have some food.'

'What's the time?'

'Nearly eight. You've been asleep for thirteen hours.'

'Mmmmmmmm.' No cat ever had such a stretch. Did I dream that beautiful pool surrounded with pine trees, the turquoise water? No, I didn't. For the first time in months, despite a low-down gut-ache, I couldn't wait to go training.

'You were out cold last night,' said Zoe, brushing her long hair. 'You just died. I've never seen anyone drop off so quickly.'

'Were you here?'

'Don't you remember?'

'No.' I must have sleepwalked too. At the pool, with me upright, but only just, we'd got a taxi after some lengthy pidgin English-Italian chat and a long wait. There'd been a small problem with Italian money, because neither of us had any. I had to grovel to borrow some temporarily from an official at the village, while Mrs C stayed with the upset taxi driver. I think.

'What day of the week is it?'

'Sunday.'

'Can we go to St Peter's?'

'Tiger for punishment, you are,' said Mrs Churchill, shuffling a folio full of papers.'You've got training and we'll talk about it over breakfast. I remember reading . . . yes, there's a special audience next Sunday for all the Olympic athletes.'

Next Sunday! It seemed a year away. My side of the room looked like a bomb went off. It had looked pretty bare yesterday when we walked in, like a school hostel. There were no pictures on the pink walls, and the furniture was mostly built-in, with a big mirror above the dressing-table. Zoe, one of those tidy types, had already got herself organized into drawers and taken up more than half the dressing-table space with her bottles and junk.

During the night something else had also happened. As I began to get out of bed, I felt, smelt, and saw that my first period in over six months had well and truly arrived, explaining the gut-ache. 'Shit.'

'Alex!'

'Oh hell.' I pulled the sheet back quickly and leant over to pull my dressing-gown from my exploded bag. Thank God Mum the nurse hadn't listened to me when I did my packing. I'd shouted at her *I'm not going to have a period ever again*, but she'd insisted that I bring the proper equipment.

'What's the matter?' asked Mrs Churchill.

'Cramp, I think or . . .' I wobbled my calf muscle from side to side, and flexed my foot up and down convincingly. 'Might have pulled something.' Five minutes later Mrs C had satisfied herself that I didn't need Mr Upjohn to find a physio immediately, I wasn't out of the Games, and I probably would walk again. Eventually I persuaded her and Zoe to go on over to breakfast, after she'd given me detailed instructions on how to get to our dining hall.

Despite the mess, I was pleased that my new slim body — my clothes told me I'd lost a few more pounds on the journey over — was in working order again. It's a bit odd, when you're nearly sixteen and as virginal as it's possible to be, to go without a period for over six months. Stress, Mum had said flatly, but I knew she'd worried about it.

It took me a while to clean everything up. Along with myself I washed the sheets in the shower. I hung them in the wardrobe, and scrubbed at the blood on the mattress with my face flannel and plenty of cold water. Most of it came out. It would dry quickly, in this heat. *Very* embarrassing, but . . . at least my period would be well over by my first race. My body was obviously telling me something.

Even at 8.30 in the morning the sun was fierce, and rock 'n roll music was blaring out across the brown grass. There were lots more people strolling round in track suits than yesterday. Mostly men, I noted, keeping well away from anyone. You could walk underneath the brown buildings — they were built on these funny legs. Everything, buildings, trees, grass, looked dusty and dry and brand-new, only just finished off in time.

I found our dining hall easily. It was bigger than a school hall and about as plain, and seemed to be for us Kiwis and two or three other teams. Mrs Churchill waved at me from one end of a long table full of our men in black track suits, tucking into breakfast. Zoe had found her athletic mates. I walked over, my gut-ache worse, remembering just in time to limp slightly.

'Morning, Alex,' a few voices cried, waving breadrolls or forkfuls of sausage. 'How's your leg?' asked Mrs Churchill, looking anxious.

'Not too bad. Where's Mr Upjohn?' I said, before she could go on about it.

'Probably still asleep. He had a managers' meeting last night.'

'Ah,' I said cynically. I'd heard about managers' meetings, with a few drinks.

'Alex, he was very tired,' she said indignantly, but she knew what I meant.

'Of course he was.'

She grinned. 'Go and get some food, dear.' I looked at her plateful of goodies and suddenly realized I was *ravenously* hungry.

I had never seen such food. To get the cooked part of the breakfast you had to queue army-style in front of a long serving area manned by middle-aged Italians acting as pantomime cooks, in white tunics like dentists and tall picture-book baker's hats. But they knew about food — there were nutty cereals and fresh fruits, huge jugs of juices, cooked eggs and bacon and tomatoes and meat and sausages, breads and sweet rolls and jams and coffees, laid out like a banquet. '*Wow*,' I said, and a tall brown man in front turned and grinned. He had the blackest, tightest hair I'd ever seen.

'Who are these people?' I said as I unloaded my tray of some oaty/nutty mixture called muesli, fruit, bacon and eggs, bread roll, and coffee.

'The very dark handsome ones are Moroccans,' said Mrs C.

'The handsome white ones in the green track suits are South Africans.'

Interesting! Someone in this village was either ignorant or had a sense of humour. Even I knew that our All Blacks and their Springboks were currently slogging it out in South Africa; you couldn't avoid knowing, front page stuff every day at home, all about a few games of rugby. One win each, including a very strange game in Cape Town with the crowd of Coloureds cheering for the All Blacks, not for their own country. A draw yesterday and the deciding Test in two weeks.

I tried my muesli. It was a bit floury, but chewy, and good too. I wondered, as I chewed, if the fair-haired South Africans over there knew about the protests in New Zealand. I'd walked with Keith Jameson and two thousand other people up Queen Street, on a march organized to protest against the team going to South Africa without Maori players to keep the South Africans happy. For my pains I got my cheesecake picture on the front page of the paper and an official reprimand. That was three months ago. The team still went.

Even here we couldn't get away from the damn game. 'Yeah, okay, a draw, but the Springbok pack's bloody walking all over us,' I heard from the table behind me. I looked around, and saw a group of our men hobnobbing with a group of South Africans, and guess what they were talking about!

'Damn,' I said. 'They'll talk about nothing else all next week but bloody rugby. Or fight about it.'

'Alex, dear,' Mrs C chided me, yet again.

'The All Blacks should never have gone.'

'Not here, please. It's a dead issue.'

Light blue touch-paper, retire. 'Tell that to the Maori players who got left behind because their skin's brown.' The two hockey players opposite glanced up from their plates, surprised.

'They said, no Maori players were good enough to go.'

'Convenient. It's the principle, don't you see?'

'I see people round us, different colours and different races, all talking, all here for one thing, the Olympics,' she said firmly. 'We'll have no more talk of rugby.'

'Suits me, Mrs C,' I said.

'Much more to the point — we've got ten days to get you fit.'

Right on cue, Mr Upjohn appeared with his tray loaded up with cooked goodies and bread rolls, like there'd never be a lunch. 'Morning Alex, and how are we today?'

'Fine,' I lied, because since I began to eat my gut-ache had got considerably worse. He didn't look too good himself, but then track suits don't look all that good on older people with barrel chests, big bottoms, wet hair from showering, and a hangover. He'd also cut himself shaving.

'She's got a leg problem, maybe a pulled calf muscle,' said Mrs Churchill.

'No, it's okay, really,' I said hastily.

'Should we ask to see a doctor?' said Mr Upjohn.

'No truly, it's not that bad. It might have been cramp. I was half asleep.'

'Well, keep me posted, Alex.' He attacked his fruit with enthusiasm. 'I hear the third Test at Bloemfontein was a great game.' I grinned *I told you so* at Mrs Churchill. 'That's one each,' he said chewing away, 'and a draw. What a game the fourth Test will be! An absolute classic!'

The man was in Rome for the Olympics, thanks to me, and now he wishes he was in South Africa watching rugby! There was no pleasing some people.

'It's not a proper New Zealand team. I won't spill any tears if the Springboks win. We shouldn't have been there in the first place, and it's a rough and disgusting game anyway,' I said riskily and apparently loudly, because now a number of surprised faces along both sides of the table were looking at me.

'Alex, you really must . . .'

'Hear, hear,' said the hockey player opposite, a skinny chap with thin gingery hair. Well, support from a hockey player would figure. Andy once told me that rugby players think that anyone who plays hockey is a poof. Actually I think it's a much more intelligent and skilful game than rugby. He raised his coffee cup in a sort of toast. 'I was in that march up Queen Street too. That picture of you in the paper . . .'

'. . . was very embarrassing,' I said quickly, because Mr Upjohn had written me a snotty letter complaining about it, threatening that I might find myself withdrawn from the Rome team if I continued to get involved in controversial issues like protest marches. I couldn't resist adding, 'I think it was rigged.'

Mr Upjohn glanced up, then at Mrs Churchill, while the hockey player looked interested, but was tactful enough not to pursue the subject. There was a long silence while we all concentrated on digging out our melons and munching on our muesli, which I have to admit was much more interesting than Weet-Bix. The pain in my gut had gone from bad to worse. I'd rather lost my enthusiasm for beginning training today.

'Now, dear,' said Mrs Churchill finally, doing what women always do when they're feeling uncomfortable, i.e. rummaging around in her handbag. 'Now let's talk about today. Where's that list of training times?'

'I'd rather rest today. Or go to St Peter's or somewhere.'

Mr Upjohn got on his coach's look. 'Your first swim, Alex; don't you think, after that long rest yesterday, you should be getting to grips with your schedule?'

Conspirator Mrs Churchill put her head down and started to rummage in her papers again.

'I've got my period, Mr Upjohn. It came last night. Actually it's the first for six months and rather heavy and giving me a gut-ache.'

'Alex *dear*,' said Mrs Churchill, so embarrassed she didn't know where to look. Girls don't talk about periods in mixed company, particularly at breakfast in front of strange hockey players. Why not? He was wearing a wedding ring and presumably knew about these things? Mr Upjohn had grown-up daughters and grandchildren too. Why shouldn't men know about something which happened to females twelve moontimes a year for most of their lives? And Mrs C, you're the worst, because you were more concerned about the men being embarrassed than you were with my gut-ache and what you could do about it. I flashed them all a brilliant and unrepentant smile.

'I'd like to just . . . well, go for a long walk, by the river. Walk round the village, look at the stadium. Tomorrow I'll start, promise.'

She tried to hide it, but her face dropped at the prospect of a long walk with me. She sighed. Duty called. 'Over to you, Enid,' said Mr Upjohn, very embarrassed, also relieved it wasn't him who had to put on his walking shoes. He pushed his half-eaten plate of bacon and eggs away. I think I might have put him off his breakfast.

Actually, wanting to go for a long walk was for a more primitive reason than simply keeping out of the pool with a very heavy period. I'd always trained, raced, whatever through periods, no problem. Some girls had old-fashioned mothers who thought it was bad for them and unhygienic, but I think that's old wives' tales; it's not cupfuls of blood, only teaspoons, if that, and cold water stops it, and anyway, think of all those small boys peeing in public pools, I bet!

I could have fixed the gut-ache with a codeine, and ignored the heavy bloated feeling. After all those days sitting in aeroplanes, I just wanted to stake out the territory, walk on the warm earth, smell the trees, absorb the sun through my skin, work out where everything was, so I knew where I was.

Begin to feel — because I don't feel it yet — like an athlete whose whole life has been working towards being here, a competitor at La Grande Olimpiade.

Mrs Churchill, who Zoe had dubbed the Bulldog, wasn't a bad old stick to spend a day with. We changed some money at the Banco di Roma and bought stamps at the Ufficio Postale. To my astonishment, there was a letter for me! From Mum, saying how proud she was, they all were, how she just *knew* (written well before I left, when things were looking pretty grim for both Maggie and me) that things would be all right. She loves me. More than enough to bring tears to my eyes. There was also a 'Welcome to Rome' telegram from darling Mr Jack which had the same effect. We bought postcards and writing paper from the souvenir shop; we couldn't *believe* the prices posted outside the beauty salon and Bulldog decided she might shout herself just one hair-set while she's here, and I decided I'll stick with my wisps.

We walked through the recreation areas where athletes, black, white, and every colour in between, were lounging around formica tables drinking Coke, keeping the juke-box going. I persuaded Bulldog we should have a Coke and one song, a new Elvis Presley 'It's Now or Never', which I thought pretty soppy and Bulldog couldn't *stand*. Then we wandered out through the main gates. We decided we knew only seven of the dozens of flags flying above the gates, and headed across the bridge towards the stadium. It was already too hot for walking, but we're stubborn Kiwis who don't mind a bit of sun and we wanted to see the stadium.

Empty theatres have always fascinated me, school halls, pools, wherever you get performers and audiences. They're full of memories, ghosts, music, people laughing and crying, if only you stand for a while and listen. This stadium was different. We found an entrance, showed our identity cards to an attendant who spoke English and understood that we just wanted to have a look. He showed us through a corridor, up some steps, and pointed us towards the sunlight.

I know I gasped. I'd imagined *nothing* like this. We were surrounded by stands, four tiers high, with groups of flagpoles around the rim. In front of us was a grassy football field, dwarfed by the red running track and another circle of grass. A gigantic scoreboard loomed over one end. We turned around slowly, speechless. It was brand new; there were no ghosts, no music here yet, but it was waiting. 'Blimey Charlie!' Bulldog said finally. 'And we think Eden Park is the centre of the universe!'

That wasn't all. We were even more overcome when we wandered into the smaller stadium next door, through the red brick buildings next to the Piscine Coni I had discovered yesterday. White paved courtyards led us on through an avenue of white twice-life-size male bodies, carrying cloaks, wearing sandals, with veins in their marble legs and rib bones showing through, and figleafs on the skimpy side. I think it was a bit much for Bulldog. In the stadium itself, a whole circle of huge statues stood white against the trees behind and looked down on a low oval of marble seats and a terracotta running track. We hadn't expected this. We found out later it was the 'severe Greek-styled' Stadio dei Marmi. It was my classical history books come alive. Children were training on the track. On the grassy square in the middle they were practising long jumps, throwing the discus, javelins. If I imagined them naked and glistening with oil, I was back in ancient Greece. It wasn't a film set, it was for real, a real living classical Greek stadium here and now, a beautiful space for beautiful free bodies.

I stood there like a stunned mullet and thought, what *else* was there for me to discover, jewels like this which weren't even in the guidebooks? I knew about the Colosseum, but what else? Below us five boys, about fourteen-year-olds, lined up for a race, dancing around as runners do. I could feel my own limbs twitching, longing to be back in my element, which is water. I could forget the throbbing ache in my lower tum. I was beginning, just beginning, to feel like an athlete again.

By lunch time we were both wilting badly, and decided to walk back along the road above the river. If I'd thought breakfast was amazing, lunch was out of this world: unknown vegetables and fruits in salads, olive oil and wine vinegar that you pour on separately, great trays of red-flecked salamis, pizzas dripping with mushrooms and stringy pale cheese, meats with green-flecked stuffings, something called pistachio, purple figs and apricots, rich cakes dusted with icing sugar, cut into small pieces, not like Gran's hunks of orange sponge-cake squelching cream. We had three weeks of this! Now I knew why they had siestas in Italy, and it wasn't just the heat.

When I woke my gut-ache was gone. It was after five. I thought of the statues around that elegant Greek stadium, the inviting blue of the pool, and shivered with excitement.

Now it was time to get out my folio of programmes, papers. Tho' it was all in Italian, the swimming programme was clear enough, with the events and competitors' names after the usual pictures of the chairmen of this and that committee.

Venerdì, 25 agosto, the swimming starts. Famous names leapt out at me: Dawn Fraser and Lorraine Crapp, Ilsa Konrads, Jon Konrads, Murray Rose, John Devitt — Australians all. Dawn Fraser's main rival Chris Von Saltza and the fourteen-year-old wunderkind Carolyn Wood, both U.S.A., a few famous Dutch and British names I knew — what the hell was I doing there? A little foreign fish of very ordinary species about to get chewed up and spat out by all the famous sharks.

There was my name, Sig. Alexandra B. Archer (N.Z.), in the fifth and last Batteria of the women's 100m Stile Libero, 15.00 to

16.00, which probably meant 3 to 4 in the afternoon. Not good for me, that was my sleepy time, my lowest ebb. I'd have to adjust my body-clock in the week to come — somehow push all my routine forwards or backwards so that I could be wide awake, up and running ready to hit the water around 3.45 p.m.

The Semi-finale, sixteen fastest times, *if* I made it that far, were on the following day, 20.40 to 21.20. Night-time — better.

The Finale, eight fastest times, why was I bothering, the *Finale* was on Monday, August 29, at 21.00 - 21.20, best time for me 'cause I'd always been a night person. Ha ha, Alex — you in the final, don't be bloody silly. You're off your rocker. Oh yes? The 400 metre Stile Libero, not really my event, had heats on Wednesday 31, at night. The Finale was the following night. Well, at worst I'd swim twice in the Rome Olympics.

I was dreaming impossible dreams when Zoe bounced in, full of the great training facilities in the village, trampolines and the like, and meeting the Aussies and Canadians she got to know at the last Empire Games in Cardiff. She'd made arrangements for sightseeing, restaurants, the lot. Bully for her.

After dinner, another banquet listening to our team men swopping training experiences, Bulldog and I went for a short stroll round the village in the pink twilight. It was obviously a custom, tho' Bulldog told me that half the teams, especially from other European countries, hadn't even arrived yet.

In the recreation areas the juke-box was going flat out, 'Let's Twist Again Like We Did Last Summer', and a few couples in American track suits showed me what the Twist looked like. I watched my first television but the novelty soon wore off 'cause there's a limit to how long you can watch an oldish man gabbling away in Italian. The main events of the Games were to be televised, but I didn't suppose I'd see any 'cause I'd be *there*. I'd have to wait for the film later. I saw a few of our men walking around, easily spotted in our black track suits. They were friendly enough, said hello, howyadoing lass, alright? but by the time I went up the stairs for my second night in my pink bed I wondered how I was going to last five more *weeks* of feeling younger and lonelier than anyone in the village, in Rome, in the universe.

Only five days away from home, and I never thought I'd feel such an aching hungry need to talk to someone the same age as me, from the same country ... who talked the same language ...

A letter from a friend

It was undoubtedly a most strange coincidence that I should have been at the airport yesterday when the team arrived. They reminded me of much I've left behind: the dour quasi-English manner, the plain creased shirts, the baggy grey trousers and appalling short-back-and-sides haircuts I also once wore; indeed that women should form so insignificant a part of a national sports team. Altogether, they looked more like a third-grade brass band hurriedly outfitted at the local branch of Farmers and sent off to a world convention in Kentucky, than the world-class athletes they supposedly are.

Equally strange was this morning, while unpacking, finding the letter I had received the day we left Milan and had tossed unopened into my bag. I get little mail from New Zealand these days. My uncle wrote once before his stroke, a last plea to come to my senses; aunt, rarely, my cousins, never. Last Christmas, some cards from my old piano teacher, from varsity friends keeping me up with gossip and earth-shattering events like the bridge opening in Auckland and television starting this year. They made the ludicrous assumption that, with the Games in Italy, I'd naturally be in Rome to cheer my countrymen on.

Against my own inclinations, nevertheless, I am here. I wouldn't have known who was in the team, nor their chances of success, nor even remembered seeing them at the airport, had it not been for the letter I opened this morning.

It came from a teacher in Auckland, a woman called Marcia Macrae, reminding me that she met me two years ago after a University Drama Club performance of *Julius Caesar* in which I played (against my physical type) a deviously smooth and menacing Cassius. My name had intrigued her. Afterwards we established that I was indeed the bastard son of her pre-war drama school friend from New Zealand. She'd been devastated by my mother's death.

Having since heard that I was studying in Italy, she was writing simply to say that a pupil of hers, Alexandra Archer, from Auckland, was shortly to be in Rome with the New Zealand Olympic Games team. (The letter, from the postmark, had taken full twelve days to get here.) She was the only swimmer in the team — the other chosen swimmer, Alex's close rival, having sadly been struck down with peritonitis just before the team left.

If I happened to be in Rome during the Games, we might meet. Alex would, she knew, be very appreciative, would enjoy meeting someone who knew Italy. As for her chances in the Games, Marcia knew little about swimming, but Alex was an unusual young woman; she would not be the slightest bit surprised if she burst on the world sporting scene like a firework. As for the rest, the local papers were predicting that Murray Halberg, the distance runner, was about the best and only prospect for a medal.

Today, Sunday August 14, I have luxuriated in a morning spent sleeping late, investigating the apartment's large collection of long-playing records and the considerable virtues of the German baby grand; also some practice, a pleasure in this high-ceilinged resonant room. My practice disturbed Turandot not one iota. She spends most of her time curled up in a basket, asleep. Wearing my newest straw hat, I went for a walk to find a local trattoria for a late lunch, enjoying my anonymity and the familiarity of waiters who no longer pick me immediately as a foreigner but (I think) accept me as Italian-speaking, Italian-dressed, Italian-born; from the accent, Milano, somewhere in Lombardy. After just eighteen months here, that's progress. I must see how long I can keep this up.

A firework? That would fit the burning grey eyes, the buoyant step into the bus of the tall girl I saw at the airport yesterday. Alexandra Archer, pupil of someone who knew my unknown and unlamented mother. I have to admit to a slight resentment; these are the very obligations I left home to avoid and forget.

I have spent the whole evening, this first Sunday in Rome,

listening to a new recording of *Aida*. Zinka Milanov and Jussi Bjoerling, utterly marvellous. Tomorrow I must get a ticket for the production under the moonlight.

Strange, if I hadn't found that letter, I would probably have forgotten the luminous fine-boned girl in the white shirt and grey skirt.

Let it here be recorded, I have tonight been listening to *Aida* and I have not thought about Alexandra Archer at all.

A hot and dangerous place

'Sorry Alex, no training this morning,' said Mr Upjohn flatly, unloading his repulsive breakfast tray across the table. 'You've got another obligation.'

Between mouthfuls of muesli and melon, I'd been going through the programme with Bulldog, explaining about adjusting my body-clock to be fighting fit at 3.45 p.m. on venerdì ventisei agosto. My training sessions were at 9.30 each day, along with the Aussies, Brits, Canadians, and some European teams.

I'd vaguely registered that some of our men seemed to be rather well-dressed for breakfast, in uniform trousers and shirts and carrying blazers, but Mr Upjohn was actually wearing his, *and* had put brylcreme on his hair. What obligation? I was starting training this morning.

'Our flag-raising ceremony is at ten, in the main compound.' he said.

'Do I have to go?'

'Naturally,' he said, shocked. 'The whole team goes. It's our first time, marching together as a team. The press will be there. Reporting time is 9.30.'

'I wasn't told about this,' said Bulldog.

'I'm telling you now.'

'It's a little late, isn't it?'

Mr Upjohn munched his breadroll, said good morning to several of the other managers, heartily. Bulldog looked at me, obviously very annoyed, warning me against saying anything rash. 'Eat up, Alex,' she said. 'We'll have to go back and change.'

We made it back in time, togged out in blazers, white high heels and all, but only just. Zoe had been out training and

Alessandra   385

forgotten her watch and had to climb into her uniform all flushed and sweaty. Out in the main compound ringed by flagpoles, the managers put us in lines, four abreast, the officials first, then us six women, then all the men. We marched in like an army, left right, another novelty for me. I was still thinking this was a waste of good training time, and sweltering in my black wool blazer, but there's something about a flag when you're a long way from home. Our flag with the four stars of the Southern Cross was slowly raised while the small band played 'God Defend New Zealand' (badly, the trumpets flat, sounded as though they were sight-reading it). No one actually sang. I was too choked up to sing, mighty patriotic and homesick all at once.

After that, we stood while the band trumpeted up the Japanese, Ethiopian, and Chilean flags too, their teams likewise ninety per cent male. Afterwards we could only shake hands and grin stupidly at each other. They didn't speak a word of English, nor us a word of Japanese or Spanish or whatever it is Ethiopians speak. Various people tried speaking pidgin English very loudly and distinctly, as though to idiots. It didn't work. We bowed and scraped. The Japanese nodded like dolls, the Chileans grinned, and the Ethiopians looked solemn.

Then I heard a female voice close by: 'Shake a Japanese hand? Never.' Bulldog joined Zoe and me, rummaging in her handbag. 'Don't ask me. Never!' she muttered, looking extremely flushed and unhappy. Behind us a group of our officials with two blank-faced Japanese bowed carefully at each other. The Japanese went to join their team. One of our officials came over to us, loosening his tie. 'Enid, that was inexcusable.' 'I'm sorry,' she said, 'but I will never . . .' 'For Chrissake, Enid, you must, it's fifteen years . . .' Behind her hanky she said, 'My husband, aged twenty-four, died in Burma at the hands of those people and you tell me I *must?*' Zoe and I were looking at each other. 'This is no place for politics, harbouring grudges,' he said, mopping his forehead. Hadn't she said the same to me about the South Africans? 'No, then what about Hitler's games in Berlin and that water-polo match between Hungary and Russia, drawing blood, only four years ago?' she shot back, surprising me. 'We fought the Italians too,' he said, 'and I was one of them, in the Western

Desert, at El Alamein, liberating Rome. According to your . . .'
'The Japs were different,' she said defensively. 'I'm sorry, I know it's not logical . . . I'll avoid them, we don't get Japs in Christchurch, not in Riccarton, but don't you tell me I must . . .'
On the verge of tears, she looked at me. 'I can't expect you to understand, Alex, you were just a baby.' I didn't understand. My Dad came home from the war; lots didn't, from Egypt, France, Crete, Singapore, Burma, all the other places I'd heard over the years. Italy too, so what should I be feeling about the Italians? I looked at the small backs of the Japanese team and wondered how they felt under all these cheerful flags; confused, angry, helpless, like me?

I'd noticed a few press people standing round, no one from home I recognized. We were interrupted by a lanky British reporter, the *Daily Mail* on duty in immaculate white shirt, club tie, crinkly hair, big sunburnt nose, panama hat. What did it feel like, ladies, to be the team that had travelled the longest distance to get here? 'Sick of aeroplanes,' said Zoe distantly. Were we homesick? 'No,' I said. Had we left behind boyfriends? I thought a British reporter might have asked more sensible questions. Zoe mumbled something about her fiancé in Wellington.

And what did we Kiwis think of the All Blacks' chances for the all-important fourth Test in South Africa? I was about to say who cared, when Bulldog coughed very loudly; so I told him I'd be glued to the BBC live broadcast even if it cost me sleep or training time, and absolutely *devastated* if they let the country down. Don Clarke was my absolute hero, my pin-up boy, not forgetting Whineray and Pinetree Meads (I knew a few names because how can you not, when they're plastered all over our papers?) The national pride of the entire country was at stake. I watched rugby every Saturday, didn't everyone, the sheilas too, Ranfurly Shield, club matches, whatever; and by now, tho' the *Daily Mail* was lapping it up, the group had got bigger and several of our guys were beginning to look at me rather strangely; Zoe was trying to keep a straight face and Bulldog was desperate to stop me, which she did eventually by pretending to see Mr Upjohn in the crowd behind the *Daily Mail*. 'Oh yes, coming . . . you'll be late for training,' she cried. 'Excuse us, Alex has to . . . I'm sorry, but she simply must . . .' leading me off by the elbow.

'Oh you scamp! You absolute scamp! You know how that will get back home, I can just see it, Olympic swimmer Alex Archer is the All Blacks' greatest fan, she sleeps under a picture of Don Clarke. I never heard such *nonsense.*'

'No one cares what I think, Mrs C. Stupid questions get stupid answers. He wasn't interested, you see.'

Wrong again, Alex. It did get back home, in an N.Z.P.A./Reuters round-up from Rome: *Rugby rivals share Olympic dining hall; South African and Kiwi athletes are shaping up over meals in the Olympic village for the final showdown between their rugby teams. Water-baby Alex Archer admits that 'The Boot' Don Clarke is her hero, will be among those listening to the live broadcast and cheering on their countrymen.* I didn't see the actual piece until someone sent the cutting in a letter, but I knew something must have appeared because I got a terse telegram from my university friend Keith Jameson who took me on the protest march three months ago.

TRAITOR, it said. YOUR FORMER MATE KEITH JAMESON. I went to the post office and fired back one of my own A JOKE THAT MISFIRED MI SCUSI MI DISPIACE CIAO and signed it LA BAMBINA DELL'ACQUA, much to the amusement of the post office clerk. But even that was communication of a sort. I stood in the Ufficio Postale and thought, I must be getting desperate if even the gnomish boorish randy hard-drinking fast-driving but somehow not entirely horrible Keith would be a welcome friend here. In all my swimming trips away from home, I'd never once been homesick. That was for miseryguts who didn't know when they were well off.

Never again would I be rude about people being homesick.

We got to the pool in time for a shortened training session. Mr Upjohn had discovered there were shuttle buses laid on. I took one look at the pool and thought: this is where it begins in earnest. The Aussies were the most obvious in their green and gold togs, brown as berries, swaggering and confident. I knew they'd all been to a training camp in Queensland. The world's top swim team no less, here to defend themselves against the strong U.S. team. I wasted a good ten minutes just sitting with Mrs C on the stands under her baby-blue umbrella, changed and ready to go, but turned to stone. For quite a while neither of us said a word.

This was the Olympics for real: about fifty world-class swimmers (and that wasn't even half of them) going like the clappers, churning up and down the blue water. No one looked tired; they all looked so horribly *fit*. Lots of officials, coaches with stopwatches, a few photographers getting action shots of Dawn Fraser training with two of the men, Lorraine Crapp, the famous Konrads Jon and Ilsa, Murray Rose; I recognized them all from photos but there were unknown younger Aussies, and Canadians in their red togs, and Brits with Union Jacks on theirs, who all looked just as fast and strong. No one looked younger than twenty. All the women looked like Amazons, but it was the men who knocked me out, because most of the 'men' swimming in men's events at home were not much older than me. These were all muscly, hard, proper *men* with crew cuts, no body hair because they shaved it all off, perfect outsized Greek gods like all those statues in the Stadio dei Marmi next door.

'Well,' I said eventually. I couldn't afford to sit in the sun any longer. 'Once more unto the breech, Mrs C . . .' Mr Jack's carefully typed schedule stipulated a mile and a half today, but I'd be lucky to get in half that. 'Chin up,' she said. I gave her the gold chain with the single pearl I always wore, all I had left of Andy, and slunk down to the concourse in my wrinkly black togs, a pale grey slug, an impostor.

No one was watching; everyone was watching. I found a slim space at the edge of the pool, as far away as I could get from Dawn Fraser. I'd swim in the same event in nine days' time. The nerve! The exhilaration of my first swim had gone. Today I felt heavy and sluggish, a boring little junior strayed into the wrong race. Every length, weaving through the bodies, seemed about a mile long.

I was hanging on the side at the end of my first quarter when someone surged up close by doing breaststroke. Male, tall, panting with hands on hips and looking at me. 'You must be Alex of the Antipodes.'

He was one of those smooth, hard men. From the pale skin,

the accent, and the Union Jack on the bathing cap he was taking off to reveal longish fair hair, an English one.

'Why must I?'

'Because you're wearing the silver fern and the black of your truly marvellous All Blacks . . .'

'I'm wearing the black of the New Zealand Olympic team, if you don't mind.'

'And because you're the only New Zealand swimmer. You have a respectable 63.8 hundred free to your credit, and have therefore been considered a possible finalist. Your rival Maggie Benton was also selected but is alas recuperating from peritonitis. You are, I see, still suffering the effects of your unenviable air journey from New Zealand.'

'Anything else?'

Grandly sweeping back his hair, he bestowed on me a dazzling smile. 'Meet me after training and we'll swop notes. Over a cappuccino and a piece of torte.'

I had thought I was boring, a mere anonymous kid! Yet here was this handsome British hunk with a very posh voice smoothly summing me up. His information was remarkably up to date, God knows where from. He was the same type as Andy. Too smooth, too fast, and too soon.

'Are you chatting me up?'

'Ah, you antipodeans! So amusingly direct. Since you ask, Alex, yes.'

'You don't waste any time. I always thought the English were slow. Gentlemen. Who didn't rush . . .'

'We are, we don't,' he laughed, lying through his handsome teeth. 'I'm Matthew, by the way. Twice British breaststroke champion, current record-holder. I'm reading History at London. I play squash for my college, chess, and know good wines from bad. I've just taken up gliding.'

'You mean those planes with long wings and no engines?'

'Exactly.'

A paragon, but mad, in other words. 'I've someone, at home. Doing engineering, not a swimmer . . .'

'We're in Rome, aren't we?' They talk about women giving seductive smiles! But why had I said that much, why had I off the top of my head, conveniently described Keith as my 'someone'? He'd be pleased, no doubt, very!

'For the Olympics,' I said priggishly, with finality. I climbed out and paused only momentarily on the starting block, aware of scrutiny from below as I called to Bulldog to time me. 'Quarter, 90 percent effort.'

From all the Esther Williams types in the pool, it was *me* he'd chatted up. Nothing like a handsome guy making a pass to make you feel somewhat less like a slug, even if you've decided you can do without boyfriends. Later he swam alongside for several lengths, fast bobbing breaststroke, but he wasn't there when I finished. I didn't see him again, and (mostly) didn't want to. What was torte, anyway? And how the heck did he know about Maggie and her peritonitis?

I managed to get in my mile and a half, change without speaking to anyone other than a hi! to a couple of Australians. Under her umbrella, Bulldog was chatting with the Aussie chaperone like long-lost pals. The Aussies were pretty worried, it seemed, by some of the reports coming from the American camp. Dawn Fraser knew she was going to have to tramp to beat Chris Von Saltza in the hundred free, and John Devitt likewise to beat Lance Larson in the men's event.

'Who was that young man, Alex?' said Bulldog.

'A Brit, no one,' I said sharply. She surely wasn't going to vet every single person I spoke to?

'Sorry to hear about your mate Maggie,' said the Aussie to me, in a voice like an Australian version of Donald Duck. 'I saw her up in Townsville. Promising lass. I hope she goes on next summer after this knock. You any good?'

I was trying to think of a suitably jocular reply when I saw Dawn Fraser get out of the pool and look as though she might be heading our way. 'Sorry, um, just remembered, lunchtime, got to meet someone, Mr Upjohn, some reporter, gotta go, come on Mrs C.' I headed off across the terracotta paving. Bulldog caught me up by the main gate, grumbling in her beard that she didn't know what I was talking about, she wished Mr Upjohn would keep her better informed and she'd love to have met Dawn Fraser. Well, I wouldn't. I had to meet Dawn Fraser sometime, but not today, not yet. I'd had enough excitement for one day.

It was only when I was sitting in the bus going back to the village that the full impact of the three words hit me. 'A respectable 63.8 to your credit. You've been described as a possible finalist.' That was what he said, my pommie history-reading friend. By who? Where? When? A possible *finalist*? Really? You're *nuts*, whoever said that. Go on, pull the other one.

Alex Archer, Olympic Finalist. Well, why not?

If I thought the new Olympic stadium was grand and vast and overwhelming, I ain't seen nuffink yet. We'd driven past the Colosseum on Saturday when we arrived, but no amount of Latin books or guidebooks or postcards could have warned me just what it would be like when you walk towards it as the Romans would have done.

'You should be resting, Alex,' Bulldog grizzled from under her baby-blue umbrella. 'We both should be resting, in this heat. You should have put something with sleeves on. You'll be getting sunburnt. You're already peeling, look, your shoulders. You're a naughty girl, you should have brought a hat. Alex, please slow *down*.'

We were halfway up the Via dei Fori Imperiali, dancing round slow, dawdling tourists who were getting in our way. The Colosseum sat planted at the end of the road, getting bigger with each step. Bulldog moaned on.

'We shouldn't have got off the bus so soon. A free bus too.' We'd waved our identity cards happily at the driver, and got off at the Piazza Venezia, by that ugly great white thing called the Victor Emmanuel II monument. 'Can't you walk a little slower, Alex?'

'Mrs C, don't you realize where we *are*?'

'Of course, but . . .'

'The Via dei Fori Imperiale, down there, look, the Forum, Julius Caesar walked up that street, the Via Sacra, Mark Antony stood on those steps, just *think*.' I knew she was regretting that she'd allowed herself to be hauled out of her siesta to go sightseeing, when only tourists were silly enough to be walking around. I thought teachers would be interested in history.

'You'll be the death of me, Alex,' she grumbled. 'It's not right. You'll never catch up on your sleep at this rate, never mind me, and I don't have to swim.'

'You can sleep when you get home, Mrs C. Now is now.'

We had one more wide crescent of road to negotiate, which nearly saw the end of the Bulldog. While I was gazing dumbstruck at the sheer size of the Colosseum, she forgot yet again that the traffic comes from the other side. She looked the wrong way and very nearly stepped under a bus. The driver threw on the brakes and all his passengers got jolted forward out of their seats. Bulldog scuttled back to the kerb. A Kiwi bus driver would have muttered a bit about bloody tourists, but this one put his head out the window and really yelled at us and waved his arms around. Bulldog was now rattled as well as grumpy, and the driver overacting so much that I yelled back 'You'd probably do the same if you came to our country and people wouldn't scream and shout and rave on at you.' Before he had time to sit down and put his bus into gear I grabbed her elbow and marched her firmly across the road, looking the bus driver in the eyes, daring him to move, just remembering halfway that traffic came from the right, not the left. Even so, my head swivelled to the left out of sheer habit.

Rome was a hot and dangerous place. We'd arrived at the Colosseum.

Later, I remembered noticing Tom outside the crowded entrance, among all the tourist buses, the tourists, horses, horse-dung, souvenir and gelato stalls, balloons, flags, and traffic flying past. It might have been the hat. Just another young Roman, black sunglasses, not quite tall enough to be really elegant. A white linen jacket was slung casually over his shoulders in a way that would be considered highly dubious at home; black linen shirt, sharp white trousers; but the wide straw boater banded in shocking pink was definitely flashy, even by Italian standards.

He was standing by the stalls that sold postcards and slides and cheap-'n-nasty miniatures of the Discus Thrower and Michelangelo's David. As Bulldog stopped to have a look, something about the angle of the hat told me that he was listening, and had read on my shoulder bag that I was in some way connected with the New Zealand team for the Olympic Games, Rome 1960. He didn't look up, as most Romans did (I knew already) to leer at my tallness; yet I do remember that uncomfortable, vague feeling you're being watched, until . . .

I was standing there, just inside the entrance, sheltering from the blinding sun, from the busloads of yabbering pushing tourists, feeling very queasy. We'd walked slowly around the great oval. The jagged remains of the basement area where they kept the animals gaped at me like a mouthful of rotten teeth. The Colosseum could seat fifty thousand people, Bulldog read out. For the opening festivities in AD 80, nine thousand wild beasts and two thousand gladiators were killed. Sometimes they filled the arena with water and had naval battles. They let loose tigers, elephants, crocodiles, lions, hippos, gladiators, and Christians. Teased them and killed them all for pure pleasure. Our guidebook showed a model reconstruction with the tiers of empty seats and the oval sandy arena bare and waiting for blood. I could hear the crowd roaring, hungry.

Bulldog was sitting in a shaded alcove, fanning herself, complaining about sore feet and badly needing a drink. I wanted to go too; but something about the place was holding me; I was hating it, but fascinated too. She was weary enough to give me grudging permission to walk around once by myself. I had ten minutes.

Alone, it got worse. I weaved in and out of these great archways, noticing more than a few scraggly half-dead cats lying round, and found myself going up a steep flight of uneven steps. A surly ticket seller wanted me to buy a ticket. The view from the higher tier was even more eerie. I noticed a large but pathetic white cross below me. Bizarre. Terrified gladiators and animals had waited in those gaping tunnels. The crowd noises in my head got louder and the weight of this whole magnificent horrible place became heavier and I knew I had to get out.

People got in the way. I nearly tripped over two cats and down the steep flight of steps, and completely lost my sense of direction. I walked fast round some groups of people and rudely in front of others taking photographs. I passed a Roman crackpot giving a speech across the arena, to no one. The entrance must be where all the people were. 'Alex, *wait*,' I heard behind me.

Crowds blocked the entrance, slowed my escape. I didn't mean to react at all; well, no more than deliver a fierce glare. I knew about bottom-pinching. It was supposed to be a sign of Roman approval, accepted in good humour. But this wasn't a genial squeeze in the fleshy bit. This was a good, hard nip near my hip bone. I turned furiously, stumbled on the uneven stones, overbalanced, my arms flew out — so it appeared that I'd hit one of a group of obviously Italian youths, right where it hurt.

It's just not the sort of thing which ever happens in New Zealand. Here I was, two days in Rome, and starting a riot. The boys, greasy Elvis carbon copies, were coming at me, three of them, angry — the one I'd hit the angriest. I heard Italian, molto forte and obviously not polite, and saw their hands holding cigarettes making threatening gestures towards my face. I saw puzzled tourists staring blankly at me, wondering what on earth I could have done.

A fourth young man appeared on the scene, as well dressed as the others were sleazy. The black shirt and sunglasses, white linen jacket, the boater with the bright pink ribbon hanging off it. He must have asked what's the problem, because instantly he became the focus of their abuse. The only word I recognized was inglese. 'I'm not inglese and it was an accident,' I shouted back, because now I was getting a bit mad myself. I hadn't started it. The man in the boater put a soothing hand on my arm. 'Un momento! Da dove vieni?' 'What?' 'La Svezia? La Germania? L'Olanda? Australia?' 'Oh-strarr-lia!' I choked. 'Okay, la Nuova Zelanda,' he said, in a voice like chocolate sauce. Then, to the curious crowd, he proceeded to give what I can only describe as an aria. It was like a crowd scene in a musical where the hero comes on and sings and the chorus has to look interested, as though they haven't heard it fifty thousand times before. I stood and gaped, and watched the anger seep out of the faces of the three Italians. From the suave torrent of Italian I picked up only La Grande Olimpiade, Nuova Zelanda, la signorina, giornalista.

It was all over in a minute or two. The youths began to bow

and scrape, offer handshakes which a stern nod from my protector told me I'd be wise to accept. Bulldog found her voice and suggested shakily that we leave. My protector, close enough for a whiff of Old Spice or something similar, took my hand, no kidding, and kissed it, looking up at me with such a wicked gleam in the large brown eyes above the sunglasses I knew immediately we'd be wise to leave, now. I might have jumped out of the frying pan . . . I waited till he'd let go and said, haughtily, without smiling, 'Molte grazie, signor.' 'Prego,' he said, obviously amused at my attempt to freeze him off. We got outside the main entrance and I led Bulldog a merry dance around the gelato stalls, the horses and the Discus Throwers, but we were still followed. I turned around, wondering if my phrase book told me how to tell an Italian to get lost. But he beat me to it. In the split second I took to find any words at all, he took off his sunglasses and grinned.

'Gidday, Kiwi,' he said.

The greater disguise

It has been an eventful day. Historical, even.

I began this morning greatly regretting my decision to come to Rome this week. I've grown used to the leisurely walking pace of Italians around their cities, but here one can walk only at the uncertain dawdle of tourists consulting maps, taking pictures and generally constituting a continual obstacle race to ordinary pedestrians. I caught a bus to the Piazza del Campidoglio, which seemed as good a place as any to begin my explorations, had not all the world's tourists also had the same idea.

Well, I suppose this was always part of it, the Ancient Olympics where people travelled over barren hills for months to get to the Vale of Olympia; once there, they lived cheek by jowl, bought their food from an army of camp followers, stood all day around the stadium in the burning sun to watch the events and lined the rocky pathways to watch the processions. Here, one can at least escape into a bar at regular intervals. As I walked up the Via dei Fori Imperiali, I pondered the idea of looking up one of my Milanese contacts, to pursue the offer of a battered Vespa, which raises the question of whether sun-stroked tourists or Roman traffic is the greater challenge.

There was no mistaking the tall girl, standing with her dumpy chaperone on the kerb, about to cross over to the Colosseum, shouting angrily at a bus driver. I'd heard a screech of brakes. I looked across to see a nearby bus bounce back on its springs and the driver leaning out the window being remarkably abusive, as only Italians can. I remember my own confusion when I first walked around Milan, the constant danger of traffic hurtling at you from the left. Few people would take on Roman bus drivers or Roman traffic other than foolhardy locals, but this girl did. Having momentarily quelled the bus driver, she marched across the road, holding up the flow of traffic by sheer will-power, dragging her companion by the hand.

Presumably, Alexandra Archer and chaperone, going to visit the Colosseum.

The coincidence I do not find, in retrospect, so very strange. We both arrived on Saturday. A day of rest — she may be a churchgoer, a Roman Catholic? — then one of the first choices for sightseeing would naturally be the Colosseum. She would probably have spent the morning training, as I spent some time practising, learning some more of my *Figaro* score.

The greater disguise today was the linen jacket slung as Italians do, over the shoulders. (It appears my absent landlady has a peripatetic son who uses the apartment as his Roman base; handily, he is about the same build as me, with a flamboyant and expensive taste in clothes; I shall have anything I borrow dry-cleaned.) I digress — back to the Colosseum — supposedly examining the Italian guidebooks, I caught a glimpse of her airline bag inscribed with New Zealand Olympic Games Rome 1960. She took charge of buying an English guidebook, clearly several steps ahead of her shaken companion in dealing with lire and stall-keepers. She was not wearing uniform, but an unremarkable cotton skirt, striped in beige and turquoise, white blouse, probably home-made specially for the trip, sandals, not a trace of cosmetics. I saw the pink of new sunburn on her winter-pale shoulders and arms; she caught me looking and glared. Before I moved away, I heard an unusually low-pitched voice, telling her chaperone to stop looking at postcards and come and look at the real thing. I heard, Alex.

I followed them discreetly, giving thanks for the long sight which runs in the family. My own reaction to the Colosseum was coloured by watching her, even from twenty yards, register first disbelief at its size, and then a growing repugnance. I saw her wrap her arms around herself as though cold, even though the temperature must have been approaching a hundred in the shade. She stood for a long time in one shaded alcove, as though listening, and later I saw her looking down at the white cross, as though marvelling at its incongruity in that barbaric place; discordant it certainly is. Then she began walking, quite fast for the heat, around the upper circle. I lost her, so made for the main entrance only to hear some raised voices: a disturbance, and an angry young New Zealander at the centre of it, standing her ground against a group of three or four hostile Italian youths.

I could either be an uncomprehending Italian bystander and let her sort it out for herself, or reveal myself as an interpreter, or a fellow Kiwi gone italiano, or . . .

Rome was not built in a day, Tom.

Tommaso

'Just how long can you keep this up?' I asked, exasperated to the point of wanting to scream. 'What about me? And the Bulldog, who's about as green as they come, so square she's cubic. You can't for much longer.'

'I can, for as long as I choose,' said Tom. 'And you can. Mrs Churchill will keep it up because she thinks I'm rather a lad. She's a good sort who likes a bit of fun.'

'It's going on too long. I think you're a poser and a fake.' That amused Tom greatly. 'I don't like covering up for fakes, having to keep acting a part, a lie, really.'

'Don't you, Alex?,' he said, feigning surprise. 'I thought you were doing it rather well.'

Four days after the Colosseum, five days before the opening ceremony, several things were driving me mad.

One, the heat had got beyond a joke. It was now officially a heat-wave, the worst for decades. At least the swimmers were the best off, by far, for training. Two, being in Rome and barred from sightseeing was torture. And three, Tomas Alexander was driving me absolutely bananas and he'd got beyond a joke too.

He was now established as Tommaso, the unofficial honorary self-appointed interpreter to the New Zealand team, on hand daily to sort out any little administrative problems we might have, available for advice on bus timetables, menus, brochures, training times. How he got hold of a press pass to get into village remained a mystery. The trouble was, all our team thought he was an Italian who'd spent some time in Australia and once toured New Zealand, loved 'your *beau*-tiful country' so very much. His papa, he told us all with deep sincerity, his dead papa had been captured by New Zealand soldiers in the war. Had been treated like a gentleman, and got Christmas cards from two of them in Tau*ran*-ga and 'ow you say, Titi*ran*-gi? He pronounced both names with a hard G sound and the accents all wrong, relishing it. Had at his own expense come down to Rome from Milan, where he worked in a travel bureau, to see if he could be of help. Our team men goggled at his hats and sharp clothes, which every day were different, and grinned tolerantly when he arrived during breakfast and went round *Buon giorno, signorina, signora!,* kissing the hands of all the women in the team — mine in an offhanded way, and the Bulldog's warmly. His English was 'ow you say? stilted, with bad grammar and a sing-song accent, frequently breaking in frustration into Italian. They all thought he was Italian bloody marvellous.

Whereas — Bulldog and I knew otherwise. What do you do when a dashing Italian with gorgeous brown eyes, who apparently can't speak a word of English, rescues you from hostile locals about to punch you in the face, then comes out with 'Gidday, Kiwi'? You assume he's an I-tie trying to be smart?

You'd be wrong. Under the linen jacket and pink ribbon he was all solid Kiwi, originally from a farm near Taihape, more recently from four years at Auckland University would you believe? Walking back along the Via dei Fori Imperiali, and over my first experience of gelato and a very small aperitivo in a bar near the Piazza Venezia, we learnt that he was living in Milano. He'd been there for eighteen months, studying Italian. He'd come to Rome for the Games. He seemed more interested in asking about us, the team, what was I competing in. Who was going to win the New Zealand elections in November and whether the Twist had reached there yet! How would I know, when I hadn't been to a single dance all year, not since Andy died.

Why, I asked, had he passed himself off as Italian? 'Because I've been speaking nothing but Italian for eighteen months. I've worked hard at it. I wanted to see if the locals could pick an accent. They didn't, at least not a foreign one. It was necessary to dress like an Italian too, down to the sideburns, the eau-de-cologne. 'The rest,' he said, with a chilling smile, 'is pure wickedness, with a touch of revenge thrown in. Kiwi blokes are generally rather humourless. It amuses me that they'll accept flamboyance from an Italian, but not, I don't doubt, from a Kiwi.'

I asked him what he'd said to the youths at the Colosseum.

'That you were an athlete from New Zealand . . .'

'How did you know?'

'I read it on your shoulder bag, earlier. You were here in Rome for the Games. They should be understanding of people who spoke no Italian. You came from a country where harrassing and touching a young woman was considered most anti-social and unacceptable behaviour. That I was a journalist from Milan working for the international press. I would hate to report that young Romans were making life unpleasant for their Olympic visitors. Have another aperitivo, Mrs Churchill. Alessandra, try some cassata!'

Honestly!

Four days later I thought the joke was wearing a bit thin and told him so. He joined the team for most meals, and often came with me to afternoon training where he flashed the press card about. He had stamina and he didn't overact. My team-mates were totally hoodwinked. He was discreet Italian charm itself, not a false Kiwi note anywhere; except once, when he slipped and fell heavily on wet tiles as we were leaving the pool and swore, though softly, in very full-blooded Kiwi. We never saw him without a hat.

I found myself at breakfast each morning watching the dining hall doorway for his arrival. I felt resentful when he was collared by one of the managers and spirited off to do something useful. He never once looked at me as he left, indeed he rather ignored me, but I somehow knew that he was saying 'back soon' to me. By the weekend, with the Games opening next Thursday, I was becoming highly frustrated that it was Tommaso the fake Italian I was seeing most of the time, the genuine Kiwi article only coming and going to the pool with me and Mrs Churchill.

He said he was living near the Terme di Caracalla, in an apartment belonging to the aunt of a Milanese friend who'd fled to Scotland at the doubly appalling prospect of an August heat wave *and* the Olympic Games. I couldn't imagine any circumstances in which I'd be allowed to see him alone.

Bulldog was like a leech. Perhaps he didn't want to see me specially.

Sightseeing in that heat was out. Bulldog and I had come back so exhausted from our Monday afternoon trip to the Colosseum, full of cassata and aperativos, that Mr Upjohn had issued an Edict: there'd be no more sightseeing for me until after my events were over.

Though it was terrible to be in Rome and seeing nothing, I knew he was right. By the time I did my early training and had breakfast, it was half past ten and already too hot and too late to go catching buses into the city. Everything took longer in the heat. You tried not to, but you just got slower. I spent the mornings writing letters home, wandering round the village shops, trying not to think of my race in a few days, trying not to hope that Tom Alexander would come round the next corner. His services were in demand elsewhere.

Lunch late as possible, at 1.30 or even 2.00, long siesta tossing on hot sheets, in the bus to go training again at 4.30. Wander back over the bridge in the yellow light, leisurely dinner, early bed. The swimming events were all in the first week; I had a week afterwards to see Rome. Sunday would be the exception, when the Pope was to give a special audience for the Olympic athletes in St Peter's square. We'd all be going, in full uniform of course.

The only good thing about training was Tom sometimes sitting up in the stands, under his own large golfer's umbrella. Most of the time I felt heavy and tired. It was taking me longer to get over the trip than I thought. Some ning-nong might have said 'a possible finalist', but I still felt like a silly junior amongst all those strong, gorgeous bodies. I identified some of the other freestylers I'd be swimming against. They all looked so effortless, fast. English Matthew made a couple more passes, then gave me up as a bad job and turned his attentions to one of the Aussies. Apparently he'd read about me in an English swimming magazine, previewing prospects for the Games. A possible finalist, an outside chance. Not bloody likely; my times, when I could get in a complete time trial without having to swerve around someone, were *awful.* Mr Jack's notes, which I opened day by day, told me to expect this, not to worry. By then, he had written, 'Day 4, 3, 2, you must concentrate on speedwork, starts, turns, rest. Day 1 will be the opening ceremony. Relax and enjoy it, conserve your energy. D-day, think only of your race plan.'

I was thinking more and more of Tom. None of the others, preoccupied with their own training, knew he was coming to the pool to watch my sessions, even Zoe who told me daily what a *dish* he was, 'that Italian guy with his hats. I think he quite fancies me,' she said. 'Lucky you,' I said.

Oh for a simple life! Instead, count-down training, an attack of diarrhoea, restless and sweating at night, again dreaming of crowds, animals, blood, races where I ran and ran and ran and moved not an inch, while something nameless and dreadful got closer.

On Saturday afternoon (four days to the opening ceremony) a familiar face turned up at the pool. My friend Norm Thompson from the *Herald*, just arrived from New Zealand, looking very old and very tired. He'd not told me he was coming to Rome; he said he didn't know himself until ten days ago. He brought letters and news from Mum and Dad, letters with pictures from Debbie and Robbie and even Jamie, from Gran with a pressed flower inside, from Mr Jack. Everyone was fine. It'd done nothing but rain since I left.

Last week, he heard that Maggie was going to live in Australia as soon as she was completely better, ending our rivalry of many years. She was finished with swimming, said Norm. I looked at all the bodies churning up and down the pool and wondered, for each one of those, how many hundreds were there like Maggie? Those who cocked up the one crucial race that mattered, or got peritonitis five days before leaving. Who missed the bus for a big Games and wouldn't go on asking for punishment. Oh Maggie my friend, you should have been here. You deserved it. It's not fair.

And how did I find the pool, asked Norm, getting out his notebook wearily. A fast pool? Turning ends good? Those yellow lane markers looked pretty substantial — could I see over them? How was my training going? Time trials? How was I coping with the heat? The rich food? Sleeping okay? And first international competition, how was I feeling about that? Missing my coach? Did I feel prepared? Any injuries, pulled muscles, ligaments, eye troubles? My chances? Would sub-64 win me a place in the semi-final? Apart from Fraser and Von Saltza, who were the threats? Did I feel intimidated by these vast stands? How did I think I'd feel, when it came to standing on those starting blocks?

Well, I'm used to being interviewed, and Norm had always been on my side. Mean or not, I didn't tell him about 'a possible finalist', though. I knew enough about the sort of thing reporters wrote, even (or especially) Norm. I could just see it. U.K. EXPERTS PICK ALEX ARCHER FOR ROME FINAL. Anyway, it was codswallop.

I got the impression that Tom, though he'd been only casually introduced to Norm as our honorary interpreter, was all ears as he gazed across the pool. 'I'm filing my first piece tonight, if I can stay awake that long,' said Norm. 'Update on you and the runners, Halberg and co. They need something at home to balance the hysteria coming out of South Africa.' The country, he said, was in a ferment over the fourth and deciding test being played against the Springboks next Saturday. Well, a virtual world title was at stake.

'How incredibly dreary,' muttered Tom, then remembering, 'Rug-bee, not — 'ow you say? — a patch on zee football.' Was that Tom or Tommaso speaking? Norm, it appeared, had turned down an offer to cover the South African tour. Unlike all his colleagues, he said, he believed the protesters — 'people like you, Alex' — would turn out to be right. 'I couldn't go, could I, thinking that?' I saw Tom's eyes flicker. 'You are protester, Alex?' he said. 'Si,' I said. 'Congratulazioni!' He turned to Bulldog who was sitting fanning herself drowsily, smiling at Tommaso.

'Domani, Signora, posso — can I?' He looked up at the hazy white-blue sky. 'No, there really comes a point.'

He'd cracked. I loved it. Norm Thompson's eyes popped out of his head as Tom went on, 'All that talk of home, and the bloody All Blacks. It's nostalgia in reverse.'

'Home?' said Norm. 'I thought you were a dinkum I-tie.' Bulldog was now awake, chuckling away heartily.

'You're a journalist. You don't reveal your sources,' said Tom bluntly. 'At the Olympic village, I'm from Milan, the team's honorary interpreter and general factotum. I work in a travel bureau. My father was taken prisoner-of-war by New Zealanders in Libya. I learned my English in Australia. I once went to New Zealand, your beautiful country,' this in stage Italian English, the vowels stretched out like chewing-gum. 'I bumped into these good ladies at the Colosseum. Alex was in trouble, being threatened by hostile elements.'

'What's new?' asked Norm, drily. 'Packet of trouble, always was. What had she done?'

'Been pinched by a randy Roman and retaliated,' said Tom.

'Oh dear, yes, she would,' laughed Norm.

'This man's a fake,' I said. 'He comes from Taihape. He likes charades.'

'I intend to keep up this charade, to the end of your stay,' said Tom with a warning edge to his voice. 'If they find out, the men especially, they'll go for me. Good Kiwi jokers don't go in for fancy dress, charades, tricks on their mates. Not one that goes on for three weeks. I'd be labelled a cheat, impostor, all the way through to camp as a row of tents, which I'm not. Especially if they knew what I was really doing here.'

'What are you doing here?' I asked curiously.

'Learning Italian. And singing.' He turned to Bulldog. 'Can I take Alessandra for lunch tomorrow, after the Pope's junket? It will be very leisurely. I know an excellent restaurant, clean and quiet. I promise to have her back by four, in a taxi, in good time for training. I'll see that she eats the right things and not too much. You'll say yes?'

Clever Tom, he'd anticipated all her conditions. How could she say anything else? The child could go.

The trattoria was in a small piazza not far from St Peter's, with tables set up on the pavement outside. He'd obviously booked, because we were shown to the only remaining table, and the best one, in a corner shaded by trees and a dazzling bougainvillaea, exactly the same pinky-red as the one climbing over our verandah at home. I was surrounded by greenery and things pink: the waiters' pink aprons matched the tablecloths. There were pink roses on the tables and fuchsias hanging above us, and there sat Tom in a pink shirt (cyclamen, as in Gran's favourite pot plant) and his Colosseum boater with the pink band, almost as if he'd planned to match up with it all.

'I thought *Karachi* was hot,' I said as we collapsed onto our pink wooden chairs. A polite old waiter came and took my hat and blazer away. They don't do that at home. I was feeling very dowdy and gawky in my grey uniform skirt and white shirt which was sticking to my back. My nose was peeling horribly. The pool was my territory. This was his. He'd said very little since we left the team behind in St Peter's square and slowly walked about a quarter of a mile down empty streets with everything closed up, marvellous heavy doors, shutters, shop windows. It was a nice silence, though, just the sound of our feet on the cobblestones and occasional music or voices from an apartment five stories above. At this time of the day people were either eating lunch or already sleeping.

He had a brisk exchange with the waiter, while I drank all the water on the table. Bottles of beer and orange juice and a basket of thick holey bread arrived almost immediately. It was the first time we'd been alone and face to face. He carefully poured the beer, but he'd taken off his sunglasses and was looking at me. I took refuge in looking round at the families behind me, eight or ten at a table, with toddlers whose chins poked just over the table, eating and talking with gusto. My family had never ever been out to a restaurant together, Gran, Debbie, everyone . . .

'Your orange juice, signorina.' When I looked back at Tom, the boater had gone. For the first time in a week he was hatless, studying the menu but clearly waiting for the inevitable reaction. With the cyclamen shirt, the bougainvillaea behind, the effect was spectacular.

'Why do you cover it up?' I said finally.

'People can't take their eyes off it. Even now.' A quick glance behind me confirmed what he meant. 'People don't believe it's natural. As a child it was corn blond. Most people's hair goes darker and duller. My late grandmother was Irish, curse her Belfast bones. They still talk about her hair, in Taihape.'

'I'm not surprised. Is that what you call Titian?'

'Among other things. I've worn hats since I was in prep school. My trademark. Like Edith Sitwell.' He parodied the supercilious pose I remembered from a book about English poetry, making me laugh. 'Hats save me from the knobbly fingers of old crones accosting me in shops. And they do, believe me.'

It wasn't only the incredible colour, which the patchy sunlight through the trees was setting alight with streaks of copper and gold. It was wavy and very thick, and longer than any Kiwi short back 'n sides. It explained the bronzy eyebrows, the coppery freckles which had made me wonder earlier whether his hair might be reddish, and all the hats. Used to being stared at myself, I could understand the hats. His level gaze was very disconcerting. I took a long swig of orange juice.

'What was the Pope talking about?' I asked.

'The usual platitudes — brotherhood of nations in friendly rivalry and so forth. But that was quite a special occasion, make no mistake. Usually he appears at an upstairs balcony.'

The Pope and his party in gorgeous reds and magentas and purples on a bright blue stage in front of St Peter's, the dome and columns and statues above us, the square packed with all the Games athletes in their uniforms, and tourists and pigeons, the morning heat, the amplified single old voice, the bells at the end — I had stood feeling totally dwarfed. 'It was amazing,' I said lamely. 'Makes New Zealand look . . .'

'Don't compare this with home, Alex,' he said sharply. 'This place has two thousand years of history. Ours is only just beginning. Though God knows I couldn't get out fast enough.'

'Why?'

'Alex, Alessandra, let's get this bit over,' he said, dodging the question and picking up the menu. 'Then we can relax and enjoy our lunch.'

With the waiter hovering, I thought he meant helping me choose from the long and rather dog-eared menu. I recognized a few words — spaghetti, scaloppine, gelato — but what on earth were calamari, verdure di stagione, fritto misto? 'I think I'll need some help.'

'I don't mean this.' He said a few words in Italian which sent the waiter sidling away. 'I've decided to go away for a few days. It'll be a week.'

I again took refuge in the menu, knowing I was being

watched. 'Oh?' I said casually. 'I thought you'd come to see the Games.'

'And Rome. That was the original intention, yes.'

'You've been very . . . translating and stuff.' Why couldn't I talk proper? 'The managers need, well, little things . . .' Even that morning, there'd been a muddle with the bus. It was Tommaso, with much hand-waving and shrugging, who'd calmed down the officials and sorted it out.

'They'll cope,' he said. 'There are interpreters in the village, on tap.'

'Yes, but . . .'

'I am recalled to my ufficio, urgente.'

'Any more of that Italian accent, I'll scream. You don't work in an office.'

'You're sure about that?' he said slyly. No, damn it, I wasn't sure of anything about him, nor why I should be feeling so let down. Six days, then he just ups and leaves.

'After my . . .'

'For a performer there's only the here and now,' he said gently. 'Tonight's performance, or in your case Thursday's first and most important race. You can't afford to think of after. It seems to me that as an Olympic athlete you're required to be a performer, a professional.'

'I am not,' I said indignantly, recalling past slurs on my reputation, evil attempts to have me declared not an amateur.

'You are in the classical Greek sense.'

'I'm at — I'm a student more hours than I train.'

'You're being supported to pursue your sport, just as Greek athletes were by their city-states.'

'Only temporarily. It's cost my parents a bomb.'

'You may not get actual money, but if you succeed . . .'

'Let's see. A Hollywood film contract, the second Esther Williams. Offer of a scholarship to an American university. Three cheers in assembly at . . .' Again I stopped short of saying school. I didn't want him to know I was still at school. 'Where's all this leading?'

'How old are you?'

I wondered how much Bulldog had told him.

'Eighteen, nearly nineteen. And you?'

'Twenty-three. Could you still be around at the next Olympics?'

'Possibly,' I said playing for time. 'You've been sitting with Bulldog at training, what did she say?'

His slow smile acknowledged the loaded question and the possible advantage of knowing a good deal more about me than I about him. My age, for starters. 'Not much,' he said, too lightly to be the truth. 'But I've listened to you, and that reporter, and watched you training. I had no idea what was involved. That's what I mean, you have a professional's attitude. That's why I'm leaving you to it.'

I must still have looked puzzled and unconvinced.

'If *I* was preparing for my international début . . . well, you just don't need any distractions.'

'Distractions.' I played with my knife on the pink tablecloth, feeling very much on the back foot. 'Presuming?'

'Rather a lot, I know. That we might have enjoyed exploring Rome together.' Ah, he was backing off until my events were over. I was on my own. Again. Our eyes met briefly. 'Most of my time has been spent in Milan.'

'Where you're studying singing?'

He nodded, but didn't seem inclined to enlighten me further. He signalled the waiter over. We went through the elaborate business of translating, explaining, deciding on antipasto for both, followed by fish grilled in a special Roman style, peperoni, and verdura mista. A white chianti — I thought chianti was always red. I had the feeling that the previous five minutes had been vaguely unsatisfactory. What did he expect me to say: see ya later, alligator? or, please stay, I need your dry humour to get me through this week, someone under sixty and sane outside the team? Someone to raise a little cheer for the New Zealand team of one when she stands up in front of that monstrous crowd next Friday afternoon.

'Nevertheless,' he said, when we returned to the table with our platefuls of antipasto, 'I shall be sad not to see you swim.'

'And the opening ceremony. Pity. You're going back to Milan?'

He seized, I thought with some relief, on the subject of Milan. Through the antipasto, the mussels and peppers and pesce, the whole slow fantastic lunch, he treated me to the glories of

Milan, the Gothic cathedral, the arcades, fashions, cake shops, the Lombardy plains and the lakes not far away. Most of all the opera house, La Scala, where he watched performances with other students from high up in the sixth tier. He was boarding with a large family: Papa was a teacher, and three women — Mama, Nonna, and Nonna's younger sister Carla — together ruled the family of five sons and two daughters with a great deal of noise. It was very cheap because Nonna had a soft spot for aspiring singers, but difficult to get peace or privacy. From various teachers he was learning singing, musicology, theory, opera history, Greek and Roman history, stagecraft, movement, fencing. His main singing teacher was a noted baritone, his fencing master a former European champion, now a nimble fifteen stone, cunning as a fox and still unbeatable. Then he got onto Florence, the only other city he'd spent any time in. I listened, and sipped my white chianti, and tried to eat as slowly as he was (since he was doing all the talking), and basked in the pink warmth of it all.

'And now Roma, La Città Eterna,' he said as the waiter put minute cups of black coffee in front of us. 'Don't be deceived by the tiny cups. It's thick and powerful and all you need. I've got two weeks here.'

'But you're leaving.'

'Where I go is beside the point.' His eyes were on his coffee as he said, 'Alessandra, you're within three days of your life's ambition. I'll not ever have it said that some expatriate Kiwi arrived in Rome and . . .' A long silence hung between us.

'You've got a press pass, haven't you?' I asked softly.

'So I have.' He smiled and somehow, putting on his hat adjusting the angle of his pink collar, he turned into an Italian before my very eyes. In a hilarious mixture of Italian and terrible pidgin English he informed me that his name was Marcello Mastroianni from Milano, lika zee filma starra, lo stesso, ma no lo stesso, capisci? He was a giornalista 'ere in Roma per La Grande Olimpiade, ma specialmente per osservare la Regina della piscina, la bellissima nuotatrice Dawn Fraser dell' Austraaa-lia when she swim i cento metri, 'ow you say, freestyle? also i quattrocento metri freestyle. This was not the discreet Tommaso but the journalist at the Colosseum again. But he was molto arrabbiato "ow you say, angree — my Eenglish is verra verra bad' because he could not 'geta zee pressa passa per il villaggio Olimpico'.

He was telling me that he would watch me swim from the press box, but would not come near the village for a week, until it was all over.

'Ho-kay, Signorina Archer? he said, taking off his boater and putting it to his chest like a minstrel tap-dancer taking a bow.
'Ho-kay?'
'Ho-kay,' I said.

The cry went up the next morning. 'Where's Tommaso?' Faces around the breakfast table looked blank. 'Anyone seen Tommaso? Someone must've seen our dago ponce.' It was one of the managers, cycling or something, a fat little fellow dashing in, puce in the face, about to have a heart attack.

I held my tongue, metaphorically speaking, and then found I'd done it for real. 'Ouch!' Dago *ponce*! How dare he, going on to all and sundry that one of his boys needed a physio quick-quick and there wasn't a village physio to be found for love nor money, and where had that I-tie gone. 'Yeow.' Heads turned. 'How should I know?' I said savagely. 'I bit my tongue.' There was blood on my bread roll.

I was already in a bad *bad* mood. I'd had to go to early and very crowded training because today at eleven hundred hours there was a compulsory rehearsal for the opening ceremony, where we'd be put in our lines and practise marching, and I'd wanted to see the Olympic Stadium when it was the real cheering thing, not empty.

Zoe, who was nagging me nightly to put my bed light off because *she* wanted to sleep, had been woken at six this morning by Bulldog coming in to wake me and falling over something on the floor, and had gone berserk. English Matthew, out of luck with the Aussie bombshell, so patronizing and clean-cut and confident he made me puke, had made another pass. Someone's fingernail had sliced a 14-inch groove down my thigh. Then the French owner of the red nail came and abused me for getting in her road, and I was too amazed and too slow to point out that I had as much right to pool space as her.

There was no mail from home today. My period was finished, but I was still permanently tired and hot, and my bowel workings permanently odd. My nose and back were peeling badly. I came and went from the changing-room without any one of the females in there saying anything more than 'Hi'. I wasn't so much a small fish in this pond as an invisible one. There'd been no mail for three days.

I had to swim my best race ever on Friday.

After breakfast, with an hour and a half to spare before the marching practice, I propped myself up on my bed and confided in my diary. Written down, it looked like the whingeing of a spoilt brat. Then I wrote up yesterday:

> **Sunday** Went to St Peter's in the morning, saw the Pope, audience for all the Games athletes. Went to a pink restaurant with Tom, tried squid (calamari) and mussels (cozze) and white chianti. Caught a taxi to Borghese Gardens, walked a bit, taxi back to training, felt lousy, tea, bed.

I looked at the bland words. That's what a ten-year-old would write. Come on Alex, you could do better than that. Which Alex? Aye, there's the rub. The one who isn't quite telling the truth most of the time. The one who is feeling totally overwhelmed by everything: the pool, all those fabulous female bodies, officials, the village, Rome, everything? The one who stuttered and stumbled her way through lunch with a young man called Tom yesterday, feeling about thirteen; who accepted his unilateral decision to go away for a few days; too proud and too scared to say please don't, I think I'll swim better with you around.

Why? What did I know about the man, except that he was apparently a Kiwi here learning Italian and singing, with a penchant for playing serious jokes on people, and an amazing head of hair.

He'd given nothing away over lunch, except his present life in Milan. Hints: he came from a farm near Taihape, he'd been to prep school, therefore his parents had money. He'd been to Auckland University and wanted to be an opera singer. He couldn't get out of New Zealand fast enough. Why? He'd not asked me one single question: about my family, what I was doing, school or work, the usual things people want to know about so-called champions. So either he knew it already from Bulldog or some other source, or he wasn't interested in me, just himself and how great and cosmopolitan he was, learning how to be an Italian. I didn't like either thought much.

After the lunch, he'd suggested a short stroll in the Borghese Gardens, as Romans do on a hot Sunday afternoon. We had an hour before I had to be back for training. The taxi took us past the Castel Sant' Angelo, by the river. I recognized it, with the angel on top, from the cover of the long-playing record of *Tosca* we had at home. I didn't tell him I knew the music backwards. I got the full story, how the last act was set on the battlements of the castle, 'up there, look!' How Tosca and her lover both came to a messy end, and the famous story about the soprano who jumped to her death into a mattress sprung like a trampoline and rebounded back into view of the audience. The police chief Scarpia, he said, was one of the best verismo baritone roles written, a scheming sadist with wonderfully oily, melodious music to sing. By Byron's statue at the entrance to the Borghese Gardens, I got a quick run-down on Byron in Italy, and Keats and other Romantic poets who'd also been obsessed with Italy. He read the extracts from *Childe Harold* written in English on the base of the statue, beautifully, like an actor.

> Oh Rome! my country! city of the soul!
> The orphans of the heart must turn to thee,
> Lone mother of dead empires! and control
> In their shut breasts their petty misery.
> What are our woes and sufferance? Come and see
> The cypress, hear the owl, and plod your way
> O'er steps of broken thrones and temples. Ye!
> Whose agonies are evils of a day —
> A world is at our feet as fragile as our clay.

Then followed the Borghese family, the gardens and art collections they'd left to Rome. I don't think he'd swotted all this up or was specially trying to impress me; it welled up from sheer enthusiasm. We walked down dry earthy pathways under the pine trees, past a lake and statues and a small grassy stadium where they were getting ready to have some of the Olympic horse events. There were small groups of boys playing soccer, and young families pushing babies and admiring daughters in gorgeous old-fashioned dresses and black patent-leather shoes. Old men snoozed on the park benches, courting couples walked along with the boy's arm over the girl's shoulder. By a rotunda, children were taking rides in a trap drawn by a Shetland pony. He talked about soccer as Italy's national game, and Italian family life and courting customs, and the Shetland pony he'd once had as a child. The grass was brown and parched and everything a bit overgrown, but it was a park for people. Our parks at home, the Domain or Cornwall Park, seemed too well kept, pretty but empty.

At ten to four, in another taxi outside the village entrance, he thanked me for the day. I thanked him. He wished me luck for Friday. I said thanks. We got out of the taxi and walked to the entrance — now very crowded and busy because, with only three days before the opening ceremony, all the teams had arrived. He said 'Ciao, Alessandra'; I said 'Goodbye, Tom'. He took my hand and kissed it formally, but this time he did not look up. I felt his lips on my hand, just half a second longer than polite. Half a second will be the difference between a gold medal and nothing. Something inside me went 'help'. He walked straight back to the taxi, Tommaso tossing his white jacket over his pink shoulders. At the taxi he turned, and seeing I was still watching, doffed his hat very briefly, so that the last sight I had was a flash of copper.

I wondered if I'd ever see him again.

Present laughter

How my musician friends in Milan would be laughing! I came to Rome primarily to have a break from work and see the city, secondly, to see something of the Games; I have ended up interpreter to the New Zealand team, camp follower at the Olympic village, familiar with the venues for the cycling, the boxing, training venues for the runners, familiar with the Olympic pool and the area around the Piscine Coni, an instant expert on prospects for the women's freestyle events, caught up in the heat and fever of it all.

A giornalista, no less, sporting a smart wardrobe courtesy of my apartment's absent owner and a press pass, gained after some very fast talking to a flustered junior at the New Zealand Embassy and another at the Olympic press office, trading on the respected name of Norman Thompson and his paper.

I cannot believe that Alex is not yet sixteen; a birthday late October, Mrs Churchill said. Her training sessions would cripple an average man, yet she tells me these are light. Tapering off is the expression, I believe. The week has put colour in her face, a light tan on those long legs and across the square shoulders; taken the skin off her longish nose. Among the most wonderful female bodies I have ever seen, she moves — I can think here only in clichés — like a cat, poised, precise, controlled, slightly imperious, distancing herself from the other swimmers, and it has to be said, from me. Some of the other girls appear to flail and fight the water; she goes through it, sleek and rhythmic, beautiful to watch. She swims with the relentless tireless perfection of a Bach fugue. Poetry, no, music in motion. Clichés again.

I think she understands very well the reason why I involved myself with the team. Do I imagine that behind the studied indifference, the unusual and perceptive reaction to my crowning glory revealed . . .? Also, why I have removed myself. Perhaps I should have expected that her response to my announcement of departure would be nonchalance, an air of I can take it or leave it, I have a job to do. Surely I didn't really expect her to collapse in a heap and say, Tom, don't go, I need your support, I'll swim to a gold medal for you! That is the stuff, the corn of light romances. The young woman I saw holding up three lanes of Roman traffic, or bailed up in the Colosseum, needs no one. She would have managed without me, probably shouted some school Shakespeare back at them. I should write here and now: friendship, or romance, will not be won easily.

Contrary to my expectations, I have enjoyed talking with Mrs Churchill and Norm Thompson, watching Alex train. News from home has not been unwelcome, especially as told by Norm, whose job as a sports reporter belies his wide knowledge of what is happening back home. He expects Walter Nash's Labour Government to go out at the end of the year. Television, he says, is coming next year and will transform New Zealand utterly, particularly in view of its isolation. Twenty years hence, elections will be won or lost on television; look at what's happening in the American elections, Kennedy and Nixon's planned TV debates. It's a long way from the rural village meetings I remember as a child, uncle rampant as local chairman.

About Alex, though, both have been curiously reticent; vague references to a rival, one Maggie Benton, to a swimming career not unmarked by injury, problems; not elucidated.

Without my press pass, without our tacit agreement that I'll be watching her swim from the press box, I'm not sure I could have stood it, remaining in Rome knowing that Alessandra was here. I think I should have scuttled back to Milan and buried my head in learning some more Hugo Wolf lieder or 'Das Lied von der Erde' or something equally soulful; saying to hell with her and with the Olympics and let Rome wait for another, less potent, occasion.

Won't it come to this anyway? An airport parting, separation by half a world. Irreconcilable distances, ambitions. Better gently, ruefully, to retire, now?

None shall sleep

Tuesday, Wednesday dragged past. Hiding from the sun, sleeping, writing letters, training only once a day, mostly sprints, dreadful times. Both the main Olympic pool and the nearby indoor pool with the horse murals were crowded now. There was less chat in the changing-room. Bulldog heard rumours there was trouble in the Australian camp, scared to death of the Americans. Their coaches had trouble getting past security guards into the pool. I didn't even *have* a coach. I checked the press box above the starting area for people under forty wearing hats. Niente.

Besides letters from Mum and Gran, a steady trickle of telegrams from all sorts of people started to arrive. Zoe and I didn't have much to say to each other, and the heat had got to Bulldog. About five thousand times a day I thought of standing up on the blocks sometime after three on Friday, and shuddered. I tried not to think of Tom at all. I'd gone into a sort of limbo.

We had a final marching practice, and got issued with bits of paper to tell us the programme for the ceremony. Basically, we marched in behind our flags, stood in the middle of the arena during speeches, anthems, raising the flag, lighting the Olympic flame, then marched out again.

The Olympic flame, our village newsletter told us, had arrived in Rome, carried by 1500 men and boys all the way from the sacred grove at Olympia. Down Greece, across the Adriatic to Sicily on an Italian sailing-ship called the *Amerigo Vespucci*, and up through Italy. Tonight it would be kept alight at the Piazza del Campidoglio designed by Michelangelo. Tomorrow it would be carried at the appointed hour into the stadium by a

Alessandra   421

young athlete, his name kept a secret, Italian and male of course, though I couldn't see whyever not a girl, like Diana or Atalanta in the Greek myths.

Today Mr Upjohn arrived at the pool to give me time trials. Important time trials. Bulldog and I looked at each other and winked. What did he think she and I had been *doing* this past week while he went off to all those managers' meetings or was just generally absent?

After I'd done two lousy 100 metre time trials and some 50 metre sprints down crowded lanes through churned-up water, he put forward the monstrous idea that I should not take part in the opening ceremony tomorrow. It was a long march to the stadium, over two miles; there'd be a lot of standing around. Apparently there were rumours that some people competing on Friday would be resting, not marching.

'You only get the one chance,' he said. 'You think I don't know that?' I said angrily. Below us the American girls had taken over a lane and were lining up for 50 metre sprints, one sleek golden body after another. I just didn't, surely, swim as fast as that. 'If I don't march tomorrow, I don't swim.' He looked startled, opened his mouth to tell me off and decided to grind his teeth instead. Our few exchanges of recent days had been quite friendly.

There was still no significant hat in the press box.

I went into the changing-room after that last session feeling sort of helpless, resigned. It was up to the fates now. I'd done hundreds of miles, twice a day for a year, just about non-stop since my broken leg. If I ever needed a friendly face in the changing-room, it was then.

The girl with the Union Jack on her track suit no doubt thought she was being friendly; she did me a favour in a funny sort of way.

'Oh you must be Alex Archer from New Zealand!' she said, matching up my black togs to my New Zealand bag as we both began to strip off. 'The only swimmer. You're supposed to be quite good, aren't you!' She must have read the same magazine as her lecherous team-mate Matthew. She was in the same events as me; I'd vaguely heard of her, as a 63-plus sprinter. She'd had a good season, swum in international meetings in

England and Europe. This was her first Olympics and her whole family had come to Rome too. She came from Cambridge, that's the university town (I *know* that), and she had an uncle and aunt who went to New Zealand about five years ago, to a rather grim little place somewhere, called Hamilton. About eighty miles south of Auckland, I said. 'They emigrated, but really they said it was like England in the 1930s. No culture, you know, theatre or concerts, no proper pubs, nothing to do at weekends. They came back.'

By then I'd realized two things had happened — she'd asked nothing about me, and she'd been rude about my country, and it wasn't even psychological warfare, she didn't even know she was doing it! I listened smiling as she prattled on in her high ra-ra voice, complaining about the ghastly Italian heat, hard beds, and oily food.

'My aunt couldn't get over the food in New Zealand.' Oh? I said. 'Well, you send over all that lamb and butter, but she said the restaurants were terrible, you couldn't have wine with your meals and there were no fish-shops to speak of. And the natives ate nothing but hogget.' I smiled back, thinking *we call people like your aunt whingeing poms.* By the time she left, friendly to the last 'Ciao, Alex, see you heats Friday,' I knew I was a colonial and not really to be taken seriously. When I see you heats Friday, Miss Britain 1960, don't expect me to smile again. There was only one answer to Brits who saw me as colonial and Aussies who saw me as a little sister, if they saw me at all, and that was to forget the whole lot of them. Get on with it, do what I had to do, as well as I could, alone.

Wednesday night a sort of hush hung over the village. People lingered over the evening meal before going off to press their uniforms or write letters before early bed. The juke-box I heard in the distance from my window most nights was silent. Even the traffic seemed to be grow quiet earlier.

'Hey, kiddo, when you going to turn that light out?'

The nightly nag. Zoe, while I was staring at my diary, had finished her bedtime routine of cleansers on face, cream on hands, elbows, legs, large brush rollers in her dark hair. How she slept at all with those things pricking into her scalp I had no idea, but she'd snored soundly every night since we arrived.

'Ten minutes?'

She made a great show of turning away from the light, burrowing her head into the pillow to find the least painful position for sleep, which appeared to be face down on her tummy. 'Five?' She didn't even have to compete until next week! 'By the way,' she mumbled. 'What happened to our Italian friend? Haven't seen him for days.'

'Someone said he had to go back to his office, in Milan.'

'Pity,' she sighed. 'Italian men sure know how to dress. And how they look at you, wow-ie . . . I hoped . . . *please*, Alex, it's half past ten, turn it *out.*'

Her timing was terrible. I'd spent three days forgetting our Italian friend; I was frantic for sleep but here I was remembering how he'd looked at me, straight and warm, as though I *mattered.* I could have thrown something at the body under the sheet. Her enlarged head looked like a mine, in one of those British war films set in the North Sea with actors in white polonecks being heroes. She might be the best high jumper ever produced in New Zealand *and* on her second Olympics *and* six years older than me *and* working in an office with a lovely boss who'd kept her on full pay while she was away *and* engaged to be married with a diamond ring and glory box and all but . . .

'O-*kay*,' I said, snapping my diary shut, gathering up my cotton dressing-gown, turning the light out. 'See you.'

She didn't even reply as I left the room. She probably thought I was going to the loo.

Outside, I put on my shortie dressing-gown and looked up and down the long corridor. I could hardly go downstairs looking for somewhere to write. The thought of the toilet and shower area didn't appeal; nor the laundry room which was usually locked anyway. I tiptoed up the concrete stairs to the third and top floor. The hall lights were dimmed right down. The athletes behind those doors — who were they, Dutch, Russian, Brits, Aussies, Hungarian? — were dreaming of gold medals. I'd decided to go back and sit under a light halfway down the stairs like Christopher Robin, when I saw a door marked USCITA DI SICUREZZA. Emergency exit.

Wasn't I just one big fat emergency, very much in need of fresh air? The handle turned easily. Outside was a small iron landing, with a staircase going down to the ground and a short ladder going up to the flat roof for a view of . . .

You read about people gasping at some wondrous sight, a breathtaking view. Well, it's true. I turned slowly, literally breathless. The moon, nearly full, was fabulously bright, but it was a soft pink moon with hazy edges; the moon at home is hard and white and windswept. The air felt pink and soft too, warm on my bare neck. I shut my eyes and listened. Cars still hooted, wheels squealed around a corner, a bus roared by. Horses' hooves clip-clopped, a courting couple in a fancy carriage. Italian voices, male and two female, argued somewhere below. Music, opera, a man's voice, a tenor, came quite strongly from someone's record player.

But when I opened my eyes . . . the black shapes of the village apartments, the lamps of the streets between, lights in the windows. Under the dark shadow of the Monte Mario was a ring of lights: the stadium, where tomorrow . . . the Olympic pool was just to the left, where on Friday . . .

Close to both ran the Tiber, which if I could fly like Wendy I would see below me as swift-running ancient silver. The bridge I went over every day was outlined with lamps. The moon was so bright that it caught the curved tops of the pines and the points of the cypress trees around the whole stadium area. And last, the best: along the horizon were white perfect domes rising from the straight line of the city's lights into the blackness. One much larger than the rest I imagined to be St Peter's. It was so unbelievably beautiful that I stood and laughed. Now I knew why they called it the Eternal City. Whatever happened, if I was last in my heat and/or never saw Tom Alexander again, if the Olympic Games were cancelled or if the plane crashed on the way home, I'd never forget this, the pink moon and the floodlit domes.

Hugging my knees on a concrete ledge, I thought of another moonlit vigil: sitting on the gravelly beach at Napier at one o'clock in the morning last February, gazing across the breaking white surf at the moon and an endless ocean. It was the night before another special race, the one I *had* to win against Maggie to have any chance of selection for Rome. Somehow the idea that Andy's spirit was out there somewhere in the night had made me feel strong. I'd stood my ground against a mean attempt to have me disqualified, and I'd won. It was my gift to him.

Six months later, another moon, another sleepless night, another first and last chance race. Another Alex, who wasn't proud of her memories of the past six months: bitching at my friend Julia, fighting with my family, rude at school, to a stand-in coach who rubbed me up the wrong way. Passing out legless, drunk and disorderly at a family wedding. Fighting with Andy's friend Keith, using him to damn near drown both of us. Not proud. Something kept all those people from locking me up while I trained on . . . and on . . . Without them all, I wouldn't be here.

I began to feel sleepy. It must be getting on for midnight, witching hour. Rome didn't seem a city of witches; rather one of solid Roman ghosts in battle armour, Caesar and Brutus and Cassius, the evil Caligula and Nero. Ghosts of bleeding gladiators and Christians. Ghosts in togas: men gossiping in the Forum, women cloistered inside their atrium houses. Tosca's ghost, bloody on the castle battlements, and the scheming Scarpia. It was time I went to a proper bed.

I should have thought that a fire escape would open easily from the inside, but be locked to anyone who might try to enter from the outside.

Not again. Admit it, Alex, you're a walking disaster area. Accident prone. Stuck on a rooftop the night before the Games. I peered down the fire escape but I wasn't game to try that. The security guards and dogs prowled round the wire fences of the women's quarters during the day, and logic told me that at midnight the security would be more, not less. If I got caught trying to get down, it would be the Italian carabinieri who carried guns, and total embarrassment, an international incident even, and Mr Upjohn crowing that he knew all along I'd be nothing but a nuisance in Rome.

So I kept a vigil, like knights used to keep in churches. An unavoidable vigil until morning, in what felt like a church of a sort. Strangely, I was quite calm, not cold, not unhappy. I thought of Andy walking along the beach at Muriwai and Tom — somewhere in Rome. I snuggled into a concrete cranny and watched the pink moon slide across the sky. At some point in the night the distant domes became fainter and vanished. The few lights in the apartment blocks went out, though the traffic never completely stopped as it did at home.

Later, when the moon was low in the sky, I woke chilled, stiff, a bit damp. I needed to move around, to do some calisthenics. I padded across the flat rooftop, around the circular structure which sat in the middle. The black shadows it threw put me in mind of temples, pillars, a courtyard, a stage: gymnasts, drummers, musicians. Exercises turned into dance movements, glorious stretches to the black sky. A procession, slow, measured, solemn. Alex in a short tunic of fine linen, her long hair plaited with gold thread, her calves braided with soft leather, silver round her ankles and wrists, kohl around her eyes. She moved in time to the slow drums, a stately dance requiring perfect balance and control. Leslie Caron danced around the fountains in *An American in Paris*, so she would dance around a rooftop in Rome (softly mind, as a cat) in her shortie pyjamas. Low arabesque, attitude, a beautiful port-de-bras, but no risky jeté. Moving figures on Greek friezes, Alexandra in the lean body of a Greek athlete, now in her tunic and now naked, feeling the soft air on her torso, the freedom of nakedness in the dark endless space, stretching to the stars, pulling down strength. Alexandra watched the dance, a small part of her laughing at the scene, at herself.

At length the procession passed. The vision faded, the dancer dressed and sat down as the moon fell slowly behind the hills. She slept, smiling, and when she woke the sky was at its darkest, with just a hint of light behind the hill to the east.

Four o'clock, five? The best bet would be to climb down the fire escape just before dawn, hoping like hell that I wasn't eaten alive by a Dobermann. Pretend to be an athlete out for an early run.

And that's how it worked out, when I woke again and saw the sky turning pale lemon. I took off my dressing-gown and wrapped it and diary into a small bundle. With top tucked into pants, my shortie pyjamas could pass for running gear. Bare feet

— well, some runners trained in bare feet, that marathon runner Abebe Bikila from Ethiopia for one. I crept down the iron staircase, my ears peeled for guards' footsteps, dogs, any sign of life. I had to jump the last bit, a good ten feet, taking care to jump squarely and land with cushioning knees. A broken ankle would be the last straw. I jogged once around the building trying to find the main entrance.

The funny end to this tale came when I found the door locked, so I had to go around several times, and do some exercises until at last there was enough light for a runner to come down the stairway inside. I was genuinely puffed enough to fool her that I was the earliest bird. As she came out I went in. She said something incomprehensible in Swedish or Hungarian. She was short and strongly-built and probably threw something. (A couple of days later I found out it was a javelin she threw, and well enough for a medal. She recognized me in the reception area and hailed an interpreter. I had to explain that I wasn't a runner; that swimmers sometimes went for a run to relieve boredom or sore eyes — which was a load of old nonsense. Like most swimmers I couldn't run to save myself, and I'd never given in to the pain of sore eyes in that terrible pool at home.) I jogged up the stairs to the second floor, heady with relief. The door opened without a squeak. My alarm clock said ten to six. Zoe didn't stir as I wiped off my sweaty brow and armpits with a towel, climbed into bed and started, silently, to laugh.

Nessun dorma

Two days into my self-imposed banishment — I've been unexpectedly lonely. Something's missing. So I've been, despite the incredible heat, walking; through the Trastevere, the Borghese gardens, yesterday out at Tivoli, through Hadrian's villa, the Villa d'Este, the Canopus valley. All wonderful . . . yet I keep thinking of a certain pool where the swimmers, surely the only people in Rome comfortable in this heat, have been having their last training sessions before the historic ceremony tomorrow and the swimming events the day after. Alex's first race, her début. I'm sure it will not be her last and only one.

I have just come home, on the eve of the opening ceremony, exhausted, having walked from the Campidoglio. Maybe three miles, though it felt like six. It's 2.00 a.m. The apartment bedroom, though large and with the ceiling fan going, still feels airless and is probably well over 90°F. With sleep eluding me, I have got up and sung through some gentle Schubert pieces, some Cole Porter, played some Bach preludes, some two-part inventions, some Debussy, Chopin nocturnes, the slow movements of two Mozart sonatas, Schumann's little Kinderszenen, to little avail.

I'd be surprised if Alex, or indeed any of the athletes, can sleep tonight. *Nessun dorma.* Turandot, Pekingese version, has been so comatose in her basket that I have several times in the past few days thought she had died. I understand the quarters in the village are not air-conditioned. I hope her room is fitted with a fan.

I had not intended to go to the Campidoglio, but the crowds seemed to be gathering in that direction and for want of any other commitment, I went with them. Soon after dark I understood why. With operatic pomp, all sorts of dignitaries and uniforms were assembled, lamps were lit, bands played, the equestrian statue of Marcus Aurelius and the encircling statues splendidly floodlit; something Italy does as well as any country. Eventually a lone runner came springing up the steps carrying aloft the Olympic flame, from, I understand, Olympia, via the Peloponnese, Athens, Sicily, and up through Italy, carried by a multitude of young runners. I wish Alex had been here, to share it — especially when the boy prodded his torch into the waiting bowl and lit the leaping orange flame; ancient Olympia come to Michelangelo's Rome, too much for a humble Kiwi. I think she would have shared my tears.

From the balcony I can see the moon, rosy and soft-edged, unlike a New Zealand full moon which I remember to be a hard dead white. *Nessun dorma.*

A long march

Alex, you've been here before!

It wasn't just the rehearsal, when we'd marched past the silent empty stands. There was something weirdly familiar as we went into the tunnel. Into the blessed shade, and the image clicked: the procession at ancient Olympia, going into the arena as one of the athletes would have seen it: inside a square tunnel with the parade walking ahead, some naked, others wearing armour and carrying spears; and ahead, the first glimpse of crowd waiting in the stadium. I could see, sharp as a photograph, the page in my classical history book, the caption under the artist's impression: "The parade of athletes assembled in the courtyard in front of the Temple of Zeus and then marched through a narrow tunnel into the adjacent stadium."

'This is it folks,' said a voice behind, male trying hard to be unimpressed, laconic. 'The light at the end of the . . .'

'Shut up, Gary, you silly bastard,' said others. This tunnel was much bigger than the one in the picture, and *we* all had clothes on (far too many, near-dead after two miles in high heels) but surely those Greek athletes had felt just like me, swept along, faces wet with sweat, hardly breathing, numb with excitement. Our footsteps echoed left-right left-right off the sides as we marched towards the light and the sound of the bands and that vast roaring crowd we knew was in there.

It must be about four o'clock. By rights, I shouldn't still be standing. From my night under the pink moon to no more sleep, tiny breakfast, loosening-up swim only before a tiny lunch. Put on uniform, assemble with teams, blazers of every colour under the sun, flag-bearers, placard-bearers out on the roads around the village, interminable wait, buy drinks, more drinks in the blinding heat, but not so many that we'd need to pee. There'd be no comfort stop, once we got going. Curse the people who put us in thick black blazers and high heels. Finally move off, march down riverside road (I was stiff from my dawn jog, tomorrow will be worse, *tomorrow* — aaargh — I have to swim), through the Ponte Milvio over the Tiber with helicopter above, through the Stadio dei Marmi with its huge white statues peering down and stands full of people, cheers, crowds, music, bunting, flags — this was what we came for.

And then we were through the tunnel and the sunlight hit us again, and the first sight and noise of a hundred thousand people, surrounded by a gigantic sweep of faces, and I felt, for the first time, yes, we *are* special, me and my mates marching around this red track behind our flag, we're athletes, and the best. All you people have come to honour us, honour the spirit of the Games, just as they used to at Olympia.

I wondered where the press box was. Up behind the V.I.P. stand, no doubt.

Burning a ring around my wrist, contrary to a silly rule which said no jewellery with uniform, was a new silver charm bracelet. It had been mysteriously delivered that morning, by special messenger. A black velvet box wrapped in shiny pink paper. Inside, on grey satin, was the bracelet, with a single charm. A musical symbol, a bass clef holding together five lines, the music stave. His signature. Zoe and some of the others had bought charm bracelets in Singapore. They were clunky; this was very classy-looking, with an Italian name from Firenze inside the lid. There was no card, and no need for one. Baritones use the bass clef. He'd asssumed I knew that. I hadn't told him I learnt music.

If you're up in the press box, I thought, as we marched down the long straight track in front of the main stand, I'm the young one in the second row, with the taller women, second from the right. You might be able to see a glint of silver round my right wrist. I'm not going to turn my head, because this is eyes-front left-right stuff, and I am, as you said at lunch last Sunday, a professional in attitude if not hard cash. I am Alexandra, at the Olympic Games! I made it!

Around the red curve of the track, we heard special cheers from Kiwis up in the stands. Behind us the noise surged, loud for the huge U.S.A. team, loudest of all for Italy as the host, in sky-blue blazers. From the grassy centre of the stadium, lined up with the other teams, I could now pick out the V.I.P. stand facing us and yes, the press box with rows of desks. Behind us, the bowl stood on the skyline, where the runner would light the flame. Under the scoreboard, bands, orchestras, choirs. Around me people took photos and let off steam about the size of the crowd, the heat and sun, the people back home who chose our uniform, sore feet. The runners rejoiced they didn't have to compete for a week, forgetting that some did. I'd have given *anything* to sit down. One clever man, a yachtsman, produced one of those folding seats on a walking stick, and perched on it, grinning smugly.

They trumpeted the V.I.P.s in for speeches in Italian and English. Eight sailors in white sailor-suits escorted in the Olympic flag. They handed over the flag from the last Olympics in Melbourne. They fired off the loudest cannons I'd ever heard in my life, and let loose about nine million pigeons. Everyone ducked, but no one actually got bombed before they headed off to the hills. The sun dropped below the rim of the stadium, giving us shade.

The arrival of the Olympic torch finished me off. The announcer said something in Italian. There was a complete hush apart from distant cheers outside the stadium, and then we heard the cry swell from those near the entrance. We'd been told not to break rank on pain of death, but how could you not; everyone did spontaneously, officials and all. We just *had* to see. I got only a glimpse of the dark boy in white running shorts, the torch held high. The noise, already incredible, got louder and louder as he ran past the athletes jammed around the inside of the track and up the steps towards the skyline. He paused while the crowd roared, then plunged the torch into the bowl. The flame burst upwards. I wasn't the only one with a wet face as we were herded back into line. Someone who knew said the boy was the Roman secondary school athletics champion.

The rest — the flags being paraded, and an Italian competitor taking the oath on behalf of all the athletes, the Italian national anthem, all seemed a bit of an anti-climax. Then we were on the move again, marching out, taking the short way back to the village.

The other women chose to amble and buy drinks and talk to people from other teams, but I told Bulldog that I was going on ahead. She was too tired to argue and I kept going like a robot, because I had to swim tomorrow and if I didn't take off my blazer (against regulations) and keep walking, I'd fall over or seize up completely. My dawn jog was the maddest thing I'd ever done. The Aussies and Canadians, being among the first out, would have been the first back to their quiet rooms. To think about Tomorrow.

Halfway across the bridge the white concrete started to go blurry and black around the edges. I was going to pass out. We'd been told that blazers were to stay on, all day. The thought of an ambulance was worse than being told off. I pulled my shirt out of my tight skirt and hung gasping for air, my mouth dry as sand, over the rail. Slowly the river scene in front of me came back into focus. The Tiber surged around the piles of the bridge, white swirls in dark turquoise. I could see the tops of the pool stands. My stomach lurched.

I thought of another bridge: the Auckland harbour bridge being opened last year and Andy and I walking with the crowds. He'd quoted Kipling at me and we'd talked of death, whether you'd live if you fell off. This bridge was not nearly as high. Fifteen months, was that all? Andy was dead, and I was here.

A small thanks-offering was required, to him, to Rome. I slowly undid the chain of his only gift to me, the pearl tear-drop I always wore. I didn't hesitate, just let it gently drop into the turquoise. It flashed milky-white once, his tear, my tears. Perhaps it would be carried to the sea, or stay in the mud on the riverbed. Quite fitting for a pearl.

I walked the last half mile back to the village in a daze through the crowds of ambling athletes, and the last bit through the village in my stockings because my feet felt as though they had been amputated. I staggered up the last stairs. The room was absolutely suffocating. It was about 6.30 p.m. Throw open the shutters. Take off all clothes! Bed! Horizontal! I hadn't sat down for seven hours! Tomorrow!

'Telephone!'
It was, of course, only a bad dream.
'Telephone, wake up. For you, Alex. From New Zealand, quick.'
'Go away.'
'From home, Godzone . . . cripes, Alex, home, *New Zealand*,' someone yelled in my ear. 'Gee, what a gorgeous bracelet, where did you get it!'
'Mind your own . . .' The words slipped sideways out of my mouth as I slid back into the void.
'Listen, it's the *telephone*.'
'So what.'
'Telephone, for you, person-to-person, long-distance. Someone called Mrs Young is spending good money to talk to you, God knows why.'
'It's probably my Gran,' I said loftily, 'rung to wish me luck.' My eyes would not open. 'It *is* my Gran.' I staggered onto the floor. 'Where? Lead me.'
'Put something on, for God's sake.' Zoe found my dressing-gown. 'If you went to bed earlier . . .'
'Nag, nag.' I vaguely knew the phone was downstairs, and that I needed Zoe's help to get there. She pushed me stumbling out the door, and led me down the stairs. It seemed to be night-time.
'Hullo?' A voice asked me if I was Miss Alexandra Archer, then I heard . . . Gran, sounding like she was round the back of the moon. 'How are you, my pet?'
'What time's it there, Gran?'
'Never mind the time. Tell me about . . . we were listening on the wireless, on shortwave.'
'You sound all blurry. It's an awful line.'
'Tell me, pet.'
'It was amazing, incredible. I cried when we marched around, I felt so proud. When the boy lit the flame I thought I'd die. Rome's *hot*.' I suddenly felt dirty and completely disoriented.
'What's the time there, Gran?'
'We just, on the midday news.' She sounded a bit breathless. 'They said the New Zealand team looked very smart, and

marched beautifully. I wanted to say good luck for your race. God bless you always, Alex.'

There was a slight pause, then I heard Mum's voice, and Dad's in the background. No one said anything special, really, except hullo, how are you feeling, fighting fit I hope, had your bottom pinched (Dad) and how's your Italian (Mum), how's everyone at home, we're fine, the kids send their love, they're at school, of course, Mr Jack sends his love, good luck and gofurrit, bye Alex, swim well, thinking of you, love you.

The line went static, the thread broken. I wished they hadn't rung, because I stood in that dim empty hallway, not knowing what time of the day or night it was, gone from thrill to misery. Zoe took the phone out of my hand and silently pushed me up the stairs. My travel clock said quarter to eleven, apparently night-time.

'Odd time to ring,' said Zoe, taking off clothes, not her uniform.

'Where've you been? Weren't you in bed?'

'I was just coming up the stairs when the phone rang. Bit of a party developed in one of the recreation areas — dancing to the juke-box, doing the conga. All *sorts* were there, Americans, Africans, Japanese, Aussies.'

Only high-jumpers and the like, I thought sourly, who still have a week before their events. Not swimmers who'd all be stiff after the march and desperately trying to sleep. 'At least it didn't wake you up,' I said, pointedly.

'No, but they woke you, from the dead. I'd have thought, the night before your big race . . .'

'Probably they didn't want to miss me tomorrow, knowing I'd be coming and going to the pool. They know I'm a good sleeper,' I lied. By the time I'd washed away the day's sweat and grime in the shower, I'd nearly convinced myself that this was true, that the timing wasn't a bit peculiar. It was a long and desperate night that I had to get through.

Overture

Since I can't sleep again, I must sing or write.

The music, I thought, was the least impressive feature of the opening ceremony this afternoon. For a nation passionately devoted to music of the dramatic ceremonial kind, it was distant and uninspiring. The British do these things better.

As spectacle, though, true to Baron de Coubertin's prescribed format, it was breathtaking. I had, from the press box dead centre of the main stand, a ringside seat! I arrived early, because it had occurred to me, jolting awake at 4.00 a.m., that Norm Thompson didn't actually know that he and his paper had acquired me as his personal interpreter/copy assistant. He was, as I hoped, in the face of a certain amount of disarming honesty, more amused than put out. The man looks seedy — he says he is not coping well with the heat, or his hotel food. I felt only slightly an opportunist.

Or perhaps he understood the deeper reason. When the New Zealand team marched through the tunnel into the arena, their black-and-white colour scheme smarter among the many-coloured uniforms than I might have expected, he silently handed me his binoculars for a brief look. I haven't seen her for four days. I picked her immediately in the second row, the tallest woman, walking distinctively and superbly erect. Even from that distance her eyes burned; a sort of solemn 'I don't believe this is happening to me' incredulity.

Above his retrieved binoculars, Norm gave me a running commentary as the team passed below us. He'd covered three Olympiads and five Empire Games, he said, but the parades always churned him up. He knew most of the athletes pretty well — Alex when she first started swimming lessons, a small,

Alessandra   437

determined kid aged eight or nine. Her coach saw her potential, even then. That dark horse Peter Snell too, a promising tennis player before he took to pounding round that lethal circuit of Arthur Lydiard's out at Titirangi.

To my question: what chance did Alex have tomorrow? he replied that it was impossible to say. She was fitter, and tougher, than she herself thought, but she'd not raced since April. She could go either way — sink without trace, or rise to the occasion. Today's long march wouldn't help.

I enjoyed watching the world's top sports reporters working at their microphones and Olivettis, two-finger typists many of them. Norm wrote his copy as the ceremony proceeded and I was able to earn my keep, securing a long-distance line for him back to Auckland. I lost all sight of Alex, despite the binoculars, when the athletes broke ranks to see the torch-bearer do his triumphal circuit. I thought I might have glimpsed her among the teams as they returned to the village, but I was defeated by the crowds; and I have made a promise.

As dusk fell, I slowly rode the Vespa, borrowed this morning, alongside the river. The apartment is mercifully cool and solitary. I'll not watch any of the television coverage; I've seen the ceremony, I have a treasured memory, I don't need the facsimile.

Today, though magnificent, was merely the overture; tomorrow is the first act. I wonder how she is sleeping, if at all. One day I'll face the same ordeal, the night before a début in a small role in — where? a major house in Rome or Milan or London, or more realistically, some small repertory theatre in Germany? — knowing that I have done everything in my power to prepare myself, and can humanly do no more.

Those burning blue-grey eyes do not tell of failure and are beginning, as I sing through some Schumann, to haunt me.

A ruddy miracle

So, it's actually going to happen. You're going to stand on the block in front of twenty thousand people for the race you've dreamed of for five years.

It'll be a ruddy miracle if I get into the semi-finals tomorrow. I didn't sleep a wink. My calves were sore from all the walking. I felt sick over breakfast, got mad at Mrs C and madder at Mr Upjohn both wanting to organize me. I had diarrhoea. All that brave talk about adjusting body-clocks for a mid-afternoon race went out the window. I couldn't face either food or rugby talk at lunch. Bulldog brought me a doggy bag, I gnawed on a bread roll. I shaved my arms and legs, and checked my gear seventeen times over. Mr Upjohn brought me a huge pile of telegrams from home, which merely made me weep. He gave me a sealed envelope from Mr Jack. 'Go out hard, but leave something for the run home, 110 per cent effort in the final 25 yards. Remember Napier, you did it then. Remember you start as equals. Good luck, Enjoy it. Ta-Ta For Now. Your cuddly friend, Bill Jack.' *Enjoy* it?

A second parcel arrived, smaller. Inside was a black velvet box from the same jeweller. A tiny silver kiwi sat on grey satin. Did you have it specially made, Tom? Firenze jewellers wouldn't even know what a kiwibird was, or why. I clipped it carefully into the silver strands of the bracelet. Two charms, two messages around my wrist. You are a Kiwi, you have a friend here, don't forget it.

To the pool at one-thirty, half a bread roll sticking in my gullet, calves still stiff. Warm-up in the covered pool with the naked horse murals felt like I was swimming in treacle. No one talked much in the changing-room. Even Dawn Fraser looked tired and grim in her corner, and she was supposed to be an old hand at this. Which would be worse being defending Olympic champ or a scared shitless first-timer?

Ten to three. Thirty grim females from eighteen countries in the marshalling area, a large bare room near the changing-rooms. We had wet hair from our warm-up, and track suits with Union Jacks, or Stars 'n Stripes, maple leaves, Aussie maps, lots of different flags. Miss Britain 1960, for all her earlier aplomb, was positively grey around the gills. Some looked like grannies in old-fashioned towelling dressing-gowns. It was just like home really. Same elderly officials with clipboards, same wrinkly chaperones clucking about, same restless bodies, same fear.

They called the first heat, la prima batteria. Being in the last, at least I could get some idea of the times. They filed out five or six zombies at a time, 25 left, then 19, 12, then six. I counted. We could tell exactly what was happening by the crowd noises filtering in through the open door — four times over, the names being announced, claps and cheers, the hush, the gun, the rising roar of the race, the climax, the results, applause. Dawn Fraser won the second heat, 62.1. Cripes! First and third heats, over 64s, encouraging. Chris Von Saltza the fourth, in Olympic record time of 61.9. Double cripes!

The last six, a Brit, East Germans, Canadian. Me, lane 6, good for me; on the return lap the field would be on my breathing side. So I was the last female to walk, towel around my neck, through the dim tunnel into . . .

Such *blinding* light that I couldn't see anything for about a minute. Tom, you up there, I don't want to see either. I kept my eyes on the heels of the girl in front, all the way up the long side of the pool staring at the pink paving until I realized she had stopped at lane 5. I had to move on to lane 6. When I looked up, I very nearly ran pronto for the tunnel.

I knew the pool well enough with empty stands. Full was another matter. This was what 20,000 people looked like, buzzing with excitement 'cause they'd just seen an Olympic record. The sunlight was coming onto the pool twice over from the white sky and reflected from the white crowd. The pool looked like a shimmering transparent turquoise stage.

Blinking, my heart g-donking away, I tried to think straight. Around the starting area were about four hundred officials in grey blazers and panama hats, the judges in tiers above the finish. At the far end, the scoreboard showed 4^a Batteria, ranging from Chris Von Saltza's 61.9 to someone who'd done 69.0. Well I could beat 69 with my legs tied! What I had to beat was 64. Swim faster than I'd ever swum. It wasn't possible. If I walked away now, if I swam a 66s, people would understand. I was still only fifteen.

I deliberately did not look up towards the press box, above the starting blocks. I knew I could probably pick out a flashy hat, a pink shirt. I knew he was there. I would not look. I was here to swim, not to flirt, and swim I would, damn you. I am Alex the pro, getting on with the job. Thank you for the silver kiwi.

Finally, introduced to the crowd — Signorina Alessandra Archer, dalla Nuova Zelanda — stripped to racers, smoothed limbs, bareheaded or in caps, we stood on the steps of our blocks. As I drew in lungfuls of air, I thought of Maggie, our show-down race in Napier. I had five Maggies to beat this time.

You've not seen me *really* in action yet, Tom, my Kiwi friend, you with the hat on.

A whistle, a hush. *Al posto!* The crouching wait, toes curled, feet ready to thrust, knees to straighten, arms to fling. No one is trying to break. I'm feeling steady. Finally, my Olympic gun.

It was my first proper race for five months. I didn't deserve it. It was one of those few races where everything went right. A great start, felt smooth, rhythmic, easy. Keeping up, from what I could see of the bodies under the water to my right. Turn perfectly timed, push-off strong.

Now I could see the opposition. Still keeping up. Still double-breathing comfortably. *Still* keeping up? Look again, Alex. Bloody hell!

Halfway up the return length I saw only one head was actually level, the others were behind. I had a chance. The time might be okay too. I gave it everything I had.

Above me the timekeepers drew back, the noise of the vast crowd fell over me like a breaking wave. I flopped back into a slow-motion backstroke. They were using special stopwatches started by the gun and stopped by the timekeepers; the first time at a Games.

The list flashed up:
 1 STEWARD, G.B. 63.5
 2 ARCHER, N.Z. 63.8
 3 . . .

I shook the water from my eyes.

2 ARCHER — I turned and did a dolphin dive. When I came up it was still there. ARCHER, N.Z. 63.8.

It wasn't possible. I've never swum faster. Tom, my friend up there, did you *see* me? I think I might have qualified.

'You've qualified,' said Mrs C, glowing all over with disbelief.

'You've qualified,' said Mr Upjohn, even more incredulous. 'Well done, child,' they choroused as I found my way back to the changing-room.

'*You've* qualified,' said Miss Britain 1960 with the voice like the Queen and the aunt who hated New Zealand. It turned out she was the seventeenth fastest, in a time one second off her best, of course in the *toughest* heat. So she'd just missed out on the semi-final. I was the thirteenth fastest, she informed me, with just the slightest hint that somehow it was all wrong, that I'd upset the natural balance of things.

Not bad, I thought, towelling my hair dry, for a colonial hick. 'Sorry, Sheila,' I said in the broadest New Zealand accent I could muster. 'That's not my name,' she said. 'Oh, but it is,' I said. 'All girls are Sheila in New Zealand. Didn't your aunt tell you, of course she wasn't really there long enough to find out, was she?' I gathered up my bags. She didn't know what I was talking about. 'Ciao, Sheila.' I don't like being patronized.

'You're through, kiddo,' said Dawn Fraser, clapping me on the shoulder as I sidled past her in the corridor. 'Good swim, Alex Archer.' She knew I existed, my *name*? I wondered if she could see my whole body going red as I mumbled 'Thanks. Great swim of yours, too,' and fled.

'You're in, Kiwi' said a delighted Norm Thompson waiting for me outside the pool, with Mr U and Mrs C. 'I might have known you wouldn't be satisfied, coming all this way for one race.'

'No comment,' I grinned.

'I've a message,' he said, while Mr Upjohn was diverted by a passing Australian official. 'From a certain I-tie journo who was watching the race with me. He sends, let's see — he made me write it down.' He found an entry in amongst a page of untidy shorthand notes. 'Saluti auguri e congratulazioni!'

'No comment,' I grinned again. I was wearing the bass clef and the silver kiwi on my wrist.

My British friend was right in one thing: the balance *had* been altered. At dinner that night some of the New Zealand men who'd not said two words to me since we left home suddenly came out with 'Great stuff, girlie', and 'You beaudy', and the like.

Telegrams — FANTASTIC, KEEP IT UP, BEST LUCK FOR SATURDAY — poured in, much better than GOOD TRY or more likely nothing at all, had I failed the first post. Mr Upjohn was conspicuous by his presence and rather politer than before. New Zealand didn't have too much to crow about at Olympic swimming level. Jean Stewart won a backstroke bronze in Helsinki '52 and Marrion Roe, who was a senior when I was just starting, reached the sprint finals in Melbourne four years ago. Could I pull it off again? 'A possible finalist', a British magazine writer had said.

Instead of filing remarks like 'Fifteen-year-old Alex Archer swam gamely in her heat but was outclassed', Norm Thompson was now writing back things like 'Fifteen-year-old Alex Archer rose splendidly to the challenge with a heat time equalling her best. The achievement of this, coming from winter training and suffering from mild dysentery and sunburn in Rome's 104°F afternoon heat, cannot be underestimated.'

I didn't know that at the time, of course, only later when I saw Mum's scrap book. But I'd jumped out of the frying pan into the fire. I could hardly force two mouthfuls down my throat at dinner, and the small print of the paperback edition of *War and Peace* I was trying to read kept blurring before my eyes. Zoe didn't even nag me to turn out the light. I must have slept, because I dreamed a Hollywood production number, me in ridiculous white gloves in a water ballet one minute and swimming a race the next, while around the pool marched an army of identical young men with lurid red hair carrying flaming torches. The Colosseum came in somewhere, too, like that film *Quo Vadis*, lions and blood, the bloodthirsty crowd . . . Around five I woke for about the tenth time, sweating.

I wondered what the dawn looked like from the roof, my special sanctuary. This time I took a sandal for the emergency door, to make sure it stayed open. This was about as silent as Rome ever got — an occasional car, a set of faint church bells on one note, roosters, a baby crying. I hadn't sat long in the cool hush before the black domes appeared against grey, lemon, pink, orange, and finally crimson streaked with black.

I spent the next three dawns on the roof, soaking up a sky so beautiful I sat in tears, telling myself that it was all worth it. I could have been the seventeenth fastest and saved myself some of the agony.

You've left behind country, family, friends, your coach. Mr Upjohn greases and Bulldog fusses, and you're indifferent. The telegrams are nice, but they don't touch you — you have trouble remembering who half the people are. When you left home you knew trouble was brewing in the Congo. Now World War III could have started somewhere for all you knew. You hadn't heard any proper news for two weeks. You don't hear the gossip and you don't look at anyone in the changing room. They thought you were a snotty bitch.

I felt aged eleven again, and on my own. Completely and utterly.

The one person who mattered, I'd let walk out of my life without a protest. Saturday lunchtime another charm arrived in a black velvet box, this time a silver fern like the emblem on our blazer pockets. I come from New Zealand. I am swimming for my country. He is still around somewhere. I will not look up at the press box.

The semi-finals were scheduled for 8.40 Saturday night. I dragged myself through the morning swim, re-ran the endless suffocating hours between token lunch, tossing siesta, reading without seeing, token tea, the deliberately slow showering/

shaving ritual, not because I needed to, but because it was something to *do*.

In the bus to the pool Mr Upjohn gave me another sealed letter from Mr Jack. *ALEX ARCHER (N.Z.) — 100m SEMI-FINALIST* it said on the outside. *To be opened on Saturday, August 27.* Oh Mr Jack, you believed! I read it in the toilet, through tears. I could almost hear his cuddly Aussie voice, telling me that I *can* win a place in the final, I have done the work, I proved yesterday I have the speed, I must give this one everything I had, go out fast, and stay out.

By 8.30 the world's sixteen fastest female swimmers, representing ten nations, were pacing around the call area. You could have cut the air with a knife. At 8.45 the first eight filed out, heads down. I'd drawn lane 2 in the second semi-final, a disaster for me because on the return run I wouldn't see a thing. I'd be swimming blind. Dawn Fraser was in lane 4. She had big rings under her eyes. She didn't talk to me or anyone.

We stood in line, one to eight, began to walk towards the tunnel. I saw the pool spread out in front of me, the water dramatically blue under the strongest floodlights I've ever seen in my life. Yellow lane ropes, red flags, pink concourse, white officials' trousers. Unreal colours, like a very clear dream. The stands soared upwards into the black. I heard the girl behind me muttering to herself as we began that long lonely walk up the length of the pool, walking the plank to watery doom. Maybe she was a Catholic, praying.

Tom, I'm the one in the black track suit, second in the line, with inadequate wobbly legs like the Scarecrow in *The Wizard of Oz*. I was the Scarecrow once, not so long ago, with a silver face. I made a great fool of myself. I'm about to do it again.

We were introduced (this time I registered some New Zealand cheers from the stands) and again faced the scoreboard. 1^a Semi-finale. 1 C. VON SALTZA, U.S.A. 62.5. The slowest time was 65.6, the cut-off point at fourth was 64.7. Mine could be the faster heat. It had to be under 64 for me to have any chance at all.

Well, I thought, this might be the first and last time I ever swim against Dawn Fraser, so I might as well make the most of it. She looked reluctant to move to the blocks.

I was just about to take my track suit top off when I realized I still had Tom's charm bracelet on. I couldn't get it undone. Then it got hooked up in my track suit sleeve. A woman official came to my aid, but by this time I was just slightly keeping them all waiting, and bright scarlet. If Tom had binoculars, he'd have seen why. Okay, I thought angrily, glowing like a Christmas tree, my nerve ends jangling like bells, watch me, matey.

What did I expect, really? This little pipsqueak upstart aged fifteen from the colonies? Halfway up the first length I could see Dawn Fraser, two lanes away, already slightly ahead, going like the proverbial Bondi tram. I felt tight, no rhythm. I might have been third or fourth to the turn. That, at least, wasn't too bad.

The trip home was one of those endless nightmares, blinded by lights, fighting the water, buffeted by the wash, swallowing water. But I sure as hell wasn't going to throw it away. I tried to ride up on my bow-wave. I really did try for you, Mr Jack, heart, soul, and every bit of puff I had. My arms hurt, my legs hurt, my chest hurt and I had no idea where anyone else was. When I touched and looked across, I knew at least I wasn't last.

A great cheer went up. FRASER (AUST) 61.4, new Olympic record. Flash bulbs were going off all over the place. Then the other names came up on the board.

    ORDINE DI ARRIVO: 1 FRASER (AUST)   61.4
                                 2 ARCHER (N.Z.)   63.5

What? This time I followed Dawn Fraser and went for a long wind-down swim, feeling the pain seep out of my muscles, telling myself I was seeing things, cruel tricks of the night. They'd got it all wrong. They'd announce a correction, the new system had broken down. Ladies and Gentlemen . . . there has been a terrible mistake. Or whatever it was in Italian.

When I could bring myself to look again, halfway up the pool and that much closer, my name was still there, large as life, and second down. ARCHER 63.5. Personal best ever. After such an excruciating race, I don't believe it. Dawn Fraser looked across at me as we both hauled ourselves out together, and grinned and nodded. She'd just set an Olympic record, but she knew I'd come second. So it must be true.

I think I am an Olympic finalist.

Everything changed again.

So recently ignored, how do you now cope finding yourself being congratulated by people who should by rights have been in the final? The champs of Britain, Hungary, Italy, Sweden, Germany, Canada? Some could shake your hand and smile, ruefully, with eyes that said where the hell did you pop up from? Others wouldn't even look but turned away, their whole bodies drooping with despair. All that work . . . you knew the feeling.

You didn't cope well at all. There was too much emotion charging around. You started to shake uncontrollably and escaped to the toilet to throw up what little food was in your stomach. You dressed in there too, numbed, fumbling in your haste to escape. You had a moment of panic when you couldn't remember where your charm bracelet had gone. You found it in your track suit pocket. You'd nearly swum the jolly race with it on!

Out of the changing-room, you got no further than Mr Upjohn and a group of ancient reporters, several from home, including Norm Thompson, four Aussies. You got confused, you answered their stupid questions like a dumb twelve-year-old, you bored them, you bored yourself. How many brothers and sisters, Miss Archer? Boyfriends, Miss Archer? Do you know what do you want to be, Miss Archer? Three, no and no.

You longed to see someone you knew under the age of sixty, preferably male, 23, and red-haired. You were on the verge of asking Norm Thompson if you could come up to the press box, when he gave you a note with a single word: *Bravissima!* You stood, tingling, poised, in the middle of the entrance hall with the naked bronze statues. You heard Bulldog say 'Alex, what do you want to do?' You walked out, down the steps. He could wait, you could wait.

You sleepwalked through two days of dreamy white heat. You saw the dawn and the sunrise and heard church bells on Sunday. You stacked the telegrams around your dressing-table mirror. You went late to meals, to avoid your team-mates' teasing, and their endless post-mortems about the All Blacks losing the

Alessandra

fourth test and the series to the South Africans who sat crowing loudly at the other end of the dining hall. You went 'training'. You 'slept', dozed, looked at the ceiling, stood under cold showers for half an hour at a time. You 'read' *War and Peace.* You still couldn't believe it. Even if you only came eighth, you'd always be 'an Olympic finalist'. Did Tom, who knew nothing about sport, work that out too? His Sunday message came via Norm Thompson at the pool. It was the Olympic symbol, five interlocking rings, in silver and enamel, barely half an inch across. You put it on the bracelet. You could wait.

Monday's message was unmistakable: a tiny medal with a wreath around the edges. Engraved on one side was *La Grande Olimpiade, Roma, 1960*, and on the other, *Sig. Alex Archer, New Zealand.* The point was, it was bronze.

At first, you were angry. What did he know about it? It was obvious that the battle for the gold would be between Dawn Fraser and Chris Von Saltza. But third, bronze? Did he, anyone, really expect you to beat all those seasoned Europeans into third, the bronze?

You dreamed. You had already, God knows how, lowered your own personal best twice. Could you pull it off a third time? Perhaps, a 63.0 might just do it? It was unlikely. It was possible. Okay, Tom, it was *possible.*

At Monday lunchtime, you took two calls, person-to-person from home — Mum only, on behalf of the family, and Mr Jack. There was a conspiracy going on. 'The bronze?' she said. 'The bronze,' he said. You laughed. It was one o'clock in the morning over there. They must have been on the plonk together. You had nine hours to go.

Your body refused to sleep or take food. You shaved it, showered it, prepared its bag, read its telegrams once more to give you some Dutch courage because you had none of the real sort, and finally you walked it out of your room to meet a stranger in a blazer called Mrs Churchill; out of the women's quarters, over to the main entrance to catch the bus to the pool. Your race was at nine. You still had three hours to go.

You walked past the bronze statues — why was everybody obsessed with bronze? — down to the silent changing-rooms. You had a 'warm-up' under the murals, in the pool made of marble. Your arms felt like they were attached to someone else. You wished, again, passionately, that you'd been the seventeenth fastest and saved yourself three days of agony.

In the toilet you read Mr Jack's final message to *ALEX ARCHER, FINALIST,* which reduced you to a sobbing mess. He'd thought even then that you could get this far? *This time, Alex, you must swim the race of your life. T.T.F.N.*
You endured half an hour in the call area. Dawn Fraser looked even more miserable. Chris Von Saltza, now that you were seeing her up close, was very blonde, Scandinavian-looking. You were called in lane 7 (very good for seeing on the return lap, for what it was worth), and you walked seventh into the strong light, beginning that march up the side of the pool for a race you never in your wildest dreams thought you'd swim.

There are only two races I remember so clearly I can run them in my head like a movie, in gorgeous Technicolor with all the dialogue, crowd noises, and background music complete.
One was that night in Napier, when I knew I had to beat Maggie to have any chance of getting to Rome. I remember so clearly those dreadful false starts, the thin rope across my chest, the shocking turn, my thoughts up that despairing last lap almost as though Andy was talking to me, egging me on.
The final in Rome is the other. I remember the little procession walking up the side of the pool, eight tall strong women in track suits, towels around our necks. The roar of the crowd as we appeared, the many Aussies in the crowd already shrieking 'Go Dawnie'. I remember the dozens of officials in their grey blazers, the tier of judges, the yellow lane-ropes, the sheen of the water, the floodlights shining down onto the pool from the very top of those vast stands.
Being introduced: *Cento metri stile libero, donne . . . dalla Nuova Zelanda, numero sette, la signorina Alessandra Archer,* with the rolled rrrs, and smiling at not a bad clap from all those people for the youngest competitor in the race. Smiling in the

direction, way up the top, of some special cheers and yells, the sort you hear around rugby fields: 'Go, Kiwi.'

I remember looking up at the scoreboard at the other end, my name unbelievably there, lane 7, and thinking: let's see how high I notch it up the Ordine di Arrivo, to five, to four, to . . . I remember looking across at Dawn Fraser, standing quite still, hunched, her fingertips quivering, and knowing just from the murderous way she was staring at the water that she was going to win. I remember smiling, the very idea of beating *Dawn Fraser* is too cheeky for words, but I'm going to do better than seventh.

I remember taking a quick look up at the press box as I slowly peeled off my track suit, without seeing anyone special. But I knew he was there.

I felt tall and dangerous as I walked over to the block and stood on the first step in my black togs and stretched my arms to the black sky. I remember Bulldog's bulging eyes as she took my track suit, the lipstick on her teeth, the announcer calling for *Silenzio!* I remember those twenty thousand people falling to a rustling silence, the long whistle, someone coughing, *Al posto!* the long steady crouching silence, we are all experienced here, no one trying to get a flier, the final gun.

The race itself? The blue water and yellow lane-corks sleeking past. Feeling superb. Black sharks on my blind side. Through my bow-wave noting the girl in lane 8 already behind as we approach the turn. A perfect turn, coming out to see several heads level with mine. Only one clearly ahead.

I remember thinking, I'm dreaming, this is an Olympic final not an inter-club carnival in Auckland and I should already be knowing my place, which is to come in seventh. Instead I can see one head ahead and three others level with mine. Already only five, jostling for three medals.

Halfway home, keeping rhythm through the churning water, through the growing disbelief that still only one head is clearly ahead, or maybe two, but no more than two. I kick into my absolute top gear. A voice from the past says *Reach for a star, Alex, the one with Rome written on it.* Another says *The bronze, Alessandra.*

Well, it was Dawn Fraser's night, but you could say it was Down Under's night too. The undisputed champion of the world, Dawn Fraser climbed onto the victory dais, waving her koala bear to the vast cheering crowd. 'Dawnie, Dawnie, Dawnie,' they chanted. She set a new Olympic record of 61.2, and became the first swimmer ever to retain an Olympic crown.

I touched the wall, and died. When I looked across, Chris Von Saltza was already hanging over the lane ropes, congratulating Dawn Fraser. Other heads came raggedly home. The timekeepers above me had pulled back. I couldn't look at the board. I went for a swim. Twenty yards up the pool I turned and came back. I still couldn't look.

Then I heard a very penetrating voice from not very far away that didn't carry above the crowd noise but somehow came underneath it. 'Bravissima, bellissima, Alessandra.'

Bravissima for what, Tom, oh bronze man? Fifth? Even fourth? FRASER, VON SALTZA . . . I knew the board didn't lie, and there were no tricks.

3 A. ARCHER (N.Z.) 63.0. I was third?

I'd won the bronze?

He was right there on the concourse, among the officials who swarmed around as I climbed out. I hardly recognized him at first. With an identity card pinned to a pale grey blazer, tie, and hair parted in the middle and wet with enough water to tone down the colour, he looked like just another official, though younger and greasier than most of them.

Before Mrs C came surging up with her screams and tears, he'd already taken my hand and solemnly kissed it. And with me in racing togs, chest heaving and hair plastered to my skull, this must have looked fairly odd. I fought back a ridiculous urge to play my part in this pageant and begin dancing a minuet with him, stately in dripping black racers, imagining the full, hooped skirt, the white wig. 'What are you *doing* down here?' I asked.

'Saluting you, before you get ambushed,' he said. 'Norm said it was on the cards. Woman, you *were third.* Believe it. You won the bronze. You'll be standing on the victory dais. I'll see you after your 400 metre event.'

Alessandra 451

I gulped. He expected me to remember my 400 metre event, *now*? He stood aside for Bulldog, who was weeping and ecstatic and obviously didn't recognize him. I was conscious of his eyes watching as I put on my track suit and had my hand shook over and over in Italian and every other language and began to believe it and waited for the pandemonium to subside.

Dawn Fraser had her own victory party going already among the green blazers and track suits. The American group around Chris Von Saltza was quieter. I'd gathered up Bulldog and Mr Upjohn, and unbeknown to them, a ghostly, smiling watcher. Eventually I was asked to come to the other end of the pool for the victory ceremony.

With the main lights turned off, we were just three in the spotlight, waiting for our names and to step onto the dais, with the Olympic flame burning in a bowl nearby and the pool, now calm, stretched out before us.

After trumpets, announcements in Italian, a little parade of V.I.P.s and girls in grey dresses carrying the medals on cushions, 'Dawnie' and her koala stepped up for gold and Chris for silver.

I heard my name called out. I stepped up onto the box marked 3, and bent down as a Very Important Man in a suit put the gleaming medal, hung on a chain of leaves, around my neck. As they played the Australian anthem, we turned to watch the three flags go up: the Australian Southern Cross with five stars, and lower, the New Zealand one with four, and the Stars and Stripes. All red, white, and blue, floodlit against the black sky.

Need I say, I was thinking of family, Mr Jack, Andy, Maggie, even Maggie's sad Mum, even Miss Macrae, even Keith, my whole parade of people, and a man with his Titian hair parted in the middle, watching. My eyes were dripping water and I couldn't stop smiling.

What then do I remember? The crowd breaking out again, Dawn Fraser leaning down to congratulate her arch-rival and then the kid from Down Under. About a million flash bulbs went off. The picture they used on the front page of the paper at home showed Dawn centre, arms around Chris on the right, me on the left — grinning like the Cheshire Cat, clutching my little Maori doll, a present from my sister Debbie — all of us wearing our medals around our necks. The pool lights came up. Time for the next race, to move on, exit centre back. We were wanted in the interview room. I might have caught a last glimpse of Tom by the tunnel entrance. Or was it some other official with a clipboard and a centre parting? Or, in all this drama, had I imagined the minuet?

States of exile

Like Eliza Doolittle at the ball, 'I knew that she could do it, and indeed she did!'

I watched, with increasing delight and tension, her first two races. She could match her rivals for sheer speed, and could outdo most of them when it came to sorting out the winners and losers in the final twenty yards. Simple observation and logic told me that the bronze medal was not out of her reach.

Beside me, Norm Thompson, laconically recording her progress towards the final, had reached the same conclusion: that behind Fraser and Von Saltza, 'the bronze is up for grabs'. But by Monday night, the watching from afar and sending of notes (and charms for her bracelet I cannot really afford) had become intolerable. In the excitement of the men's semi-final event prior to hers, it took only the quick swipe of an official blazer discarded on the back of a chair, borrowing the tie from around Norm's neck, a clipboard from a desk, a rearrangement of hair, to gain admittance to the concourse.

Down there, among a small army of grey-blazered officials, it was the difference between watching an opera from the dress circle and being on a vast stage in the second row of the chorus. She walked in seventh, virtually unknown except to those few of the vast crowd who declared themselves from the floodlit heights as New Zealanders. I knew I should not, must not let her see me, but she had gone into a private world, a trance which could have been concentration, or just sheer terror.

How I felt for her! States of exile: the indescribable loneliness of the singer waiting for an entry, an actor for a cue, the student to begin an exam, the athlete about to throw five years of

Alessandra   455

back-breaking work into one race, one jump, the woman beginning labour. Adrenalin pumping, and no escape.

Alessandra, standing motionless behind the block, unlike your restless rivals, you were well named Archer. You were Diana as archer and bow, her glorious arrow.

It took every bit of self-control I possessed not to fling my arms around her when she finally climbed from the water. I could see she had suspended belief in the result. The grey eyes registered amusement when she recognized me. In the uproar of the finish, kissing her wet hand before Mrs Churchill came panting over, I was able to tell her that she'd better believe it, because it was obvious she didn't.

I long for her second race to be over, to find out what goes on behind those deep-set grey eyes; what sort of a fifteen-year-old comes to her first international meeting and, apparently unperturbed, walks off with a bronze medal; what she will make of problems which, like Eliza Doolittle's, are only just beginning; why she stirs in me thoughts of my homeland better left forgotten.

Aftershock

For days, everything blurred. It's my diary that tells me I went to the interview room and talked to Norm Thompson and lots of other reporters that night. Talked into a microphone for someone from the New Zealand Broadcasting Service. Talked and tried to describe my medal to the family and Mr Jack laughing down the phone from home: there's this boy being carried on people's shoulders through a crowd, it's lovely, the colour is, well, *bronze*.

According to my diary I did go training the next day, and again on Wednesday morning, trying to hide from gushing people like the Australian chaperone with the voice like Donald Duck. I really tried to raise some enthusiasm for the 400 metre heats. It'd never been my distance. Maggie had won the last one I'd raced, back in February. This time everything caught up with me. My heat wasn't until nearly 10.30 at night. There were two false starts, I got a mouthful on the dreaded fifth lap and my legs just about dropped off. My time was 1.2 seconds off my best, tenth fastest, respectable enough. I tried, but I'm a sprinter. They give the men a 200 metre race, why not the women? I didn't tell my diary I was not sorry to be watching the final from the competitors' stand. I'd done my dash.

Imagine the bliss of waking very late, that morning of the final I didn't have to swim, knowing I didn't have to go training today, tomorrow, or even too seriously next week for the Naples carnival on the 13th. No training, I wanted to shout out the window. NO TRAINING. YaHOO.

Thursday, nearly noon. I lay dozing. I've done my job, Tom, what magic thing is next, this first of September? How long can you stay floating about on cloud nine? It had not all been a fantastic dream; I had the medal and fifty thousand telegrams hanging over the dressing-table mirror to prove it. Tom had not been a figment of my imagination; I had yesterday's laurel wreath on my bracelet. He'd only sent a message via Norm Thompson after my 400m heat — 'A valiant swim. Sleep well. Lunch tomorrow.' Why not here, now, in person, damn you? I remembered the sleek Italian who'd been there at the finish. God knows how he'd talked his way onto the concourse looking like just another official. A chameleon — that's it, a lounge lizard. Perhaps the music student from New Zealand didn't exist either. Why should I believe that any more than the two Italian versions I'd seen already? Impostor, rich English boy good at accents, playing jokes, looking for an easy girl and a cheap thrill to remember the Olympics by? Perhaps the bracelet was cheap silver plate in a false box? The hair a wig?

Enter Tommaso. I'd just sat down to lunch and was downing a huge glass of Coke when he sauntered into the dining hall, looking more Italian than ever, carrying a vast bunch of gold, orange and bronze flowers. Carnations, roses, orchids, done up with gypsophila and greenery, bronze-coloured ribbons, everything but bells and whistles. This joker in his canary yellow shirt with paler hat to match didn't do things by halves.

'Lover boy himself,' murmured Zoe across the table. The men, except for Mr Upjohn who went on eating and looked askance at the flowers, hailed him like a long-lost friend. 'Tommaso, mio amico, where ya bin?' He bowed and scraped and shook some hands. 'Flowers for the little lady,' they teased, because there was no doubt who they were for. I might be youngest in the team, but mine was the only medal so far.

He waited till I stopped choking, then I was treated to another kiss on the hand, his eyes as bland as butter. He saw the race on television, he explained to everyone. He came directly from his office in Milano. 'Alessandra, bambina mia, you were magnificent. A star! Una campionessa. Magneefica!'

I was too furious even to say grazie. Bambina mia! The flowers were too big to put on the table or even across my lap, so I propped them against the window and listened to him say his lines. Alas, he must work for the Rome office of his company, but tomorrow, 'tomorrow I go to watch Signor Halberg and Signor Snell, another one 'oo is big surprise'. He apologized for Rome being so unusually hot for her visitors, and asked about the team's fortunes so far. Having given the child her flowers, he sipped discreetly at a cup of cappuccino, listening, ignoring me; paying, if anything, more attention to Zoe who wasn't acting at all like someone engaged.

'You can come with us,' Bulldog said suddenly. Her mind worked rather slowly in the heat. 'Alex and I are going to the athletics tomorrow. We've got a spare ticket.' He'd be delighted, signora. They arranged it all between them, Bulldog flirting, in on the joke. Mr Upjohn looked unimpressed. The bambina sat and fumed. I'd thought he might work up enough enthusiasm to come with us to the 400 metre finals tonight, but it wasn't mentioned. I didn't dare, myself, unless we could get alone somewhere, and that looked unlikely. I gathered up my bouquet and made a grand exit. I had, I said, some letters to write.

Perhaps, I thought angrily, he'd forgotten all about Roma out there to be explored.

Well, the 400 metres was Chris Von Saltza's triumph. Like Dawn Fraser, she'd had years of local, state, and national events, fighting off challengers all the way up. I'd had an easy ride, one rival only. I could never swim like that, or like the men in the other events. They all looked so tough and battle-scarred. For the first time I found myself wondering how much longer I wanted to go on.

At breakfast the next morning Murray Halberg, our best chance for a gold, and Peter Snell, who had unexpectedly made the 800 metre final, sat silent, apart from the team. They just nodded when people said 'good luck, guys'. I had a message to wait for Mr Upjohn. He wanted to see me, something very important.

The Bulldog, clucky over Tommaso's reappearance, and pleased that I'd given her some of the flowers for her room, went off to do her washing. We were to meet up with Tom at the main entrance later. I found a sunny corner of the hall and dozed deliciously. Five minutes before closing time Mr Upjohn came through the doors and piled up his tray as usual.

'Morning, Alex,' he said, looking pointedly at my bare legs. I pulled down skirt and crossed legs in a manner proper for Listening to Important Messages. 'I had to wait for a call through to New Zealand.'

Porridge, followed by sausages, eggs, and bacon, in this heat! I could hear his jaws going, between bursts of talk. This was going to be a long conversation. Two weeks of Italian food — he'd put on weight.

'How would you like to go to America, Alex?' he said, at last, as to a five-year-old.

'When?'

'I've been approached by a top administrator from a Californian university. There's talk of offering you a swimming scholarship. We're to meet him and a Mr Hoover, midday at the pool.'

'Sorry, I can't.' He spluttered on his sausage. 'Not at midday, I'm going to the athletics today.'

He put down his knife and fork and looked at me. 'Alex, this is a serious offer. I said you'd be available to discuss it.'

'I'm not, at least not . . .' American swimming scholarship? What every swimmer dreams of. Was I barmy?

'I can't go back and say you've just gone to watch the athletics.'

'It's not just the athletics, it's Murray Halberg and . . .' It was also seeing Tom again.

'I've just been on the phone to New Zealand. You're still very young of course. The proposal is for next September, when their college year starts. That won't interfere with the coming season in New Zealand. We're planning a team — this is highly confidential, Alex — to go to one of the Australian state meetings in January, and possibly their nationals in February. Of course, you'll be number one choice. I presume you're back at school next year, but leaving in September wouldn't . . .'

'What if I want to sit scholarship?' I said, simply to stop him.

'Scholarship? You mean at home? But we're talking of *America*. It's four years. You'd do a degree. You'd have to spend some holidays at home, to qualify for Perth in '62 and of course

Tokyo in '64, but I'm sure we can cope with that, when the time comes.' He smugly finished off the last of his croissants as I stared at him. 'These Yanks are very keen.'

And you've got it all worked out, I thought. 'Tell him I'll think about it.'

This time he really did splutter over his coffee.

'Alex, you don't just tell Americans you'll think about it!'

'They can't expect me to say yes *today.*'

'But they want to talk today.'

'I'm going to watch Murray Halberg.'

'They might see that as a casual and childish way to treat a good offer. They believe you have enormous potential for the gold in Tokyo.'

Back to his old pompous tricks. My head was in such turmoil — excitement, fright, *four* years more training, California here we come, what degree would I do, could it be law, Australia, Perth, Tokyo, four *years*, leave family, leave Mr Jack, leave school? — that I couldn't say anything. He thought I was just being difficult. He sighed, wiping the grease from his lips. 'Very well, Alex, I'll meet Mr O'Reilly and say . . . heaven knows what I'll say. Tell me a time when you will meet him.'

I couldn't have chosen a better day to have a vision of gold, and what it cost, waved in front of me.

I knew that both Murray Halberg and Peter Snell had trained for years with Arthur Lydiard round the Scenic Drive out at Titirangi, about twenty miles like a roller-coaster through native bush. I'd been out there a couple of times with Andy in the Vee-Dub. You get some great views of the city. They said only the toughest runners survived the circuit.

What would be my 'drive' for gold — eight, ten miles a day? Five hours in the water and no scenery? In a sunlit all-year pool in California or various dreary pools in Auckland? Or not at all?

'You're quiet today,' said Tom as the stadium, nearly full for a big day, shimmered around us and just below, the runners prepared for the 800 metre final, one of the glamour events. 'Snell must be the big muscly one in black?'

I nodded. It was true I hadn't said much as we walked over to the stadium. Bulldog grumbled about the heat as usual. Once away from the village, Tommaso was Tom. We were politely distant. I should have been on top of the world.

Watching first Peter and then Murray run to golds had a most strange effect on me. Peter was only 21, with big ears and not forthcoming at the best of times, an outsider. No one in the seats round us thought he had a snowflake's chance. At one stage he was only fifth. Then he moved up to third. Sprinting for the finish the miracle happened — he found a gap between the two leading runners and hurtled between them towards the tape like a bullet. Once through, his balance and rhythm came completely unstuck. He changed from champion to gawky kid trying to stay upright, then wrapped himself around a flagpole, looking stunned. The runner who came second hunched himself up on the ground and cried.

At the end of the 5000 metres, Murray Halberg took two steps across the finish and collapsed. He'd gone from last, to second, then with three laps to go, into a huge lead. I heard people round us scream, 'He's gone too soon, he's mad. They'll get him in the last lap.' It was torture to watch, as Murray kept looking back at the second runner catching him, but he still had about ten yards to spare at the finish. The whole stadium was on its feet, bellowing. Peter Snell in his black track suit and a panama hat ran over and knelt down to congratulate our second Olympic champ of the day. It was the first big-time running I'd ever seen, so much more exposed and changeable than swimming. I could see how judging pace and tactics were as important as mere speed.

And in the end, wasn't there also a special 'something' that separates the champions from the rest? These two runners had it, Dawn Fraser had it, and Chris Von Saltza. Did I? Or was my bronze a flash in the pan? Could I go to America and spend four years working towards Tokyo and find I didn't have what it took?

I hadn't actually wept when I'd stood on my bronze dais. Nor since, not real teeming buckets. Now, the Olympic fanfares sounded that trumpet tune we were all getting to know rather well. Twice within an hour, two small black figures out there had stepped up onto the victory dais. The same people who sat staring at their breakfast this morning, now heroes. Our flag went up and our anthem rang out twice.

By then, I was a mess. A stadium full of people from all over the world stood to salute the winners, our winners. You could see small pockets of New Zealanders waving flags and going berserk. We'd never had an Olympic day like it. Two of the big events in quick succession. Possibly we never would again. People from big countries like America and Russia and Britain and France and Japan and Germany and Australia *expect* their athletes to win lots of medals — they could *never begin* to understand what it meant to people from a little place.

As the tumult died down, people in front of us were turning round to stare. Was I a sister, a girlfriend? Tom handed me a hanky and Bulldog tried to cuddle me. Behind my straw hat I cried for what those two athletes had just done, and what I had done, and what it had cost them pounding for years round the Scenic Drive and me up and down the Tepid Baths. I cried because I was surrounded by strangers and scared stiff of the whole new world of choices and responsibilities I'd opened up. America, university, school? Another season, Australia, or retire now? Trust Tom, or not? Trust myself? Wait for him to make the next move, or not?

'Better now, dear?' asked Bulldog, oozing sympathy. 'Do you want to go home?'

'Yes. No. Home, where's that? I don't know.'

'I think,' said Tom finally, as some huge Russian women heaved black steel balls into the air, and my embarrassing waterfalls dried to a trickle, 'I think what you need is a fair dinkum holiday.'

'Someone wants me to go to America,' I sniffed. Out of the corner of my eye, I saw him look away, as people do when they don't want you to see their face. 'Next year. A swimming scholarship.'

'Congratulations,' he said; without enthusiasm, I thought. 'That's terrific.' It was only later, as we ambled across the bridge back to the village, that he finally got around to suggesting that next year would take care of itself. Perhaps tomorrow I could think of myself as being on holiday, and what about starting with the Forum?

Full-length on the warm grass beneath a headless statue of a vestal virgin, I listened to the rich voice. No training. No Bulldog. Just me and Tom, the sights of Rome and/or the rest of the Olympics to pick and choose from. I wiggled my toes. I could smell roses, hear doves cooing and water trickling into the three marble pools in the courtyard where once the vestal virgins walked.

' "There were only six vestal virgins at one time," ' read Tom, fluently translating from an Italian guidebook. ' "Aged from 15 to 45, they were selected from aristocratic families, and lived in a spacious atrium house in the shadow of the Palatine hill." Up there. "Their primary function was to, ah, tend the sacred fire of Vesta in the nearby circular Temple." That's the white ruin with the four pillars, over there.'

'How did you manage to persuade Bulldog that she didn't have to tag along?'

'I'm very convincing. I come from an old Taihape farming family. She knows my aunt in Christchurch, a city councillor, JP, pillar of the Anglican church. She trusts me. "The Virgins were, um, bound by a strict rule of chastity. Punishment for failure of duty was harsh . . ." '

'She's a gullible old snob. You're also male and breathing.' He smiled as he went smoothly on.

' ". . . earning a beating by a priest if the sacred fire was allowed to go out, or death by burial alive if a Virgin broke her vow of chastity." '

'Yuk. Like Aida and whatsisname.'

'Radames. You know it?'

'We listened one night at home, Mum's crash course in Italian opera. The whole three hours. I had the words. Fantastic.'

'In that case, you will accompany me to see the open-air production at the Terme di Caracalla next Tuesday.'

I giggled. 'You do me much honour, sir.' The sky above was blinding blue, and the dry grass prickled my bare arms. I put my hat over my face. Opera in Rome!

' "The Virgins were not however secluded like nuns. They enjoyed the rare privilege of driving around Rome in carriages, and were honoured guests at all public functions and spectacles. They were" ah . . . "confidantes of the Emperors, and used their considerable power to influence public affairs." '

'Sounds a pretty good sort of life,' I mumbled sleepily. 'Perhaps I was a vestal virgin in a previous life. Mixing with the nobs on the Palatine, best seats at the Circus Maximus, driving around in a carriage.'

'What about the chastity bit?'

'What about it? I'm not going to marry either. Or have sprogs,' I said propping myself up on my elbows. 'I like this place. It feels, well, female.' There were dragonflies hovering about the pools, red roses and bougainvillaea climbing over ruined brick walls. Behind the row of female statues (even if only one of them had a head) were lots of trees and pink oleanders. This corner of the Forum was quite different from the rest we'd already explored with the aid of Tom's guidebook. I'd walked on the stones of the Via Sacra, and touched a sandalled foot, just a foot, growing weirdly out of a block of marble, and taken pictures of the pillars against the sky. I had to keep reminding myself where I actually was.

'How did the American interview go?' Tom asked softly.

'Oh okay.' I flopped onto my side, away from him. I met Mr Upjohn and two Americans first thing after breakfast, which was taken over by a crowd of reporters and photographers after Snell and Halberg. 'It was quite strange, really. This old American guy from San Francisco, he spoke so softly I could hardly hear him. He asked me all sorts of questions about my family, and my interests, and how Mr Jack would feel if I went. Training schedules, the pools I trained in. What I want to be . . .'

'Which is?'

'Lawyer. I've always wanted to do law. Anyway, Mr Upjohn kept interrupting and asking about contracts and expenses and money, and this guy just quietly kept asking me questions about school and stuff. He was so polite and old-fashioned he should have been English. Kept calling me Miss Archer and offering me coffee.'

'They're not all loud of mouth and tie, you know.'

'I really liked him. He said because I was so . . .' Did Tom still think I was eighteen? '. . . relatively young, I'd stay with a selected family for the first year, then I'd stay on campus. They'd pay for all my tuition, books, everything except travel to and from the States.'

After a long pause he said 'Sounds great. How can you refuse.'
'Are you here on a scholarship?'
'Not exactly.'
'What does that mean?'
'After I finished my degree, I worked for seven months. Seagull on the wharves, waiter, night-watchman. Hospital orderly for a few weeks. Piano and theory teacher, which I detested. The brats never practised. I saved quite a bit, I had to. It was quite something to be accepted as a pupil in Milan, but no money went with it.'

Something didn't add up: the poor student one minute and now the smooth Italian clothes, the bracelet around my wrist, the air of money.

'Did you accept?' he asked. 'The scholarship?'

'I wasn't asked to, really. They're going to send the details. After this summer, Australia, all that . . .' I felt more tired than excited by a prospect that was too big to even contemplate. 'No one's interested in me anymore,' I said sleepily. 'They all want to talk to Snell and Halberg now, thank goodness. I'm a has-been.'

I was on holiday, and at eleven-thirty in the morning in the Forum Romanum underneath a headless vestal virgin I must've drifted off to blissful sleep. '*Sic transit gloria mundi,*' I heard him say quietly. 'Wait till you get home.'

Notes of caution

It has taken Alex these past four days to wind down, and even then I don't think I am seeing more than a glimpse of the real personality. She is too far away from home, too precariously suspended between the climax of her unexpected success yet having to continue training, between the restrictions of middle-aged guardians and wanting to be on holiday in Rome. As far as I can tell, no real friends.

Except, if she will allow it, me.

The 400 metre heats were, frankly, a tiresome procession; eight lengths and the winners clearly obvious by the end of the first two. In the third and last heat, very late at night, she looked tired, as did Dawn Fraser herself, swimming with none of the fire of her sprint events. Norm, beside me, watching her struggle over the eight lengths of very rough water, said she'd never liked the longer distances. Cyril Upjohn had told him she was finding the inevitable feeling of anticlimax difficult. She had not taken kindly to his insistence that she must keep training for the invitation meeting in Naples the week after next.

She certainly received my salutation of flowers coolly enough. I could think of no alternative to resuming my Tommaso role if I wanted to get into the New Zealand dining hall. Telephones and messages in the village office are a less than reliable way of making contact. At lunch she was offhand, giving me no chance to make any arrangements before making an admittedly grand exit; and again at the stadium until the victory ceremony for Snell and Halberg. I have no idea what accumulated tensions were finally being released; from Mrs Churchill's guarded comments and her solicitude, from Norm Thompson's hints of a bumpy ride in the run-up to Rome, I guess they were considerable. One forgets so easily that she is not yet sixteen. She is not someone who makes life easy for herself, and never will be. I still long to find out what makes her tick — these precious days in Rome will be too short.

And how does one reconcile her returning to school, the prospect of America next September, with my staying in Milan next year and Europe possibly for ever? Her obvious and untested love for our homeland and my abhorrence of it? Her tender age and my worldly 23? Her declared ambition to do law, meaning five straight years at varsity, and my musicial ambitions, a capricious career at best.

Since I can see no way through this tangle, some caution, some other masks are called for.

A walking encyclopaedia

Everything about the man who had just parked his motor scooter under the flagpoles and was now walking my way yelled Australian.

The wide-brimmed bush hat, the garish green shirt with the Sydney harbour bridge plastered all over it, the jeans, the boots, the swagger with arms swinging like an ape. As he got closer he tipped his hat slightly back, revealing a thick gingerish moustache and sunglasses. There were plenty of Aussie males loose in Rome for the Games. About three yards away he stopped. I could feel his eyes behind the sunglasses swivelling up and down, then he gave a soft whistle. I was just about to tell him to clear off when he said, 'G'day, Kiwi.'

'Oh God,' I said. 'Not again. Will you stop doing that!'

'Any self-respecting Aussie . . .' said Tom.

'You're not an Aussie and you're late.'

'Yes, apologies. No excuses. I had to iron my shirt.'

'Where *did* you get that gear? It's awful.'

'Glad you approve. I came here by ship. The *Fairstar*, Italian. We stopped at Sydney, Perth, Colombo, Bombay, Aden, Suez, and Port Said.'

'I suppose you bought Indian . . . what do you call them?'

'Dhotis? Shalwar kameez?'

'And Egyptian robes and those silly red hats like flower pots . . .'

'Fez. Oh yes, I could have gone to the ship's fancy dress as a white slave trader . . . As a matter of fact, I went in drag. The thought of joining the usual corps de ballet doing *Swan Lake* in crepe paper didn't appeal. I upstaged all of them by going as a tiddly over-the-hill opera singer, singing *Carmen* in falsetto.

You can do that sort of thing when you're alone. That gear I *did* have to borrow — the wig, the frilly frock.'

'I should hope so.' I saw two of our team men come out of the village entrance, notice me and wave. 'Look, if you expect me to get on the back of that scooter incognito, you'd better go somewhere less public.'

'I'll wait round the corner,' he said, moving swiftly to fire up the machine and roar off as the two athletes came over. They wondered if I needed rescuing! Perhaps I did, I thought, though not quite as they imagined.

It was ten minutes before their bus came and I could walk round to where Tom was waiting under a tree, still sitting on the Vespa and reading an Italian newspaper. 'Aussies can't read Italian papers,' I said.

'Aussie Italians can. Or should that be Italian Aussies?'

I looked at the scooter doubtfully. It didn't look too new or strong. 'Where did you get this thing?'

'A friend. It won't do more than 20 miles per hour, but it'll get us around for the next week. Hop on.'

'Bulldog wouldn't like it.'

'Bulldog's not going to get it. Hop on.' I climbed on the back. 'Have you never ridden pillion before? Grip with your knees as in horse-riding and grab me round the waist. This city has lots of cobblestones and bumps. Tighter.'

Apart from frequent hand-kissing, it was the first actual bodily contact. If I'd expected from his stocky shape that he'd be slightly soft and cuddly around the middle, I was totally wrong. The stomach muscles under the thin shirt were rock-hard, as hard as any athlete's. All those singer's breathing exercises, I supposed.

Over his shoulder, I saw his hand go out to turn the key, and hesitate. He half turned in the seat. Our faces were very close, his hand was under my chin and he was after a kiss.

'May I?' he said very softly, his eyes already half closed in anticipation.

'It's only nine in the morning,' I said, recoiling.

'Does that matter?'

'That silly moustache does.'

He ripped it off, and rubbed at where it had been with the back of his hand. 'Now, is that better?'

'No.' Why? I thought. Why not?

He turned back, paused for a long moment, stuck the moustache back on, started the scooter, and we moved off. He was right, it wasn't Speedy Gonzales. I gripped him round his rock-hard waist and thought oh hell, what happens now? Am I hanging onto one of those guys who think that money spent on taking girls for meals and movies equals kisses, and more? Is that the week shot to pieces already?

'So where are we going?' he shouted.

'I'm paying my own way this week,' I shouted in his ear. I could feel my breasts hard against his back, and no doubt he could too.

'You don't have to yell. That's what I expected.' Then I saw his wrists working the handlebar controls and we puttered to a stop under another tree. We hadn't even gone two hundred yards. He didn't turn around.

'We'd better set some ground rules, Alessandra. Okay, we're going Dutch, money-wise, museum tickets, Cokes, everything. That's fine by me. You can make the next move, kissing-wise, if you want to. I don't see why it should always be the male. Frankly, it's caused me no little embarrassment and distress over the years. I'm sorry, I moved too quickly. I won't again.'

'That's okay,' I mumbled, still acutely conscious of my front pressing hard against the picture of the Sydney harbour bridge, the warmth of his back, the fresh smell of shampoo. Perhaps we'd have been safer getting around Rome on a bus, in more ways than one.

'Can you teach me to drive this thing?' I asked.

'Why not?'

Bulldog would have a double fit!

That Sunday was two weeks after our first lunch date, six days after my bronze medal and two days after I became convinced that Tom was, for whatever reason and whoever he really was, serious as in *serious* about me.

We went back to St Peter's and explored it properly, along with about four million other people. I was glad he'd told me last night to bring a cardigan, because women with sleeveless dresses were not allowed in. Some, looking sheepish, wore their husband's jackets to get past grim-looking men in robes posted like police under the huge bronze doors. We stood and listened to a service going on in Latin, with the organ and male choirs singing loudly and flat. People around us crossed themselves frequently and whispered in Latin and went up to get the Communion. Tom stood very still, his face politely blank; so he wasn't a Catholic. I noticed lots of pale teenage boys in robes with their heads shaved, and thin girls in veils and dowdy dresses; trainee priests and nuns, I supposed. We walked on marble of every possible colour, grey, green, pink, brown, black, orange, and marvelled at the mosaics, and stood speechless and misty-eyed in front of the Pietà, so much smaller than I'd imagined, and climbed up 330 steps to the very top of the dome.

The city lay around us in a haze of heat, the buildings all earthy-pink and the Vatican gardens and the hills all tree-green. I thought of my nights on the village rooftop, looking at this very dome like a pearl against the black sky.

'How do you cope with it, all this glorification! Are you a believer?' he said suddenly as we leant, still sweating, over the railing on the side shaded from the sun.

'In what?'

'God. The Trinity, the Virgin birth, Christmas, Easter, all that. *In hoc spero.*'

'Are you?'

'You haven't answered my question, but no, I'm not, despite years of church schools. I sang in choirs, from boy soprano down to bass, every part and all the solos. High Anglican church music is unsurpassed. But I grew tired of ritual, signifying nothing. Those medieval mysterious services going on below us seem worse.'

'Life after death?'

'It seems like wishful thinking to me. People live on in their children, their memories, their life work. A genius like Michelangelo leaves behind a little more.' He waved at the great open arms of the square below, where the people looked like ants and buses like toys. 'I shall leave satisfied audiences and recordings of my voice.'

'I've got a bronze medal,' I said lightly. 'So far.' We laughed. This surprising conversation was getting too close to questioning my conviction that Andy's spirit still lived somewhere. 'I think . . . making the most of what you've got, or been given . . .'

'Then you're a humanist.'

'I wouldn't know. I don't want to be anything "ist".'

'A free spirit.'

'I suppose so. I hope so.'

'They'll clip your wings, when you get home.'

'That's the second time you've said that. Why?'

'Our homeland is suspicious of success. Especially those who make it big overseas.'

'That's nonsense. Think of Ed Hillary. The papers will be full of Snell and Halberg.'

'For a few days. You will have your moment of glory. I'm not actually talking about the newspapers. Despite all their noble intentions they deal in half-truths, half-lies, and all the shifting sands in between. As you probably well know.'

'What then?' This was serious stuff for the top of St Peter's dome.

'Sufficient unto the day.' From his back pocket he brought out a small book. 'Lord Byron again. *Childe Harold's Pilgrimage*, a journey through Europe, published in its entirety, 1818. I read it last night. Listen to what he says about St Peter's dome, upon which we stand . . .

> Thou movest, but increasing with the advance,
> Like climbing some great Alp, which still doth rise,
> Deceived by its gigantic elegance;
> Vastness which grows, but grows to harmonise —
> All musical in its immensities;
> Rich marbles, richer painting — shrines, where flame
> The lamps of gold — and haughty dome which vies
> In air with Earth's chief structures, though their frame
> Sits on the firm-set ground, and this the clouds must claim.

What do you think of that?'

'Not bad.' Actually, I couldn't quite understand it. 'Read it again.' He did, while I looked down at the curve of "the haughty dome". If it was plain old *awe* Lord Byron was trying to get across, he succeeded. Tom finally broke the spell.

' "Some great Alp" — well, this climber needs a beer, and badly.' We walked once more round the circular balcony, and then set off again down the curving stone staircase. *Silence=death* was scratched on a wall. And lower down, *JFK for President, I hate Dean Martin,* and *Giorgio è stupido.*

As we walked across the main steps, I noticed Tom was chewing gum and had slipped into his Aussie cowboy walk, which may have been because, in all those thousands of people, we banged into five of my New Zealand team-mates. Next thing, he was shaking hands and introducing himself as my Aussie cousin Dennis ('on her mother's side, she's my father's sister, her mother that is, gettit mate!') in a convincing Oz accent. He was living at Earl's Court in London, working as a barman, but had to come and see his little cousin swim in the Games. 'Went like a bomb, didn't you, cuz,' slapping me on the shoulder.

'And how did youse guys get on?' They were hockey players — weren't doing too bad, considering, might end up fifth. 'I bet youse guys are proud of my little Kiwi cuz. Ran rings around them, didn't you girlie? Except for our Dawnie of course, and that American sheila. Got what it takes, I reckon, eh guys?' Sure, sure, they said, hot and tired and embarrassed by his enthusiasm, even from an Aussie. And from behind his sunglasses I caught the look which said *See what I mean?*

Tom made this deal with Bulldog. That we had to be back in the village each night before dark, unless we'd made special cast-iron arrangements involving taxis and times. She'd teamed up with Mr Upjohn and one of the Australian women to go sightseeing, so she was happy.

I made a deal with Mr Upjohn. Now I was worth asking, we'd been summoned to Naples for a special invitation meeting on Tuesday week. It meant I had to keep training, but we agreed I could go every morning at 6.30. Actually, walking over the bridge was no pain, with the river golden and misty in the new sun, and by the time I got there it was so hot and close that the mile in the water was pure pleasure. Only a few swimmers turned up each morning. I kept telling myself: I am the third fastest woman in the world!

I was stuck with the Australian Tom, though I was relieved that for the rest of the week he toned it down to ordinary shirts without the Sydney harbour bridge, and only a slight hint of the cowboy walk. I thought he was overdoing the bit about Tommaso not getting found out. It was only a joke, but he was dead serious. 'What I start, I see through,' he said. Or perhaps he just enjoyed dressing up. I got quite used to the moustache. It was amazing how completely different he looked.

After our St Peter's day we had Monday to Saturday to explore Rome. We did all the touristy things, rode down the Via Condotti and sat on the Spanish Steps and threw our coins in the Trevi Fountain, visited the Vatican and the Sistine Chapel, the Pantheon and the Campidoglio and museums until even I felt I'd had enough of marble statues and friezes and sarcophagi.

Well, I saw them, and smelt them, and took photos on my Zeiss Ikon to prove it. But my diary doesn't record the extras — the piazzas and side roads we explored, the little cafés and trattorias we discovered.

Tom said it was his first time in Rome, and I suppose this was true, but armed with his books and knowledge of things Italian, and getting into easy conversation with waiters and shopkeepers, it was like having a private guide. I obviously had a partner, so no one tried to pinch my backside. I was used to people staring more or less rudely because of my height, but here they stared and smiled and said 'Buon giorno, signorina', or 'Bellissima', and seemed to approve.

Tom talked a good deal of the time: facts, history, anecdotes connected with this or that building, statue, painting, fountain, piazza, villa. What he didn't know, he insisted on translating from his guidebooks. Pushing the bike down narrow lanes, well off the tourist track, he pointed out shady courtyards of private houses; decorated bronze doors and wrought-iron lamps; female figures with bare breasts, or male ones with muscles, carved into buildings, holding up archways or roofs; a bougainvillaea blazing against a brick wall; a tiny altar with lighted candles and a picture of the Virgin Mary built into a gateway. We wandered around markets full of strange vegetables, fantastical scarlet and gold peppers, red lettuces, baskets of nuts, figs, melons, chestnuts, and dried fruits. Even ordinary old lemons and peaches and cherries seemed bigger and brighter under orange canopies than they ever did in our boring shops at home.

We wandered in and out of cheese shops, delicatessens, and cake shops, fish shops and butchers' shops and wine shops and leather shops and shoe shops. I came out reeling with the ripe, sweet, dusty smells, utterly amazed at how many varieties of cheeses and salamis and fish and pastries, wine and shoes and leather bags they could pile into shops that looked so insignificant from the outside.

Tom would get into conversation with the shopkeepers, telling them about emigrating to Australia after the war, when he was just a boy of ten. I was introduced as an athlete from Nuova Zelanda who'd just won a medal at La Grande Olimpiade. That would set off much handshaking and noisy comments about (I think) my height and my youth and (possibly) my looks, while Tom jabbered away, and translated enough to keep me vaguely in the picture. Then we got to talking about the shopkeeper's family and we tasted this and tried that. I bought some goodies to take home as presents, and quite often I was given little goodies myself — jars of chestnuts in syrup, and gold-wrapped chocolates filled with liqueur. Family members were brought out from the back to meet us, and several times they asked Tom if he knew of long-lost relatives who had emigrated to Sydney in 1948. Sometimes it was half an hour or more before we left, glowing with heat and goodwill.

At frequent intervals we found small cafés for Cokes and big, crusty rolls filled with smoked ham and sweet tomatoes, followed by a gelato. How did one choose from fifty different flavours? Pale green pistachio? Pale yellow citron? Brown rum or mocha? *Liquorice?* We sat outside where we could. Tom consulted his books about the peculiarities of each district, while I listened to his rich, clear voice, and around us arguments, laughter, babies crying, horns and radios blaring; city life being lived, noisily and very publicly compared to home. I saw street artists and street cleaners, and rows of ripped posters from the recent election, and fat Italian mommas and creased old men in berets, overdressed plump middle-aged women. Girls my age who looked like tarts, and slim teenage boys who, Tom told me, were the male version, and real ragged beggars. Many cats, and even more pigeons. I wondered where all the children were.

Once, after walking through the Borghese gardens, we went mad and paid a small fortune for a cup of coffee, just so we could sit at the yellow table of one of the smart outdoor cafés at the top of the Via Veneto. Tom had told me about the café society shown in a marvellous new film, *La Dolce Vita* — and here it was: bored old men in pale suits with young women in linen dresses, gloves, and hats like pillboxes or lampshades. Lonely Jewish ladies with wrinkled arms and lots of bracelets. Elegant young men in summer suits smoking thin cigars. Others, like us, pretending not to be tourists.

We sat for over two hours, analysing why some people looked elegant and others a mess, trying to guess their jobs, their families, their interests. Tom had a sharp eye for dress, I discovered. My own home-made blouses and skirts suddenly felt very simple and young and boring. I wondered what it really felt like to be 23 and made up like a film star and preening yourself in couturier clothes in the Via Veneto. They didn't look much happier for it.

Most days we had a late lunch in a trattoria, each time trying new antipasto, pasta, carne, pesce, vino, formaggio, caffè freddo or cappuccino, until we staggered sleepily back onto the trusty iron horse for the next short journey.

As well as his guidebooks, Tom bought Italian newspapers and translated extracts over lunch, so that I had a vague idea of what was happening in the Congo and the rest of the Games. Armin Hary, the German, and Wilma Rudolph, the tall American Negro girl I'd seen once or twice in the village, were winning the sprint events, and the Russians the gymnastics. A Greek prince had won a gold medal for yachting.

Oh yes, the Olympics! We thought of dropping in on the athletics or the weightlifting or the water polo down at the EUR complex, but in the end we just floated around Rome on our little motor scooter in a dream, not caring about the crowds or the sweltering heat or anything except the next drink or gelato, the next place to sit under a tree or umbrella, the next perfect little piazza or fruit market or gardens or unexpected small cool church.

He didn't once offer to help me off the bike, or hold my arm as we crossed roads, or attempt to hold my hand or put his arm around my shoulder Roman-style. He was a walking encyclopaedia on Rome, a closed book about anything to do with New Zealand, but easy to be with when neither of us felt like talking. Most nights we got back to the village as the light was fading, sticky and exhausted. At the gate, he kissed my hand, very formally, under the smirking gaze of the security guards; that was all.

One night I remember specially. You can blame the weather for lots of things.

On the Tuesday, we'd planned to walk down the Appian Way, visit the Catacombs and then come back to the Terme di Caracalla for the opera in the evening, all in the southern part of the city. I packed my best jacket-dress and some decent shoes to wear to the opera. Even at ten in the morning, even under the high stone walls and overhanging trees on either side of the Appian Way, the heat was incredible. After nearly two miles pushing the scooter over the stones worn smooth by Roman soldiers, we arrived at the catacomb place to find hundreds of people coming out. Presumably because the monks who ran it had to have a siesta, it was closed until four.

'I wouldn't mind a drink and just sleeping,' I said, and we did just that because it was too unbearably hot to do anything else. We flopped under a cypress tree in a wheat field next to the catacomb gardens. Real picture postcard stuff, families spreading picnic tablecloths among the wheat-stalks in the sun, except for fat grey cumulus clouds building up along the horizon. I dozed off listening to the children and dreaming of the impossible comfort of having my head on Tom's lap.

When I woke up the sky was grey all over, brewing up for something. Tom was sitting, staring into space, looking rather glum. I didn't dare mention the opera. Walking down the

Appian Way, he told me the whole plot of *Aida*, about the première in Cairo in 1871 for the opening of the new opera house and the Suez canal. Famous productions had three hundred extras, and elephants and camels walking across the stage for the Triumph scene.

I hated the Catacombs, which turned out to be underground cemeteries, not the hiding places I'd always thought they were. They smelled of death, and that's without any dead bodies! We went down with a whole bunch of English-looking people behind an English-speaking monk. Tom was unusually silent and I panicked about getting lost. I suppose the actual excavation was amazing, miles of deep, narrow corridors and alcoves for bodies, lit with gloomy red lights, but I couldn't wait to get out.

When we finally came up the last long flight of steps, it was nearly as black as it was below. We walked in silence to get the scooter. Tom tripped over a large stone in the road, bent down and threw it with surprising force into a hedge.

'Maybe it'll clear,' I said.

'Not a chance. Hundreds of chorus, dancers, musicians, the instruments . . . not a hope in hell.'

'Why don't we just go back to the Baths. Wait and see. Find a café or something? It might . . .'

'Sorry, Alex, but it won't. We'd better head back, take you home.'

'Isn't it worth . . .'

'No.' He was astride the scooter and firing it up. 'Hop on.'

'No,' I said. Tom was beginning to sound very like the uncouth Keith, ordering me around rudely. 'I still think . . .'

'Al*right*. We'll go to the Baths and see what happens.'

'Right.' But he knew Italian weather better than I did, and by the time we arrived at the Baths the sky was black, and thunder was rolling away. We rode around the outside of the ruins, already deserted. A large sign on a wire gate announced that the performance that night was *Annullata*, cancelled. The first fat drops of rain fell, with two fierce flashes of lightning, right over the city.

'We'd better go to my place,' he shouted over his shoulder as he set the scooter up a fairly steep hill. Halfway up, the sky fell in. The water was actually bouncing off the road. 'This is going to last for a while. We won't get back to the village.'

'How far, your place?' The thunder was directly overhead and continuous. There was one fearful flash of lightning, forking down between the trees. I was grabbing his waist *very* tightly. 'How *far*?'

'About a mile. I think I can find the way, coming from this direction.'

You'd better, I thought grimly, because Auckland doesn't have thunderstorms like this and I'm terrified. We were in streets of apartment buildings of four or five stories, with balconies and geraniums and climbing roses, wrought-iron gates, cars outside; no shops, cafés, any shelter except under dripping trees. The next flash of lightning, followed by a great thunderous crash like fifty million kettle drums, really worried me. I hung on tighter still and tucked my head in behind his broad back. Three more flashes and crashes, and I heard the motor slow down. We swung sharply over a kerb, to a stop.

'Hop off. Inside,' he said. 'Through that gate, turn right.' I dashed up a narrow alley towards a set of steps. He threw the scooter against a wall and ran up behind me. We looked at each other, drowned rats, shirts sticking, hats hanging down our backs, and laughed. Amazingly, the moustache was still firmly in place. He ripped it off, grimacing, and from his tight jeans produced two very large keys.

The entrance hall was gloomy, the lift antiquated, and the door to the apartment like a fortress. 'Go in,' he said, pushing the door open. 'Don't worry about the drips. It's all wood. Parquet.'

I went straight into the most beautiful room I'd ever seen, dark and formal. Tom took off his shoes, then padded round turning on some green and yellow lamps. The floors were honey-coloured wood, the walls and high ceilings pale gold. Each bit of furniture stood in its own space — chairs, a sofa, tables, a baby grand piano, a golden harp, wooden cabinets for music, hi-fi equipment, records, books. There were several Persian rugs, landscapes in gilt frames. The windows had long, draped, gold curtains and wooden shutters.

'You told me . . . I thought you meant a grotty student flat.'

'This belongs to a musician. A flautist, aunt of a friend in Milan. She played in one of the Rome orchestras.'

'Lucky you.'

'Sure. You'd better get those clothes off. I'll get you a dressing-gown.' He went off into another room, came out shirtless, carrying a cream cotton kimono and a towel. 'I'll ring the village, get a message through if I can. The bathroom's through there.' He was as full-chested as a surf swimmer, and somewhat browner than I'd imagined, him not being an outdoor person.

The bathroom was similarly huge, tiled, with built-in mirrors and cabinets. Basic toilet things inside the cabinets gave away nothing about the owner, or about Tom. I used one of the tortoiseshell combs, and wondered how I could look elegant in the kimono and not like an overgrown kid in a dressing-gown. Did I catch a look which said I'd succeeded without even trying, as I walked back into the living room?

'Does she live here alone?' I said.

'A son comes and goes. I gather the husband died in the war. There was money somewhere in the family.' Tom had put on clean beige trousers, a cream shirt. The hair I hardly ever saw was still wet and dark. We both looked rather sleek. He held out a tall glass of pale yellow wine. 'Wrap yourself around that.'

I tried not to giggle. Drinking wine in a kimono with nothing on underneath, alone with a sexy young man in a Roman flat? Bulldog would be having fifty thousand fits.

'I can't get through to the village,' he said. 'Power failure somewhere. Hardly surprising.' Even inside this solid room, the thunder was fantastically loud and the room was lit up every minute or so by the lightning. I walked over and peered out the window. The street below was flooded and the trees thrashed about in the wind.

'Sit down while I get some pasta cooked. The news comes on about now.' A cabinet turned out to be a small television, and after the newsreader, the first picture was the Olympic stadium, deserted. Tom listened to the announcer, then they showed maps of Italy and he snapped it off. 'They've had to stop the decathlon. They say they'll resume when the storm abates.'

The Olympic Games seemed a million miles away from this

room. I plucked a few strings of the harp, and looked at the baby grand. The music on it was a score, *Le Nozze di Figaro*, with lots of pencil marks on the singer's part — breath marks, > marks and < marks, *dim*s and *rit*s and various other reminders. Tom came back with a pottery bowl. 'Have a nut. Play if you want.'

'I'm rusty. How did you know I played?'

'Mrs Churchill mentioned talents besides your swimming, ballet, piano . . .'

'Only Grade 6! She's exaggerating.'

'Is she? Cin-cin!'

The wine was yellow and sweet. I wondered what else she'd let slip of my chequered past. What about his own?

'Will you sing something for me?' I asked. He walked away to the window. I thought, if you really are a singer, perhaps that's not the done thing, perhaps real students don't just sing for newish friends, like that. But he closed the shutters, turned on another two lamps, and went to the piano. After looking at the keys for a while, he picked up a music case sitting beside the stool and took out several books. Probably his own special music, brought from Milan.

I knew immediately, from the arpeggio accompaniment and the first few bars of the song, that he really could play and he really had a voice, a beautiful one. Whatever else, the singing student was for real. Sitting through all those recordings at home, I'd heard a fair few opera singers in the past year, and Tom's voice sounded as good as any of them. It was warm and seemed to be effortless, and made me think of rich, dark chocolate. He sang seven serious songs, one in French, two in German then four in Italian that sounded more operatic, although scaled down, taking the high notes in a sort of half voice.

Then he looked over at me, grinned and launched straight into 'I got Plenty of Nuttin', and 'Begin the Beguine' with a rumba-ish sort of accompaniment and his left foot tapping on the floor, and finally that Winnie-the-Pooh song 'How sweet to be a cloud, floating in the blue' . . . and by this time I knew he loved to sing as much, or more than, I loved to swim.

It was part of him, as much as the red hair or the smooth brown hands on the keys. I lay back on the settee in my cream kimono, sipping wine. Julia-at-school would be laughing herself silly, it's like something out of a *Woman's Weekly* serial, she'd be saying. But she'd be impressed too, the mellow Italian room, the bronze-haired man at the piano and his music, the storm outside. And envious. And scared stiff. What if I was twenty, not fifteen! What if . . .

This melting ache in my stomach. It was not what I expected to find in Rome. Or wanted ever again caused by someone who was too old for me, too smooth, too clever, too likely to fire me up and leave me swinging. From next week simply too far away. Not again.

'Who wrote the first ones?' I said.

'In order, Fauré, Schubert, Schumann. Mozart, Puccini, Verdi.'

'Do you know anything from *Aida*?' I asked.

'Ah. *Aida*.' He looked down at the keys. I knew the aria, 'Celeste Aida'. He sang it from memory, the accompaniment too, but quite softly. It sounds like a cliché, but I went gooseflesh at the high notes, especially the final one, dying away around the large room.

'I thought that was for a tenor,' I said, eventually. 'You said you were a baritone.'

'I sing the odd tenor piece, for fun.' Did I imagine that he went red under the freckles? 'When do you go? I'll see if I can get two more tickets.'

'Naples, on Monday, for three days. Back to New Zealand on Thursday. It'll have to be this week.'

'Damn the weather,' he said softly. If he was trying to get rid of some frustration, he chose a good piece to do it, loud and showy, Beethoven I think. He leapt off the stool. 'Recital's over. You play while I cook some pasta.'

The storm raged on for ages. I didn't play, not after what I'd just heard. We ate some spaghetti, with bolognese sauce out of a tin, drank more wine. A funny motheaten little dog with a pushed-up nose waddled in from the kitchen. 'Meet Turandot from Peking,' said Tom, 'the resident guard dog.' She seemed to like me. With Turandot on my lap, Tom on the floor, we listened to records of Maria Callas and especially of Tito Gobbi, Tom's total hero.

He also he showed me the music of the pieces he had sung, Schubert's 'Wohin?' and Schumann's 'Dichterliebe'. 'Non più andrai' from *The Marriage of Figaro*, Figaro sending Cherubino off to be a soldier. Don Giovanni's famous serenade, 'Deh, vieni alla finestra'. From *La Bohème*, 'Vecchia zimarra senti', frozen Colline parting company with his old coat to buy food for the dying Mimi. From *La Traviata*, Germont reminding his son about the beauties of their home in Provence, 'Di Provenza il mar, il suol'. None of them looked nearly as easy as he had made them sound. When I read the English words, and remembered the voice, I knew why they had all made me feel so sad.

Was it deliberate, that to show me the music he didn't sit beside me on the sofa, but knelt on the other side of the low table? That our hands met once on the music, his warm over mine, but I pretended not to notice? We both looked hard at the music and Tom went on with the involved plot of *Don Giovanni* and the moment passed.

He tried to contact the village again, and eventually got through to a distraught Mrs Churchill. She'd got caught in the storm in the Via Veneto, been robbed by a taxi-driver, and soon after she arrived a bolt of lightning had struck the village, ripping bits of concrete off the women's quarters, frightening the living daylights out of everyone.

He didn't quite tell her where we were. We both knew she would have flipped her lid, because people of her age always imagine the worst, young gels alone with a man, rape and such. 'We're having tea at a friend's place down near the Baths of Caracalla, in the area of the Monte Aventino,' he said, just slightly implying other company. I smiled, and kissed Turandot on her squashed nose. He'd call, he reassured her, for a taxi, but it might take an hour at least. Everyone would be wanting taxis after the storm. She was not to worry. This man was not dumb.

'We can go on the scooter,' he said, putting the telephone down. I started to say it was going to be a long ride for him, there and back, but he interrupted. 'Rome at night? After a monumental storm, the sort of storm that used to terrify the ancient Romans. It might be your only chance. Do you need any dry clothes?'

The Colosseum floodlit was literally out of this world. The

reflections and steam rising off the wet empty streets made it look like something out of an ancient dream, floating and ghostly. I was slightly steaming myself, in the damp and creased opera dress pulled from my bag and a jumper borrowed from Tom. I noticed he'd put on a jacket and scarf, as well as a sporting sort of cap. It had stopped raining, but the air was wet and cool, not good for singers, I imagine.

Without asking, Tom rode us around the Colosseum twice, and then very slowly along the road above the Forum, where the pillars shone silver and the archways of the Palatine ruins were all outlined with light, and past the white 'wedding cake'. Cars splashed through puddles and under trees weighted down with water, and the streetlamps cast pink and brown shadows.

The Via del Corso took us almost straight north to the Olympic village, or would have done. We did slight detours into fairyland, over the Tiber towards the Castel Sant' Angelo reflected in the river; twice around Saint Peter's Square, around the fountains, in and out of pillars and puddles; and back along the river up the Via Condotti to the Spanish Steps and back to the Piazza del Popolo, around the archway and the obelisk in the middle. We could have gone straight up the Via Flaminia, but somehow we found ourselves taking the long way up the right bank of the Tiber, crossing over the Ponte Duca d'Aosta, my bridge, to look down into the dark Stadio del Nuoto, my pool. Finally we walked over the Ponte Milvio, where I'd marched with the Olympic parade, and puttered the rest of the way to the village.

Tom only had to stop once to consult a map. I hadn't realized, at that stage, that Rome was so easy to find your way around. I hung on to Tom's strong singer's chest from which I now knew beautiful music soared, and watched the most beautiful buildings and ruins and piazzas and streets in the world float by. I wished the ride and the week would never end.

An enigma

Saturday, September 10, 5.00 a.m. I have neglected you, my journal. Five whole days without an entry, falling into the huge canopied bed, neglecting also my practice, the work I had intended to do on *Figaro*. Sightseeing is hard, exhausting work. On the train tomorrow I must make amends.

Notes I must make, reminders for later expansion . . .

Tuesday, especially: the catacombs, the gathering storm, her unspoken but transparent pleasure for my music, that drawn-out and unforgettable ride back to the village, Rome's ancient and dramatic shadows, water and light on stone.

The Sistine Chapel, the Michelangelo ceiling and Last Judgement impossible to appreciate, ruined by noisy tourists and the strident voices of polyglot guides. Ditto all of the Vatican and St Peter's and the Pantheon, and all the museums. I must come down again in the winter months for less frenzied viewing, if I can afford it.

Yet: Alex will have no such chance, not for some years; she has drunk Rome in with an evident and avid thirst for its splendours, conscious of her short stay. If I've grown used to, even blasé about Italianate riches, her innocent wonder has been like a breath of fresh air. Many times I caught her impulsively running her hand over a pillar, the drapery or sandalled foot of a statue, the hewn chips of a mosaic; lost her briefly in the crowds as I went on ahead before she had drunk her fill of something — a painted ceiling, a tapestry, a circular staircase, a shop window full of beautiful shoes — that particularly took her fancy.

Yet: lost in wonder, maybe. Naïve, no. Only fifteen, hardly! I know Italians of twenty who, apparently sophisticated, are more naïve than Alex. Apart from the interchange on religion, (surprising, usually a no-go area for Kiwis) I know little more about her than I did at the beginning of the week. That ill-judged but understandable blunder of attempting a kiss, upon feeling those superb small breasts hard up against my back, cost me dearly. I've been grateful for the useful European custom of kissing a woman's hand. We've talked of everything — Rome, Italy ancient and modern — and nothing — of anything personal. An ephemeral expedient friendship, is that *all?* She seems — unconscious of her striking appearance, despite, or perhaps because of, her simple style of dress; is it antipodean innocence or a calculated worldliness? I don't know. Behind that again, a coldness, a reserve, disconcerting. If I had translated all the compliments passed by shopkeepers and waiters, she'd have written me and ordinary Romans off as flatterers, fawners, and creeps. Despite the apparent honesty of insisting she pay her own way, that her favours were not to be bought, I cannot read her.

Except: my risk in giving her a fairly demanding recital Schumann, Mozart et al — did, surely, come off. I remember girlfriends at home who would have been, by such an intimate recital, embarrassed, nonplussed, or bored to tears. You can always tell, in such intimate space, whether your audience is captivated or merely being polite. Yesterday, I managed by pure luck to acquire two costly tickets for *Aida* tonight, my last in Rome. The weather has settled down, Rome is again basking in its usual golden light, a little less hot. I'm relieved our drenching on Tuesday didn't result in a chill or sore throat — I have lost ground to recover next week.

The thought of breaking the spell, of saying goodbye to Alessandra after the opera tonight has begun to disturb me, more deeply than I bargained for.

Seats at the opera

'The opera?' said Zoe from her sleepy Saturday morning bed.
'You poor *thing*. What opera?'
'*Aida*. About an Egyptian princess. She gets buried alive.'
'Gawd. What are you wearing?'
'Does it matter?'
'Course it matters. What else do you go for, and don't kid me it's the music. Little black dress, pearls, high heels, loads of eye make-up, knock 'em for dead. Wasted on Bulldog, though. Pity you haven't got a nice guy. In a tuxedo.'

If she thought I was going with Mrs Churchill, fine. As for the nice guy, little did she know! Not nice, but interesting.

'My black dress wouldn't go anywhere near you. Tell you what,' she said, sitting up in all her hair-curler greasy-face glory, 'borrow my off-the-shoulder black top, that should stretch around your great shoulders.'

'Thanks.'

'Only joking. Seriously . . .'

'It's outdoors, and I've got a perfectly good jacket-dress.' Her enthusiasm to help was a relief — lost with Tom in the back streets of the Trastevere for lunch on Thursday, I'd forgotten all about going to her event on Thursday afternoon, and had to invent a feeble excuse about a press interview. She wasn't impressed. She ended up tenth, not bad out of twenty-three, and jumped 5 foot 4¾ inches, half an inch off her best. Iolanda Balas had, she said glumly, jumped only five inches higher than anyone else — what could you expect of someone who was six foot tall with legs up to her earholes and who jumped like a man? — none of the eastern Europeans or Russians looked much like women at all. She was equally disgusted that she had ended up behind her Aussie rival, and that I'd not come to cheer her on.

To humour her, I put on the black top. It looked a bit strange with no bra and my pyjama bottoms. 'Pull the sleeves down. Lower. *Lower.* That looks great. With one of your better skirts, some earrings . . .'

'No thanks,' I said, though I'd been tempted by the slinky reflection in the mirror, my shoulders bold and bare. Would it knock Tom out, or would I merely feel embarrassed? Both, probably.

'Your funeral,' she said, lying back in bed. 'Be boring.'

I went training later than usual and met Tom outside the village gate at eleven, wearing the coral pink dress which had needed a good iron after the other night, with the bolero jacket and some court shoes in my bag. *This* time the weather looked perfect. I had strict instructions from Bulldog; straight home the minute the opera finished, in a taxi, and no hanky-panky, mind. She'd not sleep until I was back safely.

Outside the main entrance, Tom looked different again; he'd left off the moustache and was wearing normal clothes — light navy trousers, white shirt, panama hat; he could pass for English or a normal, boring Kiwi. We'd planned a quieter day, walking in the Villa Borghese, a long lunch, visiting a couple of the less touristy churches. From the Games village down the long stretch of the Via Flaminia to the Piazza del Popolo, plunging into the crowded Rome beyond — hitching my leg over the scooter, impervious to the traffic, to hooting cars and screeching tyres — I was beginning to feel like a real Roman moll.

Our late, long lunch in a rather swept-up ristorante near the Pincio started off unpromisingly. We both knew that time was running out. Sometime in the next three days he'd kiss my hand for the last time and we'd walk off in different directions.

'Tell me, Miss Alexandra Archer,' said Tom across the orange tablecloth. He picked up the tall pepperpot and held it out: a mike. The voice was rich, flat, monotonous American. 'Olympic bronze medallist, the only woman of the New Zealand team to win a medal. One of the youngest ever Olympic medallists in any sport, how do you feel, about to return back home to fame and glory? Tell the listeners Stateside, how will it feel?'

'According to you, it won't be much fun.' Tomorrow was the closing ceremony. Monday, I was off to Naples. I wasn't in any mood for games.

'Of course it will. At first,' he said, dropping the accent. 'Interviews at the airport, flash bulbs popping off, honour at school, family parties, showing everyone your slides. Presumably some public appearances, speeches to Rotary, prizegivings, Country Women's Institutes.'

'And then?'

He hailed the waiter and studied the menu, diversionary tactics. Now I knew what lire were worth compared to New Zealand pounds, I was shocked by the prices on the menu.

'I don't know why we came here,' I said.

'Being our last lunch, this one's on me,' he said.

'No it isn't. And why's it our last?'

'It would give me great pleasure.'

'But not me. I'd rather keep it down the middle. I'll have antipasti first and then the tortellini, thanks. E una birra.' I looked around the crowded ristorante as Tom did the ordering. The usual people were staring at his hair. At one table, two females in arty black clothes were almost nose to nose saying an intense goodbye, snarling softly at each other. One swept out, leaving the other staring at her red wine.

I said, 'You were going to tell me . . .'

'No I'm not. You don't need me to tell you it's going to be hard to settle down to training, school, family routine. Two months till accrediting exams.'

And afterwards, in December, playing Joan in three scenes from *Saint Joan*, one bright speck on the horizon. The beer arrived, pale gold in a tall frosty glass. I drank half straight off in one ice-cold sluice. So he knew all along I was only a sixth former, a schoolkid, a fraud.

'I don't even know what school you're at,' he said. 'You've been rather reticent about your life back home.'

'You also,' I shot back. There was an uneasy silence. 'Do you know what I miss here? The sea. Knowing it's close by, just a bike-ride away. I don't think I could live away from the sea.'

'We could have gone out to Anzio or Ostia. I think you'd have been disappointed, if you like beaches clean and uncrowded.'

'I'm looking forward to Naples.' I said, lying brightly.

'Alas, I'll be back in Milan. I have to catch a train in the morning.'

'I thought . . . aren't you coming to the closing ceremony?'

'I'm sorry if I gave you that impression. Much as I'd like to, I'm expected back on Monday. Which is why I've dispensed with Tommaso and Dennis the Aussie. They served their purpose. Shall we?' I followed him to the antipasto table, the most colourful array yet. At a nearby table, the abandoned woman in black was staring at us. Tom said, 'I've got to start regular practice again. I've Figaro and Marcello in *Bohème* to prepare, a Schubert and Schumann lieder recital. Some more arias, hopefully for an audition or two.'

'What for?' My plate was becoming rather full. 'What's that?'

'Calamari. Squid. Try it. Experience and practice, mainly, at this stage. To impress a conductor, a manager, an agent, anyone who might give me a small part somewhere.'

In other words, he's never coming back to New Zealand, not for ages, so what's the bloody point. As we took our loaded plates back to the table, I tried to sound casual, not too eager.

'Couldn't you come tomorrow night, go back on Monday? Fly or something.'

Half of me recognized the shake of the head. It was the shake of someone locked into their own private system of what they'd set themselves to do, no compromises for girlfriends, flu, or anything else. The other half of me said, if he was really serious, he'd give up *one* day of silly old exercises and arias, and come with me to Naples.

'Mi scusi.' At first I thought it must be some Italian friend of Tom's. Then I recognized the abandoned woman in black. She was standing over us, swaying slightly on very high, black heels, with her handbag tucked under her arm, a full bottle of red wine in one hand and a glass in the other. 'Please, I think you are English.'

'Yes,' said Tom.

'I would like so much to join you. May I . . .' She didn't wait for the answer. A passing waiter was ordered to bring her chair.

I thought it was a bit of a nerve just interrupting complete strangers, and people half your age at that. She was at least forty, with lots of bangles, black hair carelessly back-combed up to the sky. Her face was drawn on: black cat's eyes like Sophia Loren, but smudged, more rouge on one side than the other, all except the outline of her lipstick worn off. She was smiling at me, very friendly.

'I hear you speak of Marcello in *Bohème*... you are a sing-ger, un baritono?' she said, turning to Tom. Her voice was deep, like gravel on a beach.

'Not me,' he said smiling, the voice of a BBC announcer. 'We're English. I'm an accountant, and I know absolutely nothing about opera. I have a musical second cousin who is playing the role at Covent Garden next season.'

'Ah, Covent Garden. But I hear you say...'

'You must have been mistaken,' he said politely. She poured herself a full glass of wine, and refused to take no for an answer when Tom said we didn't drink red wine in the middle of the day. Glasses were summoned and filled, another bottle ordered. Tom and I began our antipasto. She watched us with her painted cat's eyes from above the glass of wine.

'Such a handsome couple. The one so bless-ed,' she gestured at Tom's hair, 'the other so fresh and young. I think you are an athlete, my dear?'

'My sister is a well-known tennis player in England,' said Tom before I could open my mouth. 'Next season she will play at Wimbledon.'

This could have been quite funny, except that our friend was in rather a bad way. Her voice was slow and slurred, her hands shook slightly, her mouth smiled but her eyes stared. I had never seen a woman who you might call an alcoholic. There was something else too.

'You English, so obsessed with sport. ' 'Ere it is music, l'opera.' Her gravelly voice took on a sing-song lilt. 'Venezia. Roma, Trieste, Spoleto, Palermo, Firenze — I 'ave sung in them all. Verdi, Puccini, Donizetti, Rossini, Mozart, Gluck, Bellini, Offenbach, Mascagni, Leoncavallo I 'ave sung.'

'You're lucky,' said Tom.

'Not lucky,' she flashed. 'Hard work. You don't know who I am.'

'Should we?' said Tom smiling carefully. She had not told us her name.

'Many great mezzo roles I 'ave sung,' she said sadly, rattling off the names of a good many, and where she sang them, and with which conductor. As we ate our tortellini, she informed us that a growth on her vocal chords six years ago had finished her career as a soloist. Operations and what the doctors said about nodules the size of marbles didn't go too well with the tortellini.

So, she had retired. Now she sang, she said, only occasionally, a little chorus work, some teaching. Her friend sang with the opera in Rome, she was a soprano, but her friend had left, she had been so cruel, so very cruel, she had left.

'Let me get you a taxi,' said Tom suddenly.

'Your friend understands, he is so sweet,' she said to me. 'You have Diana's arms, so strong, powerful, so beautiful,' and to my horror she ran her hand up and down my upper arm. Her hand was hot and not smooth. Then — swiftly, before I could move away — down one side of my face. By this time Tom was at the back of her chair.

'I've called a taxi,' he said in her ear. 'Stay there, Alex, order a pud, this may take a while.' He virtually pulled her off the chair. There was a three-way uproar in Italian, bringing in the waiter, which started at our table and continued at the desk by the door. I guessed it involved her bill, her outrage at not being allowed to take away a nearly full bottle of wine. By this time everyone was looking. Eventually Tom escorted her out the main entrance. Another ten minutes went by before he returned. The waiter must have decided I was bored and a soft touch for pudding. He trundled over a trolley of the most fantastic rich-looking cakes and glistening fruit tarts, and to pass the time I chose a monstrous piece of a torte absolutely smothered in almonds and chocolate flakes and cream and ordered un caffè.

'What does she do for an encore?' I said. I could still feel her fingers on my cheekbones. I wasn't quite sure why it had made my skin crawl so.

Tom gave me a searching look, then ordered a coffee from the hovering waiter.

'Have some cake,' I said. 'Fantastic.'

'No thanks.'

'Does that sort of thing happen often?'

'In big cities, yes. Desperate people, lonely as hell. She knew she couldn't pay the bill. Her lover went off . . .'

'But she was with a woman.'

Tom shrugged. 'Takes all sorts. Italians are generally more relaxed about such things. Her own word — lovers, amante, she said, for four years, today finished. She must have been very good, once. Only the best get to sing big roles like Amneris in *Aida* and the gypsy Azucena in *Trovatore*.'

In other words, that's how you end up if you get nodules on your vocal chords or for whatever reason don't last the distance: alcoholic and lonely and scrounging help from tourists in restaurants. 'Did you help her, with the bill?'

'Some.' He smiled, ruefully. 'You could call it insurance money.'

'I'll shout you a piece of cake, cheer you up.'

'Alright, since it's our last. Thank you, Alex,' he said, surprisingly. He chose a large, flat piece of raspberry tart, and ordered some gorgonzola for us to share as well. It was getting on for four o'clock. Tonight we'd get caught up in the opera. I decided it was as good an opportunity as any for some straight talking.

'What time is your train in the morning?'

'9.30, I think.'

'I'm sorry you're not staying for the closing ceremony. Perhaps I could send you a postcard.'

He smiled. 'I'm sorry you're not coming to Milan. Perhaps I could send *you* a postcard.'

We formally got out our diaries and swopped addresses, mine in Auckland, his in Milan, care of a family called Bargellini.

'If you're ever back in Auckland . . .' I said.

Aida was everything I imagined and hoped for, though I was close to tears all night. We arrived early, before dusk, and wandered round the ruins, admiring the archways and the green and white mosaic floors, the small, flat, perfect bricks they'd made so long ago. Slowly the crowds arrived, the light began to fade from blue to streaky orange to black. We found our fantastic seats on the huge temporary stand, right in the middle, facing the stage between the two highest towers of the ruins. Nothing would persuade him to let me pay for my ticket. It was a prize for doing so well, he said, a small gesture from a proud expatriate. With his white shirt, a lightweight tweed jacket, a hat which he took off as the lights went down, I thought this was about as close to the real Tom as I was going to get. The night was still, the trees around all floodlit in blue. I felt like a five-year-old at her first pantomime.

The music really was only half of it. The sheer size of everything took my breath away — the orchestra, the Egyptian scenery, the stage itself, the chorus, the march with horses and *camels*, the strapping soprano who was Aida, and the even larger tenor who was Radames. Tom sat in his seat through the whole three hours like someone electrified, and was one of the first on his feet after the final terrible chords with the two lovers waiting to die in the tomb. Bravo! we shouted happily, along with everyone else.

I think we'd already started to pull apart, as we drifted out of the ruins, found the bike, and started on the return journey. It was after midnight. He didn't suggest a last drink or gelato, even if you could get one that late. He drove slowly, three times round the Colosseum, a detour to the Trevi Fountain, twice around the Piazza del Popolo, and a detour into part of the Borghese gardens. He sang all the way, some songs I knew like 'They're Changing Guard at Buckingham Palace' and 'Three Coins in the Fountain', and 'Some Enchanted Evening', and even my favourite Maori songs 'E hine e' and 'Pokare kare ana' (which surprised me from someone who didn't have anything good to say about New Zealand). Not loudly, but I could feel the resonance vibrating in his solid warm back.

It was 1.30 when we arrived at the village. At the gate, things got awkward, as I knew they would. I got off the bike and stood looking down. He had not had a hat on for hours now. The amazing hair glowed in the lamplight.

'You never did give me a driving lesson,' I said.

'We forgot. Too many other things.'
'Thanks for the opera. Everything.'
'It's been a great week. Thank *you*.'
It's up to you, kissing-wise he had said, six days ago. He'd stuck to his side of the bargain. My heart was bursting, but I just couldn't move. We should have done it earlier, if at all. He broke the terrible silence by leaning forward, taking my hand and bestowing a last kiss, lingering, as they say in those soppy serials. He *lingered.*
'G'night Kiwi. Take care. Have a good flight home.'
'I will.' I heard him say something in Italian. Then I couldn't stand it any more. 'Thanks again,' I said, walking quickly past the guard. I didn't look back, because I had tears in my eyes and couldn't have seen anything anyway.
After I reported to Bulldog, I spent the rest of the night on the roof.

Sunday September 11. Slept late (three hours sleep), went training late, last time in my beautiful bronze pool. Keep thinking about America next year. If I go to Aussie in January, they'll expect me to beat Dawn Fraser, if she's still swimming, if I'm still swimming, if . . .
Bulldog is annoying me, making pointed comments about keeping her awake last night. Haven't told her that T. has gone, caught a bloody train, gone back to his beloved Milan and his beloved singing. Music at closing ceremony tonight best part, that and when they put the Olympic flame out. Stadium went dark, and then someone lit a small flame, probably their programme, and then the idea spread and the whole stadium lit with tiny pinpricks of fire, pure magic. Teams all sitting together in stands, not on field, only flags paraded there. Tears, for various reasons. Then fantastic fireworks and choir and orchestra belting out something operatic, programme said 'Hymn to the Sun' by Mascagni from an opera called *Iris*, ended on repeated high note, cymbal crashes, the works. I'm giving up opera.

Monday September 12. Train this morning to Naples — me, Mr U, and Bulldog. SAW THE SEA. In the distance, not very often. Longer trip than expected, mostly inland, train crowded. What coastline we did see, so *pretty*, houses on rocky hillsides, fishing villages in little coves, boats. Naples huge, smoky, quite different colours to Rome, yellows, whites, blues, the bluest SEA absolutely ever. Taxi to hotel, view of the famous harbour, and Mount Vesuvius, palm trees, more tropical feel than Rome. Found a trattoria, Bulldog and Mr U *hopeless*. Haven't learnt a thing. Couldn't be bothered telling them what calamari were, or fragole. Tired. Lonely. Want to go home. Period coming? Have I been away a month?

Tuesday September 13. Swam this morning in pool, old-fashioned place, lots of pillars. Most top swimmers here, including Aussies. Kept my distance, still uncomfortable, odd. Rest in afternoon, very hot. Want to go for swim in sea, BADLY. Carnival a washout, packed stands but most swimmers just going through motions, joke. Swam in 200 metres, felt dreadful, period still coming, lousy time, came fourth. Dawn Fraser didn't finish for some reason — maybe got mouthful or cramp, looked upset later. Can't imagine why I bothered to keep training. WANT TO GO HOME.

Wednesday September 14. Day sightseeing, bus along famous waterfront, fishing boats and castles and enticing boat trips to Capri and Ischia. Bulldog and Mr U wanted to go to Pompeii instead, so we went to Pompeii. Glad, though, fantastic view of whole bay, amazing ruins, roadways with grooves for sewerage, baker shops with actual ovens and millstones, atrium houses, temples. Some horrible plaster bodies: people smothered by the eruption, a dog with its feet in the air. They filled in the spaces left when the bodies had decomposed, and got these awful impressions of what it was like. Clever guide spoke in English, French, Italian and German. Adored the paintings, that beautiful soft red. Some rude paintings only men allowed to go and see. Women hung about feeling stupid, Mr U and other men went, came back red in face, wouldn't say what they saw. Guidebook says they show couples, being erotic. Takes two to tango. Nowhere to swim in sea, no beaches, no sand, couldn't stop in bus anyway. Want to swim in sea, so BADLY. Naples overrated. Washing hanging out of windows and poor kids in streets.

Caught night train back to Rome. Period arrived. Joined up with rest of team in hotel, near airport. Could be anywhere. Daren't think of the Colosseum, the pool, the village, the river, the bridge, so familiar, so near yet so far. Only memories. My three races, dancing a minuet on the concourse, seeing my flag go up. The pink trattoria after St Peter's, the room with the harp where he sang Schubert and 'How Sweet to be a Cloud', the Colosseum after the storm. Dancing naked under the moon on the roof. Want to scream. Can't sleep. Writing this 3 a.m. Going home today, same way as we came.

They still had the Olympic flags flying at the airport, but no bands, no buzz.

We had half an hour to wait after checking in our bags. Bulldog wanted to buy some last minute presents, and Zoe was off with her athletic mates. I couldn't bear the thought of either the airport shops or sitting down. We had five *days* of that ahead. I wandered over to a window where I could see the planes, ours with TEAL written on the tail, fuel tankers around it and men in overalls with clipboards and earmuffs. There was no colour in the scene — just grey concrete, grey planes, grey grass, hazy, bleached-looking sky, grey hazy Rome in the distance. Suited just how I felt, washed out, my uniform scruffy already. My hair needed cutting and I'd got badly sunburnt on my shoulders walking around Pompeii in a sleeveless dress. I had a bronze medal in my handbag and a huge hole where my heart should have been . . .

Five minutes to go, five days cooped up in a tin tube. I turned around to look at the departure lounge. Our men were standing around in bored groups, their cabin bags between their feet. European-looking people came and went through the swing doors, smart women travelling in high heels, trailing porters with sets of baggage, men in suits, men in bright shirts. One erupted through the doors, took a wild look around, and started walking over to me. It couldn't be. He was in Milan, for ever.

'I thought I was going to miss you,' he said, stopping two feet away, his powerful chest heaving, and in a split-second decision, deciding to be a devil and give me the Italian-style double hug. 'Some fool of a girl at the Embassy told me the wrong time. I wanted to be here earlier, when you arrived.'

'Did you fly?'

'Hitched. Long-distance truck down the autostrada, nearly six hundred kilometres. I left at dawn.'

'Just to say goodbye?'

He didn't deny it. He was wearing the same clothes as our *Aida* night, except for the Italian straw boater. With the team around — Tom or Tommaso? I was feeling exhilaration and anger, in about equal parts.

'Well,' I said, 'can I ask why you bothered, when I'm about to get on a plane for New Zealand and you're about to go back to some gorgeous Italian opera-singing girlfriend who's about to sing Madame Butterfly?'

'I don't have one of those,' he said, exasperated, taking his hat off. 'I just wanted to say, oh how much I've wanted to say.'

'Like?'

'Like — oh, God, thank you for that wonderful week, Rome illuminated by your . . .'

'Cut it out!'

'It's so easy to get blasé in Europe. Look, I just wanted to tell you, I don't know when I'll be back in New Zealand, but . . .'

'Never, from the sound of it.'

'That's what I said when I left home. The whole place was beginning to appall me.'

'Why?'

'Too many reasons . . . this is not the time and place.'

'I'm interested.'

'In a nutshell, the feeling of suffocation, the hypocrisy of a small, boring, humourless, unmusical, and generally cultureless desert run by small, boring people obsessed with sport, philistines to a man.'

Behind him I could see Mr Upjohn wave, and a general bestirring of the team near him.

'I don't agree and I think that's our . . .' I began.

'No, listen. I've been thinking . . . I might be . . .'

'Tom, at the risk of presuming rather a lot' — I heard an echo from a lunch somewhere, 'don't you *ever* come back to New Zealand for a woman. She's not worth it.' Mr Upjohn was on his fat way over.

'If I come back next year it wouldn't . . . '

'She doesn't want the responsibility, when you find out what an ambitious bitch she is and it all goes wrong.'

'I'm not giving her that responsibility. I swore I wouldn't go back to New Zealand except . . .'

'Alex?' Mr Upjohn had arrived. I could see his eyes on Tom's extraordinary hair. 'Excuse me but . . . gracious, it's Tommaso, our interpreter, without his hat.' He couldn't quite bring himself to say anything about hair; Kiwi blokes don't talk about personal things like hair in public. 'We thought you'd gone back to Milan. You were immensely helpful.'

'My name is Tom Alexander, Mr Upjohn. I'm actually a Kiwi, living in Milan.'

'But you speak Italian!'

'It is possible to be both a Kiwi and speak Italian.' The gentle sarcasm was utterly lost on Mr Upjohn. 'I'm studying here. Tommaso was a rather prolonged but I hope quite helpful joke.'

I noticed he didn't explain or apologize, as such. I saw Mr Upjohn's eyes go cold. He turned to me. 'Mrs Churchill told me you'd been sightseeing all last week with a cousin, nephew of a Christchurch city councillor, a Tom Alexander in whom she had complete confidence. Is this him?'

'Yes,' I said. She must have added the cousin bit for extra reassurance.

'I do not appreciate being made to look foolish, Alex,' he said. 'Presumably you knew about this charade.'

I couldn't help smiling. 'Oh yes.'

'And Mrs Churchill?'

'Well, um . . .' I couldn't lie quick enough. Mr Upjohn shot Tom a look of intense dislike. 'Excuse me, Mr Alexander, but our flight has been called.'

'Of course,' said Tom evenly. Mr Upjohn led off. 'Believe me now?' he muttered, putting his hat back on. I could see what was going to happen. Others, straggling towards the departure gate, recognized him. Tommaso! they cried, genuinely pleased to see him again.

I think Tom had arrived determined to come clean with the whole team, but pompous old Mr Uphimself had run true to form. There just wasn't time to explain and enjoy the joke. So he was stuck with Tommaso. They shook his hand and cried Arrivederci, grazie, Tommaso, and Tom shrugging helplessly for once, slipped back into his stage Italian English. I straggled to the end of the team, with Mr Upjohn sticking to me like a leech, until we were the last three.

'Arrivederci Tommaso,' I said. 'Grazie tanto per la bellissima settimana.' It probably wasn't grammatical, but who cared. Mr Upjohn's eyes popped out of his head.

'Prego, Alessandra la bella, la più coraggiosa,' Tom said, with a desperate, defeated look in his brown eyes. 'Remember me to Auckland. Oh, and greetings to Marcia Macrae.'

'Who?'

'Isn't she one of your teachers?'

'Oh, Miss Macrae, yes. What's the connection?'

'Alex, we must go,' said Mr Upjohn.

'She and my mother were at drama school in London together, before the war. She wrote to me about you coming to Rome.'

'So this whole thing was jacked up by Miss Macrae?'

'Not jacked up,' he said, beginning to realize his mistake. 'A helpful gesture, that's all.'

'Am I sick of helpful gestures. People organizing my life for me, even ten thousand miles away.'

'Alex?' said Mr Upjohn.

'I'm *coming*.' I was feeling ill with disappointment. It had been my first ever true week of freedom, the two of us completely free from people pulling strings; or so I'd thought. 'So we were dancing to Miss Macrae's and your mother's tune, were we?'

'My mother's been dead for years, and no we weren't. Oh God, how do I convince you, her letter only came during the week, after . . .'

'Alex!!' Mr Upjohn, agitato.

' . . . after we'd met at the Colosseum, even that wasn't the first time I . . .' In a mixture of anger and defiance and bloodymindedness and mischief, I took off his hat and kissed him full on the mouth, stopping any more words coming out. It was brief, beautiful, and final. I shut my eyes and thought: 2.5 seconds can be a long, long time, ask any swimmer. Put that in your pipe, Mr Upyourself, angry with the both of us, and Tom, who'd hitchhiked on a truck all the way from Milan but just spoiled everything. I had nothing to lose. I'd lost him already. I'd never see him again.

'Ciao, Tommaso, Tom, whoever you are,' I said. I put his hat back on, took a last look at the face I'd thought I'd got to know rather well, and the startled brown eyes, and walked blindly through the gate. The beautiful voice followed me.

'Ciao, Alessandra.'

Sweet sorrow

I am left staring at a grey screen just inside a gaping doorway framed by two uniformed and interested guards. They, not hearing all that ridiculous carry-on with the men of the team — 'Molto grazie, Tommaso, ciao', their ten words of local lingo, with me bowing and scraping 'prego, prego signor' — and assuming I am English, exchange some lewd comments pertaining to Alex's height and long legs, to certain rumours coming out of the Olympic village regarding the athletes, those perfect bodies coupling, to the happy abundance in Rome this summer of free-wheeling girls. I tell them coarsely to keep their filthy tongues to themselves, provoking an accusation from one: hadn't the tall girl just shown me she was in love? why was I, an Italian, letting her go? what was wrong with me . . . ?

They and the empty doorway mock me. An Italian — the irony of it. I'd certainly not get past them. The powerful urge to let fly with a straight hook, to wipe off that knowing Latin smile, would result only in being removed by airport security. I walk away.

I can smell something sharp — the stick of 4711 eau de cologne I've seen her use? My mouth tastes faintly of lemon. Tom, thou *fool*.

I can see the plane marked TEAL, maybe a hundred and fifty yards away. Technicians and trucks still work alongside; something that looks like a movie camera is set up by the gangway, but as yet no passengers are walking out from the final departure area. I rest my forehead on the glass, one arm curved above my head, and watch tears form in ragged black circles on the concrete floor.

Nineteen months in Italy, nary a twinge of homesickness for

a country without passion, history, warmth, or generosity; bleak, raw, mean, Victorian, materialistic, and suspicious . . .

Till now, when I'd sell my soul to be getting on that plane. To fly in five days' time over the rugged western coastline, over the beaches where I've dug toheroa from the black sand, over the green farmlands and orchards and inlets of water surrounding Auckland, to walk under the oaks in Princes Street or along the sands of Takapuna after a ferry ride across the harbour. I forget: the bridge has been completed. She lives in Epsom, near One Tree Hill, Cornwall Park with its avenue of olive trees . . .

The loudspeaker is playing that banal and infernal song again. 'Arrivederci Roma, it's time for us to part . . .'

It's forty long minutes before I see the first passengers struggle unwillingly across the tarmac, about half of them carrying black blazers. Several people have materialized around the camera, and are filming their departure. She comes among the last, with Mrs Churchill, head erect, never looking back.

She is laughing?

She can forget me, my six hundred kilometre journey to see her, even that wretched last conversation, so quickly, easily? If I, if our Olympic time meant anything at all . . . Alessandra, are you so self-contained, so hard? Alessandra!

At the foot of the gangway, then standing at the open doorway into the plane, she is being filmed. The film star's wave, posed, contrived, trite, no doubt required of her. But even from here (curse my long sight) she looks extraordinarily happy to be leaving. Perhaps she is? Or an act? She laughs at the camera crew below, looks once briefly at the airport buildings (did she think I might still be here, watching?) and vanishes.

I see the door close, the plane fire up its four propellers, move slowly away, taxi to the end of the runway, and take off to the south. The wheels go up. It's soon gone, into low grey cloud. I feel anger, disenchantment; utterly desolate.

Melodramatic, perhaps, but I need to sing of my pain to forget that dumb show of farewell, to strangers, forget those grey disappointed eyes, that lemon-tasting kiss. Private music to express what words alone cannot.

Parting is not such sweet sorrow. It's the price of ambition. It's a reminder of why I choose to stay here, why I must forget

Alessandra, Rome, the whole bitter-sweet Olympics, why Maestro will be waiting for me at ten o'clock tomorrow morning.

I wander outside and begin to walk back to Milan.

Arrivederci Roma

'My dear, but we don't mind tears at all,' says the dark-haired interviewer dressed in best British tweeds and an old school tie. 'Arrivederci Roma' comes clearly out of the loudspeakers. 'The music is exactly right, too, as we requested. If you will just . . . over here.'

I shake off the hand which is cupped around my elbow, about to steer me in the direction of a camera and lights set up in a corner alcove of the departure lounge. 'No,' I say again, the tears still rolling. And I am sick to bloody death of that song!

'Alex, you'll do as you're asked,' mutters Mr Upjohn behind me, angrily. 'This is a British television crew, making a documentary programme on the Games.'

'If you knew they'd be here, why didn't you give me any warning?'

'I hardly got a chance, you and that bogus young red-head. I shall protest to Mrs Churchill in the strongest possible terms.'

'Why? He didn't do you any harm, he just showed me round Rome — we saw lots of things, I learnt lots, a perfect gentleman . . .'

'I knew there was something odd about him . . .'

'And just what . . ?'

'Mr Upjohn,' said the interviewer smoothly, 'Excuse me, I'm sorry, but we don't have a great deal of time, maybe twenty minutes before your final call.'

Behind him, as he speaks, I see Mrs Churchill searching through the crowd of people standing around. She spies us and comes bustling over. Close behind her comes Norm Thompson, hat pushed to the back of his head, notebook in hand, looking creased and worn-out.

'Alex, dear, where did you get to?' she cries.
'I was saying goodbye to Tom.'
'Yes, I shall have something further to say to you, Enid, on that score,' says Mr Upjohn.
'The cat out of the bag?' Bulldog asks me, smiling.
I nod, also smiling through my tears, to Mr Upjohn's fury. His eyes fall on Norm Thompson's face.
'Norm, did you know about this, too?' he demands.
'Miss Archer, please?' says the interviewer.
'Alright,' I say, because anything will be better than this stupid conversation. Who cares? Tom played a lengthy trick on them, all clean fun, so what? He is on the other side of that screen, he isn't worth worrying about any more. 'Lead on. But no sloppy tears,' I say, sniffing hard as we walk towards the lights.
'Has Rome been the city of romance, then?' he says archly. He is boringly tall dark n' handsome, at a guess a bit older than Tom, as BBC and smooth-tongued as they come.
'No, it hasn't, and please don't ask me anything about boyfriends and men 'cause I won't answer, there's nothing to tell anyway and have you got a handkerchief?'
'Of course.' It's Irish linen, unused. 'Keep it. My name's Michael Harrington-Jones, by the way. I'm so pleased to meet you.'
'Thanks.' I blow my nose as I see two chairs, one with a microphone on it, set out under the lights, and realize what I am letting myself in for. 'How come you got permission to be here?'
'We simply asked. We wanted the youngest Olympic medallist before she flew home to fame and glory. Sit here, make yourself comfortable. The proximity is necessary, I'm afraid, for the small screen. May I call you Alex?' He has picked up the microphone on its stalk and consulted a clipboard, and is looking at the girl and five men dressed in jeans behind the camera, waiting for the signal to start. We are uncomfortably close, our knees practically touching. 'Derek, get them to turn that music down a bit. Now, Alex, just relax, don't be nervous.'
'I'm not. Hell's bells,' I say, recoiling as someone thrusts another light practically into my face, blinding me.

'Sorry about the sun gun. You'll get used to it. Your first time in front of a camera?'

'No,' I lie, swiping the hanky across my nose and eyes again.

'Good. I'm very friendly, I won't bite you. Ready? We've adjusted the sound for all this noise, but try to speak up clearly.'

After a long pause he must have got a signal. I still couldn't see anything but lights, glaringly white.

The microphone goes back and forth between us. I keep wanting to lean back, put a more comfortable space between us so that I can't see the gold fillings in his front teeth, but of course I can't, there's nowhere to go. Trapped!

'Alex Archer, you came to Rome a completely unknown young swimmer from New Zealand. You're going home with a bronze medal in your pocket, the youngest competitor of the Games to win a medal.'

'I still can't believe it.'

'How did you feel, standing on the victory dais with Fraser and Von Saltza?'

'Sort of numb. I don't remember much at all.'

'You were so overcome?'

'I must've been. I do remember the spotlight on the flags going up, all red white and blue — and grinning like a Cheshire Cat. Dawn Fraser wearing a white track suit and waving her koala bear around, all the Aussies screaming Dawnie.' (I remember being utterly aware of Tom in the shadows nearby, several times meeting his smiling eyes.)

'Dawn Fraser's your heroine, obviously.'

'I think she's amazing. She knew who I was even before the heats.'

'How many years of training has it taken, to stand on that dais?'

'About five or six. All through this winter at home. It's winter there now.'

'So I believe. But how was it possible, coming from virtually no competition in New Zealand to an Olympic bronze?'

'I had plenty of competition. A certain girl called Maggie Benton, for years.'

'A famous rivalry, in New Zealand?'

'I don't know about famous. She usually won, up till last summer.'

'So you won the place in the Olympic team?'

'We both got in. But she got peritonitis just before we left. She should have been here too.'

'How do you think she would have swum?'

'I've no idea.' (Yes I have, I think her mother would have made life impossible for both of us, and neither of us would have got past the heats.) 'I think she'd have done well. I never beat her easily.'

'What will it be like, getting off the plane in New Zealand?'

'After five days of sitting bolt upright, wonderful.'

'I mean the reaction to your medal?'

'They'll say, not bad, kiddo.'

'You don't mean to say that literally. Surely, that's a New Zealand expression for . . .'

'Flabbergasted. Amazed. Pulled a swiftie.'

'By that, do you mean a swift one, a fluke? But surely it wasn't a fluke, was it? Your times improved with each race.'

'Yes, they did, actually. But no one was more surprised than me.'

'Gold in Tokyo?'

'That's too far ahead.'

'People are saying that you look set to take over Dawn Fraser's world sprint crown when she retires.'

'Are they? I don't know about that. She hasn't said anything about retiring, has she?'

'They're saying you have the same degree of killer instinct necessary to win races.'

'I like to win, 'course I do. But killer instinct — I hate that expression, sounds like you're a shark, eating people. I don't eat people. I think I'm more a dolphin. I think I was a dolphin once. I bet, if I looked it up, dolphins swim faster than sharks.'

'I believe there is a possibility of an American swimming scholarship next year?'

'There's lots of possibilities for next year.' (How do people find out these things? Mr Upjohn?)

'Such as?'

'It's too soon. I haven't decided. Maybe swim in Australia.' (Oops, is that a state secret?) 'Last year at school, probably.'

'And then?'

'I want to study law.'

'So you couldn't accept the American offer?'

'I didn't say that. I just said I wanted to study law, somewhere, sometime.'

'I imagine you were quite a grown-up young woman before you came to Rome, Alex.'

'I think that sounds a bit patronizing.'

'I'll rephrase that question. What do you think coming to Rome and doing so well at the Olympics, so surprisingly well, has done for you personally?'

(Gulp) 'Well, I've met lots of fantastic people. The Olympic ceremonies, I'll never forget those, the boy with the torch and the little fires at the closing ceremony. Or Rome, of course.'

'The Spanish steps, the Colosseum, the Catacombs . . . of course, to a New Zealander . . .'

'I don't think it matters where you come from, it's still fantastic. Learning all that Latin and ancient history seems to have some point, now.'

'Your impressions of the Olympic village?'

'Well, mostly it was great, everyone in together, people from all different sports, all different colours. Tho' the women's quarters were a bit like being in prison. Guards with guns, truly. And having to eat with the South Africans.'

'Tricky, you mean, because of the rugby series being played? Which they won?'

'I mean because I don't like the idea of apartheid, and our rugby team shouldn't have gone at all.' (Ohmigawd, here we go again.)

'Alex, would you show us your bronze medal?' His voice changes. 'Take your time. We edit the film, of course. I really don't want to get into politics, m'dear. My apologies, I meant to ask you earlier to have your medal ready.'

I get the box out of my handbag, relieved to have a break from our knees touching and looking into his staring blue eyes and gold fillings. I don't much want to get onto politics for British television either. I am beginning to wonder which is worse, interviewers who try to trip you up, or those who flatter you to the skies, or those who do both, like this one. I drape the chain of leaves over my hand. Under the harsh lights the burnished bronze perfectly matches the miniature that hangs on the bracelet around my wrist. To my dismay, I feel my eyes grow moist, and things happen at the back of my throat.

'Would you hold it a little higher, Alex? It was all worthwhile, do you think, all those years, all that winter training?'

'Yes, of course it was.' (I am swallowing. How do you stop tears? Will-power? I will not cry. I will not cry.)

'And Roma, la Città Eterna, the city of music, opera, song, and romance? Wonderful memories for a beautiful young woman to take home?'

'Yes, wonderful.' (A flatterer — what's that lovely word — sycophant, and turning out to be sneaky too, and my will-power pathetic and eyes now full of water and no doubt glistening and very obvious to the man holding the light in my face.)

'Romantic memories?'

'Lots.'

'And when you get off the plane in Auckland, a New Zealand national sporting heroine?'

'No, I'm no different, I'm not a heroine, never will be. I'm just me. Look, I'll have to stop this because I'm beginning to talk like a parrot and say things I don't mean and I'm going to cry again, and you must have other people you want to interview.'

I put the medal back into the box, coiling the chain into place, and stand up, knocking against his well-tailored knees and tripping over the microphone cord. 'I'm sorry, it was my first time with a camera and I'm no good at witty, pithy quotes, and don't use that last bit, please.'

Michael Harrington-Jones stands up too. 'But you were splendid, Alex, splendid,' he says untruthfully. 'Just what we wanted. I shall follow your career with great interest. You've a fine future in front of you, I'm sure.'

'I've got five days in an aeroplane, assuming we make it,' I say through my tears. 'Coming over, the wheels got stuck, coming into Karachi.'

'How very alarming.' We both listen to an announcement: our flight being called. 'When you go out to the aircraft, we've got a camera set up by the gangway. Will you give the camera some happy or tearful waves, whatever, we don't mind.'

Posing like ruddy film stars do for newsreels, I think, as I escape from much handshaking, many thank yous, good luck, happy landings with all seven of them. In the toilet, my eyes look a mess, I look a mess, the film will look terrible, and I have just gone on record as an uncouth kid from the colonies. When I come out, the first people are walking out to the plane. I wonder if Tom is already on his way back to Milan, or if he's still waiting, watching out of a window. He loathes airports. So do I, now.

Happy or tearful? In a funny, complicated sort of way, I'm both. I'm still angry, but I'm going home, and I have to admit listening to Michael Harrington-Jones carry on about me 'taking over Dawn Fraser's world sprint crown', though crazy and scary, has done wonders for my very weird state of mind.

So, happy it is, the best performance I can muster, in case . . . Walking out to the plane, Bulldog telling me about her ticking-off from Mr Upjohn while I was being interviewed, and I am certainly laughing. I wave happily to the camera at the foot of the steps, and again from the top. I look once over towards where people are crowding at the windows of what I think is the main departure hall, but my eyes aren't that good, and I can only see a blur of figures, no one special.

The plane is stuffy already, our seats cramped, Bulldog's fear of flying after the Karachi episode has made her not nice to be near, and this is only the beginning. The take-off is noisy and bumpy, the airport below a conglomeration of dull buildings and parked aeroplanes, and my ears are popping already.

Flying through the low cloud, while the terrified Bulldog beside me still has her eyes closed tight, I get out my bronze medal and stare at it in total wonderment.

I'm shivering slightly, though it's anything but cold. I rock my hand slowly back and forth to catch golden-red glints of light on the engraved figure of the athlete victorious, on my name, on the name of my country, cut in formal Roman lettering on the other side, on the thin leaves of beaten bronze.

When we came in to land, five weeks ago, I didn't even know if I could swim at the Olympics. Now, I hold this beautiful heavy burnished thing in my palm and I know damn well I'm going home to a whole lot of fame and glory. Only woman medallist of our team, youngest of the whole Games, et cetera. For a few days — alright, even a few weeks, off and on.

They'll clip your wings when you get home . . .

For the rest of my life, I'll always be Alex Archer, the Olympic bronze medallist. An Olympic medal — that was what any athlete wanted, more than anything else.

Wasn't it?

We are banking, altering course, I suppose for the first stop, Cairo. Suddenly we fly out of the cloud, into pure blue sky. The afternoon sun shines straight in my window. Looking down, through shreds of cloud, I can see the coastline against a sea so blue it makes my heart ache. On my hand the medal catches the sunlight, the athlete gleams intense coppery fire. He's so bright I have to shut my eyes.

Songs for Alex

Songs for Alex, the fourth book of the Alex quartet, fulfils a six-year commitment to Alex.

Thanks are due to a number of friends, singers, actors, teachers, notably John Hurford, for his strong cover portraits of Alex; Janice Webb, Elizabeth Macrae, Jeremy Bell and English Department staff at Waikato University, Dr Pam Laird of Westlake Girls' High School, Ted Malan, Diane Hebley, Alan Bunn, Dr Libby Limbrick, Frank Graveson, Mona Williams; and Geraldine Brophy, who played a memorable Joan in the Court Theatre production of *Saint Joan* in Christchurch, 1991.

G.B. Shaw's great play has fascinated me since my schooldays. I also acknowledge a considerable debt to Marina Warner's *Joan of Arc, the Image of Female Heroism* (Weidenfeld and Nicholson, 1981).

In 1960, New Zealand schools operated a curious system of accrediting most Sixth Form pupils for the University Entrance examination, based on internal assessment and examinations in October–November each year.

This accrediting system remained until the mid 1980s. It was, to my mind, tough and unfair on that small minority of students who were — like Alex — deemed marginal, and required to sit the external examination in December. To those who were put through this hoop, as was one of my daughters in 1983, a special salute.

Though set firmly in Auckland in 1960–61, this final book of the quartet remains, as were the others, a work of fiction.

Rude shocks

In a noisy, rattling aeroplane with four propellors and two stewardesses who speak with New Zealand accents and serve dinky little meals of New Zealand lamb chops and Watties' peas and Anchor best creamery butter: going east, going south, going cold, going home.

I have dreamt them all: warm Italy, pink Rome, blue Naples, rocky Vesuvius and ruined Pompeii, the Olympic pool, the New Zealand flag rising floodlit into the night sky, for me. The runner with the torch at the opening ceremony, the ring of fire at the closing ceremony, the brutal Colosseum, three moonlit hours of *Aida*, a certain voice, a certain kiss, certain goodbye, certain pain . . . I dreamt them all, except the pain and my winter skin tanned Roman brown under my white shirt and a bronze-coloured medal in my bag.

Somewhere over India, I dragged *Saint Joan* from my cabin bag. I stared at the words without seeing them, making no sense of them. JOAN: (bobbing a curtsey) *Good morning, captain squire. Captain, you are to give me a horse and armour and some soldiers, and send me to the Dauphin.* Over the Bay of Bengal, I couldn't even remember which scenes I was trying to learn. Over vast red Australia, I decided to give it away, the whole thing. Sorry but not sorry, Miss Marcia Macrae, thou Teacher of Speech and Drama, traitor, meddler, no friend of mine, go find yourself another Joan of Arc.

Over the Tasman, Mrs Churchill, otherwise known as the Bulldog, was burbling on beside me about seeing her lovely boys again. The six weeks we'd been away, they'd been staying with friends; one sits School Cert this year; of course she was flying straight on to Christchurch, she had to start teaching again in two days, she'd done her job as chaperone to the New Zealand Olympic swimming Team of One, got me back in one piece, *scamp* that I am . . .

'Message from the pilot,' announced Mr Upjohn loudly in his Manager's voice, standing in the narrow aisle so that everyone nearby could hear too. 'He's been talking to air traffic control at Whenuapai. There's the Mayor and five hundred people at the airport, about twenty reporters and photographers. You'd better smarten yourself up, Alex.'

'I have,' I said. 'I washed my face and under my arms in Sydney, and changed my shirt. I don't smell, at least not much. And my damn silly shoes won't fit.' The tops of my feet had swelled up even more than they did on the way over. This time we hadn't stopped for a night in Singapore, just three hours for refuelling, then kept going. After three — or was it four or even five? — days and nights, about six steamy airports, up and down like a yo-yo, sleeping on hard airport benches or even the floor, *anywhere* to get horizontal, I'd ceased to have any interest in anything except getting out of this tin tube in one limp piece.

'They'll want to see your bronze medal,' he said threateningly. As if I didn't know that already. He still hadn't forgiven me for the scene at Rome airport, kissing strange men and being less than co-operative with a BBC interviewer. 'The only woman medallist and . . .'

'They'll want to see Murray Halberg and Peter Snell and the golds more,' I said, turning away from the repulsive sight of Mr Upjohn about a stone heavier, newly shaved, hair slicked across his bald bit, blazer and tie already on. Pity he didn't use a deodorant. The view out the window was the same as it had been for the past everlasting three hours: beyond the whirring white circle of the propellors, navy blue sea flecked with white, the occasional cargo ship, clusters of cottonwool clouds. We were about ten minutes away, on our bumpy way down through the clouds to the Mayor and five hundred people at the airport.

Of course it will be fun, at first, Tom had said. And after — *They'll clip your wings,* he had said, *when you get home.*

Bugger you, Tomas Alexander. I'd sobbed all the way from Rome to Cairo and into the darkness beyond for wasted opportunities, frustration, disappointment, beautiful bitter music, 'Arrivederci Roma', and Ciao Tom. They will *not* clip my wings. Bugger you.

'The Manukau Heads, the bar. Look, that's impressive, to starboard,' I heard someone cry. Below, out my side, surf was breaking like lace on a narrow black beach; beyond, a patch of rough broken water and a small mountain guarding the entrance to the harbour; beyond that the black beach and sand dunes faded endlessly into the mist. We were already quite low, over clumps of native bush and windbreaks of macrocarpa trees and farmland that suddenly looked very green and comforting and familiar; sheep tracks on the hills, cows in the paddocks, apple orchards and vineyards.

Violins and all that — but tears in my eyes, Home, and a family waiting.

Then farmhouses, sheep, more orchards, the outskirts of the city, houses, gardens, cars and trucks driving down long straight roads, the creeks and boats of the other harbour, beaches for swimming, with clean sand, no people, tingling white surf, everything so *green*, the sheep so white, and finally we were touching down roughly for the last time and taxiing towards the terminal. The colours in the spring sunshine were bright, the edges of everything sharp and hard. Rain had left large black puddles on the concrete.

'Christ, look at the reception committee,' I heard, as the plane swung around side on to the crowd and everyone began to crawl out of their seats and try to look as though they hadn't been sleeping in their uniforms for four days. The propellors whooshed and feathered and stopped, the engines died away and stopped. They wheeled up the gangway. They opened the doors. I heard a band playing. I heard people ask 'What's the local time here? Anyone know?' The time! I didn't even know what day of the week it was. I simply couldn't get my shoes on.

'Ready Alex?' said Bulldog. 'Dear, what *are* you doing?'

'Taking my stockings off.' I did it surreptitiously, in my seat, unhooking my suspenders through my grey uniform skirt. 'My shoes have shrunk.'

'You'll have to squeeze them on somehow.'

'I can't. Look.' The tops of my feet and ankles were so puffy I could press them and make a dent. I rather liked the idea of getting out barefoot.

'You can't go barefoot,' Mr Upjohn said flatly. The man has no sense of humour. We could hear cheers as the first team members went down the gangway.

'I can't do anything else. Not even Chinese foot-binding would get my feet into those shoes.'

'You should have packed some others in your cabin bag.'

Should have, *should* have? — there were lots of things I should have, Mr Upjohn. Like told Tomas Alexander the pretentious red-haired farmer's son from Taihape to get lost, beaten Dawn Fraser and brought home a gold medal, what else do you suggest?

'You must get them on, Alex, just until we get inside the terminal,' fussed Bulldog. 'Mine were a terrible squeeze, but I managed.'

She would. I picked up my shoes. 'Sorry, no can do. I didn't choose these stupid things.' The hockey player who like me had been a protester against the All Black team going to South Africa was standing back, waiting for me to swing out into the aisle. 'Thank you, Des,' I said sweetly, gathering up blazer, handbag, cabin bag, shoes, gritting my teeth. 'Blazer, Alex,' said Bulldog. 'On, please. It'll be cold out there.'

It was. The wind whipped across the open doorway, the sun glared, the crowd clapped and cheered, the band played, and I said goodbye to the stewardess and walked down the steel gangway, and felt the cold grey tarmac of *home* with my bare footpads. The wind was chilly on my cheeks, pink from the stuffy inside of the plane. The air smelt differently, of trampled grass, farms, raw wind on the sea, the black surf just over those bushy hills. Snell and Halberg were already being mobbed by photographers.

The first face I recognized behind the waist-high barricades was not the one I would have chosen. Keith, Andy's mate; my sort-of mate, in a duffle coat and varsity scarf shouting 'Attagirl,' grinning from ear to ear like a garden gnome. Behind his new beard, he was pale, but everyone looks pale here. The only other person I have kissed or been kissed by apart from Andy. And Tom. Why can't I have a normal boyfriend, one who isn't dead, or a garden gnome, or in Italy?

I padded on through the icy puddles; some good-natured laughing. I waved my shoes at them. Photographers danced about. Flashbulbs went off.

There's Mr Jack, the coach I left behind, wearing the usual grey raincoat and a round triumphant smile. Glory be, beside him, Maggie, on her feet again, so thin, scrawny even, *very* pale, hair longer, smiling manfully — making me feel, even from this distance, healthily huge and brown. I thought of the last time I saw her, ghostly white in a hospital bed, hooked up to tubes. I thought she'd gone to Australia already, to live. No sign of her mother, thank God.

In amongst all those raincoats, the waving arms, the cheers, where are my family?

Then, a phalanx of black school blazers which look familiar — heavens, at least the whole Sixth Form, screaming fit to bust as I pass them, waving flags and banners: WELCOME HOME ALEX, and GO ALEX, ALEX THE CHAMP, and ALEX IN BRONZE. They must have hired a bus! Can't see friend Julia, but can see Miss Gillies' felt hat towering above them, and squat treacherous Miss Macrae with her medieval haircut and uniform grey suit. I've a bone to pick with you, Miss Macrae, meddling in my Roman affairs, writing to a certain music student in Milan, suggesting he show me round Rome, which he did, no doubt hoping we'd hit it off, which we did. Or I did, I'm not so sure about Tom Tomas Tommaso Alexander. I would never be sure about Tom Tomas Tommaso Alexander.

Where's my family?

Just before we filed into the passport and customs place, I saw my family at the front of the barricade, not screaming, just smiling proudly — tall Mum and taller Dad, and jostling for space in front, two pesky brothers and one sister. Robbie's grown, Debbie looks prettier, Jamie taller. Little Gran must be somewhere in there. Mum looks — older, tired . . . dare I say it, a bit colourless after those Roman women.

'I can't wait to see my boys!' said Bulldog chattily as we were doing all the boring bits through Immigration and Customs and Agriculture. I declared I had not been on a farm and listed all my presents, remembering with unwanted clarity those I'd bought in Tom's company, in the

Trastevere, the Campo dei Fiori, the Vatican, and the Zeiss camera I'd bought on the way over in Singapore, but the customs man didn't seem all that interested, and no one actually asks to pay duty. Finally we were free to go out into the arrival lounge. I heard the first applause, then great shouts as Snell and Halberg went through the door.

'Got your medal ready, Alex?' said Mr Upjohn. 'You should put it on.' I always knew the man had no taste. I didn't even answer. There was no other way out of the airport, though there must be a back door for stretcher cases. I was not quite a stretcher case. 'Okay, Mrs C,' I said, oddly nervous. 'Andiamo.' Mr Upjohn was waiting for us; he was My Manager.

This time my family mobbed me first, along with Mr Jack, who was actually crying, and Maggie who up close looked so pale and tired I felt really guilty to be so healthy and successful. 'Fantastic you,' she said, generous as always, hugging me so hard I could feel her rib bones. '*And* you,' I said. 'You won too, your battle. I'm sad you're going away.' She didn't say anything, but her expression and the tears in her eyes spoke volumes.

My head was spinning. So many eyes smiling at me. Where's Gran, I haven't seen Gran. 'She's waiting at home,' said Mum, 'She's a little poorly, she wanted to have tea waiting when we got back.' 'Perth '62, Tokyo '64?' said Mr Jack, his moonface beaming and eyes gleaming, and I nodded, knowing it wouldn't happen.

Then I got swamped by my best friend Julia and a tidal wave of screaming black blazers. Whether I liked it or not, I had to produce my medal for the photographers, and put it round my neck for pictures, with family, with coach, with Mr Upjohn and Bulldog, with Maggie. ('The tear-jerker,' I heard one reporter say to his photographer, 'that's the rival, the kid who didn't make it'); then with a whole group of my squealing schoolmates basking in reflected glory; then with Peter Snell and Murray Halberg and the other bronze medallist, in the marathon, Barry Magee. The various managers all stood at the front while the little mayor with his red robes and big chain and bristly white moustache made a speech into a microphone about the most successful team ever to leave these shores.

With Debbie and Robbie clinging to me like limpets, reporters wanted answers to not-so-silly questions. I wasn't the water baby of the team any more; I was the bronze medallist, the only woman medallist, who'd gone away just the kid, not even the dark horse, and come back ranked third in the world.

'What's your next goal, Miss Archer?'

'A decent night's sleep in a real bed with a hot-water bottle and a break from training.'

'The gold in Tokyo?'

'Four years is a long time in swimming.'

'What about Perth?'

'So's two years.'

'Are you saying you're going to retire before Perth? Maybe only one more season?'

'No, I'm not saying that.'

'There's a rumour you're being offered an American swimming scholarship?'

'I am?'

'You'll take it, of course.'

I wasn't so tired as to be caught out so easily. 'I'll consider any official offer, naturally,' I said pompously, 'if it comes and when I've had time to think about it.'

I recognized a canny young reporter with a big Adam's apple who waited until the rest had given me up as a bad job and panted off somewhere else. 'Grant Davies from the *Herald*,' he said, reminding me, shaking my hand. 'It's my day off. I just wanted to say, congratulations. I always knew you'd do something spectacular over there. You've come a way since Napier.'

'So have you,' I said, remembering the night in February he and I accidentally overheard Mr Upjohn and the other selectors pondering what to do about me and Maggie, which to nominate for Rome, either or both. He was just a small-town journalist then, new to sports reporting; now he worked in the Big Smoke with the famous veteran sportswriter Norman Thompson.

'Norm's due home on Friday,' he said. 'We heard he was pretty sick in Rome, with the heat and a terrible hotel.' I didn't like to admit I hadn't been aware of Norm's problems while he'd been at the pool, watching my races with Tom (can I never forget the man?!), or hanging round the Olympic Village chatting up me and others for his stories. 'He got all his copy back, though,' said Grant. 'I used to whip it off the teleprinter, a pleasure to read. A great old pro, is Norm. He said some nice things about your bronze. You must have a great chance for the gold in Perth. Dawn Fraser's not getting any younger.'

'I don't think I'll still be swimming then,' hearing myself say carelessly what I'd hardly even been thinking. Shut *up* Alex, numbskull. 'Sorry, Grant, that was off the record, please. My brain's addled by aeroplanes. I haven't really decided what I'll do.' 'Sure,' he said, and I knew he meant it. He'd kept faith with me last time, not scored a scoop or told tales out of school, as far as I knew. I said, 'You and Norm would be the first to hear if . . . well, you know.'

'Thanks. And how was our oily friend Mr Upjohn in Rome?' he grinned. 'Not so bad,' I said, 'I didn't see too much of him at all, only during my actual events; he was the Manager, of course.' 'Did you see much of Rome?' he asked. 'Quite a bit,' I said, the memory both wonderful and painful. 'I had a week after. Naples too. Pompeii, and Vesuvius. A nice train trip. I've seen Naples, now I can . . .'

Suddenly I'd had enough of all this, the strangers coming up, their eyes gleaming, touching me, their voices saying Alex, congratulations, over and over, great stuff champ, well done champ, congratulations champ. I'd hardly seen my family, and I wanted to see Gran, be back in my own quiet house. I'd had enough of airports to last me a lifetime. Grant read the signs. 'Go on,' he said to Debbie and Robbie hanging on my arms, 'take your big sister home. She's had it.'

I found Mr Upjohn to say goodbye and Bulldog to say thank you for being My Mum in Rome, and couldn't find Zoe to thank her for being a great long-suffering room-mate in Rome before she also flew on south on the same plane, and finally allowed Debbie and Robbie to drag me out after Mum and Dad, through the crowds, across the wet carpark, to the car.

On the way home I gave the kids my medal. They put it around their necks, trying it out for size, and silently fingered the necklace of leaves and the engraved figure of the athlete borne aloft on one side and my name carved on the other. I answered Mum and Dad's questions, but only in short bursts. There was so much to tell them I didn't know where to start. Compared to Rome, the houses flashing past looked small, plain, dull, wooden, temporary, not built to last; the gardens bare, the pavements empty of people.

Apart from the space, what else was so different? I'd never noticed before how much wire there was around Auckland, wire fences and poles and telephone wires and electricity wires looping and stitching all the roads and paddocks and farms and houses together. There were some white and dusky pink cherry blossoms out, some of those brassy pink rhododendrons, some white tulip magnolias, but everything looked plainer, smaller, raw and wintry. The afternoon light was harsher than I remembered, harsher than Rome.

End of the journey: under the pepper tree in our driveway, looking up the wooden front steps to the porch where a leafy bougainvillaea climbed and they'd strung up garlands of garden flowers and a large banner, WELCOME HOME ALEX in huge red letters. I had yet more tears in my eyes as car doors were flung open and Robbie, hefty as five-year-olds go, climbed off my knees. I wanted to rush in and see Gran, but

Mum turned around from the front seat and said firmly 'Sit tight, just wait a minute, Alex. Please understand, there's a reason.'

Dad and the kids got my bags out of the car, and went in the front door. From the serious tone of Mum's voice, I guessed it wasn't going to be a nice reason, a pleasant surprise. I understood why the kids had been so quiet on the way home. I could just hear them being told 'Now don't you tell Alex!' whatever it was. My bare feet were suddenly very cold.

'Before we go in . . . come and sit closer, Alex, in the driver's seat?' She lit a cigarette, and blew a long trail of smoke out her window.

'Gran's been, well, more than a little poorly while you've been away. She had a coronary two weeks after you left, three days before your first race. She's better, there's no need to panic, but she was in hospital until last week.'

Gran? I'd known all along something was odd. I gripped the steering wheel, thinking illogically, I'm well over fifteen, it's about time I got my driving licence. 'I should have come home.'

'Absolutely not. She didn't want that. She's made a fairly good recovery, after a shaky start.'

My aeroplane-ridden brain was desperately trying to sort out the dates. 'You rang, she rang, the night before my first race, I was asleep, or trying to sleep, about eleven? Was she in hospital then?'

Mum nodded. 'We knew we were probably waking you up. She got it into her head that she wanted to wish you luck, that she wouldn't see you again. Things that day weren't looking too good. The staff were wonderful. They wheeled her, bed, machines and all, to a telephone. But she's made a better recovery than the doctors anticipated.'

Mum the strong, Mum the ex-nurse who'd seen it all, seemed near tears.

'She's been home a week, just getting out of bed for a few minutes each day. Seeing you will be the best tonic she could have.'

I put my arm around her, and hugged her close and heard her begin to cry. 'I've so missed you, Alex, Dad has been just marvellous and the kids, but . . .'

'Mum, don't cry, don't . . . I'd have come home, course I would, you know I would.'

'No you wouldn't. You couldn't.' She pulled away, wiped her eyes with the back of her hand and smiled. 'Gran made Dad and me sign a declaration, a codicil to her will. Under no circumstances, even her death, were you to be told *anything* until you got back, with the team, as planned. Legally binding — I don't know, but morally we were bound hand and foot.'

What could I say to that? Inside in a bed lay little indestructible Gran, who'd been part of the family for as long as I could remember. Who fed her chooks and grew all our vegetables and sewed baby clothes for extra money and on top of all that made me a whole wardrobe of summer clothes for Rome. I was just about to ask if we could go in now when a woman in slacks, a neighbour, came running down the front steps. She stopped by the open car door.

'Welcome home, Alex. My word, everyone is so proud of you, clever girl! I've practically had to hold your gran down, chain her to the bed: she can't wait to see you. She's fine, Helena. Excuse me, I must dash, I have to pick up a child from school.'

'Thanks, Gracie, sorry we were a bit late. We hadn't quite anticipated the fantastic welcome at the airport. Off you go.' Mum had stubbed out her cigarette and found a hanky to wipe her eyes. 'I wasn't keen about leaving Gran in the house by herself. She's in your bedroom. I'm hoping you don't mind . . .'

'Of course I don't!'

'I wanted her to be closer to the action than she was, out in her bed-sit — and so did she. I swopped the two of you over. It was very odd with both of you away. I won't say I was lonely, how could I be? . . . it was just odd. Jamie and Debbie — now don't laugh — they've organized a special afternoon tea.'

The house, as I ran through in my bare feet, was full of telegrams, posters, flowers, the trolley set up with teacups and fancy biscuits and sponge-cake. My untidy room was now Gran's tidy sick room, warm and cosy, full of flowers, with Gran propped up against four pillows, in a turquoise bedjacket, begging to be hugged. By the bed were her little treasures, the radio, the well-thumbed Bible, the jars of Pond's vanishing cream, the *Woman's Weekly* open at the crossword, her current knitting.

Of course it was plenty tearful, Gran and Mum and me and Debbie joining in, and the rest standing round the bed — but happy, because Gran was going to be alright, I'd been to the other side of the world and got back safely, and here's my medal, Gran, isn't it beautiful? Everything would soon be back to normal.

Gran didn't look sick; if anything, she looked as though the rest had done her good. 'You can't kill a weed,' she laughed. While Debbie played mother with the tea and Jamie handed round the creamy, squelchy sponge-cake, she wanted to know everything, about my races and my medal, and the single best thing about Rome, and all about the American scholarship I'd briefly mentioned in a letter which had arrived only yesterday. Slyly: did I meet any nice young men (nobody nice, I said truthfully), and oh, tell me all about the opera, Alex, you said it was outside, some Baths or other, opera in a Baths, tell me, was it *wonderful*?

It suddenly struck me: she'd never been out of New Zealand, she hadn't even visited the South Island. I couldn't tell her enough. The kids got restless and Mum had to go and start the dinner, but Gran's smiling watery eyes kept me talking, talking. Yet, back to normal? Had I stopped to think for even ten seconds, I'd have realized everything had changed, absolutely.

After dark that night, Dad, wrapped up in his Swanndri, protesting but trying his best to understand, drove me down to the beach at Mission Bay and watched while I had a swim in the beam of the headlights, and some courting couples gaped incredulously out of their car windows.
    The wind was freezing and the water at half-tide and wintry cold, probably about fifty degrees Fahrenheit, if that. I had to wade out a fair way to reach even waist-depth water. The whalelike shape of Rangitoto lay facing me, the two humps behind a silver cloud. I wanted to feel my body washed clean of travel, in the most opposite way to golden Italy and sunny inland pink Rome I could imagine: in dark icy Pacific water. I had to reconnect myself to my particular ocean, to my city on the edge of it.
    Tom's ship would have sailed right past here, nineteen months ago, bound for Italy. The *Fairstar* — or was it the *Fairsky*? they both came here, into Auckland, tied up at Princes Wharf by the Ferry Building. They left at night, with tugs in attendance and bands playing, people throwing streamers. First stop Sydney where he bought a garish green souvenir shirt with palm trees and the harbour bridge. How can you ever trust a man who carries around a fake moustache, and not the cheap sort amateur actors use either? Across the channel, beacons winked, jeered at me, red and white.

If I thought I could wash Tom out of my system so easily, just by getting numb all over, I was kidding myself.
    I'd been looking forward to one day at home, at least, quietly with Mum and Gran. Mr Jack was coming for lunch to hear the whole story. I had my bags to clean out, telegrams to read. Presents and souvenirs and guidebooks and Games programmes to show everyone, a new room to make mine own. I reckoned I'd got the best of the bargain — the room had been tacked onto the back porch when Gran had come to live with us all those years ago. It had windows on three sides, with peach trees in bud just outside. Mum had not only done an amazing job moving all my stuff in, but had put up new curtains, a bold pattern of cheerful red poppies, with matching bedspread.
    But all through lunch with Mr Jack the phone kept ringing. Neighbours kept popping in. Several reporters rang wanting appointments, interviews,

bringing photographers of course. Debbie clung so much before and after school that it began to irritate me; ditto Robbie, home tired and whiny from kindergarten. Jamie reverted to his crude twelve-year-old self: asking how many times I got my bum pinched, and did I see any gangsters, you know, Mafia guys with guns, and was the Colosseum really that fantastic? How could I tell him it was, horribly so, a place built to kill things just for entertainment, but utterly spectacular and romantic at night floodlit after a storm, when viewed from a Vespa motorscooter.

Everywhere I turned: the posters of Rome they'd put up before I left, fruity baritone voices singing 'Funiculi Funicula' from the radio, the pile of programmes and maps of Rome, Mum's scrapbook full of newspaper clippings of the whole Games day-by-day. Dawnie and Chris and me on the victory dais, huge and smiling on the front page of the *Herald*; Zoe, me and Mrs C in the dining hall, tucking in; me congratulating Peter Snell at the Village the day of his amazing win: 'KIWI DARK HORSES. At the Olympic Village in Rome, swimmer Alex Archer (15) surprise bronze medallist in the women's 100m freestyle, congratulates runner Peter Snell (21) after his historic win in the 800 metres.'

He'd been there each time, playing Tommaso the interpreter from Milano, in the hat, watching me say 'cheese' as the flashbulbs went off. Apart from the pictures in my brain, and a few slides gone to be developed, all I had was a silver charm bracelet which I'd angrily taken off my wrist as we took off from Rome. It now sat at the back of a drawer, with the bass clef, the kiwi, the Olympic symbol of rings, the silver fern, the medal, and a last charm, a little silver sombrero which he'd secretly given to Bulldog to give to me in the plane. Even the bracelet had remained a mystery between us. He'd never mentioned it and I'd somehow been too embarrassed.

At school I'd get away, forget, revert to shiny black gym-tunic and exams. Run the gauntlet of a dreadful, inescapable assembly and Turd Formers hanging round corners, sink myself in accrediting exams in six weeks, Miss Macrae's Evening with George Bernard Shaw, scenes from *Saint Joan* in December, the last week of the term.

I think it was that first morning back I first thought of leaving school. I rang Julia at 7.30 and told her I was coming. Would she ride with me? She briskly told me she'd call in but I was nuts, I should be sleeping — and of course, sorry about your Gran being so sick, Alex. I briskly told her that I was perky as a spring chicken — and thanks about my Gran. And no I was not bringing my bronze medal to school, even if Miss Gillies had thoughtfully *specially* asked Julia to remind me.

From past experience, I knew only too well what to expect. I stick out like a sore thumb in a crowd of girls. Even just walking down the long drive was an ordeal. Even the school caretaker and secretaries saw me coming.

Songs for Alex 529

That was just the start. At assembly they dragged me up on the stage, and a press photographer in a raincoat materialized from somewhere. Then I found that Julia had persuaded Mum to put my bronze medal secretly in *her* school bag if you please, giving Miss Gillies the perfect opportunity to talk about our quite unspoiled and modest champion, Alexandra. Then she put the medal around my neck and the place screamed and yelled and they sang 'For sheeza' and then, getting totally sloppy, the school song and 'God Save the Queen' until I thought I would puke.

I was absolutely *furious* with Mum and Julia, not to mention Miss Gillies. That medal was mine, mine to do what *I* chose with, and I did *not* choose to flash it about to huge congregations of schoolgirls. I vowed and declared this was positively the last school assembly I would ever attend. EVER.

Miss Macrae sat on the stage smirking with the other teachers in their black gowns and thick stockings and crêpe-soled brogues. I hardly looked at her, the grey-haired old meddler, writing to the son of an old friend to show the child around Rome. If Tom's mother had been dead for years, how did she know where to . . .? I have sworn not to utter, whisper, think of, his name *ever* again.

Then, when I was back in history class wondering what possible relevance the first Afghan War in 1839 could have for my life, I got a summons. If I thought that all Miss Gillies wanted to do was talk platitudes about Rome, I was in for a rude shock.

The study smelled of books. Miss Gillies flapped across the faded carpet in her faded greeny-black gown, and gave me a double hug, European style. Since she is taller even than me, and thinner, it was like being embraced by a large, musty, bony, black bird.

'Your success in Rome has given the school so much pleasure, so much joy,' she cried, hoisting her gown back on her shoulders. 'We are all so proud of you, so very proud. Now, sit down, Alex.'

'Thanks,' I mumbled. Something about the way she sat down behind her massive desk, put on her glasses, and leaned forward, warned me that this was not a social chat.

'I don't beat about the bush, Alex, as you know, and neither do you. I thought it only fair to inform you of our decision sooner rather than later. Though I must say I'm surprised to see you back so soon after your no doubt gruelling flight. Yesterday's *Herald* amused me. I hope the swelling in your feet has gone down?'

It had, but the barefoot picture on the front page had not amused me one bit. And she was beating around the bush.

'Your parents know about our deliberations, Alex. You know we pride ourselves on our academic achievements. The University Entrance examination forms part of those standards. We do not accredit people lightly. Every case is taken on its merits.'

I knew then what she was going to say.

'Your situation is very unusual. If only the Games had been earlier in the year. I have been sorely tempted to take the easier kinder option. I could have said, give me a hard term's work and reasonable marks in the school exams, and you'll be accredited. However . . .'

'I only missed three weeks,' I said. 'I was away during the school holidays.'

'That's true. But your work in both the first and second terms was not notable for its consistency. I know you went through a very difficult winter, Alex. Your teachers tell me many assignments remained uncompleted. Your mid-year exam marks were poor. On those grounds alone, I cannot in all conscience put you forward as an accredited candidate.'

So I had to sit the bloody exam, meaning two sets of exams, school and external, swot right until mid-December and results not till mid-January, while *all* my friends would be accredited and footloose and fancy-free halfway through November. I needed those two free months for training for Australia. Her eyes were searching my face for clues.

'Alex, you must understand my position. I'm trying to make this as easy as possible for you. I could have waited until next week, even next month to tell you, but I know you don't flinch from facing hard decisions. You'll do well once you settle down to work, of course you will. Your teachers will provide extra tuition, should that be necessary.'

Latin after school. Yuk.

'You'll appreciate I'm jealous of the school's good name with accrediting. I could not have it even whispered abroad that here a pupil's excellence in sport allows a different set of standards to be applied. Even, or especially, an Olympic medal.'

They'll clip your wings, he whispers. I looked at the solemn Coronation picture of Queen Elizabeth II on the wall behind her, and sighed. I couldn't wait to get out of this place. I felt somehow too old for all this.

'I'm sorry, Alex. We did try to warn you back in the first term.'

'I don't remember.'

'You weren't receptive to anything very much, least of all advice. From the Slough of Despond you have risen to great and well-deserved heights.'

'At a price,' I said bitterly.

'Of course. Nothing that is worthwhile in this world is achieved without travail. You, of all people, know that. Now, Rome was full of delights? Of course it was. I spent a whole blissful summer in Italy once, during my student years in Cambridge. Would you give a talk to the school sometime?' She began to look at the diary open on her desk. 'Friday?'

'I'd rather not, Miss Gillies. Please don't make me do that,' I said quickly. Standing up to talk in front of that lot would be worse than 20,000 people

in Rome. I excused myself from her study before she could start any
waffle about my obligations to the school. As far as I was concerned,
she'd just knocked those on the head.

So, once I've sat these damn exams, if I can't bear the thought of going
back to school, what am I going to do next year? Go to varsity, or not?
Keep swimming, or not? Go to America, or not? Australia, or not? Get
a job. Stay at home and help Mum look after Gran. Go back to school
and help Mum.

At tea that night I told Mum and Dad exactly what I thought of Miss
Gillies and her conscience and their part in making me sit UE. I snapped
at the kids, and took the phone off the hook, and complained loudly
when Mum announced that my Auntie Pat and cousin Virginia were
coming up from Hamilton for a night, for hospital tests or something.
Debbie was being thrown out of her room, onto a camp bed in with
me. I didn't know why Virginia's boring little husband wasn't bringing
her up himself and going to a hotel, since they have pots of money. She's
family, said Dad, needing help. Auntie Pat, Dad's sister, was very worried
about Ginnie; her pregnancy was not going as it should. Auntie Pat wanted
to talk it over with Mum, who'd been a midwife as well as a nurse.
I snorted and muttered something about shotgun weddings, and Auntie
Pat and Mum hardly being bosom pals, remember at Ginnie's ghastly
wedding, how *rude* she'd been to Mum and to me.

I knew I was being unkind and obnoxious and I couldn't help it —
until Mum started crying and then I felt guilty as hell, and we both wept
until Dad quietly led me out to my new bedroom with the red poppy
curtains and stood over me until I had forced a sleeping pill down my
throat. Mum came in and read me a chapter from my favourite dog-
eared copy of *The House at Pooh Corner* while I remembered my arms
around a powerful chest and the vibrations of a rich voice softly singing
'How Sweet to Be a Cloud'. Then, as I did the first night in Rome,
I slept for over thirteen dreamless zonked-out hours.

You were right, Tom. Two days back — the party's over.

Postmark Milano

Casa Bargellini
Milan, Sept. 17, '60

Dear Alex,

    I don't regret for a minute coming down to Rome to see you off yesterday, but I am bitterly regretting that the name of Marcia Macrae slipped out in the awkwardness of our farewell. Nothing had gone right that day, from the time I made a 4 a.m. decision to hitchhike down to Rome, to the realization that I might indeed miss you completely. I loathe airports. Despite the stereotype, the flaming hair, I'm not often flustered. Mr Upjohn is a regular Mr Toad — no, better, a Malvolio!
    It's true that Marcia Macrae wrote to me, suggesting that if I happened to be in Rome for the Games I could perhaps get in touch, show you around, normal enough hospitality for a fellow Kiwi a long way from home? But *please* believe me that I opened her letter only after our chance (and admittedly rather fun?) meeting at the Colosseum. It had no bearing on the time we spent together. Had it never arrived, had the letter remained unopened in my bag, nothing would have changed.
    I've no particular reason to feel obliged to Marcia Macrae. She shared digs with my late unlamented mother at drama school in London, mid 1930s, before the war. I met her only once, about three years ago, when she introduced herself after a varsity play, curious to know if I was the bastard son, with my mother's spectacular colouring, grown up. The connection, as you can see, is tenuous.
    Enough earnestness! By the time you get this, allowing for Italian mail, you'll have been home a week or more. I wonder, still walking on air, fêted at school, by the press? I remember some sporting hero, a new All Black I think, once returning for a school assembly like the Second

Coming. I imagine it could have been rather dreadful? However, I do hope your return was a happy one, that you found your family in good spirits. You didn't ever tell me very much about them. I seem to remember passing mention of several siblings and a wonderfully spry nonna?

It's not so hot in Milan, mercifully. Luckily I found a truck at the airport going all the way back to Milan that night, so I missed but one day of study, and passed it off to my teacher as food poisoning, not uncommon in the summer. Having the constitution of an ox, I'd no previous reason to look up the Italian: un avvelenamento da cibo. After two long journeys, I looked convincingly seedy the next day. But my lessons are going well. After eighteen months with only five days stolen last winter to go skiing in the Dolomites, the voice has benefited from the rest. Maestro is pleased with me, I think.

I should like to have talked to you more about New Zealand, since you are undoubtedly under the impression that I'm rather sour in my memories. When I left I'd had four years of varsity, combined, as I think I told you, with any number of very odd jobs. I was deathly tired of both irreconcilable worlds. The social/intellectual snobbery of the one which refuses to allow that the nephew of a wealthy sheep-farmer might have to pay his own way through varsity, every last sordid penny of it. And the absolute contempt of the other — the world of waterside workers, mail sorters, factory hands, hospital orderlies, and the like — for students, for anything connected with what they see as élitist and unnecessary activities such as learning, books, music, theatre, anything creative.

Here, by contrast, as a student, a music student, an opera student, I feel completely at home, encouraged and even honoured at every level. My surrogate family happily withstands hours of practice that at home resulted (it's true!) in complaints to the police.

One development in the few days I've been back is the probability of an audition in November. After that, who knows? I wish I could be more optimistic about a trip home next year. I hear good reports of the local opera company's productions, a good *Butterfly*, competent *Barber of Seville* and *Tosca*. It would be good to spend some time together, not as travellers, but on home territory, as opposed to the overheated and artificial atmosphere of Rome in high summer. From the vantage point of more elegant Milan in the north, Rome and the Olympics now seem like some brilliantly-lit, overpeopled, noisy dream. I may be disenchanted with New Zealand, but I must say the sight of the Southern Cross high above the Piscine moved me more than I would have believed. I shall long treasure the memory of you just after your final — seemingly ten feet tall, shining and wet, remarkably untouched by the exertion of the race, the silver fern badge on your togs blazing proudly in the lights and your face still solemn with disbelief and triumph. Forgive me if my prose seems purple, but you did present a most incandescent image.

Will you be in California this time next year?

Ciao,

Tom

P.S. Tommaso sends his love, back at his desk in Milan filling out air tickets and wishing most fervently he could have his time in Rome again.

In the real world

I'll say one thing for Miss Gillies and her stupid exams — I knew where I stood. That's more than I could say about the entire rest of my life in those first few weeks back at home. For instance:

Julia, my loyal non-sporting scientific-leaning asthmatic friend with the knobbly backbone and a brute of a father.

I refused to talk to her for two days after she sneaked my bronze medal to that revolting school assembly. Then she told me she was also sitting UE exams, as well as the internal exams. You're utterly crazy, I said. *Why*, when she didn't have to? Because she had this deal with her father, surely I remembered: top marks in all her external exams, a university scholarship next year, and she'd be allowed to go to medical school; in return for keeping quiet about a certain Italian Aussie cousin who'd tried to flash his whatsit at her last year. Proper UE marks were better than school exams, and besides it was good practice. She's crazy.

Her father, she said, had bought a boat, a big posh gin palace, and a runabout you could water-ski behind. I must, she said, come out sometime, when it was jolly boating weather and we'd both finished exams. I suppose I was quite glad not to be the only one sitting UE apart from the bird-brains. But I noticed while I was away she'd got very chummy with Rebecca, another wheezer. She wasn't much fun, Julia, she did nothing but swot. And she didn't seem all that interested in Rome. Her fingers smelled from poking around inside a disgusting huge fish sitting on a white slab in the bio lab with all its guts revealed, and her head was full of digestive systems and chemistry symbols and equations.

And Maggie, my dark-haired, dark-eyed old sparring partner. About whom I'd never really decided: all those years she'd swum, all those miles, all that pressure, who really called the shots, her or her charming Mum?

She turned up at home after school the day after my Great Sleep. Mother, she said, would be back to pick her up in an hour. This actually was goodbye. She gave me an envelope. Inside was an expensive Congratulations! card. The only thing written on it: From Harold and Joyce Benton. I wondered which of them had done the signing. From an old foe, it was something.

The family, Maggie said, was leaving in two weeks, for Aussie, for good. Her father was going to start a new company in Melbourne, she'd be going to a posh school there. She ran her thin fingers with their nice pink-varnished nails over my bronze medal and looked at the programmes and brochures with a wistful expression that tore me apart. She showed me her tummy scar, about six inches long, still red, some of the stitch marks still swollen, not quite healed, like meat, horrible. She had bruises on her arms where the drips and blood went in, and tired bags under her eyes.

I asked her if she might get back to swimming next season; who knows, swim for Australia, she was good enough; who knows, against me again? No, she said, never. She wanted to be a nurse, had already written away to enroll in Australia. I thought you wanted to work in travel and such, I said. That's what Mother wants, she said; a gentle little job in an airline office until I get married, but I'm going to be a nurse, whatever she wants. There was a lovely Scottish nurse in the hospital . . . I know, I said, I met her. I came when you were still in a coma, two days before we left. You looked, well, terrible. No one told me you came, she said. We both had tears in our eyes. While she went in to talk to Gran, I wrote a stiff card to Mrs Benton, thanking her for contacting her friend Josephine Bailey who'd helped me buy my camera and was very kind to me in Singapore. Yours faithfully, Alex Archer. A sort of truce.

But I didn't go out with Maggie to the car. We hugged goodbye on the front verandah. I'll ring you before I go, she said. We're flying over sometime next week, when mother's got all the Chinese vases packed up. I thought of the great mansion I'd only visited once, all the porcelain and Chinese rugs and black carved furniture. Good luck, Nurse Benton. *Sister* Benton, matron even, one day? She laughed. I saw only Mrs B's haughty profile in the black Super Snipe as they drove off. Perhaps it was Maggie calling the shots all along. (Years later, I heard she'd done nursing, then physiotherapy as well and become a famous sports medicine person, official physio to Aussie teams.) But for now, end of chapter, four years, end of book.

And garden gnomish Keith, on the phone the next night after my Great Sleep, asking if he could come around and see my medal, but frankly scared stiff, he laughed, to face my Old Man. After, well you know, Alex, that day we went sailing in the rain and capsized — he was bloody angry with me, *ropable*. He'd kept well away from Dad at the airport. You can sneak round the back, I said, I'm out in the bed-sit, wondering why I was bothering to wait up till eleven just for Keith, and whether Mum would approve and too bad.

So he crept round the back very late, and no one knew except the next door's dog. He gave me a clumsy peck on the cheek. His head was also full of equations and physics and whatever else they learn in first year engineering. His beard was soft and did have a few red streaks as he'd once promised, being a Scotsman. It was rather an improvement, hiding most of the scar left from that stupid car accident last year (the one I missed by the skin of my teeth, by being pig-headed); it made him look older than eighteen. The medal was a beautiful bit of work, he said. Did I know that bronze is an alloy of copper and tin, one of the earliest known to man? Yes, I did — thinking, from a certain bronze man walking round the Museo Capitolino designed by Michelangelo.

Dangling the keys of the infamous Jameson pale blue Morris Minor, he got a little coy. Varsity exams started in four weeks, he said. Perhaps after that, we might do a film, or some varsity parties? Perhaps, I don't know, I said, ashamed to tell him I had to *sit* UE. He said he'd ring. I wondered what colour it would be if Tom grew a beard.

If Mum noticed the fat letter with the Milano postmark in amongst all the other letters still pouring in, she didn't comment. He'd covered almost the entire envelope with a fancy selection of the Olympic stamps, the Stadio Olimpico, the Palazzo dello Sport at the EUR, the Discus Thrower, all in nasty dull greens, browns, blues, even a murky purple; not the warm pinks, golds, rich browns, piney greens I remembered from Rome.

He'd written! My heart sang. He existed. He'd not just hitched off back to Milan, a fiery figment of my imagination. The letter was bulky, nice paper, not that awful flimsy airmail stuff. His handwriting (a proper fountain pen, not a ballpoint) was large and flash, difficult to read at first. It was quite long, eight pages, interesting, revealing in small ways, a touch priggish, mocking . . . condescending?

What didn't he say: well, anything about his heart being rent in two, or me (ha-ha!) being the woman of his dreams. But I still wanted him to be my own exotic discovery, my own 'find'. Miss Macrae's meddling *did* matter. Though I knew she'd be wanting to start rehearsals for the scenes from *Joan*, I'd deliberately stayed away from drama class the first week back. So he'd got an audition, had he? Whatever he might have said at the airport about coming home was history, forget it. So I'd be in California, would I? I hid the letter under my mattress. I might reply. Then again I might not.

Though not yet back at training, I was still waking each morning at five: partly from habit, and my body-clock still haywire from the journey, but mostly because I was feeling crowded, pulled this way and that, torn.

Besides trying to cram a year's schoolwork into two months, I had a gigantic and growing pile of letters-from-fans to answer. Every day people wrote or rang wanting me to speak somewhere, open a pool, present prizes. If I thought it had been bad when I got in the Games team before I went away, it was *nothing* in comparison.

I turned down nearly all of them — sorry, I have exams, I have family commitments, I have school commitments, I have exams. Some, especially the toffee-nosed ones, tried to bully me by suggesting alternative dates. Just come for an hour, Alex, we'll send someone to pick you up, we'll book you a flight home early the next morning, our children/club will be *so* disappointed if we have to tell them you can't come, they were *so* looking forward to meeting you . . . I learned all the ploys and to keep saying, quietly, thank you for asking me, but no.

Actually, some of them made me exceedingly angry. I was not public property every day of my life, I'd done lots of these things in the past, I had exams to sit. And how would they know about the housework?

Housework? *Alex*? Well, what else could I do? With Gran in bed for six weeks at least, it was all hands to the pumps. Dad was doing a lot of extra overtime at his Post Office job because we needed the money. When she got sick Gran had to hand all her half-finished baby dresses over to another worker. So I pegged out the clothes before school, folded them when I got home, ironed too, the same boring clothes three days later, boys' shorts and men's shirts and school blouses *ad infinitum*. I vacuumed carpets, washed floors, peeled spuds, learned to make stews and puddings, bossed the kids around to do their jobs too. I put flowers on Gran's food trays before I took them in to her. Mum did all the nursing things, and talked to the doctor when he came every second day. Gran was doing well, but must take it very quietly. It was too soon to see if she'd be left with angina.

Outside, Dad took over the vegetable garden and I did the chooks — thirteen black Orpingtons. I mixed up the mash, and cleaned out the run, and stroked their sleek black feathers and brought in the large brown eggs to show Gran. I loved those chooks.

Housework is soothing, a good excuse for not doing other things, a refuge, but it gets boring and gives you far too much time to think.

Can you really *stand* another year at school, Alex?

If you want to go straight to varsity, if you don't pass this UE exam (and I've missed so much, it's possible), you're right up the creek without a paddle.

Australia in January — they'll expect you to give Dawn Fraser a run for her money, or beat whoever's the latest whiz-kid.

The nationals in February — they'll expect you to break a record or two, repeat your Rome times, draw the crowds. (I've been to Tauranga several times — it's a nice place, but that's all.)

Two summer seasons, two winters of fiery eyes, all the agony again for the Commonwealth Games in Perth. Not as an underdog but as top dog. A gold prospect.

Two *more* summer seasons and winters of pain until Tokyo '64? Can you do varsity and train, Miss Archer, for four years? Can your family afford you not to have to work too? Is getting back to Europe a totally impossible dream?

And what about this American scholarship, wonderful and scary, which would put paid to school and varsity and take me away from home for four years and turn me into an American; think of those people who come home talking pure Yankee from *one* year as American Field Service scholars, what the hell did I do about that?

I was waking before dawn each morning, shall I, shan't I, perhaps ... How do people make the really *really* big decisions? Formal meetings with Mum and Dad? Put the motion, all those in favour say Aye, to the contrary No. The Ayes have it, Alex, you have just decided to leave school/return to school, continue swimming/retire from swimming. Or do decisions just somehow happen, sneak up on you, one day it all becomes clear.

For the first time in my life, nothing ahead was clear, no obvious path to follow. Up till now it'd been school, training, aiming for Rome. Now I'd done Rome, and I'd left part of me there, what next?

Late one night, the day I got my Rome pictures back from the chemist, I wrote to Tom, an aerogram, chatty, non-committal and my heart breaking into a million pieces. I wished him luck for his audition in November, said that though I still wished she'd kept her sticky beak out of it, I did understand about Miss Macrae. I found myself writing, she was putting on a G.B. Shaw evening in December. I was playing Joan in three scenes from *Saint Joan*. Miss Macrae had played her once, in London, in the West End, so she knew it backwards. I thought as I wrote, I should thank him for the bracelet. (Perhaps I should offer to return it). Thank you very much for the bracelet, a lovely memento of Rome; stiff as a kid writing a bread-and-butter letter. Ciao, Alex.

I thought, as I looked at the slides through my hand-viewer yet again and wrote the address, Tomas B. Alexander, c/- Bargellini, Via Domm. Scarlatti, Milano — that's probably the end of it. (Scarlatti — 'born Naples

1685, musical director of St Peter's for a while, wrote marvellous piano sonatas, fresh quirky harmonies, have you played any? If not, you *must*.') I wasn't playing the piano at all these days; to touch the keys hurt. Funny, it really hadn't struck me until now, until I wrote it on the outside of the aerogram, about his surname.

What I didn't say in my letter was that, also that day, I'd learned more in ten minutes with Miss Macrae about Tom Alexander's past than I'd learned from him during the whole week in Rome. She chose a wet lunchtime to buttonhole me in the hall. 'A word, Alex?'

She led me off to a little alcove beside the stage, away from the general noise of gossiping schoolgirls. Her back view was even plainer than her front: brogues, straight-skirt suit with a kick-pleat over a broad backside, thick but grey hair I swear she cuts herself with garden shears and a pudding basin.

'I haven't really congratulated you properly on your great success in Rome. I hear you're settling back very well to work. I assume you'll appear in my classroom this week?'

'Yes, well it was kind of Miss Gillies to tell me so soon I had to sit UE,' I said acidly. 'She could have given me a couple of days grace, before dropping me in it.'

Her gesture indicated that she thought Miss Gillies had bungled. 'If I'd had any say in the matter . . . but you've no worries there, really. Nothing a couple of months of solid work won't fix. Tell me, did you get to any opera in Rome?'

'*Aida*, at the Terme di Caracalla.'

'And? Was it wonderful?'

'Great.' I wasn't about to tell her who with. She was looking at me with narrowed eyes.

'You didn't happen to bump into a young man called Tom Alexander, did you? A music student in Milan?'

'Oh yes, I forgot. I was going to tell you. He took me sightseeing a couple of times. St. Peter's, the Vatican. He told me you'd written. I wasn't quite sure of the connection.'

'His mother and I were at drama school together. I caught up with him two or three years ago, when I went to an outdoor production of *Julius Caesar* at the university. He was quite the best Cassius I've ever seen, John Gielgud aside. Charming, manipulative, a viper, poisonous as a snake. With his mother's name, the same unusual colouring, I knew it had to be Dorothy's son. Then I heard he'd gone to Milan for singing tuition. As well as being a fine actor, he's thought to have huge talent as a singer, for a career in opera. He's won several major aria contests in Auckland, Christchurch, I think one in Australia.'

'I didn't go for him much. He seemed rather pleased with himself.'

'His mother was known as the wild colonial kid, the mad New Zealander, an outstanding student until she tragically stupidly got herself pregnant. She died in childbirth, having Tom — I suppose it was '38, the year I finished. The father was killed early in the war, in France. A Pom.'

'So where did he grow up?' I asked, despite myself.

'Dorothy's brother in Taihape and his wife made a special trip to England just before the war started, to collect the child and take him back to New Zealand. The real father was only too pleased to be shot of him. I gather he grew up on the farm near Taihape, as their adopted son. They had two other children, both girls. Tom was, indeed still is the heir apparent to the farm, but all he's ever wanted to do is sing. I believe he cut adrift from his family, put himself through varsity — music and English. If the uncle is your typical dyed-in-the-wool farmer, he's just waiting for the prodigal son to fall by the wayside and crawl back into gumboots.'

Not, she added, that Tom himself told her all of this the night she met him. 'One of his former teachers gave me his address in Milan. Went on at some length, spoke highly of his talent and drive. Very ambitious.'

That figured. The dedication, the reluctance to talk about home, at least this much added up. I would still liked to have found this out for myself, if at all.

'I hope you didn't mind my writing to him?' said Miss Macrae, I think a touch irritated by my lack of response. 'He seemed a personable young man. I daresay his Italian is pretty fluent by now.'

'It is.' The bell for end-of-lunch rang through the hall.

'We should really have been talking about Joan, Alex. Now, I've decided, we'll do only the trial scene. Better to do one scene well than three badly. Rehearsals in your absence have lacked enthusiasm. I don't suppose you've even opened the book for six weeks.'

She might have told me, staring blankly at the lines of the Court scene above the Bay of Bengal. 'I sort of know it.'

'We've got ten weeks, but exams will intrude. When are you back at training?'

'Week after next.'

'What's in store this season? Any overseas trips?'

'Nothing definite.'

'I do hope that your Upper Sixth Form year will be happier, Alex.' She looked frustrated. 'We could choose a full-length play that will suit you. Give it some thought. A co-production with one of the boys' schools. I'd like to have a crack at a Shakespeare: *As You Like It*? *Twelfth Night*?'

With hairy-legged schoolboys in short pants, all pimples and half-broken voices! Don't bank on me being around, Miss Macrae.

Despite going studious and domestic, everywhere I turned, willy-nilly, I was reminded of the man.

Latin lessons took on a whole new meaning. I heard 'Celeste Aida' sung (marvellously) by Nicolai Gedda on the radio. I heard a local singer do (not very well) some Schubert lieder on 1YC and knew exactly where I'd heard them much better before. I saw a Pekinese puppy walking down the road, and thought of the moth-eaten Turandot on my lap.

I got my Rome slides back. Before I showed them to the family, I carefully removed nine incriminating shots, mostly of us together taken by passers-by — sitting like bookends on the grass in the catacombs gardens, being statues among the ruins at the Terme di Caracalla, exhausted beside a pillar in St Peter's Square, posing for *Vogue* by a rotunda in the Borghese gardens, being gullible tourists outside the Pantheon and bored Romans sipping wine in an off-beat trattoria with loaded plates of antipasto. These were all the Australian Tom, with the bush hat, jeans, boots, loud shirts, and bushy moustache. There were two I'd taken: Tom striking a heroic operatic pose in front of the pillars of the Teatro dell' Opera in the Via del Viminale, singing 'a little something from *Figaro*' as he did, to the amusement of even Rome's passers-by; and one close-up of him, as himself, when I'd impulsively snapped him across the table on our last expensive lunch together, just after we'd exchanged addresses. The face was slightly out of focus, but just looking at it, the smile, the eyes, made my insides melt. The colours of all the slides were strong and clear, and brought back heat, smells, noise, my days of wine and roses.

I was haunted. I saw a harp in a music shop window; that golden living room. We had a torrential spring storm one night; I was back on a certain Vespa. I walked out in the garden in my pyjamas and allowed the thunder to scare me as it scared the ancient Romans, and got soaked to the skin.

Someone asked what a philistine was in class, and I thought of the airport — 'Philistines to a man,' he'd said bitterly, describing the New Zealand he hated and had left behind. 'A person who is hostile or indifferent to culture, or one whose interests or tastes are commonplace or material,' said the Oxford dictionary. We studied Mozart in music class; I saw the pencil-marked score of *Figaro* on the baby grand and heard Don Giovanni's serenade. I saw frequent newspaper reports of Snell and Halberg's doings, which reminded me of the day we'd been at the stadium and seen them both win gold medals and I'd bawled like a baby. I saw reports of other older New Zealand opera singers winning big roles overseas, doing well. How many years would he take? Not if, but when. I saw reviews of the latest films: *Ben Hur* with a chariot race to end all chariot races, and *La Dolce Vita*, people upset by Anita Ekberg in wet, sticking clothes wading sexily in the Trevi Fountain. We'd sat on the rim and paddled, and splashed each other, and thrown in our coins — also at 1 a.m., just the two of us.

Which one will the fountain bless . . . which one will the fountain bless . . .

I was haunted by Rome. I remembered Tom telling me sharply not to make comparisons, but how can you not? Our buildings looked so grey and heavy, or just jerry-built, cheap wood, temporary. The streets looked dull, cold, empty; the clothes shabby and creased and drab. I tried to imagine Auckland with sidewalk cafés, pigeons walking around the squares, open-air fruit markets under orange canopies, water rushing over fountains, millions of trees, pavement artists like the ones I saw painting perfect copies of 'God Creating Adam', lots of people enjoying themselves. I couldn't. It was all too prim and neat. People got paranoid about parked cars here, but in Rome they parked anywhere they pleased, up on pavements and across corners, and people just shrugged their shoulders and laughed. We went to watch rugby and turned off the lights, went to the flicks or to sleep at weekends; they ate outside and floodlit their ruins and used them for opera.

My cousin Virginia and Auntie Pat turned up as promised from Hamilton, and slept a night in Debbie's room. Three months ago Ginnie got married in a cathedral. Now she was five months preggers, huge and miserable. After the various disasters of her wedding, everyone tried hard to be pleasant, including me who'd actually behaved rather badly. The next morning Auntie Pat took Ginnie to the hospital for tests. When they came back in the afternoon, Mum and Auntie Pat talked over cups of tea, but I found myself looking at pale blotchy Ginnie and wondering about girls dying in childbirth. Surely these days, in the twentieth century, people didn't die.

Tom's mother had.

Ginnie wandered out to my bedroom, and seemed inclined to talk. She told me she was coming up to Auckland to have the baby, to a private hospital and a specialist. She was absolutely terrified. She'd felt lousy and sick from the start. Darling Merv had refused to go with her to classes to learn how to breathe. She was alone all day and most nights because he'd started playing bridge *and* gone back to his ballroom dancing with a new partner, joking that there was no use dancing with someone he couldn't get his arms around.

And, she said bitterly, he'd not turned out quite the Romeo she'd expected. This little Hitler refused to eat rabbit food (meaning salads), insisted she make a pudding *every* night, and told her off for not ironing his shirts well enough. Her mother didn't know but he'd thumped her a few times, she said airily, usually over the head, around the shoulders, but once or twice hard into her belly.

'You've got to tell her,' I said, appalled at what she was telling me, never an intimate cousin. 'Tell *someone*.'

'I'm telling you,' she shrugged, 'but you're not on pain of death to tell your parents. I'm sort of stuck, you see, there's no point, really.'

I said I wouldn't stay two minutes in a house with a man who hit me. 'It's not as simple as that,' she said sadly. His parents had helped them buy the house, had set up a trust for the baby, oh there were all sorts of ramifications. 'When the baby comes, it'll be different.'

'It'll be worse,' I said. I've seen heroines in headscarves in Westerns with the same pathetic resigned expression. And dogs.

I couldn't believe it was happening here in my bedroom. 'Promise you won't tell your parents,' she said, scared. '*Promise*, Alex!' I promised, hugging her tight, feeling her fat tum up against mine, reserving to myself the right to tell if I heard he'd ever touched her again. She'd never been anywhere, had no qualifications, no say in anything. She was eighteen. When I'm a lawyer I'll know all about the rights of babies and women, I'll change them so they *have* some rights. She made me put my hand on her tum and feel it kicking; I looked at her sad smile and thought, you look sick, poisoned, awful, you might *die*! Inside her, another baby without a mother and a pathetic worse than useless father. She was an only child. Who'd adopt this one?

They left for Hamilton without mentioning the Olympics; no, I lie, once when they first arrived when they asked to see my medal. After what I was hearing about the real world these days, of abandoned mothers and family feuds and formerly-slightly-boring Maggie going nursing next year, my little medal was rather a trivial matter, a nine day wonder. If only the next Olympics weren't four years away.

Maybe poor, beaten, hang-dog Ginnie had something to do with my peculiar mixed-up feelings about Joan.

At least the first rehearsal wasn't in the school hall, cold turkey straight onto the stage. Now that 'our Joan' was back, said Miss Macrae, today we'd just read it through in class. Those who thought they knew their lines could put aside their books and see how they went.

It went, down the plughole. We made the trial scene as dull as ditchwater. It stopped and started, while people forgot their cues and hummed and ha-ed and said, giggling, 'Miss Macrae, I know this bit, I really *do*,' when it was perfectly obvious they didn't. I thought, I don't want to be in a disaster. I couldn't wait for the bell to ring.

'Are you sure you want to do this, Alex?' said Miss Macrae, planting her backside on a desk as the others cleared out for lunch. I looked at her, thinking of exams, the whole muddle of my life between now and Christmas. 'Please give me an answer. Shall I ask Nancy instead? It's not too late.'

'I know more of my lines than most of them.'

'Maybe, but you weren't enjoying it.'

'How can you enjoy being tortured . . .'

'Joan was never tortured,' she said swiftly. 'Beaten up in prison, possibly raped, but never officially tortured. History aside, I'm talking about the challenge of getting inside Shaw's Joan, communicating her genius to an audience. I'm asking again, and finally, are you sure you want to take her on?'

Exams, training, helping Mum, the build-up to Australia, to the nationals. Everything alone. Once again, biting off more than I could chew?

'Alex, you're rather surly these days. You need this distraction, this challenge. What do you really know about her? Have you read anything apart from the play and the preface? No?'

I shook my head, tired. Here goes. The woman played Joan in London once, and she was a maniac for research. Even when we did the *Wizard of Oz* last year, she'd made us all read the book and had a special screening of the film in the school hall. Not that it did me any good. I still blushed down to my feet when I thought about the *Wizard of Oz*.

'You can find out the accepted biographical details, Domrémy, Orléans, Rheims, the campaigns and the rest for yourself. She was virgin, but also, she never menstruated. That could have been stress, or because she was known to eat extremely sparingly. She was said to be strong, but was probably thin, by our standards.'

'She fought with a sword.'

'A wiry type, then? They knew she was virgin because she was examined, several times.'

Who by?'

'Powerful women of the King's Court. Can you imagine that — spreading your legs to the eyes of curious strangers? Her virginity was crucial, because of the prophecy that a virgin would come from the forests of Lorraine and save France. There's some evidence that about a week before she died she was raped in prison by an English lord. Of course, by then it was really all over. Shaw talks monumental nonsense in the Preface when he maintains she had a comparatively fair hearing. By the final days of the trial, she'd been in a civil prison for six months, guarded by English soldiers who were no doubt brutal. She should have been in a church prison, with women. In the last month, May, she was worn down enough to sign a recantation and to agree to wear women's clothes. Once reduced to the female state, she was probably raped. Three or four days later she put on the male clothes her gaolers obligingly provided — I always found that most sinister — and died for it.'

'Why died though, just for wearing trousers?' I could see her looking at her watch and reluctantly deciding here endeth the lesson. I knew she could go on for hours. She looked at me, as they say, quizzically. 'Ah. Find it myself.'

'Exactly. Get yourself to a library. Read the transcripts of her trial and Jean Anouilh's play, *The Lark* — not as great as Shaw's, but worthwhile. Anything else you can find. You still want to do it?'

I'm a sucker for history made as interesting as this. She knew the answer.

The days drag past. Joan rehearsals are in school time, otherwise I rush from class to class to housework to swot to writing thank-you letters — how am I going to fit three hours training into this? My three weeks' holiday is nearly up. Alex, tell me, what am you training for, exactly?

Every day I hurtle out of school on the dot, pedal alone along the broad streets, and stroll nonchalantly, but with beating heart, into the kitchen. 'You're home early,' says Mum automatically. For years I've had rehearsals, hockey practice, extra lessons of one sort or another; she's not used to me turning up at 3.42 p.m.

'How's Gran? Any mail?' I ask extra nonchalantly. Gran's always fine, beginning to get up in the afternoons now, potter round the kitchen. There's always mail for me, fan mail from kids, requests for this and that because I'm supposed to be a celebrity. I flip through the pile, already sick with disappointment.

There's never the one letter I want.

House of dreams

Milan
October 13, 1960

Dear Alex,

Did I ever tell you I'm rather partial to thirteenths? We missed September 13 — you'd already gone to Naples. A month on, I wonder how you're coping with the anticlimax, personally? professionally? (I mean your swimming.) The growing chances of Jack Kennedy for US president next month leaves me with a modicum of hope for the world. You too?

My audition — the date is yet to be finalized, but it looks like this side of Christmas. We've settled on a programme. Two of the pieces I sang that stormy night in Rome — from *Don Giovanni* and *La Traviata*. I'm also trying, ambitiously, one of the bigger arias, from *Trovatore*, which might prove to be a mistake. My teacher is not entirely convinced it's right for me, but I persuaded him that I must take a risk. He's been unwell recently, and seemed unwilling to argue. The indecision re the date is unsettling, but must be expected; after all, I am one baritone among many, a young and foreign one at that. In Italy we are two a penny. Tenors are rarer.

The season at La Scala starts early December. *Tosca*, *Trovatore*, *Così Fan Tutte* are among the offerings. I'll be up in the top balcony, the sixth tier, as I was regularly last winter, with the binoculars given me for peering at sheep. Unimpressive from the street outside, the house inside is majestic, literally breathtaking, though I'd always imagined the auditorium to be deeper. Yet it seats 3000. It was faithfully rebuilt after extensive damage during the war. Audiences here are knowledgeable and tough. I was quite astonished, the first time, to hear the low murmur of approval that accompanies a favoured singer, where utter silence indicates approval elsewhere. In the balconies are the feared loggionisti, the claques whose power to make or break a singer is much feared by the management. I've only once heard them in full voice of boos, hisses, and whistles against a singer. It was a chilling experience for me and undoubtedly devastating for the hapless soprano. In New Zealand audiences would politely, briefly applaud, then drive home in their English cars for a nice cup of tea. Perhaps New Zealand audiences don't know a poor performance when they hear one?

You mentioned you're being required to sit UE — my condolences and good luck. You'll be in the throes the next three or four weeks. Isn't it hard to be swotting with spring beckoning through the winter? Here winter approaches, time to become moderately neurotic about coughs and colds. I doubt I'll get any skiing in the Dolomites this season, for simple reasons of finance (the lack of).

And what about *Saint Joan*? I tracked down a copy in an English-language bookshop. It's a wonderful play, a marvellous part for you, tailor-made. You say our mutual friend Marcia Macrae once played it in London? I find that intriguing — if she was good enough for Joan, why did she not go on to the grander classical roles — Shakespeare, Ibsen, Oscar Wilde, Chekhov et al. Yet she teaches at a girls' school in distant New Zealand?

You may laugh, but I'm about to exercise my constitutional rights and send off a postal vote for the forthcoming NZ elections. Surprising for a disaffected expatriate? Well, you reminded me that there are yet people of courage and talent among our generation, not totally lost among the philistines and sheep. I'm voting Labour, partly because I'm a natural socialist and became more so at varsity (despite my upbringing or perhaps because of it); and partly because my hidebound adopted family belongs very publicly to the local National Party Rump dominated by farmers and stock agents.

By the way, haven't you had a birthday recently? I should very much like to have seen you as Joan. You'll bring a great freshness and honesty to the role.

Ciao,

Tom

P.S. I've just realized. I've mentioned swimming but once, and you not at all in your letter! I assume you are continuing this season?! Have you decided about America? T.

Sour sixteen

Knock knock, who's there? Dad. Dad who? The overworked Dad who takes you to training, remember . . .? Oh, gawd. My holiday was over and 5 a.m. Monday October 10 was upon me.

'Can I drive?' I asked, lurching out to the garage. 'There's absolutely no one around I can hit.'

'It's a while since you had a lesson.'

'I'm sixteen in two weeks, *please* Dad. When I've got my licence, you won't have to drive me around.'

'But I like getting up at sparrow. I like my early swim with you. Okay, but I'll back her out into the street.'

I snorted. No one likes getting up at 5 a.m. I stood shivering under the lamplight at the front gate and watched the red tail-lights come down the drive. I'd forgotten how damp and raw the air was before dawn. There's no pink through to scarlet magic in the dawn here, at least not in these flat, boring streets. No windswept moon either.

I was rusty, to put it kindly. I stalled, and bounced and stalled again and graunched the gears and finally got going at 20 m.p.h. through deserted Newmarket, down Parnell Rise and through the empty downtown area to my absolutely least favourite indoor pool, where the water was cloudy salt, heated, chlorinated, and lethal. If I thought that after Rome I could just slip incognito back to training, I hadn't thought hard enough.

'Sorry we're late. I drove,' I said to Mr Jack waiting on a bench with his usual *Herald*, thermos of tea, stopwatch, and raincoat, watching the ten others already in the pool. With him was a press photographer getting flash gear out of a black camera bag. I even remembered his name: Graham Wills, responsible for an insulting front-page picture of Alex Archer hugging arch-rival Maggie Benton like a gorilla the day after we were both finally selected for Rome. May 25, engraved on my brain. He'd been lying in wait at the pool just as he was now.

'I remember you, Mr Wills,' I said as he got up and offered a pudgy hand which I ignored. 'You did the dirty on me. How did you know I'd be here today?'

'A little bird,' he said frostily. Mr Jack's face told me it was not him. 'I've been asked to get a poolside shot. I didn't ask for this job.'

'I wish people would mind their own beeswax. I'm already late,' I said peeling off my track suit. 'How much, maestro?'

'Half-mile straight,' said Mr Jack. 'Twice. Then we'll see how you're feeling.'

'Hang on a mo',' said Mr Wills, fiddling with the connections on his flash equipment. They all looked the same, these blokes, in Italy or here: ferrety seen-it-all-before eyes, baldish, untidily dressed in raincoats. 'I want a poolside shot of you diving in for the start of the new season.'

'Last time you wanted Maggie and me to pose like pin-up girls. It was embarrassing, to say the least.'

'And if I remember right, we actually used one which was unposed and spontaneous, but in your eyes unflattering. You can't have it both ways, Alex.'

'Alright,' I said, conceding, giving him a small grin to show that I was human. 'I'll buy that. But honestly, whoever saw any female in real life actually standing like Marilyn Monroe.' I cocked a knee and bent a hip and put one arm in the air and pouted. The view-finder went up to his eye and a flash went off. Dad, Mr Jack and Graham Wills all burst out laughing. 'Not fair!'

'You'll sue me?' he chuckled. 'Let's see, who can I sell it to? Next week's *Truth*! The *Daily Express*!'

'You wouldn't dare.' But he made sure of that, himself, rather drastically. He took a perfectly normal shot of me about to dive in, and another in mid-air, and it seemed to me I'd made my point about the cheesecake, but he rang again after school, sounding gloomy. After he left the pool, he went straight out on the pilot boat to meet a P and O cruise ship coming in to the harbour, but getting up the ladder dropped his whole camera bag in the drink, including the film of me and the candid shot he could have sold to the *Daily Express* for hundreds of pounds. I *think* he was joking. It was probably out of focus and unusable anyway. Would I mind, he said, if he came again with some borrowed gear. His illustrations editor had nearly fired him on the spot for messing up two assignments, not to mention a large insurance claim. Tomorrow morning, same effing awful time, and he had to take his hat off to me: how ever did I do it seven days a week?

Tomorrow morning was when my eyes began to react badly to the chlorine and hurt like hell, my arms to feel like lead, and — had I but known — the whole season began to go sour.

Graham Wills was late, so that by the time he was aiming his borrowed camera at me doing a racing dive, all the early-bird public swimmers had arrived and there was quite an audience of gawking males. Then, leaving the pool, I saw a large notice stuck to the window, handwritten black capitals stating that Olympic bronze medal winner Alex Archer was swimming in the first carnival at this pool at 7.30 p.m. tomorrow night, Wednesday October 12.

'No she's not,' I said to Dad. 'Who put my entry in?'

'Don't look at me, Alex,' said Mr Jack. 'Some one compiling the programme and suffering from wishful thinking. Ignore it.'

Easier said than done. When I got home I found the morning paper also announcing to the world: 'FIRST OUTING FOR OLYMPIC SWIM STAR'. Some junior hack, obviously not Grant Davies, and some clueless official, not bothering to check.

Then a few phone calls started flying around, between me and Mr Jack and Mr Upjohn and a chap who Mr Jack said was the new official big cheese, someone called Maurice D. Smythe. Grant Davies got in on the act. The end result was a piece the next day saying that Alex Archer was unavailable for any club meetings before December, because she'd been having a break from training and had UE exams to sit.

Not a tiny piece, mind, but a great feature at the top of the sports page, with a grinning photograph: 'BRONZE GIRL NOT AVAILABLE. No Appearances for Olympic Medallist Yet.' I was angry that Grant had felt obliged to include Mr Smythe sounding off: 'Club organizers hoping for good early season crowds will be most disappointed by her decision. After her great success in Rome, Miss Archer represents a considerable draw-card. It is indeed a great pity that her Auckland public has to wait so long to see the form which earned her an Olympic medal.'

My Auckland public! That's just bullshit, I haven't got an 'Auckland public!' But even when the outdoor pool opened and I was able to bike there at 5 a.m. and save Dad having a heart attack every time I got behind the wheel of the car — even then I'd not settled down to any sort of pleasure in my training. The lengths seemed longer, the half-mile straights more tedious, the spring winds which ripped up the pool icier on wet skin, the eyes of spectators more critical. I found out early in the piece that for some stupid reason the boys were reluctant to do time trials with me. So I told Mr Jack I'd rather swim by myself and went back to training alone.

Ploughing up and down in the half-light, sometimes in the rain, with the tips of my fingers going numb, I heard voices: is this really what you want to be doing for the next four years, either here, or in California? Basically, Alex, are you scared of going to Aussie in January to swim against Dawn Fraser and/or all those Aussie brats who yap at her heels all the time and who will bite you off at the knees?

If I stay here, have I got four summers of this? Overhearing snide comments that Alex is a stuck-up bitch, thinks she's Christmas, too grand now to swim in the club meetings, hasn't got time to have an ice-block or a toasted sandwich after training and chat to her old mates; you'd have thought wearing a New Zealand blazer, winning a medal in Rome might have rubbed the raw edges off her. True, I wasn't hanging around these days between training and wherever else I was going, home or school, but changing rooms are cavernous spaces and voices carry.

I haven't changed, I wanted to yell. I'm me, an oversized and lovesick schoolgirl in a shabby, short, gym-tunic, not quite sixteen, from a very ordinary house needing a paint in Epsom, with a sick Gran, and chooks to feed, sitting exams like anyone else, wanting to leave school, hating training. Back in jeans and sandshoes all the time because basically I hate dresses and slippy sandals, even if some silly people think I should have picked up some fashion tips in Rome. I'm just a swimmer, not a film star.

Tom Alexander — you're a performer, Alex, only as good as your last appearance. And, Alex, you have changed. I changed you.

My birthday, squeezed in between swot and training, was a low-key affair. I thought of asking Julia but her swot had turned her into the most boring person on earth, and I didn't think the suggestion of Keith would go down very well with Mum and Dad. Anyway he was swotting too, and he wasn't really all that special, not *special* special.

Gran made her first appearance at the dinner table, in proper clothes and her old string of pearls, so it was her party too. 'Sweet sixteen, never been kissed!' she cried as they sang happy birthday and I blew out in one puff the sixteen white candles on Mum's never-fail iced fruitcake.

The laughter round the table had a mocking edge to it. I thought of exactly the same scene last year. We had the white Irish linen best tablecloth and two whole chickens roasted with mushroom stuffing and bacon strips, early season strawberries and whipped cream, and Andy very sheepish as I opened the little red box with the gold chain and single tear-drop pearl inside.

I had got up and kissed him openly, even in front of the kids, who clapped and chortled. He'd fastened the chain and pearl around my neck. Now it lay at the bottom of the Tiber, and Andy's ashes in a grave somewhere. I had a bronze medal and a silver charm bracelet in the back of a drawer, and a hopeless yearning for music in my heart.

I suppose birthdays make you dreamy or maudlin, or both. Being let off the dishes, I walked Gran into the living room and fetched her knitting for her. I put the radio on, 1YC, the classical programme: a woman singing, sounded like Mozart. I sat cross-legged on the floor and watched

Gran consult her knitting pattern and count up some stitches and start click-clacking away. This was a jumper for Jamie, cable-stitch, green, for next winter. Gran was the one person in the entire world I could tell, help get rid of the real bursting ache which got worse by the day.

'I met someone in Rome.'

Her smile said, I knew, I've been waiting.

As I told her about Tom, I felt my eyes fill up with water. She listened and she listened. At one point her eyelids drooped, the rhythm of her fingers slowed and I thought, I'm boring her to death. 'Gran, you're tired, I'm sorry . . .' but her eyes flew open, and she protested vehemently that she wasn't at all tired, go on, Alex.

'I've had one letter, but . . . what's the *point*, Gran, if he's in Italy and never coming home. He has no reason to come back, no family ties, hates the place, loathes it. If I go to America . . .'

'You'll meet other young men, equally glamorous.'

'He's not glamorous — well, yes, perhaps, but . . . just wait there.'

'Do I have a choice?' I heard her chuckle as I ran down the other end of the house to my bedroom, put the little box in my jeans pocket, and ran back. Debbie had wandered into the living room in her pyjamas to say goodnight. I took her back to bed and tucked her in and said I'd read a story another time. Gran was still click-clacking her green ball of wool into complicated cables.

'He gave me this.'

She turned the fine silver chain over her gnarled fingers. 'I suppose these charms all mean something.' I nodded. 'Was it a nice letter?'

'Different. Not a soppy love letter, different.'

'You'll meet other young men. You might continue writing to this Tom for years. You *can* do both, you know. Your letters will either become a constant joy in your life, or gradually fade away. Have you written?'

'Once.'

'Did you tell him you loved him?'

'Gran! Of course not!'

'Why not? Don't you?'

'I . . . don't know.'

'Are you afraid it was just the romance of Italy? You've experienced love. You were in love with Andy.'

'It was different.'

'Why? Wasn't he going off to naval college in England for five years?' Yes, I'd told her that once. 'So what's the difference?'

'Just, I'd known Andy since primary school. With Tom, three weeks and I only know what he's told me.'

'And you don't trust him?'

I thought about it, the easy disguises, the accents, the steady gaze, the challenging half-smile, the utterly confident air, the tall stories and those which *might* be true. 'No.'

'I think trust has to be earned. So let him earn it, bit by bit. It might take years. But you can't say he'll never be back. Everything has its proper time, its season.'

The music was Mozart, I was sure.

Gran said, 'Sitting round that table a year ago today, could you have seen Andy dead a month later? Or you winning the bronze medal in Rome? Neither thought would have entered your head.'

We sat for a while and heard the announcer say we'd been listening to Elisabeth Schwarzkopf singing concert arias by Mozart.

'Love is not love which alters when it alteration finds,' she said softly.

'Who said that?'

'Shakespeare, one of the sonnets, in this week's *Woman's Weekly*. You learn lots of wonderful quotes lying in bed doing the crosswords.'

I laughed. 'I've got some pictures of him.'

'Which you took out of your Rome slides.'

'No flies on you, Gran. Yes.'

I ran out to my bedroom again and got my hidden slide box and the little hand-viewer. I could hear from the kitchen that the dishwashing wasn't nearly finished. I shut the door firmly. Gran peered into the viewer against the table lamp beside her chair, while I told her where we were and to imagine him without the false moustache. Sorry the one close-up was out of focus. Finally she said, 'Interesting, very interesting.'

'Is that all?'

'He likes hats. And clothes. Unusual in a man.'

'He's got this amazing, deep bronzy-red hair. Titian. Most people don't believe it's real.'

'I love this one. My little Alex drinking wine!'

'It was called Lacrimae Christi. The tears of Christ.'

'Lacrimae Christi!' She put the viewer down and stared at me over the top of her glasses. 'I'll make you a prediction. He'll be out here within the year. By the end of the summer.'

I could hear Jamie and Robbie arguing in the hall outside. We were about to be interrupted. 'Bet you five shillings he won't.'

'Done!'

'Look, I know you all find me highly embarrassing, but I can't help that,' I said to the stageful of gaping, giggling Sixth Formers during a temporary halt. 'The rest of you will all be in long churchy gowns. I've got to feel different. I just can't rehearse Joan being tried in a *dress*.'

At the second rehearsal in the hall, waiting for the Court at Rouen to get through twelve endless pages of script before I got dragged in, I'd changed into a pair of black ballet tights, an old black T-shirt of Dad's, and tied my girdle around my waist. It felt something like the 'page's black suit' in the stage directions. It felt right. I knew what all the sideways glances meant: Alex over the top, again.

'Don't you lot realize Joan actually died for the right to wear what she pleased, as much as for hearing voices or being a heretic or anything else. She wasn't just playing games, getting a cheap thrill. She was a soldier. She stuck with men's clothes in prison because she knew once she put on a dress, she'd get raped. In the last week of trial she did put on a dress, and she did get beaten up, and was probably raped as well. So she got back into men's clothes and got burnt.'

That wiped the smiles off their faces. Then I looked down into the hall and saw Miss Macrae sitting on the front bench with some strange woman. Both of them were smirking faintly.

'Take that entrance again, Alex, now they've got over the shock of seeing your legs,' boomed Miss Macrae. 'Give her the cue, Ladvenu?'

"Let her be brought in",' said Julia, who was Ladvenu, the only decent one among them. I tried how I thought you'd walk having been raped and with chains around your ankles, and heard a few giggles, which I ignored.

'Settle down girls,' called Miss Macrae sharply. 'Give her a chance.'

I'd read, late at night, five complete books on Joan of Arc, including excerpts from the transcript of the trial. Though I couldn't understand some of the long-winded theological bits, her blunt voice made my hair stand on end. I read that Shaw had telescoped several days' events into the trial scene, for dramatic reasons. I didn't have many moves to remember, just to concentrate on her defiance, her terror of the fire, her final blaze of courage.

'Going well, girls,' said Miss Macrae walking forward when the bell went, just as I was warming up for the final speech before getting hauled off to be burnt. 'Next time we must work on pace. All of you are far too slow on your cues, Alex excepted.'

I'd been conscious all afternoon of the woman sitting next to her. Something about the way she was following the rehearsal (script and all) and was now looking at me, was making me feel nervous. She was an arty sort, in a slinky emerald shirt with lots of crafty, chunky jewellery and a thick, dyed-black, page-boy haircut despite being at least forty. Not someone's Mum, for sure; a teacher, friend of Miss Macrae? Although she looked a bit like a colourful Russian doll, she also reminded me of the strange opera woman in black at that very expensive restaurant on the Pincio hill in Rome. Same type. I had a funny sinking feeling that she was there for a reason, and would be back.

The two letters arrived on the same day, Guy Fawkes night, Saturday, so I managed to be first out to the mailbox and to sneak up the drive and round the back to my room without anyone knowing.

I recognized Tom's handwriting, the Olympic stamps, postmarked Milano, 15 Ottobre. It'd taken ages to get here. The other was from America, San Francisco — also fat, official-looking. I put them side by side on my pillow and thought, funny, the power of just words, paper, what's inside, to make my knees turn to jelly, turn my life upside down; wish things were different, wish I could see some way out of the jungle of decisions I'd got myself into.

The American one wasn't what I expected. It was a thick brochure about a university in California, full of colour pictures of lovely brick buildings among trees, and happy clean-cut students singing in choirs and peering at test-tubes. But I'd read the letter, full of flowery phrases about my enormous potential for the gold in Tokyo, me a great asset to their swim team, their team and their coach one of the best in California, in America; lists of figures (value in $US of the scholarship, which included fee allowances, living allowances, book allowances etc) before I began to realize that it wasn't from the man I'd met in Rome, that quiet man with lovely manners and an Irish name, but from someone else. It was *another* offer.

So now it's not only if I go, but if so, to which? The plot thickens. I stared at the photographs without seeing them, thinking, what's wrong with me? I've got two offers for America and all I'm feeling is bothered and bewildered.

I opened the other letter slowly. So Tom wants to know how I'm coping with the anticlimax, does he? And why Miss Macrae is just a teacher in Auckland, New Zealand, when she once played Joan? And how the hell does he know I'll be any good as Joan, freshness and honesty, what crap. I might be terrible. Tailor-made for me, why do you say that?

And no, I haven't decided about America, Tom. I haven't decided about anything except I really am leaving school and dreading the arguments about it. Exams start in nine days and will occupy me for the next four weeks after that. I'm sitting all the swotty subjects — you either know your set plays, poems, quotes, your thousands of facts, dates, declensions, verb endings, note values, the dates of Mozart and Brahms and the difference between an appoggiatura and an acciaccatura or you don't: English, History, Latin, Music. I'm sitting them all twice. *Twice.*

Nothing about missing me, coming home, nothing corny or romantic or even slightly tantalizing. He's a prig, I decided, going on about his precious La Scala and Jack Kennedy, a ponce, a stuffed shirt even if he is voting Labour. Mum and Dad are voting Labour too, Gran's always voted Labour and I will too when I'm twenty-one, so what's so special about that, even if all the papers reckon *ad nauseam* that National's going to romp home. And yes, Tomas B. Alexander, God's singing gift to women, I am continuing swimming this season and I'm going to the pictures with Keith Jameson next Saturday night to celebrate his finishing exams even though mine start two days later, despite what you or Mum and Dad or anyone thinks.

'Alex, you about?' called Mum outside my closed door. She doesn't barge in like some mothers, I'll give her that. 'Can you hang the clothes out? The basket's on the back steps.' Her voice sounded flat, tired. I shoved the two letters under my mattress. Out of sight, out of mind.

Not true.

It was while Jamie was grizzling on at lunchtime about all his mates having a proper Guy Fawkes party tonight with real rockets and cheerios on toothpicks and stuff except us, that I made the connection. Guy Fawkes = Fire = Joan.

'Sorry, Jamie,' said Dad. 'It's money up in smoke. We've got a couple of packets of Catherine wheels, rockets, emerald fires, Mount Vesuvius, the usual. Some extra sparklers for the youngsters, and that's it.'

'They've got a proper bonfire next door,' Jamie grumbled. 'I seen it.'

'Yes, crazy, and from the size of it they might end up with the fire brigade,' said Mum, plonking a tray full of soup bowls down on the table, vege broth with ham bones again. 'I'm amazed Gracie hasn't put her foot down. And Jamie, you are not to go out and buy yourself extra double happies, do you hear?'

'Mu-um!'

'I don't want those things round here. Gran hates them and so do I and so does next door's dog.'

But it was Jamie who created the diversion that meant the first time I left a pillow in my bed and sneaked out of my room I got away with it. And I didn't quite set myself on fire.

We had our pathetic little crackers even before it got properly dark. The Emerald Fires glowed well, green, and the Mount Vesuvius things burnt crimson — another unwelcome jog to my memory of Naples, Pompeii, a man missing from my life. Debbie and Robbie danced the sparklers around on tippytoes. I went off to my room 'to swot'. Jamie went three houses down the road where he said he'd been invited by a schoolmate. I heard afterwards that he'd turned up with a whole pile of double happies which had paralysed their cocker spaniel into a slavering coma; also several large and expensive rockets which he and his mate had tried to set off. One had gone straight into a hedge and set it well alight before a team of grumpy firemen arrived spraying water everywhere and complaining about damn kids out of control before rushing off to the next fire.

Well, that was Jamie's story. The other father had rung up spitting tacks and Dad had dragged Jamie home and given him a hiding for lying, upsetting the neighbours and spending his pocket money on rubbish. Mum was really upset for all the next day. They hadn't been worrying about me, out in my room swotting. I knew it must have been a bad night for the fire brigades, because for a couple of hours you could hear them, the rockets whooshing up and the stars exploding and the sirens going whoooooooooo all over Auckland.

But it was too good an opportunity to miss. Apart from next door, I didn't know anyone giving a party with a large bonfire, so it was a question of finding one, incognito. During the afternoon I sneaked an old Swanndri out of Dad's cupboard, and a woolly hat out of Jamie's. Those, plus my jeans, sandshoes, a few strokes with Gran's brown eyebrow pencil to give me heavier eyebrows, like when I was a 1930s man-about-town in that revue at school end of last year, and I knew that in the dark I could pass for a boy, someone's mate.

The drive was too risky, so I snuck up the back garden, through the hedge by the compost and down through the next door neighbour's, running bent low like people running round in occupied France in wartime movies — feeling mighty stupid. But free too, walking with big loose strides, slouching a bit to hide what little shape of bosoms I had, swaggering a bit.

It was a majestic, spectacular bonfire I was after, preferably one with a guy getting burnt up. I wanted to see what a really big fire looked like, up close. See what Joan had to face, what utter terror she felt when she first saw the Executioner in the courtroom and heard that they actually had a stake and a huge heap of wood piled up ready for her in the marketplace. She cries out, horrified, realizing for the first time that it could happen: *But you are not going to burn me now?*

I found a bonfire a block away, a big party in a back garden with lots of cars in the street, people in the driveway, huge rockets and Catherine wheels flaring off behind the house at regular intervals. This was obviously the biggest party around, but very risk territory. As I stood hesitating across the road under a bare plane-tree and watched the people still arriving at the gate, I realized this was Sylvia's house, Sylvia from my class. She had lots of brothers, younger and older than her. She was peroxide blonde, heavily freckled, wore her gym tunic too short and (out of school) tarty size 10 clothes, and was known to be fast with boys.

Up the drive was easy, no one looked twice. There must have been at least eighty people standing around: the dads, and behind their backs, boys setting light to hundreds of pounds worth of fireworks stacked deep in three open suitcases. Rockets went off from a row of empty bottles, and huge Catherine wheels spun around, pinned to a special frame. Boys Jamie's age threw double happies under each other's feet and jumped up and down and yowled with glee. Everyone was drinking beer, straight from the bottle. A barbecue was alight in a far corner, with about nine hundred sausages on it.

I got near the fire. It had been piled about fifteen feet high, but the flames were leaping up to twice that. Luckily it was a very big back garden. A guy was burning nicely — enough of a human shape to make my blood run cold. The branches and twigs crackled and hissed and sizzled. A corpse is mostly water, so we're told, but the flesh and bones and liver and kidneys would crackle and hiss and sizzle, like meat. How long would it take, when the flames caught the hem of her robe, her hair? Five seconds, ten? Two hideous minutes? She would turn her head away from the approaching heat, shut her eyes, strain backwards against the ropes tying her hands and feet, scream in agony. I got as near to the fire as I dared — any closer and I'd be singeing my eyelashes. The heat on my face was almost unbearable, even from several feet away. I thought of the blisters on roast pork crackling.

'Get back, you bloody idiot!' I couldn't see which dad had yelled at me in that nice way males talk to each other, but caught a glimpse of Sylvia on the other side of the circle of red light before I casually picked up a stray log and threw it into the fire. If I had any sense I'd have slunk back satisfied into the crowd and left there and then, but I didn't. The fire was warming and hypnotic and I'd never seen so many fireworks going off above me and around me.

'Don't take any notice of my Dad. He's half-cut. Have we met? My name's Sylvia.'

Dressed to kill in slinky black like Brigitte Bardot, Sylvia beside me in the firelight, panda black-rimmed eyes signalling come hither, making a pass!

'I'm Alec,' I mumbled in my deepest voice, slouching like every gawky youth I ever saw and wondering how skilful I'd been with the eyebrow pencil. Surely she'd recognize me. I turned away from the fire so my face was in shadow. 'Friend of your brother.'

'Which one? Dan or Bill?'

'Bill, really. Um, from school.' Frantically, I tried to remember if Bill was the one at high school or some sort of apprentice, plumbing or something. I must have picked the right one.

'He never told me about a friend called Alec.'

'We just came. To Auckland. He tells ya about all his friends?'

'Usually,' she said, fluttering her false eyelashes cutely, so that I nearly choked. 'I have lots of friends.' I thought: quiet, freckled little Sylvia in class, an absolute mouse. You couldn't see the freckles on the snub Doris Day nose for pancake make-up. Me slouching in a shabby old Swanndri and woolly hat — she obviously wasn't too fussy, as long as it was over fifteen and in trousers. I thought, frantically, what would a gawky lad do now?

'Ya like a drink?'

She said promptly, 'Pimms, a good slug with ice and make sure they put a cherry in it, thanks Alec.' Slugs of Pimms and playing a pint-sized Bardot, in her own house? She'd certainly made free with the cotton-wool inside her bra, and her cinch belt was the widest sort they made and at least two sizes too small.

If I thought I could slink away out of the glare of the fire and out of trouble, my mousy classmate had other ideas. She minced alongside me over the grass to the big trestle table loaded with drink and glasses. I grabbed a bottle of beer as boys do when it's there for the asking and took a long swig and muttered to the barman 'Triple Pimms, ice and don't forget the cherry, mate' and thought what the *hell* do I do now? At this rate she'd soon have me pinned up against a dark hedge! Do boys really like kissing girls with all that stuff on their faces?

'What do you do, Alec?' she said, daintily biting into her cherry, standing too close for comfort.

'Apprentice.'

'What as?'

'Butcher.' I saw the disappointment in her eyes. What a snob. 'I'm teasing, sweetie-pie. Medical student, second year Otago. Just up here for the weekend, having a break from swot. I'm going to be a brain surgeon.' Tom, you'd have been proud of me.

'Wow,' she said, now impressed. This girl would believe anything.

'You still at school?' I said.

'Left last year.' A liar too. 'I'm just finishing business college. I've already got a PA job lined up.'

'What's a PA?'

'Personal assistant. My boss sells cars.'

'A secretary.'

'Better than that. A *personal* assistant. You have more responsibility. You look after your boss.'

I bet. I realized that I was very subtly being backed into a dark corner against the house behind an oleander bush. I was pushing my luck. All I had to do was run off into the night. She'd never catch me in those shoes.

The fire saved my bacon. Some real maniac came staggering up the drive yelling that the fire needed some beefing up, and before anyone could stop him, threw on half a can of petrol. The whole thing virtually exploded. While people screamed and shouted and swore horribly, fiery twigs and branches rained down into the whole back garden, onto the roof of the house, the garage, the sausages, the drinks table, over the shrubs and flower beds, over everyone. A red branch dropped off the roof within a foot of where we were standing and set the oleander bush alight.

In the confusion, Sylvia paralysed with fright, I put out the oleander bush with my almost-full bottle of beer, told her roughly to go ring the fire brigade pronto if no one else had, and left. I'd played with fire long enough.

Monday morning Sylvia sat primly mouse-like in English class, freckles and bosom restored to normal. I never take any notice of babble about boys in the cloakrooms, but that day I did when I heard the name Alec. She'd met this gorgeous boy Saturday night, she was telling another tarty type pulling on bloomers for Phys Ed. A bit roughly dressed, but a medical student, the sensitive type, quite tall, with this rather soft voice and a gorgeous way of looking at you, sort of shy, under his eyelashes, a change from guys leering and slobbering. But while the fire brigade was putting out the fire and when all the panic was over she'd looked everywhere, but he just vanished. Bill didn't know of any new friends called Alec, any medical students at all, why the hell should he, probably a bloody gatecrasher. She was livid about the guy with his petrol can, because she'd been winding this Alec in beautifully. The thought of exploring inside that particular mouth with her tongue made her go trembly all over, you know Gayleen, all shivery even now. A pretty mouth too, for a boy.

Ye gods! I listened, bent double over my gym shoes, half laughing, half totally put off; also pleased I'd been so convincing. But she'd been playing a part too, dressed to kill and about to leave business college and become a personal assistant to some car salesman! And what about the parts we were both playing at school right now — her so quiet and demure, teacher's darling pet, me the cheerful popular prefect everyone thought loved school, like the tall 'popular' girls in those revolting romanticized boarding-school stories; who was coming back for another year; who was supposed to have a good chance of being Head Prefect.

Perhaps, I thought, as I (carefully) watched her comb her hair and check her shiny little nose for blackheads among the freckles, perhaps people play lots of parts, all the time. Not just Tom, or me. The trick is to know which mask, and when, and why.

Or no mask? I wore no mask at all with Keith the following Saturday night, and because I can't escape being recognized, look where it got me!

According to Permission from Mum, it was supposed to be just to see *Ben Hur*, which had just started at the Civic in town. Same place, funnily enough, where we'd gone, me also in jeans and a Swanndri (borrowed because my own clothes were wet, not dressing up) to see *South Pacific* a few months back, before Rome. This time I settled for a plain blue shirtwaister dress, an old standby, and flat shoes and a cardigan, looking not a day older than fourteen.

Because the film was all about ancient Rome and reminded me of lying in the long grass at the Forum and walking along the Appian Way, I let Keith hold my hand during the whole three and a half hours. During the amazing chariot race, our grip became very tight. He pressed a knee up close and later a thigh. In the dark around us couples clung together and occasionally kissed. Well, you didn't go to the Saturday night flicks just to see the picture. And when he tried a kiss towards the end, I didn't stop him.

Well, why not? That *South Pacific* weekend, I'd horribly embarrassed him and myself in a forbidden public bar, and we'd both nearly drowned going for a mid-winter sail the next day. We'd capsized the dinghy and both got hypothermia and had to be rescued by a fishing boat. Dad tore a strip off him, and Mr Jack wasn't too impressed with me. Keith had kissed me that day, once, hard and salty, in the water, a kiss of thanks that I'd popped up beside the boat and not left him on a manslaughter charge. He still had the hots for me. I didn't have to be a genius to see that. I supposed — apathetically, worn down by the effort of trying not to remember modern Rome from the ancient version I was seeing on the Cinemascope screen in front of me — I supposed I owed him something.

Recklessness set in. He was so amazed he'd got that far, and I was past caring if I had a late night or not, despite my first exam at 9 a.m. on Monday, that we ended up at a rip-roaring party in a grotty flat in Grafton. If this, I thought, is what varsity parties are going to be like, I'd better get used to it: smoke, record-player flat out, men lurching about, a few girls ditto, couples dancing at the close and slobbery stage, intense and no doubt intellectual conversation in corners. Keith got me a beer. He knew most of the people there, introduced me just as Alex. I could've coped with all that, feeling like a stretched fourteen-year-old in my blue dress and flat shoes, seeing people look puzzled (seen that face before?) or bored (just a kid!), but not with people like this pipsqueak, another Tom . . .

'Who's the kid? Cradle-snatching aren't you, Keith old son? What happened, ma'am, someone sch-lip you a growth pill along the way?'

A very short boy with a beard leered up at me. All in black, cigarette stuck to a wet mouth, rudely drunk.

'Piss off, Tom,' said Keith. To me he said, 'Tom's doing electrical engineering, but he likes to pass for an arts student. Heavily into drama, the capping revue, aren't you darling.' This tiny Tom went grandly on.

'Though naked, your face is familiar. Tell me why, oh pretty maid, sweet maid. Why do I know you?'

Shades of Andy's special name for me. I stared down at him, hoping he could see the disgust in my eyes.

'Alex swam at the Rome Olympics,' said Keith.

'Oh really! That explains the body tall and beautiful. But women shouldn't be allowed.'

'Where?' I said.

'Return the Olympics to their Grecian purity,' he said. 'Let us have no women, no poofters fencing, no little black fellows in turbans playing hockey.'

'You look like you might have played hockey,' I said.

'The child speaks. Listen lady, I wasch a good half-back until I cracked my coccyx, that's my tail bone, couldn't sit down for a month, darling. But I insist, women should be kept out of sport. Lady tennis-players, now aren't they exceptionally boring, those long rallies, no power, no competitive fire. And those dreadful scrawny runners with necks like chooks. Keep women out of sport, out of the Olympics, I say,' he petered out, stumbling off.

'Prize bore himself, drunk,' said Keith. 'Don't take it personally, Alex.'

'Wouldn't give him or you the pleasure,' I said loftily, draining my beer glass, seething inside. 'Perhaps you'd better take the child home. She's got an exam on Monday, and training in five hours.'

The child let Keith kiss her goodnight in the car and cup his hand under her breast. When he began to breathe rather heavily behind his soft beard and she thought, 'He's living up to his randy reputation, he'll be down the front of my dress next', she got out of the Morrie Thou without even saying thanks for *Ben Hur* and ran round the back to find in her bed an exceedingly angry mother reading a book, wide awake, demanding explanations. It was two o'clock and she was worried sick.

It was not a good night, and it was the last one I was going to be called child.

Untimely winter

I had intended to write to Alex this week, with or without a letter from her, but find myself incapable of even the smallest acts of will. I've never felt more isolated by language; by the contradictions of winter in November when it should be spring, of new courses beginning in the month I have all my life equated with exams, of hope and refuelled ambition when all I am feeling is despair.

I should have known, or guessed, or been observant enough to see for myself that Maestro was holding out on me. Until it became transparently clear, literally, that something was seriously amiss: the day he collapsed during my lesson and was taken to hospital his face had already taken on the frail leaf-like pallor of the dying. Only the hooded eyes, tired as they are, seem to have life remaining, briefly fired by the absolute need every time I visit for my reassurance that yes, my new teacher is working out well. My audition pieces are in place, I know Figaro, Marcello, have made a start on Sharpless and Giovanni, I am taking care of myself as the first light snowfalls whirl along the streets. I am in good hands. I will do the audition.

I am not in good hands. I believe I will not, cannot do the audition. I now dread the lessons which were once the highlight of my day. Sergio does not lack discretion, while Maestro lies dying; he has not directly questioned my choice of audition pieces, nor at this late stage suggested different ways of tackling persistent problems of phrasing. But there is a coldness, a cynicism I can't respond to. For Maestro, for that special interest I always enjoyed, for him I'd have braved the vast stage, taken on the loggionisti of La Scala tomorrow, had I but the chance. I'd not have minded facing the winter so drastically short of money after my excesses with Alex in Rome that I eat only at night with the family (and occasionally, when I must, a breadline lunch of pane coll'olio or pasta, cheap filling stodge), had I the daily pleasure of my lesson and the stories (of singers, operas, triumphs, failures) which followed.

I should do the audition, for his sake; arrive jubilant at his bedside with the news that I've won a further audition, a small part, a large part, any part. But it will not be like that. As the night follows day, I'll sing badly, a lacklustre performance, no offer will follow. My silence will confirm what he may already fear, that I don't have the ultimate courage in my soul vital for this career. My voice rings hollow.

I can't bring myself to do the audition, and I can't yet bring myself to withdraw from it. I feel paralysed by illness and inevitable death. What will I feel when my uncle, already invalided, finally goes? The sentimental yearning for a death-bed reconciliation, his final acceptance of my chosen profession? Bless you, my son. Pigs might fly. Meanwhile, Maestro lies, sallow on stark white hospital sheets, rapidly dying. I've never seen anyone eaten up by rampant cancer before my eyes, let alone the one I admire, respect and love most. I can't bear it.

Alex has not written again. Her one letter was a mere aerogram, on the surface light-hearted, with small complaints of unwelcome press attention, stacks of fan mail and dodging public appearances, having to look after the family chooks because her Nonna has been sick; the unrelenting round of school, training, swot for two sets of exams. I sensed a profound weariness, except when she talked about playing Joan. The postscript was interesting, viz. 'No one knows yet, but I'm seriously thinking of leaving school at the end of the term. The thought of any more vile assemblies like the last one is truly enough to curl my toes.' Her teachers will urge even bully her to stay, as did mine in response to a similar determination. She entrusted me with her secret!

Yet, write it down, Tom: there was a flip quality, a hardness, a finality about that letter. She might have been writing a duty thank-you letter (for the bracelet) to a newly-acquainted cousin. Should I also become hard: face it, I'll not hear from her again. On a second count, I cannot bear it.

I thought we had something going in Rome? Something that would survive separation, at least until we could spend more exploratory time together? Am I such a bad judge? Can I not read attraction in a girl's eyes as I once could before I began this monastic single-minded existence in Milan? Am I so hopelessly out of touch, out of tune? Should I write again?

I am paralysed by illness, separation, indecision, oncoming untimely winter.

New disguises

Mr Upjohn picked a particularly bad day to turn up at the pool. I'd had my first two lousy school exams, English and History. Keith, who'd finished his varsity exams and was on the razzle-dazzle, seemed to think two, well maybe five kisses equalled 'Boyfriend' and was ringing me every day, sometimes twice, suggesting (unsuccessfully) parties, picnics, trips to the hot pools at Helensville, which made me laugh. I always had some reasonable excuse. The mailbox was full of junk. I was still trying to be helpful at home, but Mum took several days to simmer down from Sunday morning's little row, and I couldn't do anything right.

Besides, I hadn't a clue what to do next about leaving school, or the American offers, or the rumours I was hearing about an Australian trip in January, or when I should make my first 'appearance'. Training seemed like a boring pointless slog, and I was putting off Mr Jack's mild hints that we needed to have a Serious Talk until 'after exams'.

It was the Australian trip that was the prime reason for Mr Upjohn trotting into view, the first time I'd seen him since the airport. He still looked smugly well-fed, getting on for Mr Jack's spherical shape, but smart, since he ran a business that made men's clothes. I suppose they ran up his new XXL reefer jackets with the double split at the back and the silver-crested buttons specially for the boss. I saw him through my bow-wave, standing next to Mr Jack, two black umbrellas side by side. My entire body was aching abominably, and I still had another quarter-mile time trial to go. Mr Upjohn was the last person I wanted to see.

'I don't want to know,' I called from the end of the pool, heaving and feeling more than slightly sick, as Mr Jack held his stop-watch up to eye-level to read the time. I could tell from his face it wasn't good enough. He beckoned me over.

'Morning, Alex,' said Mr Upjohn with a forced smile. No one smiles that warmly at seven o'clock on a cold spring morning. 'I'm driving down to Wellington today, so I had to catch you now if at all.'

'What for?' I said, already beginning to shiver, my frayed old towel already useless, dripping in the rain. Mr Jack had written the time in his little book, looking thoughtful.

'My dear girl,' Mr Upjohn said, still smiling, obviously dying to ask my time, but knowing he probably wouldn't be told. 'First tell me how you are. I haven't seen you since our return. We could do with some of Rome's sunshine. How are you coping?'

'I'm fine.' I didn't want to be reminded of Rome, least of all by him, that (looking back on it, hilarious) expression on his face as I'd kissed Tom/Tommaso for the first and last time.

'Exams going well?'

'Terrible.'

'And how's your dear grandmother? Her convalescence?'

'She getting up again, if that's what you mean. She's okay.' He was not here to talk about my grandmother. This was the official mask, of one who wanted something. I waited, staring at the raindrops plopping on the still, blue water, making regular circles. The concrete was like standing on ice.

Mr Jack said, 'Cyril is going down for a meeting about the Queensland trip.'

Mr Upjohn said, 'You remember I told you in Rome we were working on a trip to one of the Australian state meetings. I just thought I should check with you personally. You are available, of course.'

'Um, I suppose so,' I said like a coward, trying to sound, if not enthusiastic, at least neutral. No one sane refuses a trip to sunny Queensland, even half-fit and stale. If I said no, the can of worms would be opened. 'When?'

'January 13 to 21. We're hoping to send about ten swimmers. There'll be national trials in Wellington on December 17 but I'm quite sure you won't have to attend those. I'm delighted the trip's going ahead, after a lot of spade-work. Good, well that's settled. Excuse me, Bill, Alex, but I must be on the road, beat the morning traffic.'

And off he bustled. Mr Jack was looking at me hard as I jumped up and down on the icy concrete. My toes and fingertips had gone from white to yellow and purple blotches, and my unusually hairy legs were prickly as a porcupine. Perched on the rail in his grey plastic mack, with his unblinking sad eyes boring unanswered questions into me, he reminded me of a nice fat grey wise old toad, sitting, watching, waiting patiently to strike.

'I'd better do that last quarter,' I said, steeling myself for five minutes of pain. That, or a heart-to-heart with Mr Jack about my future, which I wasn't ready for yet.

Two mornings later, it backfired.

Mr Jack waited until I'd done my training. In the office overlooking a couple of keen juniors still left in the pool, he silently produced the morning's paper.

On the sports page I read that a team of ten was going to compete in the Queensland champs. A meeting in Wellington had announced that national trials were to be held. The selectors required all candidates to attend, without exception.

My gorge was rising.

The new chief selector said Yes, the meeting decided that Miss A. Archer (Auckland), the Olympic bronze medallist, would be required to attend the trials like anyone else. It had been reported from Auckland that she was currently giving priority to school commitments. The Association was determined to send away to Australia only swimmers who were fully fit and prepared.

'They can shove their bloody trials,' I said softly.

Mr Jack said nothing. I couldn't read his face — was he hurt, sad, just tired of me and my problems, or was he again one step ahead?

'They've got real short memories, this crowd,' I yelled. 'It's not even three months since . . . an Olympic bronze, what more do they want? I can beat any other swimmer in the country with my feet tied, blindfolded, from a push-off or a bellyflop, even butterfly if I tried, any which way.'

Still he said nothing. I looked at the paper again, my face hot. '*Who reported* from Auckland? Mr Upjohn, I bet. Did you tell him that terrible time trial the other morning?'

'No, I didn't,' he said, the patient, long-suffering, grey toad.

'I always knew I shouldn't trust him. Well, he can stick his Queensland tour up his jumper. I shouldn't have to go to any trials. I had mine in Rome.'

'Don't you want to go to Queensland?'

'Of course I do,' I cried, untruthfully. 'Lie in the sun under the palm trees. Go surfing. Get beaten by a whole lynch mob of twelve-year-old Aussies. Local junior beats Olympic star, I can just see it.'

The toad struck gently, probing me to see where it hurt. 'I'm just wondering . . . if you refuse to swim in the trials . . .' he said mildly, putting his finger in his ear like a gun, like trying to clear a passage into his brain, a habitual gesture which usually made me laugh. 'They might call your bluff.'

'This isn't a bluff.' He looked at me, his face one huge question mark. 'Alright then. I don't want to go. I want a rest from people expecting things all the time, expecting records every time I swim and photographs and speeches and being nice to reporters and teachers and kids who follow me round at school and boring busybodies who think they own me just because I pulled off a fluke in Rome.'

'It wasn't a fluke, Alex. You swam three fine races under immense pressure for that bronze. You earned it.'

'I want . . . I shouldn't have to go to the trials . . . I'll get beaten in Aussie . . . alright, I am scared . . .' I petered out.

'Alex, you've never lacked courage,' he said quietly. 'But shouldn't we be talking about the broader picture? You've told me hardly anything about the American offer, nothing of your long-term plans.'

'Rome was . . . Rome was so, well, bronze, anything else is going to feel like an anti-climax. Tokyo, four years more slog just to go from bronze to gold. And I've had two American offers.'

He looked more sad than annoyed. 'Two? Why haven't you told me? Are you really trying to tell me this is your last season?'

'I want . . . oh hell, I don't know, I want to leave school and start at varsity and learn Italian and meet people and go to operas and museums and visit places like Naples and Cairo and Singapore long enough to see them properly and earn money and . . .'

'In other words, you're ready to move on?'

'I don't *know*. I keep thinking . . . if I don't go to Aussie and have just a fun sort of season, four years in America mightn't seem . . . I might get more enthusiastic about Perth and Tokyo.'

'Have you told your parents any of this?'

'I *can't*.' Just like I can't tell them or even you about Tom and what he continues to do to me. 'Anyway, I *can't* go to Australia on what's supposed to be a development team for Perth if I know I'm retiring three weeks later. It'd be like false pretences. I truly and honestly want a junior to go, like young Jenny out there looking lonely as hell, she's ready for a trip.'

We both looked out the office window at the only swimmer still hard at it: Jenny, a short, muscly fourteen-year-old, the national junior champ, with a silently doting dad who drove her to training from Pokeno or somewhere, twenty-five miles twice a day.

Mr Jack said, 'You know, I think you're selling yourself short about how you'd go in Queensland. Dawn Fraser won't be there. You're a different swimmer from the one who went to Rome. A few hard races will see you back on form.'

'I don't feel different, that's the problem. Yes, I do — worse. Sometimes I get out my bronze medal and wonder how the hell . . . I think having to go to trials is an insult.'

He sighed. 'Very well. But my advice is simply to say you're not available, and leave it at that. And when you're pressed for explanations, which you will be, and I will be, say family reasons.'

'But that's not true and it's none of their business. It's because I don't think . . .'

'Alex, don't be naïve,' he said sharply. 'You know reporters, even Norm or Grant just doing their jobs, will count it very much their business.

They'd make mincemeat of you. You'd be publicly accused of arrogance, of wanting the rules bent. You know that, unless you put up a reason of ill health or injury.'

'That's a coward's way. Why can't I say I'm just not available? Why do I have to justify myself?'

'Because you're an Olympic medallist and you can't dodge it.' The grey toad standing by the rain-spotted window finally struck, hard. 'Why don't you announce your retirement from serious competition now? Call it a day.'

'I . . . don't feel ready for that. The nationals, yes, but Aussie . . .'

If I'd learnt anything in the last eighteen months, it was that I hate doing anything half-baked, or just to please other people, or because something thinks I 'should'.

He sighed again. 'I don't think you're doing the right thing, Alex. If you were to ask for my advice, I'd say relax a bit, for God's sake. Go to the trials, go to Aussie, enjoy Queensland, do your best. Stop trying so hard, stop worrying. We can decide about America later.'

'I don't want to go to Aussie,' I said stubbornly, 'you know how they'd gloat to see me beaten. And I really do want a junior to go. I shouldn't have to go to those trials, not when they talk like that, not when I have to read it in the paper like anyone else. Mr Jack, I am not anyone else.'

Ah, Tom, the very way you'd looked at me, smiled, laughed, had made me feel so *special*. He'd written — that he'd long treasure the memory, me ten feet tall, an incandescent image. Tommaso sends his love, wishes he could have his time in Rome again. The two letters under my mattress had grown dog-eared and tear-stained with reading. I could recite them word for word. Tommaso sends his love.

Mr Jack punched out a ticket for an old dear come for her daily exercise, and took her money. 'Ta, ducks. Loverly weather for ducks too.' He went on smiling, wearily.

'No, Alex, you're not like anyone else. You're you, and you do make things hard for yourself. But . . . okay, I'll ring Cyril Upjohn and tell him your decision. Myself, I'm disappointed. I'd planned a trip to Queensland to see you swim, then down to Sydney to see my sister. We didn't leave things too good after our old mum died.'

'You must still go,' I said fiercely. 'You must. Jenny'll get in the team.'

'Without you in the picture, yes, she's got a good chance. As far as the press goes, watch yourself. On your head be it.'

It took, as I dug myself further into the mire, only one more of Keith's parties to convince me that if I was going to keep on being recognized and mocked for being too tall, only sixteen, and my picture too often in the papers, I'd have to do something about it. I went to a chemist and bought some make-up.

It had been an awful week. Three exams bunched up in three days, half the people missing from Joan rehearsals and the performance in two weeks' time, not to mention politicians and the newspapers going bananas about the general election on Saturday.

As I dreaded, Mum and Dad didn't understand about Australia. They thought I was stubborn, pig-headed, barmy, that I had obligations to my sport, to juniors, my public. I said, don't *you* start talking about 'my public'. To ask me to go to trials after Rome was an insult, just a way of chopping me down to size, like anyone else. Anyway, I said, you should be grateful, it'll save you some money you haven't got. I could get a holiday job. They'd finance it somehow, they said. I might never get the chance again. I was a lucky girl. Et cetera. Gran kept quiet, but she understood.

Mr Upjohn rang me the night Mr Jack told him, and piled on the pressure, begging me to reconsider, apologizing that he'd not been able to persuade the selectors that in my case . . . The committee wanted me to know they were all so very proud of my achievement in Rome. Funny way of showing it, I said.

Alex, he said, the juniors in the team need your experience and leadership. Not one of them has travelled before. 'Well,' I said, 'neither had I before I went to Rome.'

Was it money? he asked, getting desperate. No it wasn't. 'Mr Upjohn,' I said, 'I'm taking a long view, I've had two hard seasons, you know that, and a long winter, and I'm tired.' 'You're not backing away from tough competition?' he asked. Since when had I backed out, all those years with Maggie? 'That's *not fair* Mr Upjohn, I'm in the middle of exams, I need some time at home. I do want to swim well at the nationals. And Mr Jack says all I'm to say to the press is that I'm not available for personal reasons.' 'They won't wear it,' he said grimly, with a certain amount of relish.

They didn't. If my friends Norm Thompson or Grant Davies had got hold of the story first, it mightn't have been so bad. But someone (Mr Upjohn, I wouldn't put it past him) slipped the word to a keen bushy-tailed new reporter from the evening paper.

Mum told him (it was Friday) I was at school sitting my last exam that very afternoon and was not available for comment. So he rang the school and bullied the secretary into tracking me down in the library where I was frantically trying to cram some last minute Latin irregular verbs into my head.

I told him I had nothing to add. I was not available for the trials or the trip, period. Surely that was clear enough. Was it because I'd lost my Rome form? No, it wasn't, I snapped. There'd been, he said slyly, a rumour since Rome I'd had glandular fever. News to me, I said. There'd also been a rumour I was angry about being called to the trials.

'No comment,' I said literally holding my mouth shut.

'Aren't you actually just hanging on in there? Waiting for the selectors to climb down off their perches?'

'No I'm not and it's none of your business,' I said.

'It's true, isn't it, the standard in Queensland could be sky high? Good as the Olympics? The Aussies have some great little swimmers coming along behind their Dawnie.'

'No,' I said, furious, stung (because it was true) by the implication that I was a coward and adding, stupidly, 'it's perfectly *obvious* the Olympics are the tops, and it's mainly a trip for juniors away and I've got an exam to sit in five minutes.'

Why didn't I put the phone down, there and then?

'So you do think the trials are only for juniors, lesser mortals. A bronze should guarantee you a place in the team, automatic-like?'

'Well, shouldn't it? What else do they need? A gold? A world record?' I said, slamming down the phone and clutching my head in horror. The Latin exam was a three-hour disaster. I took one look at the passage from Virgil for translation and went into a tail spin. It's only a school exam, I kept saying to myself, the proper exams aren't until next week. Keep calm, keep calm. I thought of the slimy, wheedling, insistent voice on the phone and imagined his fingers now pounding a typewriter and went into a cold sweat. I couldn't write.

He was just doing his job. BRONZE MEDALLIST ASKS WHAT MORE DO THEY WANT? Top of back page over about eight inches of rubbish and a large, ugly, grinning picture. 'Olympic bronze medallist Alex Archer said today that she was unavailable for the trials to be held for the New Zealand team to compete in the Queensland state championships in January.'

' "I won a bronze in Rome. What more do the selectors want?" ' asks Miss Archer, explaining her decision to boycott the trials. 'It's only a junior team anyway."

'I didn't say only, I said *mainly*,' I shouted at Mum as I read the piece on the kitchen table.

'You should have said nothing at all,' said Mum grimly.

'I never said anything about boycotting. Boycotting . . . the man's a total liar.' It got worse: that I could be available for the team provided I didn't have to go to Wellington, that I said I was the only swimmer in New Zealand who'd trained all last winter. That I was perfectly fit despite persistent rumours of glandular fever being the reason for my not competing in any early season club meetings.

Then: Mr Maurice D. Smythe, the new chief selector, regretted hearing that Miss Archer considered herself above a normal and reasonable method of selecting the best swimmers for Queensland. "We cannot have one rule for self-styled stars, even recent Olympic swimmers, and one for the rest. In America all swimmers are required to attend all trials. That's a basic fact of life fully accepted even by gold medallists and world record-holders."

In America, I thought, they have literally dozens of people within a second of each other. I've got no one within cooee of me. It finished: Mr Cyril Upjohn, Auckland selector and Miss Archer's manager in Rome, was not available for comment today. Coward, I thought. Coward. *Coward.* COWARD.

Tom says, again, *They'll clip your wings, when you get home.*

You might think, so what? I look like a stuck-up bitch, totally up myself, in one night's paper, tomorrow's fish 'n chips wrapping. Who cares, except me? Once it would have made me weep, this sort of stuff. But I still have to ring up Mr Jack and squirm. Norm Thompson gets in touch and talks about damage control.

An equally large piece appears next morning, saying that I had decided I was not available for Aussie (which is basically true) before I heard about the trials. It was true I did think that being called to trials was an insult to someone who'd won an Olympic bronze only three months ago. ('Is that what you want me to say?' says Norm. 'Yes,' I said.) The selectors could have been flexible and could have advised me personally about the trials, as the only swimmer who'd been to Rome. Mr Smythe pipes up again, saying that he understood that Miss Archer had told Auckland selector Mr Cyril Upjohn three days ago that she was available. Even if this were incorrect, or an unfortunate misunderstanding, she could still have taken the trouble to advise the selectors. Her refusal to comply with a fair selection process was setting a poor example to the country's younger swimmers. Norm gave him the last word.

A bad influence on juniors, on kids like young Jenny? I've heard that before. I don't smoke, or sleep around, or swear (only occasionally), or drink (well, hardly ever), or wear loud clothes. I haven't run away from home or fallen out with my parents, I don't ride around on motorbikes (well, only in Rome), so what's my sin? But really, who cared? Anyone? Though it was unpleasant at the time, and the backlash went on and on, this storm in a teacup did me a favour.

I didn't want four more years of this. I hardly even wanted four more weeks. Important things were the outside exams I *had* to pass to be able to leave school. Gran getting stronger, Mum having a holiday. Ginnie not dying. A new prime minister, Jack Kennedy president. Finding out more about Joan, and slowly forgetting Tom.

I won't say it was easy. People do read the papers, and were not slow in giving me their opinions. I gave in to Keith's pestering and agreed to go to an election night party with him. He had most of his exam results, all As — behind that ginger-streaked beard and those gnome's eyebrows he's supposed to be a genius at maths — and he wanted to celebrate.

Mum gave very grudging permission. My first proper exam was on Monday. I was to be home by the dot of 12.30. She was tired and preoccupied. The garden needed attention and she had to go and vote. Would I please tackle some ironing and attend to Gran and keep an eye on the kids while she and Dad nipped along to the voting booth at the school.

Tom had sent his vote by mail, Labour because he's a socialist at heart. I read his letter for the three hundredth time.

By the time Keith came to pick me up my head was swimming with *Macbeth* and the causes of the Boer War. I'd spent the gorgeous sunny afternoon doing the ironing with my history notes pinned to the wall of the laundry. I decided to wear jeans, and a skimpy boat-necked blouse, and some earrings I'd borrowed from Julia, and experiment with a bit of frosted turquoise shadow and black eyeliner — protective colouring, I thought, shouting goodbye from the porch so I didn't have Mum saying I couldn't go to a party looking like *that*.

Keith whistled, surprised, smiling as though afraid his head was going to fall off. He wasn't exactly Gregory Peck to start with, and when he said that he already had a monumental hangover from being on the piss last night, I could see he wasn't exaggerating. Since then he'd had a brunch of fizzy toothwater (local champagne), bacon and eggs, fried steak, fried sausages, fried bread, fried tomatoes — hair of the dog, he said; *asking* for trouble, I said — and then spent the afternoon listening to Johnny Mathis records and feeling sorry for himself. The Morrie Thou stank of cigarettes and the empty beer bottles clanking round in the back. We got away quickly while Dad was still out in the vege garden pulling up weeds, the kids up in the tree-hut, and Mum involved with Gran.

The party was down a side road in the gully behind the university, in a row of old wooden villas with dirty peeling paint and the window frames falling off. It had begun early, Keith explained, because the first election results came through about eight, and most of the people there were Labour, some of them party members.

Every room was full of people squashed into sofas, sitting on the floor, propped up lining the walls; the radio was going full blast with results from Sydenham, Auckland City, Rotorua, Kapiti, Christchurch Central, the announcers trying to analyse and predict what it all meant. Along the front verandah and hallway, trestle-tables were crammed solid with beer kegs, beer bottles, flagons of sherry and red wine, lids and corks no one thought to throw away, dirty glasses, empty potato-chip packets, ashtrays full of cigarette butts. Every new result brought cheers or groans; some rough language when it became clear that Labour might not be the next Government.

Keith got me some rough red wine from a Chianti bottle as we went through the hallway. I was the only girl in trousers. I'd never seen such a variety of clothing, from the truly scruffy to the arty-crafties to the old-school-tie/tweeds/twin-set and pearl brigade. Some of the men were bearded, some much older. I thought they might be lecturers.

'Who's your doll, Keith? I know this pretty face,' said a pallid, unshaven creature in maroon corduroy in the kitchen. His glazed eyes flicked down to my jeans. 'Where have I seen this fresh young face?'

Inside, I sighed, 'I've no idea,' I said.

'What course? Arts? Are you one of Prof Reid's little English Lit protégées?'

At least I wasn't being taken for a schoolgirl. The devil stirred. 'Home Science, Dunedin,' condemning myself to being one of the haughty types who went off to Dunedin to do home science but really to catch a medical student. I saw him lose interest, but puzzled because the sorts of girls who went off to do home science were usually much better dressed.

'I don't believe it,' grinned Keith, as the maroon corduroy left, carefully stirring a giant mug of black coffee. 'The wedding-ring course? You? Pull the other one. Come on, the election's stale, Labour's history already. Let's dance.'

Of course, we couldn't dance *all* night. Keith was surprisingly good at the old rock 'n roll, not stylish but quick on his feet. It suited me to dance out in the darkened backyard on the broken concrete, to scratchy old LPs on a vintage record-player, round clumps of weeds and a revolving clothesline with underpants and shirts still pinned up. Dancing in the dark, I didn't have to cope with people staring and wondering where they'd seen me before. But Keith eventually wanted a beer and we ended up on the floor in the big front room with the bay window, about seventy people jammed in like sardines and the air thick with smoke and beer fumes. After ten minutes or so of results pouring out of the radio, an even louder voice proposed the election was All Over bar the shouting. 'Turn the fuckin' thing off. This is now officially a wake, folks. Drown your sorrows. God defend New Zealand from the National Party and all its cow-cocky cronies cause sure as hell no one else will. The Right rides again. Charge your glasses. Three cheers for Call-me-Kiwi Keith!'

There was a moment of comparative quiet as everyone groaned and drank and pondered. 'Holyoake as PM, Christ,' muttered somebody gloomily. I sipped my raw wine and tried to look as though I understood about the incoming National Party and the implications of Jack Kennedy being the first Roman Catholic elected US president. Keith was taking advantage of the lack of floor space to nuzzle closer. Someone behind me slowly began to tune a guitar. 'My dog has fleas,' he sang mournfully.

'Where have I seen that tall girl before?' demanded my thin friend from the kitchen, now sitting with his corduroys crossed on a sofa opposite. The coffee hadn't done much for his sodden brain. 'She says she's only a Home Science student, so why have I seen her before?'

The entire room turned to look at me. I felt Keith beside me tighten.

'I know her, that's Alex Archer, she won a medal at the Olympics in Rome,' said a plump boy above me, Just William in horn-rimmed glasses. 'All over the papers last night and this morning, refusing to toe the party line, swim in trials, such fun. When were the Games, again?'

'August,' I said between my teeth.

'What for?' said another voice.

'What do you mean, what for?' I said testily. At the pool this morning, at the corner dairy buying something for Mum, even walking down the road — I discovered people read the papers all right, if not one then the other. And believed it. A few had said 'good on yer, girl'; most were cold, or downright rude.

'What sport?' the voice said.

'Swimming,' I said, sorely tempted to say I was a hammer thrower or a female canoeist or did Graeco-Roman wrestling, and see if anyone noticed.

'Jeez, it's blood-out-of-stone country. Lady, what sort of medal?' Bronze, I said. There was a sort of shuffle round the room; non-plussed, I think. I heard one or two voices say 'Well done, kid.'

'Ah, that's right, Dawn Fraser won the gold, didn't she?' said an older man, pepper-and-salt beard above a brown polo neck. He looked round as though he expected applause to be able to remember such unimportant things. 'Solid birds, both, *won*derful shoulders.' His hands described curves like one of those sex-starved sailors in *South Pacific* and he made a sort of Tarzan wild-man grunt.

'Don't be personal,' I said, because I'd had more than one red wine too. 'I don't point out your bald patch to the entire world.' It caused a momentary hush, and a few chuckles. The guitar player behind me had finally found his lost chords. He did a mock drum-roll across the strings.

'Ladies and Gentleman, we have a celebrity in our midst. Una — what's the Italian for champion?' Campionessa, someone said. 'Una campionessa di Roma.' he struck a splendid D7 chord. 'Oh altogether now . . . Arrive der-ci Roma,' he warbled insultingly, in falsetto. 'It's time for us to part . . . Save the wedding bells for my returning, keep my lover's arms outstretched and yearning . . .' then he ran out of words, but by this time quite a few people had joined in, humming, ya-da-da-da-da, da da-da DA-AH . . . 'God, what a boring song. This party needs livening up.'

I knew a put-down when I heard one. Despite myself, I was flushing. He found a new key and burst into the tune of Colonel Bogey. 'All together now . . . "Walker . . . has only got one ball". 'A woman with a bright orange mouth and carrotty hair joined in. "Harry's . . . got two but they are very small. Jimler's . . . got something sim-ler, and Dickson's . . . got no balls at all." '*And* again . . .'

'That's professors they're singing about,' laughed Keith in my earhole. 'It's all downhill from now. Do you want to go?'

'Why?' Now that my moment of notoriety had passed, and I'd earned nothing more from the bearded gentleman but a sharp look, I thought I might as well sip my Chianti, remember 'Arrivederci Roma' which was played all over Rome all day long during the Games — I remembered the words alright: 'city of a million moonlit places, city of a million warm embraces, where I found the one of all the faces far from home,' — and think, Tom, who never once embraced me (no, I lie — once, at the airport), must have been to hundreds of parties like these.

The songs got longer and dirtier, the lights lower, the air smokier and hotter. The guitarist and two of the other men led the singing, with gusto. Several times I heard only a new chord, a new key, the first couple of lines before voices protested — Not that, not here, cut it out, ladies present, Fred! They all seemed to know a lot of songs. Keith sang beside me, enthusiastically but in a different key to everyone else. I knew some of Harry Belafonte's, the Batchelors' songs, 'Mack the Knife', 'Yellow Rose of Texas', the old warhorses, and the cleaner ones, from travelling round in buses with swimming teams. I wondered sleepily if Tom's song repertoire included something called Eskimo Nell that people suggested and sniggered about but no one was prepared to sing, or even if he'd led the way in sing-songs like these. Somehow, I didn't think so. Perhaps he'd been the pianist. Perhaps he played a guitar. The wine bottle came round; someone kept my glass topped up.

Eventually I had to find a loo. 'Me too,' said Keith, though he was still relatively sober. Perhaps he'd finally learned that if he wanted to drive me home, he'd only do it sober.

He went off to find a bush in the shrubbery outside. Waiting in the dark hallway, trying not to pick the peeling wallpaper from off the scrim, I half-listened to a deep conversation between two slim, dark, and artistic-looking men about the merits of Christopher Fry compared to T.S. Eliot.

'Oh, by the way, they're auditioning for *Saint Joan* next week,' said one. 'This fool of a new producer, where do they get these people? She's decided on *Joan* outdoors in February.'

I sidled along the wall and pretended to be deeply interested in a large poster of Johnny Mathis.

'What's wrong with that? I should have thought it was a splendid choice of play for the quad, the trial scene among the pillars. Plenty of heraldic banners, lovely male parts for the likes of you and me. I fancy the Dauphin myself, or Bluebeard. Poor pampered Gilles de Rais. He came to a fiery end, too, for cutting up little children to offer to the devil. Very nasty.'

But it had *always* been Shakespeare, and why change, and all the stage-struck women around varsity would be queuing up for *Joan* — one great part, an understudy, and the rest only walk-ons in the Court scene and furious. They couldn't agree between Raewyn (a good Juliet two years ago), or Isabel (not bad as Portia last year), or even that young Lesley (a reasonably defiant Jessica).

Well, I thought, I'll have to come and see it. As seniors we'd gone to see *The Merchant* last year, and *Romeo and Juliet* the year before that.

'That dreadful film has rather spoiled it for me,' said one languidly. 'Why they didn't cast a proper English actress who knew how to speak, instead of that hopeless American kid, what was her name?'

'Jean Seberg,' I said. They both looked at me, startled. 'Sorry, darling, didn't realize you were listening,' said one. 'Yes, Jean Seberg. You know, you're not unlike her, to look at.' 'I'm nothing like Jean Seberg,' I said scornfully. 'She was pretty, like a pretty boy with a little snub nose. I'm not pretty.' 'No, you're not pretty,' he said, in a detached way I found quite amusing, looking me up and down like a lab specimen. 'Interesting face, though. You're the swimmer, aren't you?'

'Yes.'

'That's explains the short *short* hair. You look like a warrior Joan. I don't suppose you can act as well as swim. I always think of atheletes as people of limited IQ and tunnel vision.' He smiled warmly at me, as though he expected me to agree with him. 'But you do look like a Joan.'

Something stopped me from telling these two rude and ripple-haired young men that I was already doing Joan. For a wild moment I thought I'd ask them about the auditions, when and where, why not if I'm going to varsity next year . . . if . . .

The loo, now free, was not nice. Someone had very recently been sick in it, and the bare wooden walls were covered with some exceedingly dirty cartoons and postcards. When I came out Keith was in the hallway talking with five or six guys about the election, total landslide to National.

I noted some up-and-down looks at my long legs and some pointed comments about Keith being sober, tonight, on his best behaviour for once, and a *sotto voce* remark about cradle-snatching (again), to which Keith muttered, thinking I couldn't hear, 'Don't you believe it!'

I was going to be half an hour late home.

'That greybeard you were rude to . . .' he said in the car.

'Excuse me, but he was rude first.'

'He's a mathematician. A PhD. One of my lecturers. One of the best.'

'A mathematician! A PhD! Golly gosh!'

'He complimented me on my taste in girls. Reckons it's improving. Make-up suits, you know. You could wear more.'

I suppose it was Keith's sort of clumsy compliment. I didn't answer. I was thinking, dreaming, of Joan, the whole play I'd see in February, the scenes that I'd learned and would never play, the scenes of her when she was still buoyant and pushy and funny, before everything went wrong and she became sullen and insolent and defiant.

Anticipating (wrongly) that he'd get a bit further this time, and me drowsy and not noticing, Keith drove us straight up Mount Eden. The city twinkled below, between the dark patches of water. He came straight at me, his mouth tasting of beer, his beard smelling of stale smoke. I suppose I tasted of sour red wine. That *Ben Hur* night he'd not tried the tongue bit. Now, breathing heavily, none too gently, he did. What on earth did boys (and girls like Sylvia!) see in it? It took all my strength to wrench myself free of his mouth, his grip, and the gear lever between us. I remembered another time I'd fought him, when he'd dragged me along a street into a taxi after going into that pub. I'm strong, but he's stronger.

'Come on Alex, you want to.'

'I do not.'

'You let me last time.'

'I did not let you poke your beery tongue down my throat. And I won't ever. If that's what you remember from last time you remembered wrong. Or was it some other girl?'

Playing rough. His silence was full of menace. Beside us another car started up its engine and backed away from the edge of the hill. I wondered how far they'd gone inside their car; how far it was for me to walk home. About three miles. I'd got out of his car once before.

'Take me home.'

'D'you know I . . . well, I . . .' I wondered what this was costing him. 'I dream about you, Alex. I dream about you most nights, amazing dreams, where you . . . That's when I'm not lying awake and . . .'

'Waste of good sleep. And flattery will get you nowhere.' I thought, in the eighteen months I've been sparring with him, that's the first soppy thing he's ever said. But don't dream about me, please, ever, Keith. All we've got in common is we were both friends of Andy, we both think the All Blacks shouldn't have gone to South Africa and we're both prickly characters. You're a funny gawky sort of guy, and I quite like you, and you're the only person who asks me out, and you keep coming back for more, but you're the wrong one. My eyes were wet.

'Keith, I've got to swot all tomorrow. I'm tired.'

He lit a cigarette and we drove home in silence. I made him stop three houses down the road. I let him have a normal sort of kiss, but how he prolonged it, how his hands grabbed at my face, my hair, my shoulders, until I simply had to stop him to draw breath. 'I've got to go, thanks for the party, sorry about Labour, see ya.' I shut the car door as quietly as possible and crept up the drive, crying.

Another row with Mum for being late home, another exam on Monday, the first real U.E. external exam for those who didn't get accredited and two freaks: Julia who chooses to sit to impress her rotten father and because it's good practice, and me being made to sit because I went to the rotten Olympics.

Another visit from Auntie Pat and Ginnie; unexpected this time, because Ginnie's been bleeding and Auntie Pat is frantic with worry and thinks she should be in hospital. She looks worse than ever. I can't believe no one else has noticed where she's covering up bruises on her face with pancake and her probably bruised arms with long, unsuitable sleeves when the weather is hot and sunny and all the pohutukawas are now in full bloom along the waterfront.

She's bigger and sadder. They find out she might have something called placenta praevia and she's got to go home and creep about and will probably need a Caesarean. I asked her if Merv had stopped hitting her. No, she said, though he was hardly ever home. As well as his bridge and ballroom, he was having it away with his father's secretary. How did she know? I asked. She laughed, it sounds corny, like a cheap Hollywood movie, but lipstick on his clothes, he doesn't even both to hide it, and a girlfriend had seen them lunching smoochily together, several times. Hamilton wasn't a big town.

'Leave him,' I said. 'Can't,' she said. 'Go home to Mum.' '*Can't*,' she said, 'Dad wouldn't have me in the house.' She's too proud just to walk out and arrive on their doorstep and then beg for help and money. I ask Mum if Ginnie can come and stay with us while she's waiting, she can have my room; but Auntie Pat says no thank you Alex, it's a sweet thought but she's got her new husband to look after as long as she's able. I'm on the verge of exploding, but Ginnie looks at me like a sick pleading dog.

The brute, I think, the animal, the *bastard*. There's no word bad enough.

Joan knew what it was like to get beaten too. I thought of Ginnie when I was dragged in and sat on my trial scene stool. Our rehearsals were daily, between swot and exams. Was I *sick* of swot and even more of exams! Miss Macrae's strange Russian-doll friend turned up several times. We spent one whole session on my final speech, with Miss Macrae making me imagine what Joan is feeling as she thinks about being imprisoned for life, letting the words guide me to the right moment when the voice gets stronger, the climax . . . *if only I could hear the wind in the trees, the larks in the sunshine, the young lambs crying through the healthy frost, and the blessed blessed church bells that send my angel voices floating to me on the wind. But without these things I cannot live; and by your wanting to take them away from me, or from any human creature, I know that your counsel is of the devil, and that mine is of God.*

This is poetry really, or music, an aria. People are still forgetting their lines; they can't pick up a cue properly to keep the thing moving. I wish I'd said I'd do something else, what about that song from *My Fair Lady*: Eliza's last angry song about words, words, words, I'm so sick of words . . . so go back in your shell, I can do bloody well without you.

Can you hear me, Tom-in-Italy?

One rehearsal I got introduced to the Russian doll. She had a dark, fruity voice, an actress's voice, and liked dramatic purple eyeshadow. She waved around knobbly rings of blue and yellow glass, and played with a huge pendant of stainless steel hanging on her black bosom. Miss Macrae told her she was thinking of a combined Shakespeare production next year with the boys' school up the road.

'Alex, I'm still waiting to hear your thoughts on the matter. I'm tending towards *As You Like It*, Rosalind of course. Or even *Taming of the Shrew*. You'd enjoy Katherine.' That, I remembered, was another role she'd once played. 'Alex?'

Had she guessed, even though I'd filled in YES I AM COMING BACK on the form they'd sent round the Sixth Form recently, knowing that if I'd written NO or UNCERTAIN I'd have opened a whole can of worms about being far too young to leave and far too young for university and possibly Head Girl and other rubbish.

I think I'm stopping school for ever and maybe stopping swimming for ever. Nobody will let me make a quick quiet dignified exit from either of them. I'm a coward.

'Rosalind would be alright, I s'pose,' I mumbled, looking at the floor. A week later, standing in the same spot by the piano just below the stage, I discovered why both of them had been looking at me rather strangely.

Two more exams to go: Music on Friday; the worst, Latin, on Monday. Friday I came home from training to find a beautiful white cyclamen on Gran's dressing-table when I took in her breakfast tray. I assumed it was hers, brought by one of the old dears who occasionally visited her. Mum's housekeeping money didn't stretch to such huge potplants, done up in red cellophane and ribbon.

'That's for you, pet.'

I stroked the dark leaves. There were at least fifteen upstanding, perfect white blooms and as many buds.

'You do remember?'

I nodded, not trusting myself to turn around. One day I'll visit his gravestone, but not today, not this year. Maybe next. I looked at my watch. 'This time last year I didn't know Andy was . . . had been . . . It was a Sunday, wasn't it? When Mum told me, I went to see his parents. Then we had an awful lunch because no one knew what to say and then I went training, up and down like a robot. I think I did about six miles, straight.'

'Water under the bridge since then, eh pet. But it makes me sad to see you so restless and unhappy. What is it? Have you heard from Tom again? Have *you* written?'

I shook my head at the mirror, seeing both myself with my usual wet hair, wet red-rimmed swotter's eyes, dull blue summer gym tunic, frayed white shirt, and Gran in her turquoise bed jacket, white hair whispy, tucking into her three-minute boiled egg. After a long silence, recognizing that I was foregoing a good opportunity to get a few things off my chest, recognizing the frustration and hurt in her eyes, I said, 'Thanks for the cyclamen, Gran. It's lovely.'

'Take it with you,' she called as I hurriedly left. 'It's for you! Alex? Alex!'

Before I pedalled off to sit Music, the phone went: Keith, also remembering this anniversary, suggesting would I like to go out tonight, go to a restaurant, somewhere quiet. For him, that's a change. So were the flowers in his arms, a bunch of red carnations, when he arrived to pick me up. Dad was not quite hostile, this first time that Keith had fronted up to him, but made no bones about him having me home by 11 p.m. Alex, he said, was dog tired and exams weren't over yet.

I'd gone back to a boring, sober dress and no face paint, because that was how I felt. Not that there was much choice at all in Auckland, but Keith's choice of restaurant was one of those hotel dining rooms, with 'table d'hôte' typed on little cards, and waitresses in little aprons, very genteel and proper; no wine, no musicians, no crimson bougainvillaea, no polite old waiters and orange tablecloths and tables of antipasto . . .

Before we even unfolded our napkins, I saw a face I vaguely knew come across the room. It was someone's Mum in a pink crimplene dress, but I couldn't remember who or where, school or the pool. She pulled up a chair without asking, with a vaguely threatening air. It didn't take long to establish that she was the mother of a very untalented backstroke swimmer, and wanted to tell me in no uncertain terms that it wasn't good for the sport for people to come back from overseas with inflated ideas and expect to have preferential treatment. Her Susan had thought the world of me, once.

Keith suddenly looked older behind his beard. He asked her to leave us alone and threatened to call the manager. Rather startled, she left, but looking smug and righteous too because she'd made her point. Cow, we agreed. But that wasn't the end of it. As we talked offhandedly of exams, of his holiday job working on building sites with a big construction company, I noted my picture on the back page of the evening paper being read at a nearby table. The bald man with the pipe behind the paper very soon made the connection with the picture and me. I saw his colourless, hairless eyes gleam.

'And not before time,' he called, tapping the paper with his pipe.

'Pardon,' I said, gaping.

'Hamilton, next weekend, first competitive outing since Rome, it says here, for the girl who's refused to swim in trials. Pride, young miss, goes before a . . .'

'That's it,' I said, wondering *who'd* said I was swimming in Hamilton, bumping into the waitress with our mushroom soup with croutons on the way out. 'Sorry,' Keith kept saying behind me, 'sorry, Alex, how could I *know*, who do these people think they are, oh Jesus, this was supposed to be a night to remember Andy, look, there's a party tomorrow night, I promise not a rowdy one, nice people, not students, in Parnell, I'll make it up.'

'Okay,' I said furiously, recklessly, at the gate. At least he had the sense not to try any kissing that night. 'Pick me up at eight, but I warn you, I've had enough of being public property, fair game for people to abuse. You won't recognize me.'

He didn't either, by the time I'd rung Miss Macrae and asked if I could borrow a wig from the school costume cupboard for a fancy dress party. I got keys from the caretaker and came out with two new wigs — one brunette, one curly blonde. Stuffing my head full of Latin, I rode around to Julia's and borrowed one of her stretchy black tops, similar to the one Zoe had tried to make me wear to the opera in Rome, stretchy enough to fit my great shoulders. Julia still had two exams to go and looked as though she hadn't seen daylight for months.

I told Mum and Dad I was having an early night. I put on my jeans, and tarty high-heels, and the top which was rather tight and my black bra showing, and a wide red belt pulled in tight, and the brunette wig and earrings and a whole lot of pancake make-up and eyeliner and eyeshadow and mascara and pale lipstick — and a pillow in my bed. Keith drove straight past me waiting in the road. I intercepted him before the gate. I walked up like Marilyn Monroe and put on a high girlish voice and asked him if he knew where the Orange Ballroom was and perhaps he'd like to take me there for a drink. I had the satisfaction of seeing an interested glint in his eye before I told him it was me, Alex, dressed to kill. He gasped, literally, then started to laugh. 'You can call me Alice if you're embarrassed,' I said. 'I'm up from down south.'

Talk about frying pan into fire. The party was indeed nice people in Parnell. Keith looked stunned all night. I kept getting backed into corners, offered G & Ts (which I took), asked to dance. One tweedy fellow with crossed eyes backed me up against a wall, lent on it with one hand near my ear, talked solemnly about his huge responsibilities as chairman of the local Young National group, getting closer and closer, until I knew I was going to be kissed. So I was kissed, long and hard, then I extricated myself with great flirtatious dignity, rubbed the lipstick off his mouth and went and draped myself all over Keith. He didn't know whether to laugh or cry.

This, I thought, is what the glamour girls have to deal with, and I don't like this either. At least no one had abused me for being famous, or mentioned the Olympics. In the car going home I took off the wig and felt rather sick. I told him to stop at the corner, because Mum and Dad didn't actually know I was out. 'Ohmigawd,' he said. I let him kiss me, even a touch of tongue. Then I got out, thinking I'd one-upped Tom with his disguises, if nothing else. I crept up the neighbour's hedge and into my room. The house was quiet. In bed, ten past two, crying, remembering happy innocent dances in a sunfrock with Andy, a year dead yesterday. Unfinished business with Tom, in Italy.

Hungover. Sunday morning, training feeling like death warmed up. It was Mr Jack who'd confirmed to the paper that I'd be having my first competitive outing in Hamilton next Saturday. That's what he thought. I said nothing, but I'm not swimming. Latin swot all day. Mum and Dad had no idea about last night, the pillow in my bed. I hid the wigs and make-up in a shoe box under my bed.

At Sunday night training, Mr Upjohn was yet again an unwelcome visitor. He'd had a private letter from Queensland, *begging* for my inclusion in the New Zealand team. He couldn't do anything about the trials —

Maurice Smythe would never climb down on that one — but please, would I reconsider. I could leave it to the last minute, not tell the press, just turn up in Wellington. Mr Jack, seeing my distress (plus what he didn't know was a hangover) said firmly, 'We'll think about it, Cyril, that's all we're saying.'

Pressure from all sides. I slept through the alarm and almost missed my Latin exam. A real nasty, worse than the school one which I'd only just scraped through. If you crash this, Alex, I thought despairingly, the words blurring on the page, pluperfect endings and who succeeded Caligula completely gone from my brain, you crash U.E. and then you'll *have* to go back to school.

I avoided Julia, spent lunchtime alone in a corner of the library, more exhausted than anything else. No more exams, swot, assignments, classes. In the afternoon, a Joan rehearsal, pathetic. Dress rehearsal tomorrow, performance on Friday. Miss Macrae asked afterwards if the wigs fitted okay and what did I go as? A tart, I said. Then, out of the blue:

'Alex, are you coming back to school next year?'

'No,' I said.

'Good,' she said, not, to my amazement, arguing or cross-examining me, or telling me I was a stupid little fool. 'Well then, you remember Caroline Bracken, the woman who's been at the occasional rehearsal. She's involved in the summer production of *Saint Joan* they're doing at the university.'

'I know, at least, I know about them doing *Saint Joan*.'

'Oh? How? They've only just decided.'

What the heck. 'At a varsity party in Grafton on election night. I overheard two, well I suppose they were men, talking about it outside the loo. They weren't very polite about Caroline.'

She laughed. 'You're getting about, young woman But I guessed as much, that you were leaving. Excellent. Privately I've thought you should for some time, despite your tender years. You're the most worldly sixteen-year-old I've ever had to deal with.'

She was looking quite smug.

'Now, Caroline wants you to audition for Joan in February.'

My mind whirled off into space. Thank God I'm not going to Aussie. Or am I, should I still give in? The Auckland champs? The nationals, early February? If I blow the nationals, do I blow America too? Should I really be getting a job? Can I even stand in front of a whole lot of varsity types and try Joan?

'It's a little irregular. Normally you have to be a second-year student. But Caroline has her doubts whether the only serious candidate for Joan can manage the whole two-week session. She thinks you might share it.'

Joan! All of her! Five or six times over.

'Remember, Alex, an audition is only an audition. She wants to see you next weekend, but she's coming on Friday night too.'

'Does she have to?'

'Why do you say that?'

'It's hopeless, girls being bishops and things. I can't feel it right. How can she tell from this?' I looked around the hall whose every creaking wooden board, every jammed window, every threadbare hem of curtain and every name on the Honours Board of Head Girls since 1923 I knew so well. Which in five days time I would walk out of for ever.

'So pitch it at the level that feels right. Trust your judgement, your instinct. Oh my dear girl,' she sighed, looking up at the empty stage, still set with Miss Gillies' carved chair on a platform for the Inquisitor, the benches for the Assessors, the stool where I sat beaten but unbowed for most of the scene. 'Yes, I'll miss you next year, Alexandra Archer. One of these days I might try telling you about my Joan. Will you do the audition?'

'Yes,' I said.

Sterner stuff

I blew the audition today, stuffed it up good and proper. The thought of inviting an Italian bus to do its worst is quite appealing. All I'd have to do is step unwisely off a pavement at rush hour. They give pedestrians little quarter at the best of times. It would, with luck, be quick.

After five days of conscience and ambition wrestling with grief, conscience won. I did the audition because that was literally his dying wish. Ah Maestro, you had too much faith in me. The spirit was willing but the instrument weak. Love, death, loss — that's what my pieces were all about in the end. Germont singing about the beauties of his far-off homeland struck doubly home. So, afraid of too much emotion, I gave them too little. I committed the one unforgivable sin. An audience of three sat silently smoking in the stalls of that musty theatre — and I simply bored them. After, they were polite, but I could see boredom written all over their faces. A pupil of Maestro? No spark here. Disappointing. Ambition should be made of sterner stuff.

Tonight, if I feel anything at all, it's anger. You, Maestro, didn't tell me how to sing in the presence of real death. You changed my breathing, phrasing, you drew from me a pure legato line, a forte I didn't know I had, a pianissimo which even you said was exquisite; you changed even the way I listen to music, to its fundamental swells and silences. But today I made the music sound dead, lifeless, as you are without life.

These past weeks I've walked endlessly, through areas of Milan previously ignored, through suburbs of closed shutters and bare trees, past factories, the faceless graceless bulk of any great city, whipped along by rain, sleet, misery. The noise of the Bargellini household has become intolerable. I am precariously short of money.

The letter-box has remained stubbornly empty. One letter, one short scrawled aerogram, would have gone a very long way, Alex. It would have been better had we never met, had I never allowed my carefully erected walls against female company and thoughts of home to be even partially broken down.

The funeral was appalling, but at least that ravaged body was laid to rest. I'd not have believed it possible, the devastation wrought in five short weeks. So painful to watch that simply to walk in the hospital door took every bit of resolve: close your eyes to the pain behind the sagging yellow skin, look only into the soul, remember the music, communicate just by being there. My last visit, about eight hours before he died, I doubt if he even knew I was in the room. Remember only the patrician face listening as you sang, the small smile and nod when you got something right.

It was my first Roman Catholic funeral, my first experience of a glass-topped casket, a body so indecently snug, a face so frozen, so closed. I knew he was a widower with no children of his own; a brother's family attended. The music in the church, for this city, this country, was inexcusably bad. Where was a former pupil, any one of the notables from opera houses all over Europe and beyond who could have raised a glorious voice, an aria from a Bach cantata, a Schubert lied? He would have been sent off with something better than a tuneless priest and an inept choir.

I see no prospect of building up any sort of relationship with Sergio. If I stay here, I must find another teacher, a second job. I have no money to get home.

In New Zealand it's summer, the shops full of Christmas tinsel, the pohutukawa out in Auckland, full crimson along Waterfront Drive, the women frazzled over presents and mince pies, students still celebrating after exams. That monstrous Santa will be up on the corner of the Farmers store in Hobson Street. At home, the shearers in full cry, three thousand sheep to get through. Alex will have finished her exams, be back to training at that pool in Newmarket. I wonder if she decided to leave school in the end, if she endured the final prize-giving.

I know this entry sounds maudlin, full of self-pity, but for once I can't sing it out of my system; I get no relief even from the piano. He was only fifty-seven. My uncle, my Dad, hangs grimly on in a wheelchair, almost incapable of speech; a teacher who showed more understanding and sympathy in eighteen months than my uncle in twenty years is gone, his voice heard no more, silenced. Damn it, I'm even smudging the page as I write.

Alessandra, one letter —

Burning bridges

November 10

Dear Tom,

Yes I am still swimming. Yes I have decided about leaving school. No, not about America. No, I don't know much about Jack Kennedy being president though I've seen stuff in the papers about the White House being the new Camelot. And No, I don't know why Miss Macrae played Joan once and then stopped acting and came out here. Do you remember her gimlet gaze, she's really a hospital matron in disguise. She's my favourite teacher, but there are some things you just don't ask.

Talking of Joan, developments! We had the last dress rehearsal today, performance tomorrow, hall full of proud parents watching little darlings do their stuff. Other classes are doing bits from *Pygmalion* etc. (All Shaw, did I tell you?) I still can't get it right, I mean surrounded by a Courtful of giggling Gerties. So it's sort of scaled down. BUT it's a sort of preliminary audition too, because a woman is coming who's putting on the whole ENTIRE Joan at the university in February and there's a chance yours truly might share the part with another girl, so I'd being doing it with real MEN and able to put some real SPARK into it. I've got to see this female on Saturday morning too, a proper audition, up at the university hall. So wish me luck.

How did yours go? I'm SURE you did BRILLIANTLY and have now got a contract to sing *Figaro*, Pong (or was it Pang) in *Turandot*, or Marcello in *La Bohème*, and lots of others. Miss Macrae told me you've actually won lots of aria contests, even Australia, and you'd been in *Julius Caesar* too, as Cassius, up at varsity. Why didn't *you* tell me! She said you were very very good. You did say you loved playing villains.

Joan actually is a bit of a worry. IF I get the part, I'll be rehearsing January and February, through training for the Auckland and the NZ champs (in Tauranga). I can do both, but I think I really should be getting a job. Dad would like that, he's tired of doing loads of overtime to make up for Gran being sick BUT that brings me to another problem. I haven't yet told them I'm leaving school. I keep putting it off, the row/ argument/disapproval. I know I'm stupid, but I just can't find the right opportunity. Then there'll be Miss Gillies (that's the Head) droning on about the advisability of doing an Upper Sixth year. I had to tell Miss Macrae, of course, but she approves, cause she knows me and she couldn't have suggested Joan if I wasn't leaving!

And I've been to a few varsity parties lately, mostly fun, not always, due to my bronze-medal face which people recognize. I've turned down the Aussie trip, partly because they said (in the paper, not to my face) I had to swim in trials, which I thought pretty OFF, but mostly because if I'm giving up swimming (IF!) I think it would be false pretences to have the trip to Aussie and then retire two weeks later. But most people don't know this of course and just think I'm being very pig-headed, and keep telling me so in very unlikely public and private places. I'm a sort of low-flying Alex these days (wings clipped, but not grounded). But you'd laugh, I tried the glamour-puss look at one party, brunette wig and loads of make-up and tarty clothes. Do you know, I looked like someone else, it worked, no one recognized me, but I had another sort of problem. If I look like me I get abused for being famous, and if I look like Jane Russell Junior (and I did, sort of) I get molested! Should I go for the plain spinster church-going look, in glasses and a grey suit (like Miss Macrae!) or — now here's a thought — see what Joan felt like, in boy's clothes. That'd slay them! I might just try it, if I get the part. It's not FAIR, that men don't have to worry about their 'look' (unless you're trying to pass yourself off as an Italian!). What I CAN'T understand is, why do people seem to think that bronze medal = swelled head = the need to bring you down a peg, make sure I f***ing well know my place, young miss. (That's what one man said). WHY aren't they PLEASED I did so well for NZ in Rome??!!

I bet you were sad about the elections, National landsliding in. I was at a Labour supporters' party that night and they went very gloomy and depressed as the results came through and Keith Holyoake came on to do his Prime Minister's bit. Where are all the women? Why don't women get elected to Parliament? If not, why not? Only four made it.

Hey, it sounds as though I'm having a pretty riotous time at parties, being in shows etc. My U.E. exams went on for three weeks, eight of them, OK except for Latin which was VILE. If I've blown it — it's back to school, Upper Sixth and all that fearsome yabber about boys/diets/ clothes, and no Joan. Too terrible to contemplate. We don't find out till mid January. Tell the truth, the whole school/swimming scene has completely lost its appeal. I really can't WAIT to get out. I'm going to do Law, but Italian too, if I can fit it in.

I had these duplicates made for you. I like the one the waiter took after that crazy opera woman (the one with the nodules on her vocal chords) had gone — drinking Lacrima Cristi. Thanks again for everying in Rome. Thanks for singing for me. I could fall in love with your voice, it's truly beautiful, it does things to me, like shivers down my spine etc. I suppose lots of women have told you that. One day you really will be famous and I'll be able to say 'Actually darling, the first time I heard him, I was quite young, it was a private recital in Rome, just me and him in a golden room near the Terme di Caracalla with a summer storm raging outside, Schubert and Puccini you know, *Bohème* and *Don Giovanni* and *Aida*, fearfully romantic.' I'm truly sorry about the airport, that it was an angry kiss, not a proper kiss — actually, I've been thinking, damn it, I missed my chance in Rome because I've never met anyone like you, and if I had the chance again . . . I was a bit strange in Rome. Too many things going on. You hinted at the airport — is there ANY hope of you coming out here next year?! Preferably sooner . . . preferably . . .

Con amore,

Ciao . . .

I haven't signed it yet. Maybe I won't post it.

Unbeknown to me, Keith has wheedled up to Mum and made his peace with Dad and included himself in the family party to come to see *Joan* on Friday night. I don't find out until just before it starts, when I've got on my black page's suit and wooden leg irons, and Miss Macrae, clever with grey and putty-coloured greasepaint, has made me look as though I've crawled out from under a stone, as Joan would have, being in a dank prison, no sun on her face for twelve months. And beaten up.

'What's that Keith Jameson doing with your parents?' says Julia, Ladvenu in black gown and Middle Ages hat, peering around the edge of the dark red curtain. I shrug at her.

'Getting keen?' She doesn't know about the parties I've been to lately, him ringing me incessantly, let alone the sessions in the car. She wouldn't approve. When she heard Keith had told me the truth about Andy's accident, the driver scooting off to Australia, she said she'd never speak to him again.

'He is, I'm not,' I say, annoyed with Keith for presuming to be there, with Julia for telling me he was. My throat is dry, my stomach hollow. But it isn't like the Tinman. This time I know my lines.

'The creep, he's being very nice to your Gran,' she says, one eye to a crack in the curtain. 'Fussing over her . . .'

'Julia, BELT UP.' She doesn't know about the Caroline lady being out front too. It's Gran's first night out since her heart attack. My mouth is very dry. I've forgotten my opening line. Miss Macrae bustles on, shoos off everyone except the beginners, me too. I go and sit alone in a classroom. I've got at least ten minutes before they come to get me. For some peculiar reason, Keith's presence is making me embarrassed. I think of Caroline, and doing this scene with men, up against something solid, like real male power and anger. I will not let Keith Jameson get in the way. I think of watching Portia in the varsity quad last year, and before that (imagining) the snake Cassius, Tom in a toga in ancient Rome, in the Forum, that rich voice turned oily. He likes playing villains. Perhaps he is one, a wolf, biding his time. I'll never know. I haven't posted the letter.

It could have been worse. Keith, afterwards, playing Boyfriend, thought I was terrific. There were some prompts. Not for me. My final speech wasn't bad. I got a lot of claps, too many. Looking down at the faces, I thought — this dear old hall: Tinman with a broken leg last year, and that song after Andy died, 'Room with a View', dressed as a young man-about-town, *circa* 1930. Ciao.

'Now let's hear what you can really do,' said Caroline, the next morning. The university hall wasn't much different from the school one, fustier, colder, less used, built of stone, not wood. She had two men in tow, glory be — one of the dark-haired languid ones from outside that disgusting loo on election night. 'Good God,' he said. 'Jean Seberg herself.'

'My name's Alex Archer,' I said frigidly.

'The Olympic swimmer,' he said. My hair was still damp from training.

'With the limited IQ and tunnel vision,' I said.

'Touché,' he said, bowing. 'I'm Ray.' But reading with him and the two others was fantastic. Now I got the contrast, the conflicts seemed real. We read bits of the Court scene, Ray very funny as the weedy Dauphin which apparently he'd already bagged, and the riverbank scene where the other guy read Dunois, uninspiringly, then part of the trial scene. 'Now come on, Alex, you know this scene,' said Caroline loudly. 'Let your voice sing, let it go.' I tried. During the scene I noticed a girl standing at the doorway at the far end, slightly furtively; a bit older than me, short dark hair, sling-back shoes, pleated skirt, polo neck sweater, slim. She disappeared before we finished. I knew at once she was the other Joan.

'We'll let you know, Alex,' said Caroline.

From exams to auditions to my first 'appearance', a different sort of test. Always *tests*.

Dad was working as much overtime as he could get. Saturday afternoon double rates were too good to miss, so he'd accepted Keith's offer to drive me down to Hamilton. Mr Jack also had to work, at the pool, so he was going later, hoped to arrive in time for my event. The rest of the Auckland team was going by bus. Keith in the Morrie Thou was marginally better than the bus; especially after yet more guff in this morning's paper: MISS ARCHER SWIMS TONIGHT, Inter-city Carnival. He kept harking back to Joan, me sending shivers down his spine, tears in his eyes — codswallop.

The last time I stood on a starting block was in Rome. The old Hamilton pool couldn't have been more different — short course, badly floodlit, and packed to the doors — to see me, they said. It was spitting with rain, and cold. I waited in my New Zealand track suit with Mr Jack and young Jenny for the first of my three events. They had me down for four, but I said firmly three, and the relay. Of course I'd swim for Auckland in the relay, why did that manager think I wouldn't!

I can't say it was awful. My times were passable, though young Jenny was a bit closer than I bargained for. The announcer got carried away and sounded like he was introducing a circus act. 'Ladies and Gentlemen, boys and girls, for the first time since her outstanding success in Rome, New Zealand's Olympic bronze medallist, from Auckland, Miss . . . Alex . . . ARCHER.'

After three months of having my swollen head chopped off, I wasn't prepared for the applause. It went on and on, and on, cheers, whistles. And I won't say, can't say I didn't like it. So you get up at five every morning, even with a woolly-head hangover from too much cheap Dally plonk or gin. You grind out your three miles. You drive eighty miles (or fly ten thousand) to put yourself, heaven knows why, on the block.

This was the good bit. I knew I was glowing, Tom's 'incandescent image'. Those families under umbrellas, all the officials and swimmers too, they didn't think I was too big for my boots. No wonder I swam well. No wonder I finished the night thinking perhaps I do want to go on, perhaps I should go to Aussie, perhaps I do want a gold. Oh hell.

Perhaps I can do varsity, and Joan, and train, and go to Tokyo. What about America — who but a fool would give that chance up? All I have to find is the airfares to and fro. I'd be halfway to Italy. Oh *hell*.

I posted the letter to Tom.

Fulsome stuff in Monday morning's paper, but even Norman Thompson not past a sideswipe: great pity I wasn't leading the team to Australia. Miss Archer, showing a new authority in her performance, would almost certainly have won the Queensland state titles. Promising fourteen-year-old Jenny Hartley, also from top coach Bill Jack's squad, was inspired by her team-mate to a respectable second placing, time within O.1 of Maggie Benton's junior record. One to watch.

Four more days at school, handing in books, sunbathing on the lawn by the small school pool, sick to death of people telling me I was *fan*tastic as Joan and of course I'd be Head Girl, and on Tuesday, the interview I hoped would never happen.

'The Staff and I have discussed this very fully, Alex, and we are very happy with our conclusions. We would like you to be Head Girl next year.'

I looked across the desk at smugly smiling Miss Gillies. From the wall behind her previous Principals and Queen Elizabeth II trooping the colour glared down at me.

'Um.' I took a deep breath. 'I can't.'

'Can't? Why not?' The smile vanished.

'I'm not going to be here next year, Miss Gillies.'

She picked up her gold fountain pen and sat right back in her deep leather chair. I don't suppose anyone in the history of this school has refused to be Head Girl. The best method of defence was attack.

'I've decided, um, I want to go straight to varsity. I've given it a lot of thought, and I know I could have a go at scholarship, but I'm really ready to leave because I do find, well, apart from Julia and one or two others, I don't have much in common with my class any more.'

She twirled her pen between her fingers. 'I do wish you had discussed this with me earlier, Alex. Your parents don't agree, surely?'

'Um, well . . .' I hesitated.

'You haven't told them?'

'No, not really. But they'll agree.'

'They might. I don't.'

'Miss Macrae does.'

'Oh does she,' she said sarcastically. I'd put my foot in it.

Then it was just as I feared, all about me being only *just* sixteen, yes sophisticated in some things, but university studies are *quite* a different story. You'd have a most fulfilling year, she said, and Head Girl looks very impressive for employers on your Curriculum Vitae later on. So does Olympic bronze medallist, I said. Alex, we *know* you'd do so much better at university for this last year at school; Law is a most difficult course; you know, the university doesn't like people coming from the Sixth Form. (Slyly) Of course you're assuming you've passed the U.E. examination. Yes, I said bravely, I'm sure I have, the papers weren't that bad, I'm sure I'm okay; remembering Latin, my Achilles heel.

She rang Mum, who was similarly outraged. I ricocheted from Miss Gillies' study to Mum's kitchen; the same arguments, pleadings, reasonings.

'I want to leave,' I kept saying. The iron kept on, up and down the pillowcases. 'You can't make me go back, Mum, I've just *had* school, up to here.'

'Dad might not be keen on supporting you to do something we believe is wrong,' she said, chillingly. What did she mean by that — throw me out? 'Help me fold these sheets, please Alex.'

I heard myself say, 'Then I'll go flatting and get a job. Lots of people put themselves through varsity.' Tom did.

That shook her. It shook me too. So did the argument about the prize-giving tomorrow afternoon. 'I'm not going, I can't bear smug teachers and smug assemblies any more,' I yelled, pulling so savagely at the sheets that I nearly pulled her right over. 'Miss Gillies will go on and on and *on* about my Olympic medal.' 'Please, Alex, for our sakes . . . I'll talk to her,' said Mum. 'No you won't,' I yelled. 'Can't you *understand*?'

Well, I didn't go to the prize-giving and Miss Gillies apparently mentioned me in despatches only once in passing, hurray. I certainly had no academic prizes to pick up, I was Captain of Swimming, a swimming blue, wow. I think it was Gran who persuaded Mum and Dad not to put their foot down; I heard them talking intensely in her room after tea. On the last day, I put on my vile blue uniform for the very last time and went to school in the morning, and told Julia and a few others I was leaving, today, now.

I didn't tell them I would have been Head Girl. They all told me I was mad, looked at me with envious eyes as though I'd somehow betrayed them. 'I'll ring you,' I said to Julia.

I went to see Miss Gillies, who was still sorry I was making this decision, but resigned, and in the end gave me her blessing, a good last report, and an amazingly good reference. A studious ninny called Patricia was going to be Head Girl, and Julia deputy. Sylvia of Guy Fawkes night, the town bike, was to be a prefect! The last straw!! Outside the staff room I said goodbye to Miss Macrae ('I'll be seeing you, if you get Joan,' she said. 'Miss Gillies is furious I didn't tell her.' 'Thanks,' I said. 'Keep in touch, Alex'), and pedalled home without a backwards glance.

It's called burning your bridges.

That was Thursday, six more shopping days to Christmas. I still hadn't heard from Caroline whats-her-name about Joan. I had one more day to make up my mind about the trials in Wellington. Mr Upjohn kept ringing Mr Jack, on his knees. One-to-watch Jenny Hartley had gone down already by car with her doting Dad, shades of Maggie's Mum driving her everywhere. I'd have to watch her myself. I kept remembering Hamilton, the clapping, enjoying it. Careful, Alex, that was a first, in a short-course pool, with no real competition and nothing at stake. *You're only as good as your last performance.* There'd be bad ones, and indifferent ones; and at the next one, the Auckland champs, all the old pressures for records — repeating Rome, being the draw-card — would come crowding back. I might be miles away from my Rome times, and then they'd all start saying: Miss Archer disappoints. Pity she's over the hill already, a has-been, a nine-day wonder, pity Rome turned out to be a fluke.

If I knew about Joan, then the trials/Australia decision would make itself. I could end up with neither Joan nor Australia. Then I'd have to get a job for the holidays out of sheer boredom. I could accept Julia's invitation to go away on their boat over New Year for a few days!

Friday morning was bull-by-the-horns time. I rang Miss Macrae, said Hi and asked her about the prize-giving and had Miss Gillies forgiven her? I told her my problem and could I ring Caroline Bracken because I *had* to know. She sounded rather pleased that I was being so pushy.

I hesitated. Just as well, because in the mail was (no letter from Italy but) a letter from Caroline apologizing for the delay and the formality of this note, saying that she herself had decided to offer me Joan along with someone called Lesley Preston who played Jessica in last year's *Merchant of Venice*. It was her wish that we could share the role.

However, she hoped I would understand that there was some resistance from the production team, and from some members of the cast, to the idea of casting someone so young and inexperienced in such a key role, at least without a more general hearing. Would I therefore come to another audition next Monday, the 20th, 7 p.m. in the university hall. And be warned that anything up to forty people would be present. Could I come in jeans, and be prepared to read the first scene with Baudricourt and do the whole of the trial scene. Lesley would be there also, and another girl also under consideration.

I told Mr Jack and Mr Upjohn who came to the pool during Friday afternoon training for a last-ditch plea, virtually waving an air ticket to Wellington at me, that I wasn't going to the trials.

So I burned another bridge. I realized no one other than Miss Macrae knew about this latest little acting venture. I certainly hadn't told Mum or Dad why I'd been late home from training that Saturday morning, the first audition. Keith — now coming to the pool every night, suggesting parties, a Rangitoto special at the American milk bar, going sailing, going out to Piha; all of which I refused, pleading housework, family — Keith didn't know, nor Mr Jack. I was becoming secretive, a schemer.

On Monday morning the team for Australia was announced. Jenny Hartley was in. My slot, really. I felt jealous, glad, very lonely. I thought of the audition that night, and if I thought I knew from my Tinman days what stage nerves were, I was dead wrong. I went over and over the lines. I'd turned down Australia; they might turn me down for Joan. I told Mum and Dad I was just going out with Keith to a movie, and asked Keith would he run me up to varsity, I had to meet someone. Oh, by the way, I'm going to be at university next year, haven't I told you? He was so surprised and so, well, pleased to be asked to be helpful that he waited the whole two hours I was in there.

Two hours? Well, that's what it took. I walked in, my heart pounding, in my jeans and dull blue polo-neck and no make-up, which seemed right for Joan. Fifty people at least, mostly men, old and young, a hundred curious eyes come to see this oddity, this famous swimmer just left school who thought she could act. The lovely Ray, oddly comforting. Also the dark girl from the doorway, Lesley (Jessica) Preston herself, with a bright smile and two cold eyes, and a dumpy female with a fantastic voice in tartan slacks. No one even mentioned the Olympics.

We sat around in a circle, on chairs and the floor. I knew most of the lines, but I read from the book like the others. I read first, then Lesley, then the dumpy lady who sounded marvellous but even sitting down just looked wrong. My face burned as I listened to them both. What was I doing here? Caroline said encouraging words, but I thought, beside them I was dull, boring, my dry croaky voice couldn't be heard. I had no show!

Well, I'm used to a bad heat before a good final. That was the heat. The trial scene was the final. They put a chair for Joan inside the circle. 'You have an advantage here, Alex,' said Caroline in my ear softly, prowling round the outside of the circle. 'You know the lines, let it flow. I know you can.'

Lesley was *good*, no doubt. The dumpy one didn't sound quite so good and still looked wrong. I couldn't imagine her pear shape in armour. When my turn came, they were all getting a bit tired, but for me, it was all the men around me that did it. I took one look at the circle of men, even though that night they were more curious and tired than hostile, and thought, I'm back in that pub, a female in forbidden male territory. I let it flow. Without the book I played to their eyes and watched their interest reluctantly grow. I thought of the heat of that bonfire.

'Okay, folks, that's great,' said a male voice as we reached the point where Joan gets dragged off. 'Call it a day.' As the group broke up, I didn't look at the dumpy one with the elocution lessons voice. Surely it would be safer to try and make her look good than take a gamble with the schoolkid, no, the ex-schoolkid. It would be between me and her, I knew. 'Lesley, Andrea, Alex, thank you all for coming,' said Caroline. 'I'll ring you all tomorrow.'

Keith, who'd apparently been sitting at the back the whole way through, said 'You'll hose in.'

But when she rang, it was for another audition on the Thursday morning, just her and an older man with a beard who took me outside the hall, into the quad where I'd seen *The Merchant* last year, where Tom once was Cassius. I had to read the Dunois scene with him. Eric's voice was strong, mine seemed to dissolve across the grass before it got anywhere near the stone walls around. Passers-by watched and made me feel stupid. We read the scene three times, with Caroline standing where the seats would be, urging 'let *go*, Alex, use your chest voice, project it. I know you can. This time, when he kneels to you, it's a lifetime ambition realized, hug him as though you meant it.' A total stranger! But his eyes were kind and enthusiastic and drew me on and I did it. They made me do the final speech of the trial scene, four times, each time bigger than the last, until my throat ached. Tom wouldn't have had any difficulty making himself heard.

I sat exhausted on the grass while they talked. I thought, oh gawd, Mum will be wondering where I am, I promised to look after the kids while she did her last bits of Christmas shopping. I haven't even started mine. I'm a varsity student, nearly. I'm Joan, nearly?

'You're it' said Caroline, smiling above me. 'First rehearsal weekend of January 7th, Saturday at 10 sharp. I'll send you a schedule in the mail. I don't want you to learn your lines. Go away and forget her, have a good Christmas break. Marcia tells me you've had a hard year. I want you fresh.'

I'll come for three days, I said to Julia, still at me to go boating on the new family launch over New Year, take a few days away from the pool. Mum and Dad didn't approve much, even when I said I'd arranged with Mr Jack to do my training in the sea, behind the launch. Some sea air would do me good. I was finding the pool, and the training, rather dreary these days.

But you don't forget Joan of Arc. She was just another thing I had to tell disapproving Mum and Dad and Mr Jack who was still waiting patiently for us to have a long talk about my future, the American thing and all that.

Another weird Christmas — last year I was a mess, Andy had just died. This year, with the challenge of Joan making me go hot and cold in bed at night, a public performance, six times, not just in front of long-suffering parents — I was also a mess. At a crossroads, without any signposts.

I sat in church with the family on Christmas morning, and with wet eyes listened to an elderly baritone sing 'Unto Us a Boy is Born', very flat. I was crying mostly for Ginnie — she had a boy yesterday, Christmas Eve, four pounds, only seven months, Caesarean section and a lot of drama. He lived only three hours.

Mum seemed surprised Ginnie had gone into early labour. I told her to ask Auntie Pat if by any chance Ginnie had a few bruises; to ask that two-faced foxtrotting treacherous little bastard Mervyn where they came from. Mum did; she had. Merv had thumped Ginnie once too often, too hard. They should throw the book at him, said Dad, so angry he broke two dishes he was drying, but his ninny of a sister wouldn't even tell her husband. She couldn't face the rows and scandal. Ginnie would be returning home when she came out of hospital in Hamilton and getting a divorce. She's eighteen!

The choir sang 'See Amidst the Winter Snow' — does it snow in Milan in winter? Not even a tiny Christmas card from Tom, let alone any more fat and interesting letters. I wish, I *wish* I hadn't posted that letter. Perhaps he's gone skiing in the Dolomites. Bugger him. Forget him, Alex. Like he's forgotten you.

In flight

Two hours out of Rome, first stop Cairo. A strange way to spend Christmas Day. Every hour an hour nearer Auckland.

An exercise in memory: that toll call last week to Denise. I'd forgotten what a good Kiwi farmer's wife sounds like. Alex's accent was mild, compared. She didn't write again. Did she have a boyfriend, all along?

From Denise, the usual cold banalities: Pleasant surprise Tom, after so long. Yes, Dad's fine, as well as can be expected. Mum too. We're all getting together for Christmas, kids, the whole fam-damily catastrophe but . . .

Denise: Is this merely a social call, Tom?
Tom: Can you lend me the airfare to get home?
Denise: (Laughing) Tomas asking for money? You must be desperate. What's this — a sudden desire to see the aged parents? Be with us all pulling crackers, gorging on Christmas pud?
Tom: I can't get a flight until Christmas Day.
Denise: The children will be disappointed. You could have sung a lovely solo in church.
Tom: Let's cut the bullshit, Denise. I'm asking the only person in the world I can ask.
Denise: Why not Dad?
Tom: You know why not. Even if I was the blue-eyed boy running the farm, generosity was never his strong point.
Denise: True. (Said with feeling; I've heard nothing to alter the situation, that Dad still pulls the purse strings from his wheelchair while Denise and Harry do all the work.)
Tom: Briefly, my teacher here has just died. Cancer, of the colon, and secondaries, it raced through him in five weeks. I've had hardly a break in eighteen months. Before I find another teacher, I need to sort myself out.
Denise: Homesick, Tom? Really? I thought you never wanted to see New Zealand again.

Tom: (Gritting teeth) People change. Motives change.
Denise: Not a girl, is it? Met a nice Kiwi girl swanning around Europe in a clapped-out van? Plenty of them are doing it these days.
Tom: How could it be? I've forgotten what nice Kiwi girls look like. I need about £300. Can you send me a bank draft?
(Pause)
Denise: You're asking a lot.
Tom: I realize that.
Denise: No job, and what training you do have fairly useless. You won't be able to pay it off for years.
Tom: (What one will do for love, or infatuation, despite letters, any real clues as to what I might find in Auckland!) I may go back to teaching.
Denise: I'll have to ask Harry.
Tom: Christ, Denise! Dad aside, it's you who controls the money. (That could have been unwise, Tom). You always seemed to be the only one who had the slightest idea what singing meant to me.
Denise: What it meant to me was years of listening to you and Dad rowing. Him turning into a bitter, mean old man. He had to do with a citified son-in-law, didn't he, for the farm, and me spending my poor life banging round in gumboots.
(Not exactly poor, Denise, and positively rolling in it when Dad goes . . . . I waited.)
Denise: I'm tired. We've got the shearers here, nine of them permanently hungry. I'm sick of the sight of scones. (Pause) Even if I can sneak it past Dad, I'll still have to ask Harry.
Tom: Okay, ask Harry. I'll pay it back within a year, with interest. Here's the bank address. Can you cable it through tomorrow? But don't tell Dad or anyone I'm coming. I don't want a great family build-up.
Denise: Always one for mysteries. Little dramas going on behind that smooth mask, under those hats. But you've lost a bit of your oomph, me lad. Italy lost its appeal? (Sharp!) I suppose you speak Italian like a native. How are the singing lessons going?
Tom: Denise — thanks.
Denise: One condition.
Tom: What's that? (Tarred with her father's brush?)
Denise: Some of those fat juicy scrumptious chocolates with liqueur inside. A big, big box.

We actually laughed, an unusual occurrence. The stewardess has just brought the menu for BOAC's Special In-Flight Christmas dinner. The chocolates (acquired with my remaining lire in lieu of eating these past few days) are in the rack above. I can see the heel of Italy quite clearly below, receding into an intense blue haze.

The piper's son

I had told Julia I was glad to be having a few days' break from Keith's lecherous eyes every day at the pool, but Julia hadn't told me about Mario.

Well, actually, she had, when was it, about a year ago? That day she told me about the deal with her father. I'd always wondered what he looked like, this half-Italian second cousin lover-boy, married but separated, who'd made indecent advances to Julia, in her own home. Julia, amazing asthmatic Julia, had agreed to keep quiet — as long as she could go to medical school. Her father was furious, but agreed.

She hadn't told me Mario was over from Sydney for Christmas, visiting his wife and kids now living in New Zealand, or that he was coming away on the launch over New Year. She didn't know herself, until he walked along the marina in his Persil-white nautical gear and climbed aboard. Grey hair, fortyish, large sleepy spaniel's eyes. That made Julia's parents, her two older brothers James and Charles, Julia and me, and Mario. The boat was called the *Juli-Beth* after Julia and her mother. Ugh!

We hurtled off down the harbour, putting up a huge wake; Julia's bandy little father with purple veins in his legs, wearing baggy navy shorts and a cap with SKIPPER written on it, Mario his right-hand man at the controls, grey hair sleeked back in the wind. Her faded mousy Mum in crisp navy slacks and fresh shiny pink lips hung on for grim death, and her brothers lolled around looking nautical but basically useless. At least Andy had taught me how to tie a bowline and do a half-hitch. I wasn't expected to be useful so I didn't try. I watched them fumble.

I hated the bouncing, the slamming, the rolling as we headed off across the gulf. The launch was huge, could sleep eight, with lots of chrome and carpets and a small speedboat hanging off the back. Julia was feeling sick, her Mum too, but Mr Foxton, fascinated by his new toy, wouldn't listen to pleas that we find somewhere and stop for lunch and enjoy the perfect weather. We left Auckland behind, Brown's Island, Motuihe Island, Waiheke; lolloped across deep blue swells towards the Coromandel peninsula and ended up anchoring in an isolated bay called Te Kouma with lots of other yachts and launches.

I soon realized Mr Foxton didn't take me seriously, my request to keep up my daily stint of training. Mario just laughed too, but eventually he and a very quiet Julia came with me in the speedboat because Julia wasn't allowed to work the outboard. I swam out into the bay, trying to work out distances from how my muscles felt, trying to forget sharks, those below and above. I didn't like the lack of markers, of signposts, just swimming blindly into the green streaked with sunlight. I've had nightmares about green sea. Mario stopped laughing after I'd been swimming for an hour. He said next time he'd bring a fishing line.

There were some good things. The weather was gorgeous. Julia and I went for long walks on the hills, among cows, not talking much. The rest of the family went water-skiing, which I thought a basically futile sort of pastime, and visited other launches, for elevenses, fourses, the sun being over, or not over, or nearly over the yardarm, and came back extremely flushed and happy. Julia took me training again, with her rowing alongside.

On New Year's Eve the launch was covered with laughing people, coming and going from dinghies. My Olympic exploits suddenly became very important, for about ten seconds per group of visitors. 'Oh, Alex Archer, the Olympic girl, yes of course, you're much prettier than your photographs.' The bay was full of boats, lights, voices singing, shouting, music. Mario kept watching me sleepily from behind his glass of pink gin. We had fillet steak out of the fridge and Australian wine and French champagne he'd bought specially for tonight. At midnight people let off flares, crimson blazes hanging suspended in the sky, and we all sang 'Auld Lang Syne' and joined hands, Mario next to me and pressing my hand.

1961, here we come.

I wondered how they celebrate New Year's Eve in Italy. Not with a Scottish song, I bet. It's winter — do they have family dinners, fires, fireworks, sing famous opera choruses?

I went training by myself the next morning, while the rest of the family and all the yachts in the bay slept late. I swam past white hulls glinting in the yellow light towards a headland, landed on a little beach, lay for a while.

I was sick of men, the sleazy Mario, those boring brothers, demanding brusque father, and back home, moony-eyed Keith, and others too far away to mention. Dad's okay of course but he was working too hard and I hardly ever saw him, and Mr Jack just made me feel guilty all the time. Miles away from anywhere I tried Joan's last speech to the seagulls, as big as I could make it. *But to shut me from the light of the sky and the sight of the fields and flowers; to chain my feet so that I can never again ride with the soldiers nor climb the hills . . .*

... what would I choose, if I couldn't sit on a beach like this, with the pohutukawa dropping their red needles on the wet rocks, and the greenest, free-est hills in the world behind me waiting to be climbed over? If I faced the prospect of prison for life looking slug-like grey as I had that night on the school stage, and would again soon . . . I tried the speech again. The seagulls flew away.

Later that day we motored around to Coromandel to get fuel and a few stores. I swam part of the way beside the launch, while they looked down on me with pitying eyes. The little township was full of people in shorts. Julia and I saw notices for the Miss Coromandel Beauty Quest, 2 p.m. We were stupid enough to mention it at lunch. The men wanted to go ashore, teased us, but particularly me about entering. 'What about it, girls, put on your bikinis. Alex, with those long Jane Russell limbs of yours . . .' I told them I thought such things were humiliating, like a slave market, just an excuse to ogle legally at legs; I'd sooner die. They told me it was good clean fun, where's your sense of humour gone, Alex, lovely to see a pretty girl . . .

The girls, seventeen of them, were lambs dressed as mutton and not pretty at all. They wore fancy togs with padded bras and white high-heels and far too much make-up and had obviously walked straight out of the local hairdresser's, all with hair like the Queen's. A stage had been rigged up on the beach and a local wise-guy was the compére, and it was all extremely tacky.

'Ladies and gentlemen, boys and girls, please welcome . . . the winner, Doreen St John, Miss Coromandel 1961.' They put a shiny red sash around the weepy winner and a home-made crown on top of her stiff hairdo, and everyone whistled and a knock-kneed youth played a trumpet fanfare. I told Julia I couldn't bear it, I was going training, and I did, past all the waiting dinghies at the wharf, and the moored yachts, so far they got worried and came after me, Julia and Mario in the speedboat. Mario, Julia told me later, had been chatting up Miss Coromandel; they'd had to drag him away.

I was going to have to catch a bus home, but Mr Foxton found a launch returning to Auckland the next day. They would take me and Mario, who also had to get back. I said my goodbyes, thank yous. We climbed onto the other launch, nearly as big, but older, with about twelve people on board. Away from the family, and I suppose the embarrassment of Julia and her father (the only people who knew about his moment of weakness last year, or so *he* thought — away from them, Mario made no bones about sitting close, putting his arm around me, calling me sweetie, *cara* Alessandra. We were packed into the stern area; I moved inside, he followed. I moved outside again, so did he. I watched the city come nearer, the Grecian museum up on the Domain hill above the city. At the marina he tried to help me off the boat, as if I couldn't see where to put my own feet, and offered to take me home in his car. He was old enough to be my father. I hate men. I told him it was people like him that gave Aussies a bad name, and stomped off to find a bus, and went straight to afternoon training, feeling the cool fresh water on my sunburnt skin, glad to be back.

Except for one thing: Keith, who came *every* afternoon. I was used to being watched at the pool, parents pointing, showing their kids the Olympic bronze medallist at work. We trained half in public time, with people lying around sunbathing on the spectator stands, half when the pool had closed. Keith perched on the rail buddy – buddy with Mr Jack and watched. He bought me iceblocks when I'd finished and got hurt when I said I was riding home, thanks. He'd have handed me my towel, licked me dry, if I asked him. I had never felt so *watched*.

Which might be why I said yes, I'd go to the pictures with him Friday night, because I was going to say, in the car on the way home, Look Keith, I like you, I really do, but that's as far as it goes, please don't get too serious, I'm not into boyfriends at present, a few kisses don't equal being owned – words to that effect.

With rehearsals starting tomorrow, I wanted to be free of complications. We had the choice of *Carry on Constable*, or *The Nun's Story*, or Elvis in *G.I. Blues*. I'd quite like to see *Ben Hur* again, I said; that incredible chariot race. He booked tickets, the Civic's best seats.

I wasn't looking my best. My nose was red and peeling from those four days sunbathing on Julia's boat. I'd lost weight since Rome. I'd put on jeans, a T-shirt, a cardigan that clashed, pulled my belt in too tight and made my hair into a beehive with backcombing and hairspray; thick dark blue eyeliner, blue mascara, Audrey Hepburn eyebrows, and thick pale lipstick to divert attention from my red nose, and dark glasses. Not the sort of clothes girls-from-good-homes wear to the Civic on a Friday night. Proper nice girls mince up and down Queen Street looking at each other's best suits and long gloves and matching accessories. In short, slightly in disguise again, a widgie, a mess. Not the Bronze Medallist, just someone who looks a bit like her. Some familiar faces in the foyer looked me up and down, curious, askance, disbelieving.

You know how it is at the end of a three hour film. Your eyes are glazed, and your lipstick worn off by ice-cream and by Keith finally having his way as the credits roll. The Civic's famous star-studded blue sky twinkles above you, the minarets blaze orange and turquoise and gold and scarlet. You throw your Jaffa packet under the seat and stand up. Keith puts a possessive arm over your shoulders. You wait for your row to start moving. You might see someone you know.

You see Tom.

You see a man below you in the aisle, from the cheaper seats closer to the screen. He's alone, and unshaven, in jeans and T-shirt, and sandals. He's holding a hat. Can't be. Keith's arm has suddenly become very heavy. Your row is moving, but not you. He comes closer. He sees you.

Neither of you speak. His eyes, expressionless, hold yours as he is swept past. You see the broad back you held onto in Rome, see him put his hat on, cover the glowing and even longer bronze hair. Keith gives you a gentle push. Is he here for the same reason as I'm here, a connection with Rome, ancient Rome, any Rome, or just to see a good film?

He's not in the foyer with the stone elephants, not on the Indian staircase, not by the ticket box. He is outside the entrance, on the corner of Queen Street. By the traffic lights. Waiting. Unavoidable.

You walk out feeling stupid, exposed and ridiculous in your widgie gear. Mind you, he looks pretty terrible himself.

'Gidday, Kiwi,' I say, with my dark glasses on.

'Alessandra?' Just a hint of a question: that you, in there? He bends forward and picks up my sweating right hand, the one not still being held onto tightly by Keith, and kisses it. Passers-by look on curiously. People don't wear hats or kiss widgies' hands by night in Auckland.

'Who's this?' says Keith, sizing up the straw hat, the generally down-at-heel appearance.

'Tomas Alexander, at your service,' he says, the voice like dark chocolate, clicking his heels like a Russian soldier, bowing stiffly. He gestures at me. 'We met in Rome.'

'This is Keith Jameson,' I say. Keith lets go my left hand. They shake hands. Tom's eyes have gone frighteningly blank.

'You met in Rome?' says Keith, stupidly, bored already.

'Briefly,' I say.

'I acted as interpreter to the New Zealand team,' says Tom. Acted is about right, I think. 'I was lucky enough to see Alex win her bronze medal.'

'Interpreter?' says Keith, suspiciously.

'I speaka da lingo. I was studying there.'

Was? Was? Is he trying to tell me something? He is studiously avoiding my eye.

So we all stand looking at the traffic lights. I think, this is going to go nowhere. Here is Keith doing his hands-off-this-is-*my*-girl bit and here is Tom, large as life in Queen Street, hasn't even told me he was coming, not a single miserable letter since October 13th, since mine telling him I'd never met anyone like him, virtually that I was head-over-heels, could he please come home; no answer, two and a half months of sheer misery, expects me . . . what does he expect? Anything?

'Gottago,' I say. 'Training, never stops, you know.' It can be convenient, the commitment of training, at times. Keith puts his arm very deliberately around my shoulder, strokes the side of my neck with his fingers, pulls playfully at my earlobe. I see a very faint glint behind the watching brown eyes. 'Ciao, Tomas.'

'What a drip,' says Keith as we walk away up Wellesley Street. 'What was he studying, in Italy?'

'Music, I think.'

'That explains it.'

I was too stunned to say what I should have said to Keith that night. I made feeble excuses about training, first Joan rehearsal tomorrow, let him kiss me once and ran inside, scrubbing my face clean and climbing into my jamas before I went to say goodnight to Mum and Dad.

I lay awake for a long time. Even unshaven, even with long hair, even in Jesus sandals and old T-shirt, he still . . . I realized now it wasn't just his hair and his stocky build; he seemed to fill the whole inside of the Civic, in the street people had looked at him twice, there was something generously larger-than-life about him, an aura. What was he doing here? Why hadn't he told me? Just a holiday, or for good? Surely not, he hates this place, can't stand New Zealanders, philistines to a man. Why was he here at all? Given up singing, going home to the farm? Joining the local opera company? I had no idea how or where or even if I'd see him again.

After training I finally had to tell Mum about the Joan of Arc thing, why I was catching a bus into the university this bright Saturday morning, why she mustn't worry about me fitting in Joan with my training, the Auckland champs in a week and NZ champs in four; especially as I'm not going off to Australia with the team which flies to Brisbane tomorrow. Young Jenny was at her last training session this morning, proudly showing me her New Zealand blazer, her black shoulder bag. 'Mum, I'm not starting varsity till March, and it's mostly weekend rehearsals anyway.' She just shrugged her shoulders. 'Nothing I say . . . I'm pleased about Joan, Alex, it's a great opportunity for you. You make your own decisions these days.'

I found Gran out with the chooks and pressed five shillings into her hand. 'You won,' I said. 'He's here, the bugger didn't write, didn't answer my letter, and yes it was a love letter, sort of. Didn't tell me anything, just turns up, him with his hats, I saw him at the pictures last night, I don't know anything else, here's your five bob.'

'He didn't last long,' she said happily. The bus got me to town at 9.20, so I walked slowly through Albert Park, up the steep steps and curving asphalt paths, past the statue of Sir George Grey and the floral clock. The university tower, another 'wedding cake', loomed ahead of me, the ornate doorway, inside the echoing circular entrance hall. I'll be five years walking in this door, I thought, across these blue mosaic floors. I was still early. I wondered if I could get through, down the stairs, into the quad where the play would be done.

I could hear voices. Male, female, a friendly conversation, laughter. As I got nearer down the stone corridor with the slim arched windows, I realized I knew the voice. There's only one voice like that.

This was a Tom I hadn't met. Another one. Talking flat out, joking, relaxed, intimate, with a female voice; about Italy, Milan, his family there, operas he'd seen, a bit of time in Rome for the Olympics, saw Snell and Halberg win their races. No mention of mine. He needed a short spell at home (why?), just arrived, a week ago (why hadn't he got in touch sooner?). Not sure how long he'd be staying, but camping meanwhile with a friend in Mt Eden, remember Barry? now teaching English at Mt Albert Grammar.

Then, abruptly, it was him asking questions, hearing about her graduate work in nineteenth century novels, her holidays hitch-hiking round the South Island, her flatting arrangements, so that I knew they must have been the same year at varsity. Old friends? More?

I know the dangers of eavesdropping. After Napier, overhearing the selectors, I should. It wasn't eavesdropping, just childish leaden feet, listening to this cheerful man and a woman laughing, flirting. I stood in the cloisters, staring out at the grass, aged fourteen again and listening to grown-ups, listening just a fraction too long.

They came still talking around the corner and saw me. I'm pleased to say this time Tom's mouth literally dropped open.

'Gidday, Tom, again,' I said. He was wearing exactly the same clothes as last night, the hat too. He probably slept in them. He probably smelt. I was in jeans, but at least I had a clean shirt and a face clean of warpaint. 'Tomas.'

'I'm dreaming.'

'Nope. You want to kiss my hand?'

I held out my hand. He kowtowed, rather embarrassed, I thought. The M.A. student, twentyish, owlish in heavy glasses, but handsome, looked amused.

'What are you doing here?' he said.
'Rehearsal. What are you doing here?'
'Rehearsal.'

We looked at each other. I wouldn't know what he was thinking, but I was thinking, please help me, tell me it isn't true, is Tomas Alexander the price I have to pay for being Joan? What part will he be playing this time?

'Are we talking about the same play?' he said.
'I guess so.'
'*Saint Joan* by George Bernard Shaw?'
'Yep,' I said, making him work. The penny dropped.
'You're the raw little first-year they're bringing in to share Joan!'
'Yep.' I liked seeing this smooth always-in-control man, never at a loss for words, for once struck dumb. Good. I didn't like the broad grin that was spreading across his handsome freckled face. He took off his hat, knelt down on one knee, crossed hat on chest, and looked up. '*You command the king's army. I am your soldier.*'

'Dunois,' I said, recognizing the line. Ohmigod, I don't think I can do this, I'll have to kiss him. He stood up, and was still looking at me with glinting eyes but saying with an unpleasantly grating voice, slightly clipped, nasal and higher in pitch, an evil voice, '*I am the Promotor; and it has been my painful duty to present the case against the girl.*'

'D'Estivet,' I said, recognizing those lines too. 'The Prosecutor, Promotor, whatever you call him, a nasty piece of work. *Both*?'

'They're always rather short of men. It's a huge male cast. I think my old friend Caroline Bracken was quite pleased to see me appear out of the blue.'

'That would be an understatement,' said the woman, laughing. 'We'd better get upstairs. Alex, I'm Genevieve, stage manager, general factotum, for my sins. You'll be seeing a lot of me.' We walked up the wide curving stairs. I very nearly walked across the blue mosaics and straight out the main doorway; I must have hesitated when I saw the crowd of people in the hall, heard Caroline's loud fruity voice calling for folks to find a seat, it's five past ten, we're going to have punctuality in this production, let's get down to work.

Nerves were bad enough, Tom as himself was worse, but Tom as Dunois, Joan's only friend at Court, would be too much. 'Come, Alex,' he said quietly, borrowing a Dunois line, letting Genevieve walk on into the hall. 'Today there'll be a lot of chat, a gentle read-through, everyone settling down. Let me begin to make an actor of you.'

You've done that already, I thought bitterly.

I avoided him all that day, all Sunday, refused suggestions for lunch, coffee breaks, except in groups. I hated his unwashed stubble-faced actor's appearance, just another of his disguises, the easy familiarity with all the cast, male and female. I hated his eyes which I knew were often on me, even when it wasn't my turn to read; eyes which, when he thought I wasn't watching, were clouded and sad. Something had happened. He wasn't sad like that in Rome. If he wasn't going to tell me I wasn't going to ask.

During those first readings, I hated his voice for Dunois, the slightly gruff but generous noble soldier, and his reedy voice for D'Estivet the lawyer in wolf's clothing, out to get Joan. Both were absolutely right. I hated the fact that of all the men, his timing came so naturally that right from the start he made the lines come alive and dragged me along with him. I hated sharing the role and I hated it when my turn came to read. I hated Lesley for being so good and myself for being so bad, cowardly, holding back.

I hated him for being here, not telling me anything, why, how; not acknowledging the things I put in that last letter, not thanking me for the pictures I sent, not asking me how it'd been since Rome, nothing about what I was doing this year. By the end of the weekend I'd got angry enough to thump somebody and was ready to give Joan away. I went in Keith's car to the pool for Sunday night training, determined to ring Caroline Bracken tomorrow. The plump lady with the ringing voice and the fat bottom in tartan slacks could have the part; I've got a few swimming races to prepare for, an obligation to my public.

I might even ask Keith out somewhere, anywhere.

After-images

Sunday, Jan 8, 11.30 p.m., sleepless, restless — a weekend of torment. Why, oh Jesus, *why* did I not have the courage to confront her when she finally turned up at the pool last week (last Monday to be precise) after two days of disappointment. Where had she been? I thought athletes at her level, like ballet dancers, couldn't afford even one day off.

Why did I prevaricate, procrastinate, fatally delay what should have been a reunion of hope and potential, remain cowardly up on the stands, watching her toil remorselessly up and down, talk to her avuncular coach, talk with a younger less classically-shaped girl also wearing a New Zealand track suit, joke with that scarred, bearded, and clearly besotted boy in close attendance whose name I now know is Keith Jameson; leave with him.

Such a gallery of images I am building up! The first, in the garish half-light of the emptying cinema, under the artificial sky, Alex as rebel, playing common, as artless as the Indian decor around her, hardly recognizable as the same girl in her summer dresses in Rome. Presumably for good reasons — seeking anonymity, perhaps? Or was that the real Alex, and the simply dressed girl in Rome a pious fraud, a counterfeit? I still don't understand the coolness, even hostility of the reception. I can't believe she favours that boy.

The second image: I'm sure someone, one of the Pre-Raphaelite school, has already painted it. The stonework back-lit, that slim boyish body relaxed and in profile, face in shadow; shafts of dusty sunlight beneath the receding arches of the cloister; a study in perspective, composition, available lighting, what can be done with all the tones of blue, grey, green. A picture!

Can I put down her refusal to respond just to nerves? Was it just my dissolute appearance? Twice caught short, Angel Alexander as down-at-heel wharfie, actor, archetypal perpetual student, the *Cherry Orchard*'s worn Peter Sergeievitch Trofimoff. Not, at this moment nor in the near future, a singer. Angel Alexander back on the wharves, tedious labour but good pay. Peevish big sister Denise will have her £300 in short order.

Yet with Alex I doubt that a shave, a haircut, better clothes (could I afford any) and better food would cut much ice. At least I remain unrecognized, have to endure only uni*varsity* student taunts, bloody poofs, spongers, the usual. Nothing changes. I shall stay thinner, unshaven, stick with the starving artist look. You, Alessandra, are to a large degree responsible.

I am frankly terrified of her possible Joan. Her first readings were nondescript, overawed by the occasion. Who wouldn't have been in her shoes; maybe she was also, I'd like to think, somewhat thrown off-balance? Lesley I remember from two, three years ago. She'll be good, a traditional slip-of-a-girl Joan, but she lacks energy, fire, that compelling quality. Alex will be superb. She'll fill the stage, with persuasion, anger, despair, defiance, the full force of her personality. I've never seen her angry, apart from that volcanic glimpse at the airport. Jack Dunois will be acted off the stage if I'm not careful, made to look a wet, rather than the tough successful commander he is. D'Estivet, *vulpine beneath his veneer*, a key figure among the determined bigots of the trial scene, offers real scope, real tension. Dangerous territory? What will come of it all?

I must brave the pool, this week, before Wednesday's rehearsal. Tomorrow, if not working. Find a way past the gallant and protective Keith. Haul our relationship back to square one, clear the decks.

I must, if I'm ever to sleep again.

Caught short

Monday morning I'd changed my mind.

I would *not* ring Caroline Bracken and back out of *Joan*. I wanted to try Joan and I was damned if I was going to let Tomas Alexander or Keith Jameson or a few championship races put me off. I began to read the trial transcripts again. How she stood up to those men!

And that odd insistence on men's clothing. Why was it so important to her? Was it simply the freedom, the right clothes for the job? I could understand that. The protection against being beaten up and/or raped? Would people react as strongly now as they had then? They called her unnatural, unwomanly, dissolute, ill-shaped, immodest. If you wear jeans about the place these days, you're a tart or a tomboy, I should know; but what about a sportscoat, collar and tie?

Tuesday morning at the pool I could feel the pressure rising; the Auckland champs next week, and a large preview in the morning paper, Norm Thompson raving on about my first Auckland appearances since Rome. I was expected to win the three freestyle events comfortably with my only real opposition, Jenny Hartley, away in Brisbane; also the butterfly and medley for good measure, a lark. My pride told me I had to do a good sprint, under 64.0s, at worst under 64.5s. My time trials stuck stubbornly around 65s or above. Mr Jack didn't know about Joan, unless the ever-present Keith had told him during the little chats they had while I was training. If he had, I'd *kill* him.

While at the pool Keith didn't go swimming much. I didn't think he could swim, at least not very well. He kept asking me out sailing in his dinghy. I told him I was still having to help Mum with Gran, help mind the kids, which was partly true. Gran was much better, though slower around the house. And it was still school holidays, three weeks yet before school started. The kids hadn't had a holiday at the beach this year. I did occasionally take all or some of them shopping or to the park.

There was a letter for me when I got home Tuesday, no stamp, cheap paper but my name, Alessandra Archer, in the familiar large fancy script. Mum looked at me rather strangely. I wondered if Gran had told her that my life had (yet again) got rather complicated. So he'd identified my house, seen the family villa that needed a paint, the bougainvillaea now blazing crimson on the verandah, bikes and balls in the driveway, the letterbox Dad keeps saying he'll fix; passed by, but not come in. A short letter. *Alex, can you come early to the pool this afternoon, say 3.30? I'd like to see you without hangers-on.* Blunt enough. He meant Keith.

My pounding heart made me and him wait twenty minutes while I sat sweating outside the pool on my bike and tried to get control of myself. Look, Tom, I rehearsed, we're stuck with this play, I don't know why you've suddenly turned up in Auckland but that's your business, Rome was fun but let's just be friends, forget I ever wrote that letter, huh? I want to swim well at the nationals, I want to be a good Joan, in other words, steer clear, huh?

So who was the first person I saw when I walked in? Keith, early, perched on the rail like a blackbird. Changed and sitting on the starting block, I looked nonchalantly around the sunbathers up on the stands. He wasn't hard to pick, the burning man in the old-fashioned red togs, straw hat, sucking an orange iceblock, sitting up there above and behind Mr Jack, Keith, and the rest of the squad. He hadn't ever gone for a swim in Rome. The powerful chest I'd seen before, but the rest of him was slimmer and browner than I expected. I didn't wave, nor him. No signal. Single guys — there were always lots of them at the pool. He'd picked up quite a respectable tan in a short time back in Auckland.

Three times now he'd seen me with Keith. So Keith was the resident Boyfriend. That's what they both thought. I did an angry flip turn. Everything was aching, including my heart. Bloody hell. Through my bow-wave I saw them both, Keith on the rail below, Tom in the stands above. At some point during a time trial, just before the pool officially closed, the man in the straw hat must have got fed up. When I shook the water from my eyes, I saw the stands were empty.

Our first night rehearsal, Wednesday, I went straight from training, by bus. Dad had offered to come and pick me up at 10.15. By the time the bus reached town, it was raining hard, and I'd forgotten an umbrella, even any sort of jacket. I ran from shop verandah to tree to next tree, and used a wet towel as a shield, but by the time I'd got up through the park my T-shirt was soaked, jeans too. It wasn't warm, for midsummer. As I walked past the floral clock and across the road towards the arched doorway I saw a motor scooter parked under the trees, and someone, Tom, get up from sitting on the steps and begin fossicking round inside a pillion bag. He held out a crumpled shirt and a pair of slacks.

'Put those on,' he said.

'I'm alright. Where did you get the motor scooter?'

'Seventh-hand, for a song. It goes, just, and I'm not a bad mechanic. You should get a motor scooter. Alex, take them.' He shook the bundle of clothes at me. Today he was wearing a brown oilskin over his jeans and a cloth cap. He looked like a fisherman. 'I know you're tough as old boots, but your voice is valuable now, not to be weakened by colds. Look after it.'

I took them, but not for the reasons he thought. If I'd been wondering how it would be, in men's clothing, now was my chance. We were exactly the same height. I was probably a bit slimmer round the waist.

'Tell me,' he said, as we walked up the steps. 'Did you enjoy *Ben Hur*?'

'Fantastic. Great film.'

Casually, while taking off his oilskin, 'Keith a swimmer, is he?'

I stood looking at the mosaics, playing for time, hearing voices coming from the hall. What he really *means* is, the Boyfriend? Someone, the lovely Ray, ran up the stone steps, shaking an umbrella. 'Evenin' all,' he said. 'You look a bit damp, Jean Seberg.'

'I answer to Alex,' I said. 'Where's the ladies' loo around here?'

'One floor down,' said Ray.

Tom was still waiting when I came back. The grey slacks were a touch loose, but a belt threaded through the loops kept them up. In the mirror in the loo I didn't look much different from Katherine Hepburn, those wartime ladies in their slacks.

'What I need is a short back 'n sides,' I said when I joined him.

He laughed. 'You mean, for modern-day Joan shock tactics?'

'Right.'

'Don't, Alex. Caroline likes authenticity. She gives designers and costume people a hard time. Joan's hair, even cut like a man's, would have been longer, the page-boy crop, with a short fringe. Almost like hers. You should be growing it.'

'Jean Seberg's was short.'

'True. The look reinterpreted for the times, perhaps.' He looked at me critically. 'Those slacks look better on you than on me. I remember two girls here who wore male clothing for a while, waistcoats and plus-fours. Created quite a stir, you can imagine. As did the famous ones like the divine Sarah Bernhardt, George Sands, Collette. And Joan of course.'

Was that a warning? Tom, talking so lightly about girls choosing to wear trousers, knew nothing of my past problems. If I wanted to find out how Joan felt, I'd be accused, yet again, of being a masculine sort of girl, only worse, because it would have to be blatantly in everyday life, not in costume for a play. I wasn't sure I had the nerve for that, on top of everything else.

'Want a ride home?' asked Tom, again so casually, when the rehearsal ended at ten.

I thought of Rome, that broad back vibrating with his songs, and now the chance of seeing Auckland after summer rain as I'd seen Rome. I told him Dad would already have left, and stuck with Lesley, Ray, and a group of others chatting on the steps.

Lesley wasn't being overly friendly. We'd both read a scene each, still sitting round in a circle, talking about what was actually happening in each scene, the relationships between the characters. She seemed to know her lines pretty well. Everything about her screamed that she was definitely the senior Joan. Luckily, Dad stopped the Morris Oxford under a tree, in shadow from the streetlights, so he didn't see my odd clothing. Tom might have taken it all in his stride, but I got some pretty peculiar looks from the cast when I first walked in.

I felt like a stupid kid, being picked up by Dad, not yet driving a car, but anything was better and safer than the warm vibrations of Tom's back. I saw him packing up his motor scooter bag as I ran down the steps. 'Ciao, Alessandra,' he said.

'How did your rehearsal go?' asked Dad in the car.

'Alright. Dad, can I take my licence, *please*?' If I could have the car sometimes for these late rehearsals, plus my bike, then I'd be independent of Tom's scooter and Keith's Morrie Thou. 'With a bit of swot on the Road Code . . .'

He drove a mile or so. 'Alright,' he said at a traffic light, knocking me over with a feather. 'After the Auckland champs are over. I've noticed how helpful with Gran and the kids you've been since you got back. Even through your exams. Not easy.'

We were driving through the Domain. I looked up at the floodlit Museum between the trees, the Greek shape, the pillars, and thought, from a motorscooter it would look even better. Is that how Dad really sees me at home: the helpful oldest daughter, the packet of trouble coming to heel? Jeepers creepers — I'm a better actor, or sham, than I thought.

'But I *can't* come tomorrow morning,' I wailed to a fairly annoyed Caroline on the phone. 'It's the Auckland champs, the heats, I just can't . . . the afternoon's alright, Sunday's alright.'

'I need one of you. Lesley's got a very sore throat, she's virtually lost her voice. She's coming to the rehearsal, but she can't read.'

And I've got half of Auckland, I thought, coming to see me swim tomorrow, the 220 free and the butterfly.

'I'll get there as soon as I can,' I said, adding dishonestly, because I knew it was going to happen again, 'It's just this once.'

Keith rang before I rang him.

'Feeling fit for tomorrow?'

'As a fiddle. Look, I'm supposed to be at a *Joan* rehearsal in the morning. I've told the woman I'll be there as soon as I can, when I've swum. Could you . . .'

'Happy to oblige. I was coming to see you swim anyway.'

He would be. 'Thanks.'

'Can I stay for the rehearsal?'

'We're still only reading, it's pretty boring.' Tom and Keith under the same roof! No thanks.

'I've got some work I can do in the library. What about eating somewhere, a pie or something, between then and the finals?'

'I'll want to get home. Sorry. Could you pick me up from varsity at five? Dad's working tomorrow.'

The sooner I get my licence . . .

Tom rang five minutes later. It was the first time he'd called me. He walked outside my house, knew my phone number, he'd watched me train at least once. I wondered if he had come to the pool when he first arrived, spied on me then. Was he keen enough for that? If so, why weren't we talking? He'd said nothing about the quiet talk at the pool that didn't happen.

'I see in tonight's paper you've got two heats in the morning. Will you be at rehearsal in the afternoon?'

'Caroline's throwing a wobbly. Lesley's got a sore throat and can't read. I'm coming soon as I can.'

'They can do Scene Four in the morning, which doesn't need you. Can I come and pick you up?'

'I've got a lift.' Dammit.

'Alex, we need to talk.'

'Do we? What about?'

There was a slight pause. 'I've been thinking about the short back 'n sides, the male clothing. I've done some reading on Joan, esoteric stuff from the university library.'

'Oh yes?' So have I, mate. Keith got the books out of the varsity library for me first.

'Alex, you haven't gone and had one, have you?'

'A short back 'n sides? Not yet.'

'Can we make a time, outside of rehearsals?'

'After . . . Tom, I've got ten Auckland champ races this week.' Does he really want to talk Joan, coach me — or is she just an excuse? 'Next week maybe. Early night calls. Ciao.'

I was trying to avoid looking at the papers, but how could I when Jamie took a fiendish delight in telling me what was in there, reading bits out. The evening paper was just a free ad, picture of me in Rome with my medal, my reporter friend reminding everyone why he thought I wasn't currently in Brisbane for the Queensland state championships, though conceding the Auckland champs would have been a lacklustre affair without me.

I thought of all the kids I saw training day in and day out for the champs, four miles a day, twelve-year-olds doing as much as me, and was so angry I wrote him a letter, pointing out yet again that I was not in Aussie purely because of family reasons.

I wrote that I thought telling young competitors they were collectively lacklustre before they even started was 'an irresponsible misuse of the power of the press' (I liked that bit!) and 'no way to encourage juniors to strive for better times or spectators to come and support them'. Yours faithfully. The blighter had it published halfway through the champs. Letters to the Editor. Young Champion Speaks Out. I was quite pleased, really.

I did my stuff and waved to the crowds and won my five titles. The sprint was 64s flat, annoyingly.

Tom produced all sorts of books I hadn't seen at the weekend rehearsals and I, for at least two good reasons, took them but said I couldn't discuss them till next week. I had another little barney with Caroline when I couldn't come the second Saturday morning; this time Lesley had a stomach upset and missed the whole day. At least she had me in the afternoon.

Keith hung about the pool on the first Saturday night of the champs, the Tuesday, the Thursday, and the following Saturday, and all the days of light training in between. I used my need for early nights to avoid and/or ignore both of them.

I couldn't ignore two other little clouds gathering.

One was reports from Brisbane that young Jenny Hartley was doing an Alex — she'd gone away a promising unknown and faced with really tough competition for the first time, of her own age, had 'exceeded all expectations'. Mr Jack, over in Brisbane too, was no doubt ecstatic with his second female freestyle 'star.'

Her times, a 64.6 sprint, a 2m 17.3s for the 200, and a quarter just under 5 minutes, had won her all the junior titles and similar times placings in the senior events too. She had a marvellous week. Now Norm Thompson was writing 'Olympic bronze medallist Alex Archer will have to look to her laurels'. To retain her two national titles in Tauranga next month, Miss Archer will have to swim up to or near her Rome triumph.

That was the official story. The unofficial story I heard over tea and date scones in the clubrooms the last night of the champs was that quiet young Jenny was no easy pushover. The team had been issued with official but very uncomfortable togs which pinched around her (admittedly chunky) thighs and bagged under the arms. She wanted to wear her own familiar togs, without the official fernleaf. Though apparently she protested hard and long, she lost. Three times, so the story from Brisbane went, they made her go and change. Wrong togs = she didn't swim. Her father had been very upset.

I saw one or two people looking pointedly at me as this was told, coming to the same conclusions. My official togs for Rome had been fine. If she could produce those times after three major rows and wearing horrible togs, what might she do in Tauranga in two weeks?

If, *if* these are my last races, my last champs, I want to go out in style, my titles and my pride intact.

The other cloud dropped its load on me like a thunderbolt.

On the Monday morning after the champs, in the privacy of my bedroom, I stared at the skimpy official envelope just arrived in the mail.

I had expected it, dreaded it today, Archer being top of the alphabet. Saturday's paper had said that X thousand University Entrance exam results had been sent out and should begin arriving on Monday. I put it on my pillow. I got up and took three ripe peaches from the tree outside the window. I adjusted the curtains. I looked at the stack of books on Joan that I was going to have to begin discussing with Tom this week. I looked at the swag of medals from last week tossed carelessly into the muddle on my dressing table. I looked at Tom's clothes from last Wednesday night still over the back of a chair, not returned at yesterday's rehearsal because I hardly spoke two words to him. I thought of my old school uniforms, the sports gear, the worn-down black sandals all bundled into a paper rubbish bag under my bed, the Prefect's badge I'd worn and the Head Prefect's badge I'd never wear, the last-ever school magazine in the bookcase. I thought of the Latin exam.

'Well?' Mum said from the doorway, on her way out to the clothesline. I rather wished she'd go away, let me do this alone. 'I can't open it.'

'Do you want me to?'

'No. Yes. No.'

I threw my peach stone out into the hedge, wiped my fingers on a wet towel on the floor. I opened the envelope fast, ripping it, and smoothed the flimsy paper on my pillow. I finally lifted my hand from the neat little box of results.

The others were alright. It was Latin that screamed out at me. 48. FAILED. I knew it all along.

I handed the paper silently to Mum.

'You can go for a recount,' she said flatly.

'Yes, and if that doesn't work?'

She didn't need to say anything. She put down the piled-high wicker basket of washing, walked over and sat heavily on my bed. She smelt of soap powder, ammonia. I felt someone had punched me in the stomach, knocked all the air out of me. Every bone in my body yelled, I *can't* go back to school. A thousand curses on Miss Gillies and all her ilk!

After I'd wept my heart out on her shoulder, I said, 'You and Dad know. No one else does, not Gran, not the kids, not Mr Jack, not *anyone*.'

I began rummaging in my desk for some writing paper.

'They can all think I've passed, even Tom.'

'Who's Tom?'

'Just a friend, even him, especially him. And I will. I only have to pick up two marks, that's all. Two piddling little marks. There's a good chance, there must be. Two marks. I'll send it off this morning. Dear Sirs, I wish to apply for an urgent recount in Latin. Will it help if I say I must get U.E. because I'm going to university this year and I absolutely can't ever go back to school, the thought just makes me shrivel up and also I'll be thrown out of *Joan* because even that's a "little irregular" — oh *hell*, Mum . . .'

It was so ironic, to fail in Latin, the subject I used to loathe and still found hard but at least saw the point of, since my trip to Rome.

Mum pulled an unironed hanky of Dad's out of washing basket. 'Use this. Write your letter,' she said.

Sotto voce

Alex as the relaxed champion, winning Auckland titles in every stroke, streets ahead of any other swimmer. She waves shyly to the crowds, obviously popular, admired, sensitive to those younger and lower on the victory dais, a performer to her fingertips.

Returning, between races, to the group around her coach: a tall, good-looking man, the Ed Hillary type, who could be her father; on one occasion joined by an equally tall woman, handsome northern European features, not slim, not overly smart: her mother — together they explain the statuesque daughter. With them, the small bird-like nonna, two younger children, and the bearded Keith. The attentive boyfriend, the engineering student spied several times last week propping up the bar in the Central. Decidedly uncouth when sloshed, which is often. I can't see the attraction.

Alex unresponsive to my hand-delivered letter. (The benefit of the doubt — did she even get it? Her mother looks a sensible type.) Unresponsive at rehearsals, except to talk about Joan. The Dunois role is so horribly appropriate — he admired Joan, even feared her, but was level-headed, pragmatic, even cynical about her actual achievements. Saw her as a useful image, a comrade-in-arms; not, at her insistence, as a woman. As D'Estivet, I can't meet her eyes, I use the book where I don't need to, the words are so heavily loaded with frustration, sexual jealousy, non-comprehension and hate. The enmity which grew between these two during the months of the trial was apparently notorious.

I'm having times when I wish passionately I'd kept right away, from her, the whole varsity scene, dull city, wretched small-minded country. Stuck it out in Milan, or gone to London in search of my lost voice, the voice Maestro took with him to that rain-swept wintry grave. Instead I'm here, a stranger in my own country, in a bind, watersider by day, actor by night, and for what — deeply in debt to my sister, and lusting after a cold woman, 'an ambitious bitch' she described herself at the airport — yes, but much more besides.

Small gleanings: the widgie uniform, thank God, was an aberration. She lives in jeans, face clean as a whistle, hides behind sunglasses. Punctual for rehearsals, takes direction intelligently, chest voice developing strongly with Caroline's skilful coaching, the slight, rustic, west-country accent perfect for Shaw's rough-tongued Joan, and apparently altogether unaware of her compelling presence. Through Joan can I find Alex, Alexandra, Alessandra?

Hot January: the silly season, a new Government still sound asleep on a beach; the people likewise. A few restlessly awake: the sports community; Alex punishing her body daily, and showing signs of applying the same dangerous intensity to Joan in the next few weeks. The performer can turn exhibitionist, become an embarrassment, given the right (or wrong) climate. I know, to my cost. A thirteen-year-old boy, known variously as Blue or Angel or Canary Alexander, acting his heart out as Rosalind; Lady Macbeth at fourteen, Lady Bracknell at fifteen, Shylock at sixteen — sure guarantees of years of sniggering and worse.

Every day I stare at my well-thumbed scores: *Figaro, Don Giovanni, Bohème, Aida, The Barber*, the 'Selected Arias', the Mahler and Schubert lieder, pencil-marked by a generation of Italian singers, given to me by Maestro before he died.

I hear them only in my mind, that's all.

All in a good cause

'Fan*tas*tic!' said Julia just back from three weeks at sea and ringing to see what my exam marks were.

Hers were all in the 90s, another step nearer to medical school. Her father, whom I disliked even more after the New Year trip — asking that sleazy creep Mario along after last year's little performance — was apparently quite pleased with his bright daughter, now he'd got used to the idea!

'I said you'd breeze in,' she said, a touch sadly. 'You won't change your mind about school? We start in two weeks, on the sixth.'

'Nope.' Not unless someone in Wellington changes it for me, I thought gloomily. 'Not a chance. Have I told you about *Joan*?'

'Joan who?'

'*Saint Joan*, ning-nong. At varsity, outdoors, you know, where they do the Shakespeare every year. This year it's Shaw. The whole deal. That woman who came to school rehearsals, the one with all the jewellery, you know — she's the producer, name of Caroline.'

'Alex Archer, you make me *sick*,' she said brightly. 'March straight into a starring role, typical. People like you shouldn't be allowed.'

'I had to audition like anyone else.'

'Oh yeah! I bet Miss Macrae set it up. She thinks, she *thought*, you were just the cat's pyjamas.'

She was often proved disconcertingly right, canny Julia. But I hadn't seen Miss Macrae since the day I left school. I rather thought she might have turned up at a *Joan* rehearsal or two. I changed the subject.

'How was your holiday?'

'Alright, once we got rid of Mario.'

'He slobbered all over me on the way home. He's *disgusting*. I told him to keep his Aussie paws to himself.'

'You would,' she laughed, her wheezes turning to coughs. I waited patiently, used to her coughing fits. 'You'd think, all that sea air . . . Gosh I'm pleased about your exam results; teachers will be too.'

'Do they get told the marks?'

'The lists get sent to school.'

I'd forgotten about them, flapping black crows cackling over the list sent to school, rubbing their hands in glee in the staff room saying, she'll be back, she'll be back, she if she won't! Surely it'll leak out. I thought of 1961 hanging on a letter I'd posted to Wellington, two little marks on a bit of paper.

A million curses on Miss Gillies!

'You're amazing!' said Keith. He'd called me at the pool, interrupting my training, to find out my results. There was noise in the background, pop music, and men laughing. He must be ringing from a pub. 'What about coming out tonight, celebrating?'

'Not tonight. Not at all. These two weeks are pretty important, Keith. I've got extra rehearsals during the day, some nights too.'

'I hear your Italian friend's got a part. Two parts.'

'Which Italian friend?'

'Him with the deep voice. Tomas.'

'He's not Italian. I just met him in Rome. He comes from Taihape.'

'I've seen him in a pub or two — actually he was here, just left, cold bastard, fish eyes. His hats give me the pip. Something soft about him, poncing round on that little Vespa.'

Jealousy of Tom's life in pubs and wherever that I knew nothing about made me prickly. 'Just because you've got a Morrie Thou to cruise around in.'

'You know it's my Mum's. So, you don't want to celebrate your results with me?'

Also getting prickly were we, with a few pints down the hatch? Oh gawd, had the time now come . . .?

'Not now, I've got too many other things, little worries like the nationals in precisely two weeks tomorrow, mere trifles really.'

'He's good is he?'

'Who?'

'Your Tom.'

'I told you, he's not my Tom. Now do you mean good as in truthful and kind, good as in good-looking, good as in good works, as in good on stage, good at games, or just plain good, you choose.'

He took a while to digest that. 'I *meant*, good, in the play.'

'He's terrific, fantastic, sexy, Laurence Olivier himself. I can't wait for the bit in Scene Three when he kneels to me and I have to burst into tears and even though we're both wearing armour, fling my arms around his unshaven neck and kiss him on both cheeks without knocking his hat sideways, and then we rush off hand in hand like a couple of kids to storm the walls of Orléans, I can't *wait*. Look, I've got to go, Mr Jack's beginning to make faces at me.'

There was silence, because over the phone the poor woozy guy couldn't tell just how sarcastic if at all . . .

'So he's a drongo,' he said. 'I thought he was. See you at the pool tomorrow.' I could just see him draining his glass empty and forcing his way back to the bar for a last refill from those sordid plastic hoses. I knew about public bars with Keith, I did.

We moved from sitting round reading the lines to standing up with books, blocking in the moves around an imaginary stage marked by benches and chairs in the bare hall. People like the Keeper of the Wardrobe started to make their presence felt.

'I don't suppose either of you girls has handled a sword before,' he said loftily, a two-edged sword resting across his plump hands.

'I have,' I said. 'I was Ruth in the *Pirates* once, but the sword was skinny compared to that thing, more a fencing sword, a rapier.'

'Lesley?'

She was not impressed with Ruth or rapiers. 'No.'

'Well, darlings, you both have to be able to pull this thing out of the scabbard in one fluid movement. Fumble, and the audience will collapse in a heap, the scene with the Dauphin will be totally ruined.'

We took turns at strapping the leather scabbard on, 'suddenly flashing' the sword out, as Shaw wanted. It was quite long, as swords go, and not light. It overpowered Lesley completely, absurdly hanging alongside her tartan skirt and slingback shoes and almost touching the floor. I had to admit she already had Joan's hair, dark, straight, needing only to cut her thick fringe a bit shorter.

I would have a black wig, and look nothing like the Miss A. Archer whose face stared far too often out of the sports pages. The Keeper decided to get another smaller sword for Lesley. 'You'll be fine, dearie,' he said to me.

I felt anything but. I asked the Keeper if I could take the sword away quietly somewhere while Lesley was doing a scene, get the feel of it. In a quiet stretch of cloister, away from the voices, I tried drawing it 'in one fluid movement', which was harder than it looked, made a few thrusts and slashes. Already my wrist was beginning to ache. How could I play Joan if I couldn't even hold up her sword?

'They have her sword, in the Musée de Dijon,' said a voice. 'At least, one with a small hilt for a woman's grasp, attributed to her. Is that as heavy as it looks?'

Cornered, blushing, by the man in the black French actor's beret. He must have seen me wander off.

'Not really. I'm just not used to it.'

'If you bent your knees, created a more solid platform. May I?' He tried the sword for weight, balance, kissed the hilt as fencers do, looking as though he'd been born with a sword in his hand. Of course — I remembered a fencing master in Milan, fifteen stone and cunning as a fox.

'We spent some time with these things too,' he said. 'There aren't many sword fights in opera, not like Shakespeare, but it was thought to be a necessary skill. *Trovatore* is one, *Lohengrin*. I'll ask Rodney to bring another weapon tomorrow. I'll have one too. You should know the sound of clashing steel. In battle Joan preferred to carry her standard, so she avoided killing anyone.'

'The standard she loved forty times more than she loved her sword,' I said.

'We've been reading the same books,' he smiled. 'What about a coffee after rehearsal?'

'Sorry, training,' I said, unpleasantly reminded of time trials tonight and Jenny Hartley getting better by the day.

'Tomorrow then?' I shook my head. 'Okay, I get the picture.'

Did he? When I didn't know what it was myself.

'Come on, now really slash it across mine,' he said the next day. 'This is not fencing, it's more a downwards, cutting movement. Put some herbs into it.'

We must have looked a funny pair, both in jeans, T-shirts, and sandshoes, scabbard strapped around waists, shaping up for a fifteenth century sword-fight. I gave an almighty whack. The stone cloisters rang. Thank goodness it was Saturday and still holidays, so there was hardly anyone about.

'Less of a fencing poke, get your feet planted. More downwards, a swipe. Try to cut my arm off. And again. Again. Again. That's better. Now hold yours steady, an angle away from the body, be ready, parry mine.'

Wham, I felt my wrist give, the judder go right up my arm. Wham. Wham. 'Now a back cut, backhand, like you've got a heavy tennis racquet.' I slashed again, and again, forehand, backhand, forehand, cut and parry. I began to feel a free rhythm, my body and sword all of a piece, my blood rising. We must have exchanged forty or fifty blows, slowly at first, gathering speed. 'That's it,' he said, 'that's good, *good*.'

Probably he allowed himself to give ground, even backwards down a few steps, but then it was me slowly giving way, though I tried hard not to. He seemed to be able to anticipate what I was going to do. I felt myself being backed along the cloister.

Suddenly he lowered his sword, pointed it at my feet, neatly sidestepped my swipe. Then while I was off balance he pinned me against the wall, the point of his sword resting just lightly against my T-shirt, on my diaphragm. I felt the rough edges of the stone digging into my back. His eyes were hard too.

'Why are you avoiding me?'

'I'm not,' I said, panting. 'I couldn't avoid you if I tried, Monsieur Jack Dunois.'

'Commander, please.'

'Commander. I've got the nationals in two weeks, remember, a kid of fourteen breathing down my neck.'

'You'll talk about Joan and your bloody swimming, but nothing else.'

'I haven't got anything else. And my bloody swimming, as you put it, got me to Rome and is taking me to America in September.'

'Is it?'

'Yes it is. This Joan bit is just a diversion. I'm really a swimmer, a very boring person.'

'That's bullshit, Alex, and you know it. I think you've got more spunk and *joie de vivre* hidden away in there than any female I've ever met, you've just forgotten how to use it, or for some reason I can't fathom . . .'

'What do you suggest?' I said coldly, looking at my watch. 'We start again in five minutes. Do you want a quick seduction scene on the grass, behind a bush? Do you want to play the English lord this time, the one who raped Joan in prison a week before they barbequed her?'

He suddenly looked tired, dropped the point of the sword and turned away. 'I told you in Rome, that's up to you. I won't touch you. You want the platonic bit, that's okay by me.'

'*Right* then,' I said. We were both lying. We fought with the swords only once again, on his suggestion, but the meeting of eyes, steel, anger, disturbed me; I liked it, the clash of wills and nerve. And Tom — so light on his feet, so damn Errol Flynn — didn't even get as puffed as me and I was supposed to be the fit one, made me go weak at the knees. And I had other things about Joan to explore, with or without him.

At least she gave me something to think about other than Jenny Hartley while I was training. Mr Jack was still pounding the miles into me. I still trained alone, doing my sprint time trials with two of the boys, not with Jenny. Every day closer to the nationals I told myself I'd have it out with the ever-present Keith *today*, and every day I put it off until tomorrow.

I didn't want it to finish the way it did. I pushed him too far. Still hurt about that phone call, two days later he asked me to a party in

Epsom, not far from home; the very day I'd come from a particularly bad rehearsal and decided I had to find out about a girl in boy's clothes in the twentieth century.

No time like the present, I thought grimly. In my bedroom I ironed and put on Tom's slacks, still not returned to him, and one of Dad's good shirts. I put on some of Dad's socks and my old black school lace-ups, put one of his better ties and a nearly empty tube of Brylcreme into the pockets, and ran out to the car, thankful it was nearly dark. He didn't make any comment until we stopped outside the house, where I quickly tied the slippery tie and combed my hair greasily backwards. I got out of the car and put my hands in my pockets. 'Okay Buster. Whose party is this?'

'Christ, Alex, you're not going . . .'

'Why not?'

'It's my engineering mates, the parents are away . . .'

Good, I thought, walking away up the path towards the light in the porch, a bunch of real blokes and their very boring nice girlfriends. I knocked loudly, before Keith behind me could say anything, then we were inside, standing around among forty or fifty others, record-player going full bore.

It was a very confusing evening. My bronze medal came up, of course, but even while people were being coldly polite about the Olympics, their eyes were saying, what have we here? I knew what they were thinking, of course, huge swimmers, well we always knew but how come one-of-the-boys Keith Jameson's got himself involved with one of those girls, a real one, by the looks of her, what's going *on*; so I ignored the staring women and made a point of drinking beer and staying with 'the boys' all night. Joan had preferred male company, and I thought on the whole I did too when I overheard one female comment '. . . always thought sport attracts rather *odd* women'.

Auckland being such a small place, the same people meeting in different combinations, it was bound to happen, that I'd meet someone I knew. But Sylvia of the Guy Fawkes bonfire! She arrived late in a very tight, bright red sheath-dress, teetering on the arm of a handsome and already well-lubricated man. I saw her look at me, puzzled. In the bright light of the big family room, she knew who I was, of course. We'd sat in class together for years. But my general masculine appearance was ringing more than a few bells.

'Hullo Sylvia,' I said, with just enough beer inside me to make me reckless. I could tell from her bright eyes and flushed cheeks that she wasn't exactly stony-cold sober herself. 'Haven't seen you for a while.'

'Hi,' she said, panda-eyeing me, speechless with confusion. 'Alex,' she said, while the men were talking cricket, 'you haven't got any older brothers, have you?'

She would know.

'Have you got a cousin who looks, well, very like you?'

'No. One female cousin only, lives in Hamilton. Why?'

'Oh nothing.'

'All ready for school next week, a prefect too?'

'Sssssh,' she hissed. 'Gary thinks . . .'

'Of course,' I said. 'You're at business college, got a job as personal assistant at a car firm lined up.' It wasn't quite enough. 'I've decided to do medicine, myself, got a yen to do brain surgery.'

She choked into her Pimms. I slapped her riotously between her bare shoulder blades and just for good measure, when I knew both Keith and her revolting boyfriend and by now half the room were watching, gave her just a friendly ruffle of her peroxide hair. 'Get the lady a glass of water,' I said to the pop-eyed Gary in my Alec voice. That finished her completely. It also finished Keith.

'I'm taking you home, Alex.'

'Okay,' I said. 'I don't think much of this party.'

In the car he said, 'What the hell was all that about?'

'All what?'

'Those clothes, teasing Sylvia Parsons, honestly — if you want people to think you're . . .'

'Sylvia Parsons is a silly tart and you don't understand anything, Keith Jameson.'

'You're bloody right I don't,' he shouted, banging his door, revving up the car and screeching away from the kerb. He drove about two blocks, very fast, before he said, 'Alright, I suppose the clothes have something to do with that damn play . . .'

'That's right, they have.'

'. . . but I'm beginning to think it's going further.'

'Just what do you mean by that?'

'You like those clothes.'

'Sure I do. I feel free. Just like you'd hate female clothes if you had to wear them, yards of material, stupid teetery shoes, stockings, handbags, tight skirts, bras that cut you, merry widows, make-up you hate wearing, hair in rollers, having to choose this goes with this and that goes with this and the other thing doesn't, you'd HATE it. Men call it being in drag, and it is.'

'What are you *talking* about?'

'Slow down.' We were tearing along the Great South Road at about sixty, overtaking cars and buses. 'Look, I'm buggered if . . . slow *down*, Keith, you moron. You didn't kill me at Helensville and you're not going to now. You're the worst driver in the world. Let me out!'

'That's the . . . no girl speaks to me like that, that's the finish!' He screeched the car to the halt under a lamplight, causing a bus behind to swerve and toot angrily. I recognized the shopping centre ahead, about a mile from home. He didn't stop the car. 'Fine when you want lifts hither and yon, just fine when you want to go to parties, play the first year student, sucker Keith, . . .'

'You suggested the parties, not me.'

'Leading me on, a kiss or two but never returned, months of taking you out, trying to understand . . .'

'I've always paid for myself.'

'No you haven't. Christ, it's not the money, Alex,' he cried, rubbing at his beard. 'Money's nothing. For six months, ever since you got back from Rome, I've tried, and before that . . . Alex Archer, my girl, you wouldn't know how proud — no, shut up for once, you might be blunt, use people, but Christ, you fascinate people too and I was so *proud*, I thought it was more than just Andy, I dreamt of you, I still do, I tried to tell you once and you brushed it aside, sucker Keith and now you've got in with that drama set and anyone with two eyes in their head can see that Tom what's-his-name is head over heels and so are you . . .'

'That's rubbish. There's nothing doing there.'

'Piss off, Alex,' he said. 'Go home and grow up.'

'Thanks, I will,' I said opening the car door. 'But you can't accuse me on the one hand of having the hots for Tom Alexander and on the other of being butch. Though the way I feel about you *and* him right at this moment, it's not such a bad idea. Good night and good bye.'

I slammed the car door so hard the poor little Morrie shook all over, and walked down the road. I heard the door slam, running footsteps. He stood in front of me. I thought, I've broken the door hinge or the glass of his mother's precious car. But his eyes were wet and tired and full of pain.

'I'll drive you home,' he said heavily.

'Not bloody likely. I wouldn't get in a car with you again if it was the last thing I did. The way you drive, it probably would be. You don't own me, Keith Jameson, you never did.'

After a long moment he took a step back. I strode on. I heard the car turn around, more screeching of tyres, and drive away fast. I knew I wouldn't see him again, at the pool or anywhere else.

Funny, I was so upset, I forgot about the clothes until I reached the shops. There was a large crowd spilling out into the road from the cinema. I saw the posters, a horror film, which explained the numbers of teenage boys and men in their twenties. I tried to walk through them. The first jostle I thought was an accident; the second I knew it wasn't. I heard jeers, hoots, laughter.

The scorn in their eyes was a high price to pay for an experiment. I didn't think much had changed since the fifteenth century.

With the nationals so near, how do I explain the next two little dramas? I don't, I can't. How do you explain anything when you spend all your waking hours longing to see a certain person; and when you do, you close up like a clam?

As a swimmer, I'd been lucky, avoiding all the usual injuries: no shoulder problems, pulled muscles, back problems, only that broken leg halfway through 1959. Well, my luck had just run out.

I'd taken my driving test, given the traffic officer only one heart attack, and passed. It was the first day I'd been allowed to take the car, a big favour from slightly hesitant Mum, to drive down to Clevedon. Tom had arranged a day's riding. Simple.

The day after the sword-fight, I'd made the casual remark to Tom: how can I play Joan if I've never sat on a horse? The next thing, he's reminding me that he grew up on a farm, has a few friends from schooldays farming around Auckland. He could possibly arrange something. He warned — I can't say now he didn't — I might be a bit stiff afterwards; perhaps we should wait, go after the nationals; I didn't listen, I wanted to go now. I organized the car, to go straight after training.

Tom was waiting outside the pool. Most of our talking was about the best route out of the city, the road through Papakura then east to Clevedon. Tom navigated. I didn't admit it was my first time solo; after a while I began to enjoy the driving, the smooth gear changes around the curving country roads.

The farmhouse was nothing special, a pale blue suburban house at the end of a hard dirt road up a hill. Barney lived there alone, a nice guy, no wife yet, Tom said as we bounced up the track. Grass tickled the undersides of the car, cows stared at us, some dogs near the house barked.

Barney and the horses were waiting in a yard behind the house. It turned out Tom's nickname at school was Blue! There was some chat about varsity, Italy — very dodgy and non-committal about why or how long he was here, I noticed. More chat about our shoes; in the end we both borrowed some from Barney, Tom his proper riding boots and me some brogues with thick heels. I had to have heels, they both said, sandshoes were not safe, wouldn't do.

Horses, when you're going to ride one, look huge. Tom's was a big chestnut with a wicked look in its eye. Mine was smaller, beautiful pale gold with a cream mane and tail. Victoria was a bit special, Barney said, a palomino, thirteen-year-old mare, nearly sixteen hands. Nice amiable beast, named after Victoria de Los Angeles, the Spanish singer, you'd know, Tom.

I stood by feeling useless while Barney and Tom got the tack out of a shed, untangled bits of leather, stirrups, and did up buckles. I was given two apples and a knife, told to cut them in quarters and offer them, which I did very cautiously. Up close, horses' lips looked very menacing, especially the chestnut whose eyes rolled devilishly at me. 'Tickle them under the chin,' said Tom. 'I'll leave you to it,' said Barney.

Tom understood why I declined a leg up. He patiently explained the basics: left side, reins in left hand, grab pommel, stirrup this way, face that, now push and swing. The first time my foot slipped; the second, I pushed and swung so hard and successfully that I found myself up and sliding down the other side — to much amusement all round, including, I think, the horse. The third time I was on, sitting, it seemed, twenty feet up.

The world looked different. Tom, now astride his chestnut, a broad-brimmed Aussie hat slung down his back, jeans and red checked shirt, could have gone straight into a cowboy film. In the sunlight, his hair had a fiery intensity similar to the horse's coat. I followed him slowly out of the yard towards a gate. He didn't try to tell me everything all at once, but boy, there was more to riding than I ever dreamed. Hold the reins like this, elbows in, heels like that, grip with the whole inside of your leg.

Time flashed by, opening and closing gates between endless hard dry-green paddocks, occasionally glimpsing the sea between the folds of the hills. Riding meant you didn't have to talk. I began to feel comfortable walking, stopping, turning; then, thinking that we were beginning to understand each other, Victoria and me, we tried trotting. I got the rhythm in a few minutes, though occasionally lapsing, experiencing the bumps, laughing, catching the rise and fall again. We found Tom's clever chestnut knew how to stand so that he could lean down and open the gates.

I became cocky, wanted to canter. The wind had got up and Tom's horse was restless. 'How do I start?' I asked. 'Well, you swing your weight forward, kick, but . . .' and I did before he had a chance to say I shouldn't, and off we went, up a rising slope, at terrifying speed. I fought panic, *I'm going to break my neck.*

Tom came thundering up beside me. My horse, I think, broke into a gallop. 'Grip, use your knees, grip hard, keep forward, keep *down*,' he yelled. 'Get the reins, pull her up.' I found my hands grabbing at the coarse cream hair, pulling at the tangled reins; Victoria finally got the message and slowed to a trot along a ridge. The sea, green islands and headlands, slept peacefully below.

'Hell's bells,' I said, when we'd all calmed down to a walk and I could speak. 'Imagine doing that with a lance, towards someone who wants to poke your eyes out.'

'Not bad, first time,' he said. 'But enough's enough.' Just then his horse shied, and mine too. I stayed on by the skin of my teeth. We walked across the sloping hill, talking of Joan; our books didn't agree on whether she'd learnt to ride on that first long journey from Vaucouleurs (to see the Dauphin) well enough to use a lance in battle, or whether she'd surely have ridden as a child on her father's farm. Tom led me down rutted sheep-tracks to the beach.

As I slid off Victoria's back, I noticed the first signs. My legs, the muscles up the insides, had seized up, and my backside was tender and sore, though I wasn't going to let on. Tom produced some ham rolls and bananas from a small bag around his waist. He loosened off the horses' girths while I lay in the sun and threw shells into the water. I didn't want to talk, partly because I was extremely sore and trembling all over and he should have *told* me, and I still had to get home.

At least I didn't have to walk; I got back on the horse after maybe twenty minutes of silence; but I was acutely conscious of the hardness of the saddle and my inside leg muscles being stretched even just sitting there. We walked up the sheep tracks, along the ridges, down the sloping paddocks; at Tom's suggestion had a last spell of trotting before we walked back into the yard where Barney was waiting.

'How'd it go?' he asked, as we both got off. 'Fine, wonderful,' I said. 'Stiff?' he grinned. 'Not really. Just a bit.'

I've told some whopping fibs in my time. This was a super-whopper. I could hardly walk. My very bones ached, my legs were semi-circles of agony. I lent over a rail and watched Tom and Barney take off the saddles, chat on about Barney's farm, what stock he carried, the curse of the continuing hot dry weather, the new government's policies for farmers.

As well as being crippled for life, I was very sunburnt, nose and forearms. They led the horses over for a drink. I was given a brush to brush my horse down. Tom gaily admitted he was sorer than he expected, but it was nearly two years since he'd been in a saddle. Barney made some comment about him handling the chestnut well, not an easy beast. I'd noticed that, how relaxed he looked, in control even when the horse had galloped and shied. I brushed the dark sweat marks out of the gold, thinking: I now know the height, the attraction, the power of sitting on a horse, feeling its strong muscles under you, but I will never walk normally again.

The consequences of the second drama were worse.

I was rehearsing *Joan* at least four time a week now. All the lines were nearly in my head. I loved her bluntness, her complete lack of awe for pompous authority; to the Archbishop telling her that her voices are only echoes of her own wilfulness, *It is not true.* To D'Estivet, with scorn in her voice, *It is great nonsense. Nobody could be such a fool as to think that*; being overfamiliar with Robert de Baudricourt *You must not be afraid, Robert.* I could enjoy those lines. She wore a sword, she rode long distances with her squires, she wore a knight's clothes; I had a wee taste of the trappings of the soldier's life she'd chosen.

But the famous jump continued to worry me. My leg muscles took three days to return to normal. Except for starting dives and time trials which were agony, I ploughed up and down the pool arms only, dragging my legs; hoping Mr Jack didn't notice that I was doing a quarter-mile backstroke instead of the quarter-mile kicking only on my schedule.

I'd been thinking for some weeks about Joan's leap off the tower at Beaurevoir, trying either to escape (she'd been in prison for some months) or to commit suicide; as with her horse-riding skills, people had different theories. One book had a picture of the tower. She was supposed to have jumped at least sixty feet into the dried-out moat. She was knocked out, and took three days to recover, but amazingly broke nothing; they thought that made her evil, a witch who could fly.

One overcast afternoon I sneaked into the pool when Mr Jack was away at the bank. There weren't many people around, no training swimmers, some boys on the three-metre springboard, a few jumping off the towers.

Things look very different depending where you're standing. Watching from the pool level, jumping off the ten-metre platform didn't look so difficult. I'd seen lots of diving displays, and those clown diving troupes, the same divers dressed up doing ludicrous and reckless things from the top towers. But go up there on the platform yourself and look down!

I managed a sneaky jump off the five-metre platform. But the ten-metre, that's over thirty feet — Joan had jumped nearly *twice* this height. I couldn't do it. I slunk to the back of the platform, while ten-year-old boys came up, ignored me and leapt off. I tried five times more, telling myself firmly that thousands of people had jumped off and lived to tell the tale — I couldn't do it. Joan was braver.

Saturday (January 28, leg muscles finally calming down, *still* no recount marks) I didn't go training very early, only a light session at eight. My first race against Jenny was that night, a warm-up for next week's nationals. The top billed event (so the paper loudly said) of an Auckland Anniversary Aquatic Festival featuring invitation races with New Zealand's top swimmers led by the Olympic bronze . . . also featuring water polo, water ballet, diving display, and of course the world-famous clown divers, Dave Koroheke and his Troupe of Fearless Freds.

After training, I stood looking at the large poster sellotaped to the office window. They were already getting out the special lane ropes for tonight, putting up bunting and flags. I merely felt depressed.

Funny, I was missing Keith at the pool, still sore over some of the (true) things he'd said. Jenny had been training earlier. I hadn't talked to her much since she got back from Brisbane, other than to say 'Good kid, great times,' and 'Good for you, standing up for yourself.' Even after Brisbane, she still looked at me with the moony eyes of turd formers at the school I'd just left for ever. Moony or not, she was nuggety and strong, and getting stronger.

I had a bit of time to fill in before biking on into town to rehearsal, which is how I happened to be there when the divers arrived.

I knew them all by name, had watched them grow from boys to men over the years. Dave, Fred, Lionel, Frank, Jason, Len, Darcy — tanned, muscular gymnast types. Some of them had been diving seriously and in the clown troupe for years, taking turns to win the national titles. They were a cheerful bunch.

Rehearsal was difficult. We were without books, but I kept thinking of that night and forgetting my cues. Tom was distant and Lesley becoming more senior and superior by the rehearsal.

But the main reason was the arrangement I'd made with diver Dave, a nice guy, part-Maori, about twenty-five, a chemist in real life. Biking down Symonds Street, I suddenly thought he might help me get off that top tower, just once. I found a call box, rang the pool, dragged him away from his practice. I didn't explain why, just said it was for a bet, could he help?

One thing led to another. Hey Alex, you've been in shows, he laughed, we need someone to take Len's place tonight. Len was usually the Charlie Chaplin clown, the cowardly one with a walking stick, just did one jump at the end after horsing round the whole ten minute act. I could win my bet in grand style, I could do a Charlie Chaplin walk, surely? He, Dave, would go off with me, when it came to it.

I've got a big race tonight, I said, remember? There'd probably not be time. He told me to hang on while he looked at the programme in the office. Yours is Event 17, but there's a water ballet before us, he said, time to get you kitted out. One condition, I said, *no one* must know, before or after, no officials, reporters, anyone, only the divers. I knew they were a close group. Done.

If you know my story of the last two years, you'll know why I said yes.

It was a warm balmy night, perfect. The stands were comfortably packed, and the special flags they had flying everywhere made it look festive. Mum,

Dad, Gran, and Jamie had insisted they were coming, got a baby-sitter for Robbie and Debbie. I hadn't told Tom; I assumed he didn't read the papers. I should, of course, have backed right out of Dave's mad crazy little scheme. Mr Jack asked me twice if I was alright. I stared at the floodlit diving platform at the other end of the pool, and felt sick.

Event 17 came around slowly. 'Just back from Australia' said the announcer. 'Just back from Rome . . .'

The race went as well as could be expected, given that I'd been at rehearsal all day and still had slightly sore legs and knew I was soon about to kill myself. I led marginally at the turn, and kept it, 64.1 to her 64.6s, passable times but close enough to thrill the crowd. I excused myself from Grant Davies wanting quotes, changed into some dry togs and an old track suit, put a towel over my head, snuck through the office, and into a back committee room the divers used.

They'd already done their serious display and were mostly ready for the clown act. Dave — unrecognizable in white face, a girl's curly corn-coloured wig, huge false bosoms ('heavy-duty balloons,' he grinned), frilly pantaloons, dress and Minnie Mouse high heels — grabbed me, sat me down in a chair and covered my face with white goo. Being a chemist, he knew about make-up. In about five seconds flat I had Charlie Chaplin's round black eyes, his little eyebrows and a black moustache. I thought, this is going to be Tinman all over again. I climbed into the black suit, elongated shoes (too big, someone produced some socks to fill the spaces so at least I could walk). They shoved a bowler hat on my head and gave me a cane.

'Right on, Charlie Chaplin,' he said laughing. 'Now you come out with us. Your job: wander up to the top platform, some mime, you're petrified, prepare to dive, change your mind. Same at the 5-metre, the 3-metre, the 1-metre. Peer over the edges, back off, don't string it out too long, eh. We'll be nearly through. Keep an eye on me. I'll take you up to the top, you think I'm a sweetie-pie. The audience will love it. We'll go off together. Relax, it's not a big deal. When you come up, float as if dead; face down if you can manage, up if you can't.'

'Dave, I . . .'

'We'll all rescue you, very noisily, lots of artificial resuscitation. Someone will have a pump that makes it look as though water is spouting out of your mouth. You just lie there on your back. It might get a bit rude. Wiggle your toes. When I tell you, get up, walk off as though dazed, stagger back in here. No one will know it's you. That's all.'

'All?' I croaked.

'Cue, lads,' I heard, 'Check your gear,' and I got swept out forcibly, through the officials on the concourse, down to the diving end. Dave and the others had run on ahead, already started climbing the ladders up to the 3-metre board and the tower. While the crowd roared, I thought: Well, I'm here. I tried the Chaplin walk, feet in first position, twirling the cane, up the tower, with leg muscles complaining, to the top. They had a spotlight, sometimes on me, mostly on the others as they cavorted and shouted and did their unbelievably stupid and brave dives solo and on each other's backs, through rings, with umbrellas, tiny parachutes, cups of tea, stools, ladders, a potty, and went through a patter of talk and jokes; as I made a great show of not going off the 10-metre, 5-metre, the 3-metre and the tiny 1-metre. I felt the crowd begin to respond, laugh at each attempt.

'Give you a job anytime,' I heard. Dave, panting, his oily red mouth smudged, because this was hard work, clown work, escorting me up the steel stairs, sensing me slowing down, pulling back. 'Come on, Alex, she'll be right, just keep going, don't look down, just go.'

'I can't.'

'Do your little pretend dive, no wonder they're laughing, then step off. You can't hurt yourself. I'll come with you. Piece of cake.'

He ran, clown arms flailing, to the edge of the platform, lay down and peered over. The pool lay sparkling blue three miles below until the spotlight blinded me. I walked to the edge, thought: I can't, I simply can't, but I have to now; stood remembering with great vividness that Chaplin film where Charlie winds up his arms and dives into a pool of water only two inches deep. I wound up my arms as if to dive, hesitated, heard Dave say, 'Atta girl, *go*.' In the end the traitor heard the crowd roar, I felt a knee behind my knee and was gently pushed off.

Falling, twisting, I'm no Joan, no flying witch, the blue glass rushing upwards, pedalling in space, I'll fall on my face, split myself open, into a thousand pieces, hitting more or less feet first, plunging, drowning, another body plummeting past, quite close, blue silence, coming up, spluttering, these clothes are heavy, I've lost my hat, I'm still alive . . . a stabbing pain in my back.

Nightmare clown faces all around, panting, clothes flapping everywhere, water splashing, my hat back on, hands pulling me to the side, each pull a stab in the back. I spluttered out, 'Dave, my back,' but no one heard, the crowd was still clapping and laughing as they hauled me up over the side, each haul a long stretch of pain.

One white face much like another, then mercifully Dave's, grinning, 'Good sport, Alex, first time's always the worst, eh girl,' while I stared desperately at the white rimmed eyes coming up and down in front of me. 'My back,' I croaked, as great spurts of water went up like a whale blowing and the crowd screamed with delight.

'I've twisted . . . I can't move.' I saw dismay behind the white, he said something to one of the others, who got up and ran off. 'Fred, keep the pump going, boy, long as you can,' he said, still feinting doing mouth-to-mouth, in and out of focus, great broad and rude movements, never again will I think a clown act is easy. Someone pricked Dave's bosoms; I nearly went straight up horizontal in the air.

'Stretcher's coming, Alex, part of the act.' With remarkable speed, the stretcher arrived, I was rolled onto it, carted off, my oversized shoes sticking straight upwards like black paddles, born aloft through the laughing officials on the concourse. The crowd cheered and clapped. We went in through the big men's changing room, out the other side, the divers surrounding me, carrying me low so that I was hidden, into the back room. They put me on the floor, closed the door. The room was full of panting, dripping-wet clowns, but the only face I could see leaning against the closed door looking down at me, was Mr Jack.

I vaguely remember the doctor who was quietly found from somewhere, the subdued clowns changing, the water everywhere, the assurances that absolutely no one outside this room knew or would get to know Alex Archer's latest escapade.

I remember the sadness in Mr Jack's eyes, even when the doctor pronounced that I could try getting up, moving around, I'd probably only torn some muscle fibres in my lower back. Only! I found I could sit, stand, walk, but bending backwards or forwards was hell. Dave, feeling responsible, helped to get the suit off, put my track suit on over my wet togs, wipe my face clean.

'For God's sake, Alex, I just don't understand, *why?*' Mr Jack said. 'With the nationals nine days away, for crying out loud, why? Is your life so unbearably dull? What were you trying to prove? You've sold your national titles for a stunt.'

I was feeling too stupid to attempt to explain, even to say that I was going to swim in the nationals regardless; even to cry. Dave kept saying he should not . . . and I kept saying, Dave, it was me, my fault, not yours, nothing to do with you, I'm glad you pushed me 'cause I had to go. And I won my bet!

Eventually, I was able to walk carefully into the women's changing-room, pick up my bag with bent knees and great care. I went out to meet Mum, who'd taken the rest of the family home and come back to get me, because she knew what had gone on.

I couldn't even look her in the eyes, nor at breakfast the next morning when Gran pronounced that the best thing about last night, apart from your race, Alex, of course, you swam so well, oh, I was so proud of you — but what she'd really enjoyed was those rude clown divers. She laughed till she cried, specially that clever boy who was the Charlie Chaplin, reminded her so much, she chuckled, those wonderful old films in the twenties, do you remember, Helena, Charlie once diving into a pool, it was only two feet deep . . .

Cliff-hanging

This woman is driving me out of my mind!

At swordpoint she tells me she is going to America in September. Do I believe it? On horseback she won't talk at all, hours of dialogue under the most perfect conditions, wasted, wasted, wasted. In the pub I hear she turned up at a party in Epsom with Keith Jameson dressed in my clothes, played the transvestite to the hilt, set tongues wagging all over Auckland.

It wasn't difficult to track down Marcia Macrae, but I'm regretting it. This much I learned: she may yet have to pull out of *Joan*. Marcia knows from her mother that she's applied for a recount, and the chances are fifty-fifty. She, and even more so Caroline, are waiting with baited breath. If she's unsuccessful, they will either be persuading the cast to accept the schoolgirl Joan, which they think unlikely, or have to give Lesley the whole season (perish the thought). Her stamina, over two weeks of performance, will be suspect. She leaves this Dunois, this D'Estivet, cold.

Also from Marcia: guarded comments about Alex's difficult passage to Rome, the delays, the rival, her high profile at school through shows, her all-round sporting prowess, hockey too until she broke her leg; even more guarded suggestions, revealing in their brevity, of some malicious gossip, so often levelled at girls who excel in sport, who dare to display, openly, the necessary ambition, drive, competitiveness. I can imagine the slurs, the allegations: so unfair, ironic, untrue. So completely inevitable, here.

So almost daily now we see each other, rehearse together, deadly serious about it, but cliff-hanging. Another suspicion: Alex stiff and unusually eager to please, even compliant, this last week of rehearsals; convincingly explained away by her imminent championship meeting in Tauranga, a first night shortly after?

Or is there any connection with my suspicion that the Charlie Chaplin at the pool the other night was a woman, a tall woman, that the stretcher wasn't part of the act? Why — a back injury, a pulled muscle, injured eardrum perhaps? Dear God, if it was her, what did she do to herself, why the secrecy, the involvement at all? If not, it was acting of a higher order than I'd expect from divers. If so, why? For kicks? A bet? Sometimes I wish my eyes, my sense of stagecraft even applied to a clown troupe, were less acute. She left the pool late (after all the crowds and performers had gone home) with her mother, neither saying much; did I simply imagine that she got into the Morris Oxford with the care of an old woman with stiff joints?

After *Joan*, through *Joan*, will I ever get near to finding out? Further, will it be worth the effort, the wait, the patience, the sleepless nights? Worth being here instead of in London or Milan or . . .

Back to the wall

They kept on at me for a week, all of them, until the day Mr Jack and I drove down to Tauranga.

'Be sensible for once in your life,' cried Mum, who knew enough about backs to put a board under my mattress and tell Debbie firmly that Alex was too tired to give her any piggy-backs at the moment.

'Please, pet, everyone will understand, you're not running away, no one would say ever say that, ever,' pleaded Gran, who knew I'd pulled a back muscle but not how or when.

'Give it away, Alex,' said Mr Jack, who still looked at me with puzzled and angry eyes, trying to understand why I did it and why I was trying to hide it. 'Let me ring Norm Thompson. You've pulled a back muscle, happens to anyone.'

'You'd be crazy to swim next week,' said the physio, a young guy, water polo player, found by Mr Jack and sworn to secrecy. I lay on my front and winced as he worked away with his hard fingers and put a radiant heat lamp on the area just above my tailbone. My three days away from the pool were put down to resting for the nationals. 'Maybe a slight chance,' said the physio; I could try gentle training, 'and I mean *gentle*.' By the next weekend I could swim more or less, but starts hurt like hell and flip turns were out. 'Marginal,' he said.

I trained at different times to Jenny, to the rest of the squad. Alright, anyone who says I'd got neurotic about not wanting publicity, not admitting a small injury, not being recognized, stared at, giggled at, whether swimming or acting or merely trying to be me, is probably right, and should try being a sports 'celebrity' sometime.

I was going to be defending my two titles so hard won from Maggie last year, and despite my period due and a back problem, there'd be no excuses.

I begged lifts into varsity from Mum and Dad and moved around rather carefully at rehearsals, trying not to look as though I was rehearsing Joan aged ninety. Various scenes were being called almost daily now, especially for me since Caroline was furious that I was to be away next week for five days. I think she really expected I'd give the champs away when the time came. If she'd known why this Joan 'forgot' to buckle the sword on so that she wouldn't have to twist her body to flash it out of the scabbard . . . Several times, having to kneel and get up 'hastily', I caught Tom watching me, frowning, as people do when they know someone's in pain. He couldn't know, how could he?

Tuesday morning I packed my bag, said goodbye to the kids going off to school, Dad off to work. Tom rang to wish me luck. He'd read the morning's paper, Norm Thompson waxing lyrical about the champs, with the team to Australia expected to do well and Alex Archer on recent showings returning to the form which won her an Olympic bronze medal. 'I'd like to come down for your final on Friday,' he said. 'Don't bother,' I said.

I waited for the mail — no recount results yet, don't these people *know* or stop to think someone's entire future is hanging on this one letter?

Mum, with Robbie on her hip, and Gran with some flowers she'd just cut, stood side-by-side in the driveway and sadly waved. 'Good luck,' they cried, without much enthusiasm. 'Take care, you ring, we'll ring.' Mr Jack and I drove down to Tauranga.

All swimming meetings are the same, really. Napier last year, the Auckland champs, now Tauranga, Naples, even Rome — the same fit brown bodies, officials in their whites, worried parents and cranky coaches, the buzzing crowds, the flags around the pool, the waiting blue water neatly sliced into lanes. The same gossip, who's done what amazing times, who's coach is upset about what, who's taking what extra vitamins, who's got a period or those new pills to stop it, who's suffering from sinus or asthma or having massage for a sore shoulder, who's going out with whom.

I looked around the sunlit pool and thought, it's just like I felt about school. I want those titles back before I go, but after that . . . I chatted with Mrs Churchill, who had come up as chaperone with the Canterbury team, and Mr Upjohn, who'd been promoted to be Chief Judge (I told him I still hadn't decided about the American offer, not telling him that there were two, actually) and cleverly avoided Norm Thompson wandering around sniffing out stories.

I met Mr Smythe, the new chief selector, for the first time. If I thought Mr Upjohn was up himself, he had nothing on this one. He was very short, a lawyer, silky in his whites, smiling as he said it had been a real pleasure to watch the team perform so well in Brisbane. They expected great things this week, especially young Hartley who'd done so especially well in Brisbane, though she had a lot to learn. I knew what he was really saying. The ten who'd gone to Aussie joked and horsed about. I felt very senior, out of it, lonely. Missing Maggie. Come back, Maggie, all is forgiven!

I avoided young Jenny (to whom I was a hero and a challenge), and her silent father, and flip turns which still gave my back gip. On Wednesday morning I woke up with my period, my whole nether region aching miserably. Which were period pains and which were torn muscle-fibre pains, I couldn't tell. I rang Mr Jack at his motel, said I wanted to withdraw from the 400 metres.

He agreed, relieved I had some sense. Norm Thompson wanted to know why, so I said I'd decided to save myself for my two major sprint events. I didn't go near the pool that day, or the next. I left an unhappy Mr Jack to concentrate on sharpening up Jenny (*mean*, Alex) and put on my largest sunglasses and a floppy sunhat and went to see Elvis in *G.I. Blues*, wandered round the shops and along the wharf area, sat for a while reading picture books in the library. I heard Jenny had won the 400 heat by miles and the final in a time close to mine in Rome. Also that she'd upset a few people, again, wearing her New Zealand track suit when the Auckland officials wanted her to wear the Auckland one. Ha!

But I wasn't imagining it — people were beginning to say it's not impossible, young Hartley might beat Alex Archer in the sprint on Friday.

No one took any notice of my slow heat time, 65.4s to her 64.9s. in the first heat. Tactics, they nodded wisely. I watched her climb out of the pool, her chunky muscles quivering, and said 'Good swim, kiddo,' thinking of Dawn Fraser saying the same to me in Rome. I noticed she put on her New Zealand track suit afterwards. Brave wee lassie!

Mr Jack had wanted to give me a painkiller, but I refused. The start was bad and the flip turn sent a spasm right through me. I thought, if I faint, will someone dive in like the official in Rome when that American kid swallowed a mouthful and collapsed halfway up the second leg of the butterfly final? I was very glad to reach the end.

The floor, face down, was the most comfortable place to lie in my single room, and that's where I was lying, sweating, thinking of other ghastly, endless, hot afternoons I've spent before a major race, Napier, Rome . . .

'Come stai?'

I didn't leap up or even look up, because if I had he'd have seen the rush of blood. My heart pounded against the carpet.

'Bene, grazie. Actually, like shit.'

'*Why did you jump from the tower?*'

That's what D'Estivet says accusingly to Joan, early in the trial scene. And she replies:

'*How do you know that I jumped?*'

'Well,' said Tom, walking over to the window. I could see his feet, no socks, in once-white sandshoes. 'I have this theory. I see a tallish woman dressed as Charlie Chaplin in a clown diving act. Oh, it's a very good act, she had Charlie to a T, the comedy was very broad, even bawdy. I see a stretcher. Of course, it was just part of the act. Now I see an injured swimmer spreadeagled on the floor, whose training in the past week has been . . . shall we say, curtailed.'

'How do you know it was a woman? No one else did. Anyway, I was pushed. Why were you there at all? Do you snoop around the pool? Don't you see enough of me at rehearsals?'

'The person I see at rehearsals is Joan. And yes, I do snoop. I was there that night, and the Auckland champs besides. At the pool I see, at a distance, the Alex I met in Rome.'

'She doesn't exist.'

'Are you going to win tonight?'

'No.'

'What happened, in that jump?'

'I tore some muscle fibres. I don't know how Joan leapt sixty feet into a muddy moat. I'm nothing beside her. Mr Jack thinks I should have pulled out a week ago.'

'Why didn't you?'

I was silent. Why didn't I? From under my arms, I saw toes beating a pulse inside his sandshoes.

'Can I do anything to help?'

'Go away and leave me alone.'

'A drive somewhere? Take your mind off it? I've got a car. I came down this morning, gave away work.'

There was nothing I'd like more. Drive right out of Tauranga.

He said, 'I'll stay away tonight, if you want me to.'

'I don't care. Go and sit in the bloody press box with Norm Thompson. Watch him sharpen his claws, dip his pen in blood. But you tell him about my back, and I swear I'll never speak to you again, I'll pull out of *Joan*.'

'Opening night next Saturday, yours on Monday, all going well.' There was an edge to his voice. He couldn't know about my Latin recount. Could he? He'd known, guessed, snooped, about other things. He said, in a gentler voice, 'A rub might help?'

'Piss off, Tom. Go and sing someone an opera.'

Inside the dirty canvas, the toes were clenched and still. After a long silence, they walked out. I buried my head in the pillow. His strong hands touching me, even my back just above my tailbone . . . I couldn't even cry.

You can tell, you always know when you've been beaten, even when it's only by a fingernail, one tenth of a second. You hope, but you know.

As I stood, I heard the pool erupt around me. People like underdogs; they were cheering for Jenny. I'd been one myself last year. I'd known when I beat Maggie by a tenth of a second, and I knew now that Jenny had done the same to me. Just as Maggie had done, I turned and swam half the length of the pool.

No excuses, not even my back, which I'd not noticed in the race but which was now aching. A 64.2s wasn't bad, all things considered; it would still have won a place in the Olympic semi-final. With painkillers inside me, I couldn't really blame my back. Jenny had just swum better. That's all. Perhaps I might have won, without Charlie. But God, I'd tried. I nearly killed myself on the second leg.

Jenny was out of the pool when I got back, being hugged by her solemn father. Not manners, Jenny; I must tell you that winners usually wait in the pool for a gesture, an acknowledgement from their victims.

I carefully hauled myself out, went across and gave her a hug, knowing that every move, every expression on my face, was being watched by a thousand people. 'Good swim, kid.' I wasn't really as puffed as I made out. If you're panting you don't have to smile. Mrs Churchill was there, 'So sorry, Alex,' and Norm Thompson wanting an instant quote to catch his deadline, and Mr Jack trying to be fair to both of us; celebrate with Jenny and commiserate with me, without any mention of backs or 'I warned you'.

I looked in vain for Tom. No fake official on the concourse this time. Nowhere. A fairweather friend? And Dad, he was supposed to have left straight after work to drive here . . . where was he?

I combed my hair for the victory ceremony. We both wore our New Zealand track suits, and to hell with them. The flashbulbs went off, Jenny captured ecstatic for tomorrow's paper; me, well, you could say smiling wanly. I kept thinking, run it again, another chance, it's really me who should be up there, we've all made a ghastly mistake. Though, as with similarly short-legged Maggie, when I stood on the second level, my head was still about level with Jenny's. Tall girls should win. I was NOT going to cry like a bad sport, a sook. Yet.

The public bit lasted about ten minutes. Mr Jack told me Dad had sent a garbled message: he'd had car trouble up near Thames, and had to limp back to Auckland. I walked straight through the dressing room and, stopping only to pick up my bag, out the other side, out of the pool with my wet togs on under my track suit, almost straight into a dark green-coloured sports car parked outside the main entrance. Tom in a bomber jacket and leather cap with ear-flaps, like a World War II fighter pilot.

'Hop in,' he said. 'Where do you want to go?'
'Auckland. Rehearsal tomorrow.'
'Seriously?'
'Seriously. The motel, my things, then Auckland. Tonight.'
'Shouldn't you leave a message for your coach? What about your parents? Aren't they here?'
'No, and I'll run my own life.'
We drove back to the motel. He waited outside in the car while I threw clothes into my suitcase. I left a note for Mr Jack at his motel: *Sorry about the 200 metres tomorrow, you were right really. People will think I'm just a bad sport, can't take a beating, well tonight it's true I am and I can't. But please don't tell anyone about my back it was STUPID wasn't it and give Jenny my luck for a good 200 time tomorrow. I've gone back to Auckland with a friend. Ask Norm Thompson, he might know. Will ring. A.*

Tom, burbling on about colds and Joan and being responsible to the production, refused to start the car until I'd gone back into the motel and put some dry clothes on, plenty of them. He pulled the car hood up and took a woolly hat out of the glove pocket. He made me put it on. We set sail for Auckland.

I sneaked the occasional glimpse sideways. The man of my dreams reflected in the lights from the dashboard, smoothly changing gears over the winding road north of Tauranga, driving as well as he rode horses and scooters, a green sports car — what more could a girl want?

My New Zealand sprint title, that's what.

Somewhere in the Waihi gorge, I felt the tears coming. If he noticed, he didn't immediately show it. The car was quite noisy with the sound of the wind rushing through the black hood. I turned my head away and sobbed my heart out. Even through my tears I noticed the car gradually slow, then pull off the road and stop. In the sudden silence, my crying noises sounded loud and dramatic, but I had to get it out of my system.

Between us was a wall. I don't know who built it or why, but it was like a sheet of glass. Tom waited. I waited. For what? When it came, the slight movement that told me he was trying to break through, even though he'd promised in Rome it would be me who moved first, before he put even a hand on a knee or a shoulder, I felt myself go rigid.

'Alex, *please* let me . . .'

'I can't.' Head shaking wildly, wiping water from cheeks, I turned away even further. My back was aching. '*Can't*.'

He didn't ask why, but after a long silence I felt another slight movement which told me he'd given up. He got out of the car, whether to have a walk or a pee I don't know, but it was about five minutes before he came back, and turned the key to continue the silent journey.

We arrived on the outskirts of Auckland around two. The long trip up the Great South Road was quick. Tom took no notice of the red lights — crazy to sit there, he said, with no one around.

'Do you want to come back to my flat?'

I had a flicker of sense left. I thought of Mum and Mr Jack ringing, toll call from Tauranga, not to say I'd won but that I'd been ignominiously beaten and had run away, was apparently on my way home with some young man called Tom Alexander, no he didn't know anything else about him; her lying awake reading, with no idea where I was — besides, it was safer . . .

'I'd better go home.'

Home was where I snuck in at 3 a.m., and found them all in their dressing gowns drinking tea, including Dad who was most upset the car had let him down, and Gran, who I think was the only one who knew about Tom, especially agog.

. . . was where I got a lecture on the storm of disapproval I should now expect; and on their preferring to know the young men I was driving round the countryside with. Was he a responsible young man, this Tomas Alexander? Was he a swimmer? If not, what was he doing in Tauranga with a sports car? They'd never heard of him. Gran winked at me.

Responsible? Safe as houses, damn it, I thought bitterly. Drives beautifully and doesn't take advantage of weeping girls. Gran would not be getting a progress report tomorrow.

Tomorrow. I had to get through the dawn first. I went out to my bedroom and was crying on my bed when Mum came in. 'The pain of defeat will pass, slowly,' she said, as I sobbed on her shoulder. 'How was the back, really?'

'It wasn't my back, not really.'

'You probably did the right thing,' she sighed, 'in the wrong way; impetuous and so easily misinterpreted.' I could, of course, say that I'd swum with a back injury . . . 'No,' I said, 'that'd make it seem Jenny's win meant less. No excuses.'

'Well, *Joan* is the next thing to get you through,' she said. 'The results from Wellington must come through any day now, surely.'

The weekend rehearsals were terrible. I talked to Mr Jack on the phone, ate humble pie, heard Jenny's 200 metre time was not so hot with the competition absent! She'd won by miles, her third title, the oustanding competitor of the champs, a strong contender for Perth. 'Are you coming training on Monday?' he asked. 'Do you have any plans at all, Alex?' I think he'd already given me up as a hopeless case. 'I'll ring,' I said.

Caroline was pleased to see Tom and me there on Saturday morning unexpectedly, but found plenty to pick at, both of us, both days. Tom was moody, even brusque, with everybody; I found it impossible to concentrate. None of the cast knew or cared about Tauranga, though they'd find out in Monday morning's paper, no doubt. Images of the smile on Jenny's face, my step up onto the box marked 2, Mr Jack's sad eyes, kept reappearing. And I sat and watched Lesley do her scenes, getting better and better, making me really believe in Joan's voices, and thought I've just set myself up for another fiasco, flop, damp squib, Alexandra the not-so-great after all.

'I'm not asking for miracles,' I whispered fiercely to the painted wooden statue of Christ on the cross. I don't deserve miracles, or any help at all. Tom said, on the top of St Peter's, that I'm a humanist, whatever that means. But perhaps, just by watching these people around me with their palms together, fingering their rosaries, genuinely praying — just by being here I might begin to understand what keeps them going . . . and Joan's voices.

The early Sunday morning Mass went on around me in sing-song Latin. I watched robed priests and boys cross themselves, chant, sing psalms, ring bells, light candles, I smelt incense, I gazed at paintings, statues, sun streaming through stained glass; the scene was a scaled-down version of St Peter's. Lesley, being Catholic, knew about these things; for her it was only a short hop to Joan's voices. For me, it had begun to seem like a great impossible gulf.

Caroline's pep talk to the cast yesterday, though very complimentary, had left me feeling I wasn't trying hard enough, shouldn't be trying at all. Should try harder. She was, she said, very pleased with her two Joans. Lesley was especially successful at catching the intense spirituality of Shaw's Joan, getting across her powerful faith in her voices and her mission from God, her uncanny ability to inspire others. Alex's Joan was coming across well as the bossy, earthy country lass, the supremely self-confident girl who talked familiarly to bishops and generals and scaled walls, who stood her ground in that last act of courage.

Earthy, bossy, is that all? She's beyond me, I cried silently above the Latin. She wore heavy armour and rode a horse into battle, and got wounded by an arrow. She knew how to create an image for herself, not just with a soldier's clothes, but with a knight's white armour, rich fur-trimmed clothes in the latest fashion, squires, pages, her special white banner. Taken prisoner, she was brave enough to jump off a tower, and how she stuck to her guns about her soldier's dress and her voices, to the bitter horrible end. After all my reading, I do understand about heresy, why she posed such a terrible threat to both the power of the Church and the State, why they had to destroy her, why she chose death rather than life imprisonment — but she's beyond me.

I've tried, as Caroline suggested, to think of a spiritual experience I've had when I say the lines about the voices — I've thought of that first night on the roof in Rome, dancing to what felt like the beautiful pulse of the whole starry universe above me. I've thought of staring speechless at the Pietà or up into the dome from the marble floor of St Peter's or at the white pillars of the Forum, perfection against the blue; I've thought of the sound of Aida singing in Rome, a single voice, so pure it made me shiver and could only be a gift from God — those were spiritual experiences, so *wonder*ful I had tears in my eyes — but Joan, she's beyond me.

The congregation went up to take Communion. I watched them come back, and envied them. I kept hearing Tom's voice reading Byron on the top of St Peter's, looking out over Rome, his slightly amused voice as Dunois and his evil, grating voice shouting at me as D'Estivet, his normal voice in the car pleading, Alex, *please*, let me . . . what? Comfort, kiss, and what else besides? The voice of the announcer in Tauranga saying over the applause, 'First, the new New Zealand champion, Miss Jenny Hartley.'

On Monday my recount came through. Miss A.B. Archer. Latin 53. I stood out at the letterbox and waved the thin slip of paper in triumph and burst up the porch steps, yelling 'Ya boo, sucks to you, Miss Gillies.' I could enroll at varsity next week. I could play Joan. Mum was so relieved she dropped the iron and sat down in a chair, and Gran didn't know what I was talking about.

I'd sworn I would not read the morning paper, but Jamie left the headline lying on the kitchen table: ALEX ARCHER BEATEN Junior Star Defeats Olympic Medallist In Sensational Race.

It had to be in daylight, an ordinary pub. Tom rang and said he had the loan of the MGB for two weeks and perhaps he could be helpful with lifts, what about rehearsal tonight. I said thanks and could he pick me up at five.

I remember Miss Macrae once saying, if the coincidences in books and plays sometimes seem a bit too convenient, too pat and easy, remember the coincidences of real life are far more extraordinary. Here's one, then: the coincidence of February 13 that put Tom, Keith, me in jeans and a desperate short back 'n sides, and two fine upstanding Kiwi family men in the same pub at the same time. Recipe for a scene.

Because I am trying harder, I told the barber it was for a play, and watched him go up the sides above my ears with the clippers. Mum had a fit, Gran giggled a bit, and the kids stared. In the car, Tom looked at me aghast, but said nothing. Together with the jeans and one of Dad's sports shirts, it was all a bit much. I said, 'What about a beer, it's forty minutes before closing time, then we could get a hamburger before rehearsal.'

The pub he chose was slightly more couth and less crowded than the one Keith had taken me to last year, and the looks were different. Last time they had been reasonably sure I was a girl; this time they weren't at all sure, because only boys ever had haircuts like that. Tom seemed unconcerned. I had my glass up to my mouth when through the heads I saw the very last person in the world I wanted to see.

'Brace yourself,' I said to Tom as Keith came over, smoking, a glass of whisky in his hand.

'Alexandra . . . and Tomas from Italia, himself,' he said, elaborately tapping his ash into the peanuts on our table. 'Well, well, at last we see them together. An interesting couple, very. And no longer the undisputed champion, I see. What a shame, Alex. Some little girl beat you.' The emphasis on girl was cruelly deliberate.

'Get lost, Keith,' I said.

'I'd worry about this girl if I was you, sir,' he said to Tom. 'I'd be very worried indeed.' Tom ignored the leer, went on munching peanuts, ash and all. 'She'll eat you, you know, have you for breakfast and spit out the pips. Did the hairdresser's scissors slip, or is this the *real* Alex?' He leaned over the table. I thought he was going to run his hand up my bristles, but instead he gave me a real boys' play-shove, clenched fist hard into my shoulder. 'Bonza, boy-o!'

'Cut it out,' I said. Tom looked at his watch. 'I think we might leave, Alex. Rough elements here.'

Keith turned his attention to Tom. 'Of course, Alex, no accounting for sensitive tastes, is there? What do you keep under there, old fruit, under the lid of the music box?' He leaned over and made as if to take off Tom's beret.

I remember after, the two blokes over by the door watching us with blank faces above a table of empty jugs and glasses. They would have seen Keith punch me in a way he'd punch no girl, Tom's hand go up, enclose Keith's wrist, move him in one movement bodily sideways, spilling the whisky. Me finish my beer and get up, Tom grasp my hand firmly as we left.

Outside they must have seen us turn into the narrow side-street where the car was parked. I heard footsteps, then I felt a body alongside, shoulders force me into the side of the building. I saw two hard eyes above a fixed grin as the hand went slap, slap across my face and the boots begin to kick my shins. 'Pretty boy,' I heard.

Past him, as I began to hit out myself and kick back, I saw Tom forced backwards across the black hood of the car, struggling with the other much bigger man. The hand stinging my face became a fist, but he got in only two playful, sneering blows before I registered running footsteps, another person, the crack of bone as my attacker went down to a sharp punch on the head, from Keith.

We stared at each other briefly over the body slumped between us before he went over and hauled the giant off Tom. Both of them pushed the giant — such an ordinary man, in walk-shorts and a tie, the family man who sells you batteries in the local hardware shop — up against the building. Keith delivered a few warning punches, some choice phrases of abuse, and sent him reeling along the footpath.

It had all happened very silently, quickly. The three of us stood panting. Tom had lost his beret. He picked it up and put it on, but not before Keith had given him a long look of appraisal. 'See ya round,' said Keith flatly, wiping his hands on his jeans. He gave me a last inscrutable look and walked off.

Safe inside the car, parked outside a hamburger bar, I noticed the hands resting on the steering wheel were trembling.

'Clearly a boxer,' he said, 'from way back, your Keith. Underneath, a gentleman. Are you all right?'

'A bit shaky. Not *my* Keith.'

'I'd say you parted in anger?' I nodded. 'A memorable birthday, one way and another.'

'Whose, yours?'

'Sì. Ho ventitrè anni.'

'How do you say happy birthday?'

'Buon compleanno.'

'Buon compleanno!' I held up an imaginary glass. 'Have to imagine the Lacrimae Christi. That wasn't a bad picture, was it?'

'What picture?'

'That slide I sent you. The letter just before Christmas telling you about *Joan*.'

'I didn't know about *Joan* before I got here.'

'I wrote before Christmas. With some transparencies.'

'Sorry, but I never got it. I left Italy on Christmas Day.'

Which explained some things. Many things. Not everything.

'You've never told me why. I thought you had an audition lined up.'

'Two hamburgers, king-sized, one chips, for the lady in the crew cut,' called the burger man, kindly for a change. I went and got them. Tom put his on the dashboard. He settled back in the seat, eyes closed. He needed a shave and there was blood on the back of his hands.

'The audition did not impress,' he said quietly.

'Why? What went wrong? So when's the next one? Aren't you going back to Milan?'

There was such a long silence that I thought he'd gone to sleep. 'Tom?'

I've never seen a man in tears. Part of me said men don't, boys who cry are sooks; part of me said that's rubbish, why not, they get hurt, feel things just as much as women.

'Is this delayed reaction?' I said. 'We could have got killed. Or both in hospital, both out of Joan.'

'You could . . . partly, yes, from years of similar treatment at boarding school. Good keen men doling it out to Angel Alexander, keeping the country pure and uncontaminated.'

It was about five minutes before he could speak, five minutes where I longed for his tears on my shoulder, to run my fingers through the bronze hair. I ploughed through my hamburger, and ate most of the chips.

'It's not really that, why I'm . . . I once told you about my teacher. After Rome, he died. Swiftly, very painfully, of cancer. The audition was five days after. The funeral . . . they put him into a grave with a foot of water in it.'

It keeps coming back to death. His teacher died. Joan dies every night, every time anyone is locked up or hit for sticking to what they believe. Andy died. One of these days Gran will die. How do you live with death?

'I'm sorry, I really am sorry,' I mumbled.

'Alex — Alessandra?' I heard, I knew, I could feel he needed, longed for a movement from me, some gesture to break through this glass wall.

I couldn't do it, even if it was his birthday. I sat there rigid while the moment passed and he blew his nose and ate his cold hamburger.

Rehearsal was to be outdoors tonight, my first complete run-through. We arrived, silently, ten minutes late, Caroline already angry, not a good start. The set, painted pillars and battlements extending the stone walls of the stage area, had been finished over the weekend.

Caroline took one look at my haircut and went berserk. I'd need two wigs now. I said mine would be alright for the trial scene because actually she had all her hair shaved off only a few days before she died. I'd dye it the same colour as the wigs should be, black. It would look just right. She shouted, 'Alex, child, I decide these things, did no one ever teach you about consultation, manners, and while we're on the subject, you've kept me on tenterhooks for three weeks, your damn U.E. results. You could have had the courtesy to ring me before Marcia put me out of my misery today. Marcia, Tom, me, your mother, we've all been nervous wrecks.' 'I didn't know myself until today,' I said angrily, feeling an idiot — so they all knew? 'That's what I mean,' she shouted. And what, she said, were those marks on my face? 'Nothing,' I said, 'I walked into a door.'

Waiting to begin the trial scene, I whispered to Tom that one thing, I now knew what it felt like to be beaten up, in a minor way. He was pale, not having a good night, missing cues, more than once stopping in the fifth scene to argue with Caroline over how the cool, sensible, buck-passing Dunois would say a line when basically, he's in the process of very subtly writing her off.... *and I tell you that your little hour of miracles is over, and that from this time on he who plays the war game best will win — if the luck is on his side.* I noticed deep purple bruises had appeared on his neck and the inside of both arms.

'Your Joan will be convincing physically,' he said coldly. 'Soldier, peasant, stubborn transvestite, the externals, you've done your homework. But we both know that she often cried, she felt things intensely. She gave of herself. Remember she once leapt off her horse to comfort an English soldier as he died. Shaw's lines are full of passion, warmth, a spiritual vigour, a sense of mission.'

He didn't need to add, where's yours? That night, in the trial scene outdoors, though the proper strong lights were being installed tomorrow, there was still enough light for me to recognize real cold anger in D'Estivet's eyes.

Hail and farewell

Alex — Monday night — late —

No doubt you thought tonight I was soliticing sympathy — that through tears, I might break through the barriers between us that seem inexplicably to be growing higher daily.

I've always been able to cry. It seems to me healthy, not a sign of weakness, though few in this country would agree. Grown men don't cry: never, since the first scuffed knee, through the footy bruise, playground knock, broken arm falling from tree or bike, head kicked senseless at the bottom of a scrum. Take it, like a man. Never show the vulnerability of tears, or pity or love. Italians cry, and touch, and laugh, and live, with more passion.

Your disappointment in Tauranga, the blow to your pride, my grief for my teacher going deeper and taking longer to heal than I've acknowledged to myself — if there was anything, any compassion between us — either would have been an opportunity for comfort and perhaps some honesty at last. But I confess myself beaten, at least temporarily. You rejected sympathy for your despair and remained impassive to mine.

We have a testing three weeks ahead. As Dunois I promise I shall give you every bit of support I can, call on all my training to bring our scenes to life. As D'Estivet I warn you, I suspect I may now find it easier to pronounce the words as they should be, legal niceties loaded with implacable prejudice and intense sexual jealousy. Did you know D'Estivet was mockingly called Master Benedickte because of his filthy tongue? Also that he came to a mysterious and sticky end, his body found in a drain. At least three of those involved in Joan's trial came to sticky ends.

As for our close escape today, I once told you that I couldn't get out of New Zealand fast enough. Not conforming to our respective stereotypes, but uncompromising (brave, that haircut!), we've both had to learn to live with jealous rumours, innuendoes, knowing them to be totally untrue. Perhaps that is why you can tap so convincingly into Joan as the individualist youth against mindless authority, Joan the soldier freed from sexual games; though the spiritual side of her, at present, remains out of your reach. It was probably always too much to ask of an actress so young.

I'm looking forward to the experience, though, watching your Joan grow through performance as I'm sure it will.

I'm not sure what I'll be doing post-*Joan*. I have money to repay to my family, which may take six months. I doubt I shall stay here. I may seek a place in drama school in England. You're going, so you say, to America in September.

Keith gives me some hope — that behind these hard-drinking façades some compassion and forgiveness does lurk. Why else would he have come to rescue the wild girl who has jilted him, and the one he sees, ironically, as responsible. I don't doubt that we would have prevailed in the end — neither of our attackers was sober, you are strong and agile and I'm not entirely useless, after years of boxing and boarding school, in defending myself, but it was probably the difference between bruises we can cover and injuries (your back, especially) we could not have concealed. One of these days I'll thank him.

I remember the day I first saw you, weeping at the airport, then climbing onto the bus with such promise and buoyancy in your step. Someone luckier, more skilled at courtship, more attractive, and more patient than me will no doubt succeed one day, where I failed.

Meanwhile, the play's the thing . . .

Collision

Tuesday night was Lesley's first dress rehearsal.

I was supposed to go and watch. I spent the day reading yet another book on Joan — one that said she was really a royal bastard who lived to a ripe old age, and some other poor girl was burnt at the stake — and after tea went training instead. I bullied Mr Jack into letting me swim after hours, when the squad had gone, in the half light of dusk. After nearly a week away from the water, with only those two races in Tauranga, I felt quite good. Water through a boy's haircut felt cold and free. No back twinges, at long last. I like swimming in the dark.

Tom was right, it was my pride that was hurting, every time I thought of Tauranga, every time I thought of his letter — a farewell, or a declaration of war? Possibly both, to see which way I'd jump. What had luck, skill, being attractive or patient got to do with it? Behind all his smooth words, he either was or he wasn't. In love.

'This carnival on Saturday night,' I said to Mr Jack as he totted up money in the dim office.

'You're down for the 100 metres,' he said, startled. He'd already choked over his tea once tonight, when I walked down the steps into the office, looking, he said, like my own brother. Sackcloth and ashes the 'in' look? he spluttered. He frowned but didn't comment on the bruises. 'Jenny's swimming. Are you?'

'Maybe.'

'How was the back tonight?'

'Better. I'll come training in the morning. Not when the squad's here. Later.' Swimming, training, even getting beaten by short-legged, fitter, less complicated girls, was at least familiar territory, even if I couldn't face Jenny and all those fresh-faced curious youngsters yet.

From one extreme to the other. Pitting my body against Jenny's, my sceptical mind against Joan's voices, my earthy Joan against Lesley's spiritual one. Tom and I both changing masks, images, roles, again.

I had two full dress-rehearsals, Wednesday and Friday. While I was training, Caroline rang home and ear-bashed Mum that she was more than a little upset with me, I should have been there at the full run-through last night. Tonight I was to arrive at six sharp. Costume call, on the dot, on pain of death.

From fairish short back 'n sides to long, black, unkempt hair with a short fringe. You can't get much more extreme than that.

'I want black hair, but I can't go on in that,' I said to my reflection in the mirror and Keeper Rodney above me, poking at the wig with his sausage fingers.

'Fifteenth century peasant girls . . .'

'She wasn't a peasant, she was bourgeoise, a farmer's daughter, her father was a headman of his village, she could spin and sew as well as any woman in Rouen.'

'Dearie, don't go on,' he said tiredly, sweating above his black polo-neck. 'She didn't use shampoo twice a week nor a brush, for sure. This is splendid. Friday, some colour in your cheeks too.'

'Is Lesley wearing this?' My head felt hot.

'A similar one.'

'Couldn't I just wear a scarf over the other wig, that one?' Joan's cropped male wig sat on its block, further along the makeshift dressing-table.

'No you could not. All *wrong*, darling. You'll be quite used to it by Saturday.'

That's if I ever get past tonight, I thought, escaping from the small lecture room which was my dressing-room along with the six or seven females who appeared in the court scene and who between them had two lines to say. Long, elegant gowns with spectacular sleeves hung around the walls; steeple hats sat on the desks. I needed some air, to find myself, inside the scratchy long red dress and unkempt black hair. I vowed to get a comb, the sort you comb horses with.

Outside in the cloisters, I sidled along the stone walls towards the noise of hammers, male voices shouting. It was a different scene from Monday; other people had been busy too, all these weeks. There were several lecture rooms full of all the men's costumes, king's court and trial court, dozens of them. The sets were nearly finished, the scaffolding was up, three hundred seats. A great bank of lights had been installed above the audience; others stood at the sides.

Someone shouted, 'Quarter hour, please folks,' as I saw the stage set with a heavy table, chairs, a chest, my stool; all so ready. I turned tail, down some steps, along the cloisters where weeks ago I'd overheard Tom and Genevieve. But there was really nowhere to run to, unless it was the dressing-room, throw off the wig and dress, and go home . . .

Eventually, hearing 'five minutes to beginners, please,' I was just about able to prise myself off the stone bench and saunter back. Caroline pounced on me, and fussed. Behind her in a front seat was Miss Macrae, whom I hadn't seen since my last day at school.

'I hear it's going well.'

'You hear wrong,' I said.

'I was pleased about your Latin recount,' she said. 'So were a few other people.'

'Relieved too, I bet. That I won't be back.'

'Immensely relieved,' she said ironically. 'Is Tom here yet, Tom Alexander?'

'I wouldn't know.'

'That wig makes you look rather too much like a serving-wench. I must get Caroline to have something done about it. And you should have a cap.'

'Thanks, anything,' I said.

From the hall to rehearsing outside was one thing, but with costumes and lights as the sun went down behind the tower — entirely another. I began to feel it might just come together, the story of Joan, in this fifteenth century French world of banners with fleur-de-lis, Joan's famous white banner with *Jesus Maria* sewn on it, heavy drapes and solid rustic furniture, wonderful costumes that looked so much richer on stage than they did hanging up backstage.

I was very conscious of Miss Macrae's beady eye on me as I scraped through the first scene. The second, at court with the Dauphin, the freedom of my soldier's dress and sword, was worse. There was no sign of Tom. He might, I thought sourly, have been around to help me through the embarrassment of peculiar wigs, a dress, strange winkle-picker soft shoes, with lights shining in my eyes, stumbling over chairs, needing prompts, laughing at and upsetting Ray because he looked so nauseatingly weedy in his Dauphin costume with the wrinkly hose and long pointed shoes, and his hair shaved right up above the ears.

Unable, even after all that practice, to remember to hold firmly onto the scabbard *before* trying to get the sword out, so that it stuck halfway and when I muttered 'oh, *shit*' rather loudly, the entire Court cracked up.

'Snap.'

I'd walked crimson from the stage, sworn at Rodney and stage manager Genevieve, been looked at strangely by Miss Macrae and told by Caroline to stop making such a noise and go and change for the next scene.

Everyone had so far been very nice, don't worry about the dries, you'll be fine Alex, but now I could see it in their eyes, she can't do it, only losers throw tantrums, this inspired bit of casting was a dreadful mistake. Bring on Lesley, who's sitting there with Miss Macrae, both of them scribbling in notebooks, just *waiting*.

And now Tom walked in larger-than-life just as Rodney buckled on the last bit of my armour.

'Snap,' he said, frowning at the tears rolling steadily down my cheeks. We were both wearing, over black knitted chainmail and leather leggings, armour borrowed from a professional company who'd done the play two years ago. It was a warm muggy night; inside, I felt hot and trapped. The Tinman had been silver-painted cardboard; this was proper beaten metal, thin but still heavy, weighing me down.

'Tom, dearie!' said the Keeper, handing us both swords to belt around our waists. 'Swopped your beret for a wig tonight? Marvellous. Italian?'

'It's not a wig,' he said, looking at me.

'You're teasing me,' said Rodney coyly.

'No. All mine. See?' He pushed it back from his high forehead to show the roots.

'But dearie, the colour!' Two females busy at sewing machines looked up with interest.

'A special brew I get sent out from Milan, numero ventisei in the Wella catalogue if you want to try it yourself. I do it every week, can't bear blonde roots, can you? Eyebrows too and in the summer a touch of chest hair.' He whipped out the sword and gave it an experimental flourish into a rack of costumes. 'Expensive but worth it, don't you know?'

Rodney was so bowled over with the idea of a Kiwi bloke using hair colouring, not just for a play but for normal every day, chest hair to boot, that he was speechless. The sewing women looked at each other, impressed but dubious. As for Tom, he had the bland smile of the born con man that he is, the smile I'd seen so often in Rome.

'What about yours, Alex? Go red with me? Which twin has the Toni? Look in the mirror, snap!'

We stood together, side by side, in our identical armour, exactly the same height. He'd had his hair cut exactly the same as my wig, shaved and cropped above the ears, the rest brushed forward, thick and shiny. He was really clean shaven for the first time since *Ben Hur*. We'd been told that make-up was to be kept unnoticeable, a bare minimum. He had on just enough to look, even close-up, convincingly ruddy, a tough soldier. Jack Dunois. Gorgeous. The fifteenth century heart-throb. The experienced actor. The future famous opera singer. The man who sent me a formal letter yesterday saying it was all off.

And Joan as she is usually pictured for the first time, with short dark hair, in shining grey armour, the equal of the soldiers around her. He held my eyes, daring me not to laugh at his nonsense, not to continue crying.

'*Hither Maid! To me!*' he said quietly.

'*Be you Bastard of Orléans?*' I said, automatically. I looked colourless, like a black and white photo, beside him.

'*You see the bend sinister. Are you Joan the Maid?*'

'*Sure.*' Behind us, the Keeper was staring, the sewing machines had gone silent. We heard someone yell 'Third scene folks, let's get the show on the road. Tom, where the hell are you?'

'You know the lines,' he said roughly, not kindly. 'Avanti.'

That was all the help I got. He had stayed away during the first two scenes, he stayed away from me the rest of the night. By the end I knew that Tom, with two key parts to play, was looking after numero uno.

Dunois in armour was one thing, Dunois in scarlet, blue and gold coronation gear was another; a Renaissance painting come to life, a complete peacock, and loving it.

Throwing a tantrum himself, stopping in the middle of the scene and demanding that the people hammering backstage do it at other than rehearsal times. The whole area went silent as his voice bounced off the stones: it was bad enough to concentrate in this heat, with a Joan suffering from what we all hoped was temporary amnesia; hammering was making it impossible. Refusing to continue. Caroline arguing with the carpenters who appeared out of the stonework, Tom retiring to a seat at the back of the stand to watch, his hands nonchalantly behind his head, while people threatened to walk out. It was twenty minutes before we got going again. He was so unconcerned that it crossed my mind that it was all an act. Just so that I wasn't the only one being difficult? No, surely.

I didn't see him as D'Estivet until I staggered on in the heavy leg-irons that Rodney had produced, and then I didn't recognize him. Thirty sombre men around me in black and grey gowns, those strange felt hats, all unrecognizable from yesterday's blokes in jeans and shorts. In Tom's usual seat behind the table sat an older man, unhealthy and pinched-looking under the clerical hat, reading his papers.

It was not a very Joan-like thing to do. It wasn't just Tom looking up from his papers with a look that froze me to the stool. The effect of all those robes, all that male weight and hostility, was overpowering. I sat there stupidly and felt tears welling up. The Inquisitor, an English lecturer who thought he was John Gielgud, said 'Are you not well?' and I simply stared at the concrete. Someone said, give her the cue again, but eventually they had to call Lesley to change quickly and do the scene for me.

'Look, she knows this scene, she's played it once,' I heard Miss Macrae mutter as the words went relentlessly on, and the whispers around me said I *knew* this wouldn't work. Poor kid, give her time. But time is what we don't have. She lost her New Zealand title last Saturday, to some young upstart. Oh *fuck* the swimming, someone said viciously, Lesley will have to do the whole season.

I stared at Joan's courtroom in front of me, noting with a grim satisfaction that Tom's attention was rather more on the whispering group around me, talking about me as though I was an invalid, than on Lesley and the court at Rouen. He missed a cue and was bawled out by Caroline. Ha!

He couldn't come anywhere near me until the long scene was over. But he didn't even after that, nor after I mumbled my way through the Epilogue, nor as I agreed to come for an extra rehearsal tomorrow morning, nor as I avoided a worried-looking Miss Macrae and went out to drive myself home.

As I sat in the car staring into space, I saw Genevieve get into the MGB. He even opened the door for her.

Swimmer, actress, Joan. No wonder I couldn't sleep. Two of my three lives collided, very publicly, on Saturday.

'You're not *coming* Saturday night?' said Caroline after the extra rehearsal, incredulously.

'It's Lesley's night. You don't need me. She doesn't, she'll probably be glad I'm not there.'

'Alex, I'd have thought it was obvious, every bit of familiarization helps. You need to get the feel of an audience of three hundred sitting here.'

'I know what an audience of twenty thousand looks like,' I said loftily. 'I'm busy that night.'

'Doing what?'

'Unfinished business.'

'Alex, you've committed yourself here.'

'It's Lesley's night. I'm sorry, but I can't.'

'God give me strength,' she said.

'If you're swimming Saturday night, Alex,' said Mr Jack, unmoved, watching one of his junior classes learn kicking up against the side of the pool, 'you owe it to Jenny, to the club, to all the people who've supported you in the past, to the Olympic association who paid for your trip to Rome, to your parents and to me and to yourself.'

'It's for my satisfaction, not theirs,' I cried.

'Both,' he said. 'You'll let me contact Norm Thompson and you'll do it with good grace. Not so much splash there, young Jimmy.'

'I just want to even the score. It's nobody's business but mine.'

'It's business, that's the point. The club pays good money to hire the pool. They're very dependent on their gate-takings. Your grudge match . . .'

'*Grudge* match!'

'Well, isn't it? Your race with Jenny will guarantee a good gate. Kate, turn your toes in slightly. Alex, you can't sneak in a side door at 7.30 and just appear.'

'Why not?'

'Break it down, Alex!' he said, the first time he's ever raised his Aussie voice at me. 'If I didn't know you better, I'd say you'd got a touch too serious about yourself.'

I sucked my lemon ice block and stared sourly at all the lunchtime swimmers enjoying themselves in the sunshine, at the row of eight-year-olds kicking furiously just below us.

'Look,' he said, quieter. 'I know you've got this *Saint Joan* thing next Monday.'

'It's all those eyes,' I said. 'Watching and waiting.'

'Don't give me that. Johnny boy, your heels should just break the water. You're a performer, Alex Archer, through and through. You're used to audiences. You just don't like failure.'

'You're dead right. I've got a score to settle with Jenny.'

'Sure. I understand that.' He told the kids to have a little rest. 'But you'll settle your score in the full glare of publicity because nothing else will do, and if it's the last race you swim, you'll do it with grace.'

He waited for me to take the bait. I didn't.

'Ring Jenny,' I said. 'Warn her.'

'You'll be right, champ,' he said softly. 'Jenny might have the titles, but you're the champ.'

'Tom, come in here and talk to this girl.'

'Why me?' he said, from the doorway of my dressing room.

'Give me strength,' said Caroline, imploring the Almighty yet again. 'Here we've got a marvellous opportunity for some free publicity and the lady won't have her picture taken.'

'That's right,' I said, catching sight of myself, now with black short back 'n sides, in the mirror. I'd used the Wella rinse, supposed to last through ten washes, before leaving home. Mum's face had been a picture of despair. I looked weird. 'No one asked me how *I'd* feel about it.'

'Tom, Genevieve wants me. You've got five minutes to turn this girl around before we start. The photographer will be here at eight. They want both of you in armour.' She swept out of the dressing room, her stainless steel jewellery jangling.

Tom hadn't changed yet. I had the scratchy red dress, a ruddy country girl's face but not the wig. He sat astride a chair and lent over the back.

'You and me, we're what's known as good copy, Alex. Publicity officers look for angles. There's me, supposedly the promising singer, back from Milan, and you, the successful swimmer, back from Rome.'

'The also-ran, back from Tauranga. Why do you say supposedly?'

'Out there, they have three hundred seats to fill, every night for two weeks. Advertising costs money. A large picture in tomorrow's *Herald*, a publicist's dream, costs nothing but co-operation.'

'Why did you say supposedly?'

'We owe it to the rest of the cast, the crew, everyone.'

'I heard all that yesterday. I'm sick to bloody death of being told I owe people things.'

'And you'll go on hearing it, because you do and that's the way life works. No one operates in a vacuum, no one stands on a stage or even a victory dais and . . .'

'Stop preaching at me. I don't like being lectured.'

'You don't like plain talk.'

'I'm being used to sell tickets.'

'Just so, just as Maria Callas is used, and Murray Halberg, and any top performer. The people who run these shows need you, just as you need them.'

'I just want to be left alone to . . .'

'A junior Garbo,' he said with scorn.

'I didn't finish. To do a good job. Whether I'm an Olympic swimmer has nothing to do with it.'

'The pure artiste.' From scorn to contempt.

'Why didn't you stay in Milan?'

'Because, my little Garbo, you had got right under my skin.'

'I told you not to come, it would all go wrong.'

'It? Referring to what, now? A relationship? An understanding? I haven't been aware of any such thing, other than being mildly useful from time to time.'

'That's not fair. And I'm not having my picture taken.'

'And if you don't, I'm walking out now, tonight. I have no understudy, between us we'll can the whole two weeks, or at least postpone the opening until a quick study plucked from the ranks can swot up Dunois, and another D'Estivet in two days.'

I knew it would come to war.

'You don't know what it's like.'

'I do. I've won things too, in my time. A major aria contest in Australia, others here. I've had my picture on the front page of the *Sydney Morning*

Herald and the *Melbourne Sun*, not to mention the *Herald*, and been recognized as I walked down George Street. So what? You're not the only person in the world to . . .'

'You can tell the photographer to get lost.'

'You can tell him yourself. And Caroline. And the cast. And the backstage crew.'

With perfect timing, Caroline marched back in. 'Ready?'

Tom hopped to his feet, picked the wig off the block and held it out. When I hesitated, he swung the chair bodily around, knelt down, flipped the wig expertly forward and smoothed it on over my black bristles. His face was close enough to see where he needed a shave before he turned himself into Dunois. To kiss.

'Well?' said Caroline, impatiently. 'It's time we started.'

I closed my eyes, to blot out his angry, inviting eyes.

'You two'll make a good picture,' she said.

'I'm swimming against Jenny tomorrow night,' I said, tired at the very thought.

From anger to pure rage.

'How the hell could I have known that?' he shouted. 'I thought that you'd . . .'

'For once, you thought wrong, Tom Alexander. Read the paper in the morning.'

You'd think someone might've said, this Archer girl, do we have to have her in *twice*?

At breakfast, inescapably on page two, a picture of unrecognizable me, Tom kneeling at my feet handing up the baton as at the end of the riverbank scene. Large heading: OLYMPIAN IN VARSITY OUTDOOR PRODUCTION, and a short caption about the Olympic girl turned actress, pictured with the well-known young baritone Tomas Alexander, temporarily returned from studies in Milan, as Dunois. Opening tonight with Lesley Preston in the title role, Miss Archer on Monday, the season running for two weeks.

Well, I did look rather splendidly fierce in my armour. Tom gazed raptly upwards. I snorted. The last dress-rehearsal hadn't been much better than Wednesday, though I did get through the trial scene in my own hair. Gran picked the name immediately. 'That him?' she demanded. 'Yes, but nothing doing,' I said. 'Want another bet?' she said wickedly. 'No,' I said, too tired to work out a foolproof way of winning back my five shillings. The kids all thought I looked very funny peculiar in a black wig. They thought my own hair, or what was left of it, looked a damn sight worse.

And on the sports page, Norm Thompson having a field day about the grudge match at the Olympic Pool tonight. Major clash, and leading coach Bill Jack pleased to see both his girls in top form — should guarantee a splendid race. No, he wouldn't like to tip either to win. Miss Archer out for revenge. Both great prospects for Perth and Tokyo.

It was me and Maggie all over again.

By the time I arrived at the pool, I was so far gone with nerves that I forgot that I'd been seen by very few swimming people at the pool since I'd run away from Tauranga, the bad sport who couldn't take it. Eyes followed me as I walked down the main steps, into the dressing room, into a remote corner. I put a bathing cap on. 'She's in a *play*,' I heard juniors whisper.

Jenny was already in the pool for her warm-up. There was already a sizeable crowd, an air of anticipation. I saw Dave and a bunch of divers arrive. He made a point of coming over, asking about my back — ssshhh, I said, it's fine — wishing me luck. My warm-up felt good, my back okay.

Sitting with my whole family, waiting for Event 13, I thought of Tom, who'd at least rung to wish me luck if nothing else. Apparently Lesley hadn't been too thrilled about this morning's paper. But she was still playing the opening night, with Tom. I was glad I'd sent her some goodluck flowers. I thought of Tom in Rome, dancing a minuet on the pink concourse just after I'd won my bronze. I wished he was here.

Keith had rung to wish me luck too. He'd seen the picture. You two make a great pair. I didn't tell him there was a war on.

Jenny sat opposite, with her unsmiling father, wearing her New Zealand track suit. Event 11, 12 . . .

Thirteens are special for him. Make them for me too.

I look along the still water. We are introduced, to much applause. Jenny's wearing her old togs, mine are my Rome ones, for luck.

I remember Napier, a year ago, against Maggie. So long ago. I needed to win that race to get to Rome. I need to win this race to quit with honour. It will be no easier.

It's nearly half past eight. Joan will be in the Dauphin's court. Dunois will be ready in his armour, waiting for his entrance, too.

The water lies waiting. The air is soft midsummer, perfect for opening night. My blood is up, Jenny. You're a nice kid, and you're going to be as good as me in the end, maybe better, but this is one battle I don't intend to lose.

The start is perfect. Not a peep from my back. I'm going like a train. By the end of the first lap I'm a full body-length ahead. I feel marvellous.

The turn is perfect. Jenny is so far behind I'm wondering what's gone wrong. I finish, stand, pull off my cap not caring that I look like a black-haired boy. I watch Jenny finish.

I move to stretch an arm across the lane ropes. She gulps at my hairstyle, then grins, tired, and we hug. Two days build-up to this had been too much for her. My time is 63.2, Rome is vindicated. A New Zealand record. One great last record.

We climb out. The applause goes on. It's the only time we've met in fair competition in our own home-town pool, this season. While we put our New Zealand track suit tops on, the announcer says something very unusual.

'Ladies and gentlemen, boys and girls . . . national selector, manager of the Olympic team in Rome, Mr Cyril Upjohn.'

Plump and pompous as always, he trots out onto the concourse, looking more than ever like a well-fed pigeon. He's carrying a framed certificate and a huge bunch of flowers. Swimmer of the Year. For services to swimming. I think of all my fights with him. 'Really?' I grin. 'Congratulations,' he says smoothly. 'If I'd lost this race?' I say cheekily. 'You're an Olympic medallist, five times Auckland champion, New Zealand record-holder,' he says, as the crowd goes on whistling and clapping. 'An interesting picture in the paper this morning, Alex.' I remember him watching me kiss Tom at the airport. Unfortunately, I remember the kiss too. 'A dark horse,' he says, holding up my hand like boxers do. 'Two dark horses. I must come and see the play.'

'Our Swimmer of the Year,' sings the announcer.

If it was my last race . . . I turned around and looked for Jenny, who'd slunk back among the officials. I went over and pulled her forward, and gave her the bunch of flowers and a hearty kiss.

'Think of me in Perth,' I said. 'Nil bastardio carborundum.'

She gaped. I saw Mr Upjohn's face go puce. He knew, as the applause died away and we walked over towards the changing-room, what it meant.

'Dog Latin, one of Keith Jameson's favourite phrases. It means, don't let the bastards grind you down.'

But my smile was because I was looking over the heads of all the officials saying 'Congratulations, Alex', looking down the pool and thinking, I'll never swim another race. If the pleased crowd saw it as handing on the torch, so be it.

My mind was really on a riverbank with a handsome red-haired soldier in armour, already terrifyingly on Monday night.

Breaking point

Nearly midnight, on Marcia Macrae's doorstep. Opening night: my head in control of Dunois and D'Estivet (Lesley edgily competent, no more) but my heart completely elsewhere; another sort of stage and challenge. Her pride on the line. Did she win? The *Herald* office closed on a Saturday night, the phones unattended. At my flat, spurning the first-night party, I rang eight Thompsons with an N-something initial, but none was the Norman Thompson who worked at the *Herald* and all were half-asleep and angry. I couldn't remember the name of that slimy official from Rome. Marcia had given me her address, so there I hied; a small house out in Titirangi, set in what seemed to be almost impenetrable bush.

No fool, she. 'Ring Alex!' she said, inviting reaction. Bluntly, stubbornly: 'For a number of reasons, I can't.' 'Then I shall,' she said, and did, and came back chuckling into the small book-lined living-room. The child was still up. She won alright. The other kid folded up under the strain. To rub it in, a New Zealand record too, only point two away from her Rome time.

A two-edged sword. Sweet revenge, but sweet enough to paint the American proposal rosy, a vision of Tokyo golden. I couldn't hide my delight or despair.

'I thought there was something going on,' she said. 'Since Rome?' 'In Rome,' I said. 'Since Rome, all frustratingly platonic, but whatever there was finished two days ago, leaving me totally baffled.' 'Why?' she asked.

'You tell me,' I heard myself demanding aggressively. 'Tell *me* why she blows so hot and cold. She's not a natural flirt, but she's driving me out of my senses. Why the gestures of defiance, the posturing of shyness, the deceptions, the calculated abuse of friendship, the stunts, the obsessive driving of herself into the ground and me and no doubt other people with her?'

'Stunts?' I told her about the diving act, the resulting back injury, her insistence on swimming in the nationals, almost inviting the defeat she suffered, the need to go riding, feel a sword in her hand, dress in a man's clothing, *my* clothes!

She stared into her coffee mug. 'Alex all over,' she said ruefully. So much natural talent and curiosity she literally didn't know what to do with it all, her buoyant personality touched with a streak of exhibitionism and a total inability to say no. At school a heroine, a leader.

'That was school,' I said. What about boyfriends? Had there been anyone serious in the past? Oh yes, a tall handsome lad, though rather humourless, and beside her a lightweight. She was clearly not describing Keith Jameson.

'What happened to him, this lad?' I asked.

'Hasn't she told you?' she said, sighing, breaking a silence. 'Then you must ask Alex,' she went on, flatly. 'But take care, Tom. These past eighteen months, since she broke her leg, have been difficult for everyone concerned.' Even the chance to play Joan had developed its unforeseen problems. Not conforming to the smiling painted doll stereotypes of *Seventeen* magazine, she'd been accused of being lesbian, more than once.

'So,' I asked, 'why on earth did you choose Joan, also unfairly slandered?' 'I'm glad we agree on that,' she said. From an untidy pile in a bookcase, she produced a programme from a London theatre, 1942. Cast list and pictures of Marcia Macrae as Joan, far slimmer than the stout person in a flowery housecoat opposite me, but the same deep-set, lively eyes. They had first pulled her out after three weeks, her voice going, her confidence gone; a week later, given a final chance to pull herself together, after one terrible night when the understudy had to take over after the second scene, for the rest of that night, and for good.

With hindsight, she said, she was never really up to Joan, though she was over thirty. It was wartime; stage people were all over the place entertaining troops, trying to keep the theatres at home open. And God knows, you need theatre at such times. She'd lost two brothers and a cousin in the desert war. She went and drove trucks in Egypt, and came out here in 1950. She never acted again; *Saint Joan* and all that went before was just a bitter-sweet memory. Joan was her gift to Alex.

So a favourite pupil was to succeed where she failed; under the guise of the spinster teacher, she is merely the classical ambitious stage mother. Having nothing to lose, I told her she was risking the same failure for Alex, stretched to breaking point, on and off stage, a volcano ready to blow apart.

'She'll not fail,' she cried, provoked.

'She could,' I said, matching her anger. 'Have you seen her this week, not hiding behind one of her masks, with her guard down? No? Perhaps you should. You've set a highly-strung sixteen-year-old at one of the longest, most demanding parts in English drama, a role usually played by women in their thirties. I've been back here six weeks. She's gone from bad to worse, juggling her final commitments to swimming with . . .'

'Is she retiring at last?'

'She says she's going to America in September, on a swimming scholarship. I doubt it. At the moment, she doesn't know what she's doing.'

'I've taught Alex since she was twelve, Tom,' she said angrily, pulling rank. 'I know her strength, her resilience, her extraordinary courage, better than you. Didn't she come up trumps tonight, and in Rome?'

I don't record this exchange with any pleasure.

'A minute-long race is nothing, *nothing* compared to carrying a three-hour play on your shoulders,' I said, adding brutally because I have — when aroused, with my back to the wall — the capability to wound: 'It was too tough a test for you, at twice her age. You stumbled, and you failed, and from what I can see it has haunted you ever since. Yet you expected her . . .'

'I was not an Alex, I know that, but your mother was, if you ever want to know.'

'No I don't.'

'Perhaps you hold the key, think about it, before you go back to Milan.'

I walked out, not bothering to tell her that I was not going back to Milan, that today's paper lied when it talked of the 'promising young baritone' Tomas Alexander, back temporarily from his studies in Milan, rueing the day I'd got tied up with Alex, Joan, Marcia, Caroline, Genevieve, the whole damn lot of them.

I drove back to the party, which was still going strong, on autopilot, via the villa in Epsom; around the back a light was still burning.

Good morning, captain squire

So, now, between me and Joan, I have no excuses left.

I'm enrolling at varsity tomorrow with my U.E. certificate in my hot hand, and no regrets. I told Mr Jack yesterday that I am ready to move on from swimming, that I want to spend the next four years doing a law degree here, not slogging away for an unlikely Tokyo gold or doing a business course in California. I told Gran yesterday that it's all off with Tom (she said give him time, pet) and I rang Keith and told him ditto and thanks mate for being a good Samaritan and see you round varsity sometime.

The kids are back at school and Gran is back to her baby dresses. Mum and Dad seem relieved I've decided to finish swimming and said they looked forward, after the show, to seeing the Alex they knew around the house, with some hair.

Why did Miss Macrae ring me at midnight on Saturday? Not quite waking the whole house, because I was in the kitchen making Milo and eating toast and got to the phone after only one ring. I wouldn't have thought she cared about who won, that much. And again yesterday before Sunday lunch, to say my last rehearsal had been put off until 4.00 and would be for only an hour, with five or six key people.

I do know all those lines, those long speeches, the arias. I've tried to understand with my head if nothing else about Joan's voices, why she was seen as the most dangerous heretic of all, the first Protestant. *What other judgement can I judge by but mine own?* I understand with my head and my heart how absolutely brave and alone she was, her whole short life.

I even understand why Caroline flipped her lid at that rehearsal yesterday, demanding to know if now, *finally*, I was ready to give Joan and the play my full commitment and attention, and a few other home truths about holding back, refusing to give of myself, letting myself down, the effect on the cast, etc. Why she made me so angry I did the riverbank scene with Tom at top speed, kissing him on both cheeks as Shaw wanted and as though I meant it; why she jumped up shouting, 'At the eleventh hour, Alex, a glimpse, at last! Please, let it be all like that? *All* of it?' In my anger, I had felt myself come alive.

So, as I sit at five o'clock in a funny little restaurant with Tom playing helpful older friend, and the minutes tick away to 7.30 start, I have no excuses left. Only me.

Which was why I was already trembling. My heart felt as though it was in my throat and my voice had gone up into my skull and out the top. Where my stomach should be was a deep hole. Tom had quickly begun to annoy me by bullying me into having Fish of the Day and salad, demanding iced water *and* that the snapper be grilled, not fried, basted in a little butter, please, a slice of lemon. He then ticked off the outraged waitress for chewing gum and for improperly washed cutlery. And when I was embarrassed, he carried on grandly about protest and education being the only way to drag this country's dreary little eating houses, where you couldn't even get a glass of wine because of the fossilized drinking laws, into the twentieth century. I think it was his nerves talking too.

'So I suppose you can't wait to get away again,' I said, 'when all this is over.'

'When I can afford to.'

'Still hating this place.'

'Nothing has changed to make me revise my opinion. You wouldn't credit it, this fish is still overcooked.'

'Have mine.'

'You must eat, Alex, nerves or not. You, an athlete, know that. Food equals stamina and you're going to need plenty of that.'

'Don't be so pompous. I'm not nervous.'

'Then you should be. Lesley doesn't appear to suffer from nerves at all. It shows.'

'How was she? There wasn't a review.' In this morning's paper, there had been a Norman Thompson rave-up of my last record-breaking race. I'd not read it, and blocked my ears to Gran thinking it would be nice for me to hear about my stunning world-class performance, thrilling the large crowd with the same form that won me an Olympic medal, the mark of the true champion.

'I heard he's coming tonight, to review you both. She was good, but only that. Our scenes were dutiful rather than inspired. Not so different from rehearsal.'

'You shouldn't have told me. About the critic coming.'

'Why not? You're used to reporters. You accepted that possibility when you accepted the role.'

'I'm scared of the trial scene.'

'So am I, i' faith.'

Why went unasked and unanswered.

'I shouldn't have had that fish,' I said.

I'd escaped from Caroline and Rodney fussing over wig and make-up and all the noisy court women cluttering up the dressing-room; I'd buckled the scabbard on over my red dress and was upstairs in a gloomy, deserted corridor frantically practising drawing out the sword. Tom, having tracked me down, but still unchanged, leant elegantly against the stonework.

'It only made me feel ill, like Joan's carp,' I said hoarsely. 'I didn't want it in the first place. All that fuss, to prove a point. And for what? Two bits of grilled snapper on a plate.'

'Didn't Rome show you how fish could be cooked?'

'So embarrassing, and expensive. And made us late. And made me feel sick.'

'Knock it off, Alex,' he said with sinister politeness. 'We were not late. You are not sick. Stop talking. Stop playing with that thing. You can do it perfectly.'

'I hated Italian fish. Disgusting octopus and calamari and eel . . .'

'That's not what I remember. Anyway, Maoris eat eel. Fishy, but pleasant, texture not unlike chicken. Talking of which, you've ten minutes. Are you ready for Baudricourt's castle, the chooks that won't lay, Joan talking to the soldiers in the courtyard, refusing to go away?'

An echo came up from quad, along with the increasing noise of three hundred people outside. 'Five minutes to beginners please!' My teeth were literally chattering. I lined up the tip and shoved the sword back into the scabbard.

'No I'm not ready, I never will be ready, go and get Lesley, tell her she's on tonight and every night, I'm going to be ill, I'm . . .'

'The coward's way out. You don't mean it for one minute.'

'I do.' The stones were now going blurry. 'I'm not going to make it, Tom. I can't, my first lines . . . she's too good for . . .'

'False modesty doesn't suit you, Alex. If you didn't think you could do it, you wouldn't be standing there in costume, made-up, ready.'

'I am not ready.' As I hauled off the wig, he pushed himself off the wall and grabbed me roughly by both arms.

'You are ready, and you've got five minutes to get outside your entrance, and calm yourself down. When you get on, don't look at the audience. Give me that sword.' He began undoing the buckle. 'Give me the wig.'

I clutched the wig. 'I'll do it. Leave me alone.'

'I'll take you down . . .'

'You will not. Just go away and leave me *alone*. Don't come near me for two weeks.'

'Seriously? On stage only? Is that what you want? What about getting here, getting home, at least can't I help . . .'

'I'll have the car.'

'Is that what you really want?'

'Yes.' Freed of the sword, I walked away from him, down the stone steps, towards Baudricourt's castle and my doom.

No one, not even Tom telling me not to look at the audience, had really warned me about the sight of all those bodies squarely face on, pale ovals in rows. Swimmers go between their spectators; this was face to face stuff. Somehow I got the wig back on, drank some water from the glass Caroline handed me as I heard my cue come relentlessly closer.

Where is she now? Down in the courtyard, sir, talking to the soldiers as usual ... Hullo, you there.

The voice bright, strong and rough. My voice. *Is it me, sir?*

... She wants you to give her soldiers' clothes. Armour, sir! And a sword! Actually!

I've no idea how I took those fateful steps out into the light, into the dusky night air, curtseyed and said *Good morning, captain squire. Captain: you are to give me a horse and armour and some soldiers, and send me to the Dauphin. Those are your orders from my Lord.*

I must have been ready. Despite gulping at the audience, the words came out, the scene happened. The scene with the Dauphin happened, and the scene with Tom, and the cathedral scene and the trial scene. By then I was deathly tired but still sufficiently aware of what was going on to decide I need not look at D'Estivet at all. I looked past him, past his shoulder. The hostile words, Tom's voice turned harsh and oily, were enough. We got through the Epilogue, Dunois deserting her, revealed as a coward and a politician looking after number one like all the rest of them. I didn't feel involved. The red flickering light of the fire between the trees didn't touch me.

It's not enough just to get through *Saint Joan*, once or twice or even three of your six times. It's not enough for your family to come rushing backstage, and Miss Macrae and Miss Gillies together, and even Mr Upjohn and his wife and daughter, all surprised, thrilled, moved, impressed, or so they said; and the *Herald* critic to write (so I'm told, I refused to read it) nice enough things about the two talented young Joans in the university's annual outdoor production. It sounded like damning with faint praise to me.

It's not enough to have read every book you can find on her, or to have tried to get the feel of her soldier's life, or to have watched devout Catholics at prayer, or to keep going over and over and over those lines you've been trying to learn since last April.

Even if you spend the days in between your performances sleeping, going to the pictures, doing food shopping for Mum, taking Gran for drives, some fun training; even a whole day spent enrolling at varsity, walking around the quad with your enrolment forms and sunglasses on trying not to see a whole new crop of people giving your hair and height odd looks; trying not to see the scaffolding, the lights, the banners above the stage, the posters everywhere — even if you do all those things, nothing works.

Nothing works because at each performance you see Dunois, gorgeous in his armour, a gilded peacock at the coronation, and D'Estivet wolf-like and evil in his black robes, and despite all your best intentions you wonder who is the person inside there?

It was the gossip, you see: the court ladies in our dressing-room my first night and my second night, making themselves into beautiful fifteenth century ladies with trains and steeple hats and arched eyebrows while I came and went from a drab dress through four changes of male clothes, feeling their resentment at having to sit around the dressing room in costume for most of the play waiting for the final bow.

Listening to the gossip made me wonder if the Tom I thought I knew and the one they knew were actually the same person? The Tom who turned up very late but got spectacularly drunk at the opening night party at Ray's flat, flirting with all the women but especially Lesley. Naturally, flushed with success and a few Pimms herself, she'd fallen into his arms.

The Tom who, when asked later to sing 'you know, something we all know like 'Funiculì Funiculà'', absolutely refused, saying that his voice had gone AWOL, going off into a corner with a full bottle of whisky, muttering away in Italian until he passed out and Lesley had had to go home with someone else. The Tom who'd sat on at Ray's place all Sunday listening to the whole of *Aida* on three long-playing records very loudly twice over, sending Ray out for fish and chips, drinking several bottles of red Dally plonk, and getting more and more morose, driving Ray bananas.

The Tom who was apparently working every available minute of the day on the wharves, usually starting at daybreak even after a performance. The Tom they all thought was the most gorgeous but infuriating red-haired hunk of man ever born; a smooth-tongued flirt with a few drinks aboard, but otherwise rather reserved, and unresponsive to serious flattery and titillation. They'd all tried hard enough. He was, though, believed to be taking Lesley home in his MGB most nights.

I couldn't believe my ears and certainly didn't want a continual running commentary on Tom Alexander's love life for the next ten days. During the second performance I asked Caroline for a separate dressing room,

I didn't care where, just by myself so I could hear myself think. It raised a lot of fifteenth century plucked eyebrows, but Caroline found a nearby lecturer's office and set me up there and Miss Macrae brought some flowers and sat with me before the third performance talking about how each scene presents Joan with tests of increasing toughness — from Baudricourt the pushover, to the sly but vulnerable Dauphin, to the pragmatic but self-confident Dunois, the wily devious Archbishop and finally to the impossible combined hostility, jealousy and intolerance of the trial scene; from Scene Four, the sense of fate inexorably closing in on Joan. She was probably trying to give me a sort of map of the play.

But the damage was done. I hardly heard a word. If I was confused about Tom before, now I was totally flummoxed. The amused, controlled Tom raving *drunk*? Taking that Lesley home? Going AWOL, what did that mean? There was nothing wrong with his speaking voice, as rich, as strong as ever.

Despite all Miss Macrae's talk, my third performance, the Friday, was so bad, needing about five prompts from Dunois on stage, and the rest heavy-going, that I told Caroline Lesley would have to play all the performances next week and good luck to her. She said, 'Nonsense child, you're doing fine and you'll do better, have a restful weekend, but I want you here Monday night without fail.'

Tom, probably too busy getting sloshed at parties and getting to know Lesley, didn't come near me. Why should he? After next Saturday I'd never see him again.

By Tuesday night I'd had a whole four days going over lines, getting Gran, Jamie, Mum, anyone to hear them. But the long run of good weather broke on Sunday afternoon with a mighty Roman-style thunderstorm, rare for Auckland. Lesley's Monday was cancelled, Tuesday was overcast and threatening. I drove the car slowly to varsity at six praying that the heavens would open.

Half an hour later, they did. From the cloisters I looked out at the water pouring off the scaffolding, the banks of lights covered with sheets of plastic, the stage area one large puddle — and gave thanks. I saw Tom only in the distance, and heard people saying 'let's go out for hamburgers, coffee, to someone's flat'. I kept away from Caroline before she could suggest using the time for an extra rehearsal.

I was turning the key in the lock when I heard footsteps splashing through the rain. 'Could you give me a lift home?'

I looked up at the figure by the car bonnet: Tom, in his usual beret and shirtsleeves under a pink woman's umbrella with frilly edges.

I said, 'Aren't you partying with the rest?'

'Not tonight. I know you asked me to keep clear, but . . .'
'Where's your car?'
'The owner wanted it tonight. Anyway, I came straight from work.'

I couldn't leave him standing there, shivering; reminded by tired-looking eyes that he was working long hours on the wharves. I thought opera singers were neurotic about not catching chills. I got in and unlocked the passenger door.

'Thanks, Alex,' he said, shaking the water off the umbrella outside. 'A touch of autumn in the air.'
'Where's your flat?'
'Mount Eden.'

I didn't start a conversation and neither did he. Apart from directions where to go, we seemed to have nothing to say to each other. As I pulled up outside an old, unpainted villa he said carefully, 'Would you like to come in, go over our scenes? It'll have been six days' break, assuming the weather's cleared by tomorrow.'

'No, thanks.'
'I think you should.'

'Caroline put you up to this, did she? Because last Friday was so bad? Because you think I'm getting worse instead of better? Because Lesley is getting so good? Because if you didn't know my lines as well as yours I'd be in deep shit?'

'Because I'm concerned, we're all concerned, yes. You have two more performances. Something seems to be getting in the way.'

'Or someone. You, for instance.'
'I'm flattered.'

'Don't give me that. You know damn well it's you. Comrades on stage one minute, enemies the next, added to various Italian gentlemen I've met in the past, not forgetting an Aussie called Dennis, it's enough to drive a girl to drink. But of course it's Lesley who's the lucky one now, isn't it?'

'Alex, what happened to the boyfriend?'
'Which boyfriend?'
'Tall, good-looking, rather humourless, a lightweight beside you.'
'And whose description is that?'
'A friend. What happened?'
'Some friend. *Who?*'
'If it's that important, Marcia Macrae. What happened?'

'Her again. Having little confabs were we, little heart-to-hearts about this crazy overgrown kid Alex who's trying to play a saint and failing miserably, making a total fool of herself 'cause she isn't and she can't.'

'What happened?'

'His name was Andy Richmond. He . . . went away. Like you will.'
'That can't be all.'
'All? You've never been jilted, Tom? You tell me something, why you told the rest of the cast, when drunk, mind you, your voice had gone AWOL, which Dad tells me is army slang for absent without leave.'
'You weren't even there.'
'Neither were you from the sound of it, passing out on the hard stuff. I have my spies. I snoop too. Fat lot of good it does me. Too drunk or too proud to sing at a party? Or only recitals to single girls in Roman apartments and far too polite to take advantage of them.'
'What are you saying?'
'I'm not sure, when it's all boiled down. But if you really are, or were a singer, and even that I'm not sure of, if you've stopped singing after one bad audition, you're more gormless than I thought.' I turned the ignition switch, and grated the car into gear. 'If you want to get out here, you'd better get out now. You should have stayed away.'
I saw his knuckles on the dashboard go white. 'Right . . . you've had your chance, Alex. If Thursday's bad, don't blame me. You had your chance.' He got out, pink umbrella and all, as the car was moving. He shouted something through the closed rain-speckled window, but I didn't catch the words.

If Thursday's bad . . . too true.
The first two scenes were dull as ditchwater, and I was having trouble with a frog in my throat. Caroline came backstage and asked me what was the matter. I said it was nothing, sorry, an off night. I'd have to speak up, she said, I could hardly be heard at the back, pull myself together, project my voice, drink some more water. Then I'd pee in my armour, I said, and we couldn't have that.
I went on for the scene with Tom, supposedly in a blazing temper but more like a damp squib. When I very soon needed a prompt he picked up the script about half a page further on, throwing me completely and probably making the whole scene like double Dutch to the audience. We eyed each other on the brink of disaster and stumbled through to the end; not even the healthy make-up could hide the strain in his face. Or mine if it came to that. The rest was a robot talking, tired to its very rivets. I got through it but only just. The voices of the trial scene hammered in my ears, Tom shouting at me *She is a relapsed heretic, obstinate, incorrigible and altogether unworthy of the mercy we have shewn her. I call for her excommunication*, his bitter-chocolate voice effortless above the din, his eyes blazing in triumph and hate. I drove myself home through tears. I had one more chance.

Not that simple. The two conversations make strange remembering.

Woken at nine o'clock on Friday morning I was swiftly declining Caroline's frantic pleas to do the Friday night. Lesley had rung, she said, to say her voice was going. She may have picked up a chill on Wednesday night when the whole quadrangle area was damp, the air heavy, the grass under the audience sodden. She wanted to swop, me to do tonight and she would play the last night, Saturday. No, I said, the arrangement was she would play the opening night and I'd do the final night. Last nights were always a bit special.

'But you must do tonight, Alex,' she cried down the phone. 'She simply can't. Otherwise we'll have to cancel. We have full houses.'

'Only if I can do both nights.' What was I saying?

'Lesley won't agree to that.'

Tough, I thought. 'Sorry, but I mean it,' I said.

We agreed I'd do tonight and talk about tomorrow tomorrow.

At nine o'clock on Saturday morning it was Miss Macrae waking me out of an exhausted sleep. Miss Macrae as angry as I've ever heard her.

'Alex, I was there last night.'

Oh gawd.

'I didn't come round to see you, because I doubted I could have kept my temper. You showed scant respect for the cast, the audience, Shaw's play or Joan. You cut pages, your scenes with Tom were a travesty, without a shred of the conviction or the fire that I know you are capable of. The tension between you two is affecting the whole cast. You sent your audience away dissatisfied — unforgivable.'

What about me, weeping alone in my dressing room afterwards? Doesn't she know it's survival time? That either I get through the words, through Joan's torment, without fire, or have them and Tom overwhelm me to the point I can't talk or think or act any more?

'Lesley wants to play tonight,' she said. 'She's been on the phone to Caroline twice already this morning.'

'The last night's mine.'

'After what I saw last night, you've put that claim in jeopardy. On the face of it, Lesley's request is . . .'

'I bet she invented the cold, simply to get the last night. She's been jealous right from the start.'

'Whether she did or not, you are going to play the last night because I have persuaded Caroline that you must, and not to give in to Lesley's whinings. You owe it to yourself and to me to give one good performance.'

Part of me had been saying, let Lesley do it — the easy, simple way out. Avoid winding myself up for a third performance in a row, wondering if my voice was going to hold. Give in; slink away. I'd forget the whole ghastly experience in time, forget even Tom, in time.

'I'm not your teacher now, Alex. I'm going to tell you what only Tom Alexander knows; that Joan was my nemesis.'

'Your *what*?'

'My downfall. I failed with her in London. She was my last professional engagement. I didn't have the stamina or the voice for performing her night after night. Alright, I was a professional trying to live up to professional standards, but I'm damned if I'm going to stand by and see it happen unnecessarily again.'

'Why does Tom know? What's so special about him?'

'He came round here the night of your last race, distraught for a number of reasons. For God's sake, Alex, why can't the two of you get together and sort it out, preferably before tonight?'

'Sort what out?'

'If you don't know that, the pair of you, then I may as well go hang myself. I've never seen two young people more right for each other.'

'That's not true. And he's not young, he's twenty-three.'

'Seven years, nothing. My one serious man was fifteen years older. And before you ask what happened, he was already married with four children and I chose a career.'

'I don't even like him much. He's bossy and cynical and I'll never see him again after tonight.'

She laughed. 'Rubbish. Met your match, Alex? Now, you get yourself organized. This is your teacher talking. I'll be out front and I want a fire from you tonight, I want a Joan I can believe in. She was my gift to you. Don't let me down.'

Sitting on the deserted stage at 5.30, sniffing the warm air, seeing a clear sunny sky behind the clock tower, I think, does she know what she is asking?

Joan's banners are fluttering gently against the grey stones. Miss Macrae: is the sour taste of your failure in *Joan* as strong as mine still is from Tauranga, or is it worse, even now? What's being beaten for one swimming title compared with failing with a chance like Joan, throwing away a whole career? Is that why she once said to me, she once vowed she'd never hear Joan's words spoken on a stage again? What had it cost, to break that vow? To break it, for me?

Later, two lonely hours later, hearing along the corridor, 'Beginners, please, stand by,' knowing that Joan's story will start relentlessly rolling in three minutes; the sun gone behind the trees, the sky turned to apricot; then I am walking out from my solitary dressing-room to some odd and not very friendly or encouraging expressions from the crew.

Tom is along in his dressing room, having his armour strapped on, with all the men. All of them dreading another probable nightmare, no doubt; another disappointment, another wasted opportunity. Has Lesley spread poison about me, that bumptious kid, around the place? Pity about the '61 production of *Joan* they'll say in years to come; one good Joan but the other one weak, a dull production, didn't come off. Does he merely listen to them complaining, as they dress as courtiers, priests, knights, soldiers, about my inexperience, my incompetence, my failure, Caroline's failure to see early in rehearsals it couldn't work; or does he defend Caroline, defend me? Perhaps tonight . . .

Do you realize, Miss Macrae, what you're asking? It's not you I'm afraid of, or the audience, or even Tom, or even Joan.

For my seventh and last performance, the third in a row, desperately tired of everything and everyone before I've even begun, the last night I'll ever see Tom — tonight, letting it all go, releasing the horror of the fire inside me, the person I'm very much afraid of is — myself.

Comrade-in-arms

Alone among the debris of clothes, robes, hats, the cloying smell of powder, strapped into armour, waiting — the rest on stage for the Court scene, distant voices and audience laughter floating up the stairs. Writing as I always do, for release. Standing up, because you can't sit down in this stuff.

I should be down there, to gauge whether she is making it — or holding back as last week, perfunctory as on Thursday or plain irresponsible as last night. Whether the huge risk Marcia took in telling her this morning about her own failure in *Joan* will actually have the desired effect: galvanize her into one last shining performance.

Added to which, a risk of my own, waiting until she appears on stage, furious with Dunois for leading her to the wrong side of the river. We shall see.

Rodney, Ray, and the rest dressing in here are firmly of the opinion that the whole thing has been a disaster. The play stands or falls on the Joan. Alex, the young Olympic swimmer, the hero figure herself, may have brought the curious audiences, but she has failed to deliver the goods. That's what they were all saying, and much as I would like to, I could not disagree. In hindsight, a sixteen-year-old-girl — Caroline and Marcia should have known better. Alex may have Joan's assertiveness bordering on arrogance, her apparent huge self-confidence, her courage, her large personality but . . .

What would they know of her problems, or of mine, come to that: coping with the burden of your given talents, the willpower you must develop, the thick skin you must grow? The burden of crushing expectations that ignorant, self-seeking, but sometimes only well-meaning people lay upon you. The blows of grief and loss and disappointment which can inexplicably bar your way forward, silence your voice . . . for how long?

I am hearing laughter. Ray on form, pushing the comedy, slightly reckless this final night? Can one dare to hope that Alex is at last . . .

They were talking of a party at Marcia Macrae's house in Titirangi afterwards. Why hers — the one person in the world outside the tight-lipped family who knew my mother — why there? What did she mean, 'your mother was an Alex, if you ever want to know.' I've managed twenty-three years without her, that earlier Alex; I'll manage many more.

They were talking of what they would be doing after tonight, after these past seven intense weeks together — they start lectures next week: some teaching; most as students. I remained silent, simply because I don't know, other than the tedium of the wharves daily, whittling down my debt, seeing my music case sit unopened in my room.

And the November 10 letter, with the slides from Rome, that finally turned up this morning, sent back surface mail from Milan: oh, Alessandra, what do I make of that? See it as a declaration, of a sort? Nearly three months later, of misunderstandings, at cross-purposes, using the play, her sport, anything to avoid the issue; is that letter now outdated — where do I stand?

To get her alone, strip away the tensions of her swimming commitments, the fatigue of *Joan* deep in her eyes; find out from her alone what happened to that previous boyfriend. But if she is failing down there to bring Joan to life in the Dauphin's Court, and through two more hours of her story, I'll not be the person to comfort her. Will I? Who will?

Is a last-ditch grand gesture called for tonight, whatever happens?

Seconds out

Last chance. Terrible heats, Alex, but you can do a great final, given good enough reasons. The job in hand.

Joan the positive: doggedly waiting for her interview with Baudricourt, confiding in a stranger for the first time about her voices, coaxing him, flattering him shamelessly, sweeping him off his feet, the first step on the road to Rheims. Her energy coming easily, her words flowing at last.

Joan the determined: the female knight who rides with her escort three hundred miles across France in eleven days to see Charles, her Dauphin, to tell him she would see him crowned him in Rheims cathedral; not fooled by Bluebeard's trick, recognising the badly-dressed weedy little Dauphin from behind the sneering courtiers. Comfortable, free, in my soldier's dress — oh yes, I understand why she preferred male clothing all right. Ray playing up to me, and me to him, the audience laughing in all the right places and some new ones too. Charles tempted at last, *Oh, if only I dare!* and Joan replying *I shall dare, dare, and dare again, in God's name!* Flashing out the sword perfectly, falling on her knees, radiant, giving thanks for the huge risks she is taking and pulling off.

Joan the blunt, impetuous soldier: rushing on, in a blazing rage, to protest to Dunois about being deliberately brought the wrong side of the river to attack Orléans. Tom realising very quickly that something was different, the scene crackling, sparkling, two clear-headed strong-minded people clashing, recognising they need each other. *Dunois, dear comrade-in-arms, help me.* Him squeezing my hand as we rush off stage at the end, wanting to say something but not getting the chance before I keep on running; but not following me.

Joan, twice wounded in battle, now the seasoned hardened campaigner: after the Dauphin's coronation, angrily defending her faith in her heavenly voices, stubbornly arguing the case to attack Paris, refusing to hear the growing earthly voices of caution, resentment, jealousy, and thinly veiled hatred; older voices, harder to convince, even Dunois only barely concealing his jealousy under the guise of common sense: *But I know exactly how much God did for us through the Maid, and how much He left me to do by my own wits; and I tell you that your little hour of miracles is over, and that from this time on he who plays the war game best will win — if the luck is on his side.* In his eyes, standing with his back to the audience, Dunois' exasperation, grudging respect.

Joan the failure, the vain knight pulled from her horse by her golden surcoat at Compiègne, the prisoner for just on a year: her ankles rubbed raw by chains, bruises on her face, her hair shaven, survivor of brutal guards, a sixty foot jump of despair, and months of constant questioning. By this stage of the night, though I could hardly think, hardly hear, hardly knew what I was doing for tiredness, we all knew this last performance had taken off and was flying on a dream life of its own; not only me, everyone.

Joan defiant: just another long-winded session of the Court, until she realizes that this time, here, *now*, her time and her luck have run out. The fire is ready, needs only one small flame to be lit. Joan so worn down, so tired and so terrified she recants, sells her voices down the river for the chance of freedom. So furious to discover she has gained nothing from these learned, two-faced, self-satisfied hypocrites but life imprisonment, that she deliberately defies them all and chooses burning, suicide, instead.

Defiant of them all, but particularly the bigoted evil-minded foul-mouthed jealous toady D'Estivet, her particular *bête noire* who never calls her anything but Woman; telling him *It is great nonsense. Nobody could be such a fool as to think that*; now at last giving back to him the same blazing intensity of hatred and contempt; eyes to eyes; beyond thinking of Tom behind the mask. Recanting, but realizing she has been terribly tricked: rising, forgetting her weariness, at hearing the sentence of life imprisonment, in consternation and terrible anger. *Perpetual imprisonment? Am I not then to be set free?* My last speech, the aria, I was crying and laughing, the words just poured out of my soul.

Light your fire: do you think I dread it as much as the life of a rat in a hole? My voices were right. Yes: they told me you were fools and that I was not to listen to your fine words nor trust to your charity ...

When I was dragged off I was shaking uncontrollably, crying real tears, clutching the torn-up paper of recantation. I saw and felt the red flickering light in the market-place beyond the trees.

My skin was prickling, hot and raw all over.

The thrusting mauling eager hands of the men pushing me off the stage dropped away. I stumbled blindly over a step, felt a hand deliberately grip mine, lead me up a staircase away from the crowd noises, the crackle of a great fire burning, the smell of smoke, the voices of the conniving jealous men who planned it to happen all along; away from the sound of the Chaplain rushing in howling at the gruesome sight of a living human body tied to a stake, struggling, her hair, her clothes, her flesh, sizzling, burning alive. I wrenched my hand from his grasp and found a wall to lean against, heaving as though I'd just swum a race.

'Break it, Alex,' he said urgently. 'Break it *now*. Throw the paper away. Look at me.'

But all I saw standing in the half-light of the corridor was D'Estivet. 'You got your way. You burnt her, you schemed and lied and plotted and called it law and justice and heresy and mercy, you conveniently called her a witch and you burnt her.'

'Alex, you were wonderful, just wonderful. You acted the rest of us off the stage as I always knew you could. Look at me. Alessandra!'

'You burnt her, she is burning . . .'

'Alex, *break it*. You must break it right now. Look at me. It's the Tom you won't talk to, not D'Estivet. You are Alex, not Joan, you are Alessandra.'

'You . . . how can you watch it . . . be . . .'

'*Look at me*.'

'How can I look at you, when you look like that, sound like that, are like that? Where do you get it from?'

He dragged off the close-fitting hat, undid the top of the long priestly gown. He had on a T-shirt underneath. His hair caught a shaft of light coming from a window of one of the dressing rooms. But the face stayed the same, sallow and lined, the face of contempt for everything Joan stood for, everything she dared for. I did register make-up so clever that even close up in the dim light he looked still a different person.

'Where do you get it from?' I cried. 'How can I tell, which is masks, which is real, what anyone is thinking but especially you, how can you trust, I don't know any more.'

'I could say the same for the masks you choose to wear. I don't know either.'

'You told me you were a singer. I heard you in Rome. I know I did. Or was it all an act, your singing? Wasn't even that real?'

I began to run down the corridor, but the swish of his black robes caught up with me, and the next thing I knew I was being dragged back by the arm. I began to recognize where I was. My dressing room was at the end, around a corner. He hauled me inside. We stood blinking in the bright light, both breathing heavily, facing each other, seconds out, yelling freely at last.

'No it's not real, Alessandra,' he shouted. 'I was a singer then, yes. I'm not now. I haven't sung a note since my audition.'

'Why not?'

'Could you possibly know, what it's like to lose . . . Maestro was the nearest thing I've ever had to a father . . . Then I come all this way . . .'

'I didn't ask you to come. Don't blame me if you can't sing any more. And how the hell would you know what's happened to me in my life if you've never asked?'

'I have asked and I'll ask again, and this time you might tell me, because whatever it is, you've got to if we're ever to get anywhere. Alex, what happened with you and Andy Richmond? Did he die?'

'I'm not telling you, now or ever,' I yelled. 'I wish I'd never met you. You ruined Rome, all those games, me stupid enough to write that letter, that stupid moustache and that boring window-shopping . . .'

'Really? You fight rough. That's not how I remember you responding to Rome, or to me, come to that.'

'And you've ruined *Saint Joan*, my one chance. You hang around and you play with me like a cat with a mouse. You take Lesley home, and Genevieve, and you go drinking, and for months I've been waiting . . .' I stopped.

'For what? Just what have you been waiting for, Alex? I'd be interested to know. The passionate embrace? More? Are you Alex the pseudo-widgie, or Keith's girl, the prim schoolgirl champion swimmer or Joan the chaste? Which one are you, Alex? You'd better make up your mind. We agreed, I thought, platonic until you decided otherwise.'

'Just good friends! Such the gentleman! Passing the buck.'

'What are you saying, Alex? You really wanted me all along . . . do you want me to now, even looking like this? Even you looking like a prisoner of war? I won't take much persuading.'

'No I do not. I never want to see you again. But don't you blame me if your voice has gone AWOL, isn't that what you said, AWOL. I'd have thought, if you had any guts, if you really . . .'

'Really what?'

I heard footsteps, someone calling Tom, Alex, for God's sake. I said in a rush, 'You've got tonight — what's left of it. Sing me something, if you really . . .'

'You two, for crying out loud!' Plump Rodney appeared at the door, very agitated, 'Alex, why aren't you ready for me?' he said, marching in and fiddling with the armour waiting to be buckled on. 'Get that suit off. That was a wonderful *wonderful* trial scene, you both had me in tears, absolute buckets, but have you forgotten Shaw wrote something called the Epilogue?'

Tom and I still glared at each other.

'Tom, you've got longer than Alex, get out of here,' flapped Rodney. 'I'll come down to you when I've finished with her.'

I couldn't move. His eyes were hostile, dangerous, just like D'Estivet on stage.

'Alex, wash your bruises off,' cried Rodney, very agitated. 'For heaven's sake, both of you get moving. You got five minutes, Alex. Keep your squabbles till later.'

'Are you D'Estivet really? Am I just Woman to you?' I cried.

'You'll never see D'Estivet again,' he said heavily, walking out. Rodney chatted me out of the suit and into the leggings, the chainmail, the armour, the sword, the wig; going on about the wonderful house, aren't last nights always fun, always the best, and of course I was going to the party up in Titirangi, *everyone* was.

They carried me through the Epilogue, where the ghosts of all the major players in Joan's story come to life, the nobles, the priests, and the soldiers all explaining and justifying their part in the burning of Joan of Arc; another trial scene, of a sort, and none of them judged worthy; they condemned themselves one by one with their excuses and fancy talk. I had a lot of talking to do, but mostly on one level; the words came out automatically, my voice thick with tiredness. Perhaps Tom had told them we'd had a major row; to help me through the last scene.

I avoided looking at Dunois, even when he had to pull me to my feet and say with an ironic smile, *Half an hour to burn you, dear Saint, and four centuries to find out the truth about you.* They all made their feeble excuses and tiptoed out, leaving her alone. Basically Shaw is saying that if Joan came back now, the same thing would happen; Joan, being a threat to the established male order of things, would get destroyed all over again. At some point it dawned on me that I'd never speak these words again, that I'd never see Dunois handsome in his armour again, that after tonight's episode I'd never see Tom again either.

The Soldier from Hell said his last few lines.

Well, what do they all amount to, these kings and captains and bishops and lawyers and such like? They just leave you in the ditch to bleed to death, and the next thing is, you meet them down there, for all the airs they give themselves. What I say is, you have as good a right to your notions as they have to theirs, and perhaps better. You see it's like this. If (the first bell of midnight) — *Excuse me: a pressing appointment* —

He tiptoed back to Hell. All that was left was for me to say the last sad lines of the play.

O God that madest this beautiful earth, when will it be ready to receive Thy Saints? How long, O Lord, how long?

There was a hush as the spot on me very slowly began to fade. As the distant bell struck, that should have been the end of the play, blackout, the beginning of the clapping. But I heard something more, something that literally made my hair stand on end.

It was the voice from Rome; Tom, in the dark somewhere behind me, singing in French, something very simple, almost like a folk song, with five or six verses. The audience, already hushed, held its breath. It was the most beautiful song I have ever heard. The voice got softer and softer, until the last verse was barely there at all, as though the singer was walking away into the distance.

I suppose it was only ten seconds or so really, but after he finished, time really did seem to stand absolutely still. I was supposed to leave the stage promptly, to come on last for the bows, but I could only stand there stupidly as the hush was eventually broken and the clapping started, the tears pouring down my cheeks — so that someone decided to bring up all the lights and all the men came crowding on.

It was Tom, unsmiling, avoiding my eyes, who took my hand, and drew me into the line as was usual. I could see nothing but blurred lights, hear only the clapping which went on and on, feel only Ray's hand on one side, Tom's on the other. Everyone knew that it was him who'd sung at the end; there were special cheers for him, and for me. I heard someone behind me say another song, Tom, and him firmly, not now, enough was enough. I couldn't look at him. That had been my song.

Caroline appeared, to more clapping. There were no speeches. She had a horror of curtain call thank-you speeches, spoiling the performance. She gave me a large bouquet, a large hug, wiped my eyes and led me off, finally. Behind the set, people, laughter, confusion. All I wanted to do was sit down and sleep.

Again I was led away, but this time further, the two of us in our armour. Tom must have anticipated I'd be shellshocked and exhausted, never mind crying my eyes out. He had sung for me! I plodded behind him, up the circular stairs, across the mosaics of the foyer, out of the front door, down the stone steps, out onto the footpath.

'We can't . . . ' I began.

'We can. Sssh.' We set off down Princes Street, fortunately too soon for people from the audience to be up on the road finding their cars and blinking at these ghostly apparitions.

'Where are we going?'

'The Grand Hotel.'

'We can't go there!'

'Why not?'

'You can't afford it, for one thing.'

'Relax.'

'Are you kidnapping me?'

'Yes.'

It was only a short walk, down the oldest, nicest street in Auckland. Streetlights shone down through the oak trees. Two fifteenth century soldiers, hand in hand, with identical haircuts, black and blazing bronze, both with genuine swords, held up all the traffic at the lights. A hundred yards further down the hill, they clanked into the foyer of the most expensive hotel in town.

It was almost worth it for the looks on the faces around, especially the man in a pinstripe suit behind the desk watching a red-eyed Joan of Arc and a grim comrade-at-arms come towards him across his floral carpet. I stood by while Tom, with an air of great nonchalance, as though chainmail, armour, and a weatherbeaten face was his usual dress, signed a large book. He had booked the executive suite, no less.

'A good party, was it, sir, madam?' smirked the man. 'I must say, it's very effective. Quite hot in this weather?' I could see his mind working suspiciously. 'No bags?'

'No baggage,' said Tom firmly. A young Maori porter in a navy uniform led us to the lifts. 'I see you in the paper, miss,' he said as we went upwards. 'You're the lady, eh, from the Olympic Games. You won a medal, eh!' I grinned, wanly. Long memories, people have; even sixteen-year-old Maori boys with cheeky faces. Oh well. We went to the very top floor. He led us across an acre of thick carpet, towards double doors thrown open with a flourish.

'Anything you want, sir, just ring.'

'Thank you. After you, Alessandra.'

I went in to a room on the same large scale as the one in Rome, but with a pale blue carpet, darker blue long curtains held back with tassels, lots of elaborate floral arrangements, cosy flowery sofas, low table-lamps and prints of early Auckland on the walls. A Queen Mum sort of room. A black baby grand piano stood in one corner. Through an open picture window all the lights of Auckland blazed, the city and wharves below, the bridge to the left, the lights of Devonport, the beacons of the harbour and North Head beyond. It had never occurred to me that little old Auckland had such grand hotels and grand rooms. I went across and studied the view. I heard him move around, grunt as he began to unbuckle his armour.

'Is this some sort of joke?' I said eventually, turning round.

'Not at all,' he said, laying the sword across a chair and starting on the buckles of the main breastplate. 'It's deadly serious.'

I could only stare.

'I know stars traditionally sit in their dressing-rooms after a triumph and receive guests. However, I've come to the end of my tether and I reckon after seven months of torment my needs are greater.'

He didn't look at me as he went on, methodically working at the small leather straps.

'I've taken this room for two hours. It's the best room in Auckland. Then we're going up to the party in Titirangi. I've got someone picking us up at one. She'll bring up your proper clothes and mine. No one else knows we're here. Consider yourself kidnapped. Though if you want to leave now and catch your own taxi home, you may. I won't stop you, or follow you, or see you again.'

'All worked out.'

'A campaign, yes, to the last detail. What arrangements have you got with your parents?'

'I said I'd be home after the show. All right,' I said, before he got bossy, 'I'll ring. I haven't got the car. I'll say you're bringing me home.'

'Please do. Tomorrow. Tell them you're staying the night at Marcia Macrae's house. They should be happy enough with that.'

They were. I didn't say where I was ringing from, because the thought of seduction might have entered their heads as it was entering mine. He'd thrown the breastplate onto a chair with a sigh of relief.

'Now it's your turn.' He turned away and began examining the array of decanters and bottles on a side table. 'What would you like to drink?'

'Coke,' I said, getting rid of the sword.

'One large Coke coming up.' He stood by with two fizzing Coke and ice-filled glasses and patiently watched me struggle with the buckles as he had done. Finally I got them loosened and pulled the breastplate off.

'Here. Cin-cin!' I hadn't realized how sticky I felt, how dry my throat was. He poured another.

Then solemnly, while I watched amazed, he took off the tunic of chainmail, the leggings and the pointed boots, revealing a loose black farmer's singlet and a pair of black ballet dancer's tights. 'I found those things rather scratchy inside, didn't you?' Then he went into the bathroom. I heard the shower briefly. Then he came back, again dressed in his black, with a clean, paler face and wet combed hair and stood squarely in front of me.

'What you see is what you get, Alex. Tom Benedict Alexander, more correctly Tomas without an H but known variously as Blue, Canary, or Angel Alexander, aged twenty-three, a bastard, an orphan, born 1938 in England to a would-be actress from Taihape, who unfortunately died in childbirth. Adopted by uncle, raised Taihape, educated at various church boarding-schools, put self through Auckland University.'

He poured a glass of water and drank it in one.

'Of so-called family, adoptive father in a rest-home in Taihape, frail worn-out mother in a flat nearby, two older married sisters, one runs the farm, grandparents all dead. Bullied remorselessly through school, thus always a loner, hiding behind hats and a talent for acting. Unable to consider his uncle's prosperous but remote farm as a career. Fierce ambition: to sing in opera. Accomplishments: skiing, riding, cricket, hockey, fencing, piano, guitar, acting, singing. Drives a mean tractor, not bad with engines and sheep dogs. Languages: English and Italian, some French and German, a little Spanish, a little less Russian. No overly serious or wounding love affairs in the past, no current entanglements here or in Italy except the present one standing in front of him. That's me. Now it's your turn.'

I swallowed the last of my third Coke in horror. I had nothing much on under the chainmail, a pair of scanty knickers and a thin T-shirt, to be precise.

'In the bathroom you'll find a kimono,' he said. 'I asked for one. The ball's in your court. But if you take off the armour, let's say it's a symbolic gesture.'

I went into the poshest bathroom I've ever seen, all cream and gold. A kimono of heavy white cotton hung behind the door. I sat on the edge of the bath for a while, thinking. I took off the wig and all the heavy chainmail and the leggings, and had a glorious shower. I splashed on eau de cologne from a cut-glass decanter, and came out similarly sleek and pale of face, in the kimono, just as I had done in Rome. Tom was standing by the window. He handed me a tall glass of yellow wine. I stood at the other end of the window.

It was my turn in this game. I knew I was only going to get one chance. It was probably our last night.

'Alexandra Beatrice Archer, born October 1944 — but I think you always knew I was only sixteen. Father works in the Post Office, mother was a nurse, Gran (who had a heart attack while I was in Rome, but she's better now), one baby sister, two pesky brothers. Educated local primary, local intermediate, Epsom Girls Grammar School. Better-than-average swimmer for six years, famous rivalry with Maggie Benton. Up till last year learning piano, ballet, hockey First Eleven, school shows including *Pirates of Penzance*, *Wizard of Oz*, *trial scene from Saint Joan*. Turned down Head Girl, enrolled in law last week. Only three other girls in the course. Not quite sure why I want to do law . . . well, yes I do really — you need to know what you're talking about.'

He waited. Down in the harbour a white cruise ship, ablaze with lights, was being pulled away from the wharf by two tugs.

'I told you I was going to America in September. It wasn't true, I'm not. That's why I had to win that race against Jenny, because I knew it was my last. My coach knows, of course, and Mum and Dad, but no one else. I suppose I'll have to tell Norm Thompson sometime.'

He waited. I heard the cruise ship hooting across the water, the sound of a distant Dixieland band. Tom had gone to Italy on a ship like that.

'America would've meant four more years of swimming, being tied down . . . all that time . . . I want to do some of the things I've missed, go tramping, be in proper plays, meet people, read, go to concerts, learn piano again, travel. Going to Rome meant . . . I've been on lots of swimming trips but really, I don't know much about my own country.'

The ship was right in front of us, moving from left to right, faster now. I thought of the tearful people on it, setting off on great adventures. He waited.

'I don't trust . . . I'm often ruder than I mean to be, because I don't think first. Lots of times, I wish I'd never won that medal in Rome. People expect . . . they expect so . . . they wanted me to be Head Girl, and give talks and hand out prizes and talk to reporters and write letters and go to trials and do exams and smile being frightfully British about losing my title, be fantastic as Joan . . .'

'You were, in the end, very good indeed.'

'They expect . . . I got so *tired*. I tried to prepare Joan properly, but I meant it when I said she was too good for me. So strong, I could never . . .'

The cruise ship hooted again, twice, slowly turning left to go round North Head, about where I'd leapt off Andy's dinghy. Last summer. One of the first rows we'd had; one of the last times we'd lain together and kissed.

'If you can't trust . . . myself, you, anyone. When I have trusted . . .'

The tugs had dropped away and were coming back. I knew what he was waiting for, the thing I hadn't told him, or myself.

'I really thought I knew Andy. I knew him at primary school. We swam together. He was tall, he played rugby and cricket, he liked music, played the trumpet a bit, everyone thought we made a perfect match. But Keith said he wouldn't have made it in the Navy, and Miss Macrae told you he was a lightweight and had no sense of humour, and remembering, yes it's true . . . but I still . . .'

He waited.

'He was killed. Got knocked off his bike, a Jaguar tearing out of a driveway late at night. The driver shot through to Aussie, was never found, as far as I know.'

Out of the corner of my eye, I saw him move behind me, felt his arms come around my waist. I felt his cheek rest against my back, and his body rocking slightly. It was the reverse of the Vespa in Rome.

'Were you there?'

'No. But it won't go away . . . the driver was drunk . . . I see, it's dark, alone on a road, bleeding . . . noises . . . he was going to naval college at Dartmouth, me to do law, then we'd . . . we. . .'

After a long silence he said, 'All that anger. When?'

'December 2, year before last. Fifteen months. He was only eighteen. I found the car. I threw rocks at it, at least at the outside of the garage. I can't stop thinking . . . how can you know anyone, really? How can you know they won't . . . just up and leave you and . . .'

'I won't?'

I nodded. The cruise ship had disappeared behind North Head. I shut my eyes and tried to stop trembling at the warmth of the body hard up against mine.

'You don't know, Alex. You can't. There's no lifelong magic innoculation against getting hurt. There's only trust. If we team up, you and I, we'll often be apart.'

'How can you say 'team up'!' I cried, breaking away, but still not daring to turn round. 'You're going back to England or Milan or somewhere. How do I know you mean it? How do I know I'll even see you again after tonight? How do I know . . . that letter I wrote, the one you didn't get, just a kid with a crush, is that what you thought? Isn't that what you're still thinking?'

'No, it's certainly not. What was in the letter, by the way?'

'Nothing. I can't remember.'

'Try.' Lightly — was he teasing me?

'It's history.'

'The duplicates were very good, I thought.'

'You did get it, you knew all along that I . . .' I stopped, blushing scarlet. Of course I remembered. *I could fall in love with your voice, it's truly beautiful, it does things to me.* 'If you knew . . .'

'I didn't know. It arrived only this morning, sent back surface mail.'

'How do I know that's the truth? How do I know anything, one moment you're Dunois, the next D'Estivet, how do I know you won't shout at me just like . . .?'

'I probably will, because we've both got minds of our own, and you'll give it back to me in spades. Where did I get D'Estivet from, you asked. The same deep mysterious place as you would, playing a baddie, and you did, playing Joan. We've all got our dark side, as well as a heroic one. And don't think I wasn't enjoying the licence to shout and express emotions normally well hidden. Of course I love playing villains, the nastier the better. Cassius was fun, and Shylock at fifteen. One day I'm going to play Iago, the ultimate bastard, on a grand and sinister scale. Goodies like Joan are much harder, and can come over as complete prigs, dead boring. It takes rather special people to play goodies convincingly. That's why you did so well.'

'It was all on the surface. You said her spiritual side was beyond me.'

'No, tonight you caught it. I know the risk you took.'

'Joan believed, she had a mission . . .'

'And so will you one day, when you find yours. Your job was to recreate her spirit. God knows, with people around like the late Joe McCarthy and that bully-boy Khrushchev, we need her voice, loud and clear. You became her voice, a call to arms. One thing Marcia said: when Alex finds something to get her teeth into, engages all that energy and talent, watch out. I want to be around when that happens.'

'But you're going away again,' I said. He didn't deny it. I said helplessly, 'Tom, why are we here, all this?'

'Turn around Alex, look at me, funny fellow that I am.'

I turned slowly. The long black singlet, the black tights did undoubtedly look very comical.

'I want to get to know you, Alex, if you feel the same about me. We might even find we want to spend our lives together. And why here, this luxury? I just want to feel, if only for two hours, some of the rewards if I make it as an international singer — good hotels, being able to look out at views like that, Auckland, Naples, Buenos Aires, New York, wherever. I want you to feel it too.'

I couldn't bear his intensity. I turned and stared out at the lights. His arms slipped round my waist again. I was trembling all over. 'You might get killed in a plane crash, all that travel.'

'I might. Who knows? We can't plan our lives on such fears. I'm not suggesting a conventional arrangement, mortgages and me coming home for tea every night at five . . . I'm suggesting we might have two parallel careers, two equal lives . . . oh Alessandra, la più coraggiosa. Let me find out who you really are.'

The lights in front of me had blurred hopelessly. It was all slow motion, me turning for the first kiss of love I had ever initiated. It started gentle, then got rather rough, my hands through his damp, unbelievable hair, his hands tracing the outline of my face, eyes, eyebrows, mouth, as though drawing them on his memory.

'I've waited seven months for that,' he said. 'I knew when I saw you at Rome airport that day . . . the incandescent Alessandra.'

'The airport?'

'Don't you read my letters? Perhaps you were too angry to register. I happened to be out there when you arrived . . . some embassy type in a suit, whatever he said had you in tears for a while. I watched you get on the bus from only a few yards away. I couldn't take my eyes off you.'

'An Italian.'

'Just so. He was called, let's say, Petruccio.' He kissed me, harder.

'That song tonight, what was it?'

'A sixteenth-century French love song. A ballad of unrequited love.'

This time I stood behind him, my hands on his broad bare shoulders as he sang the song again. The piano accompaniment was all arpeggios, like a guitar. Again it made me feel inutterably sad.

'But you're going away again soon,' I wept.

He sat head bowed for a long moment, then sighed deeply. 'Go over there, Alex, the far side. Sit down and pretend you're at La Scala, the best box in the house, of course.'

'I've never been in one.'

'You will. It's *Turandot*, the curtain has just gone up on the third act. Calaf is alone on the stage. It's show-down time with the ice-cold princess, the night before he has to answer her final riddle or have his head chopped off, like all the princes before him. *Nessun dorma*, none shall sleep.'

The aria began softly, but by the time he finished I knew I'd heard something quite different. For the first time I heard his whole, complete range, the high notes full voice.

'He gets the girl,' he said as I sat stunned, weeping afresh. 'It's one of the few grand operas with a happy ending. Now you and half Auckland know my guilty secret. I've known for a year that my voice had lyric or even dramatic tenor possibilities. Maestro had set his heart on my playing his roles, Figaro, Rigoletto, Iago and the rest. But I'm a tenor, and my voice will grow. I'll reach my peak when I'm well over forty, condemned to a lifetime of playing the good guys.'

I couldn't take in much more. He'd been singing for me.

'But you're going away,' I cried.

'I think the New Zealand company may have me. I'll get the small roles I need for experience, probably more than I would have got in Europe. Maybe some bigger ones. There are good teachers here too.'

'You hate this country. We're all boring unmusical philistines, you said . . .'

'Maybe not all. An opera company exists. An orchestra exists. A ballet company, and the New Zealand Players, they struggle along. There are writers, painters, slogging away. Television is just starting, now *there's* a challenge. I'm prepared to give it another go, for a while. I might even grow to like the place with you around. People like you and me might help change it, slowly.'

We met in the middle of the room. I was so tired it was all I could do to rest my head on his black singlet; he was the incandescent one now.

'Alex, it won't all be plain sailing. You've got to get your basic law degree, then who knows, postgraduate work, politics, or a law practice, or write books, or teach in an ivory tower somewhere. I'll be coming and going between engagements, recordings, teachers. But think of the adventures, an international life, together some of the time, pushing our careers along the rest. Think of the adventures we've had already!'

'I always knew I loved you, Tommaso.'

'Even at the Colosseum? Even the Italian spiv?'

'Even then.' Even through the kiss I began to smile as I remembered Zoe, my supposedly engaged room-mate, flirting with him in the dining hall, and the expression on Mr Upjohn's face at the airport when he found out interpreter Tommaso was not what he seemed, and the loud back-slapping Aussie called Dennis outside St Peter's. 'I'll never forget, at the Colosseum, you wearing that silly boater with the pink ribbon, the very first words you said to me. . .'

"Da dove vieni? La Svezia, La Germania, L'Olanda? 'And when you objected to Australia, 'Okay, la Nuova Zelanda?''

We were both laughing by now.

'I should have known straight off you were a fake. Only another Kiwi would have known why I choked over Ors-trah-glia. A con man, you are.'

'Stone the crows, Alex, give us a break . . .' I stopped any more of his Aussie nonsense with the longest kiss on record, until we ended up on the floor, nearly knocking over a standard lamp, both completely out of breath, and I said, 'Tommaso, Blue, Angel, I don't care.'

'Tom it will be, from now on.'

I wiped my eyes with the corner of my sleeve. 'I'm starving.'

He sat up and looked at the antique clock on the mantelpiece. 'Genevieve will be here in half an hour. Shall I order something?'

'Champagne and sandwiches. Petits fours. Torte di cioccolata.'

'You learn fast,' he said in mock horror.

Genevieve came on the dot of one with our clothes, and transported a slightly tipsy and dishevelled couple and armfuls of discarded armour to the party in Titirangi. We were cheered in the door. Miss Macrae — you must call me Marcia now, Alex (but I couldn't, at least not straight off) — was in bright red hostess pyjamas!

Lesley wasn't there. She really did have the flu. At some stage early in the evening Tom was asked to sing and did, several songs including 'Celeste Aida' again full voice, looking at me, to rousing applause, in his element, finishing with a very suggestive version of 'Don't Put Your Daughter on the Stage, Mrs Worthington' and finally, gently, 'How Sweet to be a Cloud'. Then someone gave him a guitar and we all sang all night, even all the verses of 'Abdul the Bulbul Emir', even 'Arrivederci Roma.'

Around five, we lay down together on a single bed in a small verandah area with flax bushes and vines growing out of big terracotta pots, as if there wasn't enough bush around the house already, and after a few wine-tasting kisses, went very comfortably to sleep.

I was woken by sunlight on my face filtering through the creepers round the verandah. My watch said nearly eleven. I lay for a while and heard low voices and some piano music on a radio, then staggered to my feet in search of a cup of tea. My jeans and T-shirt, slept in, felt very scruffy. Miss Macrae's house looked worse, all the debris of a rip-roaring party.

Something made me stop at the French doors onto a small square of grass between the house and bush. Tom and Miss Macrae were sitting at a garden table. Maybe it was the expression on Miss Macrae's face, or the absolute stillness of Tom's broad back.

He was looking at a photograph. I caught a signal to wait in her eyes. So I leaned against the doorway and waited, maybe two or three minutes, drinking in the cool green all around, the utter quiet you get away from the city. Three fantails ducked in and out of a tree; a tui clucked and chortled, quite close to the house. Then Tom must have sensed me behind him, because he turned around. There were tears in his eyes. He handed me the photograph.

It was a very clear black and white snapshot of two young women sitting together, smiling. Probably taken on some sort of outing, both wearing coats and hats. A stamp on the back gave the name of the professional photographer and someone had also written London Christmas 1937, Marcia and Dorothy in St James's Park.

I stared at it as Tom had done. Miss Macrae was much slimmer then. Two things were obvious about the other young woman, she was beautiful, and she was pregnant.

'She's lovely,' I whispered, hardly knowing what to say. That was Tom in there, and she had died two months later. 'She's lovely. Beautiful eyes.'

'Yes, her Maori blood,' said Miss Macrae.

Tom said softly, 'Her what?'

'Her Maori blood. There was a Maori great-grandmother somewhere.'

'Then . . .' He reached out for the picture. Could I begin to imagine what Tom was thinking as he looked at it again? His mother was part-Maori, therefore so were his very British sheep-farmer uncle, his cousins and himself. Now I knew why I'd been slightly surprised by the smooth olive skin when I first saw him shirtless that night in Rome, where the wide-set deep brown eyes and the rich voice came from.

'I thought you knew,' said Miss Macrae.

'It's never been acknowledged in the family. Never,' he cried. 'Never! They only told me there were no photos. Why did they never tell me? I had a right to know.'

'I've only been in this country ten years,' she said, 'but I gather it's not uncommon. Many European families have Maori ancestry three or four generations back; some acknowledge it and some don't.'

Tom said, still looking at the picture, 'If you and I hadn't got together, Alex, hadn't come here last night, been sitting here today, I'd probably never have known.'

'I'm glad you know,' I said, sitting down beside him and putting my arm over his heaving shoulders. 'You should know who your mother is. Everyone should know that. I'm glad.'

'Next weekend, will you . . . I haven't seen my family yet . . . my sister lent me the money . . . it's a long drive to Taihape, I can borrow the MG . . . you've never been on a farm, have you? It's about time I . . . I want . . .'

I gave him a huge kiss and felt his tears on my cheeks.

'G'day, Kiwi,' I said.

There is one more image of that March day, the day before I started lectures, learning how to become a lawyer; the day Norman Thompson announced my retirement from swimming and I wrote two letters on stiff white paper to America thanking them both for their offers, but I was giving up swimming to study law in Auckland.

Lunch turned into another party, with Caroline and Genevieve, after we helped to tidy up the mess. I heard Tom make a date with Miss Macrae on Tuesday night to talk some more about life at drama school in London in 1937.

Genevieve offered us a lift home. She had to take the two sets of armour back to university, for Rodney to return it to the professional company. There was some tidying up to be done there too, quite a bit.

It was tea-time when we finally arrived home. We crept in through the back porch. I made Tom wait while I went into my bedroom and got out his silver bracelet. He put it on my wrist, gave me a smiling Tommaso kiss on the hand and a proper Tom kiss which went on for so long I had to break it off and remind him that he was about to meet my family and he'd better put a comb through his hair. I told him to wait.

They were all sitting round the kitchen table, Mum pouring tea from the best silver teapot, Dad, Jamie, Debbie and Robbie; Mr Jack and his wife were there and even Julia, all looking eagerly at the large plateful of steaming date and cheese scones straight from the oven, her speciality, which Gran was just putting on the table.

The table was set with the best white linen cloth and the thin painted teacups from the china cabinet and a bowl of garden flowers. There were home-made afghans and a chocolate sponge-cake already cut with cream oozing out the sides and cheese straws and club sandwiches and a bacon and egg pie. It wasn't a birthday but someone had been baking.

They all turned to look at me. I don't suppose my slept-in clothes looked very marvellous or my short black hair or the black rings under my eyes. But I must have looked as 'incandescent' as I felt because they all began laughing, even Jamie, and Gran was positively dancing on her tippy-toes, her hands clasped to her chest as though she was about to start singing a song.

I thought, then the penny dropped. 'That Miss Macrae has been at it again, hasn't she?'

'She rang to tell us you were coming,' smiled Mum.

'Did she say who with?'

'No, she wouldn't say. It was a surprise, she said.'

I looked suspiciously at Gran.

'I didn't tell, Alex,' she cried, her eyes gleaming. 'I didn't tell anyone. I didn't!'

I pulled him forward. My silver and bronze bracelet twinkled. It was amazing how their eyes all went upwards to his hair. He looked about as bashful as it was possible for a future famous opera singer to look.

'This is my family. Meet Tom,' I said.